GEOGRAPHY OF SETTLEMENTS

Geography of Settlements

R.Y. SINGH

RAWAT PUBLICATIONS
Jaipur • New Delhi • Bangalore • Guwahati • Kolkata

ISBN 978-81-7033-209-1 (Hardcover)
ISBN 978-81-7033-483-5 (Paperback)

Reprinted, 2023

Published by
Prem Rawat for **Rawat Publications**
Satyam Apts., Sector 3, Jawahar Nagar, Jaipur - 302 004 (India)
Phone: 0141 265 1748 / 265 7006
E-mail : info@rawatbooks.com
Website: rawatbooks.com

New Delhi Office
4858/24, Ansari Road, Daryaganj, New Delhi 110 002
Phone: 011-23263290

Also at *Bangalore, Guwahati* and *Kolkata*

Typeset by Rawat Computers, Jaipur
Printed at Nice Printing Press, New Delhi

Foreword

Mackinder's contention that geography is at once an art, a science and a philosophy comes true if one makes in-depth study of settlements. World society for Ekistics was founded with great zeal with the clear aims and objectives to study them because besides geographers, planners, sociologists, historians, economists and others are well concerned with settlement study; for these settlements work as living organisms. Keeping in view the ecumenic share of rural settlements in this inhabited part of the globe, it is essential to have deep insight into these micro-level limbs. The author has rightly selected and adopted the holistic viewpoint of the discipline which embodies quantitative as well as qualitative analytical and synthesizing approach to the study of rural settlements. Obviously, there were scattered explanations of various themes in varied volumes which created interest among students. But they could not find most of the themes with lucid exposition in one volume. This felt-need, to our great satisfaction, has been met with in the present volume. Because, it does cover wide spectrum of all the five principal themes of cultural geography and other distinct themes, viz., human settlement system, definitions, approaches, classification and allied topics; culturo-historical perspective, diffusion models; spatio-temporal models; place names versus settlements; village unit; site, situation and location; anatomy of Indian villages; transformation of villages; types and patterns; distributional pattern of rural settlements; pioneer fringe areas; morphology—its origin and growth; nucleation and dispersion; caste ranking, layout patterns; shape analysis; rural dwellings; rural service centres; periodic markets; and integrated planning and rationalization of rural settlements supported by models and their sub-topics with micro-level details.

The foundation laid during 50s, 60s and 70s for the study of rural settlements in the Department of Geography, Banaras Hindu University at Varanasi under enthusiastic leadership has been strong, firm and fruitful. The author has made a notable contribution of mature scholarship which will certainly bring both a fascination and a deeper academic satisfaction to a wide range of English-speaking readers, be it graduates, researchers or teachers. It is commendable that the author has eschewed jargon for jargon's sake but has certainly aimed at lucid exposition and explanation of facts.

I fully hope that the present work will be at once rewarding, illuminating and enriching as it would arouse interest in rural settlement geographers, cultural geographers, sociologists, economists, historians, anthropologists, scholars of rural habitat transformation as well as among rural development planners, particularly in developing countries.

R.L. Singh
Former Head, Department of Geography
Banaras Hindu University, Varanasi.

Preface

The book is the outcome of a long period of research and teaching experience of the topic in one of the most important centres (rather, the most important centre) for settlement studies and felt demand by post-graduate students as well as research scholars regarding a publication which may cover most of the themes/topics already prescribed in varied syllabii of universities in developing countries in one volume, and that too adopting a holistic view of the discipline.

The first introductory chapter provides full perspective about the discipline and its place and significance, along with details on approaches, growth of studies and classifications. The next chapter deals with the culturo-historical perspective of settlements in the world having special emphasis on cultural hearths, realms, diffusion models, spatio-temporal models and place name studies. Chapter third, devoted to village settlements, provides clear view of the villages in general, and Indian villages in particular, the meaning of site, situation and location/position, the village anatomy model, the internal social changes being experienced as well as study of sample villages.

Chapter four deals with the types and patterns of settlements, giving their proper meaning, classification and causes, supported by study of sample villages and illustrations. In chapter five, the distributional pattern finds full treatment—qualitative as well as quantitative—on spacing and dispersion and regional comparison, characteristics of new/pioneer settlements. Morphology finds comprehensive, in-depth explanation with concrete examples. Shape analysis also provides qualitative/quantitative approaches in chapter seven. In chapter eight, the core of settlements dwellings exhibits the theoretical and experience based insight into the whole spectrum of various aspects of the topic. Chapter nine is concerned not only with the treatment of growth centre concept and central place theory based identification of hierarchical, functional gaps as prerequisite for development planning but also of rural periodic markets in full detail.

The last chapter is devoted to integrated planning and rationalization of settlements having detailed account of social requisites, ecological basis and strategy of planning and feasible models of rationalization through spatial integration, functional co-ordination, efficiency of lan-duse and marketing as well as infrastructural development. Grass roots and human settlements approaches would provide new insight to the disciplines related to the developmental planning. All the references find place at the end of each chapter.

I am thankful to a great number of writers and publishers and am specially indebted to the Geographical Society of India, Varanasi. I am grateful to Prof. R.L. Singh for going through the manuscript and making suggestions. Dr. Haushila Prasad and Sri S. Dube also deserve my thanks for typing of manuscript. Dr. Om Prakash Shrivastava claims special thanks for preparing and correcting maps. The colleagues and friends who have remained helpful in many ways too deserve my heartfelt thanks. Messrs Rawat Publications' efforts in the publication of this book are commendable, hence, worthy of thanks.

I hope that the work would be gladly accepted by settlement geographers, cultural geographers, sociologists, economists, historians, anthropologists, scholars of rural habitat transformation as well as by rural development planners.

Rama Yagya Singh

Contents

1

Rural Settlements: A Culturo-Environmental Approach

Shelter is one of the most important basic necessities of human being. Even the naked saints or pygmies need sound sleep—the physiological necessity of living beings, at some place. Man also needs some sort of shelter for safe rest. For shelter, he selects tree branches, caves or pits or rock-cut hiding places. These shelter places become the most concrete expressions of human cultural activity and assume various forms as well as names. Houses, dwellings, group of dwellings/houses, abodes, habitations—all form human habitat, more specifically settlements.* With the establishment of any sort of dwelling the foundation of a civilization is laid which grows, flourishes and spreads like petals of blossoming flowers in all directions in varied tint and colour and temporal/spatial variations in the form of habitations. These become the concrete expressions of anthropogenic and later on technogenic adaptations of human being. Although all living organisms build for themselves nests, dwellings, like bees, beavers, ants etc., an animal only produces what it immediately needs for itself or its young. It produces onesidedly whilst man produces universally.[1] This universality of houses and their groupings in the form of settlements exhibit variations in size, shape, pattern and types as well as multi-distributional aspects—all being the subject matter of systematic study.

A stake, the rope, the leather cover of the tent or for igloos or felt for yurt, a pit dug in the surface, a house cut in loess or a cave cut in rocks, a wattle-daub dwelling in forest or herder's/hunter's hut—all bespeak humanization hence, interaction with environment. The more advanced the civilization, the more complex becomes interaction. This needs, for the perfection of any study, the understanding of the concerned surrounding environment as a whole. No isolated parts, if studied in isolation, would suffice to form the subject matter because the overall effect of sum of the parts remains always less than the overall behaviour of a whole. The study of a single most settlement, with its own niche in the habitat and as a subsystem of a system—both become essential. The unit of settlement, however, may range from a slum dwelling in shanty town, a herder's hut, a farm or a tribal's homestead up to ecumenopolis. Thus, any settlement can be studied in either a world or a regional context; but any settlement, if it is to be adequately appreciated, must be correlated with other facets of geography, e.g., relief, climate, geology and social and economic conditions.[2] Brunhes put houses in the first group among the essential facts of human geography. Houses, roads and fields are also the essential facts of human occupation, the

* The term 'settlement' denotes territoriality; therefore, expression like 'The Geography of Settlement' is not proper. Late Constantions Doxiades of the Athens Institute of Ekistics used the term 'human settlements' with the emphasis that study of urban and rural settlements is a unified work.

distinctive features of the landscape.[3] Transformation of original habitat by settlements is so much so that "in towns the very air itself is changed and vitiated, and everything is of an artificial character".[4] Human race has gone a longway in technogenic transformation since the French geographer wrote the cited line above. Hence, new dimensions added to the study of settlements in relation to ecosystem dealt with in the sequel in the following section.

We start here with the assumption that man is (not only) a product of the earth's surface[5] but man's relation to nature has emerged not as one of self-interrogation, nor even of simple dialogue, but of a conference with others present and in which social man increasingly has the right of veto.[6] How much rational he is in adopting or imposing the latter is explained better through the form of settlements than anything else. Hence, settlements need explanation along with the study of physico-ecologico-economic-geographic aspects in the unique noosphere.

Human Settlement System

Geography's integrating concepts and processes concern the worldwide ecosystem of which man is the dominant part.[7] Man in the context of geographical man-machine analogy is composed of a complex of interlocking socio-economic systems which operate on the above machine by means of decision-making mechanisms of great complexity and bias, not without their own important stochastic elements.[8] In the geographical context, the machine is made up of those systems structures of the physical and biological environment which man is increasingly able to manipulate together with the physical artifacts of man's activity—buildings, lakes, polluted air and the like.[9] The same notion is obvious from the writings of Blache[10] when he suggests that the phenomena of human geography are related to terrestrial unity by means of which alone they can be explained. Brunhes also emphasized interrelationships between man and environment within some complex system. Thus, the notion of a system is not new to geographic thought. It is easy to identify elements of systems thinking in the work of geographers such as Ritter[11], Vidal de la Blache, Bruhnes and Sauer[12] etc. Nowadays any suggestion concerned with restructuring of geography and its need to increase its relevance with respect to current environmental problems involves, by all means, the application of some measure of systems analysis. But the concept of system has tended to remain on the periphery of geographic thought rather than at its very centre. A number of recent publications during the second half of the twentieth century have discussed the virtues of system's approach (Bertalanffy, Hall and Fagen, Badcock, Berry, Chorley and Haggett, Curry, Mobogunje, Tansley, Stoddart, Chisholm, Wilson, Rapoport, Miller, Cliff and Frey, Medawar, Gimingham, Odum, Biswas, Haggett, King and Golledge, Stearns and Montag, Vester, Clarke, Forrester, Klir and Valach, Hugget, Chapman, Bannett and Chorley, Jeffers, Warneryd, Webber Anuchin, Warntz, Sukachev, Lindeman, Zeeman, Zipf, Barrows, Patten, and others) and efforts have also been made to define it as a set of objects together with relationships between those objects and their attributes.[13] Thus, a system is an object[14] of study which is made up of a number (usually large) of interrelated components. Geographers borrowed the plant ecologists' concept of ecosystem which was explained through models by Gimingham, Odum, Ward, Fitz-patrick, Wilson, and others.[15] Tansley and Stoddart developed the ecosystem concept and claimed that it is monistic, structured and also that it functions and is a type of general system. To take a geographical example, the system involves not only the framework of the communication net, but also the goods and people flowing through it. Once the framework has been defined, it may be possible to quantify the interactions and interchanges between the component parts, and at least in simple ecosystems the whole complex may be quantitatively defined.[16]

While Dice[17] suggested the concept of human ecosystems at successively larger scale intervals, i.e., tribe, homestead, village, town, city, national and international levels, many geographers have implied that man in society might be viewed as forming part of a complex ecosystem. Chorley states in clear terms that geographers might temper their preoccupation with the

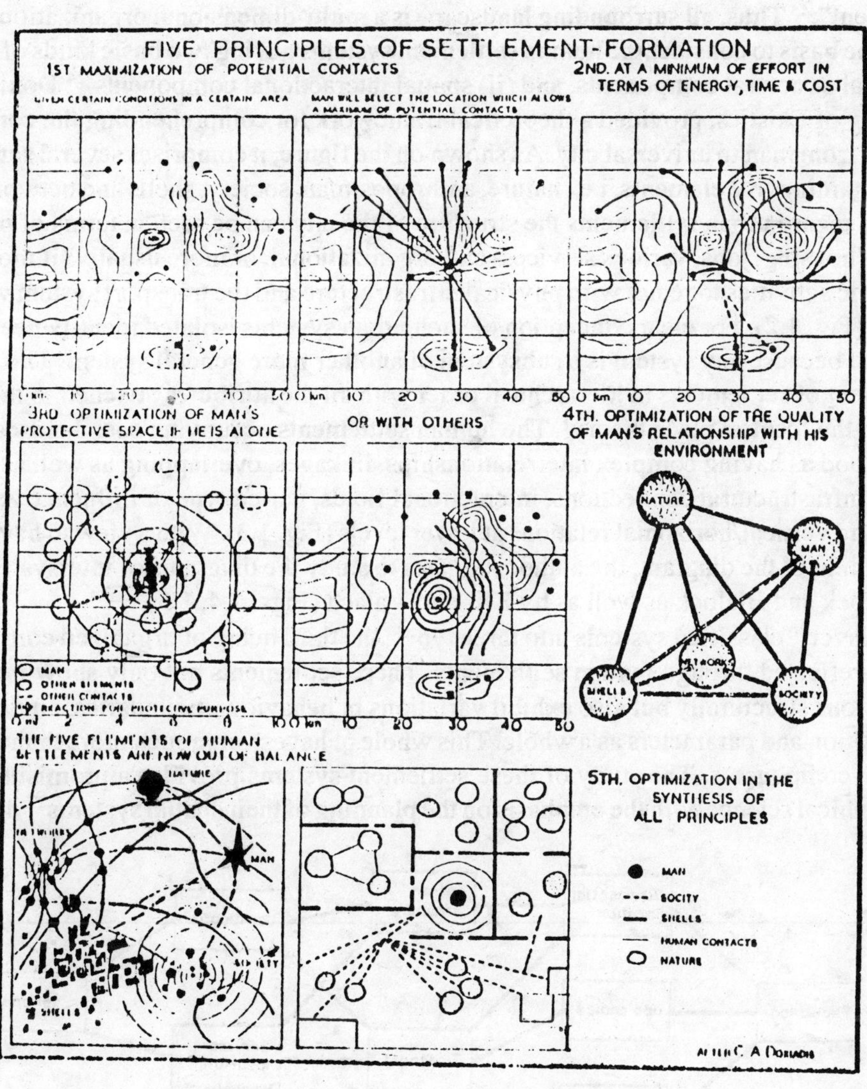

Figure 1.1

ecological type of model in favour of the application of that of the control system, so that, adapting Glacken's terminology, God's design, having been replaced by "nature's design" may be in turn supplanted, by "man's design"[18]. Berry rightly concludes: "Geography's integrating concepts and processes concern the world-wide ecosystem of which man is the dominant part".[19] Woldenberg and Berry[20] also used systems concepts to analyze central-place and river patterns. Curry,[21] on the other hand, attempted to analyze settlement location patterns in a system framework. Haggett's account of locational analysis[22] well demonstrates the use of systems approach to study spatial organizations which are actually mega-systems of "man, society and environment".[23] Thus, all surrounding landscape is a multi-dimensional organization system. This forms the basis to consider the human settlement systems having two basic kinds of components: (i) spatial structural components, and (ii) spatial interactional components.[24] Doxiadis, through the study of Ekistics, provided a theoretical framework for comprehending the complex system ranging from man to universal city. As shown on the figure, it comprises several sets, closed subsets containing five elements, i.e., nature, anthropos/man, society, shells and networks (Figs. 1.1, 1.6). As regard urban settlements the structure of the city can be seen in terms of population activities (housing, jobs, various services) and organizational, or more usually (if more narrowly), economic activities together with physical infrastructure and the transport system which support these[25] (Fig. 1.2). For clear conception of such urban systems isolated identity needs not be emphasized because any system is a subsystem of another more general system. This pinpoints arrangement of settlements in hierarchical order with all the attributes attached to them explained through the 'central place theory'. The human settlements occupying each landscape should be understood as having complex interrelationships, linkages, overlapping as well as clearly interwoven infrastructural connections, interactional fields, varied type of influence zones at higher levels and vertical/horizontal relations at lower levels (Fig. 1.3). With a view to having better understanding of the diagram, the author suggests to study the diagrams of intersystem interaction by Blalock and Blalock as well as by Klir and Valach (Figs. 1.4, 1.5).

Weaver[26] classified systems into three types; the third being of organized complexity which is well-reflected through human settlements. These settlements not only show multi-relational dimensions structurally but also exhibit variations in behaviour, boundaries, environment, state or condition and parameters as a whole. This whole behaves very much more than the sum of the parts or components. The study of these settlement systems provides a promising direction of geographical science with the emphasis on the planning of their spatial systems[27] dealt within the

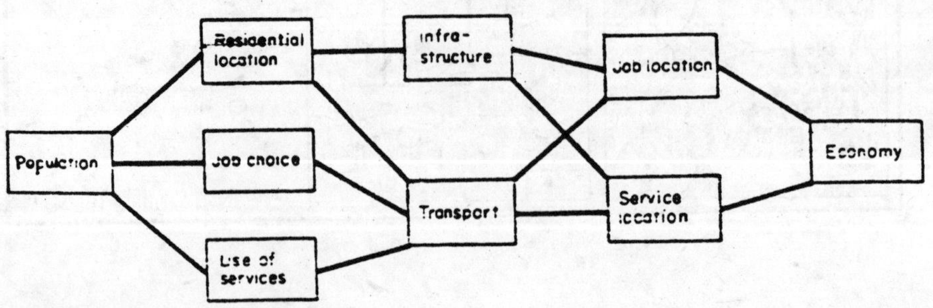

Figure 1.2. The Main Components of an Urban System (Wilson 1972b)

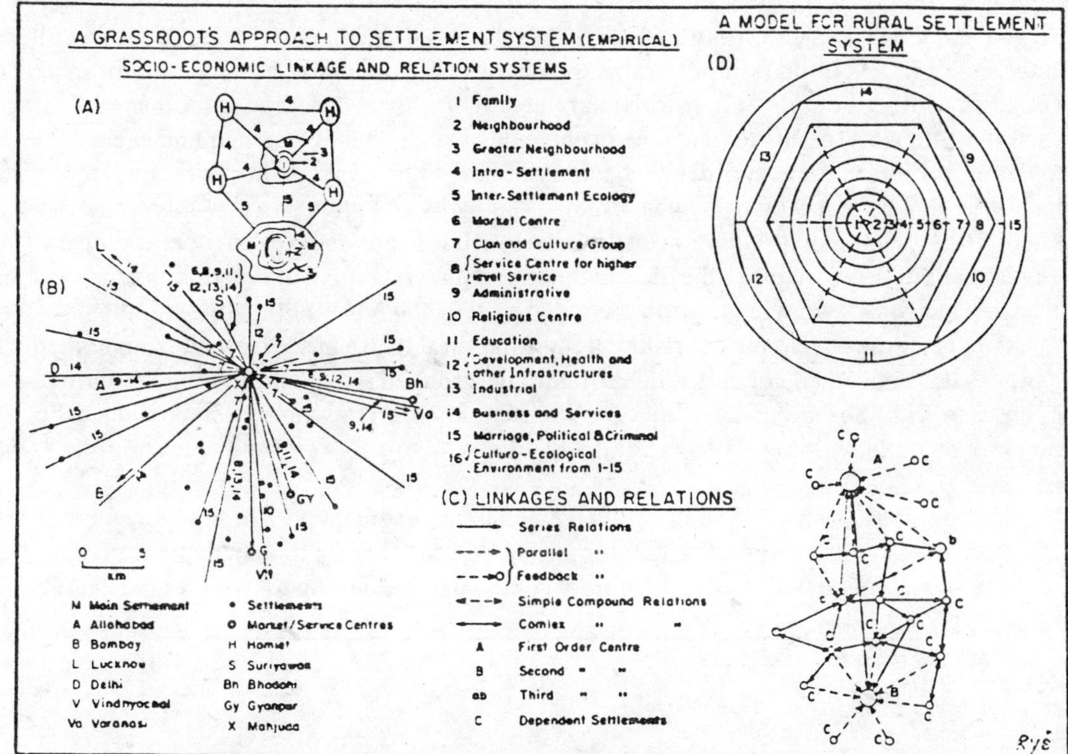

Figure 1.3

sequel. But, we should be foolish to think that we require merely to wave the magic wand of systems analysis over the subject matter of geography for all to be revealed.[28]

The discussion reveals that the separation of studies of rural settlements from urban studies should not be treated as barriers between the researchers in two fields. Rural-urban dichotomy forms only an aspect of continuum within a system. Even, distribution of settlements as service centres cannot be analyzed as a purely rural phenomenon in isolation. The spacing and function of both rural as well as urban settlements are interlinked and interdependent.

Definition, Scope and Approaches

During his adaptation with the environment, man came in close contact to various environmental features and this reaction/adaptation brought forth changes in his physical landscape. These changes are identified as cultural landscape and present man's relation to man upon earth. The author agrees with the American philosopher who philosophizes over geography, that "more than an inventory of man and things, geography at heart is a concern to depict man's relation to man upon earth, as though earth were his home".[29] In a geographer's words: "It is a way of understanding man in a matrix of human and physical relationships and interrelationships".[30] These interrelationships are best expressed through the settlements which are concrete expressions of human occupance of the earth's surface. If human geography, which depicts the interrelationships, may be defined as the study of "who gets what, where, and how",[31] the settlement geography is concerned with "who build/inhabit settlements, where and how". In the present context, 'who' means the man, a part of the terrestrial space, along with the way he has historically emerged and the processes through which he has observed the diverse waves of races, cultures and technologies.[32] 'Build' simply means the act of construction by putting parts or materials together as well as the style of construction related to the house/building and other facilities attached to it. 'Inhabit' points towards the occupance of such houses. 'Settlement' means the settlement units representing an organized colony of human beings together with the buildings in which they live or that they otherwise use and the paths and streets over which they travel.[33] 'Where' focuses immediate attention on the most sensible subdivision of territory for the purpose of investigation. 'How' requires the identification and understanding of the structure, process and causal mechanisms at work leading to a particular pattern of who build/inhabit settlements where. Thus, the discipline covers the entire hierarchy from rural to urban settlement, from nomadic to sedentary. It is concerned not only with the buildings grouped around the permanent farm dwelling, but also with the temporary camp of the hunter or herder, or with settlement clusters or agglomerations, running the scale from hamlet to village, to town, to city and to metropolis[34] (Fig. 1.6).

The geographical study of rural settlements/habitats begins with Ritter's work in the early nineteenth century. It is only since the turn of the present century that settlement geographers have been preoccupied with the study of rural settlements belonging to two groups, namely: (1)

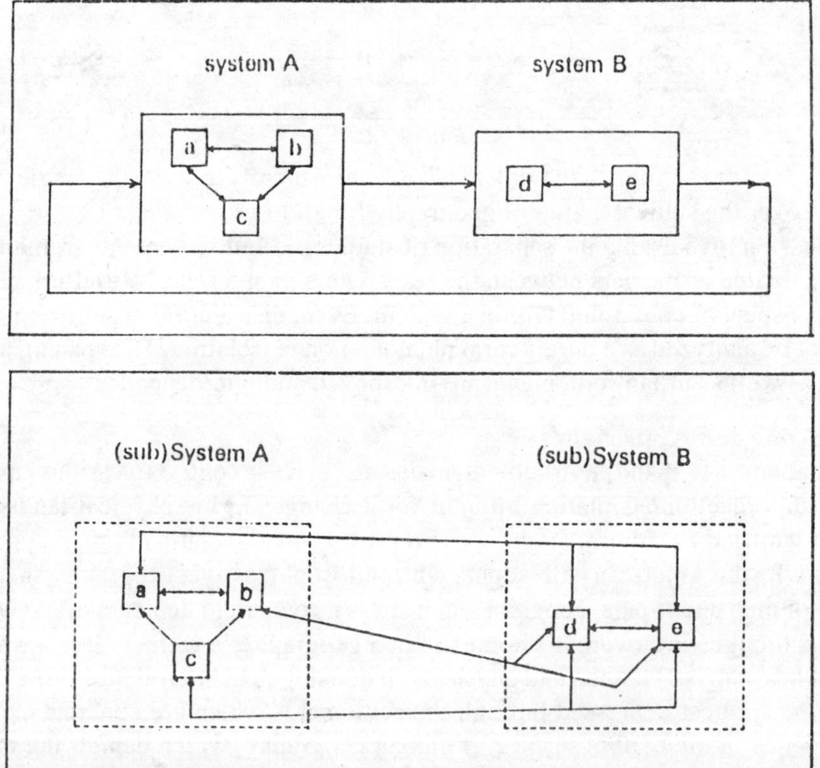

Figure 1.4: Two Different Views of Inter-system Interaction. The upper shows system A and system B interacting as units, with smaller system interactions going on within each system. The lower diagram shows systems A and B interacting at lower levels (*after Blalock and Blalock*, 1959).

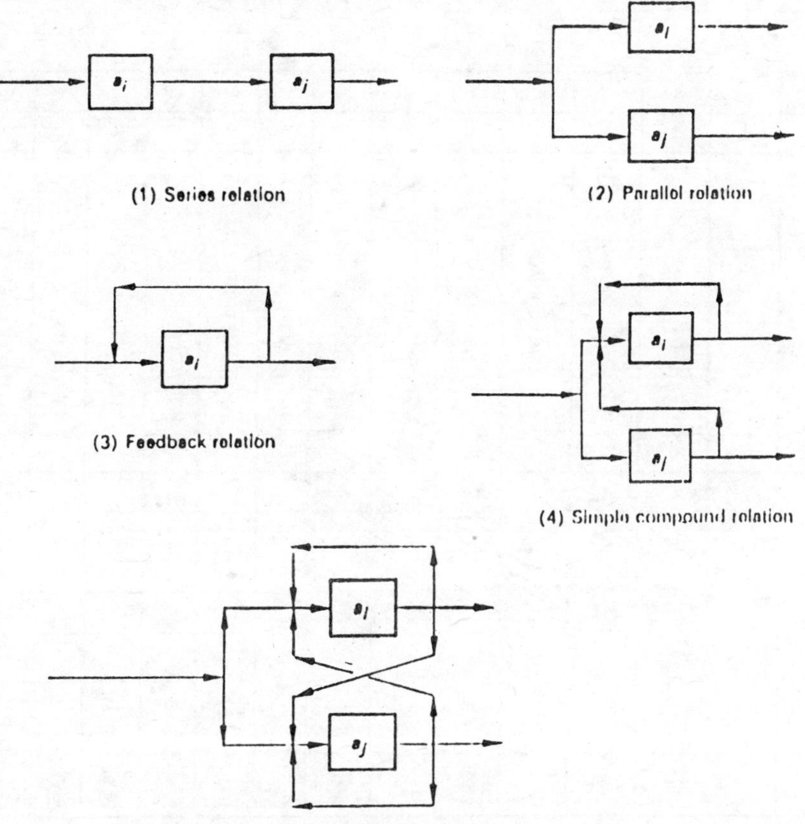

Figure 1.5: Diagrams to show the kinds of relation that may exist between the elements within system (*after Klir and Valach*, 1967).

concerned with siedlungs geographic and De L' habitat rural, and (2) that describes the process of settling and its geographical manifestations. During the sixties, Stone suggested that "geography of rural settlements be defined as the description and analysis of the distribution of buildings by which people attach themselves to the land for purpose of primary production". But he excluded some significant constituents like building materials, architectural styles, landuse and fence types. A year after, his ideas were challenged by Jordan who wrote on the 'Nature of Settlement Geography' and defined settlement geography as the "study of the form of the cultural landscape involving its orderly description and attempted explanation". Later on he emphasized three aspects of the cultural landscape: (1) the settlement patterns or distribution of farmsteads; (2) the field patterns, or the forms resulting from division of land for productive use, and (3) house and farmstead types including the building materials and folk architecture. As referred to above, the German word siedlung does indicate the process of human occupance as well as its arrangement and groupings. Obviously the main theme is to study the settlement ensembles and their spatial patterns for analyzing the sequence of change in the landscape. More explicitly, the size, form and functions of settlements and their origin are the essentials of the subject matter; their regional variations also are no less significant. Chatterjee's view is that the settlement geography deals with the size, form and function of settlements built up by man and traces their historic growth.

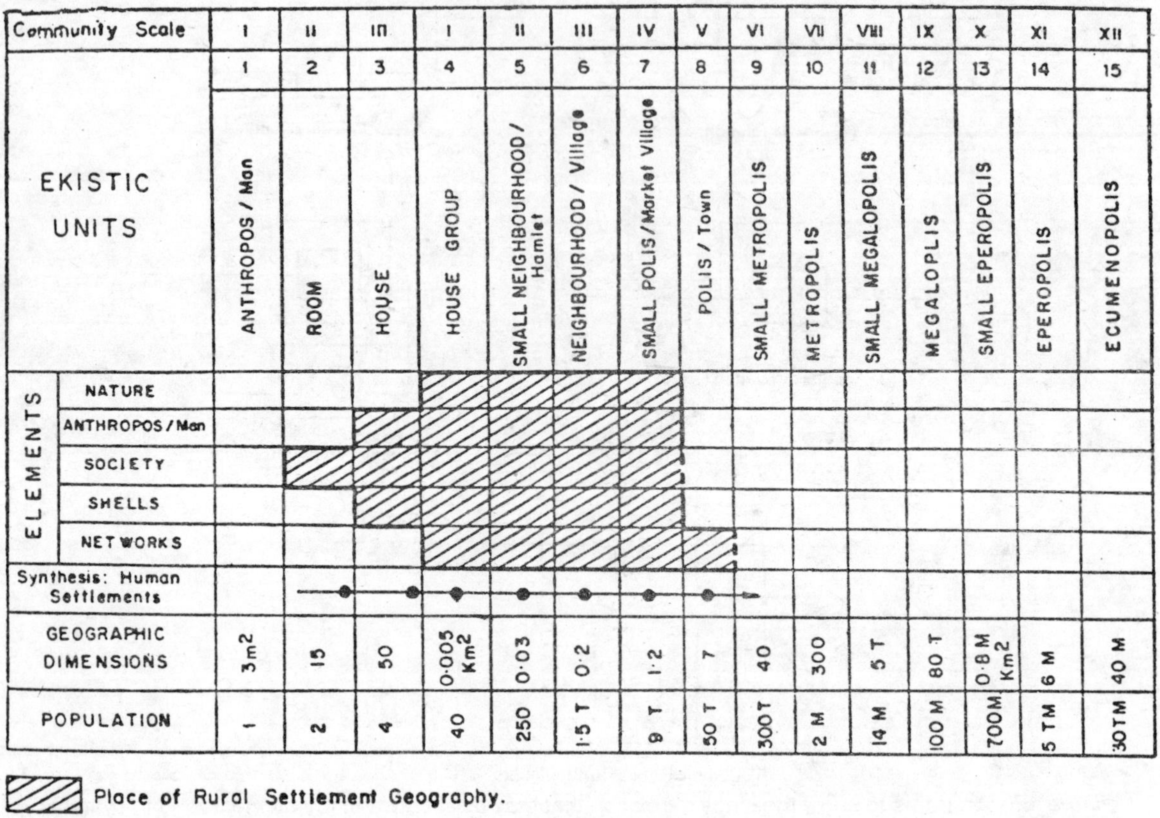

Community Scale	I	II	III	I	II	III	IV	V	VI	VII	VIII	IX	X	XI	XII
	1	2	3	4	5	6	7	8	9	10	11	12	13	14	15
EKISTIC UNITS	ANTHROPOS / Man	ROOM	HOUSE	HOUSE GROUP	SMALL NEIGHBOURHOOD / Hamlet	NEIGHBOURHOOD / Village	SMALL POLIS / Market Village	POLIS / Town	SMALL METROPOLIS	METROPOLIS	SMALL MEGALOPOLIS	MEGALOPLIS	SMALL EPEROPOLIS	EPEROPOLIS	ECUMENOPOLIS
ELEMENTS: NATURE															
ELEMENTS: ANTHROPOS / Man															
ELEMENTS: SOCIETY															
ELEMENTS: SHELLS															
ELEMENTS: NETWORKS															
Synthesis: Human Settlements															
GEOGRAPHIC DIMENSIONS	3m²	15	50	0·005 Km²	0·03	0·2	1·2	7	40	300	5 T	80 T	0·8 M Km²	6 M	40 M
POPULATION	1	2	4	40	250	1·5 T	9 T	50 T	300 T	2 M	14 M	100 M	700 M	5 TM	30 TM

Place of Rural Settlement Geography.

Figure 1.6

Various significant aspects of the study have also been emphasized by him, viz., rural houses and architectural styles; relationship between rural settlements on the one hand, and roads, farms, and field patterns on the other; type of rural settlements and their origins; rural settlements as service centres; pioneer settlements; and morphological and regional character of rural settlements. These definitions add new vista to the rural settlement geography and it is clear that the core concern of rural settlement geography is space and sequent occupance. A definition incorporating both the themes in best possible way is that "rural settlement geography is concerned with the orderly description and interpretation of processes, patterning, functions and the spatial organization of human occupance within rural environment over the earth surface".

A few more definitions present further explanation to the topic. Richthofen defined settlement as the natural manner in which man established himself on the earth's surface.[35] In Mullerwille's opinion, "a settlement might be any human overnight area whether it be that of unspecialized hunter and gatherer whose family is huddled around a camp fire and perhaps sleeps in a rock niche or under a lean-to, or the longer-used dwelling spot of a nomadic herdsman and his family and friends, or the permanent house of any city dweller".[36]

Still, as Stone indicates, there is really little agreement among geographers worldwide as to what the geography of settlement is (excepting that it includes urban geography).

Scope and Subject Matter

Settlement geography, being an offshoot of social geography[37] or a recent most sprout from the venerable trunk of human geography,[38] was mainly concerned with urban settlements before the turn of the twentieth century. The latter may be described as the hallmarks of contemporary civilization.[39] But, since about two-thirds of the world population and about 98 per cent of the total settlements occupy rural areas, many historians, sociologists and geographers have studied rural settlements as well as the problems attached with environmental aspects in rural areas. Even urbanized world still possesses varied forms of rural settlements. Thus, a comprehensive study of settlements requires explanation of site and situation, building materials, forms (including architectural style), functions, types and patterns, and characteristics. Of these, site and situation and materials need full interpretation of physical environmental aspects and cultural linkages while morphology requires in-depth study of sequent occupance involving historical background of the unit/territory of occupance as well as the man—the occupant. As the past is the key to the present and we walk to a certain degree in every village among the ruins of antiquity,[40] archaeological analysis helps a lot. Regional variations and spatial patterns present significant subject matter also for analyzing the sequence of change. The place name study serves remarkably in reconstructing the sequent occupance.

The functional analysis not only helps in visualizing socio-economic and organizational structure of rural settlements but also areal arrangements of towns as well as their distinctive zones and spheres of influence; hence, study of urban hierarchy or ranking, spacing and morphology. Thus, urban settlements are studied in two ways: (i) as an organic whole within distinctive build and structure evolved through various ecological processes, and (ii) as a regional focus and an amalgam of interconnected but disparate areas indicating the varied relationships with the region it serves. The settlement geographer is concerned with both intra-urban and inter-urban transportation[41] and with city as a functional as well as physical entity.

The range of subject matter varies, therefore, from a herder's hut in a pioneer fringe to a skyscraper in New York. Obviously, the city geography is at one end of the scale of settlement, pioneering at the other.[42]

Recently, the remarkable growth of million cities and polynuclear conurbations and irrational occupance of fields and thickets in countryside have attracted modern settlement geographers towards environmental impacts running the scale of extinction/replacement of flora and fauna. Large cities are to be studied in terms of the major aspects, viz., physico-geographic aspects, such as deformation of urban ground, state of underground water, biogeographic or ecological geographic aspects, i.e., their role as intermediaries in inter-regional interactions[43] and of the increasingly complex character. Thus, settlement geographer is also concerned with the problem of guiding and directing urban growth and development into such forms and patterns as will promote the attainment of a better urban way of life[44]. The themes proposed for international symposium held at Varanasi in 1971 outlined below form comprehensive subject matter of and approaches to the study of settlement geography in general and rural settlement geography in particular: [45]

(a) Approaches to Rural Settlement Geography:

    (i) Relation to rural settlement geography;

(ii) Field survey and first-hand observation and data collection;
(iii) Census records and maps and other historical records;
(iv) Data analysis and mapping, development of models, paradigms, hypotheses, etc.; and
(v) Other source materials, such as place names.

(b) Histogenesis of Rural Settlements and Settlement Patterns:
(i) Historic culture areas (various culture groups, mapping of their occupance units);
(ii) Systems of land division, proprietary grant systems and water rights, etc. and their relation to settlement growth patterns;
(iii) Pioneer settlement areas and their problems; and
(iv) Sequence of occupance: neolithic, bronze, iron, ages; ancient, medieval and modern periods.

(c) Basic Regional Types and Patterns of Rural Settlements:
(i) Relation of settlement types and patterns to various physical, ethnic and social factors; and
(ii) Relation to systems of agriculture water and soil management and land tenure, theories of landuse intensity, zoning, labour and input-output costs, etc., marketing of products, and other locational-spatial theories.

(d) Morphogeneisis of Rural Settlements:
Various geomorphological form patterns and their relation to various factors.

(e) Functional Pattern of Rural Settlements:
(i) Analysis of functional types of rural settlements-methodology, development etc.;
(ii) Functional analysis of service villages and service and trading centres, hierarchy of such centres in relation to general central pace theory; and
(iii) Rural seasonal migration, community patterns, etc.

(f) Rural Buildings and House Types:
(i) Analysis of rural house types and other functional buildings, their size, functions, architectural styles, building materials etc.;
(ii) Regionalization of house and building types; and
(iii) Planning of rural houses and buildings.

(g) Village Studies.

(h) Planning and Rationalization of Rural Settlements and Settlement Patterns:
(i) Planning in relation to locational efficiency of landuse, marketing, living conditions etc.;
(ii) Planning in relation to current economic well-being and social dynamics and demands of modernization;
(iii) Planning service villages and rural service centres as agents of rural change; and
(iv) Planning the infrastructural development for rural uplift.

Approaches

The two popular methods of approaches in geography as explained by Hartshorne are: (i) systematic, topical, and (ii) regional. Both types of settlements, rural-urban, have been studied in various proportions through these approaches. Rural settlements have mostly been studied systematically at micro-level—village and hamlets—along with their occupance, setting, morphology, size shape and functions etc. Such systematic empirical studies abound in all countries where geography could reach the graduation level in institutions. The second approach to study settlements of regions as a whole comprising their histogenesis, morphogenesis, spread, distribution, patterns and types, characteristics and comparative distinctiveness and regional variations also do abound in old German studies as well as in newer geographic world in terms of historical period of their investigation and development of geography. Comparative studies on regional basis did emerge during the last two decades of 60's and 70's, the study of Japanese and north Indian settlements being an example. But this type of dichotomy in approach seems to be natural, spontaneous but never deliberate. Recently, theoretical approach has been emphasized through the studies of Bunge, Haggett and so many others including those influenced by the charismatic charm of quantitative revolution.

Whatever might have been the aims—systematic, regional or theoretical—settlement geographers attempted invariably to explain the form, function and genesis inductively and deductively, sometimes applying only empirical qualitative approach while at others deductive, theoretical and quantitative ones separately as well as conjointly. Among inductive studies, Singh's pioneer work of the Middle Ganga Valley is fairly obvious. The deductive studies comprise all the works analyzed through nearest neighbour/randomness techniques and techniques applied for spacing, shape analysis and nesting, hierarchy and functionality involving various indices. We shall come to them in separate chapters. Dickinson expresses the theme of settlement geography in terms of "structure, process and stage" concept of Davis applied in geomorphology. The built up arrangement represents structure, the genre de vie of the people denotes the process and various phases of development denote the stage.[46] The explanation of the contents of the definition as well as subject matter will automatically lead to a most genuine approach concerned with the "form, function and genesis" parallel to that of "structure, process and stage".[47] With a view to having comprehensive understanding of the settlements, various strategies, frameworks and approaches have been provided by geographers since the days of Ritter. Doxiades, however, presented the most significant theoretical framework, though not applicable universally, to study the complex settlement system. He devised the Ekistic Logarithmic Scale (ELS) as referred to earlier through Figure 1.6. The ELS, having two dimensions—geographic/terrestrial and numerical concerned with population number—and fifteen Ekistic units starting from man to ecumenopolis with five elements each provides convincing framework for a better approach to settlement studies. His elements conjointly form the optimization of the quality of man's relationship with the environment. Within this framework, one can apply three basic approaches supplemented by better developed quantitative techniques: (i) genetic, (ii) spatial, and (iii) ecological.

Genetic Approach

Meitzen (1895), on the basis of historical processes, attempted to demonstrate the presence of three ethnically based zones of settlements in Europe: (i) the grouped settlements along with common field systems almost associated with Germanic conquest, (ii) isolated farmsteads associated mostly with the celts, and (iii) round and the street village form associated with the slavs. This idea of ethnic-based study was criticized variously. In the 20th International Geographical Congress Symposium (London, 1964), it was emphasized that the scientific study of settlements must be founded on an appreciation of the nature and limitation of historical perspective, whether archaeological or documentary. As the core concern of settlement geography is the spatial arrangement and sequent occupance, well denoted through the German term 'Siedlungs Geographie', the histogenetic approach is most appropriate for studying (i) the degree of continuity of territorial organization, and (ii) problems of interaction between man and environment. At micro-level, i.e., occupance unit being a homestead, hamlet or a petrol pump or a tea-stall on a crossing, during initial stage and also while grown-up into a full-fledged settlement, this approach helps in reaching the comprehensive understanding of individual characteristics in relation to the surrounding subsystem. This also includes three basic methods followed by various geographers:

(i) Retrogressive approach advocated by Bloch focuses upon the past on the basis of the evidences gathered from the recent past.[48]

(ii) Retrospective approach advocated by Roger Dion[49] focuses upon the present, the past conditions regarding settlements being considered for better understanding of the existing state.

(iii) Prospective approach focuses upon the future, past and present cultural landscape being regarded as relict features projecting towards adjustment with future needs[50].

The three approaches are not only complementary to each other but also can be fruitfully applied to understand the spatio-temporal dimension of settlements as well as their prospective planning in the environment concerned.

Place name studies, *inter alia,* are significant approach for reconstruction of cultural landscape through sequent occupance. They serve as 'fossils' of human geography[51] and their examination and mapping aid in establishing the date and the sequence of settlements.[52] Various efforts have been made by geographers to analyze settlements on the basis of suffix and prefix of place names. To cite a few may suffice to provide better reference to readers. Kemble (1849) discovered the significance of the place names ending in 'ing' and 'ingham' which was elaborated by Ekwall (1923). Alice[53], Charles[54], Wooldridge[55], Dickinson[56], Maxwell[57], Mitchell[58], Zelinsky[59], McCamphall[60], Kameron,[61] Singh[62], Jones[63], Padhye[64], and others attempted various aspects of settlements on the basis of place names in West and East.

Diffusion of settlements and the existence of early Anglo-Saxon village sites is partially revealed to us today by the frequency with which place names ending in 'ing' (people), 'ham' (farmstead) and 'ton' (village) occur in lowland England[65]. C.A. Elliot claimed that every town in Oudh and eastern part of the old northwestern provinces whose name does not end in 'pur', 'abad', 'mau' owes its origin and name to the 'bhars'[66].

Study of settlements on the basis of diffusion theory is also a significant approach followed by various geographers. This approach, however, touches the borderline of spatial and ecological approaches dealt with in the sequel. Geographers interested in settlement growth theory attempted to apply various models, popular elsewhere, to diffusion of settlements in West and East. Bylund produced four theoretical models to show diffusion[67]. On the basis of deterministic model, he sought the way in which 'waves' of settlements moved in the central Lapland area of Sweden. On the basis of stochastic processes and random numbers, Morrill[68] developed his probabilistic models. Chisholm found four factors: (i) socio-economic, (ii) defence, (iii) elimination of disease, and (iv) technical improvements in water supply, responsible for diffusion of settlements[69]. The study of social and cultural history and spatial diffusion processes also helps in many ways in explaining the dynamics of evolution of settlements. Kollmorgen discussed the evolution of cultural islands in the settlement pattern of the southern states of the United States. He also emphasized the role of these settlements in terms of cultural innovators and pace-setters[70]. Nelson, however, dealt with evolution of distinctive patterns of colonization by the Mormons and the role of social forces like leadership, ideology, conflict and cooperation[71]. Powell analyzed the pattern of moving and settling as well as the occasional process of fission or hiving off[72]. According to him, the settlement network, types, structures and functions are very much affected by the utopian social and political thinking and its diffusion over space[73]. He also explained the perspective of the evolution of compact settlements of the Mormons in contrast with the normal pattern of isolated farmsteads on the frontier lands of North America and emphasized the role of religious beliefs[74]. Bjorklund emphasized the role of religio-cultural decisions which affect the settlement process[75]. Meining investigated the Mormon influence on settlements and their territory having three zones in descending order of importance, i.e., core, domain and sphere[76]. Several studies have been made at the well developed School of Settlement Geography (Department of Geography, Banaras Hindu University, Varanasi). While R.L. Singh took the initiative many more joined the crusade. To name a few would suffice the purpose at present[77]

Within the framework of genetic approach, many writers tried to study the origin and spread of land division system and their effect on settlements. The grid pattern or rectangular land allotment system, popular in ancient China, was followed in modified form in Japan named as *Jori* system. Its numbering was based upon coordinates of *Jo* and *Ri*. The basic unit of allotment called *Ri* denotes an area of 640 square meters. The allotment system had correct numbering sequence by the coordinates numbered from north to south, i.e., one *Jo*, two *Jo* up to 37 *Jo*. Yonekura and his colleagues paid special attention to such studies[78]. The same approach is applicable to the studies on gridiron pattern of American townships, *bigha* system of India and Roman jugerium system as well as French villes-neuves[79]. Nitz[80] correlated the socio-historical factors and field patterns of northern India and Germany very convincingly.

Analysis of abandoned settlements, a new method of approach, provides conclusive evidences about the past settlements and human activities. Developed out of archaeology, it consists of three parts: (i) chemical analysis of soil phosphorus indicating human occupance, (ii) microseparation examining soil and settlement components primarily through mechanical means, and (iii) polynology (pollen analysis). Eidt presented interesting findings in his studies in the United States.[81]

Spatial Approach

Spatial organization approach is a form of system approach which helps in comprehending the settlements as a whole. A good detail has already been presented in the first section. Considering this method of approach, spatial organization may be analyzed through different concepts, among which very pertinent in rural settlement geography are: (i) type, pattern and classification; (ii) functional integration and hierarchy; (iii) local identity (e.g., village structure); and (iv) planning and rationalization[82]. In wide terms, spatial organization studies include the varied literature produced on the basis of the central place theory denoting hierarchy and rank size in relation to any environmental space. We shall come with details on this in Chapter 9. Demangeon[83] actually developed the concept of spatial organisation in context to morphological structure. He presented the classification of French grouped settlements into different types according to shape. Also, he dealt with the principal distributional patterns of rural houses. His works paved the way for geographers to produce regional classification of rural settlement types. Schaefer[84] initiated the modern orientation following the works of German geographers. Modern geographers are following him in the study of settlements through the analysis of patterns and process as they express the spatial organisations in environmental space. Through this approach the interrelationship of man, nature and society is better expressed in any cultural landscape. A number of studies on morphology, size and shape of settlements do speak some sort of organisation of space ranging from a room, hamlet, village, town to the far off settled megalopolis.

Ecological Approach

The ecological-cultural approach finds its strength through the study of plant ecologists. Plant ecology theories are being applied to explain the process of change in human behaviour and settlements over time. A fundamental work was produced by Radha Kamal Mukerjee regarding adaptation of human society and ecology in his *Man and His Habitations: A Study in Social Ecology* (Longmans Green & Co., London, 1940). The settling process as described by Hudson[85] includes three phases—colonization, spread, and competition—similar to plant communities in space. He concluded that these processes follow a cyclic way temporally. Since much of the human behaviour is of sub-optimal nature[86], people in various habitats are often satisfied with less than the ideal. Such habitats have been studied by many geographers including Kayastha[87] and Singh[88]. How people adapt their available ecological habitat finds explanation in the settlements and life patterns of Gaddis and Bhils. New studies are coming up regarding impact of dam sites, port sites, resorts and change in ecology in newly settled areas. Such studies at micro-level would help in many way and in proper geographization of ecological forecasts[89].

A few writers have described a fourth approach to study the settlements, i.e., statistical or quantitative one which should be better regarded as tool or technique applied anywhere according to its applicability and suitability. Nearest neighbour analysis has been widely used for studying the concentration and dispersion of settlements. Likewise rank size rule deals with the spatial arrangement of centres in hierarchical order starting from a primate city up to a hamlet. Birch[90], Medvedkov[91], Stone[92], Dacey[93], Hudson[94], Semple and Gollege[95], and Mukerji[96] are to be named among others. Dispersion of rural settlements has mainly been studied by Rana P.B. Singh and others on the basis of nearest neighbour analysis though the technique is not well-suited because of the variation of RN value in relation to area.

The methods of functional hierarchy and rank size rule have widely been applied by geographers. Zipf and Awerbach sought the relation between the rank of a settlement and its size and another of different level. Thomas (1961) and Gibbs investigated the problems regarding some towns and showed a positive association between the logarithms of distance and population size. King (1961), however, in his study of 162 towns and non-central places discovered that spacing of the latter was less predictable. Similar studies have been made by Stafford[97], Berry and Garrison (1958) and by Gunwardena in Sri Lanka. The problem of continuous variation, found between village and hamlet functions has been discarded by Haggett and Gunwardena[98]. Many geographers had applied the techniques based on the law of 'retail gravitation' developed by Reilly and the 'elementary packing theory' propounded by Walter Christaller (1933) and later modified by Losch (1954) and others. Thus, statistical and mathematical techniques have invariably been applied, at least to some extent, in all approaches by a geographer in true sense of the term, specially after the quantitative revolution.

Geography, being an integrating science, a settlement geographer must have understanding of being a historian, cartographer, artist, sociologist, mathematician and finally an environmentalist. The essence of his work is data collection, based on remote sensing, field study, mapping, interpretation, explanation of facts by using qualitative methods as well as quantitative techniques.

Classification

Rural-Urban Dichotomy

The rural and urban are relative terms having varied meanings in relation to the type of population and mode of life of people of a settlement. Censuses of various countries use these terms according to their own convenience and density patterns. A combination of criteria distinguish rural from urban, be it hamlet, village, town or city. Ambiguity remains in searching out the demarcation line breaking the rural-urban continuum, particularly in developing countries. In short, urban settlements are nodal in character having centres of secondary/tertiary activities and production. Moreover, they perform functions of a political, educational, social and religious character. Rural settlements, on the other hand, are chiefly concerned with primary production, be it agriculture, fishery, mining, forestry etc.

Classifications of types of dwellings and village settlements are found in *Mansar Shilp Shastra*[99] but not on the basis of any methodological study. Meitzen's classification of Haufendorfer was different from the smaller forms known as Drubbel. Such beginnings are found in the works of O. Schluter, K. Mortensen on the one hand and that of F. Steinbach, W. Muller-Wille and A. Krenzlin on the other. As early as during 1920-1940, Demangeon[100] classified French grouped rural settlements into different types according to shape. Many others tried to produce regional classifications on the basis of size, degree of compactness, shape and regularity of settlements. With the development of settlement geography, geographers also developed classification using both the morphological and functional characteristics of settlements.

Richthofen[101], *inter alia*, classified settlements into three main types as shown in the following table:

Table 1 (I)

Level	*Temperament (Bodenvage)*	*Permanent (Bodenstig)*
Low	Unspecialized Hunters and Specialized Hunters, Reindeer Nomads	Specialized Fishermen Simple Hack Farmers, Complex Hack Farmers
Middle	Transport Nomads	
High	Other Nomads	Horticulturists, Irrigation Farmers, Farmers who use Fertilizers

But he failed to point out as to where his impermanent category merges with the permanent one. Muller-Wille[102] classified the settlements according to degree of permanence as follows:

1. Ephermeral	1-7 days in a place
2. Temporary	8-30 days in a place
a. Episodic	8-15 days in a place
b. Periodic	16-30 days in a place
3. Seasonal	Several months in a place
4. Semi-permanent	Several years in a place
5. Permanent	Several generations in a place

His system of classification is more significant for the first four categories concerned with rural settlements but the fifth one being complex needs further explanation. Uhlig and Lienau,[103] in their three published volumes, have emphasized rural settlement classification as well as rural and urban relationships. They have tried to define the differences and areas of overlap between these two categories. Size[104] of settlement has been included on a sliding scale for defining terms, such as hamlet, village and town.

Thus, settlements are classified on criteria bases also as explained in the sequel. One may classify the rural settlements on the basis of mean population, mean distance, mean coefficient of dispersion and coefficient of variation[105] as given below in Table 1(ii).

Table 1(II)

Classification of Rural Settlements in Some Selected Tahsils

Tahsil	*Mean (a) population*	*Mean distance (D)*	*Mean coefficient of dispersion (Md)*	*Coefficient of variation (Vs)*	*Formula*
Indore	> 500 (L)	R	N	Vc	LRNVc
Sawer	300-500 (M)	R	N	Vn	MRNVn
Depalpur	300-500 (M)	R	N	Vn	MRNVn
Mhow	300-500 (M)	R	N	Vc	MRNVc
Barwani	> 500 (L)	R	N	Vn	LRNVn
Begamganj	< 300 (S)	R	N	Vn	SRNVn
Ratlam	> 500 (L)	R	N	Vn	LRNVn·
Malhargarh	300-500 (M)	R	N	Vc	MRNVc

On the basis of mean population (a), all rural settlements, on tahsil basis, may be categorized into three groups: (i) small size, where (a) is less than 300 (S); (ii) medium size, where (a) is 300-500 (M); and (iii) large size, where (a) is above 500 (L).

On the basis of mean distance, one may breakdown rural settlements into three: (a) relatively widespread distribution, where village distance (D) exceeds 3 km (key letter W); (b) relatively less widespread distribution, where (D) is 2-3 km (R); and (c) relatively close distribution where (D) is less than 2 km (C).

On the basis of mean coefficient of dispersion, there are two groups: (a) rural settlements having uniform distribution, where (Md) is less than 50 per cent (U); and (b) non-uniform distribution where (Md) is more than 50 per cent (N).

On the basis of coefficient of variation, rural settlements fall into two groups: (a) with centres of population concentration where vs is more than 1.00 (Vc); and (b) without any clearly defined concentration where Vs is less than 1.00 (Vn).

Sample analysis shows that Indore and Begamganj stand distinctly in two categories: Sawer and Depalpur in one; Mhow and Malhargarh in a second one and Barwani and Ratlam in another one. We may now see a few general criteria used for classification:

1. On the basis of setting, settlements are classified into plain settlements, plateau settlements, lacustrine settlements, coastal settlements, forest, desert and usar land settlements etc.
2. On the basis of spatial distance between dwellings and hamlets, settlements stand as dispersed, compact, isolated, semicompact, hamleted etc.
3. On the basis of occupations of settlers, rural settlements are often classified in relation to

agriculture, livestock raising and vegetable growing. In India, subcaste or *jati*-based villages/hamlets abound everywhere, particularly in the north plain, i.e., Koiran, Ahiran, Kewtan, etc. In urban category, manufacturing, trade and transport settlements are conspicuously found in developed countries. Such urban centres are coming in developing world too.

4. Functions-based classification includes settlements named as agricultural villages, fisherman's village, pastoral huts, etc.
5. Size-based classification ranges from a dwelling up to a megalopolis named as farmstead/homestead/pahi[106], hamlet (*purwatola, nagla, tapro*, etc. in India), town and city in hierarchical order.
6. Shape-based classifications are mainly concerned with the pattern of dwellings having varied nomenclature. In Germany, settlement forms, classified by Dickinson[107] and modified by Christaller, are as follows:
   1. The irregular clustered villages (Haufendorf or Gewanndorf).
   2. Isolated farmsteads (Einzelhofe):
      a. Irregularly scattered, e.g., Munsterland
      b. In groups around a village nucleus (Schwarmensiedlung), e.g., Osnabruck district
      c. In linear arrangement, along routeways (Kettendorfer)
   3. Hamlets (Weiter):
      a. Founded by landlords in forest clearings
      b. Grouped around large estate farms (Gutshofe)
      c. Emerging through the continual subdivision of holdings (Erbteilung)
   4. Place villages (Platzdurfer) or rundlings.
   5. Angerdorfer (two rows of farms face a wide, long space running the whole length of the village).
   6. Street village (Strassendorfer) (two series of farmsteads face each other in two rows on a road).
   7. Linear villages (Reihendorfer) are similar to the villages of groups 2c and 6, but are fundamentally different in origin:
      a. Marsh village (Marschhufendorfer)
      b. Forest villages (Waldhufendorfer)
      c. Fehnkolonien
      d. estate settlements (Gutskolonien)
   8. Estate villages, especially mining and industrial settlements.
   9. Urban villages.
   10. Sub-urban settlements.
   11. Modern industrial settlements.

Likewise, various patterns stand on the basis of forms or shapes of settlements enumerated below and dealt with in the sequel: (1) linear, (2) circular, (3) radial, (4) triangular, (5) block, (6) arrow, (7) star, (8) fan, (9) beehive, (10) stair, (11) terrace, (12) checker board pattern etc.

Taylor,[108] in an address to the Association of Geographers, proposed a classification of towns which is applicable to all settlements; various stages are as follows: (a) In the 'sub-infantile' stage, a settlement has one street and there is no differentiation into special areas of such shops as may be present amid the residences. Such a haphazard distribution of houses and shops may be cited as characteristic of the 'sub- infantile' stage. (b) The second stage is the 'infantile' settlement where the beginnings of a street-grid are seen. (c) In the 'juvenile stage' there is a fairly clear segregation of an extensive commercial quarter towards the centre of the town, including a number of streets without residences. The beginning of maturity is shown by a differentiation of the residences. (d) The various types in this 'adolescent' stage are displaced outwards as the years move on though examples of the early houses survive in the expanding zones. (e) When later the separation of the industrial portion of the city from the residential is fairly distinct, and when the residences themselves have segregated into four zones ranging from mansions down to slums, then we have a 'mature' city. (f) A 'late maturity' reaches where some indications of modern town planning in form of new diagonal boulevardes and C are cut, through the earlier grid. (g) The last stage is 'senile' and is rarely met within prosperous young nation. In this stage, considerable areas of the city are abandoned and the remainder is stagnant.

Haggett, however, treating settlements as point-like objects presented an alternative types of settlement classification in his, *Locational Model* (p. 98) as shown below in Table 1(iii):

Table 1(iii)

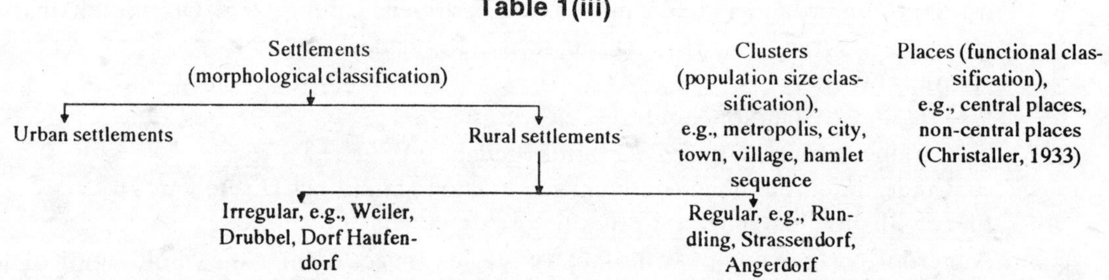

Likewise M. Aurousseau ("The Arrangement of Rural Population", *Geo. Rev.*, 10, 1920, pp. 223-240) gives taxonomy of agglomerations (grouping of rural populations) based on factors like type of pursuit, nature of water, soil, size of holdings, space economy, special physiographic conditions and topography.

B.K. Roy (*Rural Settlements in Monsoon Asia*, p. 197) gives five main and twenty-three subtypes of settlements as classified for mapping purpose:

1. Block pattern
   (a) Compact and semi-compact (other than 1b and 1c)
   (b) Rectangular
   (c) Checker-board
2. Elongated and linear pattern
   (a) Elongated settlement on levee
   (b) Elongated settlements on river fronts
   (c) Elongated settlements on ridges
   (d) Fish bone
   (e) Linear settlements along beach or canal
   (f) String pattern settlements (other than 2a, 2b, 2e)
   (g) Elongated villages along roads/tracks (one side of the road/track; both sides of the road/track)

3. Fan pattern
    (a) With convergence of lanes on a main road
    (b) With convergence of lanes towards a pond
    (c) With lanes converging on temple, mosque or church
4. Circular pattern
    (a) Hollow circular pattern
    (b) Radial settlements
5. Other patterns
    (a) I-shaped settlements
    (b) T-shaped settlements
    (c) Dispersed or sprinkled settlements
    (d) Hamleted settlements
    (e) Irregular, or amorphous settlements
    (f) Deserted settlements

These rural settlement patterns are discussed in detail in Chapter 4.

Table 1(iv)

Agglomerations

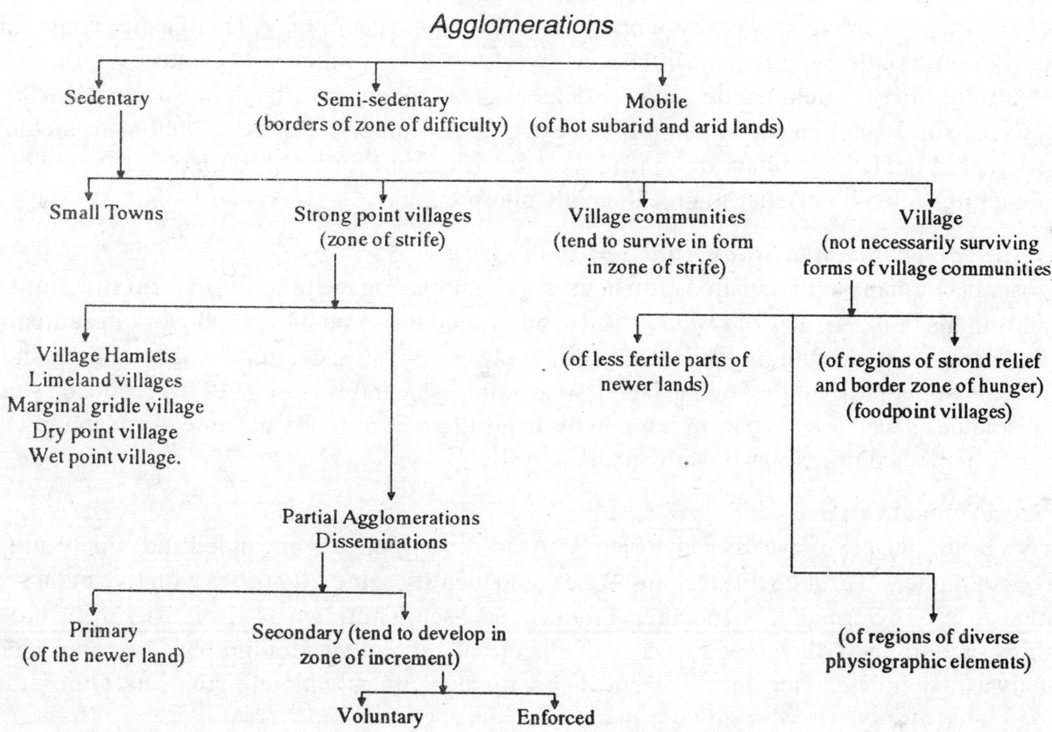

Studies in Settlement Geography

Historicity

Ancient Hindu and Buddhist literatures, like the *Puranas* and *Jatakas*, give comprehensive details about house types, *vastupadvinyas* (layout plan), village settlements and town planning as well as architectural styles but no systematic study has been made regarding the hidden aspects of settlement's study by now. In Europe, the settlement studies began with the writings of the first historians and geographers[109]. Herodotus (440-425 BC), claimed as the father of history, wrote about settled places and their dweller's customs. More cautious were the accounts of personal investigations of towns and cities in the books of Strabo (63 BC-20 AD), the first man to call himself a geographer. Romans showed interest in settlement planning and developed their well-organized quadrate system (centuriation). Caesar and Tacitus also recorded valuable settlement data concerning non-Roman systems. The Spanish and Portuguese extended Latin planning methods to the New World and information about Iberian settlement activities in America was recorded in questionnaires called *Relationes Geographicas* and in the *ordenanzas de Poblaciones of the Codigo de Indias.* With the *Voyage of Cook* came the important book by Forster in 1772 which included detailed description of settlements on some of the Pacific Islands.

According to Badcock,[110] as a specific area of enquiry, settlement geography is the product of the nineteenth century German geographers who initially were concerned with house types (including distribution, architecture and building materials) and urban centres. By 1840, settlement geography had evolved into an investigation of the relations between cities and the natural environment. During the next decade, the early emphasis on urban morphology declined and the historical approach developed to near suffocating proportions. As admitted by Stone, the developments in urban geography overwhelmed settlement geography. Though the geographical study of rural settlements began with Ritter's work in the early nineteenth century, it is only since the turn of the twentieth century that settlement geographers have been pre-occupied with the study of rural settlements belonging to two groups, namely: (1) concerned with siedlungs geographie and De L'habitat rural, and (2) that describes the process of settling and its geographical manifestations[111]. Better to give thematic interpretation.

Analytical Approach to Study Function and Form

Moser in Germany at first visited farm houses and reported on the function of farm structures and fields in his book *History of Osnabruck.* He advocated the systematic field work in settlements which helps in understanding the relationships between physical geographical conditions and the customs of people dwelling on the land. Later, Dahlmann and Hanssen (1990) produced studies on isolated as well as group farm settlements in northern Europe. By his time, form and function were established principles of settlement analysis.

Place Name Analysis

It is a technique developed by a historian W. Arnold[112] which was expanded and widely adopted by geographers. Through this technique, he could identify some fifty tribes with five main settlement groups in Germany (Alemannen, Franken, Sachsen, Thuringer and Baiern). During modern times, geographers developed a kind of historical settlement stratigraphy by name change analysis. Jager, Niemeier and Nitz have done settlement investigations on this line. Other studies completed elsewhere will find their place in Chapter 2.

Methodological Interpretation

We have discussed the approaches in previous pages. Many geographers of later part of the eighteenth century and first half of the nineteenth century contributed a lot to methodological studies through their theoretical investigations of settlement forms and structure. Ritter (1779-1859) at first stressed that man should be at the centre of geographical research activities. He also influenced his student Reclus (1830-1905), who in turn influenced. P. Vidal de la Blache (1845-1918), the famous human geographer. The latter analyzed the influence of site and situation on both dispersed and agglomerated settlements. Meitzen (1822-1970) not only investigated the development of sedentary agricultural settlements but also followed place name analysis method and explained settlement stages. His analytical work represents a model of retrogressive research. He also distinguished settlement types and emphasized the effect of cultural phenomena. Meitzen tried to classify settlements in a systematic manner and contributed much to settlement terminology.

F. von Richthofen (1833-1905) stressed the importance of fields attached with settlements. He also recognized the broad interrelationships of climate and soil conditions with settlement types. Schwartz, in her book, emphasized the relationship between dwellings and the economic area which influenced the concept of land attached to buildings by Stone in his definition of rural settlement geography.

Classification Studies

By the turn of the twentieth century, more and more efforts were made to classify the groupings of settlements into type as discussed earlier. We may revise and recollect that among two approaches dealing with classification, we are concerned firstly with the retrogressive method started by Meitzen; and secondly, the dissection of land parcels into their respective parts in order to explain development within each of these parts. The latter's proponents were Steinbach, Muller-Wille and Krenzlin.

During the current century, not only German, French and British geographers but many from the New World and Russia as well as Asian and African countries have contributed widely on varied topics. A resume would serve our purpose. Aurousseau gave a good account of site, pattern and type of settlements and human groups as early as 1920. H.W. Ahlman (1928) dealt with settlement types. Demangeon's student Le f'evre focused her attention on house in the agricultural landscape. According to her, the purpose of settlement study involves the definition, classification, and explanation of the regional distribution of house types. Dickinson (1949) dealt with types of rural settlements in the German lands. Kohn (1954) wrote on practical aspects of settlement geography in *American Geography, Inventory and Prospect* which influenced many writers in this direction. Spencer and Thomas (1954), while dealing with culture, gave a vivid account of basic settlement forms and variations according to culture they represent. Emrys Jones, in his *Human Geography*, presented examples of old and new world settlements and dealt with site, pattern and distribution. Mitchell (1960), in his *Historical Geography*, explained settlement morphology, field pattern and the land. Likewise, Money (1967), in his *Introduction to Human Geography*, depicted house types and social-cultural differences. William M. McKinney dealt with compact settlements in detail. Chisholm (1969) explained the relation between rural settlement and landuse and Everson Fitzerald presented a treatise on settlement patterns. J.C. Hudson (1969) wrote about the theory for rural settlement geography while F.S. Hudson (1970) produced a separate book entitled *A Geography of Settlements.* Bronger (1970), however, in *Erdkunde*, drew attention towards settlements and their relation with caste system.

Austrian geographers like Hassinger followed Germans and had similar concepts regarding settlements. In Scandinavia, they emphasized upon the study of settlements as geographic entities. Grano, on the basis of analysis of form and location of rural dwellings, hamlets and urban settlements, produced a classic example of Finnish settlement regions. In Czechoslovakia, the emphasis was on the applied value of rural settlements which composed the dwellings, farm premises and the attached surrounding land.

Isaiah Bowman (1925) stressed upon the science of settlement to be treated as interdisciplinary study of how to develop 'pioneer belts' of the world. Liester, in New Zealand, worked on pioneer settlements and environmental impacts. Yonekura and his students did hard field work and produced settlement studies on Japan and plains of India. Abundant literature is available on newly settled areas in U.S.S.R. A few studies have been published in African countries.

In India, the work done by historians, sociologists and anthropologists paved the way for settlement studies. The lion's share goes to R.L. Singh who produced several volumes on settlements.

Growth of Settlement Studies in India

We get references to and descriptions of various types of settlements in the past Indian literature specially those written by the great poet Kalidasa. But there was lack of systematic study on settlements till 1940's. A few historical works related to ports were produced even before 1930's. Arthur Geddes was the first writer who wrote on *A Human Geography of Bengal* in four volumes (unpublished thesis, University of Edinburgh, 1935). Likewise, M.B. Pithawalla, in his *A Geographical Analysis of the Lower Indus Basin* (Sind) (Karachi, 1936) and S.M. Ali, in his *A Geographical Study of the Ghaggar Plains* (unpublished thesis, University of London, 1939) contributed much to the settlement geography studies. A fundamental work was produced by Radhakamal Mukerjee on *Man and His Habitations: A Study in Social Ecology* (Longmans Green and Co., London. 1940). Ahmad, through his study on the *Rural Settlements Types in U.P. (United Provinces of Agra and Oudh)*, (unpublished thesis), paved the way for further studies on rural settlements. Though sociologists and anthropologists like S.C. Dube and M. Srinivas produced authentic and systematic studies on Indian village, yet pioneer work was done by Radhakamal Mukerjee in his studies of ways of dwelling in Indian communities ('Ways of Dwelling in the Communities of India' in Theodorson George, A. (Ed.), *Studies in Human Ecology*, Row Peterson and Co., New York, 1961, reprinted from Asia, Vol. 40, 1940, pp. 287-290, 375-378, 390-401, 439-442).

As referred to earlier, the lion's share for the growth of rural settlement geography, particularly, goes to R.L. Singh who produced *inter alia*, famous articles on "Evolution of Settlements in the Middle Ganga Valley" (N.G.J.I., Vol. I, Part II, 1955) and "Typical Rural Dwellings in the Inland of Banaras, India" (N.G.J.I., Vol. III, Part. II, 1957). A.N. Bhattacharya, through his *Rural Habitations in the Upper Ganga Plain and Son Valley* (unpublished thesis, Agra University, 1956), opened new horizon for comparative study. C.D. Despande applied analytical approach in his "Market Villages and Periodic Towns of Bombay" (I.G.I., Vol. 16, pp. 327-339). A.T.A. Learmonth also brought out a unique study of the villages of southern India. K.H. Buschmann, however, made a detailed study of patterns and house types in different regions of India.

S.P. Chatterjee gives a good account of studies on rural settlements in his series on progress of geography named as *Fifty Years of Science in Geography* (1963 and 1968). K.M. Subrahamanyam, in 1938, brought out salient features of four main house types in southern India. After a long gap in 1950, S. Sinha took village studies and wrote on "Bhabharia in Chotanagpur" and R. Lahiri worked on 'Ajay Valley'. M.S. Vishwanath studied settlements in Thanjavur (Tamilnadu) in 1956 while A.B. Mukherjee (1956-57) worked on Moradabad and Bijnor districts. Spatially different areas were taken for study by several geographers. Settlement patterns in the Himalayan tarai region were studied by M. Anas (1954) and L.R. Singh (1962). J. Yonekura (1961) made a comparative study of the rectangular village pattern in South India and in Japan. S.D. Kaushik (1959) worked on Dehradun district, and S.D. Mishra (1962) worked on Mathura district. B. Mukherjee worked on settlements in the Hooghly region while A.N. Bhattacharya and L.N. Verma (1957) distinguished three types of settlements in the upper Son Valley. P. Bandyopadhyay (1957) also studied settlements of eastern Kolhan in the Chotanagpur region. Among village studies, C. Nirumala (1960) did on Vittalani; R. Ram Chandran on Muhammadpuram; A.V. Thiru on Nolambur; A.B. Bose on Chirai (Rajasthan); and V.A. Janki and M.H. Ajwani on Rasulabad. V.A. Janki (1953-57) also contributed on distribution and historical development of settlements in Kerala and S.N.P. Jaiswal on Sachendi (1961).

M.N. Vasantha Devi (1962) described house types of Edakhad village; and V. Vidyanath (1962) presented the historical background of circular house types in islands of Kolleru lake in Andhra Pradesh. Likewise, T. Singh (1965) described in detail the house types of Kurali village in the upper Ganga-Yamuna Doab; G. Krishan delimited the umland of Chandigarh (1963); S.N.P. Jaiswal worked on Bindki (1963); and R.D. Dikshit described the classification of rural house types of Dehra Dun Valley in Uttar Pradesh (1965). Contemporary writings were by A. Ahmad on civilization of Indian deserts (1965), S.K. Munshi on Chiria in Singhbhum district of Bihar (1965), and S.S. Pandey (1965) on deserted villages of Vidarbha as well as on terminology and toponymy. A.B. Chatterjee (1966) has studied the settlement patterns of Birhores of Bihar while A.B. Mukerji (1964) described the pre-Reddi landscape of Telangana. In 1965, S.N. Rafiullah wrote a monograph on the geography of transhumance. During the sixties, there were some more contributions published in the National Geographical Journal of India, Varanasi, e.g. "Meaning, Objectives and Scope of Settlement Geography" (1961) by R.L. Singh, "Ancient Bhars and Their Ruined Settlements in Ganga-Ghaghara Doab- West" (1962) by S.M. Singh, also by the same author on "The Stability Theory of Rural Central Place Development" (1965) and on "Turrufs Babhnauti and Raotar in the Ganga- Ghaghara Doab-West: A Study in Land Settlement, Social Geography and Rural Central Places" (1965); "Human Dwellings in Sonpar Region (Uttar Pradesh): A Geographical Analysis" (1969) by S.N. Mishra; and "Rural Settlement Types and Their Distribution: Examples from Varanasi District, India" (1969) by R.B. Singh.

Besides the pioneer works by Enayat Ahmad and Buschmann, a few more doctoral theses were presented for award of degree in various universities as follows: "Distribution of Population and Settlement in the Ganga Plains of U.P." (1953) by N.P. Saxena; "Ranchi Plateau: Geomorphology and Settlements" (1958) by P. Verma from Allahabad University; "Regional Economy and Settlement Patterns in East Rajasthan" (1960) by Nityanand; "Types of Human Settlements in Vindhya Pradesh" (1960) by L.N. Verma, "Malwa Plateau: A Study in Human Geography" (1962) by R.K. Nigam from Agra University; "Murshidabad: A Study in Settlement Geography" (1965) by N.D. Bhattacharya; "Service Centres of the Eastern Part of Ganga-Yamuna Doab, U.P." (1965) by S.N.P. Jaiswal from Agra; "Rural Settlement Patterns and House Types of the Deccan Trap Region of Vidarbha" (1965) by S.S. Padhye from Nagpur; "Settlement in Mahakoshal" (1966) by M. Jhala; "Settlements in Dun Valley" (1968) by S. Pathak from Vikram;

"Settlement Pattern in Kumaon" (1968) by S.C. Joshi (Agra); "Land forms and Settlements in Almora and its Environs" (1968) by V.K. Asthana; "The Evolution of Settlement Pattern in Oudh" (1968) by R.V. Verma; "Landforms and Settlements of Nainital and its Environs" (1969) by S.C. Kharkwal; "Ganga-Ghaghara Doab Central, Geographical Analysis of Population and Settlement" (1969) by N. Kaushik; "Rural Settlements of Chottanagpur" (1969) by A. Prasad (Ranchi); "The Economy and Morphology of Rural Settlements in the Ghar Tract of District Saharanpur: A Regional Investigation" (1970) by Gopal Chandra (Agra); "Rajput Clan Settlements in Varanasi District (Middle Ganga Valley)" (1971) by R.B. Singh; "Cavery Delta: A Study in Rural Settlements" (1972) by K.S.G. Krishnan; "The Geography of Rural Settlements in Bihar Plain" (1973) by R.B. Mandal (Patna); "Malwa Region: A Study in Rural Settlement Geography" (1974) by R.Y. Singh (Banaras); "Baghelkhand: A Study in Population and Settlement Geography" (1974) by J. Singh; "Clan Settlements in the Saran Plain (Middle Ganga Valley)" (1974) by R.P.B. Singh; "Sultanpur District: A Study in Rural Settlement Geography" (1974) by S.B. Singh; "Palamau Upland of Chottanagpur High Lands: A Study in Landforms and Settlements" (1974) by O.P. Singh; "A Geographical Study of Rural Settlements in Rewa-Panna Plateau" (1974) by S.K. Singh; "Tribal Population and Settlements in Kamrup with Special Reference to the Concentration in the Southern Region" (1975) by Dipti Das (Bhubaneswar); "Chotanagpur: A Study in Settlement Geography" (1975) by V.N.P. Sinha (Patna); "Geographical Analysis of Settlements Planning of Zambia" (1976) by P. Nag; "The Relationship Between Functional Hierarchy of Settlements and Patterns of Information Diffusion in Nilgiri District" (1976) by N. Sivagnanam (Madras); "Landuse and Settlements in the Districts of Bhojpur and Rohtas, Bihar" (1976) from Bhagalpur University; "Rajput Clan Settlement in a Part of Middle Ganga Valley, Distt. Jaunpur" (1977) by D.K. Singh; "Champawat: A Study in Land forms and Settlement" (1977) by B.P. Gupta; "Landforms and Settlements of Shimla and Its Environs" (1977) by S.B. Singh; "Rural Settlement of Chotanagpur Region" (1978) by D.R. Nayak (Raipur); "Study of Rural Settlement in Eastern Gujarat" (1978) by Kumkum Majumdar; "Western Tarai of Uttar Pradesh: A Study in Population and Settlement Geography" (1978) by Shail Singh; "Rural Settlements in Ballia District" (1978) by A.K. Singh; "Hazaribagh Plateau: A Study in Landforms and Settlements" (1978) by S.R. Yadava; "Urban Settlements in Eastern India: Entropy Changes and Pattern Analysis" (1978) by B. Thakur; "Lower Ganga Ghaghara Doab: A Study in Rural Settlements" (1979) by Minati Singh, "Rural Settlements and House Types in the Lower Ganga-Yamuna Doab" (1979) by J.R. Yadav; "The Lower Ganga-Yamuna Doab: A Study in Rural Settlements" (1980) by R.C. Tewari (Allahabad); "Land Forms and Settlements in Mussoorie and Its Environs" (1980) by H. Prasad; "Rural Settlements of the East-Central Ganga-Yamuna Doab: A Geographical Study" (1980) by S.K. Shukla (Kanpur); "A Study in Rural Settlements in the Upper Bhima Basin" (1980) by A.S. Job (Poona); "Geographic Dimensions of Rural Settlements in Gorakhpur District" (1981) by U.P. Singh; "Transformation in the Rural Base of Azamgarh Town: A Geographical Study" (1981) by M. Singh; "Upper Damodar Valley: A Study in Settlement Geography" (1981) by J. Singh; "Settlement Dispersion in North Western Bihar: Classification and Correlation" (1982) by S.P. Yadav; "Lower Ganga and Ramganga Doab: A Study in Settlement Geography" (1983) by S.C. Gupta.[113]

A few published theses in the form of monographs include "Settlement Geography of the Indian Desert" (1972) by R.C. Sharma; "Chotanagpur: Geography of Rural Settlements" (1973) by

A. Prasad; "Chotanagpur Plateau: A Study in Settlement Geography" (1976) by V.N.P. Sinha; "Delhi Metropolitan Region: A Study in Settlement Geography" (1976) by S.K. Nangia; "Rajput Clan Settlements in Varanasi District" (1975) by R.B. Singh; "Clan Settlements in the Saran Plain" (1977) by R.P.B. Singh; "The Malwa Region: Rural Habitat System, Structure and Change" (1978) by R.Y. Singh; "Human Settlements in Asia: Public Policies and Programmes" (1979) by R.P. Mishra and B.S. Bhooshan; "Social and Geographical Aspects of Human Settlements" (1979) by Enayat Ahmad; "Systems of Rural Settlement in Developing, Countries" by R.B. Mandal, "Rural Settlements: Planning and Development" by N. Lal; "Rural Settlement System in Rural India: A Case Study of the Lower Ganga-Yamuna Doab" (1984) by R.C. Tewari; "Evolution and Spatial Organization of Clan Settlements: A Case Study of Middle Ganga Valley" (1986) by S.H. Ansari; "Upper Damodar Valley: A Study in Settlement Geography" (1985) by J. Singh; "Rural Settlements in Ballia District" (1985) by A.K. Singh; "Rural Settlements in Lower Ganga-Ghaghara Doab" (1986) by Minati; "Rural Settlements: A Cultural Ecological Perspective" (1986) by S.A. Sharma; and "Rural Settlements: A Cultural Geographical Analysis" (1980) by Neelam Grover.

G.S. Gosal and A.B. Mukerji have taken stock of the various aspects of the progress in rural settlement geography through their reviews for a period of seven years[114] from 1969 to 1975. Since then continuous efforts made towards the advancement of this branch added some significant contributions as named below: "Application of Sampling Method for Nearest Dwelling Distance" (1975) by J.K. Shamra; "Mapping and Analysis of Settlement through Aerial Photographs" (1975) by Kailash N. Singh; "Central Place Hierarchy in Bihar Plain" (1975) by R.B. Mandal; "Identification of Growth Centres and Growth Points in South-East Resource Region" (1976) by R. Ramchandran; "Intra-village Spacing: Measurement and Comparison, Case of the Saran Plain" (1976) by R.P.B. Singh and S.L. Kayastha; "Distribution, Centrality and Hierarchy of Rural Central Places in Sultanpur District" (1977) by S.B. Singh; "Spatial and Structural Analysis of the Rural Market Network and Its Relation to Society in an Indian Environment" (1977) by R.L. Singh and R.P.B. Singh; "Place Names as Tools for Reconstructing Evolution of Settlements in the Malwa Region India" (1977) by R.Y. Singh; "Analysis of Size, Spacing and Nature of Dispersion of Rural Settlements in Jalaun District" (1978) by R.K. Srivastava; "Concept of Morphological Analysis: Some Theoretical Postulations" (1978) by R.L. Singh and R.P.B. Singh; "Nucleated Settlement in South-East Tennessee" (1979) by J.K. Sharma; "Poisson Process and Cell Model Properties of Village Shape in the Middle Ganga Valley, India: A Comparative Study of Locational Pattern" (1979) by R.P.B. Singh; "Spatial Analysis of Rural Settlements and their Types in Lower Ganga-Ghaghara Doab" (1981) by K.N. Singh and Minati Singh; "Rural Settlement System of Pratapgarh District: A Study in Spatial Pattern" (1982) by R.C. Tewari and N. Uddin (*National Geographer*, V. XVII-2); "Problems of Housing Development in Bangladesh: An Appraisal of Low Cost Housing" (1987) by P.K. Gupta and M.S. Islam; and "Travels in Ethiopian Highlands" (1987) by R.Y. Singh (*Northern Geographer*, V. II-2).

Ecology, Habitat and Settlements

Geography as human ecology as indicated earlier finds its new anthropogenic significance because more than other sciences modern geography is prepared for ecological studies on an interdisciplinary basis. While ecological approach to the study of phenomena originated and developed as a special discipline within the ecological sciences it has now become a general scientific approach. Now, adapting Glacken's[115] teminology, "God's design" having been replaced by "nature's design" we may see it in turn supplanted by "man's design". The social man is, for better or worse, seizing control of his terrestrial environment and increasingly has the right of veto. The Russian school of ecologists are using the terms 'geocenosis' for the physical habitat and 'biocenosis' for the biome; the two combinedly named as 'Geoecobiota' by Gerasimov. Within this framework, the human ecosystems, as suggested by Dice, may be conceived at successively larger scale intervals, i.e., tribe to international levels. Since ecologically efficient habitable areas on the earth are shrinking the habitat needs attention. Geoecobiota is manifested through various channels and further developments result into the present rural habitat system, i.e., the settlements (Figs. 1.7, 1.8). But the habitat is not shelter. It is not the resource base which defines the limits to growth. It is not even the home which symbolizes the social relations. It is a synthesis of the bio-culturally determined pursuit of the quality of life, institutional and infrastructural basis for supporting the quality of life and the resource base for deriving livelihood[116]. The habitat provides the site, building materials, water points, foundation of

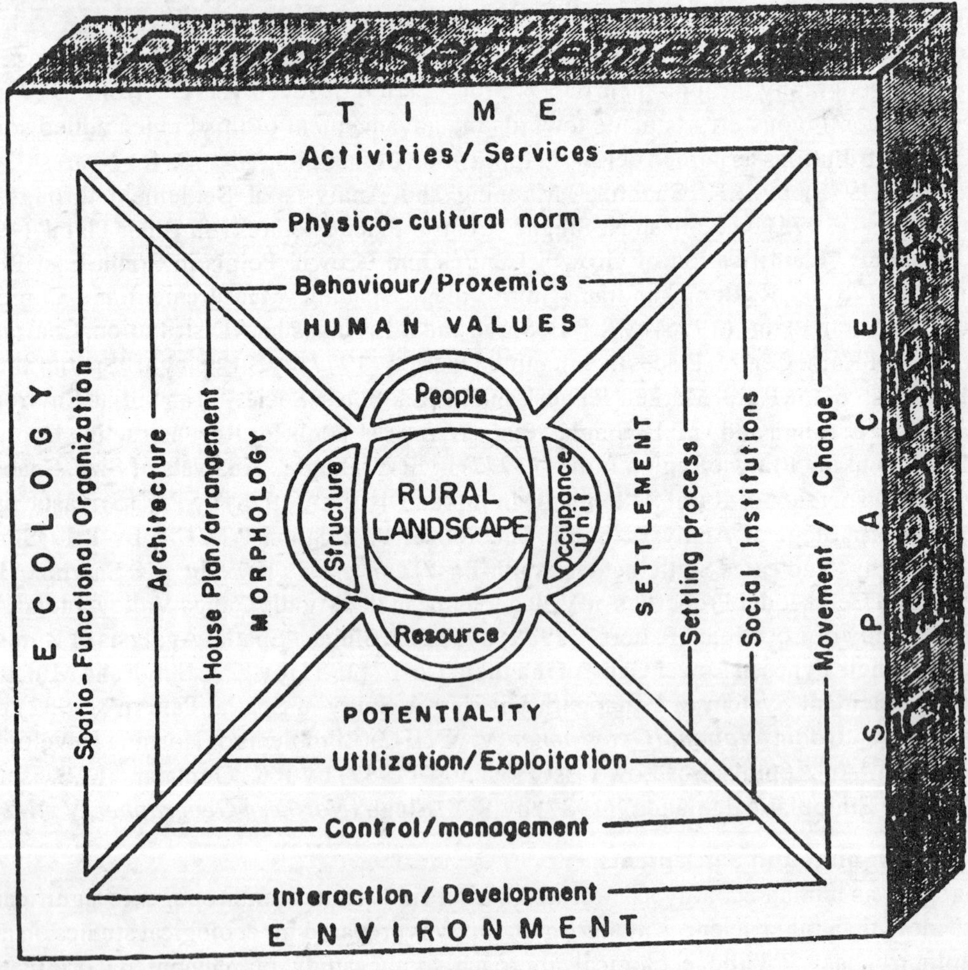

Figure 1.7

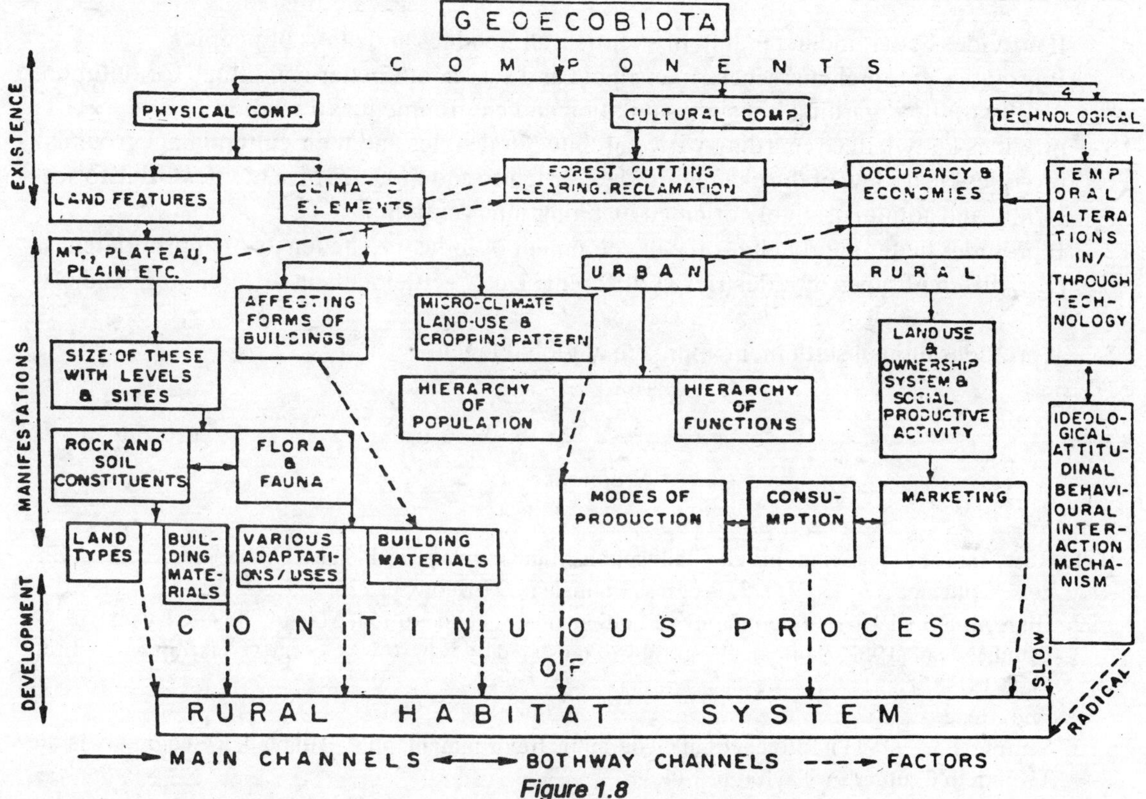

Figure 1.8

mobility and also moulds various occupances as well as settlement forms.

Human settlements are intimate bonds between habitat and culture. Thus, human ecology-man environment symbiosis is as old as human civilization.

Significance of Settlement Studies

The ultimate goal of human activity is his own welfare while settling somewhere on the earth. To seek the multi-dimensional factors involved in attaining, sustaining and improving human well-being, various dynamic aspects of settlements need to be studied thoroughly scanning all along the spectrum.[117] Hence, significance of human settlement study refers to the following:

1. It provides clear understanding of where, how and why of the people in temporal frame.
2. It provides clear understanding of division of labour engaged into type of production.
3. It provides better understanding of the modernized need in settlements themselves due to increasing number of nucleus family, gadgets and day-to-day changing behaviour of the inhabitants.
4. It provides better picture for the location and deployment of new facilities, i.e., supply of drinking water, electricity, irrigation, education, etc.
5. It provides better understanding of agriculture and pioneer settlements interrelationship.
6. It provides better understanding of impact of planned development.
7. It provides better understanding of inter-regional inter-system and intra-system relationship and arrangements to integrate the spatial structure of the economy with the settlement structure.

8. It provides better understanding of socio-cultural values and ethos of people.
9. It provides comprehensiveness to evaluate and search out better conditions for optimum quality of life regarding housing, sanitation and environment as a whole.
10. provides knowledge regarding varied architectural styles and their cultural backgrounds.
11. provides clear view of the changes in size, structure and linkages of settlements due to sectorally and administratively oriented planning intervention.
12. It provides better approach for the development of industry, the tenets of appropriateness (i.e., different types of industries in different size of settlements in different regional settings).
13. It provides human settlement approach at global level.

References

1. Karl Marx (1975), Economic and Philosophic Manuscripts of 1844 in karl Marx and Frederick Engels 'Collected Works, Vol. 3, Progress Publishers, Moscow, p. 276.
2. Hudson, F.S. (1976), A Geography of Settlements, second edition, Macdonald and Evans, 3.
3. Brunhes Jean (1952), Human Geography (Translated by E.F. Row) George G. Harrap & Co. Ltd., Plate 1, Fig. 1.
4. Ibid, fig. 2.
5. Semple, E.C., (1911), Influences of Geographic Environment, pp. 1-2 quoted in Geography in the Twentieth Century by Taylor, p. 144.
6. Chorley, R.J. (1973), 'Geography as Human Ecology' in his edited book Directions in Geography, Methuen And Co. Ltd., p. 158.
7. Berry, B.J.L. (1964), Approaches to Regional Analysis, a Synthesis, Annals of the Association of American Geographers, 54, p. 3.
8. Chorley R.J. (ed) (1973), ref. no. 6, p. 167.
9. Ibid, p. 166.
10. Blache P. Vidal De La (1926), Principles of Human Geography, (English edition, London) 7-9, see also Jean Brunhes (1920), Human Geography, ref. no. 3: 14-15.
11. Ritter, C. (1865), Comparative Geography, Translated by W.L. Gage, Edinburgh.
12. Sauer, C.O. (1925), The Morphology of Landscape, University of California Publications in Geography, 2 ii, 19-54.
13. Langton John (1972), 'Systems Approach to Change in Human Geography in Board, Chorley, Haggett & Stoddart (eds), Progress in Geography, Vol. 4, Edward Arnold, p. 128.

13.1. Bertalanffy, L. Von (1962), General System Theory-A Critical Review, General Systems Year book, 7, 1-20.

13.2 Hall A.D. and Fagen, R.E. (1956), Definition of System, General Systems Yearbook I, 18-26.

13.3 Badcock, B.A. (1970), Central Place Evolution and Network Development in South Auckland, 1840-1968: A Systems Analytic Approach, New Zealand Geographer 26, 109-35.

13.4 Berry B.J.L. (1964), Cities as Systems Within Systems of Cities. Papers of the Regional Science Association, 13, 147-63.

13.5 Chorley R.J. and Haggett, P. (eds) (1967), Models in Geog. London: Methuen, 19-41.

13.6 Curry L. (1964), The Random Spatial Economy: An Exploration in Settlement Theory. A.A.A. Geographers, 54, 138-46.

13.7 Mobojunje, A.L. (1970), Systems Approach to a Theory of Rural and Urban Migration, Geographical Analysis, 2, 1-18.
13.8 Tansley A.G. (1946), Introduction to Plant Ecology, London.
13.9 Stoddart, D.R. (1965), Geography and the Ecological Approach: The Ecosystem as a Geographical Principle and Method, Geography, 50, 242-251.
13.10 Chisholm M.D.I. (1967), General Systems Theory and Geography, Transactions of the Institute of British Geographers, 42, 45-52.
13.11 Rapoport, A. (1968), Mathematical Aspects of General Systems Analysis in The Social Sciences: Problems and Orientations, The Hague: Mouton Unesco, 320-34.
13.12 Miller J.G. (1965a), Living Systems: Basic Concepts, Behavioural Science 10, 193-237.
—(1965b), Living Systems: Structure and Process, Bheavioural Science 10, 337- 379.
—(1965c), Living Systems: Cross Level Hypothesis, Behavioural Science 10, 380-411.
13.13 Haggett P., Cliff A.D., and Frey A. (1977), Locational Analysis in Human Geography, 2nd edition, Edward Arnold, London.
13.14 Medawar, P.B. (1969), Induction and Intuition in Scientific Thought, Methuen, London.
13.15 Gimingham C.H. (1972), Ecology of Heathlands, Chapmen and Hall, London.
13.16 Odum E.P. (1975), Ecology, Second Edition, Holt, Rinehart and Winston, London and New York.
13.17 Biswas A.K. (ed.) (1976), Systems approach to water management, McGraw-Hill, New York.
13.18 King L.J. and Golledge, R.G. (1978), Cities, Space and Behaviour: The Elements of Urban Geography, Prentice Hall, Englewood Cliffs.
13.19 Stearns F.W. and Montag J. (Eds) (1975), The Urban Ecosystems, Halstead Press, New York.
13.20 Vester, F. (1976), Urban Systems in Crisis, Deutschen Verlags-Anstalt, Stuttgart.
13.21 Clarke, M. (1978), Corporate Planning in Local Government: A Review and Further Developments Towards a Systematic Modelling Framework. Working Paper 221, School of Geography, University of Leeds.
13.22 Forester J.W. (1968), Principles of Systems, Wright Allen Press, Boston.
13.23 Klir, J. and Valach, M. (1967), Cybernetic Modelling, Iliffe, London.
13.24 Huggett, R. (1980), Systems Analysis in Geography, Oxford University Press, Oxford.
13.25 Chapman, G.T. (1977), Human and Environmental Systems, Academic Press, London.
13.26 Benett, R.J. and Chorley, R.J. (1978), Environmental Systems: Philosophy, Analysis and Control, Methuen, London.
13.27 Jeffers, J.N.R. (1978), An Introduction to Systems Analysis: With Ecological Applications, Edward Arnold, London.
13.28 Warneryd, O. (1968), Interdependence in Urban Systems. Goteborg: Region Konsult Aktiebolag, (176).
13.29 Webber, M.J. (1979), Information Theory and Urban Spatial Structure, Groom Helm, London.
13.30 Anuchin V.A. (1973), Theory of Geography and also Warntz william, New Geography as General Spatial Systems Theory-Old Social Physics Writ Large? in Chorley R.J.(ed), 'Directions in Geography, Methuen and Co. Ltd.
13.31 Wilson, A.G. Rees, P.H., and Leigh, C.M. (Eds.) (1977), Models of Cities and Regions, Wiley, Chichester.
13.32 Sukachev V.N., (1958), On the Principles of Genetic Classification in Biocenology, (translated by Ramey F. and Daubenmire D.), Ecology, 39, 364-367.
13.33 Lindeman, R.L. (1942), The Trophic Dynamic Aspect of Ecology, Ecology, 23, 399-418.
13.34 Zeeman, E.C. (1977), Catastraphe Theory, Addison Wesley, Reading, Mass.
13.35 Zipf, G.K. (1965), Human Behaviour and Principles of Least Effort. New York: Hafner, 564.
13.36 Barrows, H.H. (1923), Geography as Human Ecology;Annals of the Association of American Geographers, 13, 1-14.

13.37 Patten, B.C. (ed.) (1971), Systems Analysis and Simulation in Ecology, Academic Press, new York & London.
14. Wilson, A.G. (1981), Geography And the Environment, John Wiley & Sons, New York, p. 3; see also R.J. Chorley (1973) ref. no. 6, pp. 162-167; also see David Harvey (1969) Explanation in Geography, Edward Arnold, pp. 447-480.
15. Wilson, A.G., op.cit ref. no. 14, pp. 10-17; see also I.P. Gerasimov (ed), (1983) Geography and Ecology, Progress Publishers, pp. 71-76.
16. Harvey David, op.cit. ref. no. 14, p. 468.
17. Dice, L.R. (1955), Man's Nature and Nature's Man: The Ecology of Human Communities, Ann. Arbor. Mich. pp. 251-266.
18. Chorley, R.J., op.cit. ref. no. 8, p. 167.
19. Berry, B.J.L. (1964) op.cit. ref. no. 7, p. 3; also see his 'Cities as Systems Within Systems of Cities, Pap. Reg. Sci. Ass. 13, pp. 147-163; also see Forrestor J.W. (1968), Principles of Systems, Wright Allen Press, Boston and (1969), Urban Dynamics, M.I.T. Press, Cambridge, Mass.
20. Woldenberg M.J. and Berry B.J.L. (1967), Rivers and Central Places: Analogous Systems, J. Reg. Sci. 7, No. 2, pp. 129- 139.
21. Curry, L. (1967), Central Places in the Random Spacial Analysis, J. Reg. Sc., 7, No. 2 pp. 217-238 (Supplement).
22. Haggett, P. (1965), Locational Analysis in Human Geography, London.
23. Gerasimov, I.P. et al. (eds). (1975), Man, Society and Environment, Progress Publishers, Moscow, p. 234.
24. Kohn, C.F. (1970), The 1960's: A Decade of Progress in Geographical Research and Instruction, AAAG, 60, pp 217-218.
25. Wilson, A.G. (1981), op.cit. ref. no. 14 p. 17.
26. Weaver, W. (1958), A Quarter Century in the Natural Sciences, Annual Report, The Rockefeller Foundation, New York, pp. 7-22; also see Chorley R.J. and Kennedy, B.A. (1971), Physical Geography: A Systems Approach, Prentice Hall, Englewood Cliffs; see also Klir J. and Valach M. (1967), Cybernetic Modelling, Illife, London; see Langton, John, (1972), op.cit. ref. no. 13 p. 162.
27. Zvonkova T. & Saushkin Yu (1986), Problems of Long Term Geographical Prognostication, in Geographical Prognostication, Progress Publishers, p. 21.
28. Harvey, David (1969), Explanation in Geography, Edward Arnold, p. 469.
29. Dolphin Vernon (1970), 'The Earth is the Home of Man' Education Department, Harward University, 4 Quoted by W. Bunge in "Ethics and Logic in Geography" p. 327 in Chorley, R.J. (ed) 'Directions in Geography, op.cit. ref. no. 8.
30. Garrison, W.L. "Future Geographies, p. 237 in Chorley, R.J. (ed), ref. no. 8.
31. Smith, D.M. (1974), "Who Gets What Where and How". A Welfare Focus for Human Geography 59, 289-97; Sea also for better treatment of Geographical Welfare Data Matrix (who, what, where) in Smith, D.M. (1977), "Human Geography, A Welfare Approach, Edward Arnold.
32. Singh, K.N. (1977), 'Emergence of Man, Culture and Settlement' in India", p. 4 in Eidt, R.C. et al. (eds.), Man, Culture and Settlement, Kalyani Publishers (A Festschrift presented to Prof. R.L. Singh), New Delhi.
33. Finch, V.C. et al. (eds.), Elements of Geography-Physical and Cultural, McGraw Hill Book Co. INC, New Delhi, 1977.
34. Kohn, C.F. (1954), 'Settlement Geography' in James P.E. and Clyde F. Kohn (eds.), American Geography: Inventory and Prospect, Ch. V. p. 138; see also R.Y. Singh (1978), The Malwa Region: Rural Habital System, Structure and Change' N.G.S.I., Res. Pub. No. 20, Inter Centre for Rural Habitat Studies Res. Pub. No. 1: XV.

35. Von Richthofen, F. (1908), 'Vorlesungen uber ollgemeine Siedlungs-Und Verkehrsgeographie' (ed) by O. Schluter, Berlin.
36. Muller-Wille, W. (1954), 'Arten der menschlichen Siedlung', in Ergebnisse Und Probleme moderner geographischer Forschung: Hans Mortensen Zu Seinem 60, Geburtstag, Bremer-Horn, pp. 141-163; also see Idem (1944), 'Langstreifenflur Und Drubbel, ein Beitrag Zur Siedlungsgeographie Westgermaniens', Deutsches Archiv fur landesvolks-forchung, Vol. 8, No. 1, pp. 9-44.
37. Hudson, F.S. (1976), op.cit., ref. no. 2, p. 10.
38. Singh, R.L. (1961), Meaning, Objectives And Scope of Settlement Geography, NGJI, Varanasi, Vol. 8-1, pp. 12-20.
39. Hudson, F.S. (1976), op.cit., ref. no. 2, p. 11.
40. August Meitzen (1985), Siedlung und Agrarwesen der Westgermanen... in his series entitled Wanderung, Anbau Und Agrarecht der Volker europas Nordlich der Alpen, Berlin: W. Hertz, Vol.-1, p. 28.
41. Mayer, Harold, M. (1951), 'Geography and Urbanism', Scientific Monthly, Lxiii, July 1951, pp. 1-12.
42. Bowman, Isaiah, (1953), 'Settlement by the Modern Pioneer', Geography in the Twentieth Century, Second Edition, Ch. XI, p. 266.
43. Lappo G.M. et al. (1973), 'Modern Constructive Geographic Problems of Large Cities' in I.P. Gerasimov (ed.), Geography and Ecology, Progress Publishers, Moscow (1983), pp. 144-158.
44. Mayer, Harold, M. op.cit. p. 2 ref. no. 41.
45. The idea for organising and setting a separate commission on Rural settlements was initiated by Demangeon in I.G.U. 1932 and relentless efforts continued. The proposal for setting up a commission on Rural Settlements in Monsoon Asia was voted by the General Assembly of the I.G.U. held at New Delhi, India, 1968. The Chairman Prof. R.L. Singh, with the concurrence of the commission members and the Secy-Treasurer, Prof. Chauncy D. Harris, managed to organise an International Symposium held at Varanasi in Jan, 1971 on the occasion of Silver Jubilee Celebrations of the national Geographical Society of India, Varanasi.
46. Dickinson, R.E. (1948), "The Scope and Status of the Urban Geography, An Assessment" Land Economics, August, pp. 216- 237.
47. Baker, A.R.H. (1969), 'The Geography of Rural Settlements' in Trends in Geography: An Introductory Survey (eds) R.R. Cooke & J.H. Johnson, London: Pergaman Press, p. 124.
48. Bloch, M. (1954), The Historians Craft, London, pp. 43- 47.
49. Dion, Roger (1949), 'La geographie humaine retrospective' Catriers Internationaux de sociologie', 6, pp. 3-27.
50. Julliard, E. (1964), 'Geographie rurale francaise Travaux recents (1957-63) et tendances nouveles' Etudes Ruraler, 13-14 pp 46-70.
51. Brunhes, J. (1952), Human Geography, Abridged Edition by Jean Brunhes Delamarre et al., George G. Herrap and Co. Ltd., London, p. 579; See R.Y. Singh (1977), Place Names as Tools for Reconstructing Evolution of Settlements in the Malwa Region- India, N.G.J.I., Vol. XXIII, parts 3 & 4 Sept. Dec. pp. 199-206.
52. Mitchell, J.B. (1960), 'Historical Geography' The English Univ. Press Ltd., 102 Newgate Streets London, E.C.I., pp. 88-101.
53. Alice, F.A.M. (1933), 'Place Names and History of Settlements in South West Germany' Geog., 23: 113-119.
54. Charles, B.G. (1933), 'Non-celtic Place Names in Wales, univ. College, London.
55. Wooldridge S.W. and D.L. Linton (1935), 'Some Aspects of Saxon Settlements in South East England Considered in Relation to the Geographical Background, Geog. 20, 161-175.

56. Dickinson, R.E. (1940), 'Rural Settlements in German Lands' AAAG, 30, 239-263.
57. Maxwell, I.S. (1956), 'The Age of Settlements' in Charles, Batey (ed) 'Sheffield and Its Region' The University Press, Oxford, 239-263.
58. Mitchell, J.B. op.cit. ref. no. 52.
59. Zelinsky, W. (1955), Some Problems in the Distribution of Generic Terms in the Place Names of the Northeastern United States, AAAG, 45: 319-345.
60. McCamphall, C. (1958), Texas History as Revealed by Town and Community Origin, Southeastern Historical Quarterly, 58, 91-97.
61. Kameron, K. (1959), The Place Names of Derbyshire, Cambridge Univeristy Press, London.
62. Singh, S.M. (1960), Former Distribution of Forests and Woodlands in Faizabad and Sultanpur Districts of Ganga-Ghaghara Doab West: A Study in Historical Geography, NGJI, 6: 137-158.
63. Jones, G.R.J. (1961), Early Territorial Organisation in England and Wales, Geog-Annaler, 42;174-181.
64. Padhye, S.S. (1967), The Geographic Correlation of Vidarbhian Toponyms, NGJI, V. XIII part I, p. 14.
65. Hudson, F.S., op.cit., ref. no. 2: 39-40.
66. Elliot, C.A., Chronicles of Unnao: A District in Oudh p. 26; Lucknow Settlement Report, p-42 and 216.
67. Bylund, E. (1960), Theoretical Consideration Regarding the Distribution of Settlements in Inner North Sweden, Geog. Annaler, 42, 225-231.
68. Morrill, R.L. (1963), The Development and Spatial Distribution of Towns in Sweden: An Historical Predictive Approach, AAAG, 53: 1-14.
69. Chisholm, M.D., (1962), Rural Settlement and Landuse, London.
70. Kollmorgen, W.M. (1941), 'A Reconnaissance of Some Cultural Agricultural Islands in the South' Eco. Geography, 17: 409-430; idem (1943), Agricultural Cultural Islands in the South, Part 2, Eco. Geog., 19: 109-117; idem 1945, Immigrant Settlements in Southern Agriculture: A Commentary on the Significance of Cultural Islands in Agricultural History, 19: 69-78.
71. Nelson, L., (1952), The Mormon Village: A Pattern and Technique of Land Settlement, Salt Lake City.
72. Powell, J.M. (1971), Utopia, Millenium and the Cooperative Ideal: A Behavioural Matrix in the Settlement Process, The Australian Geographer, XI (6 Sept.): 606-618.
73. Powell, S.C., (1965), Puritan Village, The Formation of a New England Town, New York.
74. Idem, 616, ref. no. 73.
75. Bjorklund, E.M., (1964), Ideology and Culture Exemplified in South Western Michigan, AAAG, 54: 227-241.
76. Meinig, D.W. (1965), The Mormon Culture Region: Strategies and Patterns in the Geography of the American West, AAAG, 55: 191-200.
77. Singh, R.L. & K.N. Singh (1963), Evolution of the Medieval Towns in the Saryupar Plain of the Middle Ganga Valley: A Case Study NGJI, 9 (i): 1-11;see K.N. Singh, 1968, The Territorial Basis of Medieval Towns and Village Settlements in Eastern U.P., AAAG, 58: 203-220.
78. Yonekura, Jiro, (1949), Historical Geography of Settlement in Japan, Teikokushyoin, 2: 411-32.
79. Dan Stanislawski, (1946), The Origin and Spread of the Grid Pattern Town, Geographical Review, 36: 105-120.
80. Nitz, H.J., (1966), Geographical Studies in the Field Patterns of Northern India and Germany, Geographer, 13: 61-74.
81. Eidt, R.C. and W.I. Woods, (1974), Abandoned Settlement Analysis, Theory and Practice, Wisconsin: Field Test Associates.
82. Singh, R.L. et al. (1975), Readings in Rural Settlement Geography, National Geog. Society of India, Varanasi, Publication, No. 14, xi.

83. Demangeon, A. (1920), L' Habitation Rurale in France' Annales de Geographie", 29: 352-375; idem, "La geographie de L'habitat rural, Annales de Geographie, 36 (1927), 1-23; "Types of Villages in France" Annales de Geographie, 48 (1939), 1-21.
84. Schaefer, F.K. (1953), Exceptionalism in Geography, AAAG, 55: 549- 577.
85. Hudson, J.C. (1969), A location Theory of Rural Settlements, AAAG. 59: 365-381.
86. Pred, A. (1976), Behaviour and Location, Lund Studies in Geography, Series B., No. 27, p. 28.
87. Kayastha, S.L. (1957), Gaddis of Dhauladhar-A Study in Himalayan Ecology, Vol. III, part 2, pp. 65-78; Also see his "Kandla—A Study in Port Development, vol. IX, part 1, 1963, 12-24.
88. Singh, R.Y., (1972), Bhils of Malwa Region-Their Habitat, Economy and Society, Vol. XVIII, parts 3 & 4, 223-239.
89. Yermakov, Yu et al. (1986), Geographical Aspects of Prognostication of the Environment Outside the Soviet Union, in Geographical Prognostication, Progress Publishers, Moscow, p. 104.
90. Birch, B.P., 1967, The Measurement of Dispersal Patterns of Settlement, Tijdschrjft Voor Econ. en Soc. Geografie Vol. 58: 68- 75.
91. Medvedkov, Y.V. (1967), The Regular Component in Settlement Patterns As Shown on A Map, Soviet Geography, Review and Translation, Vol. 8-3: 150-168.
92. Stone, K.H. (1968), Multiple Scale Classification For Rural Settlement Geography, Acta Geographica, Helsinki, Vol. 20, No. 22: 307-317.
93. Dacey M.F., (1968), Multiple Scale Classification For Rural Settlement Geography, Acta Geographica, Helsinki, Vol. 20, No. 22: 307-317.
93. Dacey M.F., (1968), An Empirical Study of the Areal Distribution of Houses in Puerto Rico, Transactions, Inst. of British Geographers, No. 45, 1968: 51-59.
94. Hudson, J.C., (1969), Pattern Recognition in Empirical Map Analysis, Journal of Regional Science, Vol. 9.2: 189-199.
95. Semple, R.K. and Gollege R.G., (1970), An Analysis of Entropy Changes in A Settlement Pattern Over Time, Econ. Geog. Vol. 46- 2: 157-160.
96. Mukerji, A.B., (1970), Spacing of Rural Settlements in Rajasthan: A Spatial Analysis, Geographical View Point, Vol. 1: 1- 19.
97. Stafford, H.A. Jr. (1963), The Functional Basis of Small Towns, Econ. Geog. Vol. 39, April p. 173.
98. Haggett, P. & K.A. Gunwardena (1964), Determination of Population Threshold for Settlement Functions by Reed Muench Method, Prof. Geographer, Vol. XVI, No. 4: 166-169.
99. Acharya, P. (1933), Architecture of the Manasara (Eng. Trans.) London, Oxford University.
100. Demangeon, A. op.cit. ref. no. 83.
101. Von Richthofen, F., (1908), Vorbsungen Uber allgemeine Siedlungs- und Verkehrsgeographie-ed. by O. Schluter, Berlin.
102. Muller-Wille, W. op.cit. ref. no. 34.
103. Uhilg, H. and Lienau, C., (1967), Types of Field Patterns, Giessen; Rural Settlements, Giessen, 1972 and Rural Population, Giessen, 1975.
104. Eidt, R.C., 1976, 'Some Observations on the Role of Geography And History In the Analysis of Settlements' in Geographic Dimensions of Rural Settlements (eds.) R.L. Singh et al., NGSI, Res. Pub. No. 16, pp. 7-18.
105. See for details Murel, V.N. (1970), 'Indicators Characterising Systems of Rural Settlements' Soviet Geography Review and Translation, March, pp. 166-173; also see R.Y. Singh, The Malwa Region: Rural Habitat System, Structure and Change, NGSI, Res. Pub. no. 20, 1978, pp. 97-98.
106. In developed Western Europian Countries and U.S.A. etc. farmers reside in their farms settlements named farmstead/homestead; in India farmers reside in the midst of their land holdings in separate dwellings called 'Pahi' or *Chhawani* or second house away from the main village settlement.
107. Dickinson, R.E. (1949), Rural Settlements in German Lands, AAAG, V. 39, Dec., No. 4, p. 240.

108. Taylor, G. (ed.) (1967), Geography in the Twentieth Century, Methuen & Co. Ltd. London; see his article on 'Urban Geography' pp. 524-525.
109. Eidt, R.C. op.cit. ref. no. 104.
110. Badcock, B.A. (1970), A Preliminary Note on the Study of Intra- Urban Physiognomy, The Prof. Geographer, Vol. XXVI, July, p. 189.
111. Examples of first type include Demangeon, Lefevre and Swartz etc. and second group includes Enquist and Norling, James, Stone and others.
112. Arnold, W. (1875), Ansiedlungen Und Wanderungen dentscher Stamme Zumeist nach hessischen Ortsnamen Marburg.
113. Sinha, B.N. (ed.) (1983) 'Progress of Geographical Research in India, Transactions Indian Council of Geographers, Vol. 11, Dec. pp. 1-28.
114. A Survey of Research in Geography, 1969-72 (ed.), Moonis Raza, ICSSR, Allied Publishers Private ltd, 1979 pp. 184-187; and for 1972-75, Concept Publishing Company, 1984, pp. 119-125.
115. Glacken, C.J. (1967), Traces of the Rhodian Shore; University of California Press, Berkeley and Los Angeles.
116. Burman, B.K. Roy (1988), Man's Expanding Home and Shrinking World, Keynote Address, Seminar on Culture and Habitat, School of Planning and Architecture, New Delhi, Feb. 88, p. 2.
117. Rao, V.L.S. Prakasa (1988), Human Settlements Development Perspectives: Search for New Horizons in Annals of the NAGI, Vol. VIII, No.1, June, p. 48.

2

Culturo-Historical Perspective

Geographic and Cultural Background

Evolution of Homo Sapiens is unique in the living world. Its singularity lies in the fact that the human species evolved culture. During the last würm glacial stage, man occupied the ice free zones and the shelters that man learned to erect also greatly aided his adaptation to living in a variety of physical environments.[1] The Mesolithic cultural revolution brought great environmental and cultural change. Within any geographic territory, men in group with a particular form of social organization and a particular level of technology, express a distinctive way of life. While categorizing culture, Julien Huxley produced a model consisting of three components, i.e., mentifacts, sociofacts and artifacts. The first includes religion, language, magic and folklore, artistic traditions and the like; the second includes those aspects of a culture relating to links between individuals and groups. At the individual level they include family structure, reproductive and sexual behaviour and child rearing; and at the group level they include political and educational systems. The third includes those aspects of a culture relating to a group's links with its material environment. In practice, however, we find aspects of culture in which the three components seem tangled into an intractable knot and others where a strand can be pulled free and studied individually.[2]

These components do have impacts on cultural variety, hence mosaic of world regions comprising spatial variations in religious beliefs. The latter is expressed through its distinctive geography having territorial limits, i.e., Christianity, Islam, Hinduism and Buddhism and their subgroups (Fig. 2.1). These beliefs also depict distinct philosophy of resource use. Chinese as well as Indian landscapes continue to have paths, structures and wood lands designed to blend with the natural landscape and never exercise domination over it. The relationship of man to environment is not just a matter of demography and economics. Beliefs and fantasies, traditions and taboos, also have their place in any interpretation of man's relations with his environment.[3]

Since the present mosaic of culture and cultural regions reflects the population growth, cultural differentiation and migration of the past, we may discuss the centres of human groups which spread on the earth in old ages. There is consensus of opinion that Homo Sapiens originated first in tropical Africa in general and in East Africa in particular. These human groups later on differentiated as races—Caucasoid, Mongoloid and Negroid—spread in various geographical regions originally evolving from centres of evolution, i.e., hearth areas (Figs. 2.2a, 2.3a, 2.3b). It is common now that human groups had spread to most of the land masses around 25000 B.C. The origin and development sequence of human culture exhibit four distinct technical stages: (1) food gathering and hunting cultures, (2) herding cultures, (3) agricultural cultures, and (4) urban cul-

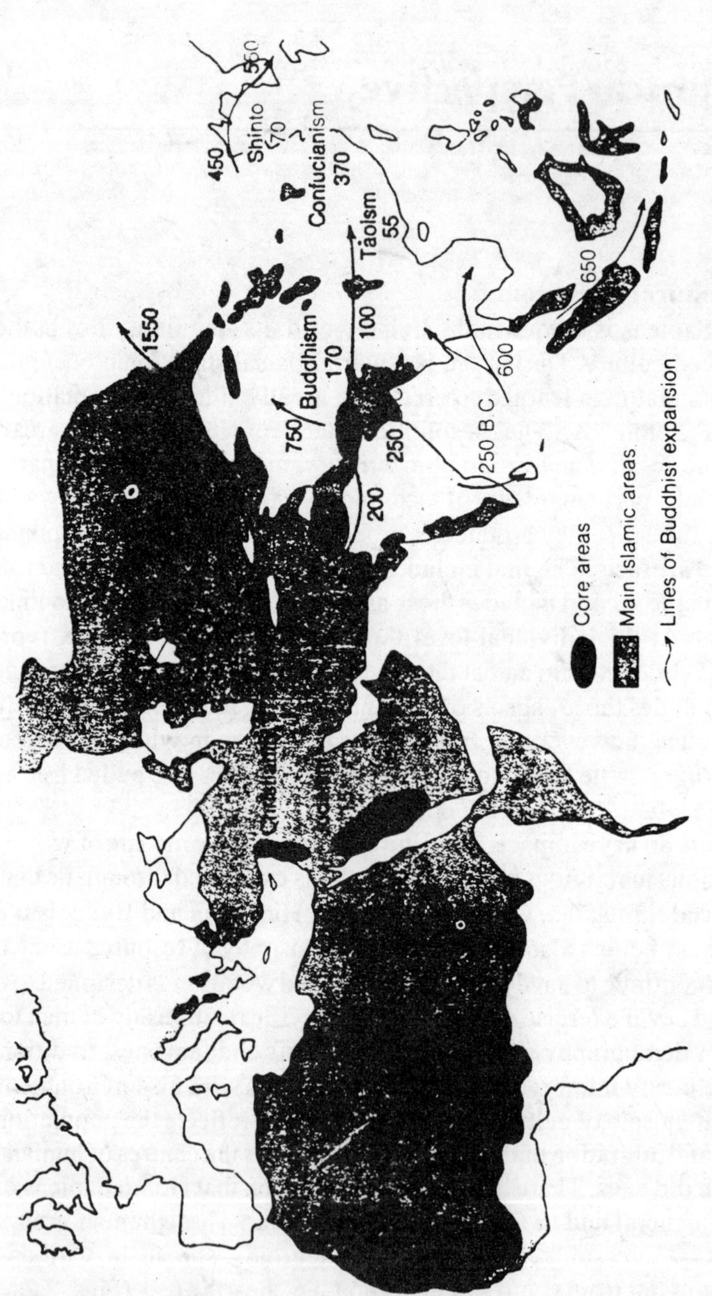

Figure 2.1: Cultural core areas. The map shows Old World core areas for the world's main religions. The figures indicate the approximate number of adherents of each religion, in millions, in the 1960s. The lines showing the expansion of Buddhism (with dates) are approximations only

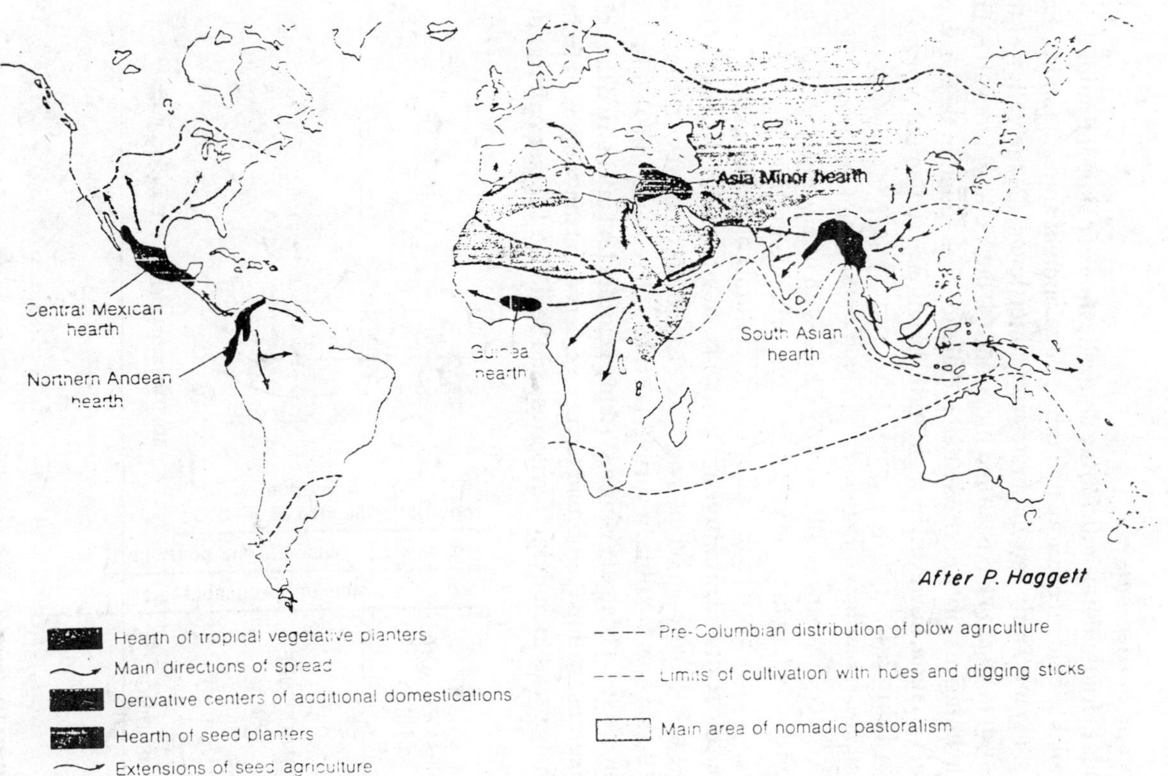

Figure 2.2(a): Agricultural origin and dispersal. The world map shows in a highly generalized form the supposed main features of agricultural diffusion in the pre-Columbian world. It is based on the views of geographers Carl Sauer and Eduard Hahn and geneticists such as N.I. Vavilov. Note that there are two main hearths shown the the Old World: (1) tropical South Asia as a center for agricultural systems based on reproduction by vegetative planting (e.g., subdividing an existing plant into several parts, each of which grows into a new plant); and (2) subtropical Asia Minor as a center for agricultural systems based on reproduction by planting seeds. The fundamental distinction between the two types of plant propagation is repeated in the two centers (again, tropica and subtropical) suggested for the New World. The probable main lines of spread around each hearth are shown together with a secondary hearth area.

tures. These are linked by the three processes of human activity: the domestication of animals, the permanent cultivation of croplands, and trading of goods (Fig. 2.2b). Settlements were, however, the prerequisites for agricultural as well as urban cultures. Sauers' old world hearth in South Asia and the later New World hearth in the valleys and lowlands of the Northern Andes were most probable environments for agricultural innovation.

Archaeological Finds and Settlements

The archaeological finds in Iraq and Iran indicate the domestication of plants and animals by 3000 B.C. Likewise, the available evidences show that urban development appears to have begun in four major river basins: (1) the Tigris and Euphrates river interfluves, (2) the valley of the Nile in Egypt, (3) the Indus system areas in Pakistan and India, and (4) the Yellow river valley in northern China. The overwhelming majority of the settled population was found in these river valley areas. The geographical variation, however, brought forth variation in settlement types. The main core areas are shown in Table 2 (i).[4]

Thus, the south Asian part having more than 40 per cent of the estimated population during the beginning of the present century, was followed by China with its HwangHo culture area and thirdly by Roman Empire including the Nile valley and Syrian concentration. The Crete, Mayan, Aztec, Inca and Yoruba cultures also speak well about old cultural concentrations of settlements obviously different from the scattered primitive agricultural settlements and also the food collecting groups. Archaeological activities in other areas, like Asia Minor, may reveal additional cultural centres where diffusion was possible in various corridors. It remains true that in a number of separate regions man did succeed in devising a system of culture that intensified the collective level of living. These regions, within their broad territories, served as the sources of traits, complexes, and cultures that spread to outlying territories, and regions of lesser cultural development.[5]

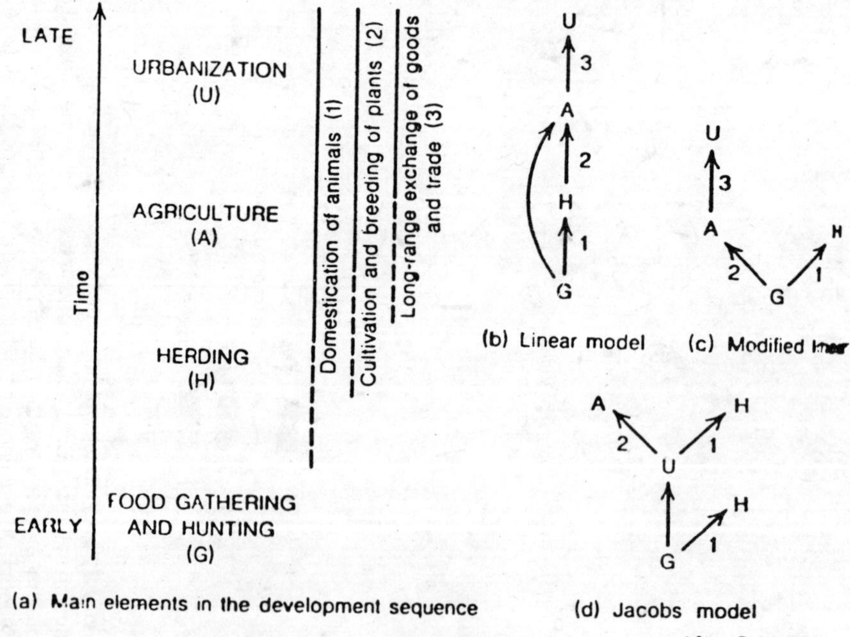

Figure 2.2(b)

Table 2(i)

Main Urban Core Areas

Zone	Location	Early Urban Culture	Representative City
Middle East (Fertile Crescent)	Nile Valley	Egyptian (3000 B.C.)	Memphis, Thebes
	Tigris-Euphrates Valley	Sumerian (2700 B.C.)	Ur, Uruk
	Indus Valley	Indus (2500 B.C.)	Mohenjodaro, Harappa
East Asia	Hwang Valley	Shang (1300 B.C.)	Anyang
	Mekong Valley	Khmer (A.D. 1100)	Angkor
Southern Europe	Aegean Islands and Peninsula	Aegean (2000 B.C.)	Knossos, Mycenae
	Italian Peninsula	Etruscan (400 B.C.	Felsina, Rome
America	Yucatan Peninsula	Mayan (A.D. 500)	Palenque, Tikal
	Central Mexico	Aztec (A.D. 1400)	Tenochtitlan
	Peru	Inca (A.D. 1500)	Cuzco
West Africa	Niger Valley	Yoruba (A.D. 1300)	Ife

* The dates are indicative of the middle period of the culture.

Protohistoric and Prehistoric Settlements

As human groups clustered in a particular landscape, the successes in inhabitation accumulated the technologies and such regions became culture hearths. With the crystallization of the most important old world hearths went through the growth and crystallization of settlements. The hearthwise spread and stabilization of settlements of protohistoric period are reviewed here in brief (Figs. 2.3a, 2.3b).

Mesopotamia

This old cultural centre lying within the larger zone of the Fertile Crescent, includes within its limits the Tigris-Euphrates valleys, the estuary of the two, the surrounding fringes of hill country on the east and north and the margins of the Arabian desert on the west and south. Due to its accessibility, the plain generated centripetal force to immigrants during the fifth and the fourth millennia B.C. This resulted into growth of a great number of centres of local settlements. By 3000 B.C., the Mesopotamian region had not only a mature culture but also helped in maturing the Egyptian civilization. The centre received many immigrant people like conquerors, settlers, slaves, and traders. The earliest archaeological evidence suggests rather sparse and scattered occupance by sedentary folk in linear patterns with shifts in locality over time during later periods having a peak in both areal occupance and population patterns in the era of Sargon-Hammurabi (2300-1800 B.C.). With the conquest of Mesopotamia by Assyrian and Persians after about 800 B.C., the centre lapsed into decadence, decline and ruin, to become again a land of agrarian villagers in riverine lowland in which the ruins of great cities became mythical marks of the past.[6] Abandoned canal systems and settlements exhibit variations in occupance.

The Nile Valley

The environmental conditions of open land along the Nile between the head of the delta and the first cataract, e.g., between Cairo and Aswan, had blooming culture and state even before the state of Mesopotamia. Though this culture never matched with the heights achieved in Mesopotamia and any few of its diffused offshoots spread beyond the eastern shores of the Mediterranean, yet it affected the latter zone during later period and served as a source for the diffusion of many

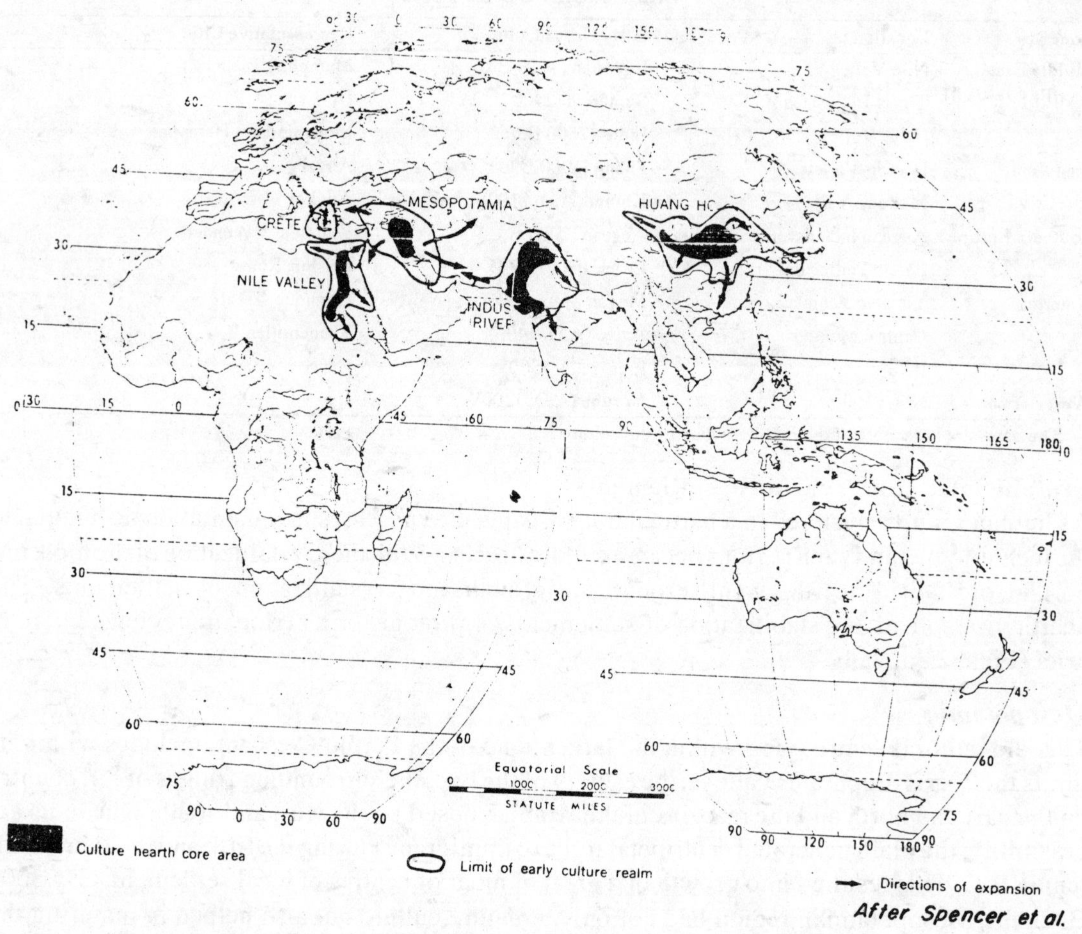

Figure 2.3(a): The early old world culture hearths and culture realms

things. Well before the onset of the Christian era, Egypt became a political pawn or a colony of outside power and the Nile valley again became a land of agrarian villagers living out an annual cycle of life framed around the seasonal pattern of the river.[7]

The Indus Valley

Excavations of new sites of Mohenjo-daro and Harappa, now in Pakistan, show evidences of urban culture having big size settlements mostly in the form of fortified palace-citadels. Intercourse between the urban civilizations of the Indus valley and Mongolian tribes, presumably already located in central Asia, is proved for the first half of the third millennium B.C.[8] Probably, there was a Neolithic continuity of occupance from the Indus lowland across to the Mesopotamian lowland, with both crop growing and animal economics widely distributed. Although similar in many respects to that of Mesopotamia, Indus valley culture exhibited a good deal of regional specialization which makes it unlike the cultures of the Mesopotamian lowland and the Nile valley.[9] The impact of Indus valley culture is visible up to Kausambi in the east and Maharashtra in the south in India.

The Yellow River Valley

The Neolithic sites of the basin exhibit this centre as a zone in which village dwelling, crop domesticating, animal using and culture developing patterns matured. Its expansion reached the Central Asian part. The walled settlement, the Chinese language system, pounded earth construction and the patterns of domestic and public architecture, both technology and forms, in bronze metallurgy and pottery and all other features have clear continuity with the Chinese Neolithic in too many ways to permit description of the North China culture, hearth as built wholesale on a base of diffusion.[10] We observe a clear historical continuity between the North China culture hearth and the later Chinese regional culture area and also between early Chinese culture systems and those of historic China. The large plain flourished with extensive settlements dominated chiefly by small regional states and city states.

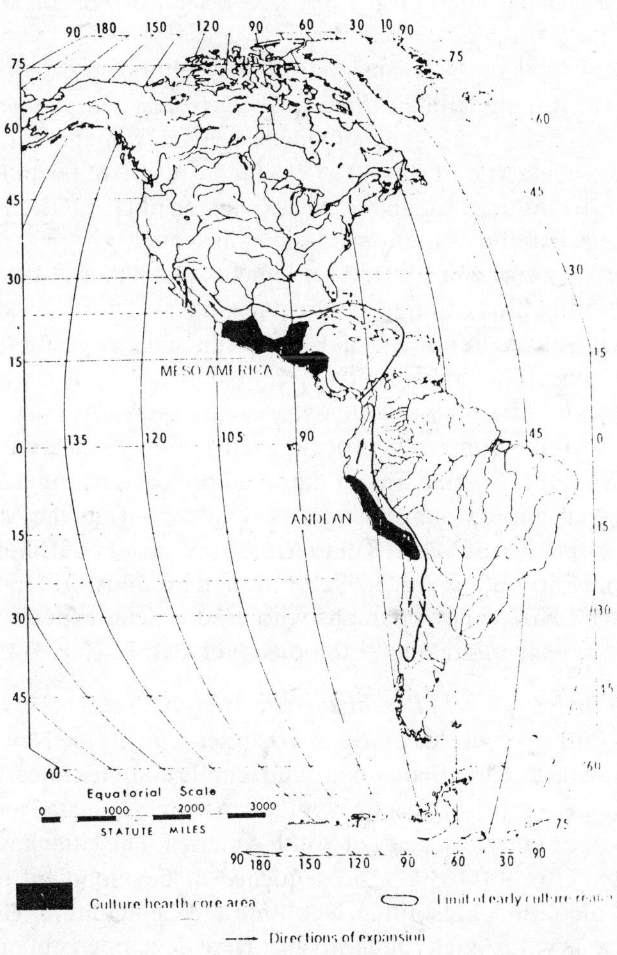

Figure 2.3(b): The new world culture hearths and culture realms.

Other Minor Centres

Besides the big hearths, there also existed minor pockets of advanced culture mostly having geographical association but a few far away from the old world hearths. As early as 4000 B.C., we observe Neolithic crop-growing clusters of villages on Crete Island plains. The Minoan culture also had towns built along the coast.

The environmental conditions of the eastern Mediterranean shores were also favourable for Neolithic crop-growing, village dwelling population. The region experienced struggle for territory among Hebrews, Hurrions, Armaeans, Phoenicians, Hittites and others. Likewise, Greeks advanced into Aegean peninsula shortly after 2000 B.C., adopted Minoan culture during Myceneaen age (1400-1200 B.C.); later arrival of Dorian Greeks was responsible for Greek civilization.

As regards expansion of Vedic cultural spread in India, there co-existed various settlement forms along with the three episodes from a geographical point of view: (a) The eastward carry of materials, technology and ideas derived from the Indus civilization during the later stages of its existence (i.e., 1500 B.C.), (b) the diffusion of Early Iron Age cultures in South Asia in the first millennium B.C., and (c) the expansion of Gangetic civilization after .500 B.C.[11] Details regarding spatial distribution are given in sequel.

The way of life and settlements in southern Manchuria, Korea and Japan were affected by North China culture in particular and that of north-western, western and southern parts in general. Of course, the border-lands of hearths settled by barbarians or semi-civilized people were also influenced in terms of village settlement and agrarian way of life.

In Africa, excavation works point towards vast areas of treasures of old cultures. Village dwelling crop-growers occupied different pockets dating from 4000 B.C. to 500 B.C. extending from the Arabian Sea to the western coast, the nuclear areas being the Nigerian (Niger basin) coast, upper Congo basin, Chad lake region and the Abyssinian highlands. With the excavations on the sites of Melka Kontoure, the pre-history of Ethiopia covers a period of time expanded from the Early Stone Age to Neolithic and protohistoric.[12] 'Punt' in Axumite culture was well-linked with Nile valley Pharaohs who used to send expeditions as early as 3000 B.C. Even the South Arabians migrated to Ethiopia much before 1000 B.C.[13] (Fig. 2.4).

The New World Pre-historic to Historic Settlements

Unlike old world centres of urban settlements the New World secondary hearths show evidences of clustered settlements around temple complex sites. One of these spread in the Meso-American zone comprising central southern Mexico, Yucatan and Guatemala and the other in the Peruvian zone of the west coast of South America. The latter hearth representing the Inca civilization dates back to 3000 B.C. The sequence of development here too is the same as in the old world Paleolithic, Mesolithic, Neolithic and Chalcolithic. The Inca Empire had close and clear connections with Azteks and Mayans. Here developed not only settlements, fortifications and political organizations but also irrigation system, metallurgy and specialization in manufacturing even before 800 B.C.

Thus, the humanization took place in old times due to complex forces diffused from primary hearths to secondary ones with a tendency to organize the space provided by ecological environment for human welfare.

The Later Culture Realms

The preceding discussion reveals that beyond the cultural centres of Western Europe, southern Africa and Australia were all peripheral areas and the Americas were colonized from East Asia at a late stage in human history. While Christianity prevailed in most part of Europe and German, Slavs etc. occupied the fertile plains and valleys, the Moslem realm took on a militant political

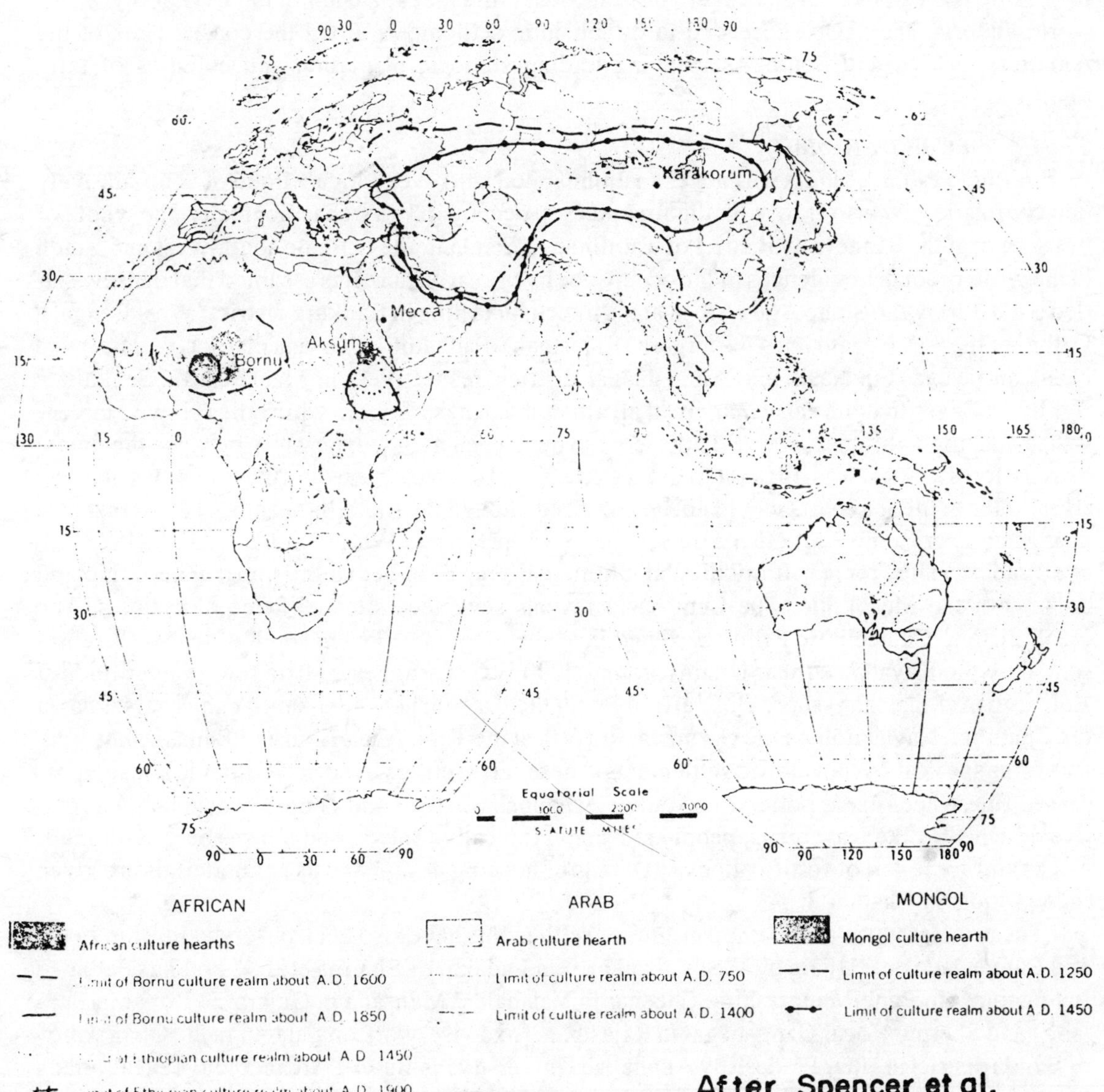

AFRICAN

African culture hearths

Limit of Bornu culture realm about A.D. 1600

Limit of Bornu culture realm about A.D. 1850

Limit of Ethiopian culture realm about A.D. 1450

Limit of Ethiopian culture realm about A.D. 1900

ARAB

Arab culture hearth

Limit of culture realm about A.D. 750

Limit of culture realm about A.D. 1400

MONGOL

Mongol culture hearth

Limit of culture realm about A.D. 1250

Limit of culture realm about A.D. 1450

After Spencer et al.

Figure 2.4: The later old world culture hearths and culture realms

and economic role and spread in southern part of Europe and most of the northern and eastern part of Africa. It gave codes of religious laws which influenced the aspects of life including the architecture and form of settlements in varied environmental conditions.

Some other culture regions did exist but basically they took the combines of culture devised elsewhere, e.g., Roman Empire, Khmer Empire, Pueblo culture region, etc. Some of these satellite regions achieved results that seemed to overshadow those of the original hearth.[14]

By and after 1500 A.D., most of the hearths expanded and humanization was complete even in oceanic islands, but Europe experienced most significant expansion in the next 400 years of world history. They also succeeded in establishing settlements along the coastal rims of the Americas, Africa and South Asia having trading stations, plantation and colonies of farm families.

The Indian Culture Realm

According to Pittard, "India was never an unihnabited land over which a flood of comparatively late civilizations was to flow with the first races to occupy it."[15] Archaeologically, the whole of India, except the Tinnevelly district of Tamilnadu, Kerala in the extreme south-west and Sindh in the west, produces evidences of the occupance by the early man. It is assumed that densely settled parts during the Stone Age were in areas like Sisunia hills in Bankura district (West Bengal), Lalitpur (Jhansi), Nagaur and Chittorgarh (Rajasthan), Padhamli, Mehsana district (Gujarat) and Nasik and Nevasa in Nasik and Ahmednagar districts respectively in Maharashtra. Sankalia[16] rightly observes that the early man lived all along the banks of rivers which then flowed in very wide beds, high altitudes, above 2,500 seem to have been avoided, possibly because they were heavily forested or it was difficult to get water easily. Likewise, very low marshy areas near the river deltas or the sea coasts would not be preferred, though the foothills near the sea, for instance near Madras or Bombay, if otherwise suitable, were preferred. While Sihora and Gonchi (Madhya Pradesh) sites represent middle Paleolithic culture, Bhimbedka the upper Paleolithic and Adamgarh the Mesolithic. The Luni basin reveals seventeen sites of Paleolithic times. The Neolithic and Chalcolithic cultures existed in Malwa region and even south of that well-represented by the Kayathans (near Ujjain) around 2000 B.C. as suggested by a few. Newer finds at Kalibangan (Rajasthan) show close affinity with the Kayathans. Other similar sites at Nagda on the Chambal, Navadatoli on the Narmada, Prakash at the Tapi, Ahar, Eran and Banas valley with rich finds speak about developed settlements. These early settlers lived in well-made houses, possessed fine wheel-made pottery, used tools, weapons of stone and copper/bronze and eat cultivated wheat. Like Kayathans, people at Nagda, typically Malwa, had houses built with mud-bricks and some sort of fortifications.[17] Details of housing design and use of materials are given in the sequel in Chapter 8.

The pre-Harappan and Harappan sites of settlements have also been observed in Bhimbetka and Dangewada near Ujjain by V.S. Vakankar,[18] in Ladakh; by Sharma et al.,[19] Prabhas Pattan,[20] Inamgaon;[21] in Pune-Maharashtra, Chechar in Vaishali,[22] Mehsana in Gujarat,[23] Ropar in Punjab,[24] and Sherpur[25] near Ganganagar in Rajasthan. Likewise, work on Lalapur in the Ohan valley of Banda district in Uttar Pradesh by Allahabad University Institute of Archaeology reveals many protohistoric and prehistoric sites of settlements. The protohistoric period would include the Harappan (2750 B.C. to 1700 B.C.); late Harappan (1700 B.C. to 1500 B.C.), degenerate Harappan (1500 B.C. to 1000 B.C.), and the Painted Grey Ware (1000 B.C. to 500 B.C.) cultures; thus, it extends from approximately 2750 B.C. to 500 B.C. The Neolithic finds may easily be categorized into three geographical zones as depicted in Figure 2.5. The first zone comprising finds from Assam, Bihar, Bengal and Orissa seems to be quite independent of the other two zones. The second zone comprises the finds from the valley of Kashmir and parts of Punjab. In the third zone comprising Karnataka, Andhra Pradesh and Tamil Nadu, there is overlapping of Neolithic with preceding Mesolithic phase on one hand and with Chalcolithic on the other. It seems that the

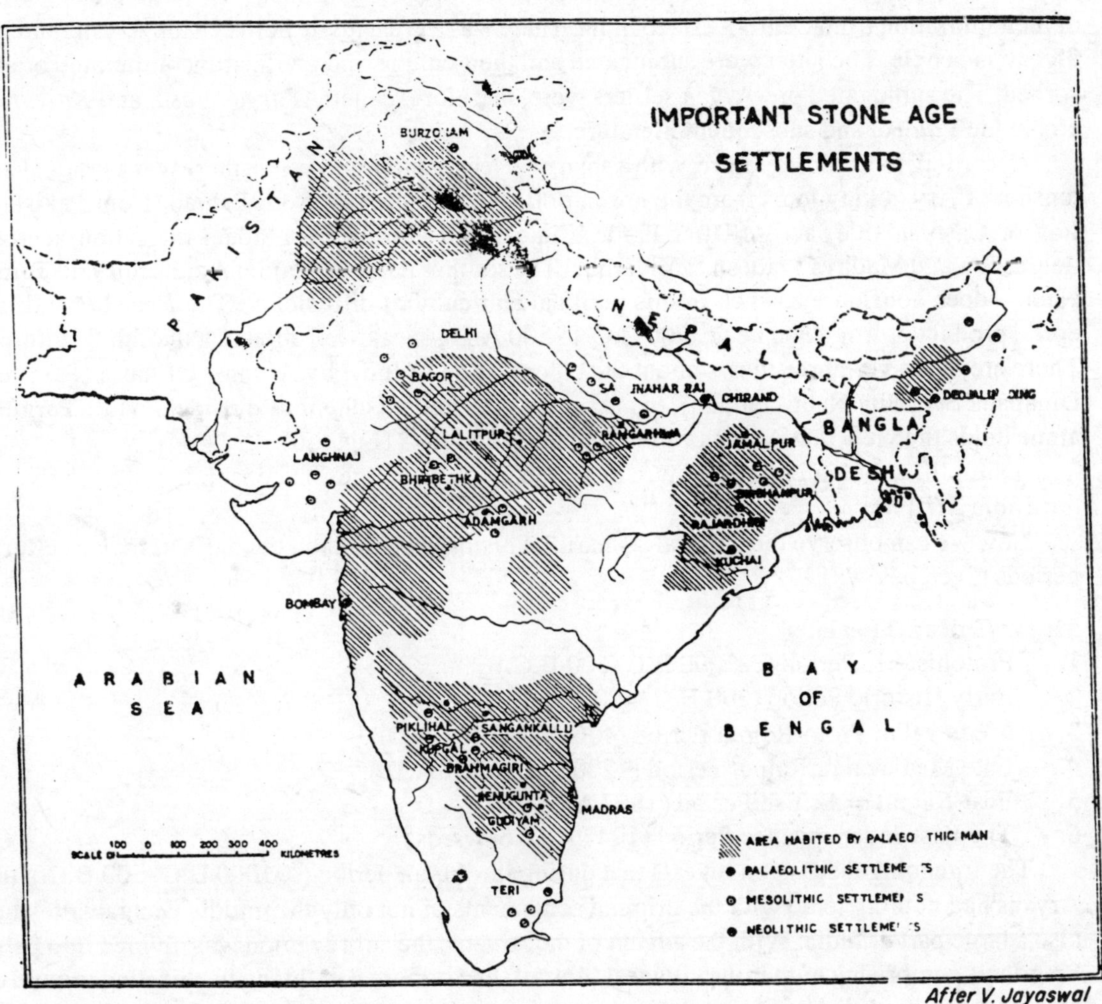

After V. Jayaswal

Figure 2.5: Important Stone age settlement

wide sweep of the Vedic and Harappan cultures extends beyond the Indian land mass. The influence did not end in Indonesia or Indo-China as commonly presumed but made itself felt in Latin America[26] There is interesting evidence of close ties between the Vedic and Indus Valley civilizations and the Maya civilization of Mexico.

Aryan Colonizations

The Soviet scholars trace the origin place of Aryans in Central Asia. According to Dube, the history of the Aryan settlement is a matter of controversy but the consensus of opinion is in favour of their migration from Central Asia to India. There was a great tussle between the Aryans and indigenous people. The latter were subjugated and their culture and civilization obliterated or absorbed. The subjugated pre-Aryan settlers were, therefore, called *Anarya*, *Dasa*, and *Kaivarta*, etc. in the *Vaidika* and subsequent literature.

According to Vedic literature, with a span of at least a thousand years, there was a gradual extension of Aryan kingdoms from the north, north-west to the east from Punjab (from Pakistan, Iran or Caspian side) across Uttar Pradesh into Bihar and then a gradual migration accross Saurashtra and Madhya Pradesh to Vidarbha. The south—Andhra, Karnataka, Kerala and Tamil Nadu—does not figure as such in this political and cultural diffusion.[27] The *Puranas* and the epics, product of Iron Age, i.e., c. 700 B.C. to 500 A.D., speak well about Chalcolithic cultures. There are, however, three views about the colonization of India by Aryans. Of these (Pargiter, Umapada Sen, Sita Nath Pradhan), the majority view regards them as outsiders while Pargiter alone holds the view that Aryans were indignous to India[28] (Fig. 2.6).

A simplified but integrated picture of Indian history emerges on consolidation as shown in the Table 2 (ii).

Now we can observe the cultural scenario of historical period on the basis of major cultural periods given below:[30]

Major Cultural Periods

1. Protohistoric Period (c. 3000 B.C.-300 B.C.)
2. Early Historic Period (300 B.C.-400 A.D.)
3. Medieval or Proto-Rajput Period (400 A.D.-1200 A.D.)
4. Late Medieval or Rajput Period (1200 A.D.-1857 A.D.)
5. Post-Rajput or British Period (1857 A.D.-1947 A.D.).
6. The Post-Independence Period (1947 A.D. onwards)

The foregoing discussion reveals that during the Aryan period (c. 1000 B.C.-500 B.C.), the Aryans had nothing to do with the original settlements of not only the middle Ganga valley but also a large part of India. With the advent of the Aryans, the entire region was divided into petty kingdoms comprising numerous villages. Most of the northern part, being the meeting ground of several races, provided good opportunity for racial admixture, not only of proto-Australoids and Mediterranean but also of Vedic Aryans and aboriginal cultures. The new Hindu culture, with its peculiar caste system, philosophy and religion, was evolved later by Aryans in the process of racial assimilation and Hinduization of the aboriginal population. As regards the political organization of the Vedic Aryans, the basis was the patriarchal family (*griha* or *kula*) reared on a decisively monogamous foundation. The successive higher units were styled as *grama*, *vis* and *jana* under the leadership of *gramani*, *vispati* and *gops* respectively. There were six types of human habita-

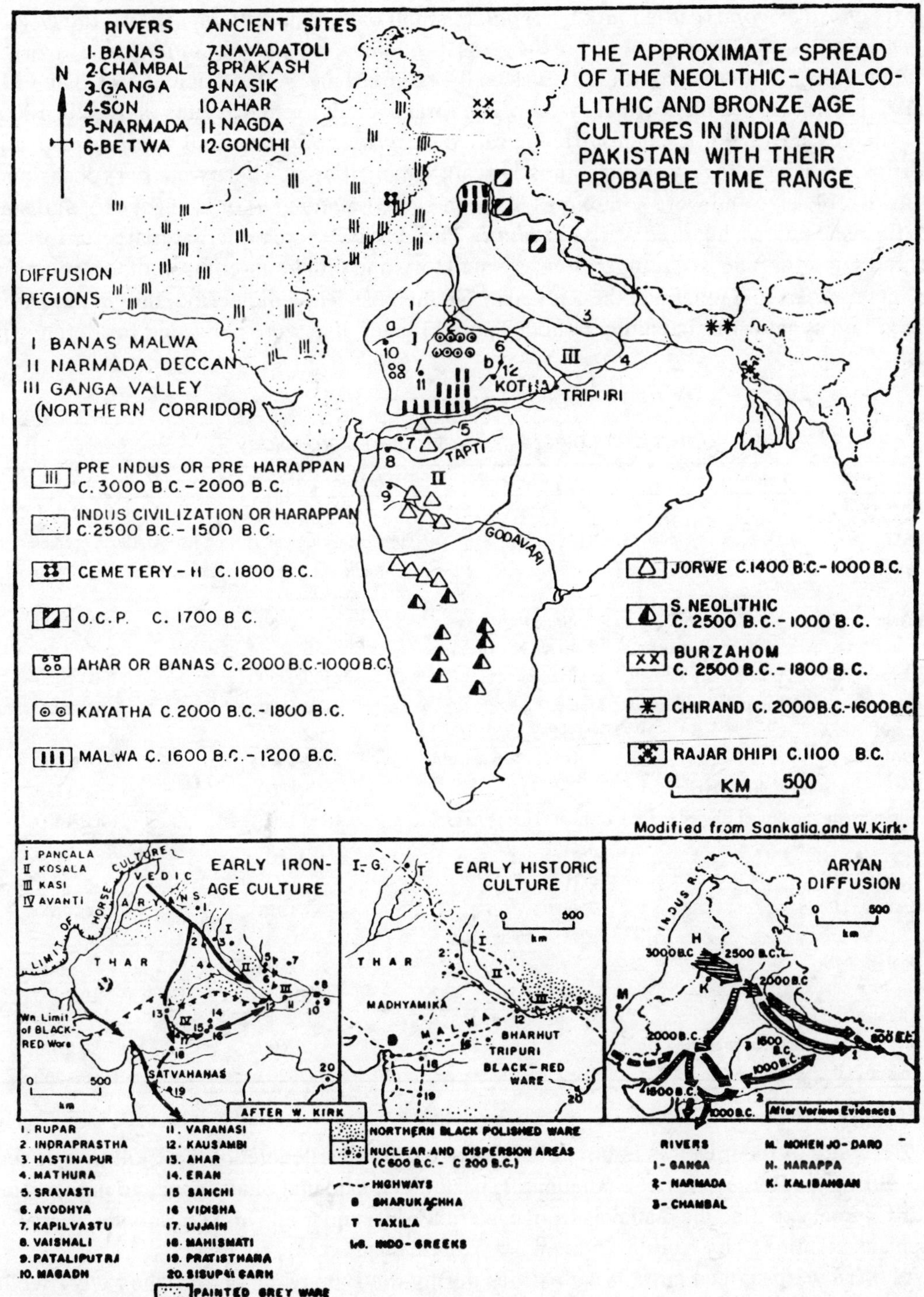

Figure 2.6: **The approximate spread of the neolithic-chalcolithic and bronze age cultures in India and Pakistan with their probable time range**

tions: (i) *ghosa* or *gopa* (cattle ranch), (ii) *pali* (a small barbarian settlement), (iii) *durga* (fort), (iv) *grama* (village), growing round the *durga* as its nucleus, (v) *kharwat* or *pattana* (town), and (vi) *nagar* (city). The rural community was well-organized and self-sufficient unit. The village organization was based on decimal system. The rural society formed groups of 10, 20, 100 and 1,000 villages, the ruler of each group being called *Dasgrami*, *Satgrami* and *Adhipati* respectively.[31] Thus, the Rigvedic Aryans were mostly scattered in villages. There were *purs* occasionally of considerable size and were sometimes made of stone (*asmamayi*) or iron (*ayasi*), and sometimes furnished with a hundred walls (*satbhuji*). These '*purs*' were rather ramparts for forts than cities and served as places of refuge. Houses, small forts and village assembly halls are mentioned as an integral part of a village in the Rigveda.[32] In the post-Rigvedic period, the '*mahagramas*' (large villages) have also been mentioned. These villages also were palisaded for defence purposes.

Table 2(ii)

Upper and Lower Limits of Indian Chronology[29]

Legend	*Legend*	*Lower Limit (in B.C.)*	*Upper Limit (in B.C.)*
Literary	Archaeological	(a) Literary (b) Archaeological (c) Radio-carbon (Uncorrected)	1. Astronomical 2. MASCA corrected RC dates
1. Pre-literary	Neolithic (Amri etc.)	3000-2500	3500-3000
2. Proto-Vedic	Pre-Harappan	2500-2250	3000-2700
3. Atharvavedic and Trans-Indus Rigvedic	Mature Harappan	2250-1750	2700-2000
4. Turmoil and War	End of Harappan Culture	1700-1650	2000-1900
(A) Dasa rajna battle of the Rigveda		1700	1930
5. Atharvaveda and Indian Rigveda	(a) Late Harappan (b) OCP (c) B & R	1650-1200	1900-1400
6. Brahmana Period	Early PGW (west of Yamuna)	1250-1050	1400-1100
(B) Bharata battle		1100	1400
7. Sutra Period	Late PGW (east of Yamuna)	1050-600	1100-800
(C) Breakdown of Sanskrit as spoken tongue		600	800-600
8. Prakrit-Pail Literature	NBP	600-200	600-200

Epic Period

Due to paucity of records, it is impossible to weave out a detailed net of the evolution of settlements during the Ramayana and Mahabharata period. It is said that Shatrughna, youngest brother of Lord Rama, expelled the Yadavas from eastern Malwa and made his son Subahu, emperor of Vidisha as mentioned by Kalidas in his work *Raghuvansham*.[33]

As there were sixteen large principalities during the Ramayana period, they were well-inhabited according to the suitable environmental conditions. The pattern remained almost the same during the Mahabharata period. The tribal areas mostly under a system of confederacy existed side by side. Though no definite rural structure is on record, it appears to be certain that the agrarian landscape maintained the continuity of Aryan settlements in *grams* (villages) to feed the warriors, cultivators and a host of other members living under the Aryanized social order. But the Mahabharata War resulted into disaster and kingdoms (mostly Kshatriya) were annihilated and vanquished. For a few centuries, the historical curtain dropped and darkened and it seems possible that for a long period the most populous parts of India saw the natural growth of flora and fauna and remained desolate, only being overpowered by the aboriginals.

Buddhist Period (c. 500 B.C. to 325 B.C.)

The curtain rises again from the early Buddhist time when we hear about flourishing cultural centres/cities of Kausambi, Kashi, Pataliputra, Ujjain, Vidisha etc.

The Rajputs, while leaving the Sarswati valley and Ganga-Jamuna *doab*, settled near Kausambi and brought with them the sacred name of Saraswati, though deserted and left over during later geographical period, and could not detach it from Ganga-Jamuna hence Prayag or Pratisthanpur (Jhunsi) as cultural centre at the confluence of the three rivers (three river valley cultures), the tri-*sangam* being the symbolic representation of the old culture. As regard rural settlements, villages appear, in those days, to have enjoyed a large share of autonomy under their headman, while class distinctions were not very strongly marked. Buildings were mostly of wood; only forts and palaces were made of stone.[34] During this period, rural settlements were of compact type mainly along the trade routes and in river valleys. Defence from invaders and wild animals played major role for their nucleation. But the aboriginals established homesteads suited to their racial characteristics. In the neighbourhood of the inhabited site stood a patch of narrow village grove, a remnant of the primeval forest and beyond this was the wide expanse of cropped land, usually comprising millet fields. Each village had invariably a common pasture land for the cattle and also a considerable stretch of jungle to provide wood for building and fuel, perhaps owned in common by village community. The entire village was enclosed by a fence of bush but the individual fields were not enclosed.[35]

Post-Buddhist or Hindu Period (325 B.C. to 800 A.D.)

Under the Sunga rule, a survival of Brahmanism took place and Buddhism began to lose the paramount position it had acquired during Ashok's period. This period was marked by the erection of temples around which revolved the rural social system of those days. Religious centres evolved at several places, particularly around Kashi, Ujjain, Maheshwar, Mathura etc. With the advent of Sakas during the first century B.C., there took place great admixture of races and significant changes occurred in the rural occupance on the line of the alien invaders who brought with them a new culture only to be gradually adopted by and assimilated with the early settlers.

During this period, the villages and townships were autonomous.[36] The regional human occupance suffered a loss since the Scythian victory in A.D. 78 and cultural changes in the rural landscape followed the political ups and downs in the north under Sakas and in western Narmada valley area under Haiyhayas or Kalchuri kings. After 390 A.D., the Guptas of Magadh established peace and the Golden Age prevailed. Even after the fall of this empire, settlements expanded towards new clearings following diffusion of human groups who were under constant pressure of the foreign invaders. The aboriginals moved towards hilly parts and reclaimed forests. Huen Tsang, who travelled India during the eighth century, has mentioned about the Hindu as well as Buddhist centres which exerted great influence on the rural society.

Pre-Muslim or Rajput Period (800 A.D. to 1200 A.D.)

This was the period of independent principalities of Rajputs showing alliances and dissensions of these clans. From the eighth to the tenth Century, by a gradual process of evolution, very imperfectly understood as yet, these tribes became Brahmanized and adopted pedigrees which, connected them with the Hindu Pantheon, probably developing finally into the Rajput clans.[37] This was the period of healthy horizontal expansion of settlements. Most of the fertile and cleared tracts were occupied by these clans. This invading Rajput culture was of a greater economic complexity than the indigenous culture of early settlers with simpler socio-economic structure (Hoffman, 1964: 45-65). The aboriginals still occupied several parts as independent principalities like Banswara under Bansia Bhil, Jhabua under Jhabboo Nayak, chief of Lavana tribe during later period. Gonds, Santhals, Oraon and others occupied separate hilly and plateau areas. It is noteworthy that aboriginal cultural landscape was at times obliterated and transformed by the superseding Rajput clans. The latter established new villages, the land was put under continuous tillage, new settlements and hamlets were founded and even the marginal land was brought under plough. The aboriginals belonging to the upgraded category found a separate part or sector in the villages. There took place no wholesale expropriation and expatriation or overnight massacre of the aboriginals as one visualizes in some clan areas of the Ganga plain. The main remarkable feature of this period was the establishment of strongholds, fortified villages, fortresses etc. as the internecine war was a common thing. Most probably, the tribal territories, occupied by the Rajputs, formed clan areas of the Rajputs who expanded them during successive period of occupance.

Late Medieval Period or Rajput Period (1200 A.D. to 1700 A.D.)

Moslem invasions from the eleventh century onwards in the northern parts of India dispersed and drove out various clans and they migrated and settled in many areas. The mass movements appear to have followed the overthrow of Hindu kingdoms of Delhi, Ajmer and Kanauj in the twelfth century. Powell[38] has rightly remarked that the Rajput settlements now known are almost all the result of later movements of small bodies or clans, and frequently originated in individual adventure and in royal grants to settlers in available waste tracts. The Rajput society of this period was cut into two distinct divisions: first, there were those Rajputs who had established themselves in the eighth century or those who had retired to the plains and plateau areas when the first rush of Muslims in India, swept away many of the Rajput chiefs from the north and west. They were the landholders and well-settled when the Moghuls established their control over most of the north and central India. After 1598, there was, however, another set of Rajputs who classed themselves as true Rajputs of the purest blood and as such purer than those of the first set. This set consisted of those Rajputs who came from royal families of Rajputana (Rajasthan), who had served the Moghuls very faithfully, and proved their mettle and were rewarded with grants of land. These Rajput grantees brought their relatives, friends and dependents with them[39] and founded states as well as new clan territories. These evolutional phases of occupation might be well understood while discussing the spatial diffusion of clans and settlements.

In addition to all these, there was the Muslim element in the population. The Afghans had scattered throughout plains and particularly in Central India in different centres while the Moghul element was limited to big towns only or to places where there were outposts of the government.

It was during the reign of Akbar (1556-1605) that peace and stability were established and clan settlements which obtained clan agglomerations were later crystallized into 'Tappa' and 'Turuf' centres. During the last decade of the nineteenth century, there were brought changes in administrative 'subah' limits at macro-level and 'mahal' limits at meso-level but there was little interference with the local Rajput chiefs who were largely responsible for the development of the rural settlements. Muslim conquest was not followed by Muslim immigration into the countryside. The Muslim villages of the interior are, in origin, mainly Rajput villages being converted later to Islamic faith.[40] During this period, out of the widespread scramble for land and agrarian unsettlement, produced by Rajputs invasions, emerged the landed aristocracy of superior Rajputs under the reigning sovereigns. Agricultural pursuit, however, encouraged social assimilation between the rulers and the ruled, the landowner and cultivators.[41]

Post-Rajput or Maratha and British Period (1700 A.D. to 1947 A.D.)

Though most of the northern plains were less affected, yet anarchy was rampant, during the eighteenth century, not merely in political affairs but also in social and cultural matters. The Maratha invasions, internecine warfare, incursions of Pindaris and *thugs* (dacoits) in Central India (Madhya Pradesh) retarded the development of rural settlements. Might was right everywhere, Rajputs still capturing weaker states or territories,[42] cultivators being confiscated of their properties be it cash or kind, and aboriginals either playing the part of predatory tribes[43] or sharing the fate of other inhabitants. There occurred changes in ethnic structure due to immigration in many parts.

But, throughout the period, function played a strong role and the groups which were quite dissimilar in ethnic origins tended to unite under its influence to continue the age-old organization of village communities. The settlement forms could not be changed before the arrival of the British because of the lack of peace and security. Most of the big villages, during this period, were surrounded by trench or canal in plains, walled or built round fortress on plateau. Forests and woodlands formed boundaries between villages and more commonly between clan areas of different local chiefs.[44] The process of making the 'parganas' more symmetrical, started under the later Muslims, was continued under the British rule.[45]

By 1811 A.D., the British rule brought peace and security and several states were formed under Muslim and Rajput rulers. Population increased, and more land was brought under plough through deforestation. New villages were established and hamlets increased. The state chiefs divided their territories among Jagirdars mostly of their kith and kin and rural settlements expanded in the far off areas of forests. With the development of means of transport and communications, technical advance, organized tenure system, security of life in rural areas, spatial expansion of old habitations and urbanization of old agglomerations in the form of administrative centres was the outcome.

A Few Examples of Protohistoric and Historic Settlements

The Indus civilization (or Harappan culture) represents the earliest known development of large-scale urbanization in the Indian sub-continent and in so far as no immediate successor civilization can be recognized the episode on the whole has been judged abortive—a glorious but false dawn of Indian urbanism.[46] Even the *vis* of the Indus culture, the *puras* of the Epic times, and the *janapadas* of the second urbanization appear to be viable stages in the development and vicissitudes of cities, towns and villages.[47] Whatever might have been the hierarchy of settlements, it is true that cities must have got support from village settlements in their hinterland. The old sites of settlements scatter throughout India in general and northern plain in particular which need mention.

Ropar (Rupanagar District, Punjab, on Sutlej)

The archaeological finds revealing the sequence of cultures showed Harappan (2000-400 B.C.), Painted Grey Ware (1000-700 B.C.), NBPW (600-200 B.C.), followed by Sunga, Kushan, and Gupta (C.200 B.C.-A.D. 500). Construction of houses was made with slabs of *kankar*, burnt lump of clay (burnt bricks), etc. Drains, water storage reservoir and soak wells speak about developed habitations. A nuclear dating of not earlier than 600 B.C. in the more eastern region of Uttar Pradesh, Bihar, Ganga valley and a shorter dating for the total range of the NBPW from 600-300 B.C. as it moved west up to the Taxila, seems well indicated by the combined evidence of Ropar, Hastinapura, Ahichchhatra and the more easterly nuclear NBP sites of Bihar and east Uttar Pradesh.[48]

Ahichchhatra (Panchala Kingdom Capital, near Hastinapur)

Here finds reveal sequence ranging from 300 B.C. to 1100 A.D. in nine stages. Mud brick buildings, brick peripheral wall and mud ramparts, once attached to the town, existed from 300 B.C. to 100 B.C. It seems that it was only in the *antervedi* between Yamuna and Ganga, virtually from Indraprastha to Prayaga, that the full advantage of the trends in polity, urbanization, onward of Iron Age metallurgy and main stream movements of the historic communities between the Indus and tributary system and the Yamuna-Ganga system were impressive.[49] Incidentally, the whole *doab* suffered heavily; the loss of battle could not bring the economic stamina as well as cultural vigour up to the fifth century A.D.

Hastinapura (on deserted bank of Budhi Ganga)

Here finds show an antecedent culture, namely, the Ochre Coloured Pottery, i.e., protohistoric (mature Harappan), then Painted Grey Ware belonging to 1200 B.C.-1000 B.C. and after a gap NBP using culture with a life span ranging from 600 B.C. to 300 B.C. Evidences of ring stones, soakage wells and brick buildings belonging to Sunga period prove it to be a well-populated town. Then afterwards up to the tenth century, it again lapsed into oblivion only to be revived in the eleventh century A.D. by the medieval Hindu kingdoms. It seems that the Kuru links were dismembered by a poetic justice through floods around 850 B.C. seemingly after Parikshit, Janmejaya and six others up to Nichakshu. The centre of power drifted towards east starting from Kausambi to Rajgir and Pataliputra.

Kausambi (near Allahabad, Uttar Pradesh, on Ganga)

The city as well as *janapada* of Kausambi exhibits sites with occupation almost continuous for nearly 3,000 years. Ramparts dated to 600 B.C. and guard rooms, bastions and stoned paved corbelled drain were constructed during later periods. The palace of Udayan Vatsaraj, later elaborated during *Kushan* times, saw the invasion of the Huna hence in ruins. Other rich finds are similar to those found in Taxila, Ropar and Patalipura. Fa Hien and Hieun Tsang also visited the place. That around 875 B.C., Hastinapura communities should have considered only Kausambi, which is more than three hundred miles away in the *anatarvedi*, as the fit migratory domicile, speak high, not only of the well-known status of Kausambi then but also its provisions for a happy habitation.[50] Kausambi represents the spread of settlements during 1500 B.C. to 800 B.C. in western as well as eastern Ganga valley. Chirand, Rajghat, Sonepur, Chechar and Belan valley sites of Koldihva, and Deoghat are other examples. Kausambi came in closer contact with Malwa during the first millenium B.C.

Rajghat (Kasi or Northern Part of Varanasi)

The site reveals various periods of settlements ranging from pre-NBP to the medieval times. Mud walls and ring wells, rampart, channel, hearths and drains in houses, brick *kunda* or tank speak about various phases of settling process. The mud rampart could have been coeval with that of Magadh, Rajgir and Patna. Kasi *janapada* was well-linked with Kosala and Kausambi. Thus, Rajghat was well-supported by village cultures spread out in mid-Ganga valley. The Buddhist ruins bespeak its antiquity which is very great but unfortunately is robbed of the glory which is justly her due.[51] It is worthy of notice, as illustrating the nature of Mohammedan rule in India, that nearly all the buildings in Banares (Rajghat or Kasi) of acknowledged antiquity, have been appropriated by the Musalmans.[52] A diligent perusal of the Kasikhand might lead to the discovery of its era because it contains at least thirty to forty epithetical designations of Banares.

Rajgir (Rajgriha or Giribraja) (South of Nalanda and Patna in Bihar)

The old Rajgir, associated in the sixth century B.C. with the Buddha and Mahavira during the formative time of the Buddhist and Jain faiths, had massive dry stone walls 40 kilometre long.[53] This Magadha nucleus was the seat of Jarasandha who fought the Mahabharata War. Well linked with Kuchai towards south in Orissa and Belan valley sites of the Son (Madhya Pradesh) and Uttar Pradesh, this zone flourished with settlements in the hoary past. Excavations at Rajgriha reveal use of stone blocks in fort, *chaitya* and monastery, pathways, and caves. The place was visited by Buddha, Mahavira, Fa-Hien and Hieun Tsang and yielded NBP ware as well as remains of Sunga and Kushana period. Once being one of the mightiest cities of the Ganga valley only next to Kausambi, it represents the power centre which also formed a sacred triangle with Bodh Gaya and Nalanda. When Udayan (459-443 B.C.) shifted the capital to Patna, Rajgriha was affected and lost supremacy.

Pataliputra (Patna—Confluence of Ganga and Son)

It was probably founded (500 B.C.) as a border fortress town of Magadha, and had massive fortifications, and ramparts. The site yielded evidences of settlements of Maurya and Gupta periods with a sequence of five such phases starting from 600 B.C. to 1600 A.D., Pataliputra was then the first most functional, innovative and wide-based urban power centre and formed a definitive phase of Iron Age urban economy.

Ujjain (Ujjaiyini, Avantika on the Bank of Kshipra, Madhya Pradesh)

The capital of Avanti Mahajanapada it was ruled by Pradyota Mahasena II contemporary of the Buddha and Vatsaraja Udayana. The site revealed four period starting from B.C. 750 having ramparts, structures of mud and burnt brick-particularly tank and canal-tile-roofed mud brick workshop as well as Malwa coins. Ujjain was well-linked with Mathura in the north, Kasi and Kausambi in the Ganga Valley, and Kaundinyapur in Vidarbha to the south. Besides being a clearing house of trade and seat of intellectuals like Varahamihira and Kalidas and republican leader Vikramaditya, it was a cosmopolitan and Versatile city of leadership. It is also associated with Sandipan's Ashram where Krishna and Sudama both stayed for study, hence, dating back to the Mahabharata period.

New studies reveal a few more ancient sites in northern *doab* area. Bhardwaj[54] describes such places existing in Haryana as representatives of the Ramayana and Mahabharata period.

Ailadhana was the old name of Ludhiana and finds mention in Valmiki's Ramayana. It literally means the 'seat of Aila or Ila's son, Ila being the daughter of Manu Vaivasvata.

Pratisthana is associated with Pururava's now identified with the town of *Patran* located near Rigvedic Saraswati. Likewise Panini's *Tausavana* is Tohana, *Vatadhana* is present Bhatinda and Jayanti of the Mahabharata is Jind.

Manusa as mentioned in the Rigveda[55] is the present village *Manas* near Kaithal. It is listed as one of the *tirthas* of Kurukshetra.

Ilaspada: It is the ruined mound site near Shergarh near kaithal *named* as *Ilayaspada* in the Rigveda and later in the Mahabharata.

Kapisthala is the present Kaithal. Panini and Albiruni also noticed it.

Asandivat is the present town Asandh about 750 B.C. old and associated with king Janmejaya Parikshita. It must have been famous during Buddhist period.

Karoti lies near Diplana railway station. Excavations contain evidence of a continuous occupation from pre-Harappan times. Sandilya[56] describes it as the place where Tura Kavaseya made a fire-alter for the gods.

Srughna was important town now represented by a small village Sugh near Jagadhari. There is mention of this place in the Buddhist works Mahamayuri and Divyavadana. The finds reveal it to have been existing during c. 600-500 B.C.

Khandavaprastha: Purana Qila site is the old Indraprastha (Capital of the Pandavas) which reveals continuous occupation from the Mauryan period. In Bhagavata Purana[57] it represents Khandavaprastha. It also finds mention in Jatakas and is associated with Arjun, Krishna as well as Vedic kings like Pururava, Nahusa and Yayati[58].

Prithudaka is the town of Pehova on the Sarasvati near Thanesar widely mentioned in the Mahabharata and Puranas. The site is associated with *Rsi Visvamitra* and finds reveal its antiquity beyond 1000 B.C. It owes its origin to king Prithu, son of Vena.

The Vedic site of *Vinosana* is represented by Kalibangan whose finds belong to Harappana culture quoted with the age of the Atharvaveda. Other notable site Ahicchatra was the capital of Panchal. Beside these, various ancient places of settlement find frequent mention in epics, Rigveda, Puranas and Jatakas[59] but need archaeological seal to be on record (Fig. 2.7)

It was in towns such as these that the cultural forms of a widespread Gangetic civilization evolved, encouraged by river and road communications and the growth of commerce and a monetary system.[60]

Stein[61] and Ghosh[62] could find evidences of flourishing old settlements of Bhatner, Bhadrakali and Munda near Hanumangarh town in Ghaggar Valley. Most of the settlements, compact in nature and having well established corporate life, were decayed due to desication during the end period of 1,000 B.C. Even up to the rule of the Sunga, Nahpan and Saka (500 B.C.-57 B.C.) there were important regional centres of commercial significance.

From Kausambi to Bharukaccha (Badodara) were located the early Buddhist sites like

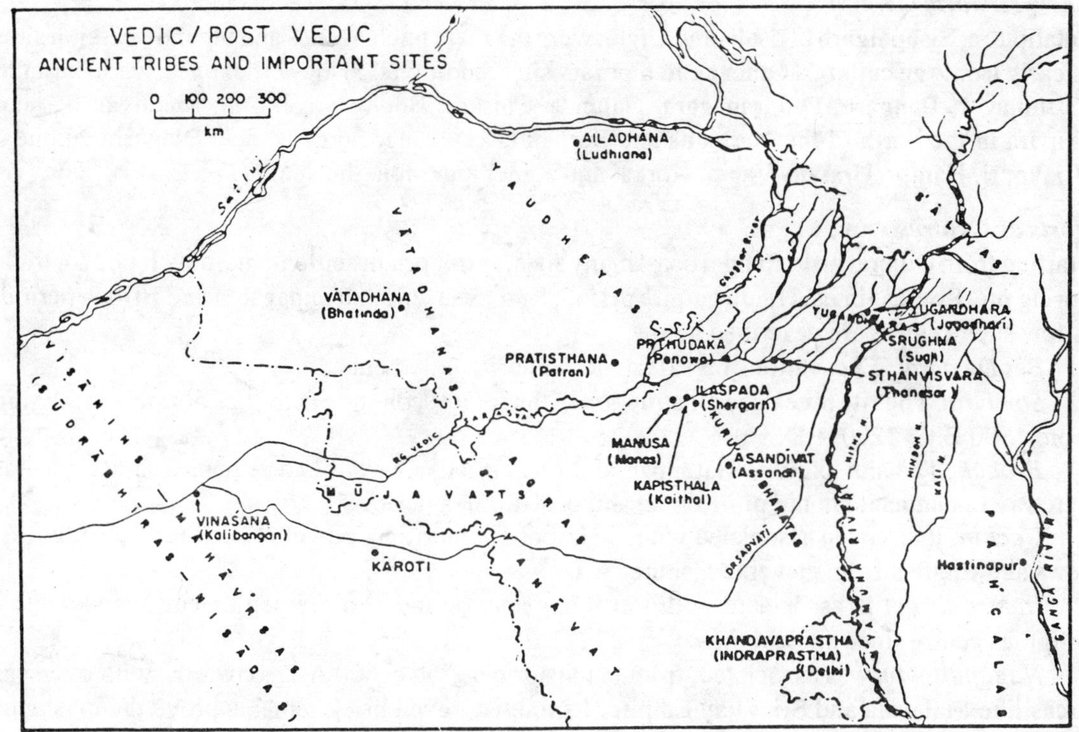

Figure 2.7: Vedic/Post vedic ancient tribes and important sites

Sanchi, Vidisha (Bhilsa) and Bharhut on the one hand and to the south existed Mahismati, Pratisthana and Brahmapuri, Hampi and Madurai. Likewise, Tamralipti was the outport of the civiliza tion in west Bengal. Now, we can name a few centres according to periods of civilization.

The Indus Civilization Centres

Starting from the north western front zone while Ropar, Kalibangan, Sandhanwala, Alamgirpur represent the north zone; Sajanipur, lothal, Rangpur, Amra, Rajdi, and Bhagatrav, the Saurashtra. Other centres influenced by these were Gilund, Ahar, Nagda and Tripuri of Malwa region; Navadatoli, Prakash, Bakal, Nasik, Jorwe, Nevasa and Sonegaon of central zone; Maski, Utnur, Kesarpalli, Nagarjunkonda, Tekkalakota, Kupgal, Sanganakal, Brahmagiri and Hemmige in the south zone.

Early Iron Age Centres

The main centres were Hastinapur, Ahicchatra, Panipat, Indraprashta, Mathura, Ayodhya, Sravasti, Kapilvastu, Vaisali, Pataliputra, Varanasi and Kausambi in the north; Ujjain in the Malwa; Champa, Tamralipti and Sisupalgarh in the east and Kancipuram and Madurai in the south. Other contemporary sites were again Ropar, Rajagriha in the north; Eran, Ahar, Vidisha, Sanchi, Nagada, Somnath, Bharukaccha and Mahismati in the central and western zones and nasik, Pratisthana, Pachampad, Maski, Bhongir, Dharanikota, Brahmagiri, Mahabalipuram and Arikamedu in the south.

Early Historic Centres

Pataliputra, Sisupalgarh (Tosali) and Ujjain were the main nuclear sites and other dispersion sites of early Iron Age cultures. Other contemporary sites, additional to the earlier ones, were Sarnath, Kushinagar, Bangarh, Pundranagara, Nalanda, Paisara, Bodhgaya, Bairat, Madhyamika and Tripura in the north of the Narmada and Sorparaka, kalyana, Jaggayyapeta. Nagarjunakonda, Vijaypuri, Hampi, Uraiyur Vanci, Korkai and Kanchipuram in the south (Fig. 2.6).

Ports as Centres

Starting from Gujarat up to Bengal coast many sites, as important settlements, developed for trade during pre-Roman times, Hindu empire period, European colonial expansion and British period. A few such centres are described below.

Bet Dwarka: Excavations reveal the pre-historic settlements.

Somnath: The site reveals reconstruction of the socio-economic activities of a period ranging from 1500 B.C.-1200 A.D.

Broach: The site exhibits Harappan and pre-Christian early historic phases and served as gateway to peninsula in the pre-Roman and post-Roman period.

Cochin: It has been associated with the important maritime powers like Dutch, Portuguese, Jews and English from eleventh Century A.D.

Rameswaram is associated with the Ramayana period and the settlement has served as religious centre since ancient time.

Nagapattinam was associated, from the historic period c. 600 A.D. onwards, with overseas areas like Malaysia and Sri Vijay Empire. Its multistoreyed brick remains prove the existence during past.

Sadras or Sadurangapattinam was the chief southern port during Pallava period and important port for Chola and Vijaiyanagara.

Motupalli was an important centre of trade and culture in the period from the thirteenth century A.D. in Andhra.

Kalingapatnam had been trade centre from sixth-seventh century onwards between kalinga and Andhra and Burma and Malaysia.

Origin and Growth of Primitive Settlements

Buildings and settlements are the visible expression of the relative importance attached to different aspects of life and the varying ways of perceiving reality.[63] In short these are the physical expression of the *genre de vie*. Man makes choice to mould space according to his cultural values, hence variations in habitations in response to environmental stimuli. He, consciously or unconsciously, through settlements relates, himself and his way of life, to the pravailing environment. Thus, settlements become physical embodiments of an ideal environment. The preceding discussion in the earlier sections regarding past stages of man who adapted through varying environments leads us to think about the primitive settlements.

Habitation Models

Evidences available reveal that man started living in a group of houses following a characteristic pattern according to his best choice. Most probably, in the first model he preferred to make round settlements with houses arranged in a circular way, the hollow space in between being of multipurpose use. Of course this strategy provided the best defence from wild animals and enemies too.

The primitive vernacular buildings, in some tribal areas in India and in rural areas in developing countries, still depict the same arche typal arrangement in scattered small settlements. The conical huts of Amharas in Ethiopian Highlands and tiled houses of Gonds in Madhya Pradesh (India) are a few examples. It seems that man being a gregarious animal naturally liked to be at one place along with his kith and kins as discussed later.

The second choice of settling design comprised the linear pattern of houses in a single row along a river, edge of the sea, lake or marsh according to the site available and the resources of the tract for earning a living.

In the third model houses were arranged in parallel rows facing each other and thus formed streets in between, the open street itself played multifarious role. This was the better arrangement not only for defence but for playing, gossiping, performing functions etc.

As the social organizations developed in time, many structures were added to fulfill the need of the society. They could add, therefore, the dormitory, the drum house, the village assembly or the chief's house, the granary, and the canoe lodge at one end of the street, the spirit house, the shrine or clan god (Dih) and the Earth Goddess or the village Mother in a dominant site, in the junction of village alleys or outside the village boundaries in the sacred grove.[64] This was the case in all tribal societies of the world with some variations in spatial arrangement of structures or place allotted to deities or ancestors. We shall study and discuss in detail the morphogenesis of Indian settlements in Chapters 3 and 4 and morphology in Chapter 6.

Diffusion of Settlements

The study of spatial diffusion occupies a central place in geographical researches. The question, which haunts a geographer, is the dynamics by which a phenomenon originally located at one place becomes transferred to another. The word diffusion from the verb 'diffuse' means to disperse or be dispersed from a centre; to spread widely, disseminate (The Oxford English Dictionary). If we look to the history of geographic literature on diffusion a rich modelling appears in agricultural, medical, economic, social and cultural branches. These are, of course, borrowings from researches in Economics, Sociology, and Epidemiology.[65]

Empirical Studies

The work on cultural as well as settlement diffusion could be traced in the frontier thesis of Turner[66] in American history, Bowman's[67] Pioneer Fringe and Zoergs'[68] Pioneer Settlement: Cooperative Studies—the Classics of that period. During thirties Sauer and Brand[69] (1930) collected archaeological evidences from pueblo-sites and attempted to deduce the culture areas and successions in South-eastern Arizona. Stanislawsky[70] (1946) traced the diffusion of the grid-pattern in the Americas. The cultural diffusion idea was propounded by Sauer[71] (1952) at world scale. Mitchell and Sandner in 1954, 1961 respectively and others in their studies have tended to recognize distinct phases in the settlement process. Chisholm[72] (1962), however, emphasized four major changes affecting diffusion of new settlements. Firstly, socio-economic changes in the land-holding system help in dispersion of settlements i.e. farmsteads on individual consolidated plots in Uttar Pradesh (India), secondly removal of the need for defensive agglomeration which lead to hamletization in several parts of India; thirdly, elimination of such factors (like lack of water and disease etc.) as improvements in water supply attracted settlers in canal irrigated areas in Rajasthan and Haryana and malaria free zone of Tarai region in Uttar Pradesh. Changes in sys-

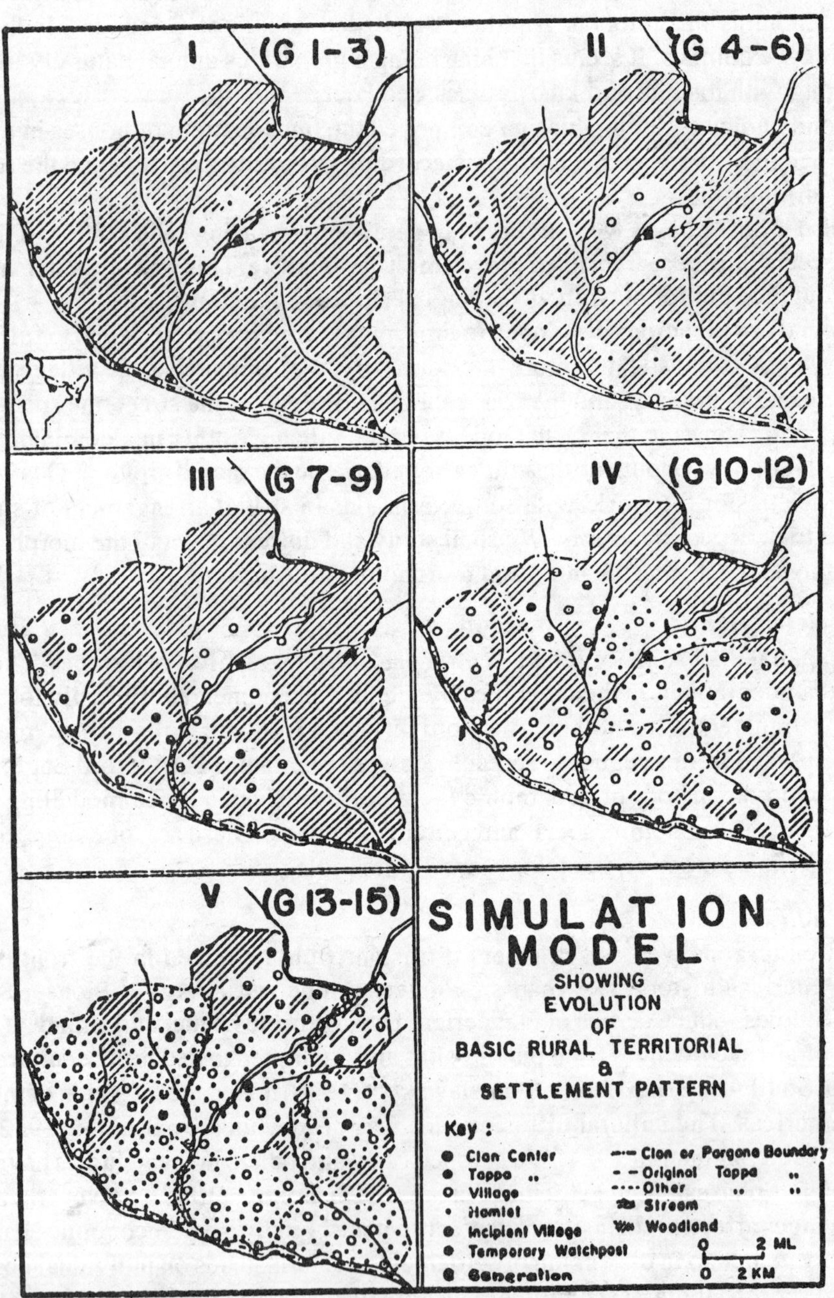

Figure 2.8: Simulation model depicting evolutionary pattern of territorial systems and settlement types

tems of land holdings are mainly responsible for diffusion in industrialized areas. Chisholms' second and third factors are effective in farm distribution in southern Italy and colonizations in the Dry zone of Ceylone (Sri Lanka). Fourth factor of technical change in terms of barbed wire and steel wind mills have allowed the dispersion of farm settlement over the Great Plains (Webb, 1927).[73] Likewise, improved water supply allowed dispersion of farmers on their chaks in northern Indian villages. Further, technical changes notably automobile and the combine harvester allowed the growth of absentee farming—the 'sidewalk' and 'suitcase' farming.[74]

An empirical study made by Singh[75] (1968) in Eastern Uttar Pradesh reveals the spatial diffusion of rural settlements. His semi-deterministic formulations based on four sets of assumptions show generationwise phases of territorial evolution of settlements. From Ist period up to Vth and generations 1-15 (about 350-400 years) the entire clan territory is occupied and hierarchical pattern of 'pargana', tappa' centres as well as several villages and hamlets proliferate to saturate the area (Figs. 2.8, 2.9).

Diffusion-A Deductive Approach

Hudson[76] applied spatial processes of plant ecology and found three components in settlement dispersion. Colonization, spread and competition, the three processes operating in three phases are characteristic features in settlement distribution. The three phases are:

(1) A phase of colonization occurs; the species invades a new area extending its habitat beyond the borders of its former environment,

(2) Biological renewal produces a regeneration of the species through an increase in numbers with a general tendency to short distance dispersal, filling up the gaps in the distribution formed by the original colonizers, and as time passes the process is checked by a third set of forcess;

(3) Owing to limitations of the environment, weak individuals are forced out by their stronger neighbours, density tends to decrease, and pattern stabilizes.

Thus, colonization is associated with the dispersal of settlement into new territory or a new environment, or into an unoccupied portion of the old environment. The spread is characterized by increasing population density, creation of settlement clusters and eventual pressure on the environment, both physical and social. Competition however, tends to produce regularity.

Hudson postulated the concept of *biotope space* for physical space wherein the variables of the *niche* space are realized (Fig. 2.10). In general, the function defines a mapping that determines the density of settlement in the biotope space and is called the magnitude function. According to him, colonization is a function of the size of the fundamental niche. As this expands, settlement may spread outward, and if it contracts, frontier settlement is abandoned. Likewise, spread is characterized by a general filling up of the biotope by settlers. Figure 2.11 shows the relationship between the first two components in a one dimensional situation; first, with colonization alone (2.11A), second with spread alone (2.11.B) and third with the two components combined (2.11C). In all three diagrams, the number of settlements varies inversely with distance from an optimal location in the environment (0 in Fig. 2.11). Under colonization alone, the area available for occupation (the biotope in ecological terms) will increase without changing the number of settlements, thereby lowering density in order to expand the frontier. Under a pure spread process, the magnitude function is shifted upwards, but not outwards, producing an overall increase in density[77].

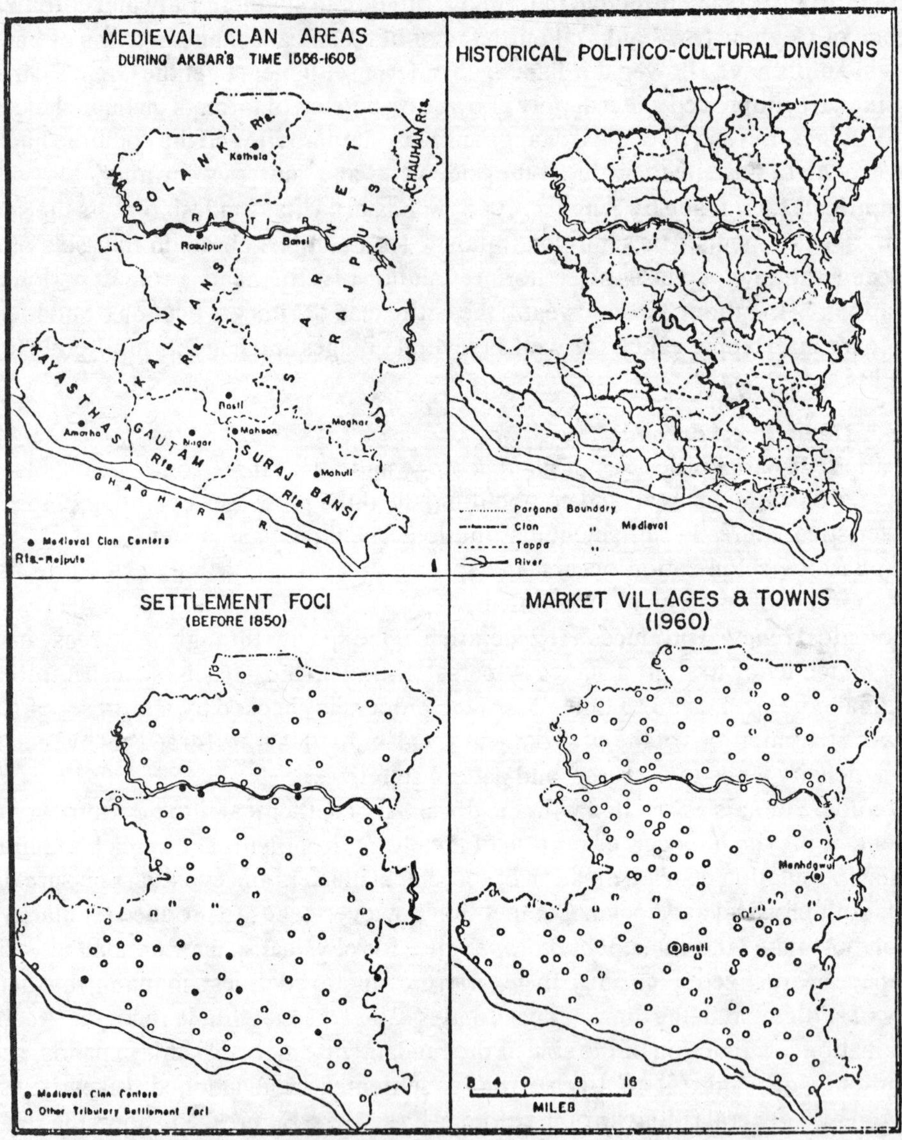

Figure 2.9: Impact of historical politico-cultural forces on the evolution of territories and diverse settlement types in Basti district, Uttar Pradesh.

A look at the diffusion of clans in various parts of India (particularly the Ganga Plain) suggests that: (i) the distance of satellite settlements from their parent villages decreases through various phases of spatial diffusion. Singh and Singh found such distances to be 13. 8 and 6 km in first, second and third stages respectively[78] (Fig. 2.12). This distance varies according to the landscape, i.e., the plain, plateau, valley or the hill in different human groups; (ii) further removed is a satellite from its parent settlement, larger is its population.

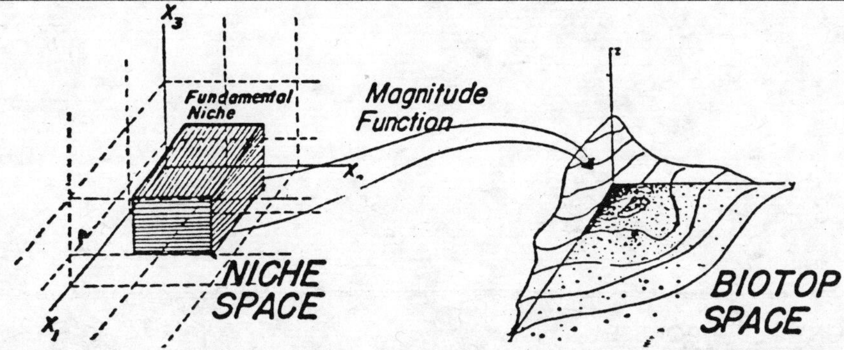

Figure 10: The magnitude function, f(x_1, x_2, x_3) determines the density, (z), of settlement in any area, dB, of the biotope

Recently, Crowley[79] studied the spread of Amish settlement in the United States since 1717 to 1976 (Figs. 2.12a, 2.12b.) It clearly shows the links between parent settlements and new colonies.

Other Approaches to Diffusion Modelling

In general, many studies in settlement geography, following the Hagerstrand approach, focus upon the processes (operating in time and space) which generate an observed distribution of phenomena. A conceptual framework for spatial diffusion research has been provided by Brown.[80] The framework is based on isomorphism. It envisages that spatial diffusion situations consist of six basic elements:

(1) an area or environment, (2) a temporal dimension, (3) an item being diffused, (4) places in which the item is located at the start of a time interval (modes of origin), (5) places in which the item is newly located at the end of a time interval (nodes of destination) and (6) paths of movement, influence or relationship between origin places and destination places (edges).

In terms of building models of diffusion, there are two basic alternatives to the use of simulation: (1) Deterministic Model concerns with formulations on the basis of empirical studies, the typical example being that of Bylund and (2) Stochastic or Probabilistic Model in which growth is simulated by random process which are restricted by the operation of certain rules based on empirical observations of settlement behaviour. The typical example is provided by Morrill who applies Monte Carlo techniques.

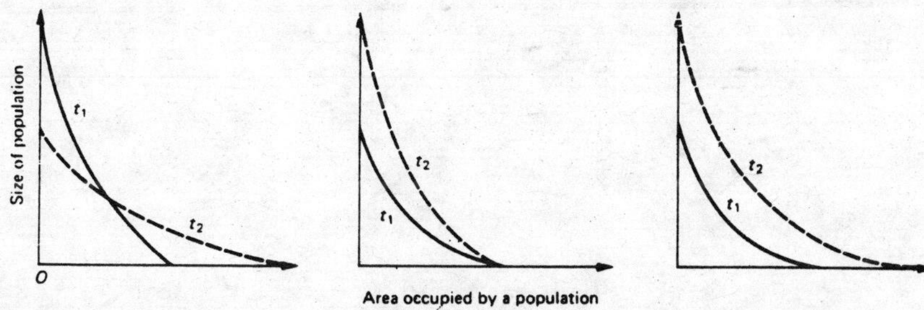

Figure 11: Relationships between colonization and spread process in the Hudson mode.
A colonization alone; B infilling alone; C colonization with infilling.
Source: Hudson, 1969, p. 369.

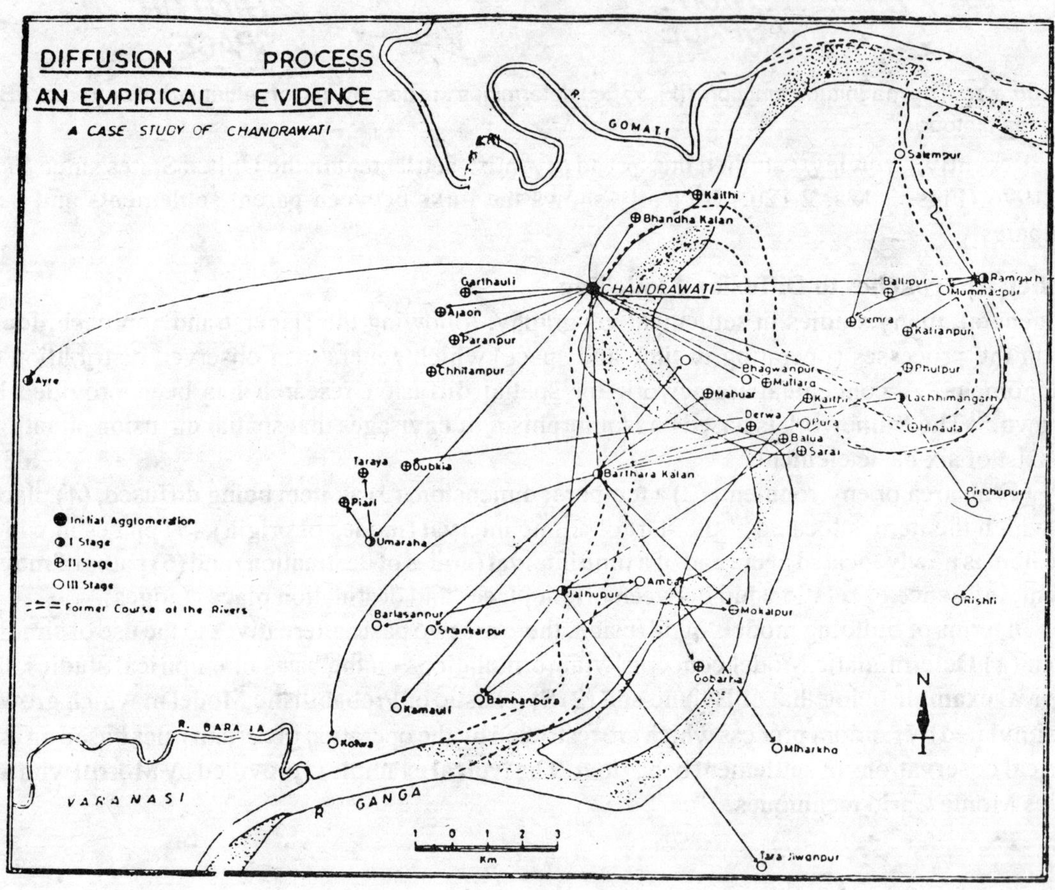

Figure 2.12: Diffusion process: An empirical evidence, a case study of Chandrawati

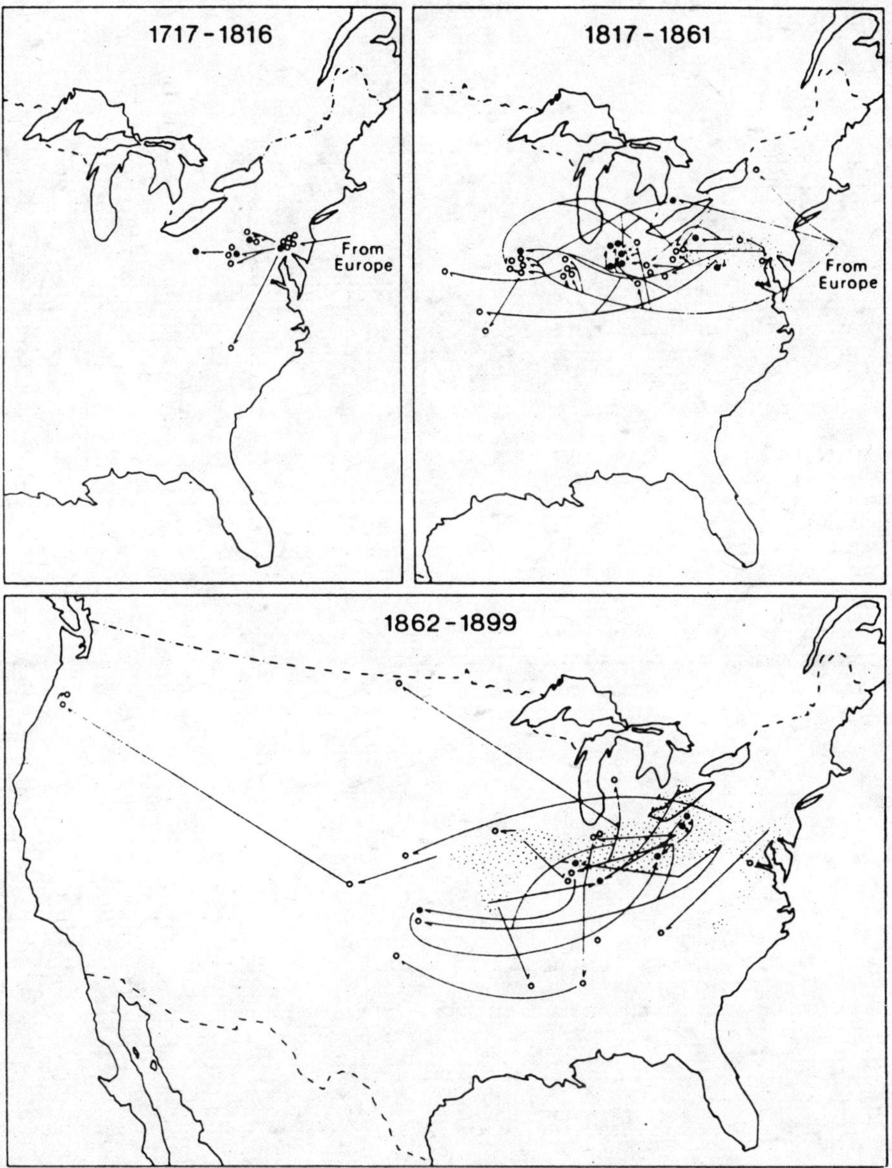

Figure 2.12(a): Spread of Amish settlement in the conterminous United States, 1717-1976. Arrows indicate known links between parent settlements and new colonies.
Source: Crowley (1978, pp, 252-9).

Other models, particularly applicable for urban settlements-gravity models and intervening opportunity models-will find place in our treatment in the sequel. We must remember the warning that the researcher's conceptualization of the diffusion process is moulded to fit the form and assumptions of existing mathematical models, rather than vise versa. The need, then, is for a model which emanates from the (latent) form of the researcher's conceptualization.[81]

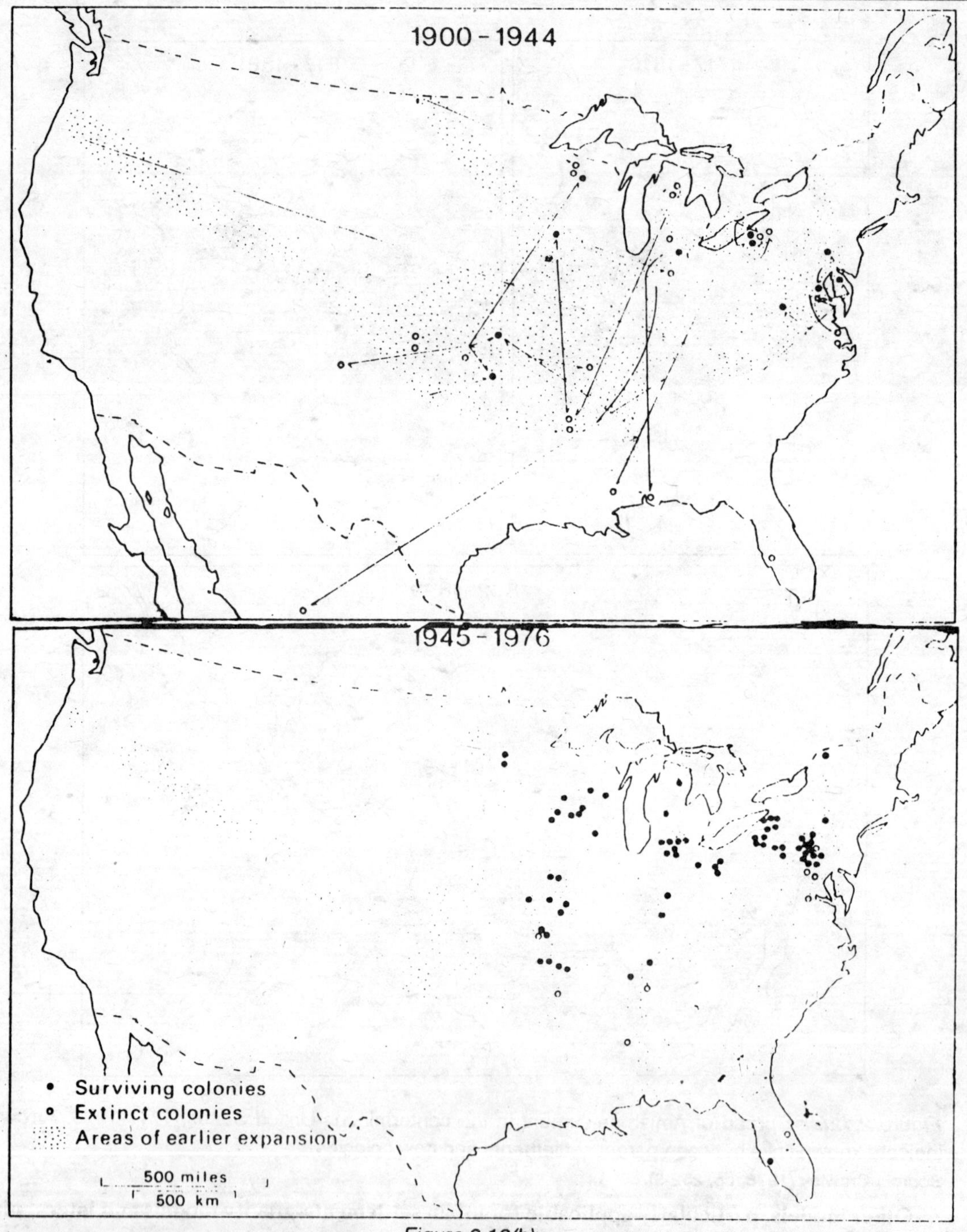

Figure 2.12(b):

Central Place Diffusion

Most of the big settlement centres named as town, city, central places etc. present a mixed hierarchical spatial contagious process of diffusion of institutional centres/office Headquarters leading

to spread of such centres running the scale downwards i.e., banks, schools, trade centres, administrative. headquarters and so on so forth. But this type of diffusion is controlled rather than natural. The supporting settlements, however, spread through spatial contagious process and help in expansion of urban centres.

Diffusion Models: An Inductive Approach

(1) Bylund[82] studied colonization process in Lappland (Sweden) and contributed four theoretical models of settlement development within a deterministic framework. The idea emerged in investigating the reason—as to why even relatively favourable natural and geographic conditions had not always attracted settlement. The problem was posed in such studies by Rudberg, Ernquist and Bylund himself. His model contained three main features. It was assumed that colonizers wished to minimize distance between their new settlement and (i) their parent settlement, (ii) a church and (iii) an available communication link. In each model the basic assumptions are that (a) the physical conditions of the land are equal in all areas, (b) further areas will not be occupied until those close to the original settlements (mother settlements) have been occupied. Each model assumes a four phase sequence (Figs. 2.13a, 2.13b) but the number and locations of original settlements differ; while first and last models assume spread from coastal locations. He simulated the spread of settlement around an initial set of settlements and found broad similarity between the simulated map and the actual map of dispersion of settlement in that areas (Arvidsjaur parish between 1775 and 1867).

(2) Morrill[83] applied Monte Carlo technique to the evolution of settlement. The basic rules followed by Morrill are: first, in each time period or generation (t_o, t_1, t_r) every place generates at least one migrant in the order of its origin with the total number of migrants from each place proportional to its size; second, any place may be settled more than once and enlarged in size, provided it does not clash with the distance-compatibility rule which restricts the size of a place according to its distance from the larger places (e.g., a settlement five cells from the origin, may increase to five and then remain stagnant); third, the distance, and direction of each migrant's move is governed by the numbers in the probability matrix[84] as shown in (Figs. 2.14a, 2.14b). The grids in A, B show a hierarchy of six settlements.

A study in the spatial diffusion of clan settlements in the Ganga plain,[85] however, suggests some minor modifications in the hypothetical models, particularly presented by Bylund (Fig. 2.12). While Bylund foresees an increasing number of satellites with the process of spatial diffusion the case study at Chandrawati indicates an asymptotic growth during the fourth phase. It seems that diffusion process is determined by, inter alia, *genre de Vie* of the people on the move, hence, deviations in actual observed patterns from simulated ones. If we are able to model a diffusion process adequately, we need one data set upon which to calibrate it and another data set upon which to test it; thus, we need a process which repeats itself in time and space in a way that cultural events seldom do[86]. The basic problems of measuring and interpreting the differences between observed and theoretical (model generated) spatial patterns of diffusion have not been adequately resolved.[87] As discussed earlier, in true geographical terms, the study on settlement diffusion started as early as 1931 when Bowman's article was published. Brown and Moore have attempted to synthesize the various approaches within a common conceptual framework. First, the culture and landscape approach concerns-with Culture origins, Culture area and Culture influence. A notion basic to the discussion is that the diffusing item is both, a stimulus to new in-

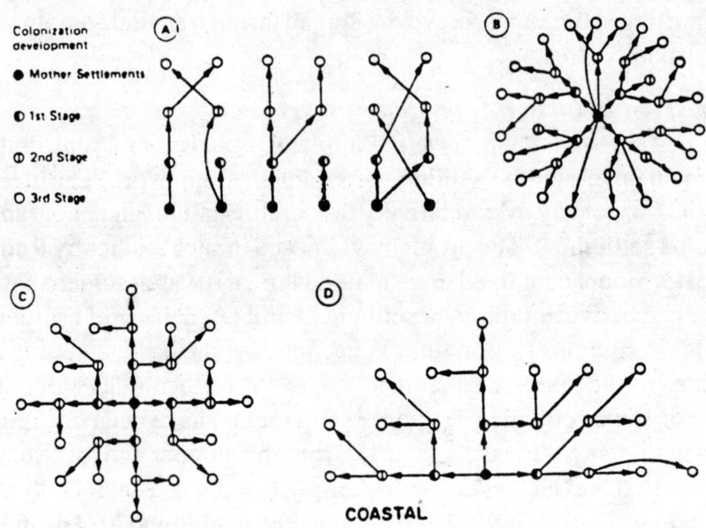

Figure 2.13(a): Hypothetical models of settlement diffusion. Source: Bulund, 1960, p. 226

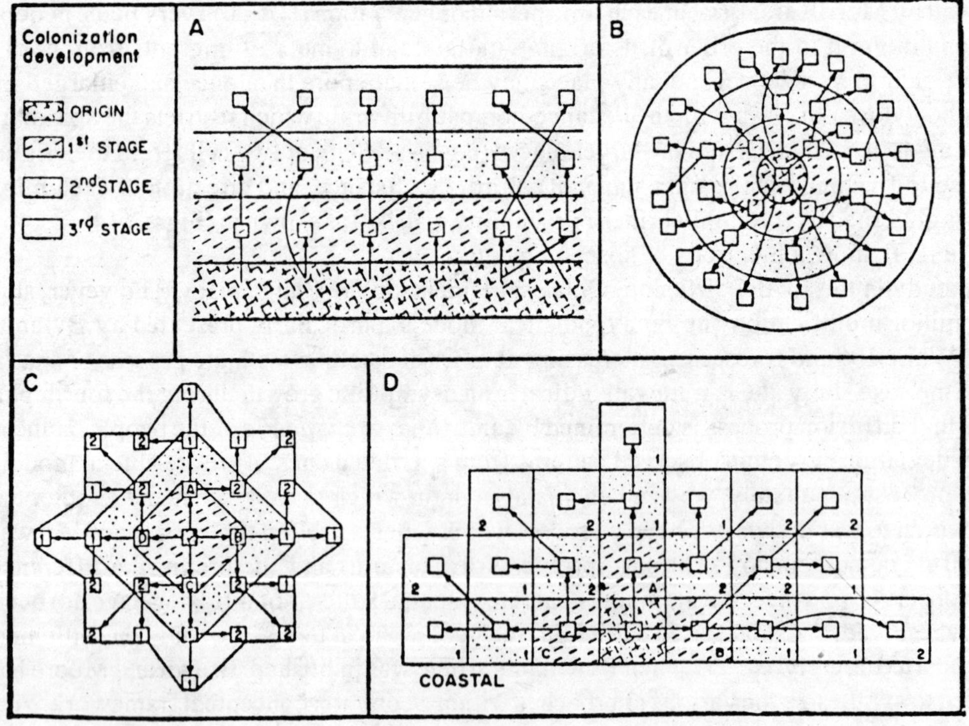

Figure 2.13(b): Theoretical models of settlement development (squares = settlement)

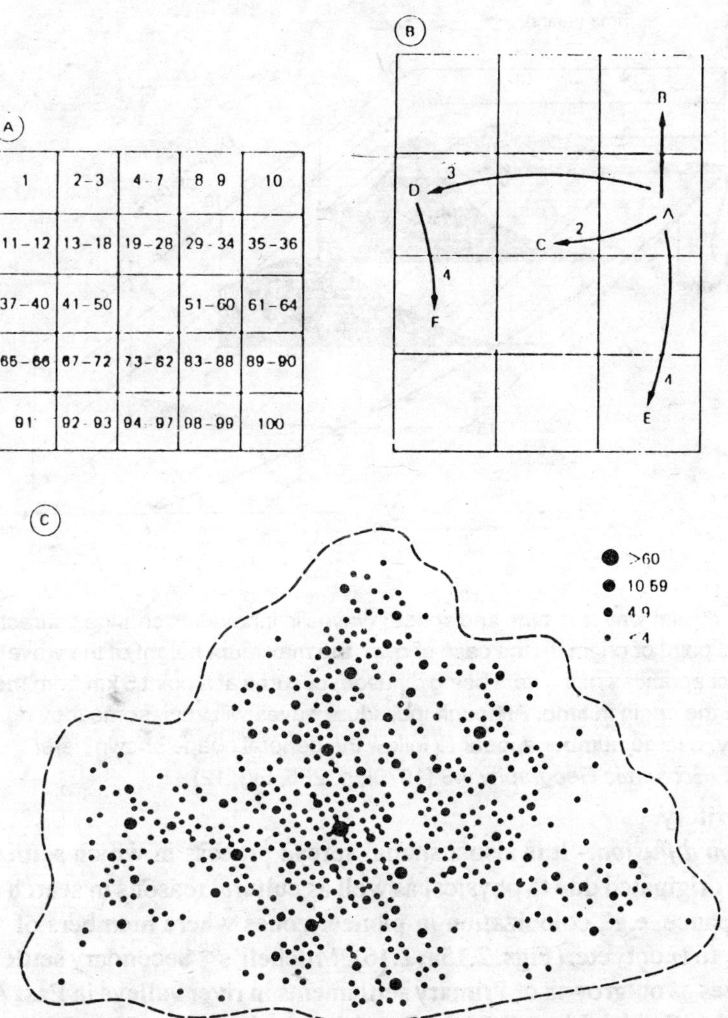

Figure 2.14(a): Simulation of settlement hierarchies. A Distance and direction probability matrix. B sample simulation sequence using Monte Carlo methods. In B, the numbers refer to generations, not size. C, Simulated settlement pattern generated by Monte Carlo methods. Source: Morrill, 1992, p. 112.

novation and itself subject to modification. The second approach emphasizes the generative processes by which the observed locational pattern of a given phenomena comes into existence. While the first approach relates, to Ssauer group, called as Landcapists or Ecologists, the second representing the Hagerstrand school as Locationists, to Haggett. We emphasise here the usage of the term in settlement geography in particular. This is of two type.

(1) *Expansion diffusion*:- It is a process whereby a settlement spreads from one big settled clan centre or tribal chiefs' cluster to another place but at the same time additional houses increase in the compact one. Spatial dimension expands alongwith temporal following growth in population in family and clan members. The clan settlements of the Ganga plain or Malwa Plateau or Narmada Valley are typical examples (Figs. 2.15a, 2.15b). This involves centrifugal dispersion

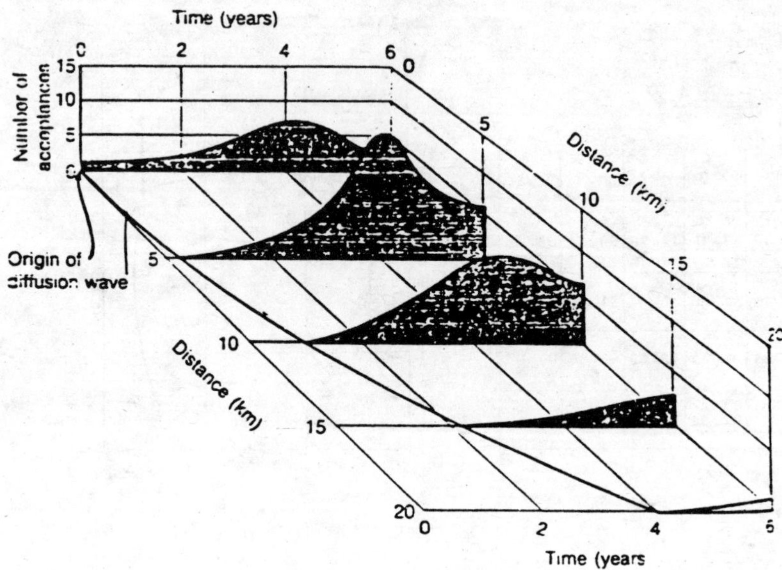

Figure 2.14(b): Diffusion waves in time and space. Waves in innovation change character with distance from the time and point of origin. In the case shown, the maximum height of the wave (i.e., the largest number of new acceptances of the item being diffused) occures at a point 5 km from the origin in space and 4 years from the origin in time. Although individual waves will vary, some moving very slowly and some very rapidly, a large number appear to follow the general shape shown here. (After R.L. Morrill, *Economic Geography*, 46 (1970), p. 265, Fig. 12).

within village territory.

(2) *Relocation diffusion*:- It is also a spatial spread process in which settlements leave the areas where they originated due to physical as well as cultural reasons in search of better habitat or place of occupance, e.g., colonization in pioneer zones where members of a group migrate from a location t_1 to t_2 or t_3 etc. (Figs. 2.15a, 2.16). Mitchell's[88] Secondary settlements on the till covered interfluves as outgrowth of Primary settlements in river valleys in East Anglia are better examples. Likewise, Sandner described the Spanish colonization in Costa Rica in which 'mother settlements' relocate their 'offsprings'.

Spatio-Temporal Models

Settlements occupy some space at a particular point of time. This occupance reflects effect of certain factors during the process of settling a particular piece of land. These are in brief as follows: (a) Land type, its fertility, spread and capability to produce depending on management and lead use, (b) Land tenure which guarantees right on use of land for a particular time period in temporal frame according to tenure system in a state or community, i.e., on lease or permanent hereditary succession, (c) Type of terrain having uniform, homogeneous stretch of land or full of barriers restricting and limiting occupance spatially as well as temporally, (d) Socio-cultural attributes related to racial characteristics, i.e., in tribals, (e) Socio- cultural factors related to ethnic, religious groups and caste (Jati) groups, (f) Political strategy of land occupance in certain well demarcated areas, i.e., Malaysia, Israel and Russia, (g) Socio-functional aspects concerned with arrangement of houses belonging to various groups, i.e., status, dominance and jati-wise, (h) Economy and its

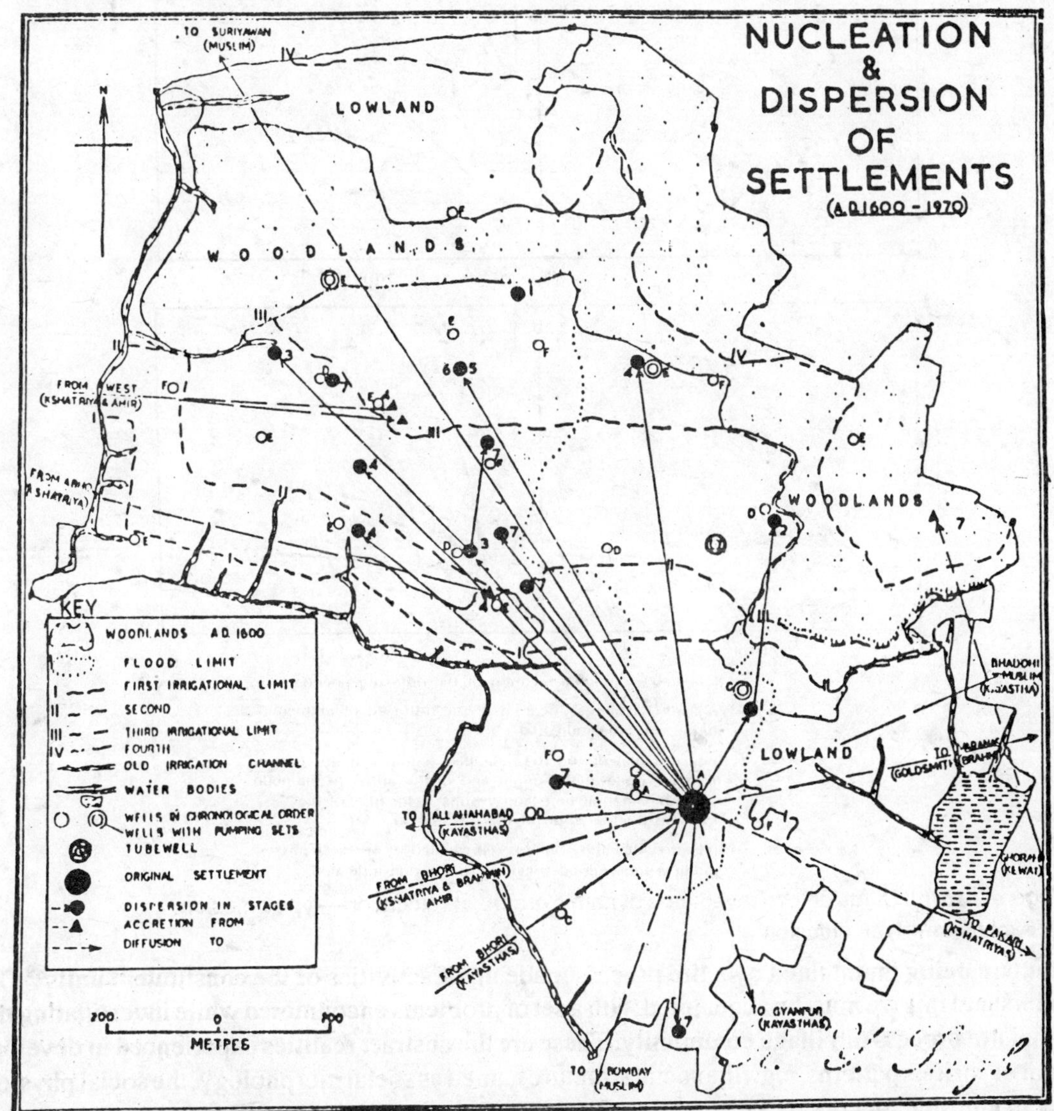

Figure 2.15(a): Nucleation and dispersion of settlements

stage, i.e., agriculture, fishing, mining, forestry in traditional or modern age, (g) Technological developments regarding use of surface, aquifer, vertical space and architechtural designs or mechanized farming, (h) Defence or security condition of social group, (i) Infrastructural development, i.e., road, rail feeder roads; institutions and appendages, and (j) colonization in pioneer areas-as village or colony on canal, dam, factory, port-sites, or forest, usar margins.

We shall elaborate these aspects of occupance in sixth chapter while dealing with morphology of settlements. Here is an attempt to present models to approach the study of morphological variations in settlements, particularly, in northern India. The morphological patterns can be best interpreted through the concepts, (i) of function and (ii) of social space. The former involves the notion of a structure consisting of a set of relations amongst unit entities, the continuity of the

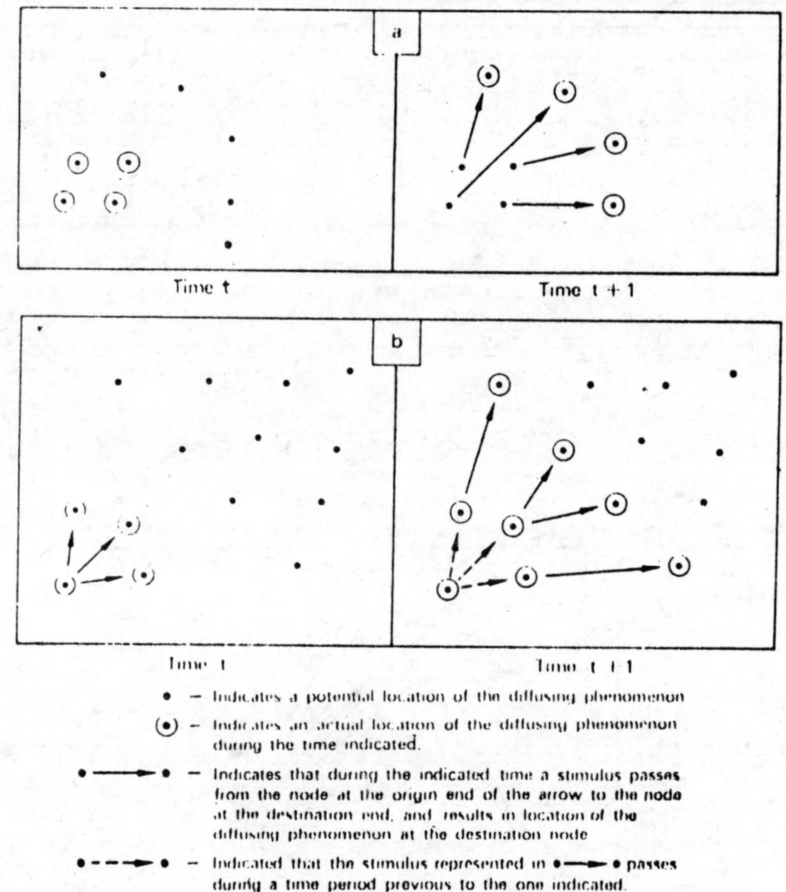

Figure 2.15(b): Diffusion portrayed as a dynamic graph. a: relocation—type diffusion. b: expansion—type diffusion.

structure being maintained by a life process made up of activities of the constitutent units[89]. To understand this we must be acquainted with a set of problems encountered while investigating the social life process of village community. These are the abstract realities experienced in development of various patterns, e.g., the social structure named as social morphology, the social physiology exhibiting how the social structures function, how do new types of social structures evolve and the period of time through which the patterns are welded.

The *second* concept is related to social behavioural and territorial spatial context better expressed in residential units, streets, and other concrete objects. This concerns with several local spaces, i.e., ritual, territorial, economic and social etc., which combinedly evolve a geographic setting. Thus, social space and functions are expressed through / in various morphological patterns which can be studied on the basis of three models in general: (i) The Religio-ritual model, (ii) Secular dominance model, and (iii) Economic space model.

Religio-Ritual Model

The village habitations have various hierarchy and ranking of jatis still practising age-old customs and maintaining religio-ritual distances in behaviour. Various levels of status as well as no-

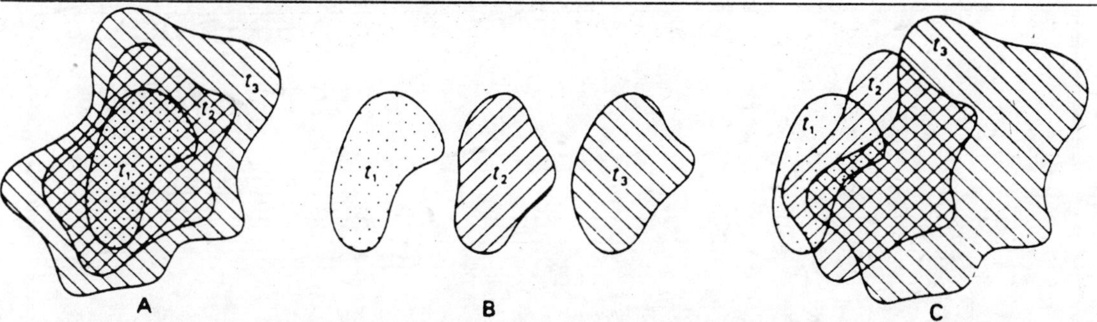

Figure 2.16: Types of spatial diffusion: (A) Expansion diffusion. (B) Relocation diffusion. (C) Combined expansion and relocation processes. The term t_i denotes the time period.
Source: Haggett (1979, p. 300).

tion of pollution (regarding out caste and untouchable people or sub-castes) are expressed through a series of ritual distances which determine behavioural, spatial system. There exists a Brahmin-untouchable ritual continuum in which all other various castes occupy different niches; these placements, however, in middle rungs of ritually determined social scale, vary in different regional and local structural models.[90] While outcastes stay separately, not to be easily contacted during daily routine, the untouchables are kept at a distance (mostly calling distance) separated by some physical barrier, a pond, thicket or waste land and without a common drinking water well in between but service class people stay nearer to high caste ones to be easily approached in time of need (Fig. 2.17). Here socio-petal force works in arrangement of houses to minimize the distance. Various caste groups occupy continuous expansive site following the Jajmani system which works through a process of steady assimilation and acculturation.[91] The directional aspect of Chamar habitations in relation to prevailing wind, determines their spatial occupance mostly found in the eastern side of the main settlement occupied by the landlords or high caste group. This is because the notion of pollution puts stigma on the lower as well as upper rung of ritual scale. Even caste taboos are stricter as one goes down in the social scale. But, this model does not explain other patterns also visible in many parts, hence a secular model was adopted.

Secular Dominance Model

It is the territorial hold by the dominant family or kin-group as the jati or the caste in the village through the control of the village land resources, which fulfills the most basic needs of majority of the villagers by providing the source of food or livelihood, shelter or house site within the village protection and security of a job, and a position or status in the village society and freedom of movement.[92] The landowning dominant caste group articulated the settling and socio-economic patterning of the village society. This dominant caste may be a Rajput, Brahman, Jat, Kurmi or Bhumihar etc. varying spatially. In the case of a typical village Mahjuda the people of diverse castes flocked together for earning their living upon the produce of the arable land under the dominant Rajput lineage supremacy (Figs. 2.15a, 2.17). But, the village pattern of the past is much affected now and explanation of the additional expansions or relocations needs a separate model.

Economic Space Model

After Independence villages experienced change in the occupance and expansion of various sites irrespective of the factors explained through the two models. The founding of separate *puras*,

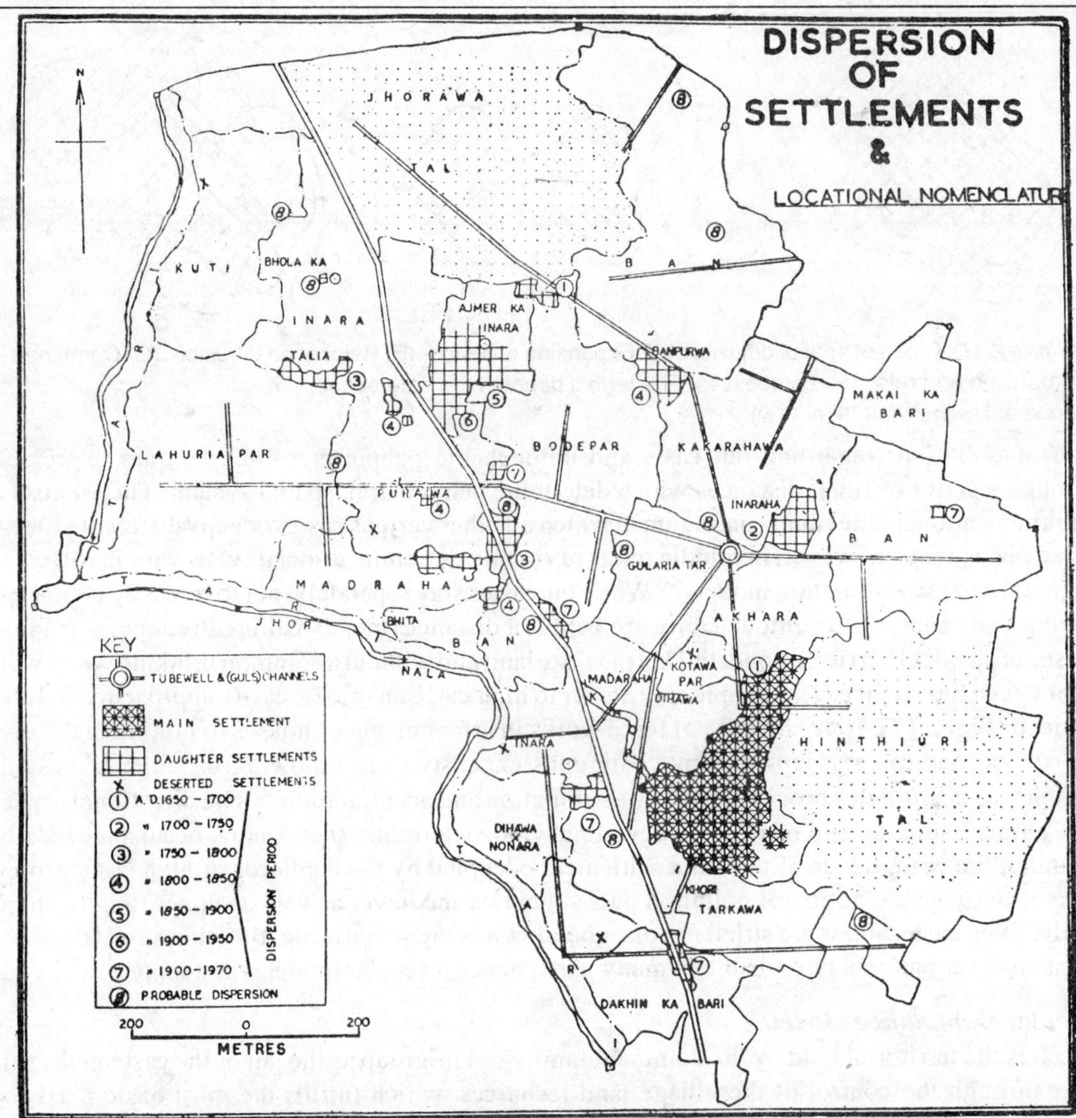

Figure 2.17: Dispersion of settlements and locational nomenclatures

tolas, purwas, tapro or pattis (hamlets) may best be explained by economic factors, hence, economic space model. In Figures 2.15a and 2.17 dispersion, leading to separate cluster founding during the last fifty plus years, reveals that all probable spaces have been either occupied or are in the process of occupation. Here socio-fugal forces are at work hence dispersion. Ahirs spread towards the *jungle* area to avail maximum benefit of stock raising and cultivation of their own fields, Nonia and Chamars came along the road to enjoy the free front of the road avoiding congestion of the main settlement and others are occupying temporary bases (pump-set locations). Road has attracted various caste people for economic gains. This road side expansion is new phenomena in rural countryside resulting from development of transportation means, hence, job opportunity. After consolidation of holdings could be completed in Uttar Pradesh, farmers shifted to their chaks, temporarily first, and lastly, permanently.

Thus, the former two models explain the pattern obtained through socio-petal forces, while the latter, through socio-economico-fugal forces, dynamically changing the countryside.

Place Names Versus Settlements

Like living beings rural settlements are also identified by some name allotted to them sometimes by inhabitants but sometimes by outsiders or neighbours. The place names, as 'fossils of human geography',[93] are an accumulation from the past, the variety and density of which depend, partly upon the density of population and nature of distribution of settlements, partly upon the length of time during which country has been occupied. Processes of settlement and nature of terrain do effect it. Thus, three elements namely ecological diversity, cultural perceptions and dialectical wealth interacting combinedly produce variety of place names. Obviously, the place names reflect all the five components of the cultural geography, i.e., culture, culture area, cultural landscape, culture history and cultural ecology. Mitchell[94] has rightly observed that the examination and mapping of the place names themselves will aid in establishing, broadly, between region and region and within one region in more detail, the date and the sequence of settlements.

Occidental geographers have studied place names in relation to settlements and discovered their significance.[95] The toponymical studies in India are very much neglected and more attention has been paid to the historical and sociocultural aspects than to the geographical correlationship.

Ivan rightly suggests that to the extent that one succeeds in interpreting them-and this is being done with increasing success-names also give, through their content and form, some information concerning one or the other, or both, of the geographer's two chief interests, nature and mankind, hence, helpful in reconstructing sequence occupance of settlements. The two broad groups in which place names can be divided are: (1) Place names associated with natural environments and (2) Place names associated with cultural elements.

(1) The settlements which have place names epitomizing various natural origins may further be grouped into (a) Geologic (b) Topographical (c) hydrographical (d) Vegetational. 1a. Names like limfjorden, Limhamn and Lima in Dalara, (Sweden) show natural influence of Limestone. Likewise, places with sand, or, mal, Malm, mo (meaning sand of various grain size), gryt (grit) hed (sandy plain) in their names depict glacio-fluvial deposits. Calcutta of today has geo-economic background behind its etymology with the Bengali *Kali* (sea shells for lime burning) and *Kata* (lime ready for slaking). 1b. Place names after miscellaneous geographical features, including various landforms having suffix *garh*, *dara* (Valley), *Ghati* (narrow valley), *ghata* (escarpment), *mal* (higher land), *khoh* (cave), and prefix *teela* (high mound) *khai* (a ditch) are densely distributed in central India. *Khai, mer, dhar* associated with place names indicate hilly nature of the place. Place names having suffix *garh* are not invariably named after fortresses or 'killa' the stronghold of chiefs. Minor features such as soil, stream meander and bank sites are responsible for lending their names to the villages in the plains and plateau with almost levelled surface (Figs. 2.18 to 2.23). 1c. Like landforms, water features and place names seem to be in direct correlationship. A village with plenty of water is named as *Sagar* and where there is scarcity as *Nipaniya* (without water). A village with more wells is named as *Kuwakhedi*, one on the bank of the river as *Ghatkheri.* Place names having epithets *Kuwa, Kund, Pani,* and *Jhira-jhiri* are concentrated in the central and Western Vindhyas and Satpura hills which have scarcity of water, examples being *Patalpani, Jamajhiri, Gondkuwa, Junapani, Menhandikund, Gaukund* and *Besarkund* etc. In Rajasthan *Sar, Sir* and *Tal* suffixes reflect such names.

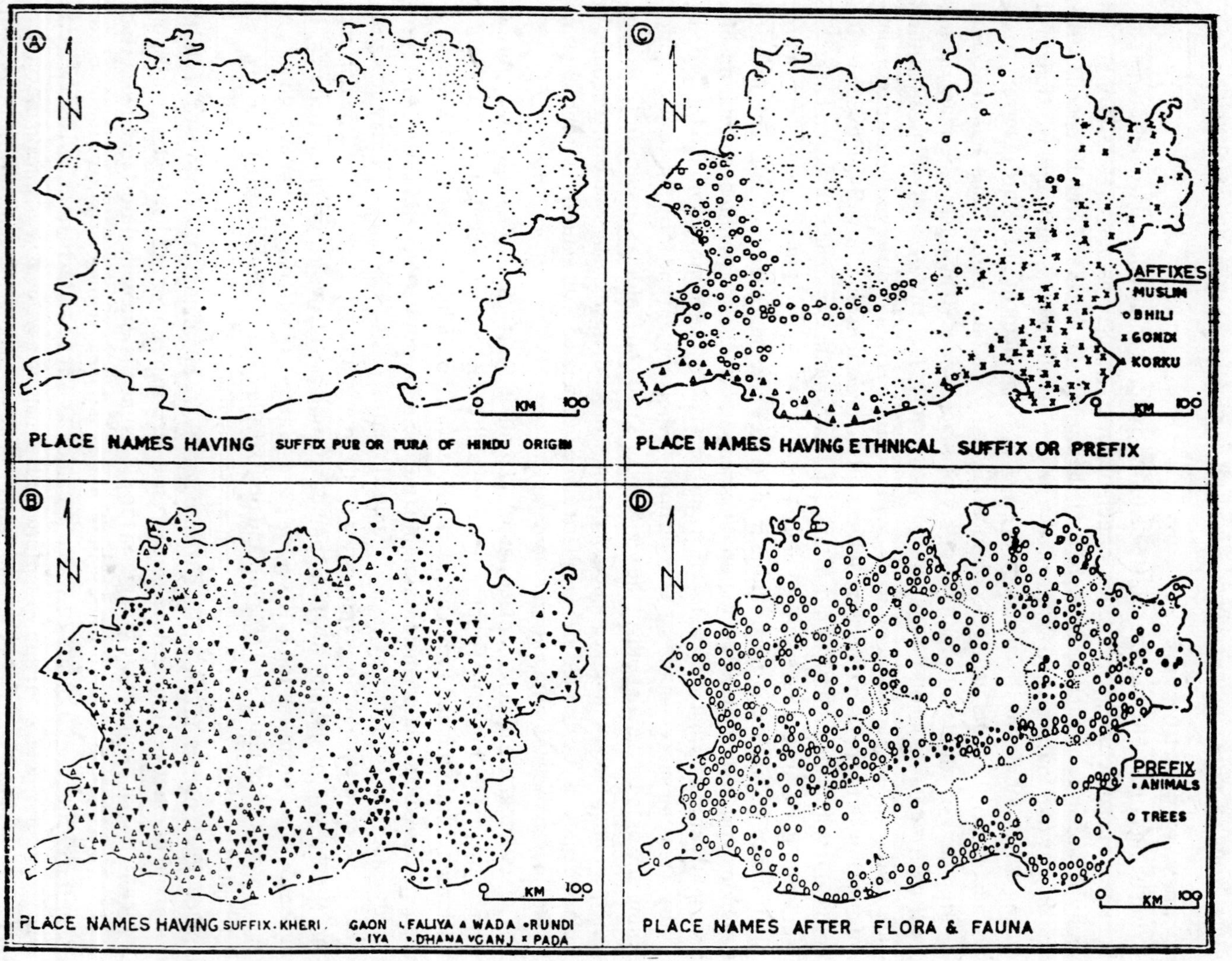
A
PLACE NAMES HAVING SUFFIX PUR OR PURA OF HINDU ORIGIN
KM 100
C
AFFIXES
MUSLIM
BHILI
GONDI
KORKU
KM 100
PLACE NAMES HAVING ETHNICAL SUFFIX OR PREFIX
B
KM 100
PLACE NAMES HAVING SUFFIX. KHERI. GAON FALIYA WADA RUNDI
IYA DHANA VGANJ PADA
D
PREFIX
ANIMALS
TREES
KM 100
PLACE NAMES AFTER FLORA & FAUNA

Figure 2.18

1d. Place names after flora and fauna (Figs. 2.18D, 2.23), cover most of the forest covered area on hills and their offshoots or spurs. River basins among the Vindhya hills are spotted with such villages. These villages are after the names of trees, flowers and crops etc. and speak about the type of vegetation during occupation. *Amkheda, Amrohi, Amliya* (after mango); ***Kamalpur*** (after lotus); *Champakhedi* (champa flower); *Jamanpur* or *Jamunia* (jamun or black plum); *Jirapur* (cumin seed), *Kesarganj* (after saffron); *Imlia* (after tamarind); *Neemkheda,* (after margosa tree); *Berkhedi* (after plums); *Kachnaria* (after Kachnar); *Karela* (after a vegetable); *Karondia* (after a wild fig); *Pipaliya*, Pipari Pipris, (after Pipal trees-Ficus religiosa) or *Khan Pakar, Khori-Pakar* (after Pakar tree-Ficus infectoria); *Semelkhedi* (after Semal); *Mahuakheri* (after Bassia Lotifolia); *Gehunkhedi* (after wheat); *Dhaturia* (after thorn apple); etc. are a few examples from Malwa Region.[96]

Other place names after birds and animals are like *Kagpur* (for crow); *Chikali* (a bird); *Suwakhera* (for parrot); Chilpahari (for kite); *Sherpur, Sherkheda, Naharkheda* (for lion) and *Kachhawa* (for tortoise). Similarly, domesticated animals like buffalo, bullock, horse, cow, sheep etc. have lent their names to villages on plateaux and plains.

(2) Many cultural factors separately or combinedly are reflected through placenames. These may be grouped as based on: (a) culture/caste/ethnic groups, (b) personality, deity, community, (c) cultural landscape/function, (d) culture history and culture area, (e) settlement process and (f) miscellaneous.

2.a Place names in many instances depict caste elements, predominating at present or in the past in a village, examples being *Dhobikheda* (after washerman), *Malikhedi* (after gardener) *Sunari* (after goldsmith), *Gondkhedi* (after gonds), *Sumesdangi* (after dangi); *Naukund* (for barbar), *Kachhikheda* (after milkman), Jaton-ki-dhani (Jats clan settlement) etc.

Many villages in northern India are named after tribes like *Doms, Cheru, Bhar,* i.e., Domiagarh, Dominganj (after Doms) Chirand from *Cheru* and Bharauli, Bharauti after Bhar. A semi-tribe Mushahar also finds place in villages like Mushehri, Mira Mushehri etc. Many a name stands after clans, i.e., Belwa Misir, Mishrauli, Dube chhapara, Jigna Dube etc.

2b. Religion stands behind many place names and examples are as follows:- Pontianak (Borneo) is the name for a dangerous spirit; Lhasa means 'spirit world'; Bombay after a Goddess (Mumbai Devi), Kanpur after (Kanha), Amritsar meaning the 'Immortal pond'; Vindhyachal after Goddess Vindhyabasini etc. With the advance of Christianity and Islam came new names after saints like Santiago and Buenaventura (after the scholastic philosopher and saint) and Rasulpur, Mohammedpur etc. Many names follow church and priest too. Gods and deities have also found their names in many villages. Some villages borrow their names from important persons, saints etc. like Yeshwantnagar, Yusufpur, Hasanpur, Jafarabad, Sikandarpur, Manpur, Jhabua, Banswara. Ivan Cites Slavic names as also Germanic ones ending in -ing, inge, ingen; the Celtic one ending in -iacum; Spanish in -ac; French one ending in -Y; Latin ones ending in -anus, -anious, -inus; Polish in -ov, -ev; Finnish ending in -Lal, -la etc.

2c. In northern plains of India the generic terms suggest the size of settlements, i.e., *gaon, nagar, majra, majri* where gaon and majri are smaller than *nagar* and *majra* respectively. Similarly, *chak, Bas* or *was, Dhani, Kalan/khurd, tola, toli, tapro, patti, pura* or *purwa*, as suffixes or independently indicate hamlets of different size and function. Place names ending in -'ing', -'ham', and -'ton' meaning people, farmstead and village occur in Lowland England.

Places with *Chak* names followed by number in Ganganagar (Rajasthan) depict irrigaticn based settlements, i.e., chak 43 GG, chak 25 F etc. Ganj as suffix in Indian plains is mostly used for grain markets (*mundies*), i.e., Gopiganj, Mahrajaganj etc. *Chit* in Middle Ganga Plain represents the larger size original settlement, i.e., Chit Badagaon, Chit Math etc.

2d. Elliot propounded that every town in Oudh and eastern part of the old North western Provinces, whose name does not and in *pur*, *abad* and *mau* owes its origin and name to the Bhars.[97] Place names with these suffixes owe their origin to the Rajputs, Muslims or other enlightened Hindus. If we see the Figs. 2.18, 2.19, and 2.20, it becomes obvious that suffix or prefix like *pur, nagar, gaon, garh* end *ghat* etc. must have been derived from the Sanskrit language mostly of Hindu origin, while *ganj, bazar, buzurg, khurd, bad* etc. are taken from Urdu and Persian. The common Dravidian word for village is *Ur* as suffix, i.e., Nellore, Indore, Gwalior—a bit deformed. Place names having affixes Dhana, Kheri, Kheda, Dhab, Falia, Tapra seem to be of Dravidian origin mostly associated with the areas occupied by tribals in Banswara, Jhabua, Satpura hills and Vindhyan range. This fact indicates that the area was once inhabited by non-Aryan settlers long before their Aryanization (Figs. 2.18, 2.20). A careful study of the map (Fig. 2.19D), containing place names mostly mentioned in early inscriptions and literatures, unravels strong proof of Aryanization of the land in India. The places with *wali* and *wala* show the impact of Punjabi culture. Ivan cites that a host of names points to a military origin. The Latin *Castica Castellum* lives on in many forms within the old boundaries of Roman Empire, from Castilla to Manchester and New castle, with the Germanic *borg* (Burgos), the Slavic *grad (Graz) Novogord*), and the Greek *pyrgos* (Bulgarian *Burgas*) as rivals.

2e. Place names do reveal process of settlements by Dravidians, Aryans, Mohammedans and other cultural groups in various parts of India. *Pur*, Gaon, kheri, garh, nagar as suffixes in Aryan settlements, khedi, kheda, pada, Rundi, Iya and Gondi affixes in Dravidian settlements and Ganj, Bad, Sultan, Sujal, Begam, Fateh and Mohammed etc. in Muslim States of the past are indicative of such processes. A notable feature of the ost of the place names of the Muslim origin is that they lie deserted. Most of these settlements along the national highways/state highways were nothing but places of temporary camps of the Mughal armies, i.e., Mughal Sarai, Gopiganj, Saidabad, Allahabad, Muratganj, Fatehpur, Farrukhabad, Moradabad etc. Place names having suffixes such as *Wadi* and *Wada* are conspicuously found in Nimar and north western part of Madhya Pradesh indicating the influence of Holkar and Scindhia, i.e., Marathi origin. Newer settlement processes are well reflected through place names like Banpurwa (forest hamlet), Mar-Kanal=mar+kanal or creation of agricultural land by felling or Dhaneri=dha+neri by burning. Place names also suggest many steps of agriculture and speak very often of 'clearings' or 'burnings' (for example, Bayreuth, Praha or Prag) and other preparations of ground (Novara, 'New fields'). Likewise, place names in Siberia and Israel bespeak new settling process. Some villages in northern India, particularly, indicated process of settlement through grants from Jagirdars or zamindars as rent-free land hence named as *Rampur birt*, *Saunhi birt* while birt=vritti (meaning source of livelihood). Likewise, Mafi/Muafi as suffix in Bihar and Uttar Pradesh villages speak about rent-free land granted to Brahmans and their settlements. The word 'math' is found as suffix or prefix in village names, particularly, in eastern Uttar Pradesh and western Bihar specifying the land donated to a saint like Karmaha-Mathia, Modho Math etc. Likewise, *Khairati* (after Charitable grant), *Nankar* (after rent free subsistance grant), Enamat (grant as reward), Nizamat (piece of

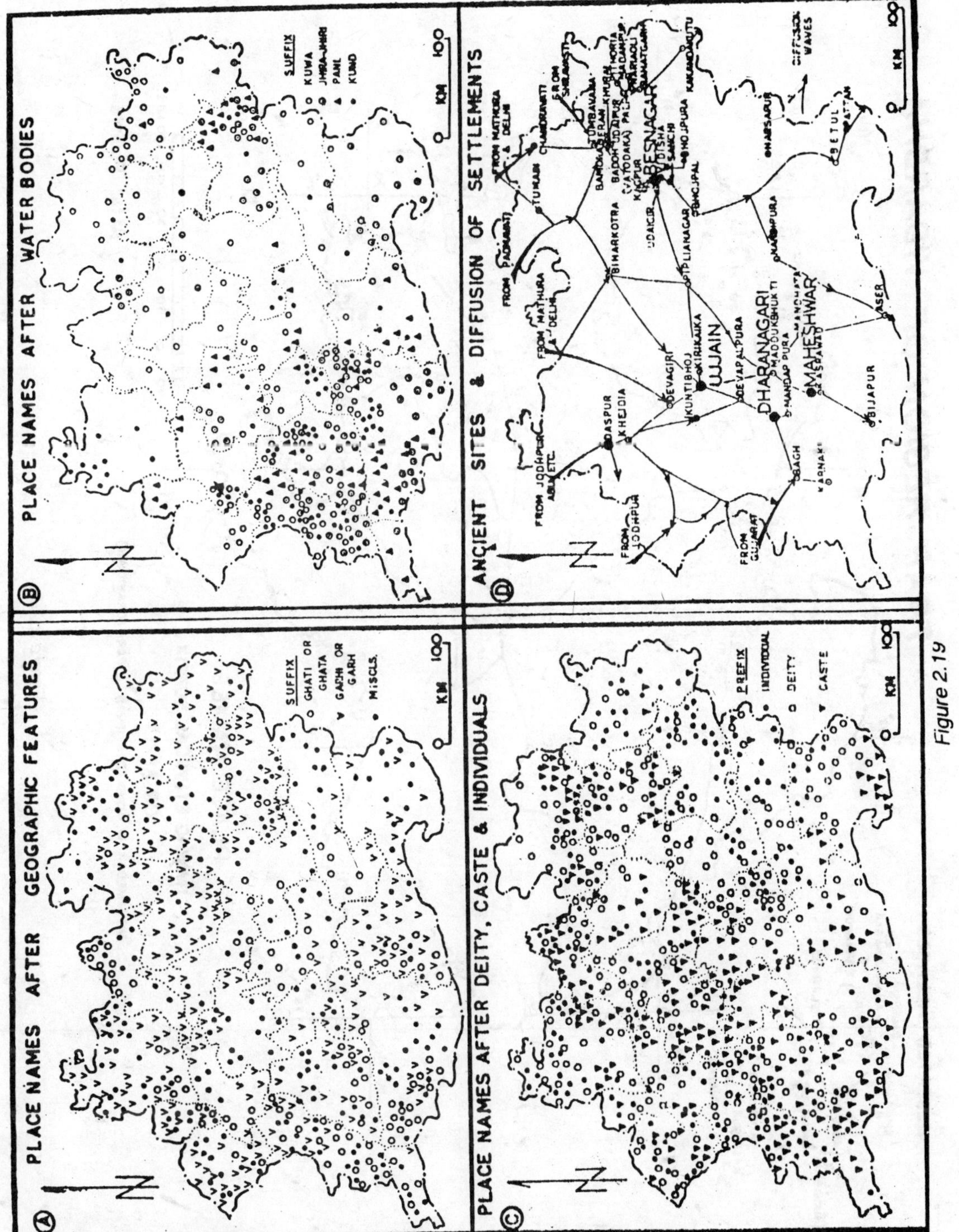
A PLACE NAMES AFTER GEOGRAPHIC FEATURES
SUFFIX
GHATI OR GHATA
GADHI OR GARH
MISCLS.
KM 0 100
B PLACE NAMES AFTER WATER BODIES
SUFFIX
KUWA
JHIRA-JHIRI
PANI
KUND
KM 0 100
C PLACE NAMES AFTER DEITY, CASTE & INDIVIDUALS
PREFIX
INDIVIDUAL
DEITY
CASTE
KM 0 100
D ANCIENT SITES & DIFFUSION OF SETTLEMENTS
UJJAIN
DHARANAGARI
MAHESHWAR
BESNAGAR
VIDISHA
SANCHI
DASPUR
KHEJDIA
DEVAGIRI
KUNTIBHOJ
DEVAPALPURA
BIJAPUR
BAGH
ASER
BETUL
DIFFUSION WAVES
KM 0 100

Figure 2.19

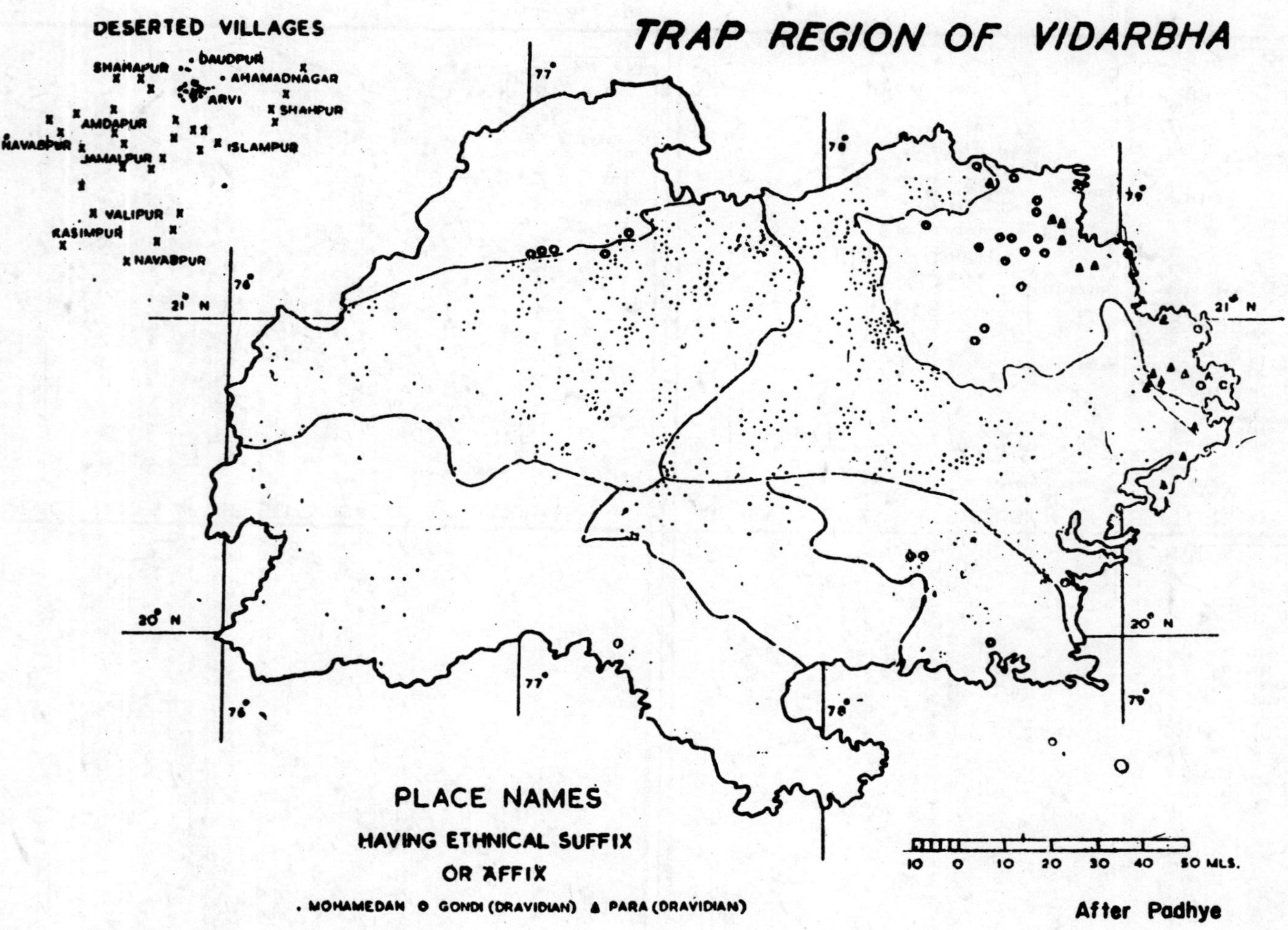
TRAP REGION OF VIDARBHA
DESERTED VILLAGES
SHAHAPUR
DAUDPUR
AHAMADNAGAR
ARVI
SHAHPUR
AMDAPUR
NAVABPUR
ISLAMPUR
JAMALPUR
VALIPUR
KASIMPUR
NAVABPUR
PLACE NAMES
HAVING ETHNICAL SUFFIX
OR AFFIX
. MOHAMEDAN o GONDI (DRAVIDIAN) ▲ PARA (DRAVIDIAN)
10 0 10 20 30 40 50 MLS.
After Padhye

Figure 2.20

land grnated by-Nizam (Muslim Nawab) find place as affixes denoting settling process through grants. Kosambi finds use of Marathi word *Vali* synonym of Hindi *auli* meaning a settlement in village names like Kandivali, Barivali etc. Similar suffixes *auli-*, *auti*, *aula* and *-aila* abound in the Middle Ganga Plain. Baden Powell refers to the use of-*ura* suffix in Northern India i.e. Banaura, Dhanaura etc., which is purely a *Chola* term met conspicuously in Canarese, Telugu and Tamil speaking areas. Singh[98], finds suffix-*dih* (Persian) used in old ruined or deserted as well as newly inhabited sites of settlements and the cult of dih having both positive and negative attributes. Likewise, Vikasnagar, Ambedkarnagar etc. are due to planning process.

2f. There are many settlements which could not be put under any of the groups identified earlier. These of multifarious origin are grouped under 'Miscellaneous' category e.g. *Diyakheri* (after light), *Palki* (after Palanquin), *Gyaraspur* after Gyaras (Ekadasi). A notorious village lends its name as *Durjanpura* and with well-to-do people as *Raispur, Daulatpur; Nehra* after girl's father's place; Motipura after *pearls*; Ratanpur (jewels); Hirapur (diamond); *Kotha* (a store); Jamnapur (river Jamuna); *Gangdhar* (the Ganga); *Himmatpur* after courage, *Patwarikhedi* (after Patwari). Similarly villages have been named after drum (Dholkhedi), doorsill (Dehri), Monday (Sombara), temple (Madni or Madhia or Mathia) and adjacent to a nala as Parwanala, on a crossing as *Chaudagara* or after ornaments like *Bichhia*.

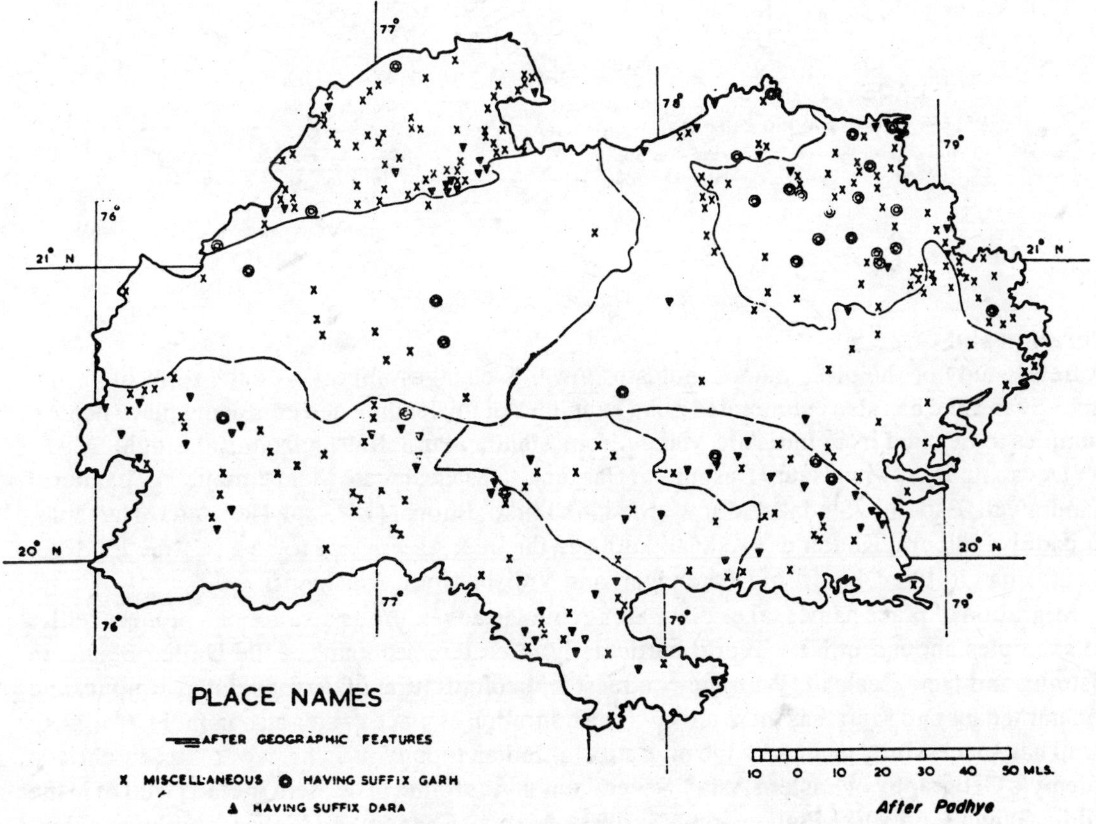

Figure 2.21: Trap region of Vidarbha

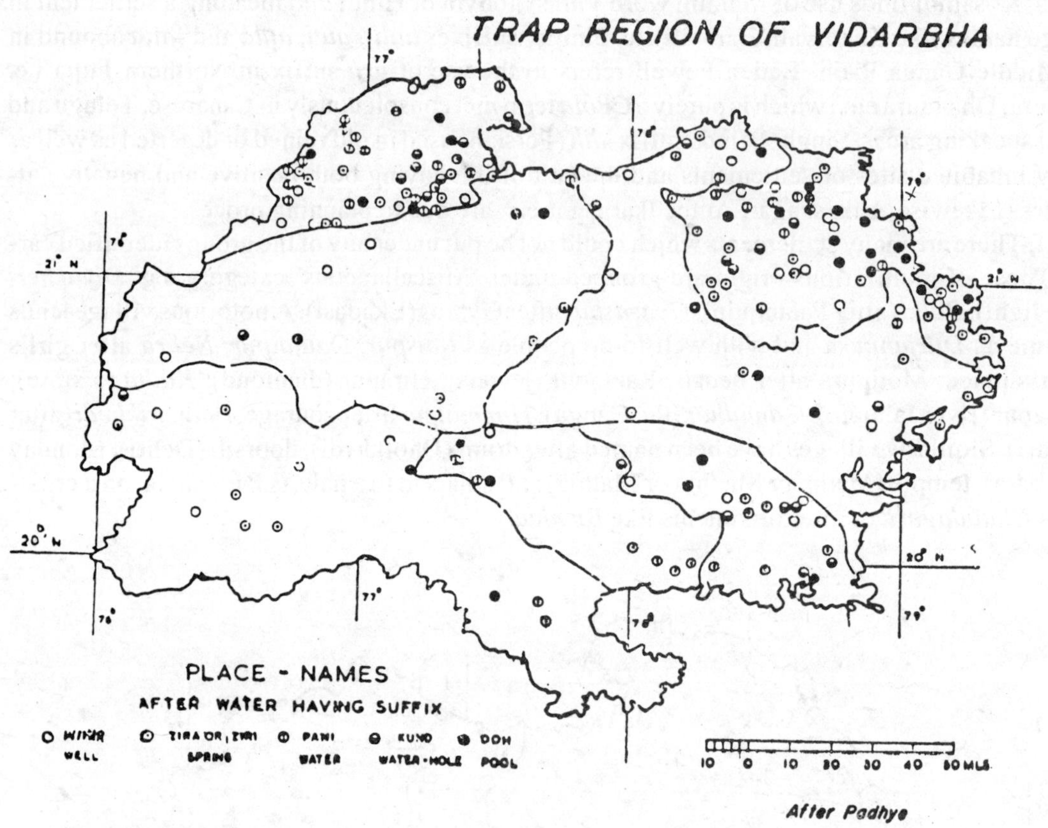

Figure 2.22: Trap region of Vidarbha

Migration and Change

A careful study of the place names indicates towards changes imposed on the form of earlier names. Ivan Lind has also enumerated good examples of misleading and confusing place names. Examples to be cited from India are Mandu from Mandap Pura, Raisen from Rai Singh, Depalpur=Devapalpur, Mandsaur=Daspur (Dasaur), Maheshwar=Mahishmati, Chanderi=Chandrawati, Badoh=Vatodaka, Mhow=Maddukbhukti, Bhopal=Bhojpal, Harsanda=Harsapur, Nandad=Nandipura, Khutunda=Kakand kutu and the like. Aser seems to be a contraction from Aswathama giri like Dhar from Dharanagari and Vidisha from Vidishagiri.

Migration of place names takes place alongwith the adventurous invader or a pioneer settler and examples abound in New World particularly in eastern seaboard of the United States, in Australia and New Zealand. With the conquest and colonisation of Aryans, later, Rajputs and Mohammedans and Marathas there took place a migration of place names also in India. Col. G.E. Gerini has successfully dealt with the migration of Indian toponyms in his work "Researches on Ptolemy's Geography of Eastern Asia". Several toponyms found in western India as well as in the Middle Ganga Valley like Pratapgarh, Mandhata, Makrai, Chandravati, Pali, Maheshwar, Bhatni, Deori, Gorakhpur and others having suffixes *pur, bad* and *Ganj*, undoubtedly and unfailingly,

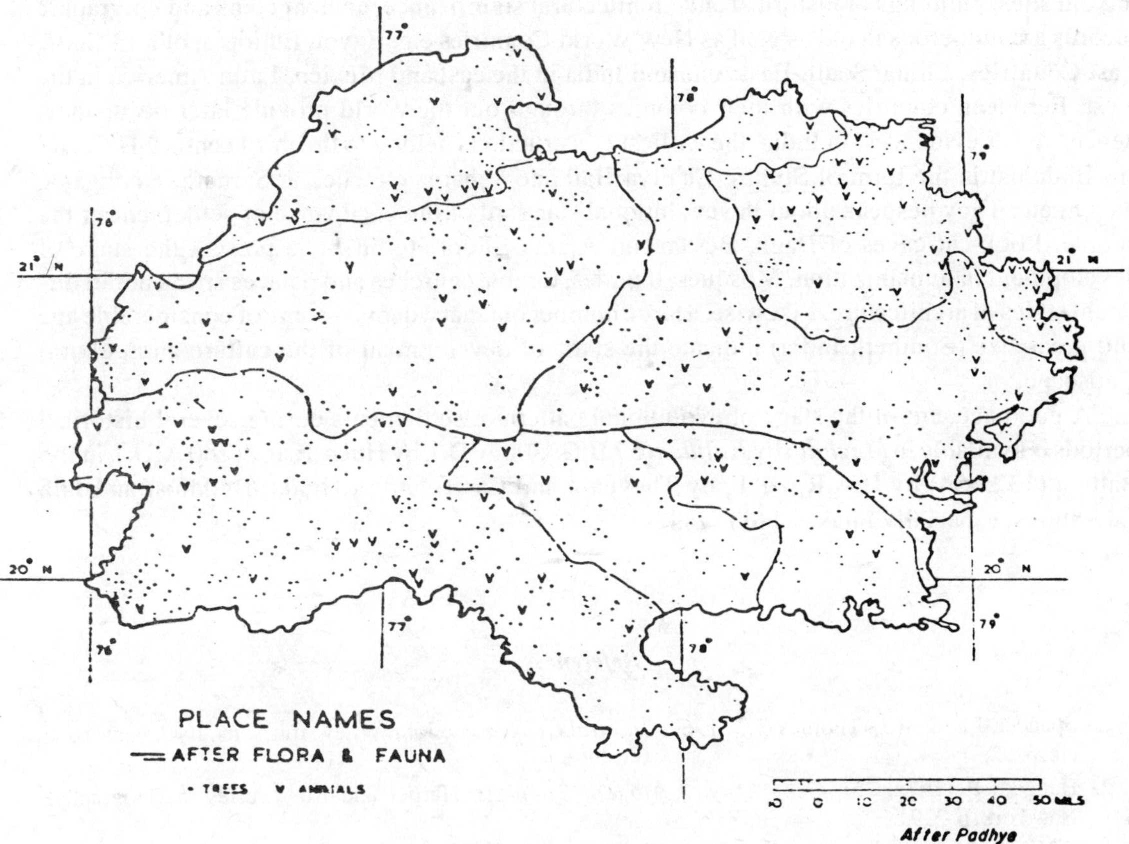

Figure 2.23: Trap region of Vidarbha

depict migration from either or both sides during historical period, particularly, Medieval period, due probably to successive alien invasions. There are geographical limits to a few suffixes like 'para' of Bengali and oriyai origin, Dhana of Gondi origin, wadi and wada of Marathi origin, Faliya and Rundi of tribal origin. Gerini mentions that one should not, in the least, be surprised at finding so many Sanskrit names of people, regions and cities transported in Burma, Malaya, Sumatra and other parts of eastern Asia from India. The second syllable in Djakarta is the persian *kert*, originally 'made' and later 'founded' (of a town). *Zanzibar* likewise, is from the Persian Zenj, 'black' and the Indian *bar*, 'land'. *Ayuthia* in Thailand is, almost surely the ancient Indian *Ayodhya* 'invincible'. According to Padhye the Melghat and the foothill zones of the Satpura form the southern limit of toponyms of Korku and Hindi origin having suffixes such as *talai*, *baodi*, *dehi*, *patha*, *iya* etc. The Yeotmal plateau forms the northern boundary of migration of the south Indian toponyms especially those of Kolami and Telgu origin. The Telegaon-Kondali Plateau and the Satpura demark the western precinct of migration of the Gondi toponyms.

Testimony and Authority

Beside the assessment of place names, it is essential to deal with the archaeological and architectural findings and various records of relevant importance. These archaeological remains, including old sites, buildings of historical and architectural significance, ancient coins and epigraphic records are numerous in old as well as New World Countries e.g. Egypt, Ethiopia, other Middle East Countries, China, South-East Asia and India in the east and Mexico, Latin America in the west. Eeropean countries with their colonies through out the world provide later occupance, hence, newer evidences. In India, the earliest constructions belong to the third century B.C. and are Buddhist in the form of Stupas, Chaitya Hall and Viharas etc., i.e., at Sarnath, Bodhgaya, Sanchi etc. They bespeak about the evolutional standard of the occupance of settlement of the people. Rock-cut caves of Bagh, Besanagar, Ajanta-Ellora etc. in India present the stage of development in humanization. Mosques, temples, tombs, churches and palaces speak about different styles of architecture. Likewise, a large number of Ghats, dams—some of considerable age and great size (Southern India) indicate the stage of development of the culture and cultural landscape.

A good account of the stage of evolutional pattern of settlements during several historical periods is available in *Meghdut* by *Kalidas* (57 B.C.-500 A.D.), by Huen Tsang (780 A.D.), in Ibn Battuta (1325-54) by H.A.R. Gibb, by Thevenot and Careri and in Hindu, Buddhist and Jain Literatures, especially Jatakas and Puranas.

References

1. Spencer, J.E. & W.L. Thomas (Jr.), 1969, *Cultural Geography,* John Wiley And Sons, INC, New York etc. p. 92.
2. Haggett, P. (1972, 75); *Geography: A Modern Synthesis,* Harper and Row Series in Geography, New York, p. 239.
3. Ibid, p. 249.
4. Ibid, p. 273.
5. Spencer, J.E. & W.L. Thomas, op. cit. ref. no. 1. p. 174.
6. Ibid, pp. 210-211.
7. Ibid, p. 212.
8. Wagner, P.L. & M.W. Mikesell, (eds.) (1962), *Readings in Cultural Geography,* The University of Chicago Press, Chicago and London, p. 214.
9. Spencer & Thomas, op. cit. ref. no. 1, p. 212.
10. Ibid, p. 214.
11. Kirk, William, (1975) 'The Role of India in the Diffusion of Early Cultures', *The Geographical Journal,* Vol. 141, Part 1, March, London, p. 20.
12. Sellassie, Sergew Hable, (1972) *Ancient and Medieval Ethiopian History up to 1210,* United Printers, Addis Ababa, p. 19.
13. Ibid, p. 26.
14. Spencer & Thomas, op. cit. ref. no. 1, p. 224.
15. Paul Masson-Oursel (Helena De Willman Gr-abouska Philippe Stern, (1967), *Ancient India and Indian Civilization,* Lakshmi Book Store, New Delhi, Foreword xiii.
16. Sankalia, H.D. (1974) *The Pre-history and Protohistory of India and Pakistan*, Deccan College, Post Graduate and Research Institute, Poona, p. 135; see also G.S. Rathore on "The Luni Basin: A Note on Pre-historic and Historic Settlements" in *Rural Settlements in Monsoon Asia* (eds.) R.L. Singh et al. (1972) NGSI. I.G.U. Pub. pp. 241-248.

17. Ibid, p. 434.
18. Pre-historic coins on Chambal banks, Indian Express Jan. 5, 1979, also see 'Indian Express' 25.2.1980.
19. Pre-Indus Valley Sites Found, Times of India, 30th March, 1989.
20. '1500 B.C. Culture excavated at Veraval, Indian Express, 18th April, 1980.
21. "Prosperity in pre-historic Maharashtra" The Sunday Standard, July 30, 1978; see also 'Excavations Reveal 3,500 year old culture' 23rd April, 1981-Jorwe Culture settlers lived in houses with several rooms and settlements had definite Plans and Layouts.
22. 'Unique Arrow Heads Found in Vaishali' Indian Express, 6.8.81-Bihar Puravid Parishad Calls this place to be Kotigram of the Buddhists.
23. "21 New Harappan sites Found in N. Gujarat, Indian Express 30.3.80.
24. 'Harappan Settlements Found in Himachal' Indian Express 18.3.81.
25. Pre-Harappan Site Discovered' Indian Express, 31.1.80 (by Rajasthan Department of Archaeology and Museums).
26. Indus-Maya Cultures had close ties, Indian Express, 2.4.88.
27. Sankalia, H.D. op.,cit. p. 353.
28. Ibid, p. 558, see also K.V. Soundara Rajan (1986) 'Mechanics of City and Village in Ancient India' Sundeep Prakashan, Delhi pp. 107-147; also G. Dongard Levin and A. Vigasin (1984) 'The Image of India'-Progress Publishers, Moscow, pp. 188-233; also Wheeler, R.E.M. (1968), The Indus Civilization, Supplementary Volume to the Cambridge History of India, 3rd edition, Cambridge University Press, p. 125; Majumdar, R.C. (1952), 'Ancient India' Motilal Banarasidas; Dutta, R.C. (1893), 'History of Civilization in Ancient India; Childe, V.G. (1926), The Aryans; Taylor (1889) 'The Origin of the Aryans; Baden Powell, B.H. (1899) 'The Origin and Growth of Village Communities in India, Swann Sonnenschein, London, 28; Chatterjee, S.P. (1970) 'Presidential Address of the 35th Annual General Meeting of the Geog. Society of India' Geog. Review of India, Vol. XXXII, June No. 2, pp. 69-70; Dube, B (1967) 'Geographical Concept in Ancient India', National Geographical Society of India, Research Publication No. 3, p. 102; Mukerjee, R.K. (1958), 'A History of Indian Civilization and Classical Traditions', Vol. I, Hind Kilabs Ltd. Bombay, Preface V., Singh, R.L. (1955), 'Evolution of Settlements in Middle Ganga Valley' N.G.J.I. of India, Vol. I, Part II; Sharma, G.R. (1960) 'The Excavations of Kausambi, Allahabad Institute of Archacology Alld. University Publications, No. 1, pp. 7-11; Wakankar, V.S. (1973) 'Bhimbedka Excavations' Journal of Indian History, vol. II, Pt I, Series 151, pp. 23-32.
29. Agrawal, D.P. and Chakraverty D.K. (1980) (eds.) 'Essays in Indian Proto-History-A Collection of Essays' or Indian Chronology, Indian Express, 7.3.80.
30. Sharma, R.C. (1972) 'Settlement Geography of The Indian Desert', Kumar Brothers, Hauz Khas, New Delhi 16, p. 85.
31. Mookerjee, R.K. (1936) 'Hindu Civilization', London; 24.
32. Rigveda VI, 286.
33. Kalidas, Raghuvansham, Canto XV
34. Imperial Gazetteer of India, 1908, p. 335.
35. Singh, R.L. op.cit. ch, 2. ref. no. 30, p. 74.
36. Pandey, R.B. (1951) 'Vikramaditya of Ujjaini', Shatdal Prakashan Banaras, 45.
37. I.G.I., 1908, p. 337
38. Powell, G.B. (1896) 'Indian Village Community', London, Longmans Green & Co. p. 124.
39. Sinh, Raghubir (1936) 'Malwa in Transition:A Century of Anarchy', Bombay, p. 13.
40. Singh, R.L. op.cit. see ref. no. 28, p. 79.
41. Mukerjee, R.K. (1938), The Changing Face of Bengal, p. 256.

42. See Singh R.Y. (1978) 'The malwa Region: Rural Habitat System, Structure And-change, N.G.J.I. Res. Pub. No. 20, An Episode was related by Sri Udai Pal Singh, M.A., LL.B. (the then Additional District collector of Jhabua in 1970) regarding capture of Jhabua State from Jhaboo Nayak, a cheif belonging to Lovana tribe. Fateh Singh (coming from Rathore family of Jodha Singh Dynasty of Jodhpur) was ruling at Badnawar (Dhar) Madhya Pradesh. He used to get melons from the former during bumper crop season out of his friendship or courtesy. Once he failed to do so due to scearcity for which Fateh Singh showed annoyance. Being communicated, Jhaboo Nayak sent hundreds of bullock load of boulder's (in shape of melons) and this resulted into fierce fighting at Hathipani (Rankhet) where the latter was killed and his Chhatari and Sati place is still there; likewise, Bhars were eliminated or shifted from Bhadohi Tahsil by Maunas Rajputs in Uttar Pradesh (Varanasi). This was the fate of other aboriginal chiefs occupying several territories throughout India.
43 Tantiya Bhil was defamed for his predatory activities and Military forces of Holkar and British could not or hardly maintain law and order.
44. The local chiefs in Malwa formed their territories within the native Cultural Zones of (i) Kanthal with its centre at Mandsaur, (ii) Bagar with Banswara as centre including Ratlam state, (iii) Rath consisting of Jhabua, (iv) Sondhwara of Sondhia Tribes with Mahidpur centre, (v) Umatwara of Umat Rajputs with Rajgarh and Narsingarh centres, (vi) Kicchiwara of Chauhans with Raghogarh centre, (vii) Gondwara of Gonds with Betul centre and (viii) Nimar with Maheshwar as its centre and hilly parts under aboriginals.
45. Singh, R.L. op.cit. ref. no. 28, ch. 2, p. 79.
46. Kirk William, op.cit., ref. no. 11, p. 20.
47. Soundara Rajan, K.V. Op.cit. ref. no. 28, p. 120.
48. Ibid, 129.
49. Ibid, p. 131
50. Ibid, p. 136.
51. Sherring, M.A. (1975) 'Benaras-The Sacred City of the Hindus', B.R. Publishing Corporation, Delhi, p. 8.
52. Ibid, p. 30.
53. Ghosh, A. (1951), Rajgir, 1950 Ancient India 7:66-78
54. Bharadwaj, O.P. (1986) 'Studies in the Historical Geography of Ancient India, Sundeep Prakashan, Delhi, pp. 193-198; see also G.S. Rathore, Luni Basin, op.cit. ref. no. 16.
55. Bhargava, N.L. (1984), The Geography of Rigvedic India, Lucknow, pp. 30-33.
56. Weber Alberecht (Varanasi, 1974), 'The History of Indian Literature' p. 120.
57. Bhagavta Purana, X 73. 32-33.
58. Mbh. Ådi 206 (Southern Recension after V. 25).
59. Dube, B. op.cit. p. 74-80, ref. no. 28.
60. Kirk, W. op.cit. ref. no. 11, p. 31.
61. Stein, A. (1942) 'A Survey of Ancient Site Along the 'Lost Saraswati River' Geographical Journal, 99, 173-182.
62. Ghosh, A. (1952) 'The Rajputana Desert-Its Archaeological Aspect' in National Institute of Sciences, India, Delhi Proceedings of the Symposium on Rajputana Desert, Bulletin 1,37-42.
63. Rapoport A. (1969), House Form And Culture, Prentice Hall, INC, Englewood Cliffs, NJ, London, p. 47.
64. Mukerjee Radhakamal (1968), Man and His Habitation-A Study in Social Ecology, Bombay Popular Prakashan, p. 18.
65. Hagerstrand, T. (1952) 'The Propagation of Innovation Waves, Lund Studies in Geography, B, 4, 3-19; Idem (1983), (1969) 'Innovationsförloppet ur Korologisk Synpunkt, Lund:Gleerup. Innovation Diffusion as a Spatial Process, Translated by A. Pred, Chicago:University of Chicago Press;

Idem (1967), on 'Monte Carlo Simulation of Diffusion', in W.L. Garrison and D.F. Marble (eds.), Quantitative Geography, Part I:Economic and Cultural topics, Northwestern University Studies in Geography, 13, 1-32; see Lösch, A. (1940), Die Raumliche Ordnung der Wirtschaft, Jena (1954), The Economics of Location, new Haven:Yale University Press; see curry, L. (1976) 'Fluctuations in the Random Spatial Economy and the Control of Inflation, Geographical Analysis, 8, 339-53; see, Edmonton, M.S. (1961) 'Neolithic diffusion rates', Current Anthropology, 2,71-102; also Rogers, A. (1968) 'Matrix Analysis of Interregional Population Growth and Distribution', California:University of California Press, also Rogers, E.M. (1962) 'Diffusion of Innovations', New York:The Tree Press; see Stuart-Harris, C.H. (1965) 'Influenze and other Virus Infections of the Respiratory Tract, (second edition), London:Arnold; also Cox, K.R. and Demko, G.J. (1967) 'Agrarian Structure and Peasant Discontent in the Russian Revolution of 1905,' East Lakes Geographer, 3, 3-20; see for cultural diffusion Sauer C.O. & Brand D. (1930) 'Pueblo Sites in South Eastern Arizona, University of California, Publications in Geography' 3, 415-48, also Sauer C.O. (1952) 'Agricultural Origins and dispersals', American Geographical Society, Bowman Memorial Lectures, 2; see Turner F.J. (1920) 'The Trontier in American History' New York, Holt; see Parsons, J.J. (1949) 'Antioqueno Colonisation in Western Columbia:An historical Geography; Ibero-Americana, 32, 1-225; Farmer, B.H. (1957), Pionear Peasant Colonisation in Ceylone: a study in Asian Agrarian Problems, London:Oxford University Press.

66. See ref. no. 65.
67. Bowman, I. (1931) The Pioneer Fringe, Amer. Geog. Society, New York; see also Brown, L.A. and Moore, L.G. (1969), Diffusion Research in Geography:A Perspective' Progress in Geography, 119-157; see also Haggett, P. Cliff, A.D. and Frey Allan (1971), Locational Models, Edward Arnold, 231-257; and also Brown, L.A. (1968), Diffusion Process and Location: A Conceptual Framework and Bibliography, Philadelphia: Regional Science Research Association, Bibliography Series, 4; also Cliff, A.D., Haggett, p., ord J.K. and Versey, G.R. (eds.) 'Spatial Diffusion:An Historical Geography of Epidemics in an Island Community, Cambridge University press (1981), 6-34.
68. Zoerg, W.L.G. (ed.) (1932), Pioneer Settlement:Cooperative Studies, New York:Amer. Geographical society; also Stanislawski, D. (1946), The origin and Spread of the Grid Pattern Towns, Geog. Review, 36, 195-210; Kudolf, G. (1955) 'Migration Probabilities' Lund Studies in Geog. Series, B., Human Geog., 14, Lund Gleerup; Morrill, R.L. (1968) 'The Distribution of Migration Distances:Papers of the Regional Science Association 11, 75-84; Bylund, E. (1960), Theoretical Considerations Regarding the Distribution of Settlement in inner North Sweden, Geografiska Annaler 52,225-231; Wolpert, J. (1964), The Decision Process in Spatial Context, AAAG, 54:537-58; Olsson, G. (1966), Central Place Theory, Spatial Interaction and Stochastic Processes, Paper of the Regional Science Association, 18, 13-46; Mikesell, M.W. (1967) 'Geographic Perspectives in Anthropology', AAG, 57, 617-34; Morrill, R.L. and Pitts, F.R. (1967) 'Marriage Migration and the Mean Information Field', AAAG, 57, 401-422; Harvey, D.W. (1966) 'Geographical Process and the Analysis of Point Patterns:Testing Models of Diffusion by Quadrat Sampling:Transactions and Papers of the Institute of British Geographers, 40-81-95; also see Garrison, W.L. (1962) 'Towards simulation Models of Urban Growth and Development' in Norlog, K. (ed.), The I.G.U. Symposium in Urban Geography, Lund Studies in Geography Series B, Human Geog. 24, Lund:Gleerup, 191-208.
69. See ref. no. 65.
70. See ref. no. 68.
71. See ref. no. 65.
72. Chisholm, M.D (1962), Rural Settlement and Land Use: An Essay in Location, London.
73. Webb, W.P. (1927), The Great Plains, New York

74. Haggett, P., Cliff. A.A. and Frey, A. (1971), Locational Models, Edward Arnold, p. 109.
75. Singh, K.N. (1968), The Territorial Basis of Medieval Town and Village Settlement in Eastern Uttar Pradesh, India, AAAG, 58, June, 203-220.
76. Hudson, J.C. (1969) 'A location Theory For Rural Settlement, AAAG, Vol. 59, 365-381.
77. Haggett, p. et al. see ref. no. 74 p. 109-110.
78. Singh, R.L. and Singh R.B. (1975) 'Spatial Diffusion of Clan Settlements in a part of Middle Ganga Valley, NGSI, Pub. No. 14, pp. 143-44.
79. Crowley, W.K. (1978) 'Old Order Amish Settlement' Diffusion and Growth, AAAG, 68, 249-64.
80. Brown, L.A. see ref. no. 67.
81. Brown and Moore, ref. no. 67.
82. Bylund, E. (1960), Theoretical Considerations Regarding the Distribution of Settlement in Inner North Sweden, ref. no. 68.
83. See ref. no. 65.
84. See ref. no. 74, p. 107.
85. Singh, R.L. and Singh R.B. (1975), op.cit. ref. no. 78, p. 146; see also R.L. Singh, Rana P.B. Singh and D.K. Singh (1976) 'Mechanism of the Spatio-temporal Diffusion of A Clan Settlement in A Part of Middle Ganga Valley, Some Comparison and Correlates' in R.L. Singh et al. (eds.) 1976, 'Geog. Dimension of Rural Settlements', NGSI, Pub. No. 16, pp. 19-32; also Gunnar Olsson (1968), 'Complmentary Models: A Study of Colonization Maps', Geografiska Annaler, B. Vol. 50; 115-132; also Singh Rana P.B. (1975) 'Mechanism of Diffusion of Clan Settlements in the Saran Plain-Saptio-Temporal Analysis, N.G.J.I., 23:182-183; see for a new model A.B. Mukherji (1976) 'Rural Settlement in Chandigarh Siwalik Hills:An Application of Multiple Collinear Fission Model' in R.L. Singh et al. (eds.) 'Geographic Dimensions of Rural Settlements', Pub. No. 16, N.G.S.I. Varanasi-54-66.
86. See ref. no. 67, p. 35.
87. Brown and Moore, op.cit. ref. no. 67.
88. Mitchell, J.B. (1954), 'Historical Geography' London.
89. Singh, K.N. (1972) 'An Approach To the Study of the Morphology of the Indian Village' p. 204; also R.Y. Singh, 'Village Mahjuda' A Study in the Morphogenesis of a Rural Settlement, Eastern Uttar Pradesh, India, pp. 234-40 in R.L. Singh et al. (eds.) (1972) 'Rural Settlements in Monsoon Asia', N.G.S.I.
90. Mandelbaum, D.G. (1970) 'Society in India, I. University of California Press, Berkeley, see ch. 12; see also Rana P.B. Singh, (1977) 'Clan Settlements in the Saran Plain-A Study in Cultural Geography, N.G.S.I. Res. Pub. No. 18, pp. 140-145.
91. Singh, R.Y. (1972) op.cit. ref. no. 89, p. 236.
92. The Concept of 'dominant caste' was first introduced by M.N. Sriniwas in 'The Social System of A Mysore Village in Marriot M. (ed.), 1955, 'Village India' Studies in the Little Community,' Chicago University Press, pp. 1-35.
93. Brunhes, J. op.cit., ref. no. 3, p. 579.
94. Mitchell, J.B. op.cit., ref. no. 52.
95. See R.Y. Singh (1977) 'Place-Names As Tools for Reconstructing Evolution of Settlements in the Malwa Region, India, N.G.J.I., Vol. XXIII, pp. 200-206; also R.B. Singh (1965), Historical Geography:Place Names and Settlements-A Review of Studies, N.G.J.I. Vol. XI, pp. 101-124; also see S.S. Padhye (1967) 'The Geographic Correlation of Vidarbhian Toponyms', N.G.J.I. 13, p. 14; Idem (1962), 'A Study in Toponymy, Bombay Geographical Magazine, 10, pp. 97-102; and Idem (1963) 'Some Methods of Identification and Derivation of Antiquity, Origin and Meeting of Vidarbhain Toponyms, Vidarbhian Journal of Science,1, pp. 30-39; see also for details Ivan Lind (1962) 'Geography and Place-name's in P.L. Wagner & M.W. Mikesell (eds.), Readings in Cul-

tural Geography, The University of Chicago Press, Chicago, pp. 118-128; also see Raghavan, V. (1943), Bodhi and Vishnupada in N.W. India and Toponymical Duplication, I.G.I. Madras, Vol. 18, p. 98.

96. See Sharma, Savita Anand (1986), Rural Settlements:A Cultural-Ecological Perspective, Inter India Publications, p. 87.

97. Bhars were the people who, inter alia, occupied Northern Indian Plain during Pre-Rajput Period.

98 Singh, Rana P.B., ref. no. 90, p. 41.

3

Rural Settlements

Village versus Settlements

The term 'village' attracts and simultaneously denounces any legal definition. It discards to be delimited by either size or population criteria. In India, officially a village stands for the area demarcated as a *mauza* meaning "parcel of ground with definite boundaries, for revenue purposes without clear and consistent regard for its population." Obviously, village, *gram*[1] and *gaon* are synonymous terms which denote a cluster of houses including the surrounding land almost self-sufficient and usually grouped at a convenient site. The houses along with the street pattern, the two essential facts of settlement geography, are relatively permanent and visible elements of the rural landscape which man has superposed on the natural landscape of a region. Thus, the village of the present day or village community, so popularly used term of the past, is a comparatively small and simple agglomeration of the houses at a favourable and convenient site. Environmental factors in early stage and socio- culturo-economic factors in conjunction with the former in later stage determine its existence and growth. Leaving aside the definition provided by the Census of India, the term 'village' used here means an administrative unit having a parcel of land, the boundaries of which are defined, cluster of houses or more than one such cluster and bearing a distinctive place name. The hamlet, locally named as *faliya*, *para*, *dhana*, *dhani*, etc., means a separate aggregate of houses within the village boundary, sometimes having name and always forming a part of the whole. But the village is not synonymous to settlement. Village in India is *mauza* (everything within the revenue boundary with a name) and settlement is *abadi*, the built-up area, be it main settlement (*abadi khas*) or other hamlets within the village boundary as demarcated through tradition or in revenue records. The Arabic *mauza* adopted into general revenue language more or less all over India, is derived in Johnson's dictionary from the form *waza*, with the meaning of founding, laying down. Often the boundary between two villages is the forest land, usar land or some physical barrier, i.e., *nala*, mound, etc. or only the (*mend*) field boundary. This boundary remains undemarcated in areas where settlement of land is not complete physically or on record. In England or similar developed counteries greens resemble the common forest land of the bygone days in northern Indian plain. The German *dorf* like the Sweedish *torp* originally meant a pioneer farm which became a village. In the same way, the Latin *villa* (farm or more properly manor) is used for village.

Origin and Purpose of Village

As stated in the preceding chapter, man wants to live along with his kith and kin and others at one place not without some purpose. Instinctly and behaviourly, he has to stay and live in shelters which best satisfy his needs. Moser and Tayler state that in south-east Colombia, the houses of

Tukano Indians, known as *malocas*, are seldom occupied by less than twenty people. C. Robequain finds that the Dyaks of Barneo, living in long houses of wood thatch, are more than six hundred persons. The type of economy in various environmental conditions enables man to live in huts, tents, encampments and big houses. In hunting and colleeting stage or under primitive economy of pastoral nomadism, man is content with encampments. It is only in sedentary agriculture that man depending on cooperative operations gets assured reward hence living together, if not in one house, in group of houses, i.e., village. Not only gregarious instinct but cooperation required in tilling soil, organizing drinking and irrigation water, controlling runoff and drainage, storing water, cutting forest, reclamation of land, harvesting, building, thatching and repairing all were conducive to living together in a best possible socially organized way of life. This form of cluster of dwellings reflects the need of cooperation in fishing, mining, lumbering and newly developing transport and market settlements. Even defence has played its role in aggregating the dwellings as a close knit-cluster. Besides these physico-cultural constraints, socio-economico-political constraints are also responsible for such clusters, i.e., the Israeli *Kibbutz* or the Russian *Kolkhoz* or industrial, irrigational, multipurpose project colonies in developing world.

As man does not live on bread and butter only, his spiritual need is met most in village living. Even the pinch of being low in hierarchy—be it caste, status or otherwise—is normalized, standardized and lastly compensated through the feeling of common hold and participation on/in one village. We shall discuss it in detail both in this and Chapter 5 and 6.

Indian versus other Settlements

Not only the Indian villages differ from others in some respects such as form, size, shape and internal structure but, have regional variations too. The varied environmental conditions in conjunction with cultural variations and many thousand years of living history have enriched diversity of settlements ranging from the tropics to temperate highest parts of the Himalayas and riparian, old Ganga valley to farmsteads of *terai*, having almost all sorts of building materials ranging from Burma, Nicobar up to Jaisalmer and Kashmir up to the coastal Kanya Kumari. The occupants' ethnic diversity is no less varied, nor the manners and customs. From Neolithic up to the modern age, the spatio-temporal variations are met with conspicuous absence of similarity. This diversity leads to differences in many aspects as under:

(i) Morphology in relation to caste sectors only in India.
(ii) Morphology in relation to religion and ethnic groups: Hindu, Muslim, Christian.
(iii) Morphology in relation to type of village: compact, disperse.
(iv) Morphology in relation to site of village: river, hill etc.
(v) Internal structure of layout of houses in various types of villages, settled according to different models, hamletization.
(vi) Green villages of England up to rock villages on dykes and hill tops—treeless surroundings.
(vii) Based on livestock raising, poultry farming and reindering, i.e., in Savannah land and Tundra.
(viii) Semi-nomads (*Gaddilohars*) and nomads of Central Asia are distinct in spatio-temporal and functional framework.
(ix) Kibbutz and isolated chaks of individual farmers.
(x) Building materials.

The villages also differ in the type of institutions, associations, tribal panchayats, party based organizations and the infrastructures ragarding all these separately and combinedly. That is why, a Japanese village is different from Indian or Italian or Canadian or Brazilian village on the one hand, and Israeli and east Siberian village on the other.

Site, Situation and Location/Position

These three terms are interrelated but easy to be distinguished. Though no consistent theory could be formulated, references abound regarding Italian hill towns, villages in Greeks' islands or sea islands, hill sites, etc. Ecological determinism is reflected through Evans-Pritchard's-Nuer settlements in Sudan and by Brockmann where she attributes settlement patterns almost exclusively to site. Dickinsons' view also is more ecology-oriented when he says that site embraces precise features of the terrain on which the settlement began and over which it spread. Similarly, Emrys Jones observes that site is the relationship between a dwelling or a group of dwellings and the immediate physical environment. It is well-known assumption that in the selection of settlement sites man is usually guided by both the attractive and restrictive forces of physical setting which is an ensemble of various elements, such as, geology, relief, drainage, soil, and natural vegetation. We need not, therefore, emphasize the significance of site which Blache thinks to be the first to be considered for the study of the distribution of human establishments. But, his statement that "nature prepares the site and man organizes it to enable him to satisfy his desires and his needs" approves of the fact that the very concept of site is inherently cultural. Moreover, the effect of site is cultural rather than physical, since the ideal site depends on the goals, ideals and values of people or period and choice of the 'good' site whether lake, river, mounation or coast depends on this cultural definition. The first settlers with their acquired knowledge make rational judgements concerning choice of sites for their habitations always based on balanced consideration of ease of conducting internal economy and external transactions. Still, the sites performing the basic functions and dysfunctional ones which failed to do so do exist. The latter, however, indicate temproal exigency or chance factor during occupation of site. For scholars like Blache, Brunhes, and Sauer, the term 'site' connotes the natural endowments in relation to their utilization by a culture group. Chisholm stressed on arable land, grazing land, water, building material and fuel as site determining factors. Thus, site provides concrete expression of the ancient and ever changing relationship of culture and nature.

The situation or setting is usually concerned with physical and cultural conditions over a much wider area. It refers to the relation of one settlement with the surrounding settlements in the country through varied linkages. Situation is partially unique and can be generalized to a limited extent.

Location indicates the place where an object or settlement is situated, i.e., its geographical address, hence extent in degree, minute and seconds in reference to latitude and longitude expressing uniqueness. A graphic model of location (settlement) is represented by a table where the rows show objects of geographical observation and the columns indicate units of geographical observation. Enrid Alayeb[2] observes that the same characteristic of an object extended to include the indications of the objects' links with its environment is traditionally called geographical position (or setting). As distinct from the term location, the term 'geographical position' carries more information (the objects' position with respect to other centres, lines of transportation, its physico-geographical conditions and so on) and for that reason is a factor in distribution or regional development. Geographical position is a graphic example of a concept accepting the method of concentric division. For instance, it is possible to describe the macroposition, mesoposition and microposition of an object (settlement), which will reflect an analysis of its geographical position on the national, regional, and local level respectively. Thus, geographical position is a historical category; naturally an object (settlement) remains in its former place but its environment, transport facilities may change with the object playing an active part in these changes.

These attributes are well-distinguished in the table 3(i), prepared on the basis of empirical studies[3]. The site types will find treatment in Chapter 4.

Indian Village

In order to study the village settlements in India, we must understand rural-urban continuum of past as well as of present. It does have a rare human plane where the town and village agree to co-exist. Rightly says Soundara Rajan that if the village is a backwater of Indian nativity, the city was the watershed of its enthusiastic *joie-de-vivre*, and the panorama of both have a mystique of related thinking for simultaneously balancing life's many needs, pragmatically and pompously. It is, thus, in India alone that village is the cocoon of the city and the city the cage of the village. One gets orphaned without the other, but one does not out himself asunder in either, from one's own typed environment. Moreover, it is the universalizing of the incipient perspectives of the microcosmic rural atmosphere that stretches its expansive ken into a well-knit bondage with a macrocosmic urbanvista and finds fulfilment therein, beyond the pinches of hunger and cold. India stood apart as a model from other world models of a city and village life, and had been able to infuse into the entire structure of the land, the impregnating blood of *dharma* and to keep human sentience in a state of suspended animation all the while.[4] If we compare the urban and rural settlements, it is clear that the desideratum in a city is almost diametrically opposite to that in a village, not because they have divergent needs indeed, far from it, they have almost identical basic needs but what distinguishes one from the other is that of the values set on time factor and coordination of effort.[5]

The village was perceived by Metcalfe as a separate little state in itself. Srinivas[6] characterizes the village of pre-British India as having generally existed in a state of isolation from the rest of the world. Each was stable, self-sufficient whole, controlling its own affairs and yielding to the outside world only a land tax through cautious intermediaries. Whether treated as isolable or not an isolated whole economically, socially or politically, the village in India may be described as a vertical entity made up of several horizontal layers each of which is a caste. The superiority and inferiority of the caste is strengthened by the reciprocal relationship often termed as *jajmani* system by Oscar Lewis or *aye* system by Ishwaran. We shall see the details regarding village organization and morphology in this as well as Chapter 6.

Emrys Jones gives a birdeye view of Indian villages true for generalization. Comparatively, few people in India live in dispersed dwellings. Even in the Himalayan zone and hill country, generally, the hamlet is the main unit of settlement. In Bengal, even the technically dispersed settlement makes a close pattern indeed. Elsewhere, the nucleated village is supreme. The market place either occupies roadside or centre of the village. Post office, police and grain store or seed fertilizer store, maternity centre or community centre find place according to availability of suitable place. Mosques and temples, schools, wells, hand-pumps and other facilities are located where need and public demands determine. Social factors, states Spate,[7] are no less important, at

Table 3 (I)

Attributes of Site, Situation and Location

Attributes	*Scale*	*Historical Component*	*Degree of Generalisation*	*Areal Focus*	*Planning Significance*
Site	Largest, topographical Map of 1" to 1 mile, 1" to $\frac{1}{2}$ mile and large scales	Most responsive to historical processes, form and area changes	Generalisation possible and valid	Settlements as area	Settlement planning
Situtation	Medium, Chorographical Maps of 1" to 4 miles, 1" to 16 miles scales	Less prone to historical stimulii	Moderately generlised partial uniqueness	Settlement in area	Micro-spatial and micro-regional planning
Location	Smallest, Geographical maps of 1" to 32 miles, smaller than 1" to 32 miles scales	most resistant to historical processes, almost invulnerable	Unique	Settlement in area	Regional planning

best once we go beyond the fundamental antithesis of the north-west (or south-west Asia) type and the thatched gable of the more humid areas. Not only the site and layout of the village, but the geography of the house often reflects age-old religious and magical traditions.

Settlements in Other Occidental and Oriental World

Being gregarious in nature, man prefers to live in family or clan. Nucleated villages result from this primary urge. During past, protection, both of man and his pet animals, played major role in nucleation. It is still the same in most of the occupied areas, e.g., like enclosures and fences in central and southern Indian house surroundings, the African *kraal*, Iranian walled villages, compact villages of southern Arabia, like mudwalls and trenches surrounding Indian plain villages of the past. In China, compact settlements, sometimes of a clan and joint family, abound in a great number; many of them have enclosure walls and square or rectangular pattern (Fig. 3.1). In delta areas, there is a vast floating population. Like Indian craftsmen and artisans, they also have such families based on division of labour. Communes and cooperative farms, wherever established, are of different plan and layout. In the smaller farming villages, there are no artisans, the farmer does the work of blacksmith, carpenter and architect too. The settlements in loess cut forms are also different from the counterpart in southern China where hamlets and fragmented habitations abound along streams. Confluences of streams attract nucleated big villages. In Manchuria, hamleted villages spread in vast area.

In Japan, site often decides the actual form of larger villages. The paddy lands have big compact villages while many of them are like street settlements along the routes. The valley floors and level lands too have nucleated forms. Hill slopes are covered with dispersed and isolated settlements. Based upon the *jori* system, the settlements often reflect square pattern, a few having two to three sections or hamlets, hence, of composite type. The cottage industry based shops find place in front of the houses. The village organization though a social unit, is well-oriented towards economic sufficiency sustainable on agricultural as well as industrial production.

The south-east Asian parts have too much variety to specify a distinct form. In north Borneo, pile villages are built over water for protection. Such is the case in many low-lying flooded areas.

In Africa, in most of the countries, isolated hamlets with separate houses of varied type prevail. The Negroes usually live in villages but in western Africa, larger villages like town do exist, i.e., in Nigeria. The pigmies have no permanent dwellings but construct rough shelters from branches of trees. The bushmen live in small groups or clans. The Hottentots, the nomadic cattle herders, live in shifting tents. In the larger, Oases in Sahara Arabs live in villages with their tall, flat roofed mud houses built close together.

A village in China, India or Egypt may occupy the same site for hundreds/thousands of year built over their rubbish dumps.

Occidental

In Germany, the rural settlement forms vary according to sequence of occupance. The irregularly clustered village groupings—Haufendorf or Gewandorf—occupy the edge of its striped arable field, meadow and pasture and woodland. The strassendorf (street village), angerdorf (in a row) and rundling etc., dealt with in the Chapter 4, show lines of contacts between Germans and Slavs, hence admixture of two ethnic cultural characteristics (Fig. 3.4).

In England, Anglo-Saxon family or kin groups formed closely tied up villages with open field

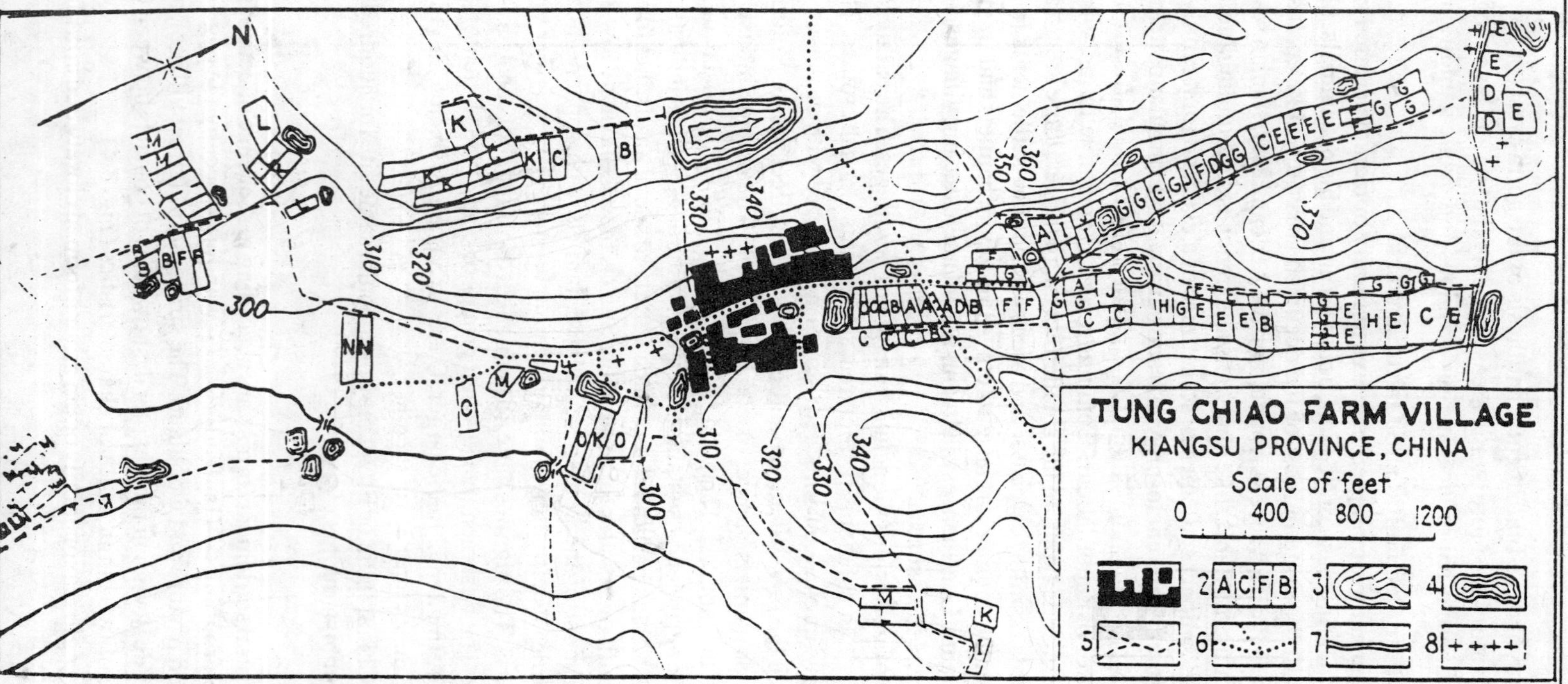

Figure 3.1: A Chinese rural village and its associated fields, ponds, temples, etc. 1, the village; 2, field plots (all marked A are tilled by farmer A, those marked B by farmer B, etc.); 3, hill lands, usually in grass and graves (contour figures are in feet); 4, ponds for irrigation and fish; 5, earth paths; 6, paths paved with stone; 7, paved road 7 ft. wide; 8, Buddhist temples (*Original map by J.L. Buck. From Jones and Darkenwald, "Economic Geography," by permission of The Macmillan Company*).

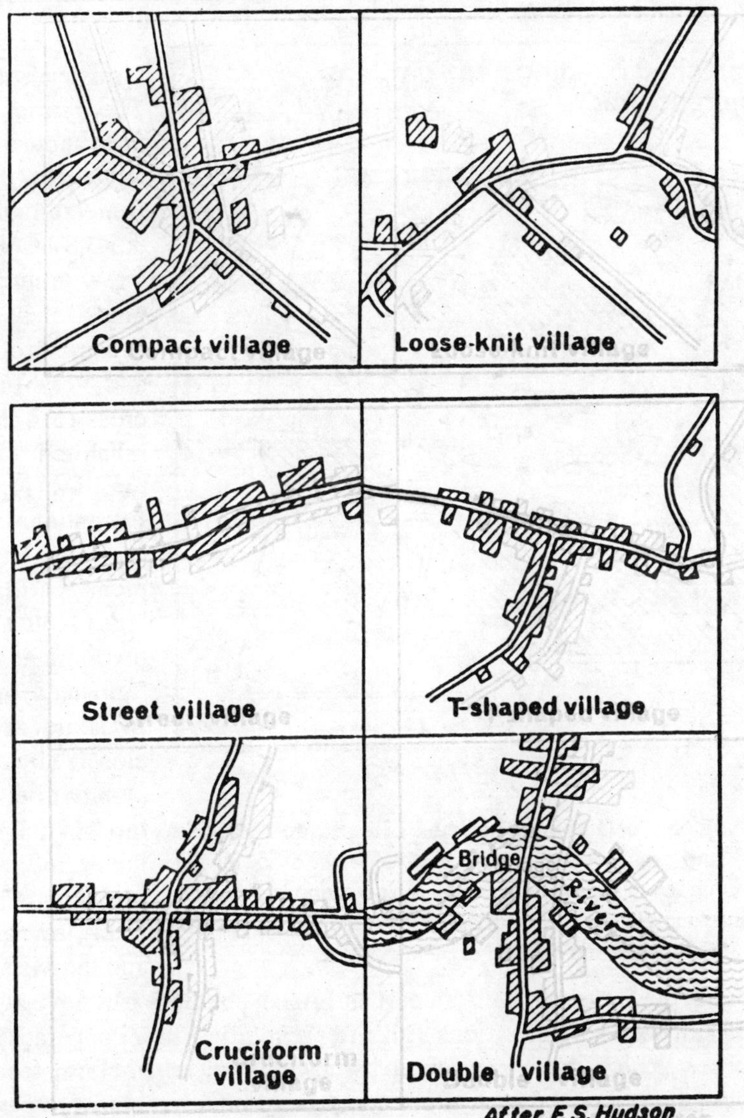

Figure 3.1(a): Typical village forms. While some villages appear to be formless, many adhere to one of the forms illustrated here. Most Ordnance Survey maps provide examples.

system of agriculture. Danes and Norsemen followed the same pattern. Normans brought new additions and variety and now the idealized English village is a closed community having green line of trees, road, church, village pump, pond and school and sometimes new community centre. Besides agricultural villages now one comes across forest villages, mining and quarrying villages, fishing villages, tourist villages, dormitory villages and industrial villages with varied social organizations (Figs. 3.1a-3.5). Europe presents variations due to complicated intermigling of the dispersed and nucleated types. This is true for U.S.S.R., Mediterranean, central and northwestern Europe too.

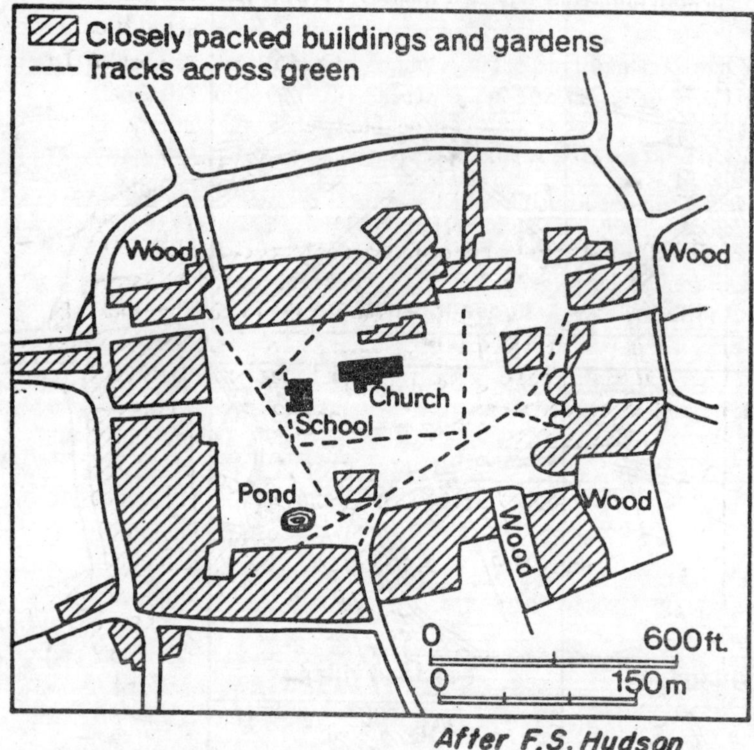

Figure 3.2: Heighington, Co. Durham. The whole of this "green" village is virtually square, and was probably built in this way for defensive purposes, the church tower providing a useful look-out and the green a refuge for men and animals. A number of buildings have encroached on the green since defensive needs ceased to be important.

In U.S.A., isolated farmsteads mark the scene. The farmer has his own farm house and attached structures in his farm at some suitable place (Figs. 3.6-3.8). Compact villages, a few in number, are composed of shopkeepers, artisans, professional men and very few farmers. A cross-road hamlet is also inhabited by non-farm families (Figs. 3.8a, 3.8b). Exceptional case has been cited by Harris[8] of Mormons who live within villages. But now dispersion predominates, hence, farmstead more common. In some areas, however, closely situated farmsteads along a highway give a picture of village organization, the examples being French settlements in the Lake St. John lowland in Canada and the Mississippi delta.

In Soviet Russia, the European western part and Asian southern part have age-old compact villages with well-knit social organizations. But, after revolution, new cooperative farm villages have farmers' houses closely, though separately, situated. They are not farmsteads of U.S.A. or Canada but following mechanized agriculture comprise similar structures like peasant houses, fertilizer and seed store, cooperative office, laboratory, laundry, school, hospital, recreation centres, granary, stables, shops, dairy, piggery, equipment garage, park, electric power house, poultry farm, cold storage and other modern appendages. The two types of cooperative farms are *Kolkhoz* or state farms and *Sovkhoz* or collective farms.

Plantation Settlements

In both parts, oriental as well as occidental, plantation settlements are different lacking in permanency and close social bonds found in other villages. Here the life-style is closely regulated by the estate owner or trade unions. Tea, rubber, coffee, banana, coconut and sugarcane cultivation/plantations in India, Burma (Myanmar), Malaysia, Sri Lanka, Indonesia, Brazil, United States, and Ethiopia have given rise to factory like colony settlements, sometimes showing temporary nature of the relationship between owner and tenants or manager and labours. The tea gar-

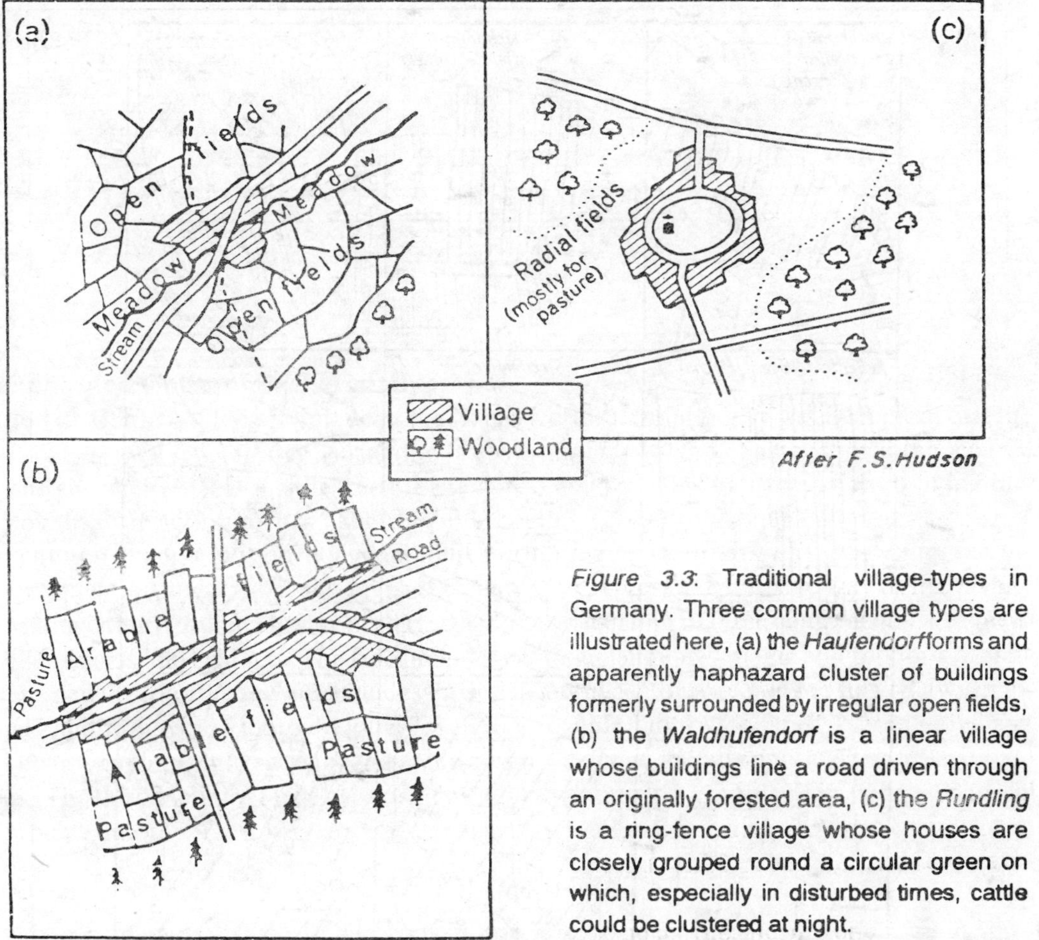

Figure 3.3: Traditional village-types in Germany. Three common village types are illustrated here, (a) the *Haufendorf* forms and apparently haphazard cluster of buildings formerly surrounded by irregular open fields, (b) the *Waldhufendorf* is a linear village whose buildings line a road driven through an originally forested area, (c) the *Rundling* is a ring-fence village whose houses are closely grouped round a circular green on which, especially in disturbed times, cattle could be clustered at night.

dens or plantations of India are different from coffee plantations of Brazil in arrangement of houses of labours and owners. In New World, the houses are separate planned while in old world, they remain huddled together away from manager's buildings. These are named as *Latifundium* (hacienda, plantation, finca, estate) by Finch *et al.* Fazenda,[9] rural hamlets of Brazil coffee plantations, present typical example. Various other village/settlements would find their place while dealing with type and morphology in Chaper 4 and 6 respectively.

Anatomy of Indian Village

Rural settlement, more appropriately *gaon* is a living system, like living organism which has since immemorial past perceived, does perceive and would do so (tongues in trees, books in the running brooks, sermons in stones and good (God) in everything) in future; because here only the human community is knit together by land and lore, by love or law. Kinship, culture, languages and tradition, all in conjunction, provide integration to the living society. That is why, the following features, as observed by Dube, characterize most of the settlements:

1. As a territorial as well as social, economic and ritual unit, the village is a separate and distinct entity.

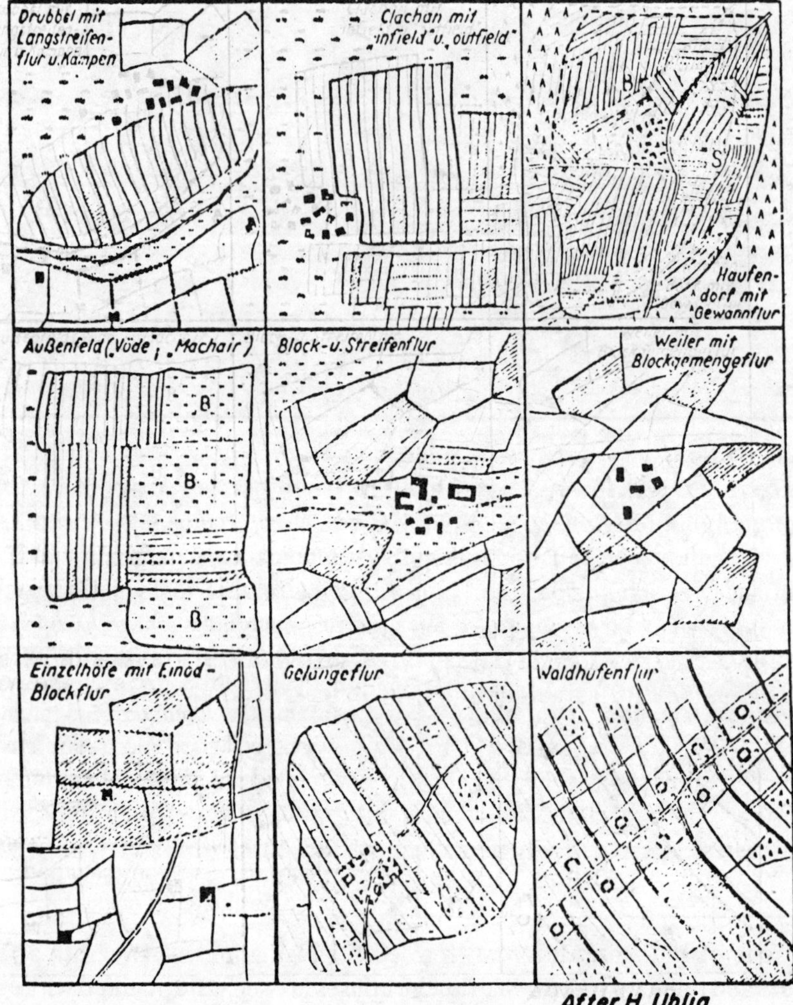

***Figure 3.4*:** Diagrams of some different possibilites of "open-fields".
1: "Drubbel" with permanent arable fields in open "Langstreifen", later addition of younger, single farmsteads with (enclosed) property in square field-plots ("Blockflur"), locally called "Kampe". 2: "Claschan" with permanent infield (in open—formerly run rig—strips, the whole infield enclosed by one common earthen bank or stonewall), outfields open—formerly also lotted in run-rig strips, periodically changing with grassland: "Haufendorf"

2. These settlements have a composite population comprising a number of groups belonging to different Hindu castes and in some cases to tribes as well as other religious groups. No caste alone is self-sufficient.

3. The members of this local group are bound together by ties of mutual and reciprocal obligations.

The interdependence of castes within the village is one of the factors making for village unity. This, says Srinivas, is the 'vertical unity' of many castes and contrasts it with a 'horizontal unity'

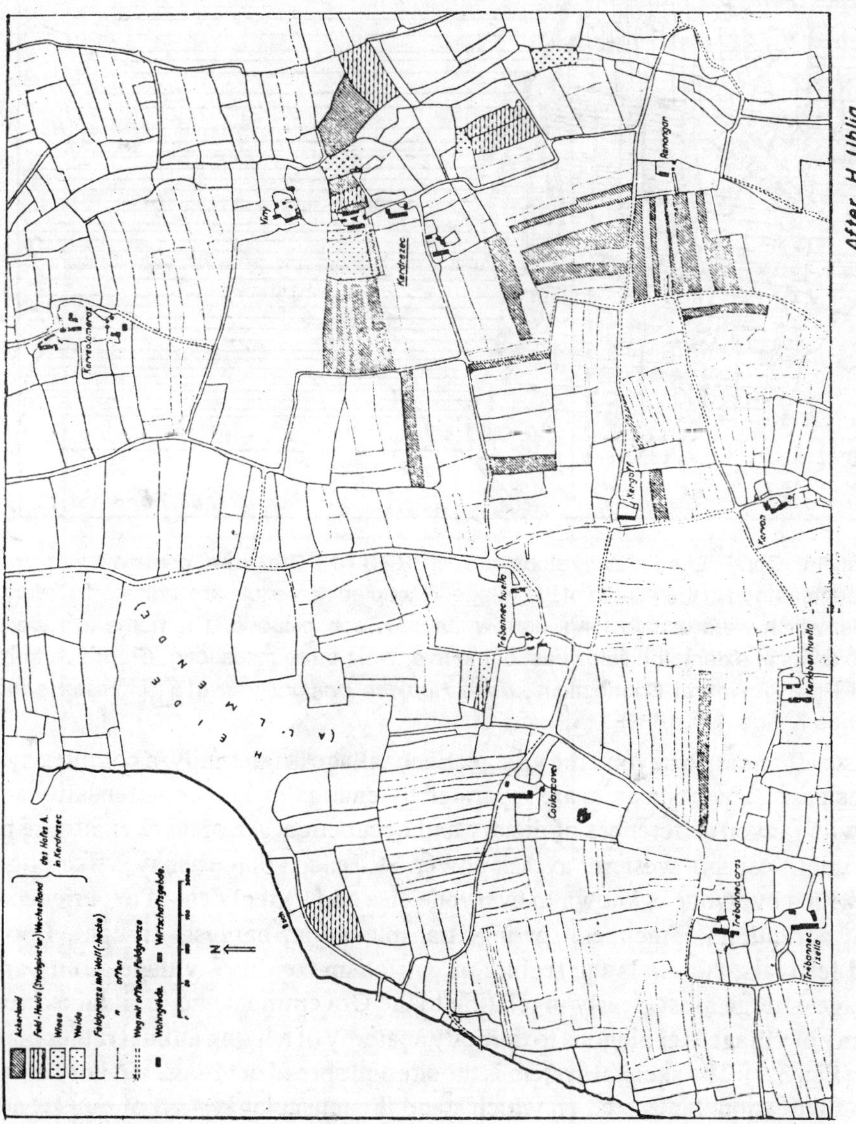

Figure 3.5: Settlement-and Field-forms of parts of Plovan (Quimper), Brittany (Copied from the original cadastral plan of Plovan, section Kerdrezec, 1:2500; 1827) property and Land Use of the example-farm matricels of 1931 and in the field 1957.—Translation of the key: Ackerland: arable land. Feld-Heide (Stechginster) Wechselland: field-heather (gorse) cultivation (changing every 5-12 years). Wiese: meadow. Weide: pasture. —All landuse symbols (hatching etc.) are given only for the property of the farm "A" at Kerdrezec, thus showing the distribution of one typical holding—Feldgrenze mit Wall (hecke): field-boundary with earthen bank (or hedge on bank). Feldgrenze offen: open field-boundary (groups of open strips, formerly of the "Mejou" type). Wege mit offenen Feldgrenzen: fieldlances with unenclosed field-boundaries, Wohngebaude: farmhouses, Wirtschaftsgebaude: byres, stables barns etc.

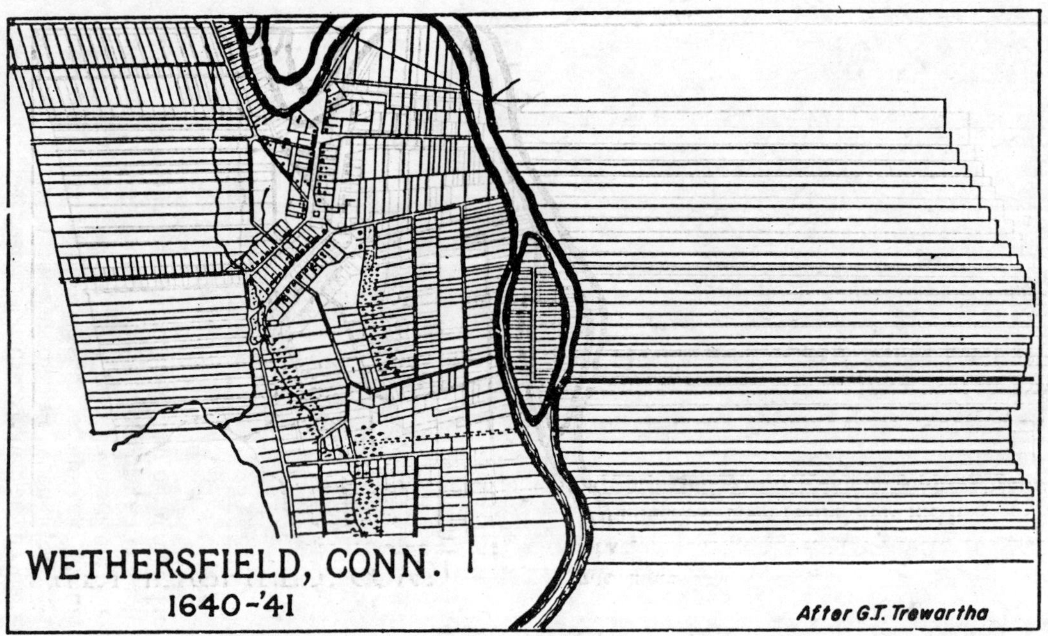

Figure 3.6: Wethersfield, Conn. Land subdivisions are of 1640-41. The town common with the metting-house at its center stood in the middle of the village. Occupied home lots are indicated. Orderly arrangement of fields, which were usually long, narrow strips, is conspicuous. The home lots were generally about three acres in extent; the fields east of the river were three miles long. (Redrawn from C.M. Andrews, "The River Towns of Connecticut", *John Hopkins University Studies in History and Political Science*, Series 7, Nos. 7-9, 1889).

of castes in which caste alliances go beyond the village. Each village is internally, a complex system of heterogeneous parts. The caste units are separated by endogamy and commensality and they are associated with ranked differences of dietary and occupation. Also, there exist side by side ritual, economic, political and 'western' axes of power. Still each village behaves like a light little community in which everyone is known to everyone else and a great deal of experience is common to all, i.e., agricultural practices, sowing, transplanation, harvest, drought, flood, epidemics, fairs and festivals, etc. So is the feeling of patriotism for one's village. Unity and solidarity of the village emerge most clearly in relation to the Government and in ritual expressions.[10] Thus, anatomy of village is analogous to the body anatomy of a living animal rather man. Let us elaborate this (Fig. 3.9). The skeletal system is the site and spread of village territory along with arteries of communication, lanes etc., on which stand the muscular system of houses and other allied structures and constructions. The nervous system through which it perceives, controls and sustains the life-line are the rituals, festivals, fairs, sports, Ramlila like plays and worship of Gods, trees etc., reflecting the nature's symbiosis or cosmic symbiosis. The endocrine and respiratory are represented by the all pervading sense of gregariousness, oneness—a common feeling regarding own village as a joining and connecting force. Traditions, culture, religion, social customs, village norms are the cardiovascular representatives. Likewise, the lymph vascular or defence structure is provided through interdependence of caste hierarchy, *jajmani* system or division of labour on one hand, and visible forms like enclosures, walls, hedge, ditches, and so on on the other. The digestive system is reflected through dawn to dust busy work rhythm of production and consumption of food materials which give life for creative activity. Various ways of cleaning and waste disposal, manuring of fuels for continuous sustenance of reproduction system represent the excretory system of body. Lastly, the reproductive system is visible through family, progeny, generation of clan in the form of sons and daughters as well as varied plantations of orchards and construction of buildings, schools, wells, *dharmashala*, and temples through which one thinks to be personified after death or recollected, at least.

Thus, *the anatomy of village is symbiosis expressed in forms which in appearance gives a holistic view called morphology*. Here, the cosmos seems to be reflected in a microcosm where man and nature remain in a state of balance. In the past, the man in these settlements was symbiotic in relation to nature but now, day-by-day is becoming exploitative, hence, change in anotomy as well as morphology (Fig. 3.9).

		Body System
	System	*Major Organs and Structures*
(i)	Skeletal	Bones, cartilage, ligaments
(ii)	Muscular	Muscles
(iii)	Nervous	Brain, sense organs, nerves, spinal-cord and glands
(iv)	Endocrine, Respiratory	Hormone producing glands, lung, bronchi, trachea, mouth, nose, diaphragm
(v)	Cardiovascular	Heart, arteries, veins, capillaries, blood
(vi)	Lymphvascular	Body's defence structure against disease etc.
(vii)	Digestive	Mouth, teeth, tongue, salivary glands, stomach, small intestine, liver, gall bladder, pancreas
(viii)	Excretory	Removal of waste organs, sweat glands, large intestine, kidneys, ureters, bladder, urethra
(ix)	Reproductive	Testes, penis, ovaries, uterus, vagina, vulva etc.
		Village System
(i)	Arteries	Streets, lanes, inter-house lanes, inter-sector lanes, ponds separating hamlets, khori-drainage/pathways/livestock route
(ii)	Houses	Temple, dih etc. morphological aspects
(iii)	*Rituals*	Festivals, fairs, sports, gossips, play and games
	Worship	Gods, trees (nature's symbiosis) or cosmic symbiosis
	Ramlila	A binding-spontaneous force
(iv)	Oneness	Common feeling regarding own village
	Gregariousness	Instinct in all—joining force or connecting force
(v)	Tradition, Culture	Religion, social customs, village norms
(vi)	Caste	Vertical/horizontal unity (interdependence)
(vii)	Production-consumption	Food material etc., work rhythms, meal, creative activity-dawn to dust
(viii)	Waste disposal	Cycle of living creatures, manuring of fields, reproductive systems
(ix)	Family	Progeny—gereration, orchards, constructions, clan

Indian Villages

Their Nature and Regional Characteristics

While discussing regarding villages in India in the preceding paragraphs, it was repeatedly emphasized that main common features of the Indian village are caste hierarchy, structural unity, the

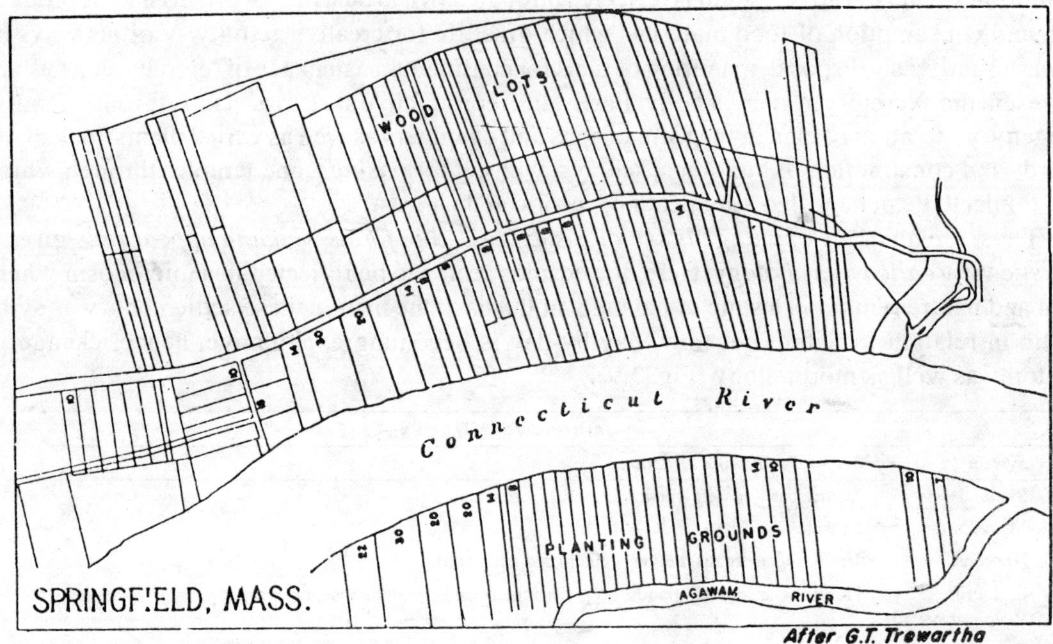

Figure 3.7: Land subdivided into long tiers, and the tiers in turn divided into regular, narrow strip fields of approximately equal size and shape, is very well developed in the part of the town of Springfield shown here. Most of the lots were eight rods wide. The Top of the map is east. (Redrawn and simplified from frontispiece map in H.M. Burt, *The First Century of the History of Springfield*, Springfield, Mass, 1898).

jajmani system operating along with the sixteen *sanskaras* of the Hindus, kinship organizations in defined territorial units of the past, rituals and myths associated with worship of Gods and Goddesses or their various forms but all leading towards a stable, peaceful life to see the infinite reality through finite celebrations. Because, man's enjoyment of pleasures in his brief span of life is a ritual and a sacrifice that conquer his finiteness and mortality. Accepting finiteness and mortality like God, says R.K. Mukerjee (*The Indian Scheme of Life*, p. 3), he yet attains the infinite, the eternal and the divine, by participation in sacrifice at the alter of life's duties and obligations.

The rigidity of caste and class, however, against which there is much hue and cry, based on heredity and wealth, is against the true philosophical meaning of *varna* defined by the universally accepted texts like the Mahabharta, Bhagwad Gita and Bhagvata Purana and indeed against the spirit and genius of Indian culture. That is why, the inherent solidarity is resisting the modernization while adapting various changes in society.

The regional scene of villages is also varied as is the landscape. Anatomy and morphology both reflect the overall effect of the distinct landscape, environmental as well as cultural and a milieu of these. The generalized picture given by Jones and Spate shows only the variation in outward appearance to an onlooker. A few examples would highlight the regional characteristics regarding internal social arrangement. Srinivas presents the social system of a Mysore village in which he observes the extent of conformity, change, flexibility, overlapping in traditional occupations, and shifting relationships. Ritual, economic, political and western axes of power reflect themselves in behaviours, occupations and their expressions as concrete forms or

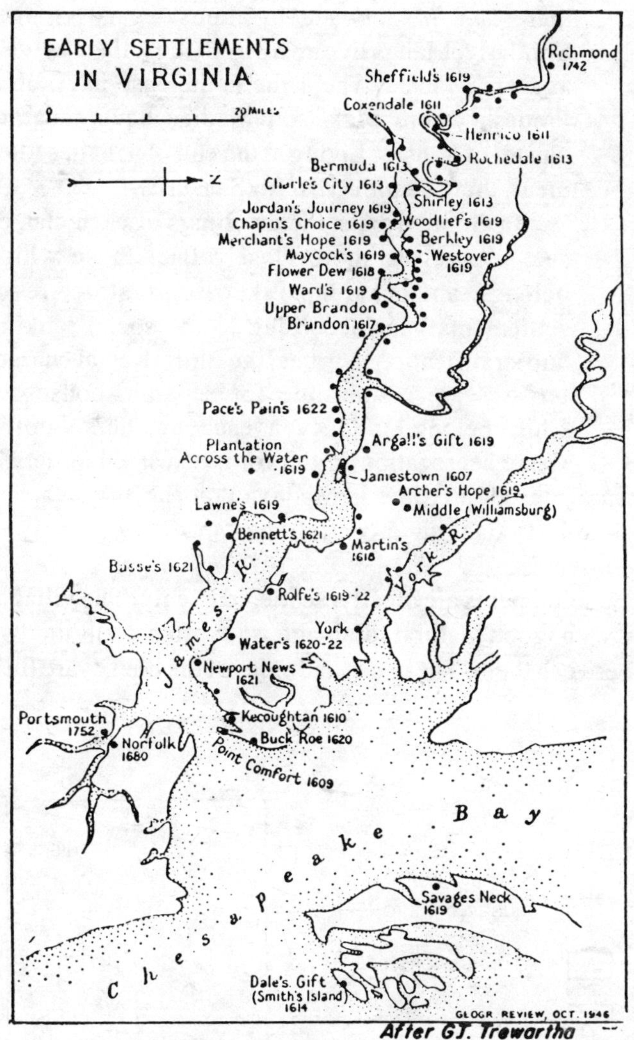

Figure 3.8(a): With three exceptions (Richmond, Portsmouth, and Norfolk) the named and dated settlements were in existence by 1622. (Compiled from data contained on map opposite p. 201 in Lyon G. Tyles, *The Cradle of the Republic*, 2nd ed., Richmond, 1906; and from maps prepared by Lyon G. Tyler in M.P. Robinson, "Virginia Counties," *Bulletin of the Virginia State Library*, IX, Nos. 1-3, 1915, following p. 124. In the latter publication there is a series of eight maps showing the progress of settlement in Virginia from 1607 to 1671).

houseforms along with their surroundings. In old settlements, each kinship group or totemistic sect has a separate quarter or hamlet. We agree with Mukerjee's view, as others should, that the division of the Indian village into caste wards is a replica of the pre-Dravidian division of the tribal region into *parhas*, *desams* or *pattis*, each having its central village. The arrangement of central village is discussed in Chapter 6. Here is given brief account of social system of settlements in several tribes. Irawati Karve's survey reveals that hamlets in Maharashtra are called *wadi*. In the same way, in Andhra Pradesh, there are clusters of huts a little away from the main village which are called *pali* or *guda* and said to belong to an *oar* (*gaon*). To the *wadi* (hamlet), people sometimes call the *gaon* to which they belong. *Kasaba* or *pethi* are words which mean an area where various types of craftsmen (Kasabi) live. In the eastern parts of Satara district, many villages have *Bangar wadis* (shepherd hamlets). Likewise, there are *Romoshi wadis*. *Wadis* are called generally after a clan, name or after a tribe or a caste, and are just like *chhawani* in the northern plain. In Maharashtra, for one caste, there is a village exogamy, while for the other castes there may be marriage within a village. In the south, multi-clan village is the rule. In the north, where there are no clans, settlements are supposed to be peopled by descendents of one ancestor for each caste and there is strict exogamy which applies even when people of separate ancestries and *gotras* come and live in the settlement. In the Dravidian South, each caste in a village is made up of more than one lineage and clan. The untouchables

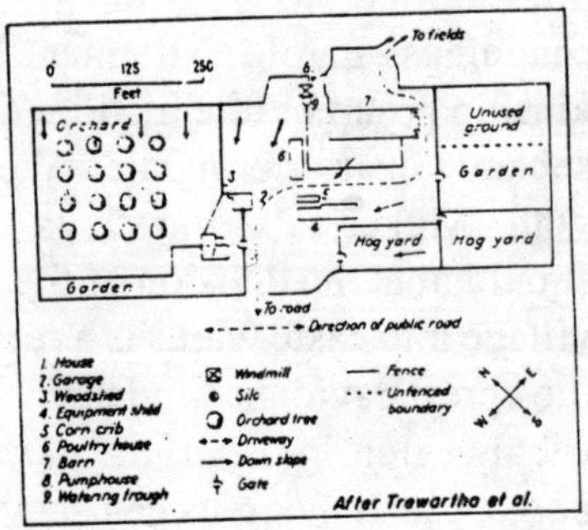

Figure 3.8(b): Plat of farmstead on a Wisconsin dairy farm. Note the large barn with twin silos and the numerous other outbuildings.

have distinct separate habitations. In Maharashtra, there is a Maharwada in almost every village. Similarly, Mangs live away from the village as well as from Mahars. The same is the case in Andhra Pradesh where Mala and Madiga have separate cluster of houses. Living at the end of a main settlement, they are *ante-vasi* (in Sanskrit).

In Gond, tribals, the dwellings of each clan or sect congregate more closely than those which belong to another group. Likewise, the structures of settlements vary according to the social ranking and stratification in tribes like Bhils. Racial characteristics are responsible for separate houses of Bhils belonging to even each nucleurs family. Caste segregation in the form of caste hamlets is common in non-tribal areas too. Even, among the Gond tribes in Madhya Pradesh, the detached huts tend to group themselves roughly into lines flanking a central open space for granary or various household operations.

In Betul (Madhya Pradesh) the village settlements are mostly, scattered evenly. The villages are usually situated on high grounds with good natural drainage and often built in two straightlines of houses with a wide road between them. The backs and sides of the houses are little

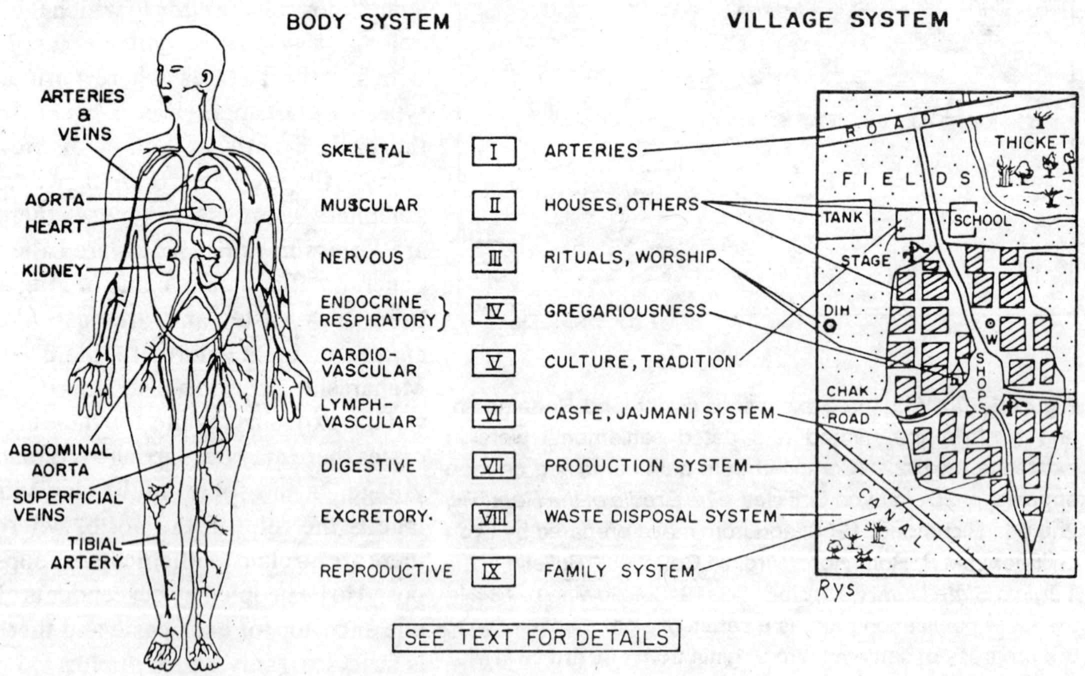

Figure 3.9: Anatomy

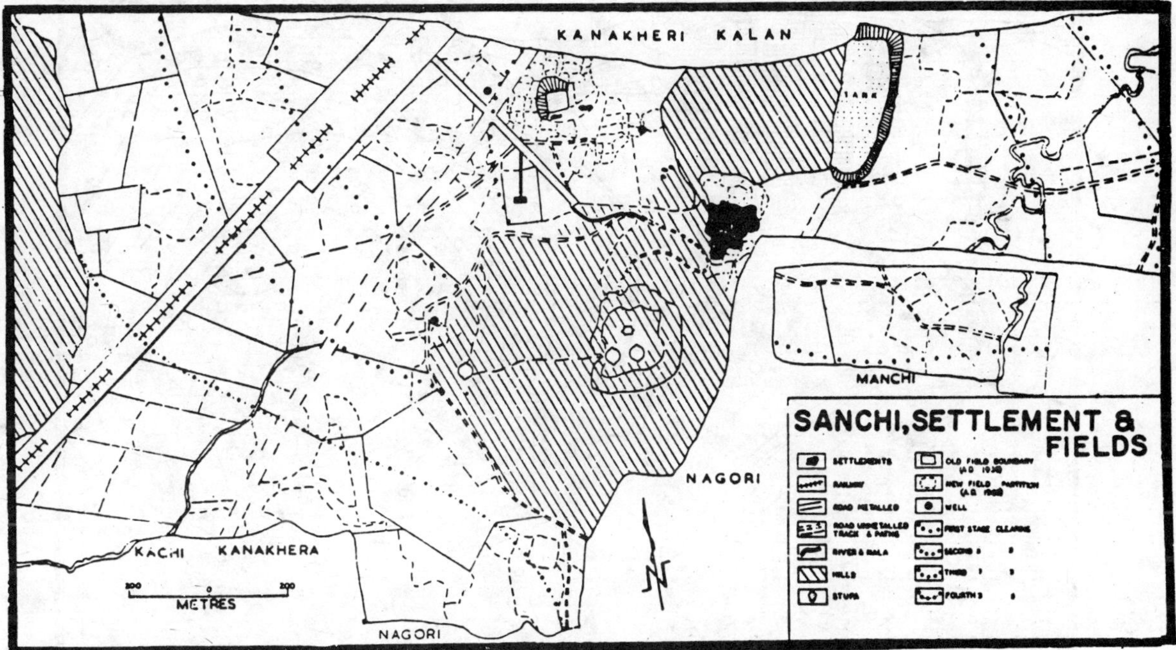

Figure 3.9(a): Sanchi, Settlements and Fields.

baries or gardens in which vegetables, maize, tobacco are grown. The village is often divided into two or three quarters called *dhanas*, inhabited by members of different castes. The Gonds and Mehras live, usually, in quarters of their own separated from the main village. In such settlements, temples are rarely seen and the village dieties are usually represented by heaps of stones, sometimes under a tree near the stem on raised ground. Most of the tribal villages in Bastar are self-sufficient with blacksmiths, artisans and other occupational groups belonging to the same tribe or sub-groups of the Gonds.

The Gonds and the Kolams in Maharashtra and Andhra, the Katkaris in Maharashtra, the Bette Kuruba and Jenu Kuruba, the Erawa and the Sholega of Mysore live in settlements of many huts. Likewise, the Warli of the west coast and the Cheachus of Nallamalai hills live either in an individual family house apart from others or in a cluster of a few huts.

The size of settlements of Kharias living in Chotanagpur and Orissa varies according to their cultural stage. Mostly they live in groups of five to ten families in huts separated by a distance of about 100 metres, scattered on hill sides. The more advanced Delki Kharias inhabit villages with regular houses, groves, dancing arenas and burial ground. The villages of Christian Kharias are more substantially built and compact. The hill Kharias also have dormitcries for bachelors and the maidens.

The Santhals, a totemistic tribe split up into a large number of exogamous totemic clans, have an elaborate territorial organization in Bihar based on Parha system. Here, the headman of a village exercises social and political authority; hence, organized settlements. The Birhors also possess the institution of village dormitory. The nomadic section moves from settlement to settlement. Among the forest cutting aboriginals, the Bhuinhar—the pioneer families—are the main occupants of settlements in Oraon or Kuruth tribes in Bihar. Other families of subsequent settlers

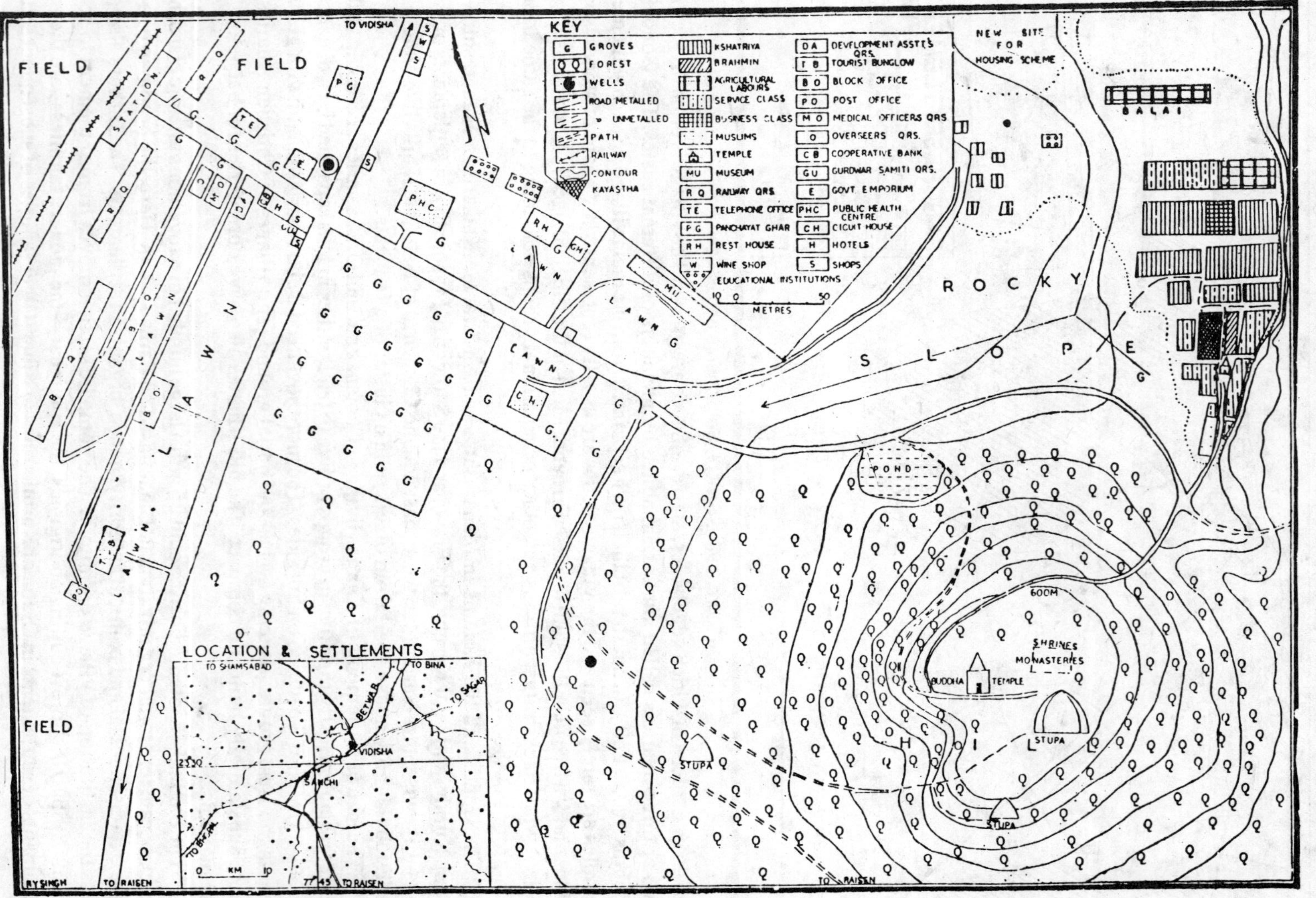

Figure 3.10: Morphology.

(Jeth raiyats or ordinary raiyats) like Gorait or Ahir, Lohar and Kumhar etc. join them later on. An Oraon settlement has three important organizing factors: *Baiga* or *Pahan*, his assistant known as *Panbhara* and the *Mahato* of the village. There is a proverb "*Pahan gaon banata hai, Mahato gaon chalata hai*". Sarat Chandra gives a vivid account of Oraon *bastis* (settlements) of the past. It consists of a cluster of mud huts huddled together without any definite arrangement with filthy surroundings. Among the public places of an Oraon village are the *akhra* or dancing ground and the *dhumkuria* or dormitory for the bachelors of the village. Outside the *basti* is the grove called *sarna* or *jhakra* sacred to all. Houses are of ordinary type thatched with straw or tiles and furnished with *manchia*, *khattis* (cot), and *pitris* (mats).

The Kuki tribe clans, in Lushai hills, live in villages consisting of four to five huts built of

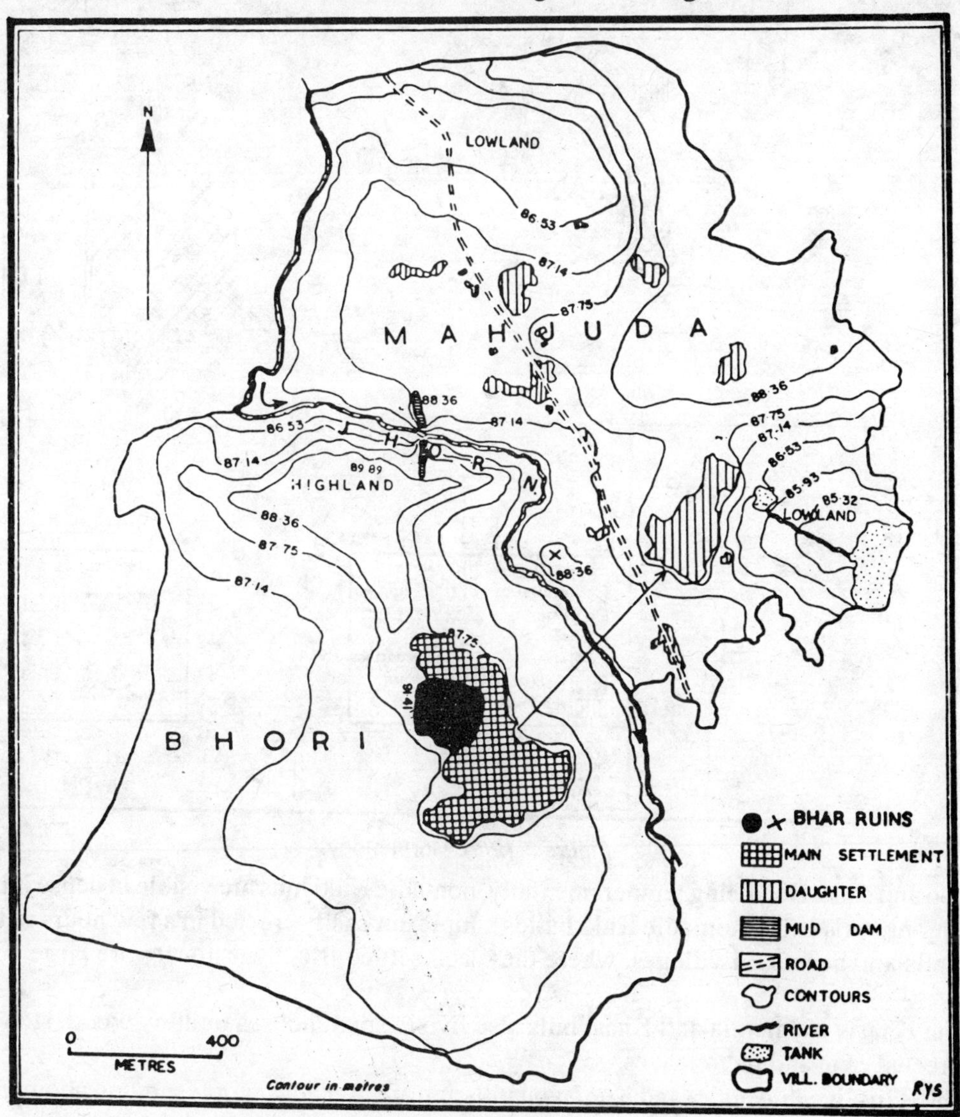

Figure 3.11: Village Bhori-Mahjuda, Location.

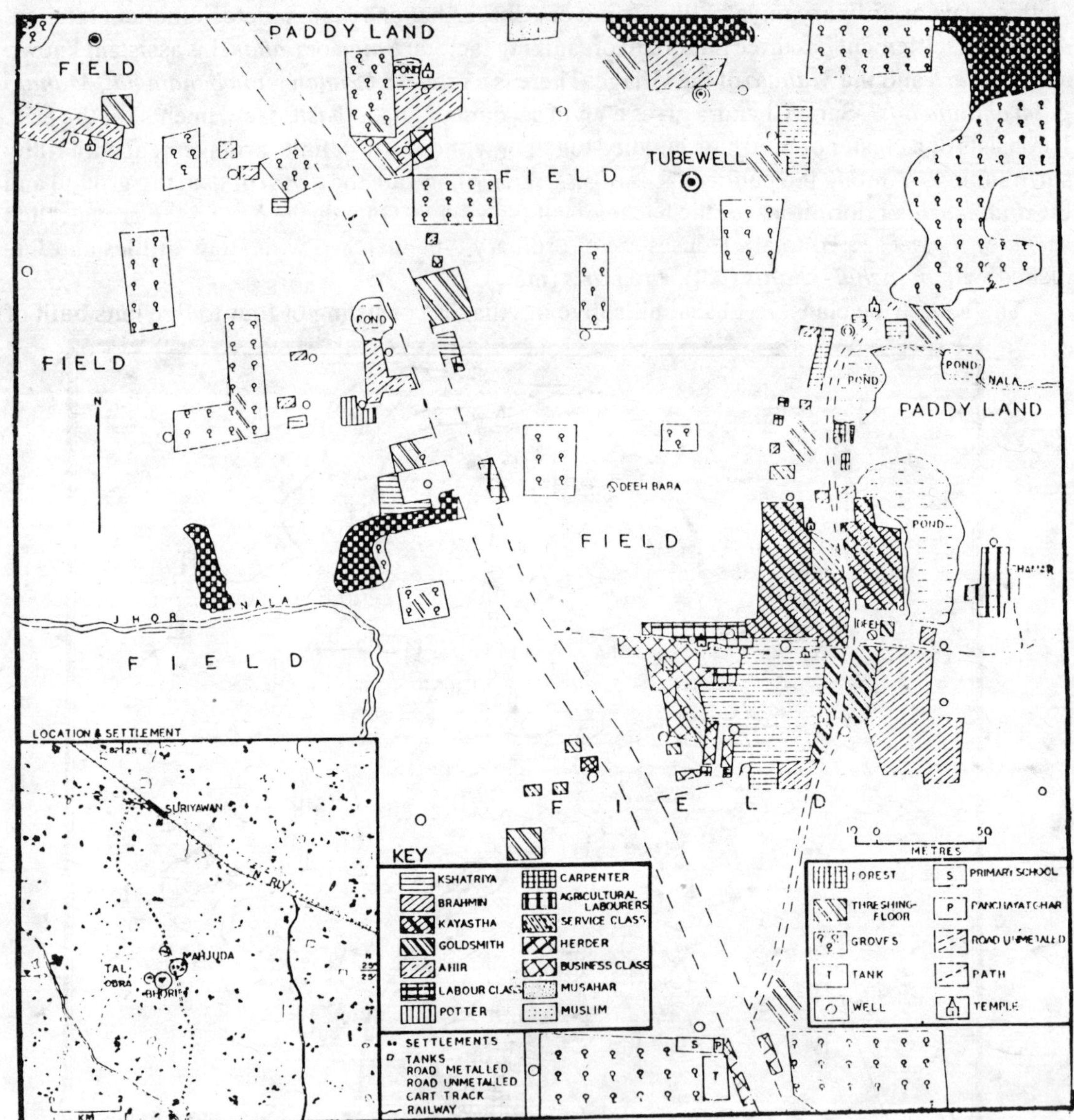

Figure 3.12(a): Morphology.

bamboo and cane. But, being temperamentally, nomadic Kuki huts are visible in dense jungles of Manipur hills also. The nomadic Kuki builds simple hut easily erected in a few hours with bamboo walls and beams. In villages, where they lead settled life, their houses are large and built solidly.

The Khasis of Jaientia and Khasi hills also live in small houses built by wood, stone, bamboos, reeds, cane and palm leaves.

The Rajis live in Almora and Kumayon hills and are nomadic people moving about in search of jungles to clear and take crops.

The Saoras of Ganjam or Tamilnadu are divided into a number of village units. They build houses with stone and mud and use thatch either of sage palm or tamarind branches.

The Chenchus live in *pentas* consisting of 15 to 25 huts in Andhra Pradesh. The Kadar of Kerala live in interior forest tracts in villages having 15 to 20 huts. These huts have enclosures in which they grow banana, yams and kitchen vegetables.

The Khasas of Jaunsar Bawar live in joint family houses. Often a group of family live together with one or more wives under the same roof.

The Mushahar, a semi-tribe mainly living in Uttar Pradesh and Bihar, inhabits in group of huts near common jungle land outside the main settlement. Mostly, they have open space in be-

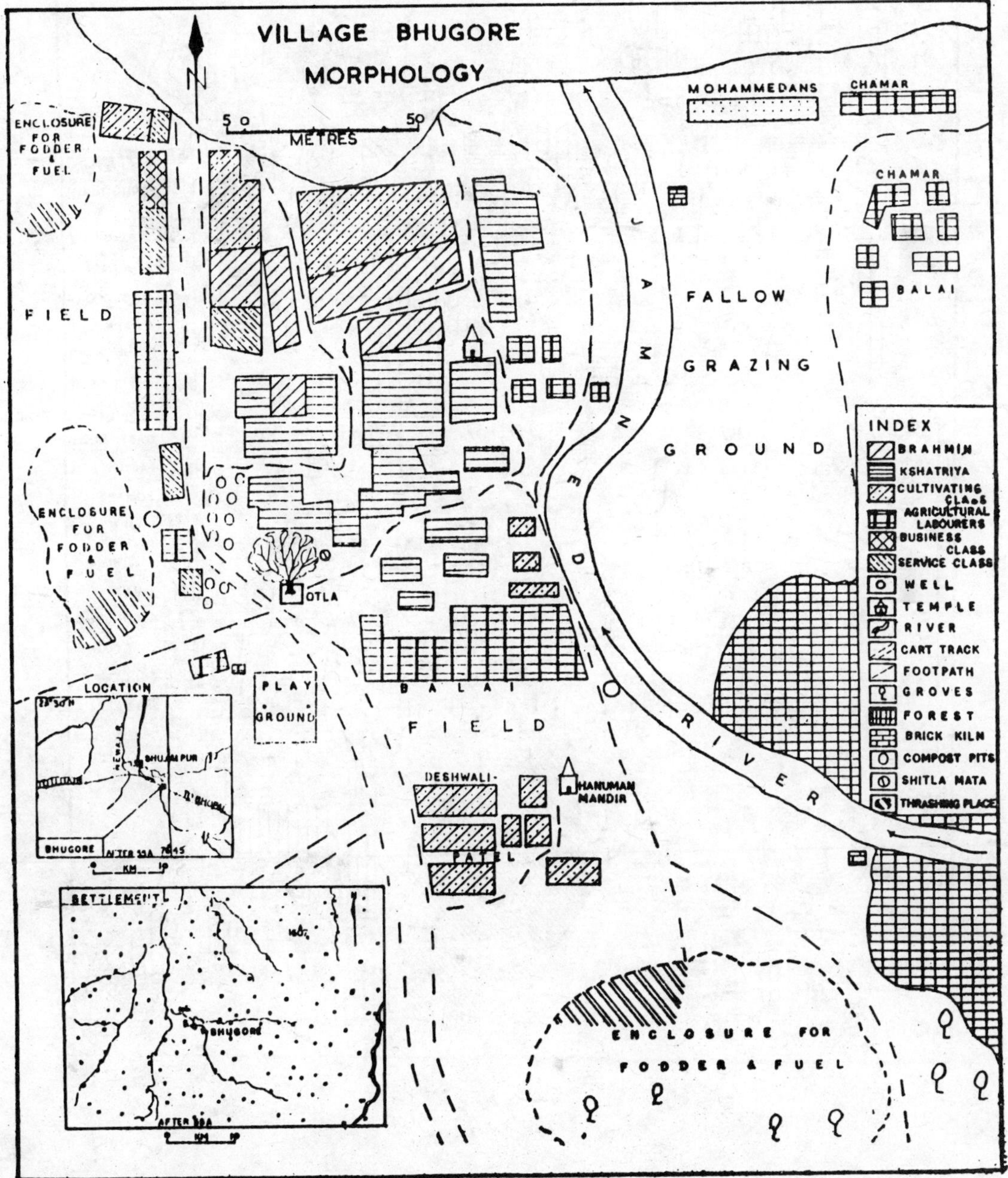

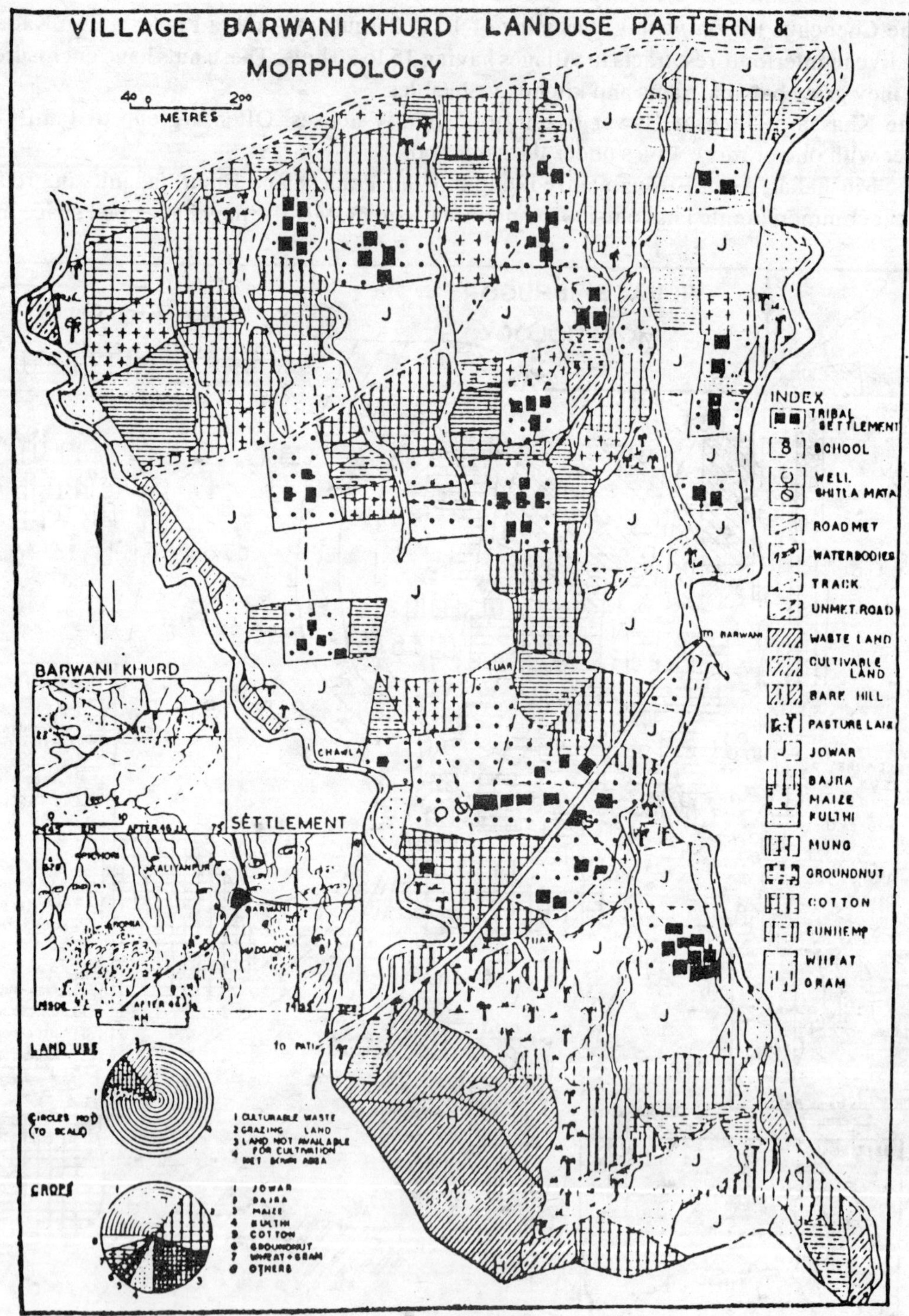
VILLAGE BARWANI KHURD LANDUSE PATTERN & MORPHOLOGY
METRES
INDEX
TRIBAL SETTLEMENT
SCHOOL
ROADMET
WATERBODIES
TRACK
WASTE LAND
CULTIVABLE LAND
JOWAR
BAJRA
MAIZE
MUNG
GROUNDNUT
COTTON
WHEAT
GRAM
BARWANI KHURD
SETTLEMENT
LAND USE
CROPS
1 JOWAR
2 BAJRA
3 MAIZE
5 COTTON
6 GROUNDNUT
8 OTHERS

Figure 3.13

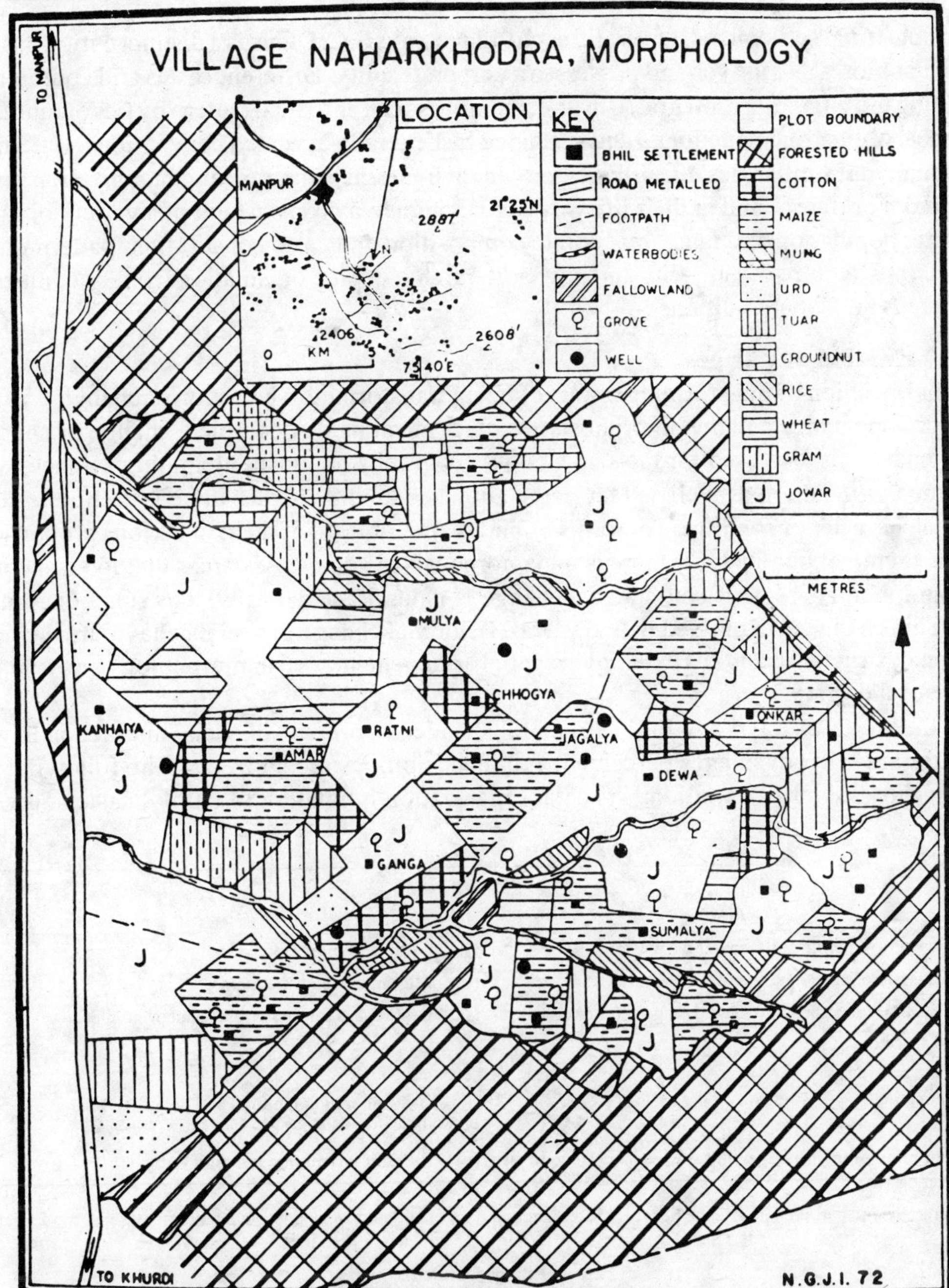

Figure 3.14

tween huts surrounding a hollow place of multipurpose use.

The Gaddi Lohars, a group of families, are found staying at the outskirts of towns in Madhya Pradesh and Rajasthan. They follow blacksmithy and live on carts (*gaddi*). These carts are covered with light thatch and tents.

In non-tribal settlements, generally each village, says S.C. Dube, is a distinct entity, has some individual mores and usages and possesses a corporate unity. Different castes and communities, inhabiting the village, are integrated in its economic, social and ritual pattern by ties of mutual and reciprocal obligations sanctioned and sustained by generally accepted conventions. But, in spite of fundamental similarities, the villages vary in their internal structure and organization, in their ethos and worldview, and in their life ways and thought ways on account of a variety of factors, e.g., size, population and land area, ethnic composition and caste constitution, pattern of land-ownership, structure of authority and power hierarchy, degree of isolation from or contact with urban areas and local traditions.

Transformation of Villages

It means on action of transforming or fact of being transformed. The action of changing in form, shape or appearance and metamorphosis are other meanings. A complete change in character, conditions etc. is also used for the same. Now, geography being an integrating science, we are concerned with action as well as fact in the above context. Whether there is complete change either in character or conditions or forms or/and shapes or in all of them in various proportions is also the theme of our study. If there is metamorphosis in some cases/areas that too is a concern of geographer. As regards settlements, change is natural, spatial as well as functional in time scale. This change is expressed in two ways: (i) internal change in social behaviours; hence, institutional, structural; and (ii) external in spatial arrangement, i.e., in morphology and functions. Let us see the first.

In the words of Raymond Firth, structural change is a product of social interaction in which pressures are felt, advantages perceived, and reponsibilities recognized.[11] The following comparison shows lines of variations in social organization in relation to family, caste and village council.

The Past	*Present*
Family	
(i) Insistence on family solidarity and cohesion	(i) Growth of individualism
(ii) Greater attachment of soil and settlement	(ii) Migrations more frequent
(iii) Intra-family relations governed by regard for age and kinship status	(iii) Less regard for these traditional principles
Caste	
(i) Occupational specialization on the basis of caste	(i) Caste no longer the final and only determinant of occupation
(ii) Prohibition of interdining with some equal castes and all lower castes	(ii) Rules of interdining less rigid
(iii) Hierarchy and permanent distance between different castes	(iii) Mild protest against social hierarchy some modifications in actual practice
Village Council	
(i) Constituted on hereditary principles	(i) Also admits people with achieved status
(ii) Little outside intervention	(ii) Considerable outside pressure
(iii) Decisions generally accepted	(iii) Defiance or avoidance possible

We shall come back to see the transitional phase of village organization in Chapter 10. The second type of change, i.e., morphological finds treatment in Chaper 5 and 6.

VILLAGE BHAGATPURA, MORPHOLOGY

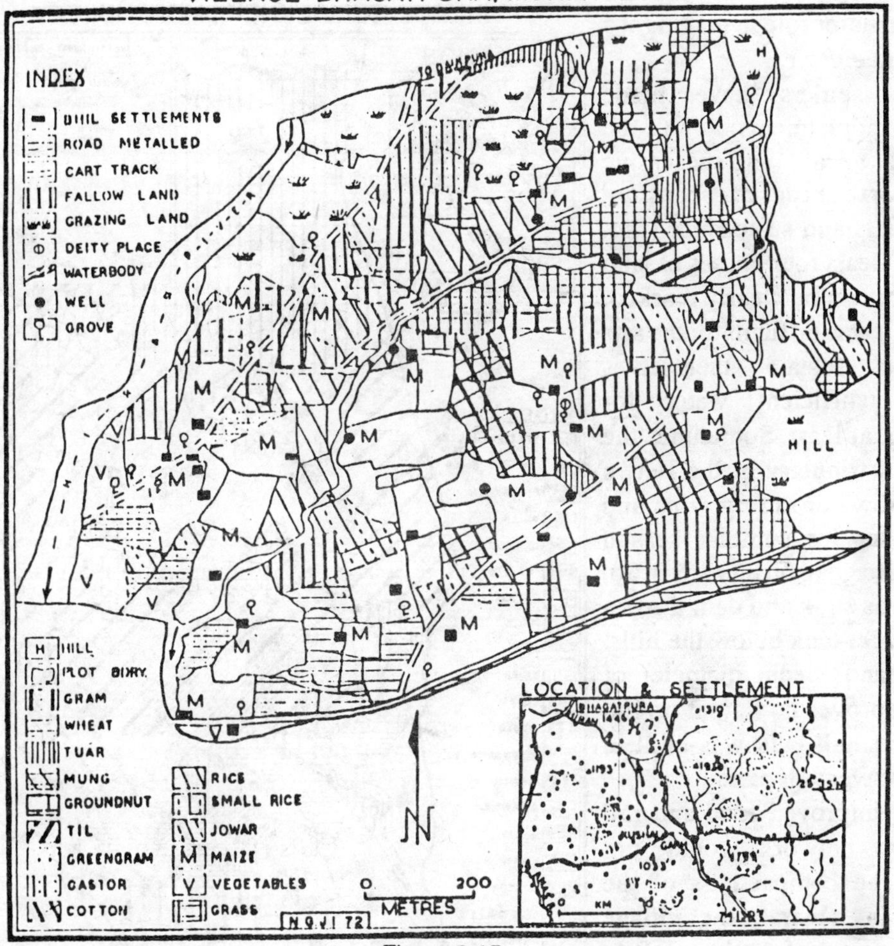

Figure 3.15

Study of Sample Villages

The study of a few selected sample villages from typical regions would present the actual picture of various aspects of rural settlements. These are: Sanchi, Mahjuda, Bhugore, Barwani Khurd, Nahardkhodra, Bhagatpura, and Semalkheri. Figures 3.17 to 3.22 are self-explanatory.

Sanchi

Lying on 23° 29'N and 77° 45'E (1,290 population, 1990) at a distance of 9 km from Vidisha and 44 km from Bhopal, it is a medium-sized village and has a station on the middle section of the Delhi-Bombay railroad. The village stands at the foot of small flat topped hill of sandstone rising 100 metres above the plain. Most probably, Sanchi derives its name from Sanchi-Manchi Bhils—the original settlers of the site, like Jhabua from Jhabbo Nayak and Banswara from Bansia Bhils. The arable land below the scarp in Betwa plain, water available from the river and lately supplemented by tanks, a suitable defensive site at the foot of a small hill in the west and a junction of old routes—all combinedly provided a suitable site for the settlement of the Chandrabanshi Rajputs, who established themselves here. Due to unsettled political conditions in the region, defence played a major role in making it a close-knit cluster.

The settlers havę made several adjustments with the physical terrain in successive phases for the needs of expansion, settlements and sustenance (Fig. 3.9a). At least four phases of land clearance can be clearly marked. At first, it was difficult for the settlers to sustain themselves without sufficient water for drinking, at least. Sometimes the *nala* or a tributary of the Betwa provided water during rains and winter but for summer season they had to go to further areas. So, a well was sunk and dam thrown to construct tank below the hills. This Chandrabedhi diameter of thê tank proves its Rajput origin. Another small tank was built in the north-western part.

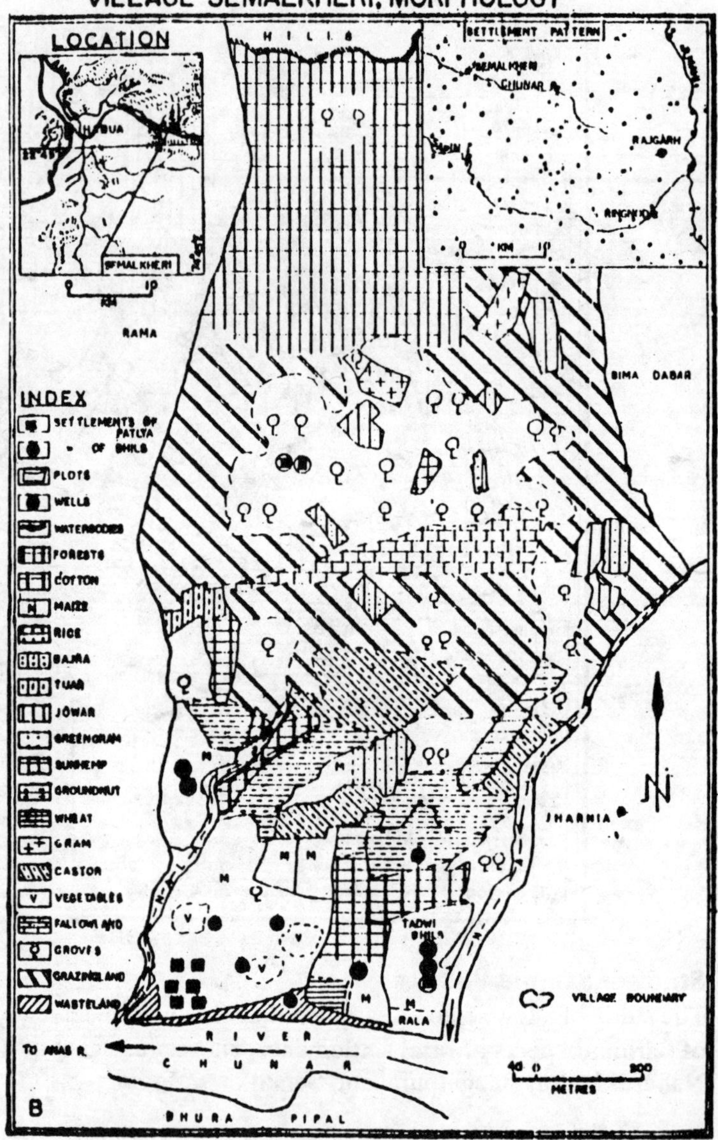

Figure 3.16

The improved road and rail transport network could not change the compactness of the village in general, the village shopkeepers preferred to shift to roadside so that they might serve the casual travellers. Others came from outside and started restaurants and hotels and retail shops. The Indian Railways established residential quarters for its staff. With the opening of N.E.S. Block new quarters and office buildings were constructed. To this were added the public health centre, telegraph office, museum, circuit house, guest house, tourist bunglow, *dharmshala, panchayat ghar* (community centre), emporium, cooperative bank, post office and other institutions, all in a planned way quite different in layout from the village. Civil facilities like supply of water through a new well, electricity, trains and bus service will, still, attract newcomers who must depend on business and industry only, as no land is now free for cultivation. The Bhil tribes still occupy separate site due to their racial character.

The scarp of the hill slopes and the arable land below gave it originally an elongated shape

BRAHMIN
JAT (Cultivating caste)
BUSINESSMEN
SERVICE CLASS
AGRICULTURAL LABOURERS
ARTISANS
CHAUPAL (Community centre)
CREMATION GROUND
TEMPLE
WELL
WATERBODIES
DISPENSARY
CANAL
THRESHING GROUND
SCHOOL
0 50 100
METRES
A
B
CANAL

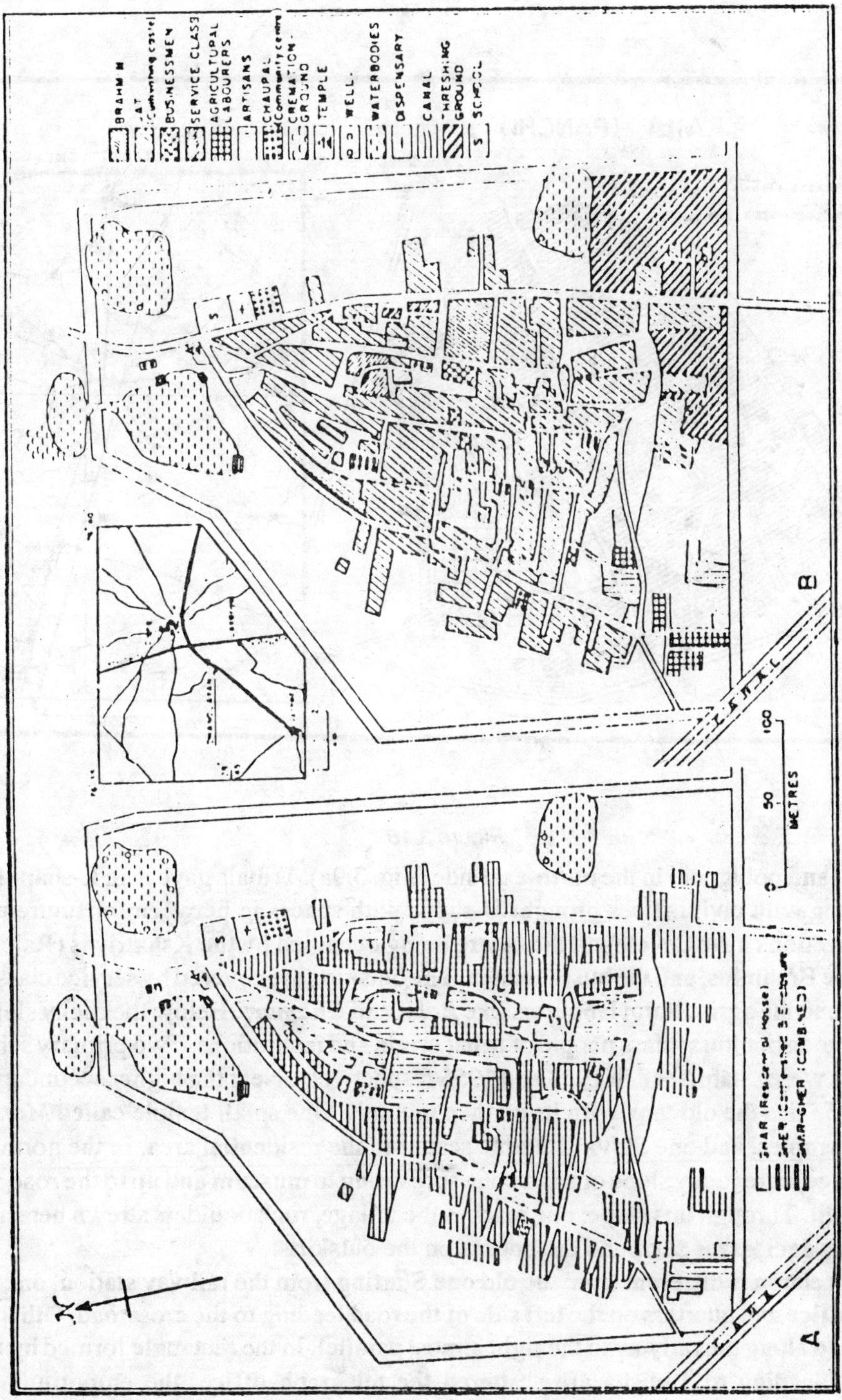

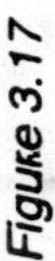

Figure 3.17

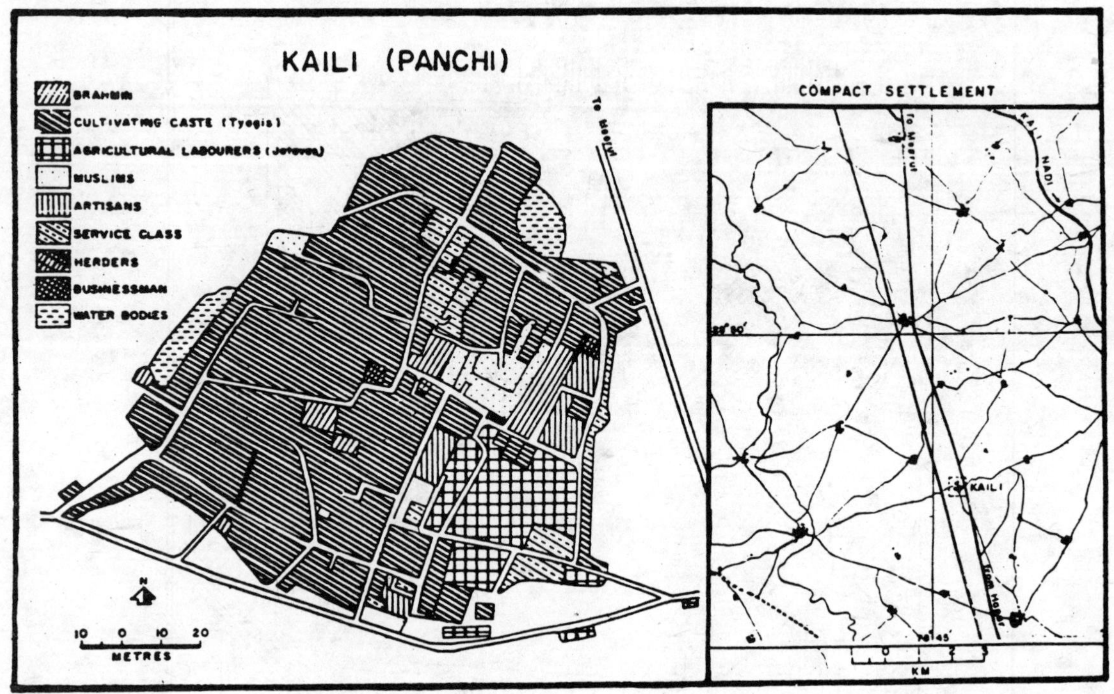

Figure 3.18

below the hill and polygonal in the north-east side (Fig. 3.9a). Tribals gave it an L-shape and new additions along with civil offices brought U-shape with spaces in between for future use. Different caste sections have developed the centre being occupied by the Kshatriyas (Rajputs), the Kayasthas, the Brahmins, and the businessmen. The outskirts are covered by service class people, the Muslims and the agricultural labourers like *Balai* and *Chamars*. Below the rocky slope in the north-west live agricultural class people of tribal origin and institutions. Two primary schools for girls and boys were established in 1953 and 1955 respectively. Near the higher secondary school opened in 1955 lies the old tank with its earthen mounds. One small temple called *Marhia*, two Hanuman's temples, and one Shiva's temple scatter in the residential area. In the north-west of the main village, bare rocky slope of sandstone spreads up to museum and up to the road skiriting the forested hill. Through this slope, one reaches the village, rock boulders strewn here and there and the thorny enclosures surround the houses on the outskirts.

The new section is different from the old one.Starting from the railway station, one may see the railway office and quarters on the left side of the road leading to the crossroad. Other railway quarters spread along the railway to the right almost parallel. In the rectangle formed by this road and the road leading to Vidisha are scattered the telegraph office, the emporium, and the *panchayat ghar*—all occupying the amidst wide open spaces and arable fields. In another rectangle formed by the Station Road and the Raisen Road are scattered, in a planned way, along feeder roads, the government quarters , the cooperative bank, hotels, retail shops, the *Gurudwara Samiti* and behind them the block quarters and the office, the tourist bunglow and the post office along the road. After the crossroad, in the left sector, lie the government orchard and the circuit house each having uncultivated space in between with lawns and occasional trees.

Beyond these are the forests and the hill, approachable by motorable metalled but circuitus road and also by a narrow path which starts beyond the high lying pond below the foothill. Beyond the hills are the magnificent *stupas*, the beautiful temple and other remains. The great *stupa*, the chief object of interest, stands conspicusouly in the centre of the hill. This building forms a segment of a sphere, solid throughout, and built of red sandstone blocks, with a diameter of 110 feet. at the base. A berm 15 feet. high sloping outwards at the base forms a raised pathway 5.5 feet. wide round the *stupa*, giving it a total diametre of 121 feet 6 inches.

Caste Structure and Houses

Out of the total 325 households, 317 belong to the Hindus, six to Muslims, and two to the Christians. About 42 per cent are occupied by the dominant caste Kshatriyas, followed by scheduled castes of agricultural labour class (31%). Others are Brahmins, Kayasthas, Banias, scheduled tribes, like sweepers, sherman, etc. Most others are government servants of various castes (Fig. 3.10).

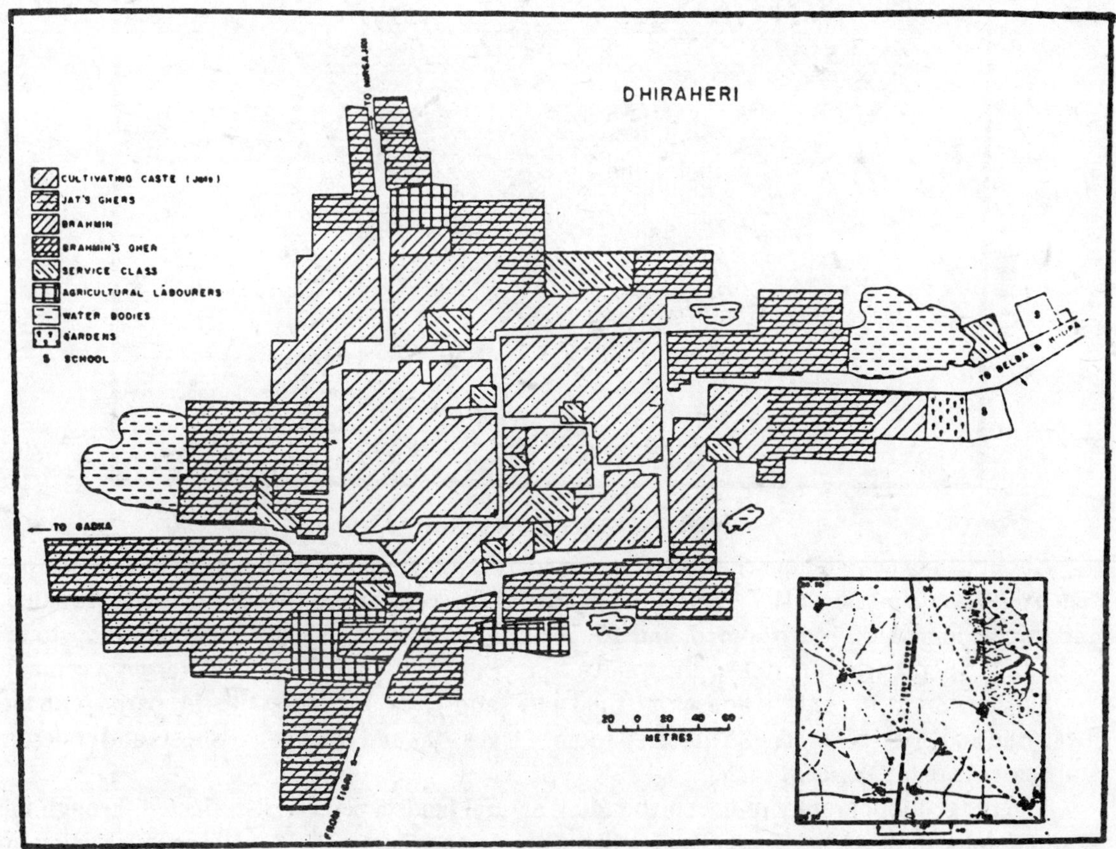

Figure 3.19

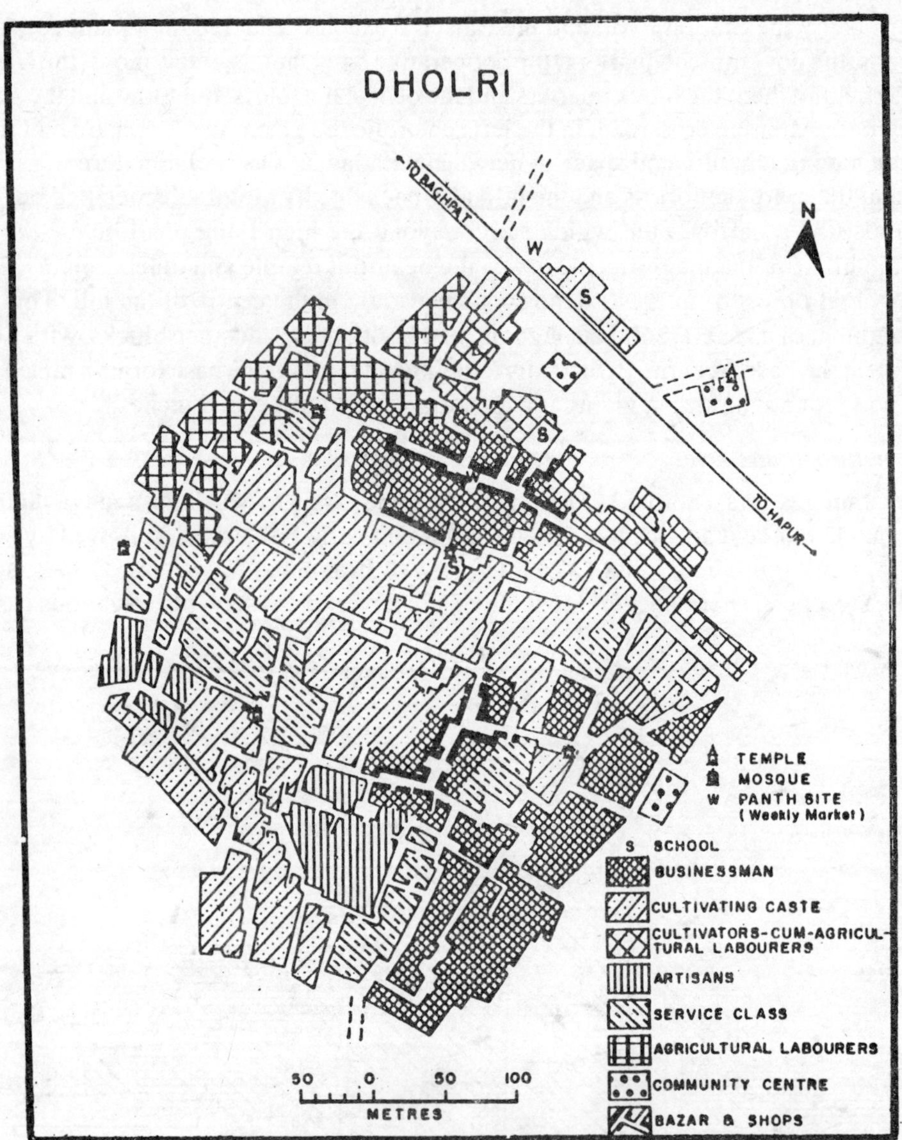

Figure 3.20: Village Morphology.

About 61 per cent of households are occupied by 2-4 members, 21.5 per cent by 4-6, 9.2 per cent by 7-9, and 7.6 per cent by single member. Out of these, 30 are one-roomed, 20 two-roomed, 130 three-roomed, 30 four-roomed, and 15 five-roomed houses, About 61 per cent are stone-walled, 32.5 per cent burnt brick-walled, and 6.5 per cent brick-walled and plastered with cement.

Further, about 76 per cent houses are tiled with semi-circular and flat tiles prepared with the local mud and those covered with thatched roofs of leves, tins and corrugated-sheets and concrete and cement are 6.1 per cent each.

The rugged topography in the surrounding natural landscape is well-reflected through the size and shape of these dwellings. There will be found no symmetry in the walls or eaves or layout of houses in relation to each other. The configuration, the length, the breadth, the geometrical shape in appearance, their openings, the slope of the roofs, arrangement of the door and windows, inter-house difference and above all their location—all are quite different and distinct in general outlook from their counterparts in the Betwa valley, the Kshipra valley or the middle Ganga valley.

But, the houses and quarters in the new sector have planned roads, rooms, windows, ventilators, layouts and locations. The developed technique speaks through their walls, roofs and the space around them.

Functions

About 33 per cent houses have separate sleeping rooms for each couple and the rest are multifunctional. About 40 per cent houses are rented. Generally, the houses vary in function according to the status of the occupants. The rich class houses tend to have separate courtyards, several rooms, a gallery for entry and a front room for guests. Rooms serve for sleeping and store for grains and other household articles. One of the rooms or the courtyard is used as cattlefold. Some houses have *bakhal* (separate courtyard) for cattle and fodder and fuel. Windows are usually small and in front walls. Muslims have small courtyards enclosed in one corner. Enclosures surrounded by thorns and woods are used for keeping fuel and fodder. Some houses have two rooms in L-shape, the front being raised with mud, usually for sitting and preparing grains. Cattle in such houses are tethered on one side at night. Double-storeyed houses have windows and are airy. Main outlets or drains open in each direction. In three-roomed houses, the front room is used for attending

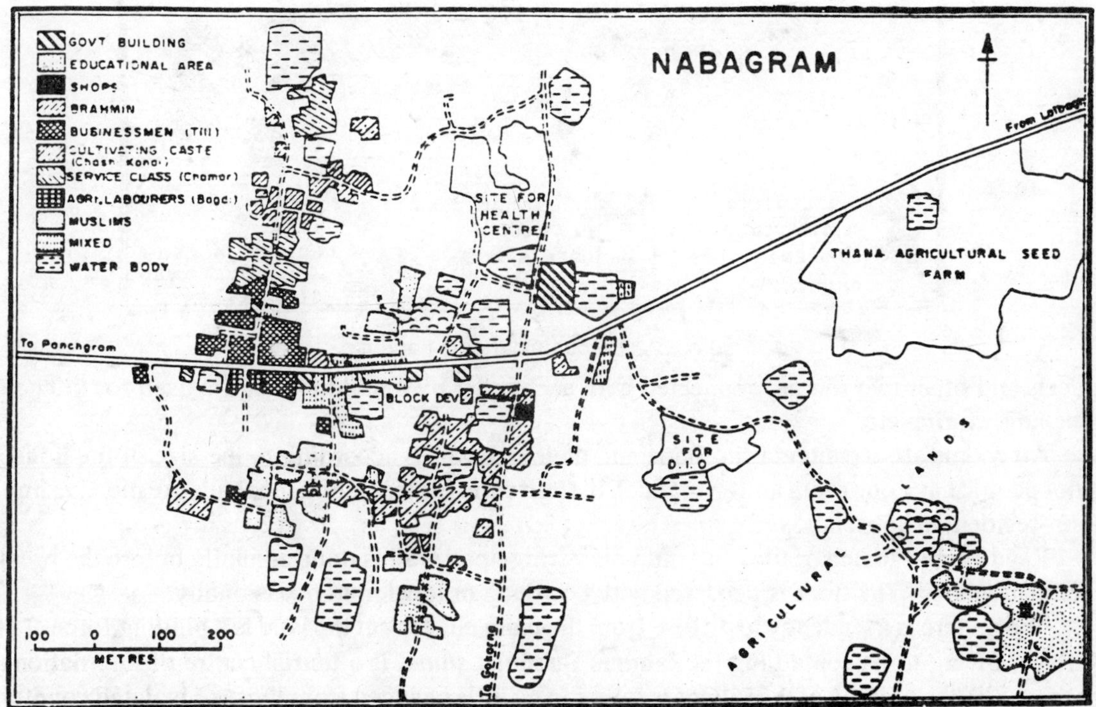

Figure 3.21: Village Morphology.

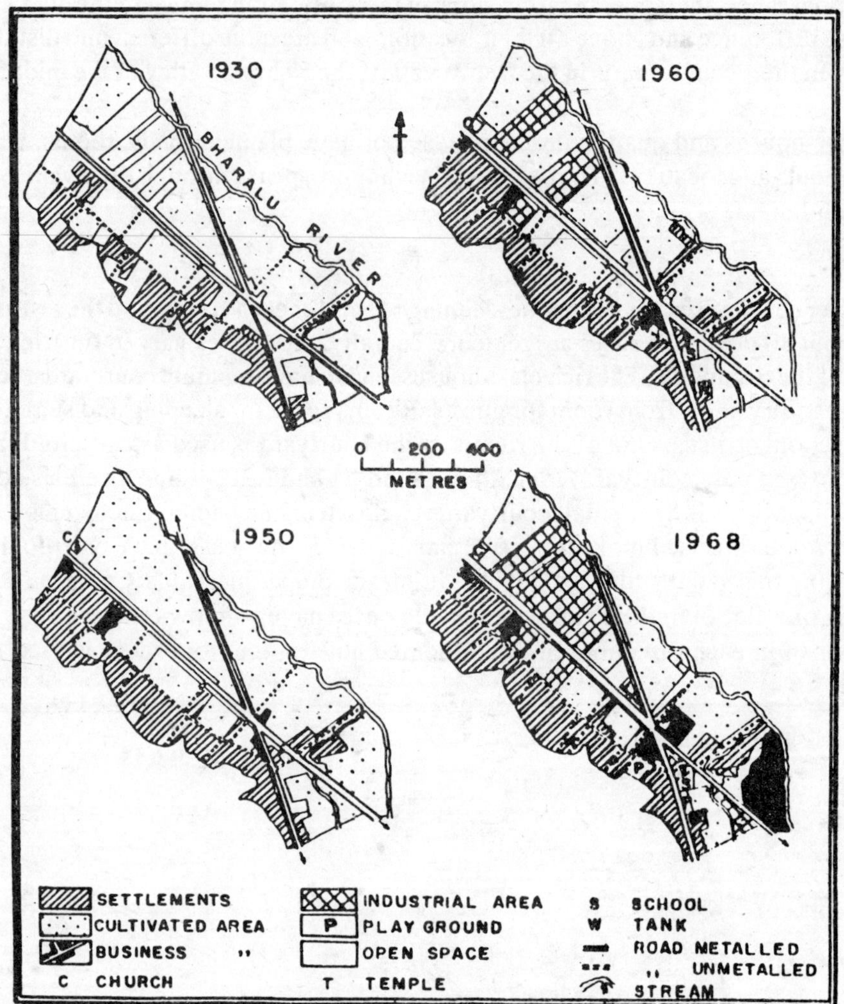

Figure 3.22: Dispur, Changing Landuse.

guests and other two rooms, connected with each other by a middle door are used for kitchen, sleeping, storing etc.

All rooms are rectangular in shape and their size varies according to the size of the house. Poor people have one room and a verandah in front side. Houses along the roads are mostly shop-cum-residential households.

Repairing of thatch or tiles and mud plastering upon wall is done annually before the break of the monsoon. The floor is plastered with cowdung or local mud occasionally.

Now, there is a tendency to diffuse from the main cluster but the land is a binding force. The village, owing to its containing the famous Buddhist *stupa*, is a tourist centre of international repute. Yet, the outlook of the villagers seems to be little changed from those of isolated counterparts.

Mahjuda

The village Mahjuda lies in the Bhadohi tahsil of Varanasi district. In the following paragraphs, we will discuss a short occupance and cultural history of the region, processes and patterns of original nucleation, formative stage of agglomeration and dispersion and diffusion as the recent trends, over a span of over 300 years of the existence of the village.

Cultural History of Bhadohi Region

Historically, the term 'Bhadohi' is supposed to derive its name from the Bhars whose cultural traces survive in many old tanks and mounds named after them. The 'Bhar Raj', whose capital was at Bhadohi, was probably tributary to that of Kannauj and with it eventually formed part of the kingdom of Jaunpur in the early medieval period. Bhars are supposed to be semi-aboriginal people by cultural historians. They gained suzerainty over large parts of western middle Ganga valley along with other such people in the early medieval ages. They had established their villages and towns, had their chiefs and knew agriculture and crafts. In the reign of Akbar, Bhadohi was made a *dastur* and included in the *Sarkar* and *Subah* of Allahabad. Eventually, these Bhars were over-powered by the Maunas Rajputs in the fifteenth century and the whole tract came under Sagar Rai, the first head of clan. Jodh Rai, his grandson, obtained *zamindari sanad* for his suzerainty from emperor Shahjahan. Madan Singh, Seo Baksh Singh and Ban Singh are important in the lineage who went into friendship with Balwant Singh of Banaras and Prithvipat Singh of Pratapgarh.

In 1750 A.D., the Maunas Rajputs having fallen into arrears of revenue, Raja Prithvipat Singh who was answerable for the arrears as security, made the whole *pargana* over to Raja Balwant

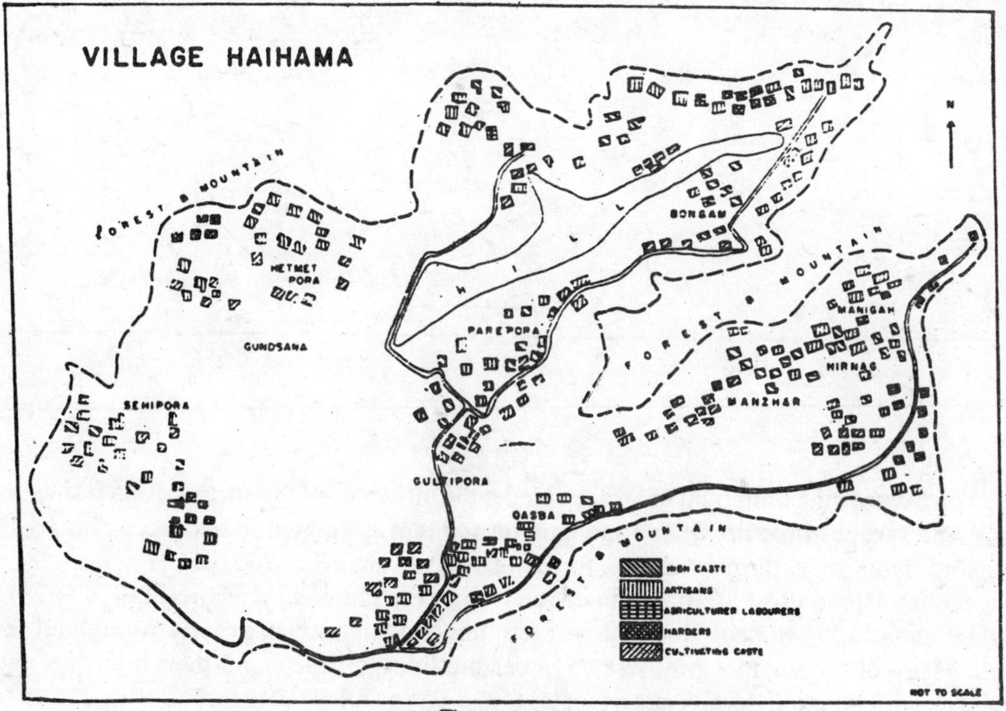

Figure 3.23

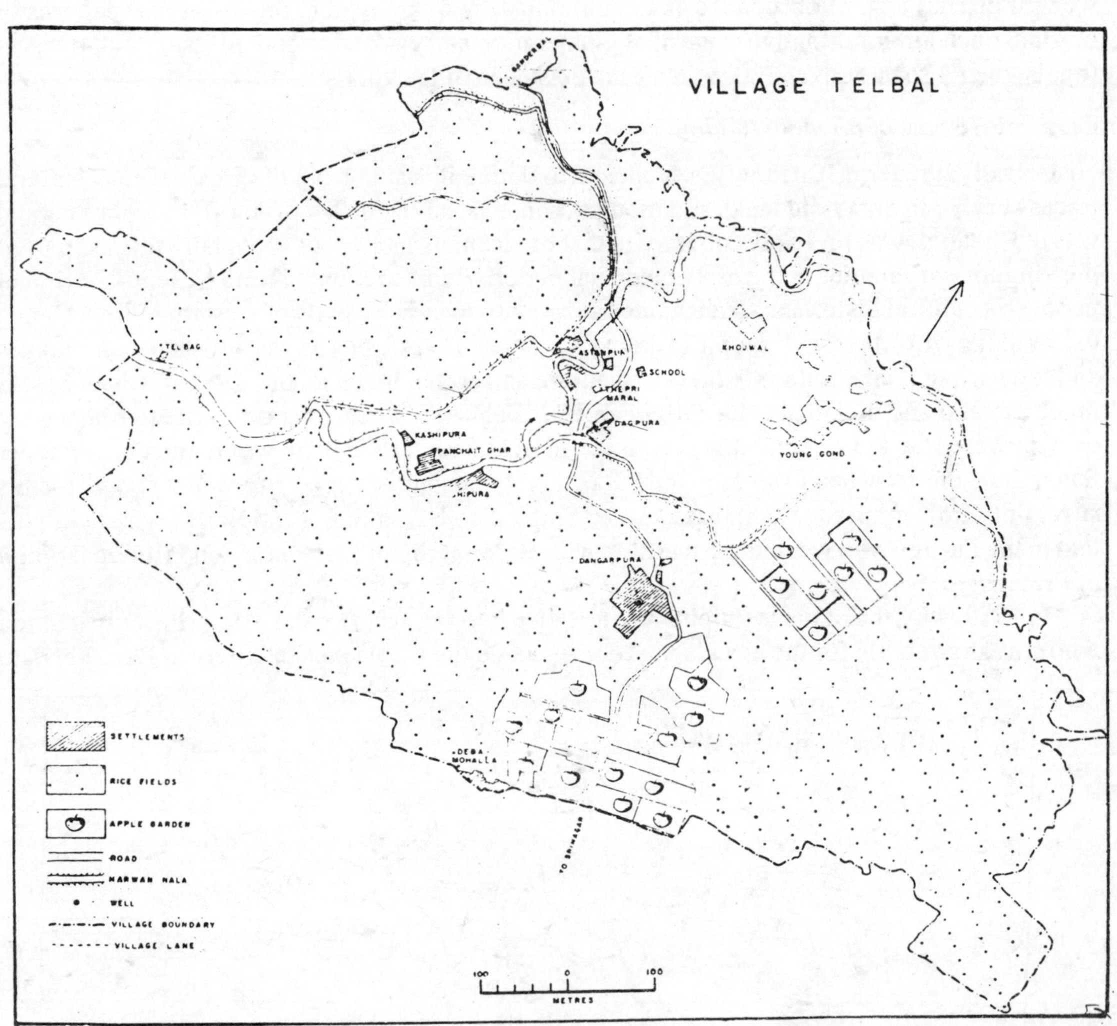

Figure 3.24

Singh on his paying the amount of arrears. Under the influence of the British, Raja Balwant Singh was made secure in the *zamindari* and later on *sanad* was granted to his successors by Nawab Shuja-ud-daula under the guarantee of the British Government in 1770 A.D. However, the period between the later half of the fifteenth century up to the fall of Maunas Raj (1770 A.D.) saw a gradual but steady segmentation and proliferation of Maunas clan groups throughout the *pargana*. Many of the villages proliferated under the lineage cadets and their branches and sub-branches with their territorial endowments.

A
DAULATPUR
0 150M
ORCHARD
SPRING
SETTLEMENT IN RUINS
SETTLEMENT AREA
CROPPED AREA
UNCULTIVATED
CURRENT FALLOW
METALLED ROAD
PATH
NALA
KANGRA
DAULATPUR
KM.
B
GADIARAH
GENERAL LAND-USE
1957-58
METRES
PASTURE
HAY
CULTIVATED
SETTLEMENT
PATH
N

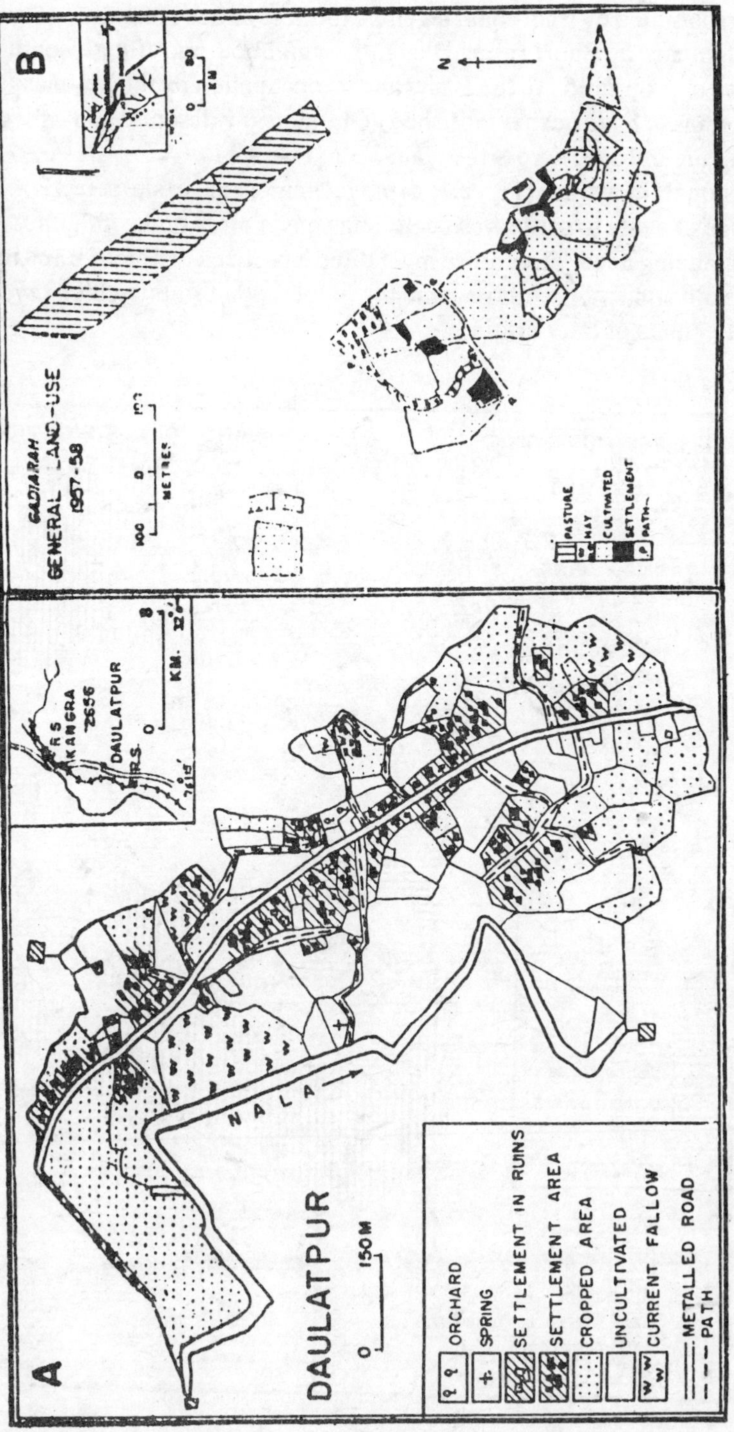

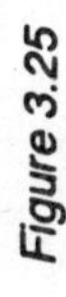

Figure 3.25

Origin and Evolution

Evidences corroborated by traditional legends, folklore and the presence of ruined mounds of the old Bhar settlements in Bhori (after Bhar), the neighbouring village south-west of Mahjuda, speak about the expropriation of the Bhars and its occupation by the Maunas Rajputs. An outpost of the Bhars seems to have been established at the site now deserted and called Dihawa and Non-ara, just facing the old site, across the Nadi Jhor (Fig. 3.11).

The occasional flood limit (Fig. 2.15a) played major role in site selection. It was just possible that "the choice of a site to settle was sometimes made more and sometimes less consciously in response to balancing need. The choice must often have been instinctive and incidental in detail." The dih or the old site, afterwards became the pivotal point round which revolved the whole activities of settlements of later origin.

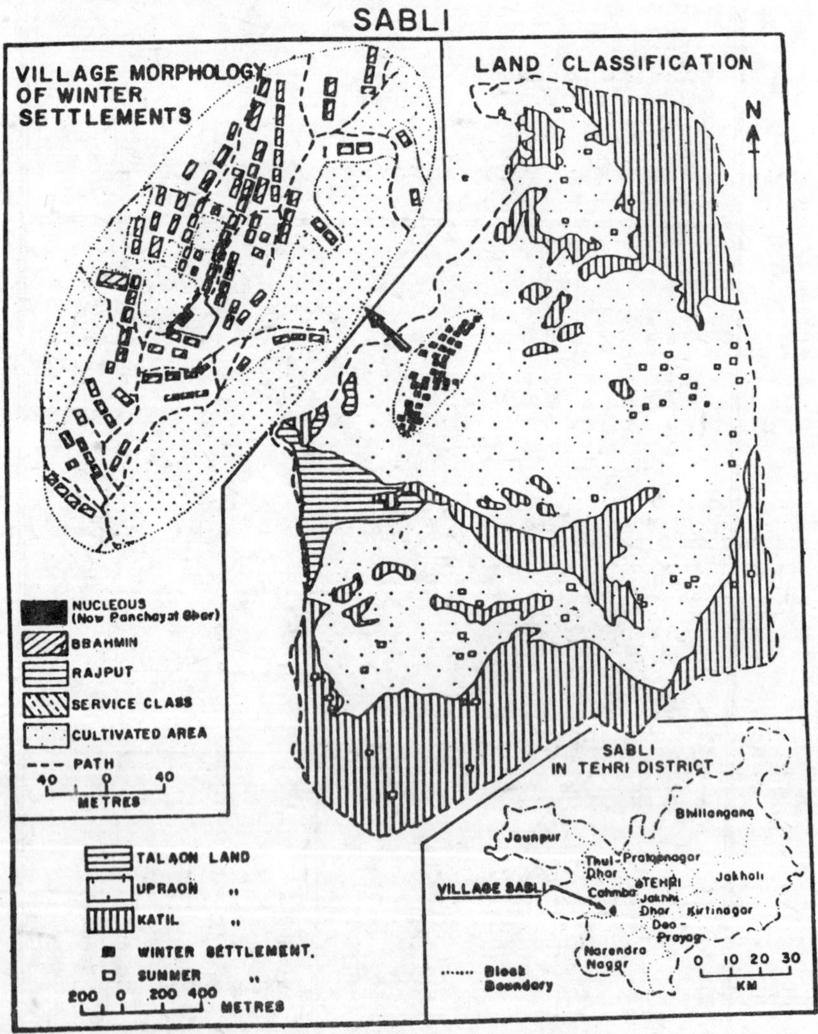

Figure 3:26

Nucleation

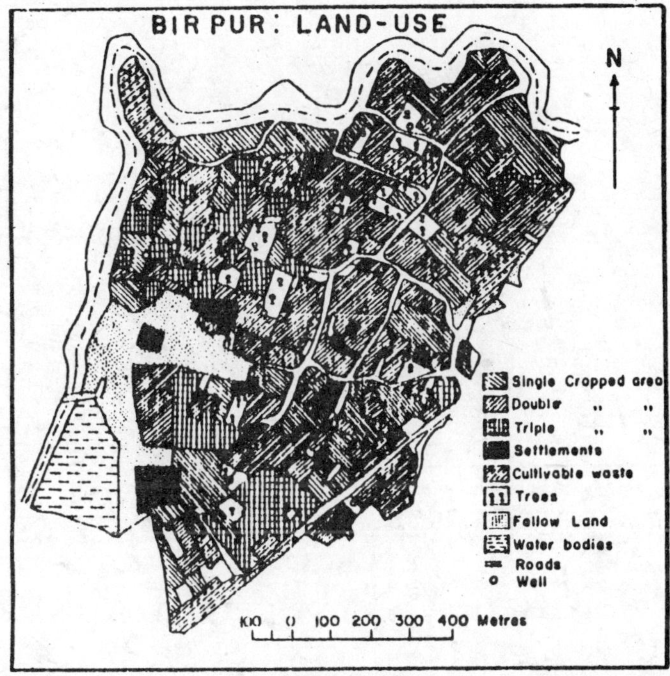

Figure 3.27

Mahjuda derived its name from 'Mahi' meaning land or homeland of the Rajputs and 'Juda' meaning separate from the same, i.e., a place or site occupied by people who were separate from their original site.

The people of diverse castes flocked together for earning their living upon the produce of the arable land under the dominant Rajput lineage supremacy, the only corporate political group in the territory (Bhadohi), and others (were) rendered to a non-corporate and non-political status.

Once the site was inhabited by diverse castes, the needs of farming and communal life articulated a strong sense of co-operation among them. The *jajmani* system prevailed and worked through a process of steady assimilation and acculturation.

Dispersion

Zoning of land existed from the centre outwards keeping pace with the irrigational limit (Fig 2.15a). Intensity of landuse varied, as still varies, as the distance from the central settlement increased (Figs. 2.17, 3.12a). The double cropped areas confirm the trend. Soil conditions and farming practices also played major role in the dispersion of settlement. We thus find isolated units of settlements (hamlets), more than 150 metres away from the next unit.

First Phase (A.D. 1650-1700): During the later half of the seventeenth century, one of the Rajputs moved towards north and occupied most of the area lying in north-eastern portion of the village territory. There followed a clash with the main clan descendants, which led to partition of the land into two sections. The newly established part was named as being located in the north. This was the period when Maunas Rajputs were involved into their local disputes and the central hold of clan solidarity was loosening.

Second Phase (A.D. 1700-1750): Further division in joint family system brought fragmentation of holdings but still the land was held by the clan members and the forest land was common land under the supreme hold of the Rajputs. The increase in forest clearing, occupation of newly cultivated land and water supply through wells gave impetus to the second unit of settlements, again of Rajputs, descending from uttar patti. Landholdings under their possession still corroborate this fact. Being settled round a well and mostly depending on the same for water supply, both for domestic and irrigational purposes, this site was named as Inaraha, meaning having a

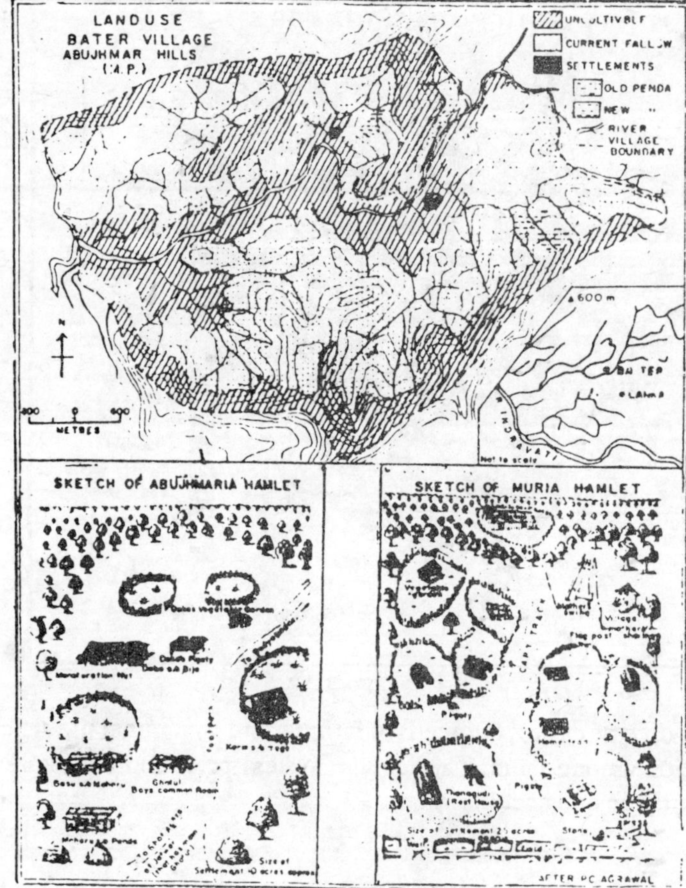

Figure 3.28

well. The wells played important role in irrigating crops.

Third Phase (A.D. 1750-1800): By the time when Rajputs of the second phase of evolution were migrating to the north, other Rajputs of the main joint family were holding their outpost or occasional homestead (*chhawani*) at the third site. At this stage, the occasional flood limit had become a rare limit and shifted west ward due to the cutting of *bhita* in the west and consequent imporoved drainage facilities (Fig. 3.11). When family members increased and irrigational limit shifted northward, it became essential to settle in the centre to minimize the production cost. Population pressure and location of woodlands and pastures in the marginal areas forced the stockraising caste to leave the compact settlement and a new hamlet grew in the centre. Such a centre, purely based upon caste (of Ahirs), also grew in the north-west. The former being settled around a member of the main clan descendant was named as Purwa, meaning a hamlet— second settlement of the village in order of importance— and the latter as Taliya being settled along a small Tal (water depression). These milkmen, mostly tenants, still cultivate the *barha* or the poorland away from the settlement. In course of time, this land became *goind* and now double cropping is practised. To this unit accreted the potters who were provided fallow land to settle around the well already built by the settlers of the third phase.

Fourth Phase (A.D. 1800-1850): When the third phase settlers were occupying the central and north-western parts, some of the milkmen were busy with their temporary occupation of the site in the north and when they became able to purchase some plots, they shifted there. Water supply was made by a new well constructed in the north on the margin of the forest and, in the central part, forest gave fuel and grazing ground in their neighbourhood.

During this period, two outcaste—Brahmins and Rajputs—made their separate dwellings as most of their land was in the western part of the village. Flood conditions had slightly improved and it was possible to take even *kharif* crop in western fields.

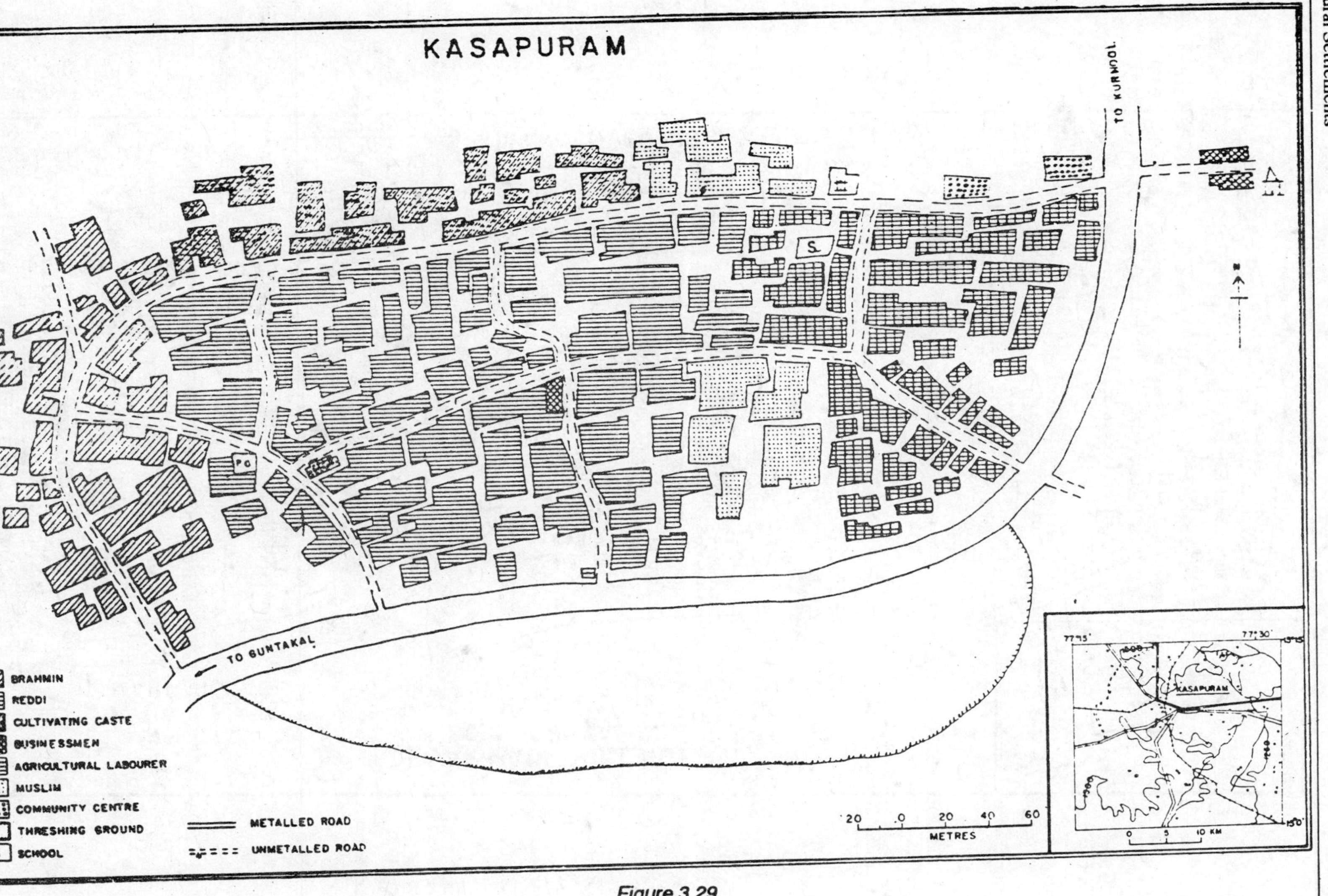
KASAPURAM
TO KURNOOL
TO GUNTAKAL
P.O
S.
BRAHMIN
REDDI
CULTIVATING CASTE
BUSINESSMEN
AGRICULTURAL LABOURER
MUSLIM
COMMUNITY CENTRE
THRESHING GROUND
SCHOOL
METALLED ROAD
UNMETALLED ROAD
20 0 20 40 60
METRES
KASAPURAM
0 5 10 KM

Figure 3.29

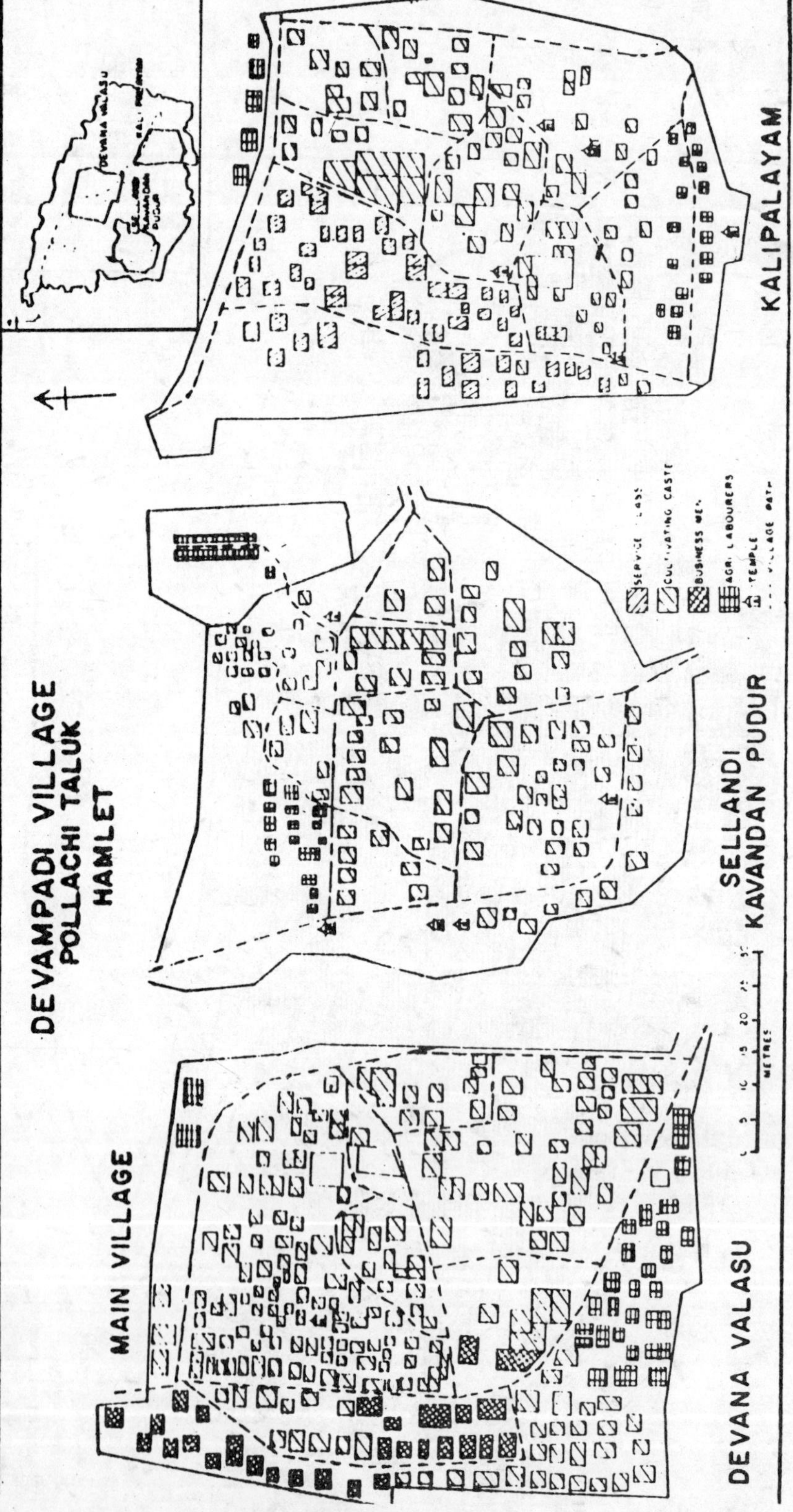
DEVAMPADI VILLAGE
POLLACHI TALUK
HAMLET
MAIN VILLAGE
DEVANA VALASU
SELLANDI
KAVANDAN PUDUR
KALIPALAYAM
CULTIVATING CASTE
BUSINESS MEN
AGRI. LABOURERS
TEMPLE
METRES

Figure 3.30

During this phase, continuous drought conditions resulted into crop failure and the Rajputs (dependent on agricultural labour) could not pay the revenue, and some of the plots were again occupied by a Rajput of higher clan hierarchy on the paying of arrears to the Banaras State offi-

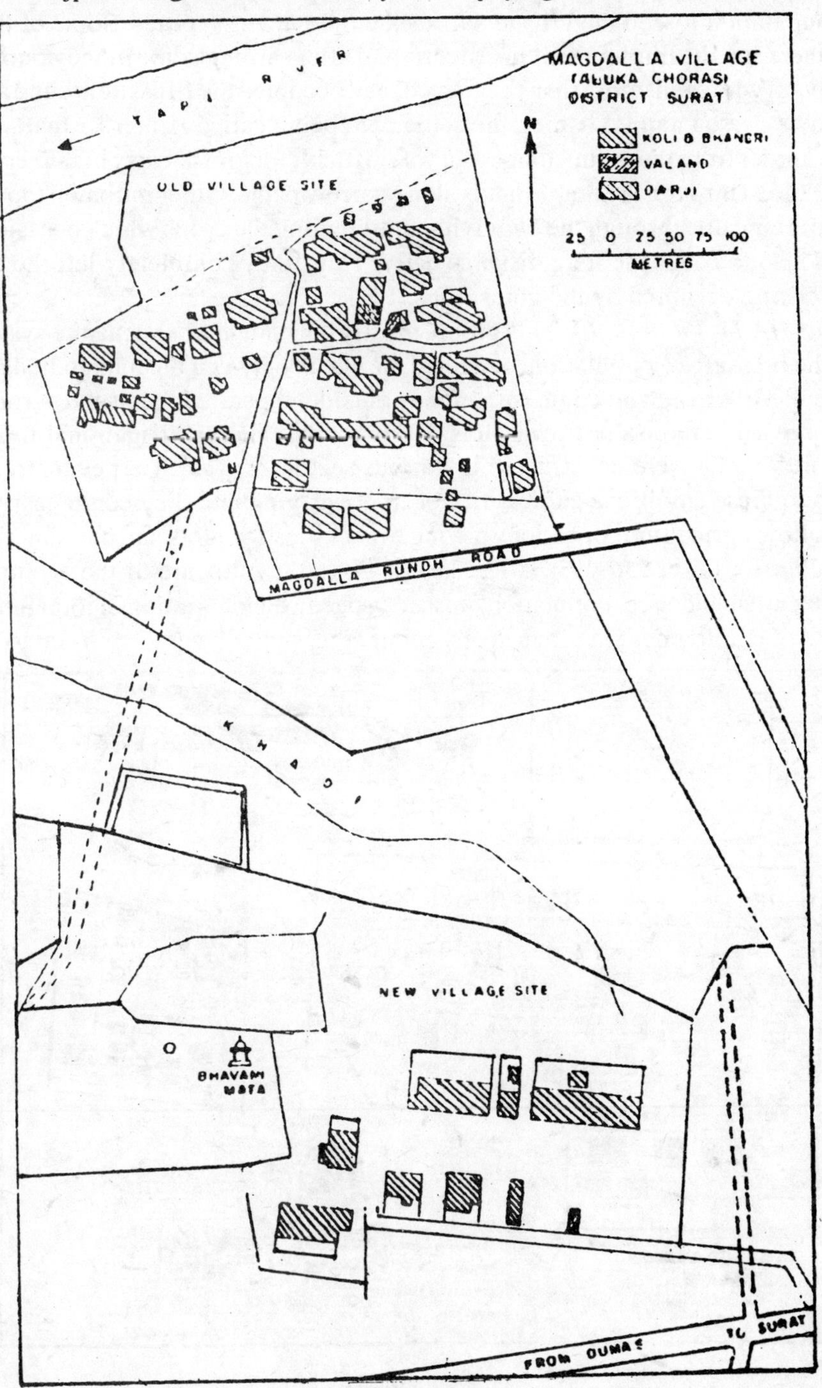

Figure 3.31

cials. Thus, a separate small unit, almost adjacent to the third central units, grew with three dwellings in course of time.

Fifth Phase (A.D. 1850-1990): During the British regime, transport facilities improved and pressure of pupulation forced the villagers to seek employment in cities. Some of the milkmen along with others sought employment in Calcutta and after earning some money purchased plots from the Rajputs (who spent more than they saved) and occupied the fifth site around a well newly constructed by a person named Ajmer, the settlement being called Ajmer ka Inara. To this site also shifted a herder from the main village as it was difficult for him to carry his sheep to and from the pasture or forest through the arable lands along narrow paths. Other milkmen too found it difficult to drive their cattle through the *khor* without trampling the crops which occasionally led to disputes, and also to cover the long distance daily. Thus, they completely left the original site which is now being occupied by the goldsmiths.

Sixth Phase (A.D. 1900-1950): This group, mostly dependent upon tenancy system and suffering from the pressure of pupulation, occupied the site in between the unmetalled road and the fifth settlement. Milkmen, who could earn money outside, separated themselves from their joint families and settled here on their own plots. By this time, the last irrigational limit had been reached and new wells were constructed in various sectors (*siwan*). Carpet centre at Bhadohi gave impetus to these ambitious earners from carpet weaving and they could easily build new houses and follow agricultural opeations paying higher bids for plots surrounding their site.

Seventh Phase (A.D. 1950-1970): The last phase is the outcome of the economic change brought in after independence. Population pressure, speedy disintegration of joint family system, better avenues of employment in urban areas, commerce, switch over to cash-nexus and change

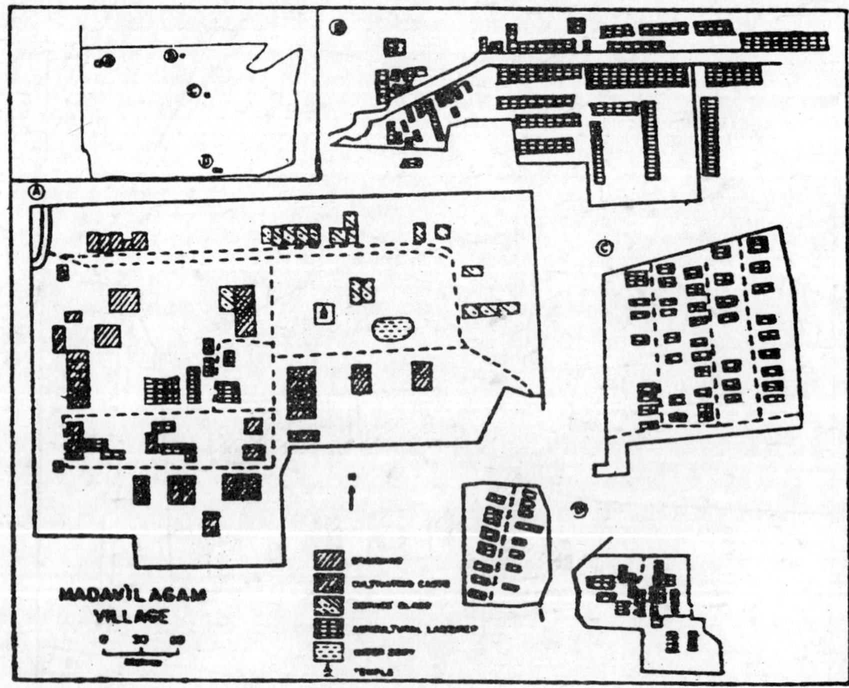

Figure 3.32

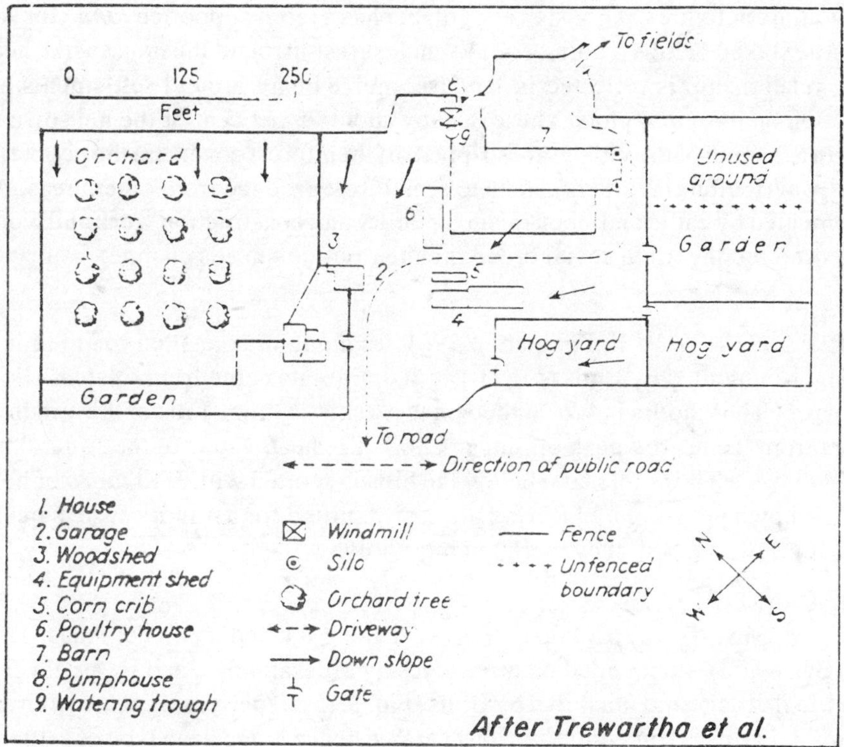

Figure 3.33: Plat of a farmstead on a Wisconsin dairy farm. Note the large barn with twin silos and the numerous other outbuildings.

in land tenure system after the abolition of *zamindari* in 1952, severally and combinedly have led to some trend of diffusion.

Bhugore

A dopple dorfer village along with the abjacent Bhilkheri in the north separated by narrow lane only, Bhugore derives its name from the Bhagoriya *hat* of Bhils who were expropriated by Rajput settlers in the area during the period of clan settlement. It is a small compact settlement with hamlets not more than 100 metres apart (Fig. 3.12b).

Enclosures (*khala* or *bara*) for storing fodder, fuel and for threshing are distinct features of the settlement, being located on the fringes.

Barwani Khurd

It (22°5'N—74°53', Population 935) occupies the lower slopes of Bawan Gaja Hills in the Satpura range, south-west of Barwani town. It is a typical tribal village dominated by Bhilala tribals (Fig. 3.13). The settlements are highly hamleted to isolated scattered on arable land avoiding water-bodies. The nearby rivers are the main sources of water supply supplemented by wells. A metalled road, running from Barwani to Patti, passes through the main aggregation in the southern half of the village. Habitations have close relation with the surrounding terrain. Houses are low, small, thatched with grass, leaves or tiles having mudwalls or wooden rafters plastered with mud. Primary school building and its neighbouring dwellings exhibit impact of social reforms and welfare activities. Almost every villager has a rafter supported *tanda* for fodder kept over it and cattle staked below. Thorn or wood enclosures surround the houses like hedge. Farm and dwelling relationship is reflected in landuse, maize being around settlements and *jowar*, *bajra*, and cotton on marginal plots. These occupy about 75 per cent of the net sown area.

The hills in the south of the village are stripped off their forest cover and the people (including women, mostly agricultural workers), have to seek forest produce from other areas. Agricuture is also supplemented by cattle and stock raising, poultry and construction work and wood cutting. Gambling has entered the tribal social order and their outlook needs change.

Naharkhodra

The village (21°24'N—75°39'E, Population 396) lies along the metalled road joining Manpur and Khurdi and is inhabited by Bhils (Fig. 3.14). It derives its name from 'Nahar' (lion) usually found in the past. Naharkhodra is surrounded on three sides by high hills of the Vindhyas sent as offshoot spurs from the nearby peak of Singar Chori. The headwaters of the Ajnar drain the village from east to west. The arable land below the hills is spotted with Bhil *tapro* or homesteads. These never occupy a permanent place and are easily shifted for a minor cause, a quarrel, a disease or some superstition. Still they mark the morphology.

Bhagatpura

It is situated (23°13'N—74°29'E, Population 363) along a tributary to the Anas, 1.5 km from Kushalgarh (Banswara), surrounded on three sides by hills, and bisected by a *nala*. The village is typically a tribal village and inhabited by Bhils (Fig. 3.15). It derives its name from some tribal leader of the past. Farm and dwellings are unseparable hence homestead type of settlement is the rule.

Semalkheri

The village (22°46'N—74°44'E, Population 166) lies along the river Chunar, a tributary to the Anas, 11 km east of Jhabua, amidst forest covered hills on fertile soil, inhabited by Bhil tribals and having two sub-castes—Patlya and Tadwi (Fig. 3.16B). Small hamlets scatter in the space nearby their farms.

References

1. The sanskrit 'grama' may originally have had reference to a tribal grouping of a limited number of families, as the dictionary gives 'clan' 'community' or 'host' 'aggregate' as among the meanings (vide Macdonell, Sanskrit dictionary' S.V. grama). In the Veda the word seems chiefly to indicate the sort of fort or protected residence site into which the cattle could be driven at night or to escape attack (see, Zimmer, p. 142 as to the Vedic *grama* or *vijana*.
2. Alayeb, Enrid (1986), Social and Economic Geography—An Essay in Conceptual-Terminological Systematisation, Progress Publishers, Moscow, pp. 64, 99, 100.
3. See Mukherji, A.B. (1974), 'Morphogenetic Analysis of Rural Settlements of the Chandigarh Siwalik Hills, Punjab University Res. Bulletin (Arts) Vol. V, No. 2, p. 66.
4. Soundara, Rajan, op. cit. ref. no. 28, ch. 2, p. 38.
5. Idem, p. 148.

6. Srinivas, M.N. (1951), 'Village India—Studies in the Little community' in Marriot Mckim (ed.) 'Little Communities in an Indegenous Civilization', p. 172.
7. Spate, O.H.K. (1954), India and Pakistan, London, Methuen and Co. Ltd., p. 177.
8. Finch, V.C. et al. (1957), Elements of Geography- Physical and Cultural, McGraw Hill Book Company, INC, New York, p. 552.
9. James, P.E. (1932), The Coffee Lands of Southwestern Brazil, Geog. Rev., Vol. 22, pp. 225-244; also see Trewartha, G.T. (1946), Types of Rural Settlements in Colonial America, Geog. Rev., Vol. 36, No. 4, pp. 568-596.
10. Srinivas, M.N., Ref. no. 6, p. 32.
11. Raymond Firth (1951), 'Elements of Social Organization, London, p. 85, See also 'The New India: Progress Through Democracy, New York, Planning Commission, Government of India, 1958, p. 42; also V. Nath (1962), The Village and Community, p. 144 in turner Roy (ed.) Indias' Urban Future, Berkeley, University of California.

4

Types and Patterns of Settlements

Elements of Settlement

Generally speaking, a settlement consists of two visible elements: (i) the man who is the dynamic one and is wholly responsible for the construction of the second (ii) the static forms. Obviously, size, shape, form, layout, types and patterns—all are elements of a settlement. While the first element is the subject matter of population geography, in particular, the forms of houses and settlements as a whole are important elements of settlement. In this chapter, two distinct elements, namely, types and patterns, will be discussed. The components of these elements like house, street, enclosure etc. are equally important and will be explained in the sequel in next few chapters. The tow elements of type and pattern are intricately woven but visible, hence, identifiable. Likewise, other attributes of settlement are also distinguishable on comparison. The type of size, shape or layout is discernible always in relation to different types of settlements in existence with various degrees of variations on the basis of certain norms. These norms vary according to landscape—physical as well cultural (i.e., small, big, amorphous)—with certain directions or fixed sites or forms in the first world or other worlds. That is why, the terms assigned to these elements convey relative meanings as well as connotation, i.e., size and shape of an English and Ethiopian or Indian settlement or even form of a farmstead or homestead in U.S.A. or in Indian northern *terai* zone and *chak* farmsteads in the Ganga plain. The number and magnitude of habitations also vary as do the appearance. Thus, the elements of settlement, as geographical terms used universally, convey various conceptual meanings and significance to a particular group of people living in various environments. A compact settlement of a country may be just equal to a hamlet of ancient country or a big size settlement of New World may be a small, tiny settlement along a road in India.

Difference Between Type and Pattern

These terms find place in geographical literature, particularly in rural settlement geography, conveying various meanings, sometimes as synonymous, at others interchangeable and yet others as one being element/part of the other. But, actually, these are neither of them. Let us see a few examples. Einch and Trewartha *et al.* refer to two primary types of settlements: (a) the isolated or dispersed and (b) the nucleated. Hudson says that the major patterns in rural areas, then, are either (a) nucleated, or (b) dispersed. There are similar references, treatments and explanations regarding types and patterns of settlements by other geographers in India like Enayat Ahmed and R.L. Singh, to name a few.

Pattern of settlement has been defined by Emrys Jones, as the relationship between one house or building and another and to isolate this relationship he refers to a large-scale map. He thinks that often pattern is unrelated to site and site may have little or no bearing on pattern. But Finch and Trewartha *et al.* attribute the contrasts in the arrangement of streets and houses, i.e., patterns to the site as well as historical causes. Thus, two identifying factors are clear: (1) pattern refers to geometric form and shape of the settlement which may be of different types; and (2) the latter refers to relationship of number of dwellings and number of sites. It is the analysis of patterns which brings before us various classified types of settlements with various shapes and forms. The intra-settlement analysis of inter-dwelling distance clarifies the occupance of village territory on one or more than one sites. This provides the picture of nucleation or dispersion, hence, types. But when we refer to a certain form of settlement depicting a particular shape, a distinct pattern gets a name according to geometrical attributes, i.e., elongated, linear, block, L-shaped etc. Pattern also refers to two dimensional geometrical arrangement of rural settlements in an area. This arrangement exposes itself through the relationship of the rural settlements to each other and the adjacent physio- cultural landscape or topographic features. This pattern clearly indicates comparison among several settlements and identification of one, i.e., linear along road, valley or fan pattern along foothills etc. But, it is different from the type and pattern observed in the form of individual settlement dealt with in sequel. The two patterns—geometric and non-geometric—are easily discernible on a map drawn or airphoto taken for/of a wider area.

Classification of Settlement Types and Patterns

Let us have a few examples of classifications of types first. D.C. Money, in his *Introduction to Human Geography*, broadly classifies as: (1) the single large nucleated village, (2) hamlets scattered throughout the countryside, and (3) single homesteads. Enayat Ahmed gives four types: (1) compact, (2) cluster and hamlet type, (3) fragmented or hamleted, and (4) dispersed settlement. R.L. Singh discerns four main types: (1) compact settlements, (2) semi-compact or hamleted cluster, (3) semi-sprinkled or fragmented or hamleted settlements, and (4) sprinkled or dispersed type. Most of the settlement geographers have classified the types according to their regional distribution patterns of such habitations on the basis of theoretical, empirical and associational considerations. In the Indian context, the term signifies the characteristic groupings of rural dwellings in that well-defined parcel of the ground which is known as 'mauza'.[1] But, in a regional framework, the term denoted the relationship between settlements within space.[2] Thus, types are to be recognized on a large-scale map through the distribution of houses on one or more sites in a defined village territory whether on record or notional. On a small-scale map inter-settlement spacing and number of sites of a named settlement would help in identifying the types. Often the inter- site or inter-settlement space is occupied by other landuses, i.e., agriculture, orchard, wasteland, water bodies etc.

Theoretically, the two extreme types of groupings of the rural settlements are: (i) the isolated farmsteads or dispersed dwellings in which the single family residence unit is the distinctive nucleus occupying its own farm, and (ii) nucleated settlement in which all the dwellings are clustered almost in the centre of the village lands. Between these two extremes there are gradations (Figs. 4.1-4.3a). We can classify them in four categories as shown in the map (Fig. 4.3) on the basis of nucleation and dispersion as well as their dominant occupation of a particular area: (i) compact, (ii) semi-compact, (iii) hamleted, and (iv) dispersed or scattered type or isolated homestead type.

(1) *Compact type rural settlements* are found throughout the plateau region of Malwa, in the

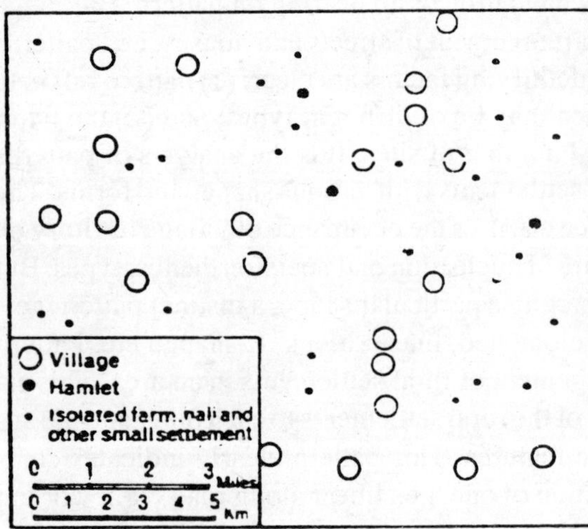

Figure 4.1: Nucleated settlement north of Grantham, Lincolnshire. This pattern of settlement—prodominantly nucleated—has been charcteristic of most of the English Plain even since it was settled by the Anglo-Saxons and Danes.

Narmada valley, Nimar upland, Great and Little deserts, paddy lands in Bihar, Uttar Pradesh, Vindhyan plateau, western Uttar Pradesh in particular and several other cultivated parts in India in general. In such villages or 'mauzas', all the dwellings of *abadi* or settlement are concentrated in one central site. The fertile soil extending through homogeneous and sometimes undulating plains attracted people since early historical times to live in groups and follow primitive type of agriculture. The existing form reflects now aggregation of such agricultural cultivators and other dependents living reciprocally under *jajmani* system and enjoying the benefits of community life. Such settlements, however, range from a cluster of thirty to hundreds of dwellings of different forms, size and functions with various types of arrangements and patterns dealt with in the sequel in Chapter 6 (Fig. 4.4). The size varies from 500 to 2,500 persons in sparsely populated parts like Rajasthan to more than 10,000 in the Ganga plain, i.e., Gahmar in Uttar Pradesh.

(2) *Semi-compact type settlements* are common features on plateau or plains according to environmental constraints as well as cultural considerations. These reflect outgrowth of later periods by the people of diverse castes during settling process, sometimes as a separate grouping by aboriginals and low caste people in the neighbourhoed of the main residential unit (Figs. 4.5, 4.6). This type also reflects modification of the compact type because here dwellings are not very closely knitted and huddled together at one common site. Also, it covers more area than the former; the hamlets occupy new sites near the periphery of the village boundary mostly the common jungle or grazing land.

(3) *Hamleted settlements*: In such villages, the entire territory exhibits hamlets spread with

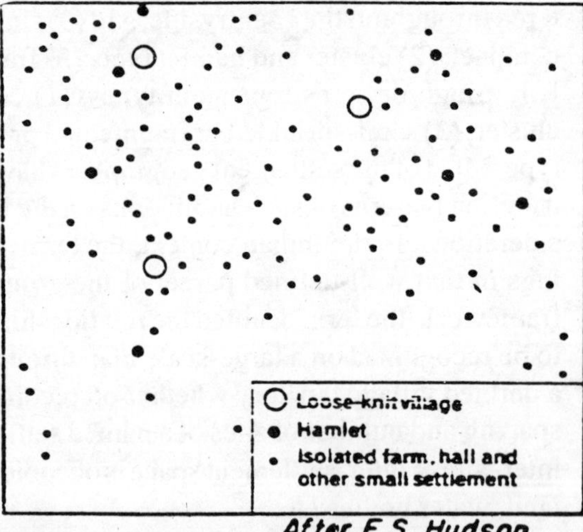

Figure 4.2: Dispersed settlement east of Llanrwst, North Wales. Predominantly dispersed settlement is characteristic of Highland Britain, and in areas such as Wales may well date from early medieval times. Above 1,000 ft. (300 m) there is little settlement of any kind, but in the valleys a structure of market towns (such as Llanrwst) came into being as farming became more commercialised.

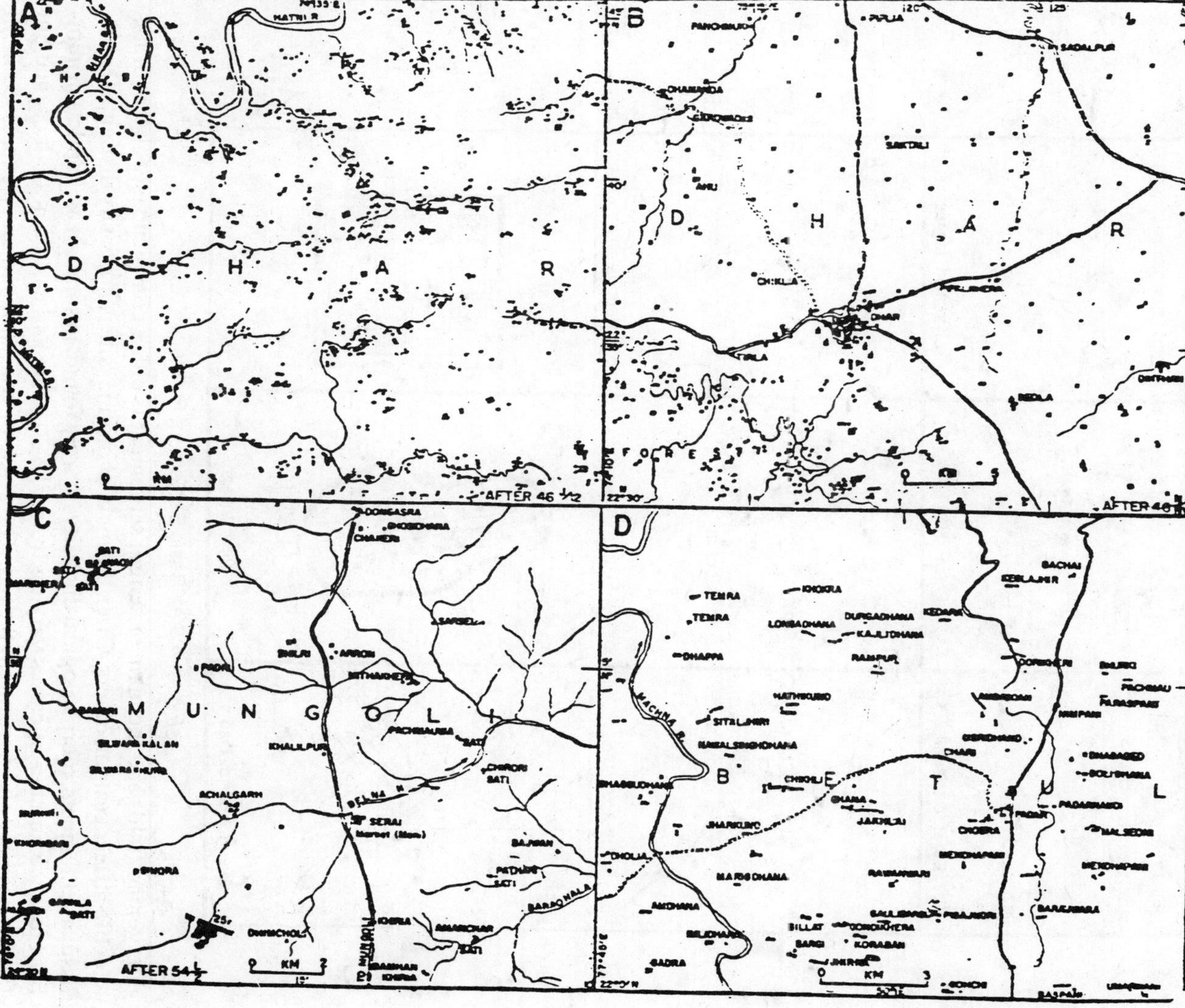
A
D H A R
AFTER 46 1/2
B
D H A R
DHAR
FOREST
AFTER 46
C
M U N G O L I
AFTER 54 1/2
D
B E T U L
MACHNA R.

Figure 4.3

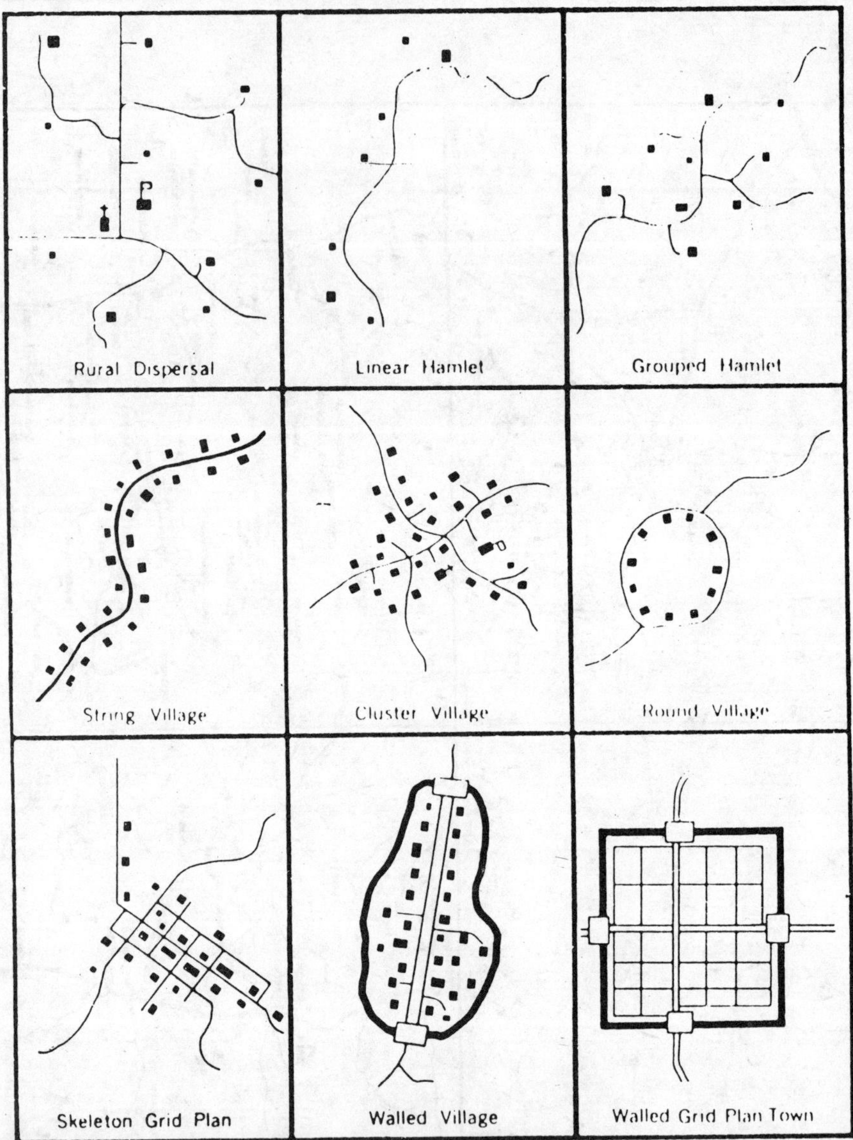

Figure 4.3(a): Basic Settlement Forms.

intervening fields and the main or central settlement is either conspicuously absent or has a feeble influence upon others. Often the main or original site is not easily distinguishable. In such settlements, morphological diversity is rarely found. In some areas, hamlets in number cross the number of castes varying from 5 to 20. Clan and caste ties are loosened but family ties become more strengthened. The sense of cohesion and unity expressed in all day-to-day behaviour in compact settlements are absent in conspicuous. Also, they are not at par with the compact ones with regard to other varied aspects of community life, such as common rejoicing on the occasion of fairs, festivals, ceremonies, weddings, worships, *keertans* (chanting of songs), dramas etc. The visible, concrete objects or morphological

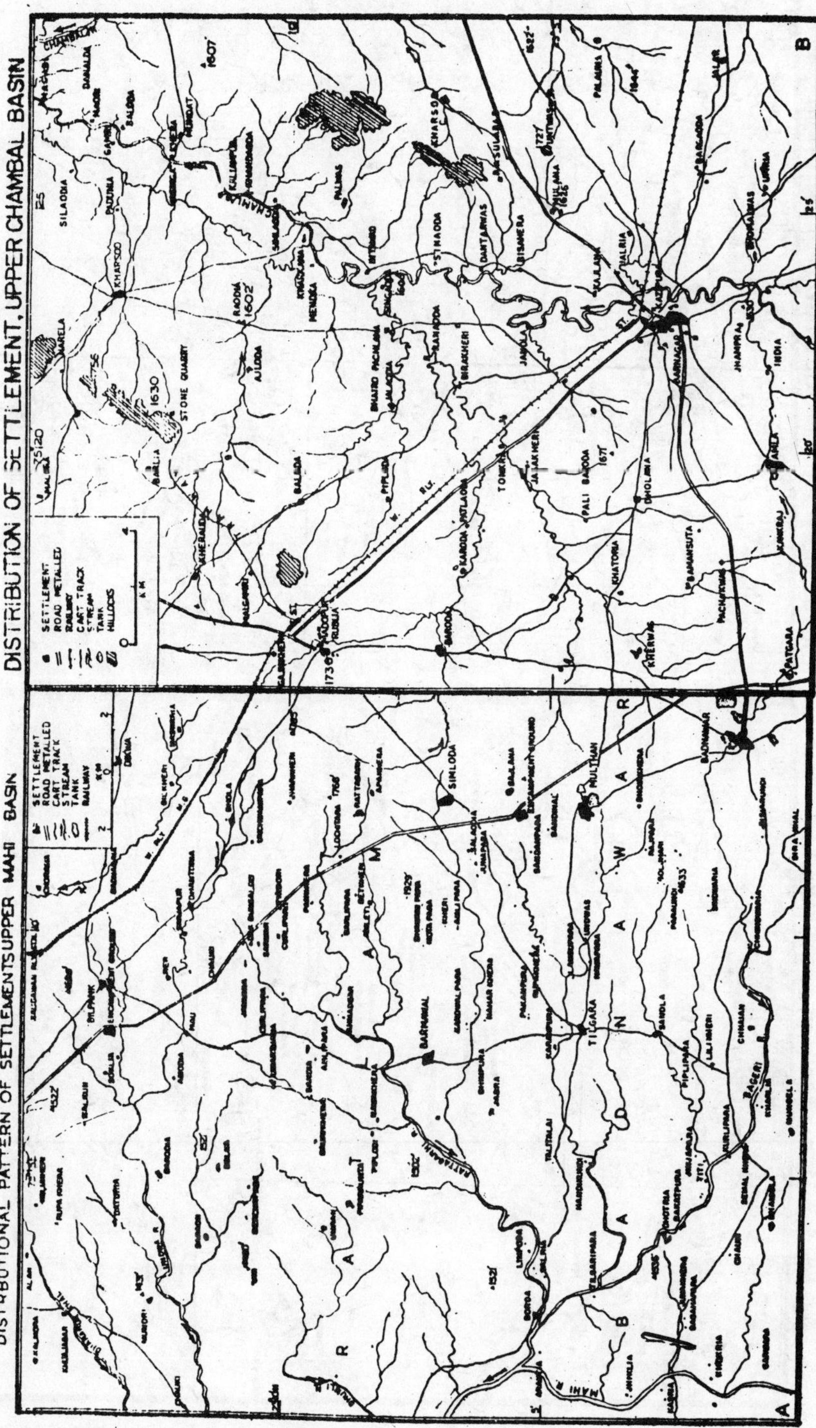
DISTRBUTIONAL PATTERN OF SETTLEMENTSUPPER MAHI BASIN
SETTLEMENT
ROAD METALLED
CART TRACK
STREAM
TANK
RAILWAY
DISTRIBUTION OF SETTLEMENT, UPPER CHAMBAL BASIN
SETTLEMENT
ROAD METALLED
RAILWAY
CART TRACK
STREAM
TANK
HILLOCKS
A
B

Figure 4.4

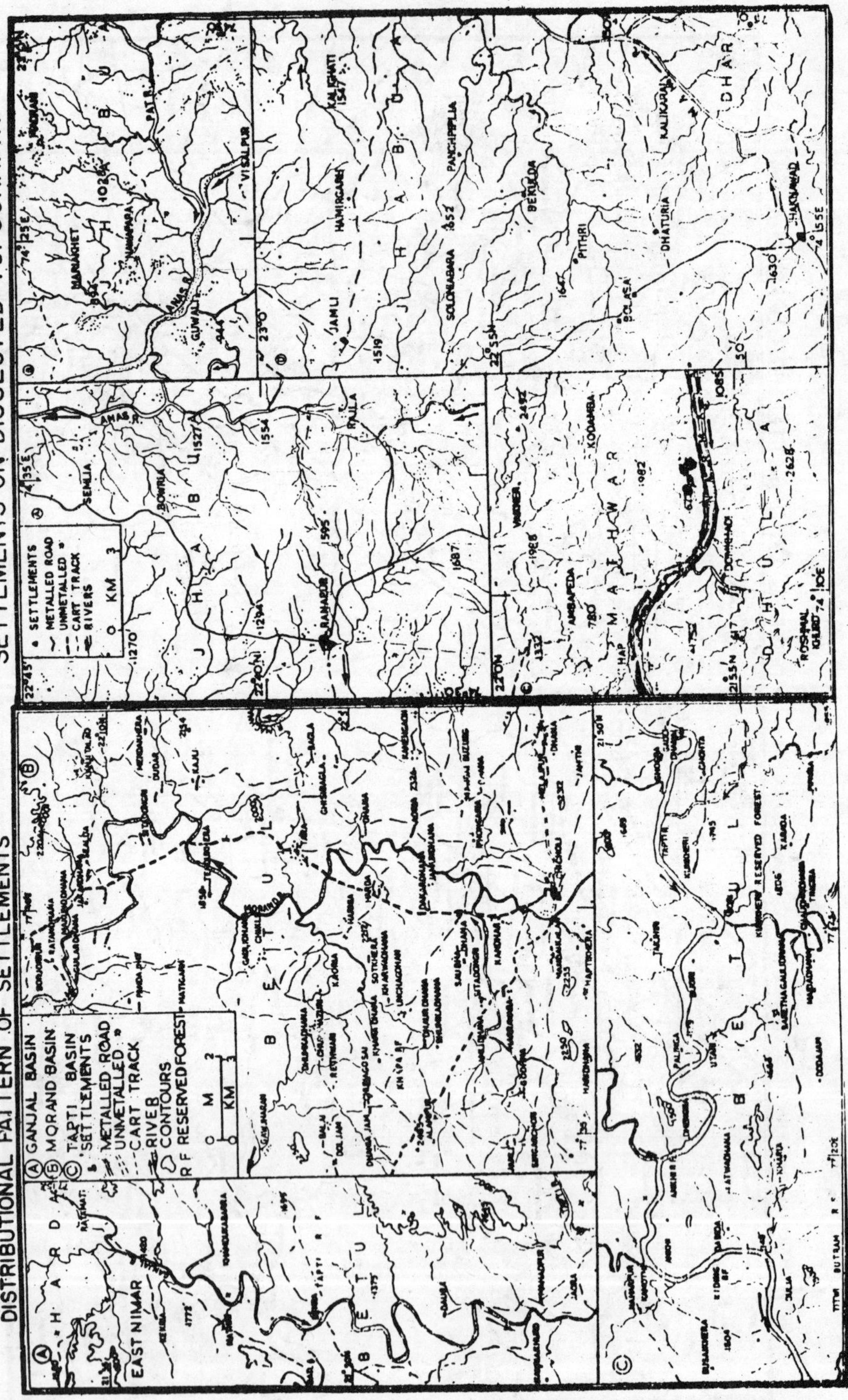

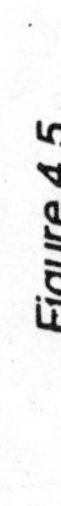
DISTRIBUTIONAL PATTERN OF SETTLEMENTS
A GANJAL BASIN
B MORAND BASIN
C TAPTI BASIN
SETTLEMENTS
METALLED ROAD
UNMETALLED
CART TRACK
RIVER
CONTOURS
R F RESERVED FOREST
SETTEMENTS ON DISSECTED TOPOGRAPHY
SETTLEMENTS
METALLED ROAD
UNMETALLED
CART TRACK
RIVERS

Figure 4.5

DISTRIBUTIONAL PATTERN OF SETTLEMENTS

Figure 4.6

details do not exist, i.e., streets, open space, community centres, schools, amenities, temples, *dih* (common worship-place for a clan or village settlers). Mostly, such settlements are found either in later occupance or fertile soil tracts or due to tribal racial characteristics (of Gonds in Madhya Pradesh), e.g., in West Bengal, eastern Uttar Pradesh, Madhya Pradesh and coastal plains. They unincorporated hamlets of U.S.A. are a combination of rural and urban functions with a population ranging from 20 to 150 inhabitants. They contain post office, church, school, general store, cheese factory, feed mill, tavern, filling station, garage, etc. The residents of these hamlets mostly are non-farmers and some are farmstead dwellings (Fig. 4.7).

(4) *Dispersed settlement*: These are commonly found in tribal areas covering the central part of India, eastern and southern Rajasthan, Himalayan slopes in India and land with dissected and uneven topography in several world tracts (Fig. 4.3b). Homesteads or farmsteads of U.S.A. and Canada or *terai* areas in India belong to this group. Here, dwellings belonging to one family or nucleus family occupy one site situated in his cultivated field. The whole (*mauza*) village territory throughout its margins receives scattered dwellings. Individualism, sentiments of living freely, custom of marriage relations are conducive to such rural settlements. Private ownership of land and its occupance go side by side. But, such isolated dwellings lack the sense of neighbourhood and communal interdependence. This type, however, is not original but secondary type of occupance in the process or humanization of the earth. Modern society too is affected to follow suit due to availability of facilities, resources, security and ambition to achieve one's aim individually.

Causes of Diverse Type of Rural Settlements

Most of the studies in settlement geography repeat the same two factors—physical and cultural—as responsible for various types of agglomerations and dispersions. A few modern studies have drawn attention towards more significant role played by culture, tradition and clan organizations. But, environmental determinists' emphasis upon various physical factors is not without weight or explanation. Empirical studies done in various areas would reveal one or the other factors more significant. Valid generalizations applicable universally are rather impossible. One has to be cautious about spatio-temporal dimensions while dealing with causes of agglomerations or dispersion in a country or even a macro region. Both, old and new world regions have historical as well as archaeological evidences of big compact agglomerations as referred to earlier. Aurousseau, in the study, *The Arrangement of Rural Settlements*, observed that the definite grouping of rural populations is a conscious human response to, rather than an actual physiographic control by a number of factors in each region, chief amongst which were: the type of pursuit, nature of groundwater supply, rainfall, surface water, soil, size of landholdings, space economy, local physiographic conditions and the topography of the region. These, in short, may be categorized as (i) physical, and (ii) cultural factors which determine the type of rural settlements separately or by their interactions and simultaneous interplay.

Physical Factors for Compact Settlements

The practice of living in compact settlements was fostered among newly settled communities (e.g., the Neolithic cultivators of ancient Egypt and China, and the early anglo-saxon immigrants into Roman Britain) by a necessity of dealing effectively with a somewhat hostile environment,

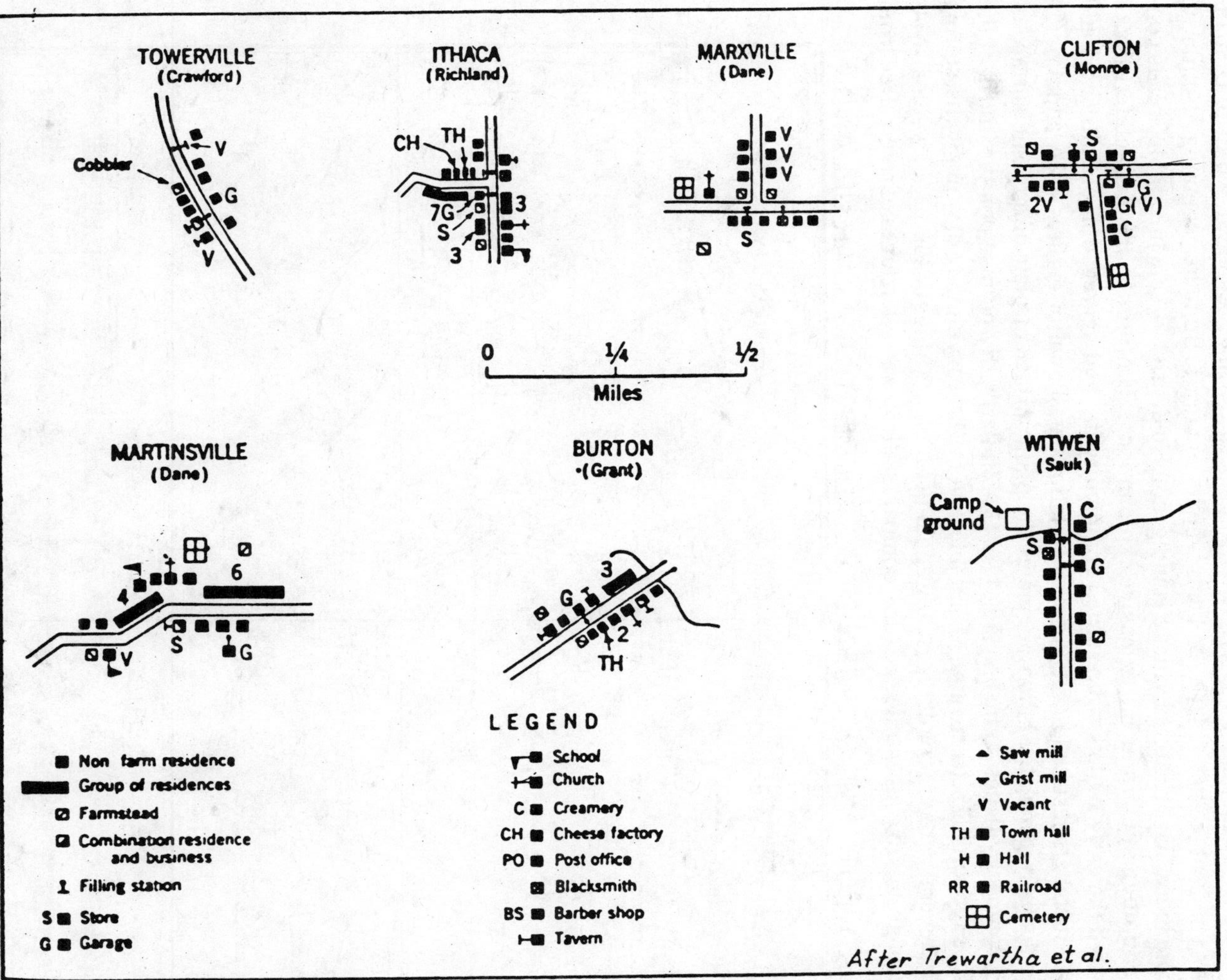

Figure 4.7. Samples of hamlet types in Wisconsin. The hamlet is the smallest type of nucleated settlement. The population is composed principally of nonfarmers.

e.g., a forested or marshy landscape, and by the advantage of organizing a permanent system of cultivation (Hudson, 1976: 64). The physical factors for compact settlements are as under:

(1) The compact farm village is the basic unit of settlement in eastern and southern Asia.[3] Such settlements are found in great river valley plains and 'will be found', in words of Demangeon, "as an ancient feature, chiefly, on lands which were fertile from the beginning.[4] Similarly, Blache concludes that "clustered village is indigenous in districts where the arable area is continuous, admitting of uniform and extensive exploitation".[5] Uniformity of relief and fertility of soil attracted the early settlers, who started community life and aggregation of cultivators and other caste members resulted into compact habitations as shown in Figures 4.4A and 4.8. (2) Wherever sparsely populated hilly tract meets the plain surface of plateau or plane surface of plain, big compact villages come up (Fig. 4.9). (3) Similarly, dry points upon the bluffs of the river valleys support big settlements. (4) Suitable water table, easy sinking of water wells, storing of water in several parts are conducive to big agglomerations. Springs or sources of water also attract human groups to concentrate and form compact settlements. Interfluves of rivers, free from

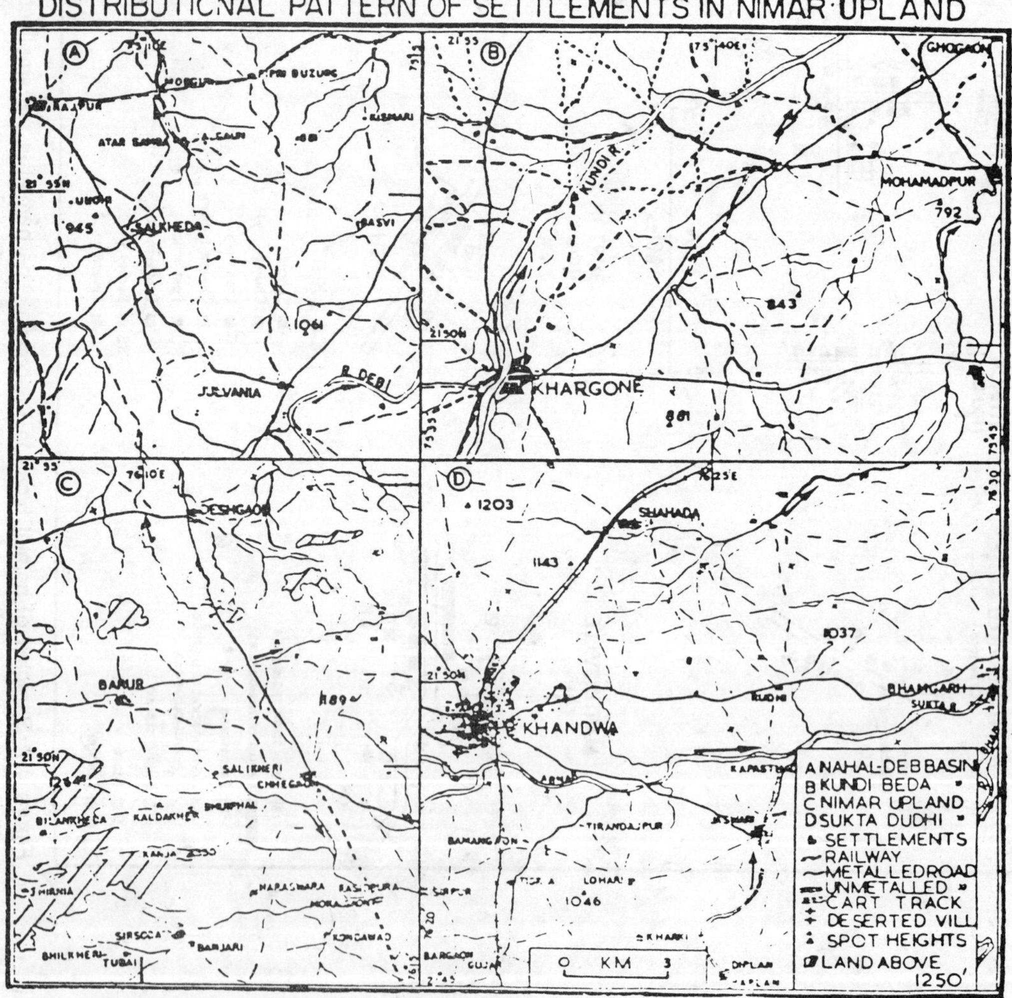

Figure 4.8

SETTLEMENTS ON BREAK OF SLOPE

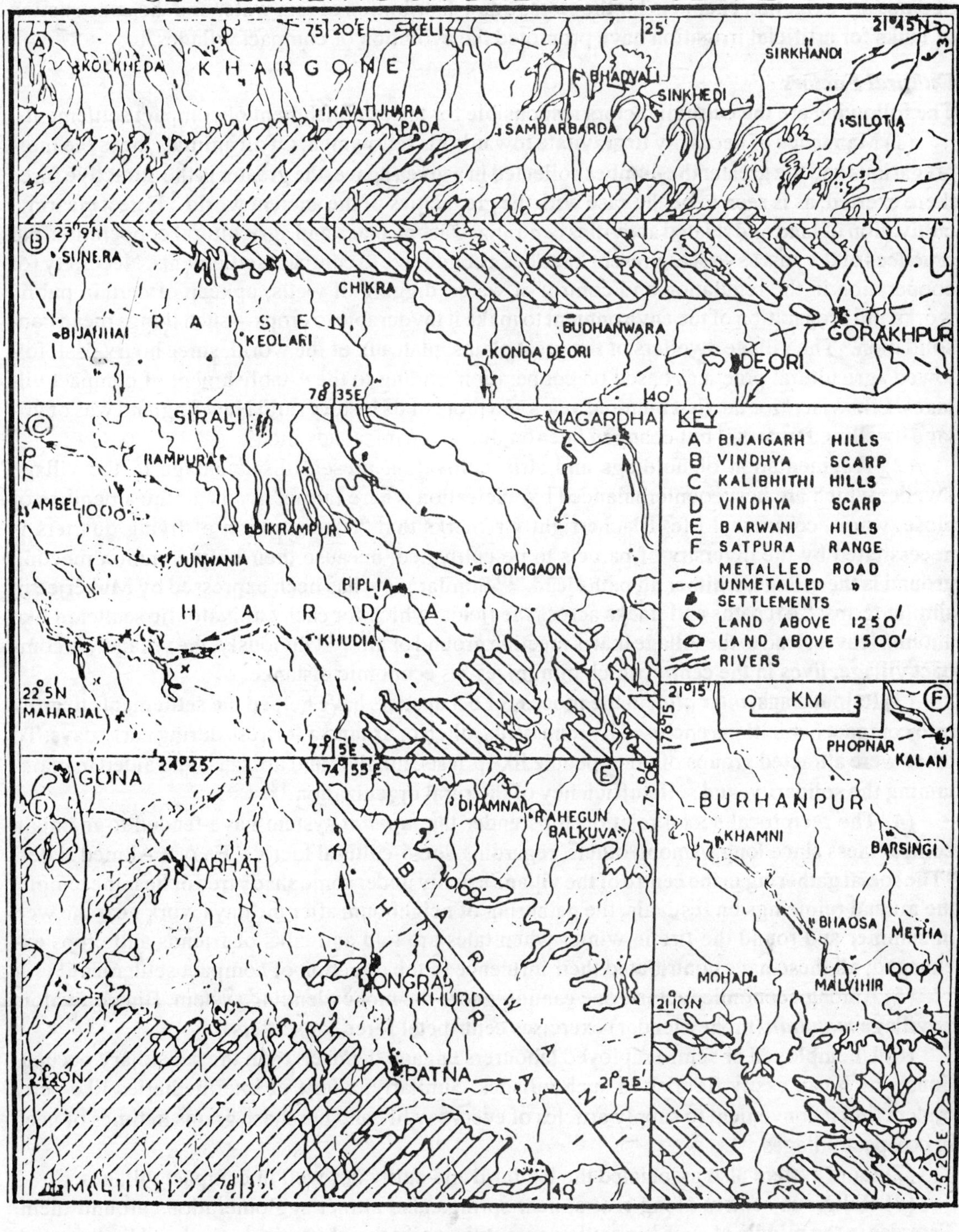

KEY
A BIJAIGARH HILLS
B VINDHYA SCARP
C KALIBHITHI HILLS
D VINDHYA SCARP
E BARWANI HILLS
F SATPURA RANGE
METALLED ROAD
UNMETALLED
SETTLEMENTS
LAND ABOVE 1250'
LAND ABOVE 1500'
RIVERS

Figure 4.9

ravines, easily support such villages (Fig. 4.4). (5) In some parts, likewise, the collective building of dams are irrigation channels for the storage and distribution of rain water and the construction of tanks for artificial irrigation have promoted the evolution of compact villages.[6]

Cultural Factors

The following are the cultural factors responsible for the establishment of compact settlements:

(1) Man tends of necessity to gravitate towards his fellowmen. Of all animals, he is the most gregarious and the greater the number collected in a given space, the greater is the attractive force there exerted, as is seen to be the case with the great cities of the ancient world.[7] Forest clearing, cultivation of land and related activities centralized at one place and agricultural cooperation and practices of the past as well as present have been conducive to compact settlements. Necessity for cooperation in the regulation and control of water, digging of wells, upkeep of certain public works and preparation of the environment to make it favourable to crops—such things mean consolidation.[8] The village dwellers of the great plains, plateaux of the world, since hoary past, followed agricultural practices based on cooperation leading to the establishment of compact villages. Likewise, "for the first hundred years and more of its history rural New England was of village dwelling farmers"[9] but changed later on due to technical advance.

(2) Fragmentation of holdings and strip cultivation present disadvantage to the village dweller which are best counterbalanced by nucleation where farmer avails all the amenities of close, warm, communal life. Blache rightly remarks that "concentration of living quarters is necessitated by the diversity of parcels to be cultivated, because their only common meeting ground is the village, whither all paths lead."[10] Similar view has been expressed by Mukerjee in similar terms: "All paths and tracks across the fields, which for each cultivator lie scattered like autumn leaves, lead to the village that is meeting ground of all."[11] Obviously, the villager, in compact village, lives in the centre which minimizes his economic distance.

(3) Rajput clans, *inter alia*, in the process of occupance, have helped the settlements to grow into compact habitations enclosed by mud walls, ditch or around a fortress during early days. To these were attracted groups of other people like priests, menials and artisans who aided in maintaining the solidarity, and self-sufficiency of the rural organization.[12]

(4) The reciprocal social relationships under the *jajmani* system have tended to maintain compactness since long. Among others, regarding socio-cultural factors, Enayat Ahmed states: "The social gathering in the centre of the village usually under some shady tree or near the temple, the mutual rejoicings on festivals, the gathering of neighbours after the days work near the well in summer and round the fire in winter when tales are told and talks of friends and crops exchanged; all these have contributed their influence in the direction of compact settlement.[13]

(5) Among economic factors, one cannot ignore the money lending system. Big cultivators or village *mahajan* (money lender) exercises centripetal force for settlers.

(6) Unemployed or semi-employed labourers engage themselves in the subsidiary occupations which can easily flourish in such villages. Similarly, a host of intermediaries like petty traders find it convenient to supply articles of everyday life and purchase grains in times of need in compact villages.

(7) Land system also associated the landlord and cultivator well in compact villages.

(8) Religious centres along rivers, near springs also attract agglomerations around them. Temples in the middle of such big settlements still signify their historical role, i.e., Vindhyachal,

Chitrakut, Pushker etc.

(9) Some villages grow as compact settlements due to definite political bias or administrative decision, i.e., Manpur (Indore) during the British rule, Mandu by Muslims and others of Hindu period, Tefki in Ethiopia with Italian stronghold.

(10) Defence plays significant role in agglomerations. Its examples are walled villages of the Hansa tribes in northern Nigeria, acropolis villages in the Mediterranean and others in Algeria, Kenya and Mormon villages of U.S.A. The internecine war, robbery, *thug* menaces and looting during the period of anarchy, particularly in Central India, compelled the people to live in closed and compact sites, still present in several parts. The presence of outer wall, ditch, *garhi* and the usual practice of erecting *khala* (enclosure) and huddled together houses exhibit the need of defence in the past and their continued use during present rural landscape.

(11) Hall, rightly observes that "the compact village form (haufendorf) is well-adapted to the mode of life of a paddy area."[14] Various operations linked with paddy cultivation generate such centripetal force.

(12) Mukerjee's remark that "the seasonal idleness of the peasant, especially marked in the rice region, contributes to the development of a large variety of cottage industries which can thrive only in compact settlements."[15] Besides, cottage industry flourishes well in agglomerations as visualized in carpet industry, i.e., in big villages, such as Khamaria, Ghosia etc.

(13) During old days, new site was rarely selected to live separately due to being inauspicious till it was approved of by a group of settlers after getting confirmation from the priests.

(14) In modern agricultural system of USSR, Israel (Kibbutzim), China etc., collective farms are conducive to compact settlements.

(15) During medieval period, open field system of farming required communal field labour which favoured agglomeration in western countries.

Factors Responsible for Dispersion

Though dispersed settlement unit is taken to be granted as synonymous with the farmstead, its main characteristic is the nucleus family along with isolation and privacy. Various factors, such as environmental, socio-economic as well as socio-psychological are responsible for such dispersion. This has its own economic advantages and social disadvantages attached with the living pattern.

Physical Factors

The reasons for disperse type of settlements seem to be different in different regions and no logical explanation of universal application may be given. However, some common factors as given below are clearly visible:

(1) A number of European writers have observed that dispersion appears to increase in direct proportion to the raggedness of the land surface.[16] Blache related such scattered dwellings to the dissected relief. In Malwa region, one finds a proportionate increase in dispersion closely related to the extent of fertile land. So, the scattered 'tapro' (homestead) of tribals is visualized along a river, a slope, on a hill top, a spur or wherever he could play his hand on plough. The poor soil strewn with boulders enhances dispersion to such an extent that one dwelling is enough for several acres. Gradation from a homestead of Bhil or Korku to hamleted *dhanas* of the Gonds well illustrates the influence of land upon concentration of dwellings (Fig. 4.10).

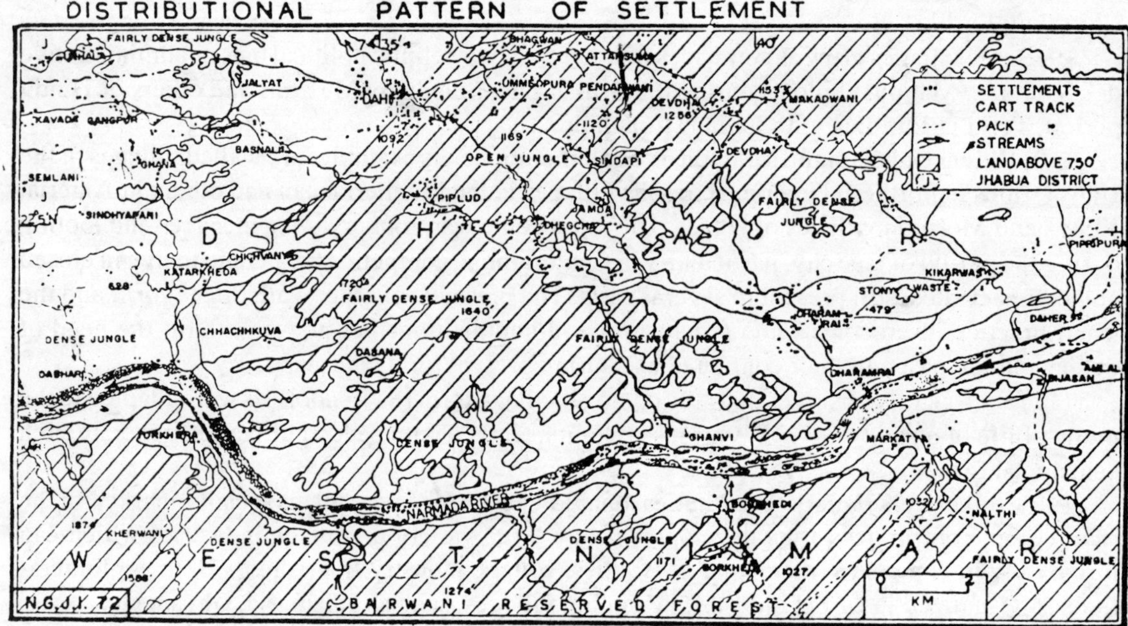

Figure 4.10

(2) In the areas of harsh climate and sterile soils, such as high mountainous lands of the Himalayas, dispersion is common according to supporting capacity of land, forest and pasture.

(3) High water table uniformly available in plains attracts settlers to form homesteads or hamlets with close dwellings, e.g., in Bengal, Belgium (with jutish land holding system), irrigated areas of Spain.

(4) In New World, the vast fertile lowlands have extensive farming land to support isolated farmer, e.g., in U.S.A. and Canada.

(5) Floods in river flood plains provide only seasonal agricultural opportunities. Temporary or shifting type of dispersed settlements grow in such areas. On higher ground permanent type of huts mark the land according to landownership, e.g., in the Ganga and Ghaghara river flood plains, such settlements are found throughout the plain.

Cultural Factors

Varied cultural factors related with land tenure, type of agriculture, individual initiative, peaceful conditions, clan affinities, and racial system have separately or jointly been responsible for various gradations in settlement dispersion ranging from a hut to a hamlet. These are as follows:

(1) The land tenure system changed to a great extent in the mid-nineteenth century in India and with the decline of feudalism later on, private landownership favoured outgrowth of hamlets and isolated dwellings. Tenants of Jagirdars were also bound to live near the field they cultivated. The land dedicated to a *sadhu* (a saint) results in *Math* type settlement. Grants of lands by *Zamindars* (land-lords) as charity also attracted people to form separate dwellings on such sites. After *zamindari* abolition the drift appears to be away from the compact village towards farm dwelling and centripetal forces are loosening hold due to change in social order. In areas of consolidation of holdings farmers are coming out of compact village *abadi* (settlement) and occupying their own *chaks* (plots). There are examples of such isolated farms and settlements in England, Ger-

many, Sweden and Denmark too. Among areas in Britain having individual ownership, fruit farms and market gardens represent dispersed settlement pattern. The trend is also visible in peasants of Egypt, Fiji, Mexico, Israel, Ethiopia etc.

(2) Where cultivable land is divided into too small fields to permit plough cultivation, hoe is the alternative used by sowing which needs intensive labour. People living in such fields do form dispersed settlements. Tribal, hilly and mountainous areas, having terraced slope cultivation, such as Himalayan valley slopes, Ethiopian highlands, also present such isolated habitations. Also, where the existing peasantry is poor, illiterate and unskilled in intensive farms of agriculture and lacks mechanical equipment, it is without question essential to locate the farmsteads on the holdings.[17]

(3) Individual initiative also plays its role in the selection and formation of isolated settlements in newly developing areas, on newly purchased or possessed plots/sites either for living, better agriculture, mining, forestry or some business. It may also be due to desire to get away from religious or ethnic persecution.

(4) Due to peaceful conditions prevailing during modern times, open country isolated living is increasing. In Italy, newly planned areas with small holdings have disperse type of new habitations. This is the trend in other parts of the world where irrigational facilities, security, eradication of disease are improved by now.

(5) Clan affinities also make the closer, kindred to live at one place quite separate from other. Blache quotes Richthofen regarding clan characteristics of Chinese who divided into clans live in little hamlets, with manners and customs differing from those of plains.[18]

(6) The type of economy and racial characteristics have determined the dispersion of settlements in tribal areas. Still, privacy of life and polygamy, two concurrent causes, have led them to live separately in scattered dwellings. Residing in his *tapro* (habitation), a Bhil feels himself safe and keeps a close eye on his wives staying at the house or working in the field in the neighbourhood. Security of crops from wild animals and birds and also theft, so common a feature in hilly Central India, compels them to make their huts separate at a central place closely related to the contour of the terrain. They can also construct their huts within some days out of woods and try to be as near as possible to their cultivated fields. Superstitions and ignorance also play their part in keeping them aloof from other members. Such is the case with other, several, tribals spreading over the world.

(7) Colonization of available agricultural land following industrial revolution in Europe has been conducive to disperse type of settlements, i.e., in Danube plains on the open flattish grasslands (Puszta). Poland, Czechoslovakia and Hungary all show such trends. After the second World War, Japan saw the same show.

(8) In areas of pastoralism and transhumance, dispersed dwellings are common. Herders in Switzerland, Austria and Norway make dispersed chalets (Almhutte) or saeter huts. Seasonal huts of Sawannah and Steppes' pastorals are other examples.

(9) New forest clearings or reclamation and occupance of user margin land have, since medieval period, encouraged dispersion.

(10) Newly constructed rail-road network has also attracted the villagers to come out along the road or near railway station to erect shops, *dhabas*, resting/halting places for trucks along highways, and later on permanent dwellings resulting into separate hamlets.

(11) Rural market (*hat*) villages have also encouraged the establishment of separate dwellings and hamlets near the hat site or fair site. The fair sites are occupied by a shopkeeper to serve the casual traveler, or a separate hamlet of priests.

(12) Caste system has also been condutive to the dispersion during recent times. Separate hamlets of Kachhi, Koli, Ghosi, Ahir, Bhils and some others of low agricultural class and service class like Chamar, Balai, sweeper and other scheduled castes and tribes, have been developed outside the main village as a satellite of the latter. *Banjaras* (wanderers), *Lauhpite* (ironsmiths) and *Patharkatta* (stone cutters) live in separate dwellings away from the main residential units. *Chamars* live generally at the outskirts of the villages or sometimes even entirely segregated from it and possessing its own tanks, wells and boundary Gods[19] (Figs. 4.5, 4.10).

(13) The headquarters of community development blocks or tribal welfare blocks and their subsidiary affiliations have also contributed to new dispersions in the vicinity of villages or towns. Similarly, big farms, ginning and spinning factories have also encouraged new *bastis* in their neighbourhood.

Other Types

We saw in Chapter 1 some general criteria based settlements. But, all varied forms cannot be explained on the basis of functional types alone. Site is the most significant factor in developing certain patterns which are discussed below. A few sites are divided on the basis of physical phenomena which prove to be more attractive factors in settling process while in others cultural factors become determining, or controlling ones. Since all sites have topographic locations, it is simply more convincing to present them with generalized categories of *physiographic* and *cultural.*

Physiographic Sites

All the physiographic sites are further discernible according to their relations to the environmental features: (1) hydrographic, (2) geomorphic, and (3) vegetational

Hydrographic

Man breaths and exists but he survives only when he drinks and eats. Water, therefore, is the sole and the most determining factor in occupance. Water containing features also serve as means of livelihood, communication, defence as barriers, cultivation through irrigation as well as climate ameliorating device. Among many minor and major factors affecting hydrographic features, a few more significant are water table depth, portability of water, its volume, seasonal fluctuations, accessibility, skill of inhabitants in making use of water from different sources and nature of reservoir, spring, or tank and stream banks.

(a) *Tanks* have played a major role in attracting rural habitations since hoary past as the water for drinking for man and his cattle was in itself an attracting force. In northern India, 'Chandravedi' and 'Suryavedi' tanks are used to decide the alignment of settlements. In hilly or undulating parts, these tanks, mostly constructed by throwing embankments on small rivers, are widely scattered on plateaus and big compact villages stick to them almost every where (Fig. 4.11 E_1-E_{10}). Construction of tanks as means of water, *inter alia*, is considered to be a step leading one to salvation. Similarly, lakes attract and give shape to settlements along the banks.

SITE OF SETTLEMENTS

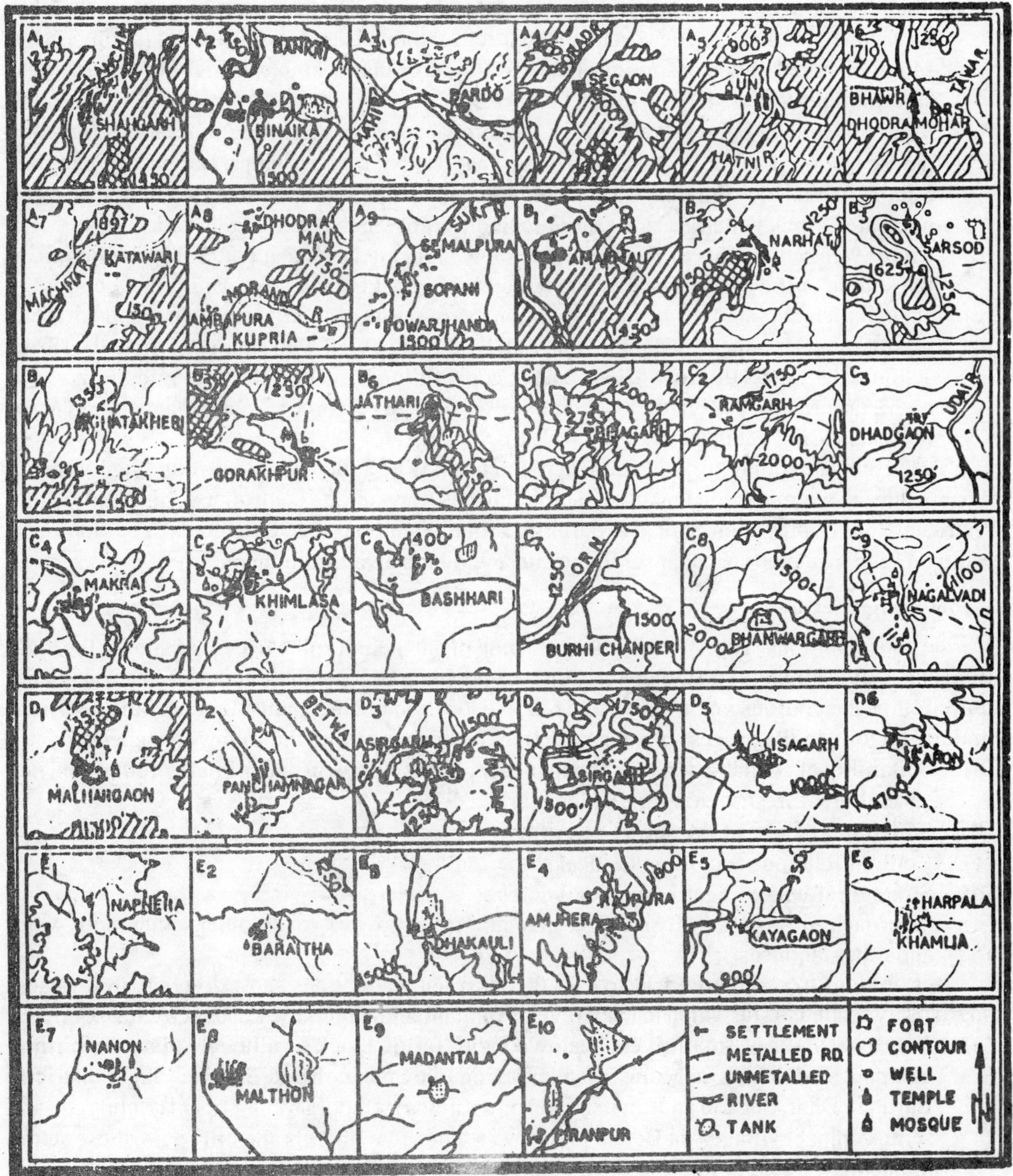

Figure 4.11

(b) *Springs* available in mountainous, hilly or plateau regions due to geological formations providing flow of natural water have given rise to several settlements rather, have influenced the social organization of sites. Artesian wells in many parts of the world, and in *terai* zone of India, have been centripetal force for human habitation. 'Ukala' (spring) in the Mahi-Chambal divide or springs of the Siwaliks are other examples which attracted settlers since antiquity (Fig. 4.12 N_1-N_3).

(c) *River Side* or wet point settlements as big compact rural or urban agglomerations mark the landscape, be it along the Ganga, Volga, Thames, Nile, Mississippi, Danube or Yangtze. Small streams too sometimes attract big human nucleation. Various elongated, linear and nucleated block patterns are discernible in different landscapes (Fig. 4.12 L_1- L_4).

(d) *Canal Side* settlements of modern times show elongated or linear pattern. New sites are at the source or the road-crossings where hamlets are taking the shape of market centres.

(e) *Well-settlements* are the original habitation. Most of the old settlements surround the wells giving semi-circular or rectangular layout. Even, number of well sites determine the site of settlements especially for various caste people in India. Tubewells belonging to government or private cultivator also emerge as attractive force for new development of farmsteads and hamlets.

To these 'water point' or 'wet point' settlements may be added others surrounding 'oases' in deserts. It is also remarkable that ownership of means of water, its control, use, distribution and restricted supply play their specific, definitive role in shaping the settlements. The dominant group or clan occupies space closer to the site and others away from them.

Geomorphic

Varied considerations are responsible for selection of any geomorphic feature as site for the location and establishment of a settlement. Settler's perception depending upon his knowledge acquired since generations on one hand and relative location of site on the other become decision-making factors. In the process of such selection, he keeps in mind the following aspects:

(a) Suitability of available land for occupance for both settlement and primary production, i.e., agriculture, forestry, mining, fishing etc.
(b) Suitability of size of the site in a territory.
(c) Contour relations according to local slope.
(d) Strategic situation regarding overall defence.
(e) Approach and accessibility linkages in relation to pathways, roads, other settlements, water and other landuses.

It is obvious from Figures 4.11 to 4.13 that different habitations show diversity in form and size closely related to site which in itself reveals fundamental diversity. Let us see with examples.

(a) *Narrow valleys* of small rivers bestowed with fertile black or alluvial soils give birth to compact settlements on Malwa plateau region like Shahgarh and Binaika (Sagar district.), Bardo in Dhar, Segaon and Un in Nimar and Kalwari, Dhodra Mau, Sopani (Betul) etc. and semi-compact villages on Betual plateau. Ensconced with hills and hill spurs, these settlements have been, in later periods, connected by routes sometimes rails, roads or age-old footpaths (Fig. 4.11 A_1-A_2).

(b) *Fort settlements* on hills, river sides scatter throughout the world reflecting compulsion of site selection for the purpose of administration and defence, i.e., Tefki in Ethiopia and Hopi

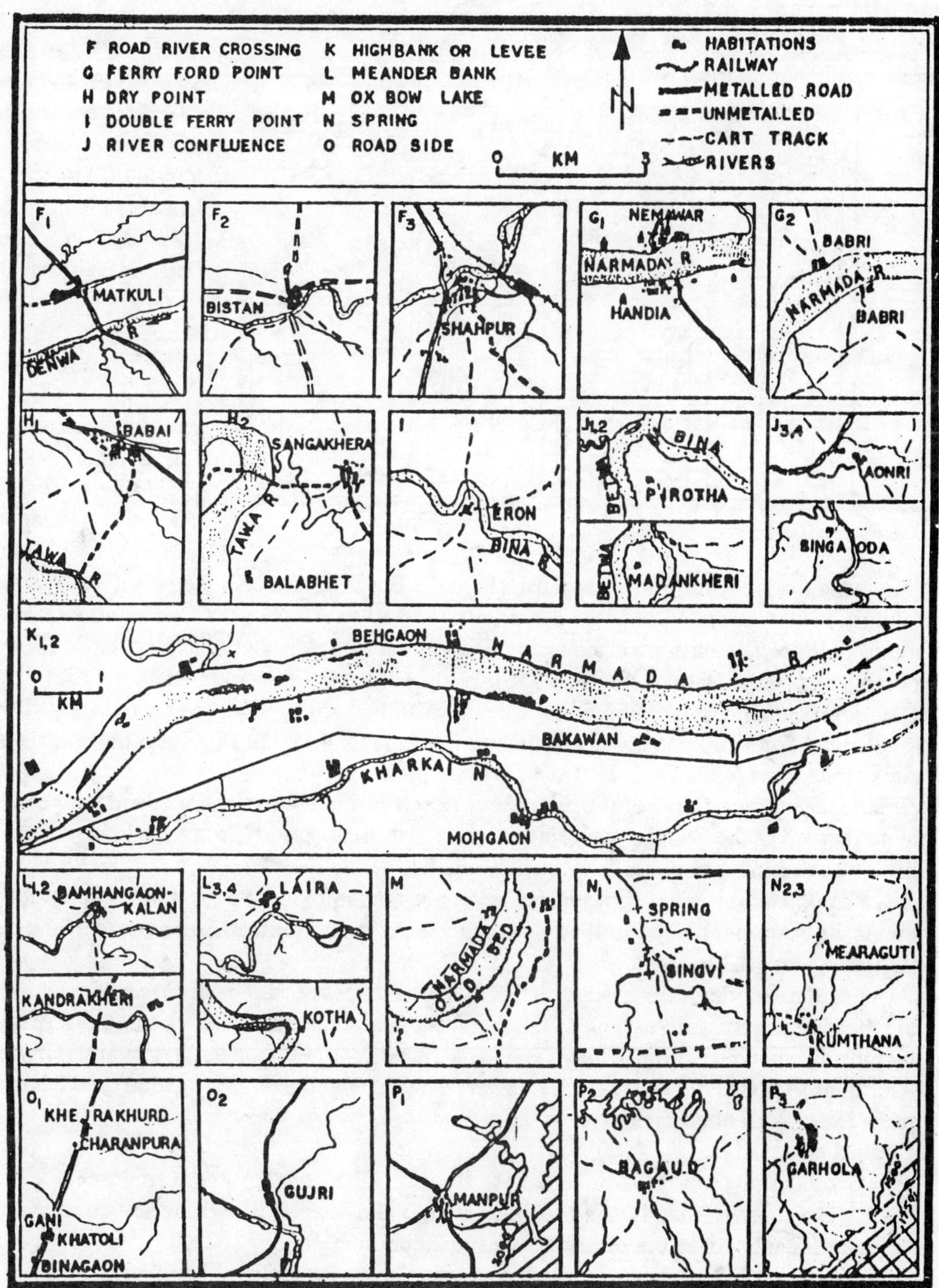

F ROAD RIVER CROSSING
G FERRY FORD POINT
H DRY POINT
I DOUBLE FERRY POINT
J RIVER CONFLUENCE
K HIGHBANK OR LEVEE
L MEANDER BANK
M OX BOW LAKE
N SPRING
O ROAD SIDE
HABITATIONS
RAILWAY
METALLED ROAD
UNMETALLED
CART TRACK
RIVERS
0 KM 3
MATKULI
DENWA R
BISTAN
SHAHPUR
NEMAWAR
NARMADA R
HANDIA
BABRI
NARMADA R
BABRI
BABAI
TAWA R
SANGAKHERA
TAWA R
BALABHET
ERON
BINA R
BINA
PIROTHA
BETWA
MADANKHERI
AONRI
SINGA ODA
BEHGAON
NARMADA R
BAKAWAN
KHARKAI N
MOHGAON
0 KM 1
BAMHANGAON-KALAN
KANDRAKHERI
LAIRA
KOTHA
NARMADA OLD BED
SPRING
SINGVI
MEARAGUTI
RUMTHANA
KHEJRAKHURD
CHARANPURA
GANI
KHATOLI
BINAGAON
GUJRI
MANPUR
BAGAUD
GARHOLA

Figure 4.12

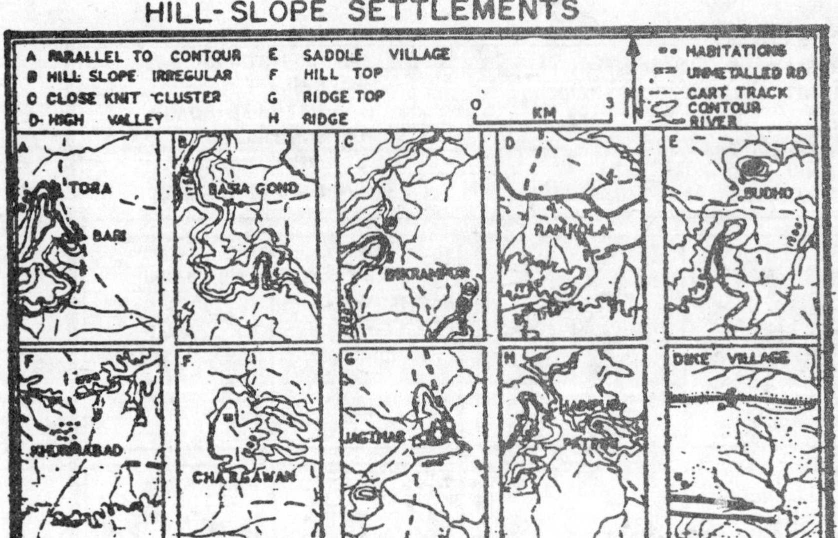

Figure 4.13

settlements (Pueblos) on mesas in south-western U.S.A. and Castle villages of England. The incessant internecine wars, a common feature of political history of Malwa region, compelled the settlers and their chiefs to establish fortresses as strongholds[20] throughout the region on suitable sites, the examples being Bijagarh, Ramgarh, (Khargone district), Dhadgaon (Dhulia), Makrai (Hoshangabad), Khimlasa, Bashhari (Sagar), Burhi Chanderi, Isagarh (Guna), Asir (Betul), Malhargaon (Vidisha) and Asirgarh (Khandwa) (Figs. 4.11 C_1-C_9 and D_1-D_6).

(c) *Ferry point settlements* are of common occurrence along the rivers. Nemawar in Dewas, Handia and Babri-Babri (Hoshangabad) are suitable examples (Fig. 4.12 G).

(d) *Dry-pointsettlements* like Babai and Sangkhera in Hoshangabad lie on the land above flood level almost one kilometre away from river banks (Fig. 4.12 H). Big rivers have also such sites along narrow banks as well as vast flood plain.

(e) *Double ferry point*: Some of the rivers have developed meanders and the land between the bends served as the best defensive site in early historical period. Eron, rich in inscriptions, lies on such a site of double ferry point (Fig. 4.12 I).

(f) *River confluence* sites have, in several parts, been inhabited in the form of compact settlements; its examples being Pirotha, Madankheri (Vidisha), Aonri (Hoshangabad), Singaoda (Ujjain) (Fig. 4.12 J_1-J_4).

(g) *Levee* settlements have developed on the high banks or levees almost free from floods along big meandering rivers like Ganga, Ghaghara, Narmada, Chambal, Betwa etc. A few of them include Godgawn, Pathari Khurd, Behgaon (Khargone), Mardana, Bakawan (Barwaha, Khargone), Ghata Billod (Dhar), Nemawar (Dewas), Handia (Hoshangabad) and Dharampuri (Dhar)—all of compact type.

(h) Contact points of *break of slope* or slope-foot sites have given rise to several big compact villages; examples being Garhola (Sagar), Bagaud (Dhargone), Manpur (Indore) (Fig. 4.12 P_1-P_3), Bargaon in Khandwa in Malwa region, in the Siwalik hills zone settled by Kanets in lower Himalayas and in other areas on such junction points.

(i) *Terrace site* settlements are occupied by mostly Gujars in the Siwalik hills and the Dun and in lesser Himalayan zone by Kanets. They enjoy the benefit of proximity of water, flat cultivable terrain good for means of transport etc. as well as for grazing. Volcanic mount terraces provide such sites up to last dividing rest line, i.e., Zuquolla Mounts in Ethiopia where settlements scatter surrounding the cone slope. Woods and easily available cultivable slopes provide sustenance.

(j) *Alluvial fan* sites have attracted people since historical times. Often many converging routes merge in one main road or street towards the apex of the alluvial fans. The three segments—upper, middle and lower—are observed as occupied by various groups of people in the Himalayan *terai* belt (Fig. 4.14).

(k) *Natural basin* settlements are commonly found in the little desert region of Rajasthan. Surrounded by sand ridges, they are located with radial layout where converge many foot paths of the area.

(l) *Amphitheatrical basin crest site* settlements occupy the space a little below the water divide, the typical example being Nashal (Fig. 4.15).

(m) *Ravined upland sites* have two diverse types: (a) edge sites having settlements younger than the ravines, and (b) interior sites having settlements older than the edge settlements and ravines (Fig. 4.15a).

(n) *Stream islands* in big rivers serve as good settlement sites, i.e., Mokalpur and Gobaraha in Varanasi amidst Ganga channels.

Such types of sites are further to be named as *hill settlements* having hilly physiographic characteristics at the base, hence separate treatment. It is rightly remarked that with its self-evident

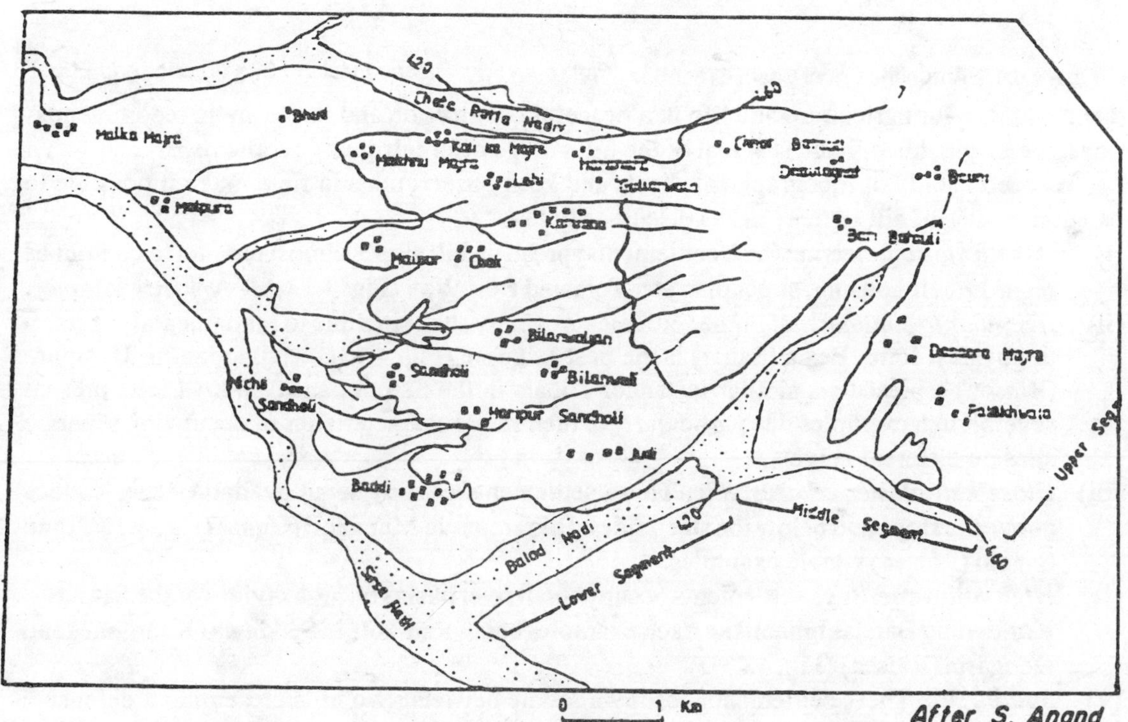

Figure 4.14: Alluvial Fan Site.

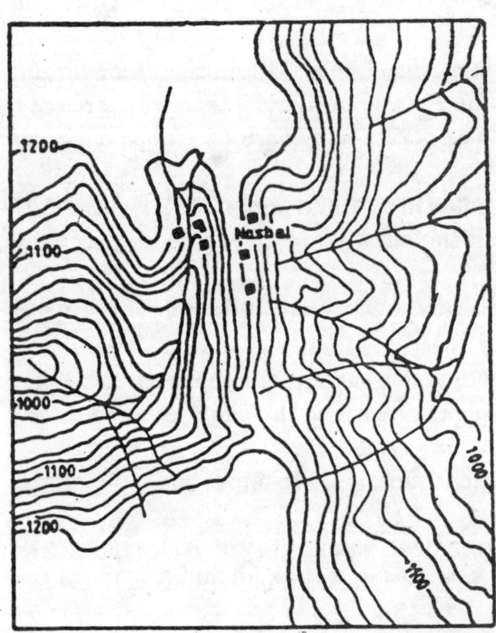

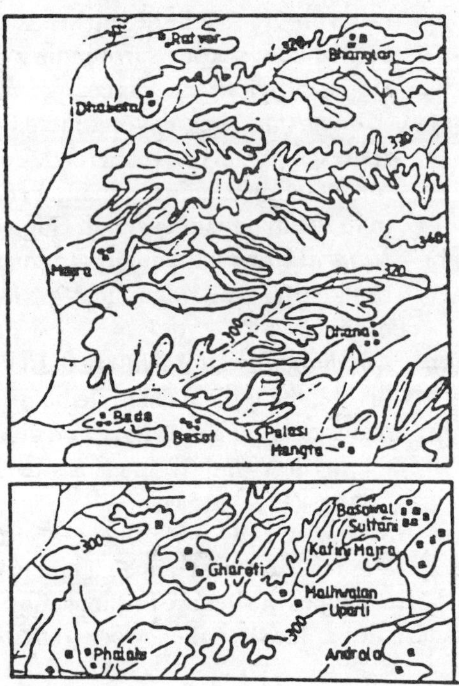

Figure 4.15: Amphitheatrical Basin Crest Site *Figure 4.15(a)*: Ravined Upland Site (Interior and Edge)

disadvantages for agriculture and life in a peaceful countryside and its aesthetic recommendations, the origin, history and survival of the hill village offer intriguing problems.[21]

A careful study of topographical sheets and keen observations in field make it possible to categorize sites of hill settlements as discussed below:

(i) ***Parallel to contour site*: Such settlements spread on hill slopes almost parallel to contour as regards their housing, street plan etc. Tora and Bori Wali (Fig. 4.13 A_1- A_2) are examples.**

(ii) ***Irregular to contour site*: Some settlements occupy such sites due to fundamental diversity in physical form. Besia (Sagar) is the best example (Fig. 4.13B). Jujharpani in Udaipura (Raisen) represents a similar instance. Tribals in the Satpura and Vindhya hills present several such examples due particularly to their racial characteristics of occupying separate sites on different heights.**

(iii) ***Close knit cluster or crest site*: These settlements occupy some available level surface above the slope and below the steep sides. Bikrampur in Mungaoli (Guna) (Fig. 4.13C) and Sanchi (Raisen) citable examples.**

(iv) ***High valley site*: Such settlements occupy small river basins on high divides of the Satpuras. Korkus and Barelas inhabit the tract, examples being Ramkola in Sendhwa (Khargone) and Dongaria (Raisen) (Fig. 4.13D).**

(v) ***Saddle site*: These settlements occupy a saddle between two hills presenting a defensive site. Budho (Sagar) (Fig. 4.13E) is the best example. The Aravalli out-crops region has**

many radial and elongated settlements on such gap sites. Such sites are in abundance in the lesser Himalayan region.

(vi) *Summit sites*: These are better suited where water is available and woods supply fuel and hunting ground. Khurmabad in Sendhwa (Khargone) (Fig. 4.13F) and Chargawan in Udaipura (Raisen) are good examples.

(vii) *Ridge top sites*: These are occupied by people during the process of settlement starting from slope foot after clearing the wood. Jagthar in Banda (Sagar) (Fig. 4.13G) and Gadra in Betul and Mandu in Dhar are examples.

(viii) *Lower ridge site or dyke sites*: These are often inhabited by people forming compact to semi-compact settlements along with the cultivated land below. The examples are Chainpura and Patpiri in Udaipura (Raisen) and Wail and Dedula of Manawar in Dhar (Fig. 4.13H).

It would be pertinent to mention here itself that the siting and distributional pattern of these settlements present a lot of disadvantages: steep approach and consequent difficulties of transporting loads to the villages and of reaching it on foot from the main road; the remoteness from the main arteries of trade and social life; scarcity of water supply; costly construction of wells and failure of this source of supply in period of drought; thin soil cover and rapid depletion on high steep slopes; lack of enough fertile lands; the general poverty of agriculture; exposure to wind and weather; and dangers of animals. Defence and religious factors in early historic and medieval period have played major role in siting and distribution and continuation of these villages. Invasions from outside compelled the aboriginals, like other parts of the world, to shift to hilly areas and occupy some fertile tracts, clear the woods and live upon the forest resources. But, now most of the rural settlements, with some exceptions, lie within the agricultural zone of altitude isolated and dispersed. Medieval fortresses are mostly deserted and inhabitants have shifted down to the small river basins. Some fort settlements on high summits, once developed into towns, lie ruined only to attract some tourists and archaeologists at present.

Vegetational

Removal of forests started since proto-historical times and humanization and occupance of suitable forests sites mentioned in epics speak about the settlement process on forest sites. Along with occupance, forest preservation seems to have been the motto of forest settlers who even worshipped trees of varied species. This shows the affection of settlers towards life sustaining qualities of forests. On one hand, they possess the ambivalent attitude of fear and mystical reverence on the other, forests are regarded as an integral element of primordial nature or even the seat of Hindu Gods and Goddesses. So, the culture trait of preservation continued since past still survives in spite of the technological exploitation. Of the varied site types, two have spatial, territorial origin and spread.

(i) *Forest edge sites* are in the areas where margins are cleared and inhabited. This may be near a spring or stream on level plain or on spurs. Such sites scatter near all types of protected or reserved forests. These lands provided easy access to woods for wood product and grazing ground and piece of tract available for construction of house, cultivation and wood-cutting (Fig. 4.16). *Terai* and Mirzapur in Uttar Pradesh, and Jhabua (Malwa) in Madhya Pradesh present various examples.

(ii) *Forest core sites* are mostly occupied after cutting by government agencies for convenience

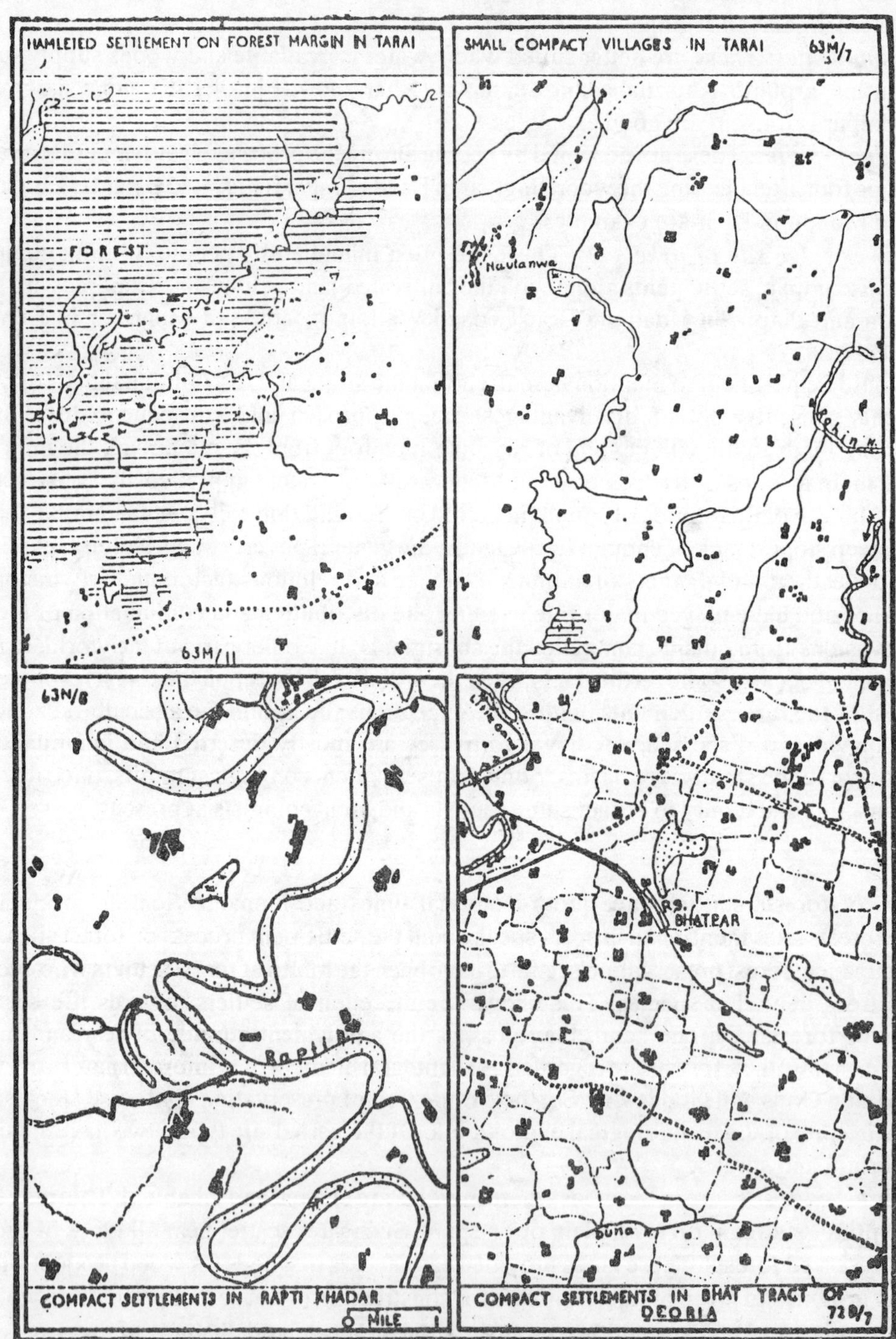
HAMLETED SETTLEMENT ON FOREST MARGIN IN TARAI
FOREST
63M/11
SMALL COMPACT VILLAGES IN TARAI
63M/7
Nautanwa
Rohin R.
63N/8
Rapti
COMPACT SETTLEMENTS IN RAPTI KHADAR
0 MILE 1
R.S.
BHATPAR
COMPACT SETTLEMENTS IN BHAT TRACT OF DEORIA
72B/7

Figure 4.16

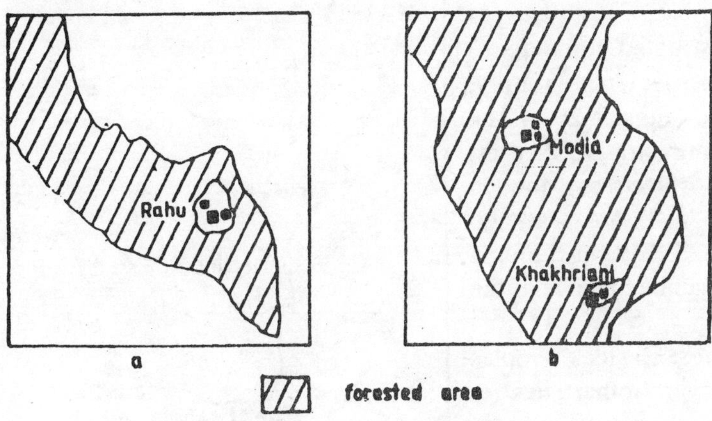

Figure 4.17: Forest Core Sites.

of administration or by tribals who naturally like to live away from the civilized part of the land. Such examples are available in forest areas of tropical zones occupied by the Pygmies, Negritos and other old primitive tribals. Newly developed areas also exhibit such sites now being changed into high hamlets (Fig. 4.17). Old *ashramas* are better examples to be named.

Cultural Sites

The man-made landscape presents many forms showing associations during the occupance of a particular area. Settlements occupy such sites which later on are so much deeply interlinked that it becomes difficult to tell which preceded what. Roads, railways, canals, dams, reservoirs, hydle projects, hydle sub-stations, factory point, wells, tanks, temples etc., all seem to have attracted settlers and settlements. A few of these cultural features have already been discussed. Now we emphasize the general cultural features easily discernible on the cadastral and large scale topographical maps.

(i) *Roads*: Many ancient routes in oriental world are associated with large settlements, a few of them converted into urban centres like Ujjain, Vidisha, Mathura etc. The pilgrim routes also exhibit settlements still existing in changed form; whether it be silk route of traders or others or pedestrians, they are proof of being antecedent to settlements. The ancient Ram-Janaki Road extending from Ayodhya to Janakpur (Bihar), Parikrama Road surrounding Ayodhaya, Kashi and other *teerthas* present clear-cut examples of such sites. Even Shahi Road (administrative highways) of medieval period too are antecedent to newer settlements, i.e., Muratganj, Jangiganj, Mirzamurad etc. along Grand-Trank Road. Halting places of old pilgrim routes are other examples. *Sarai* (inns) along routes are many in number, i.e., Khojwa in Varanasi, and Kanjari Sarai in Moradabad.

(ii) *Canal sites* are newer phenomena and attract settlers due to facilities of water, transport-road and transportation line. Many settlements clung to such sites and are developing into market centres. Defence site has also been a centripetal force to settlers.

(iii) *Canal road* crossings are other cultural features to act as sites.

(iv) *Road river crossings* present good sites showing interaction of various factors remarkably stamped on the arrangement of dwellings, layout plan, development of roads themselves in relation to water features (Fig. 4.12 F_1-F_3).

(v) *Road side halt spots*: Some newly originated and established halt spots along highways are direct results of road and means of transport, i.e., truck and bus in particular (Fig. 4.12, O_1-

O_2). Pack-track site settlements are other examples (Fig. 4.18).

(vi) *Forts*: In most cases constructed for defence such sites exhibit good settlements in hilly, plateau and plain areas too (Figs. 4.20, 4.21). Mostly they served as administrative centres. Bhar castles (small forts or fortress) now in ruined form as big *teela* (hill) are scattered throughout the Ganga plain. Tefqee in Ethiopia presents an example of Italian occupance of the site.

(vii) *Miscellaneous religious sites*: Besides temples of Gods and Goddesses, several other sites related to hero (converted into deity), *majars*, saints' church etc. get sanction from society as sacred places where tanks, *dharmshala* (resting place), school are provided, well-linked with settlements. These sites later on develop into hamlets. *Chhatri* and *satti* site settlements also develop at village settlement level as a separate hamlet (Fig. 4.19).

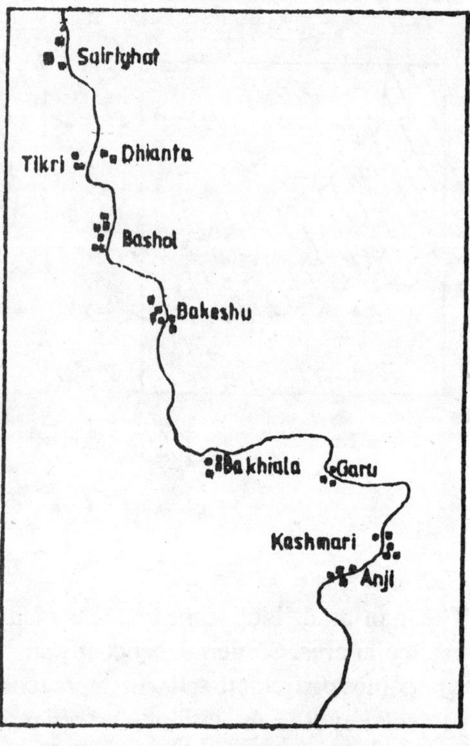

Figure 4.18: Pack Track Site.

Layout Plan/Pattern of Settlements

The external shape of the morphological structure of settlements reveals some geometrical form as a result of definite layout of houses, streets, open spaces etc. in relation to the field. This form is pattern defined as, relationship of one dwelling to another, sometimes irrespective of site. This relationship of dwellings presents, distinct form of the village which in itself is a natural growth determined by physical and cultural setting of the region. These, comprising various factors, find treatment in the sequel.

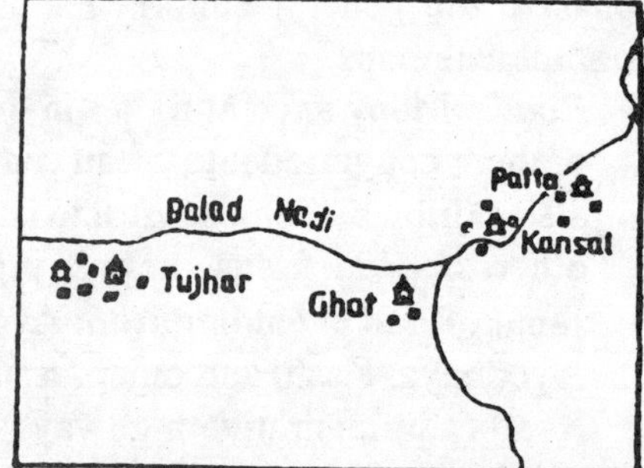

Figure 4.19: Temple and Chharti Site

Ancient

Before going into detail about the pattern of the present villages, we may have passing reference to the ancient rural settlements recognized by the Buddhist, Jain and Pauranika literatures. The Jain texts speak about Uttānamallakakara (looking like an open bowl) in *Avanmukha* (circular in pattern), *Khanda* (semi-circular), *Patalika* (avenue pattern), *Valabhi* (settlement with the trees planted at the four corners) and *Ruchak* (with uneven ground ringed with trees) (*Brihatkalpasutrabhasya* 1103, 1104, 1105, 1106).

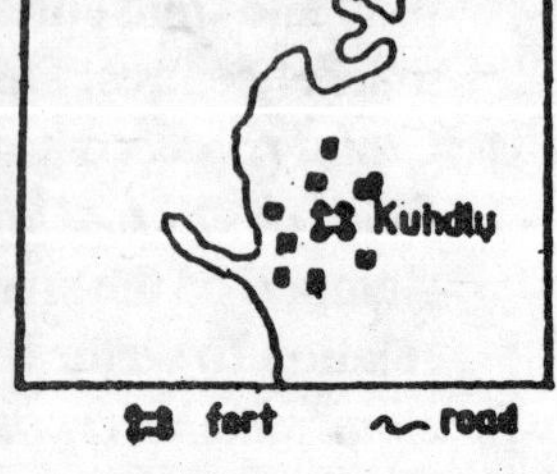

Figure 20: Fort Site

Mansara Shilpshastra and *Arthashastra* have description about

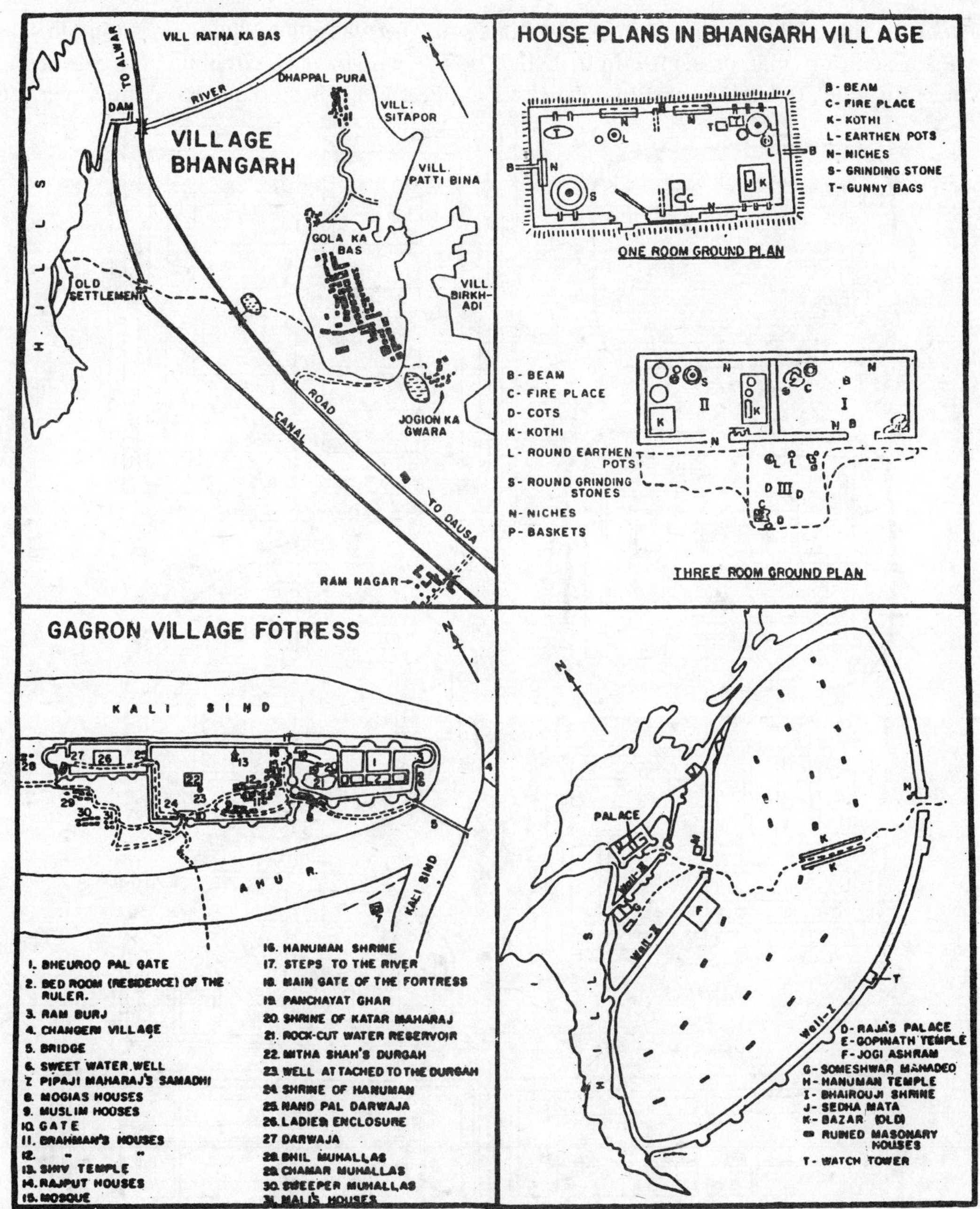

Figure 4.21

rural settlement plans which are not perceptible at present in their true form; based on the description and illustrations of Acharya and Havel these are treated below.

Dandaka was rectangular or square and possessed a rampart of the same shape; *sarvatobhadra*, having oblong or square plan—the temple of Brahma, Vishnu and Shiva being located in the centre and inhabited by the Brahmins and religious aesthetics; *padmaka* was lotus shaped;

svastika resembled the mystic figure of Svastika; *prastara* was either square or oblong in shape; *karmuka*, semi-circular or semi-elliptical like bow; *nandyavarta*, circular; and *chaturmukh*, having four gates extending east to west (Figs. 4.22, 4.23). These plans have, however, been

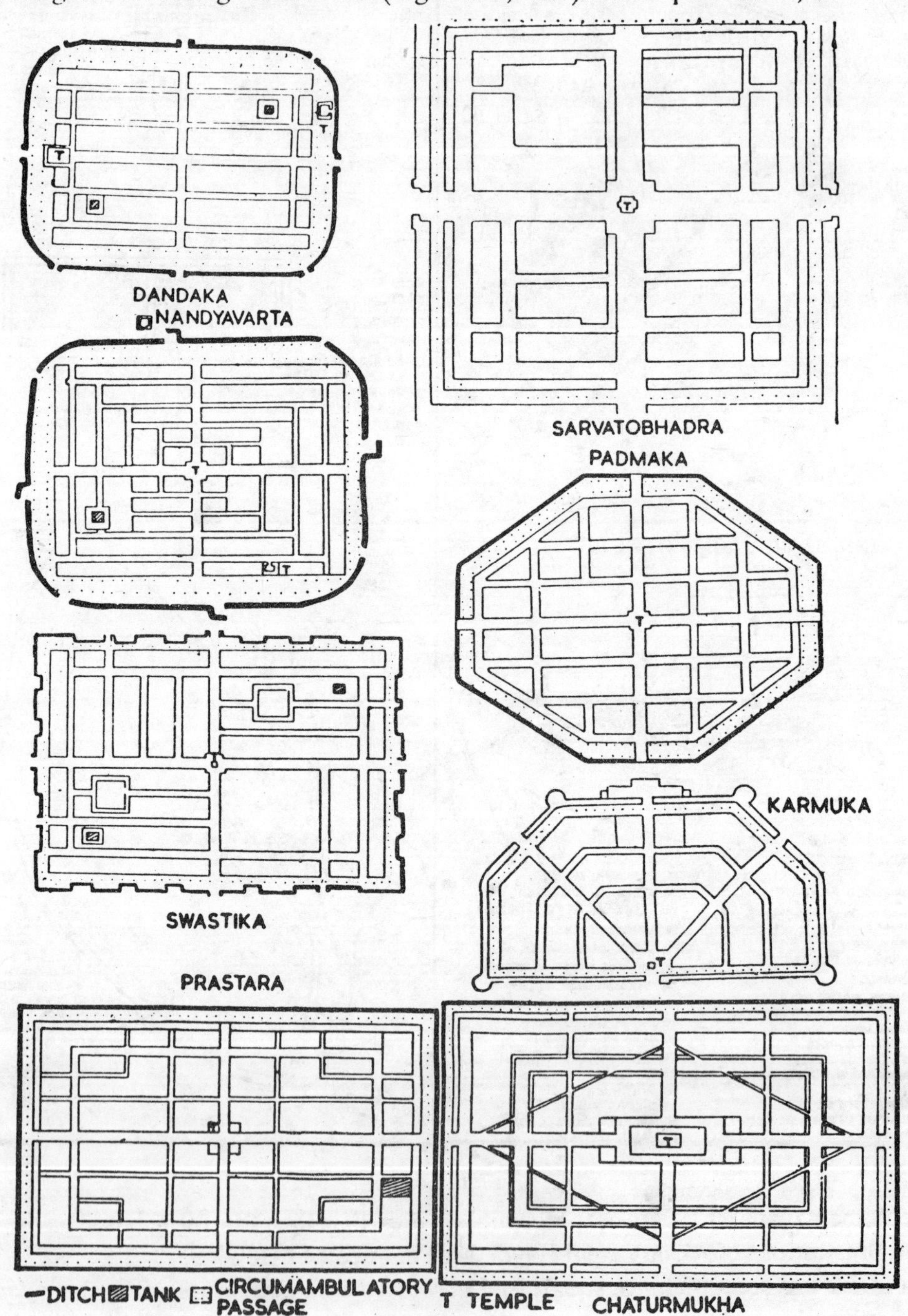

Figure 4.22 After R. L. Singh

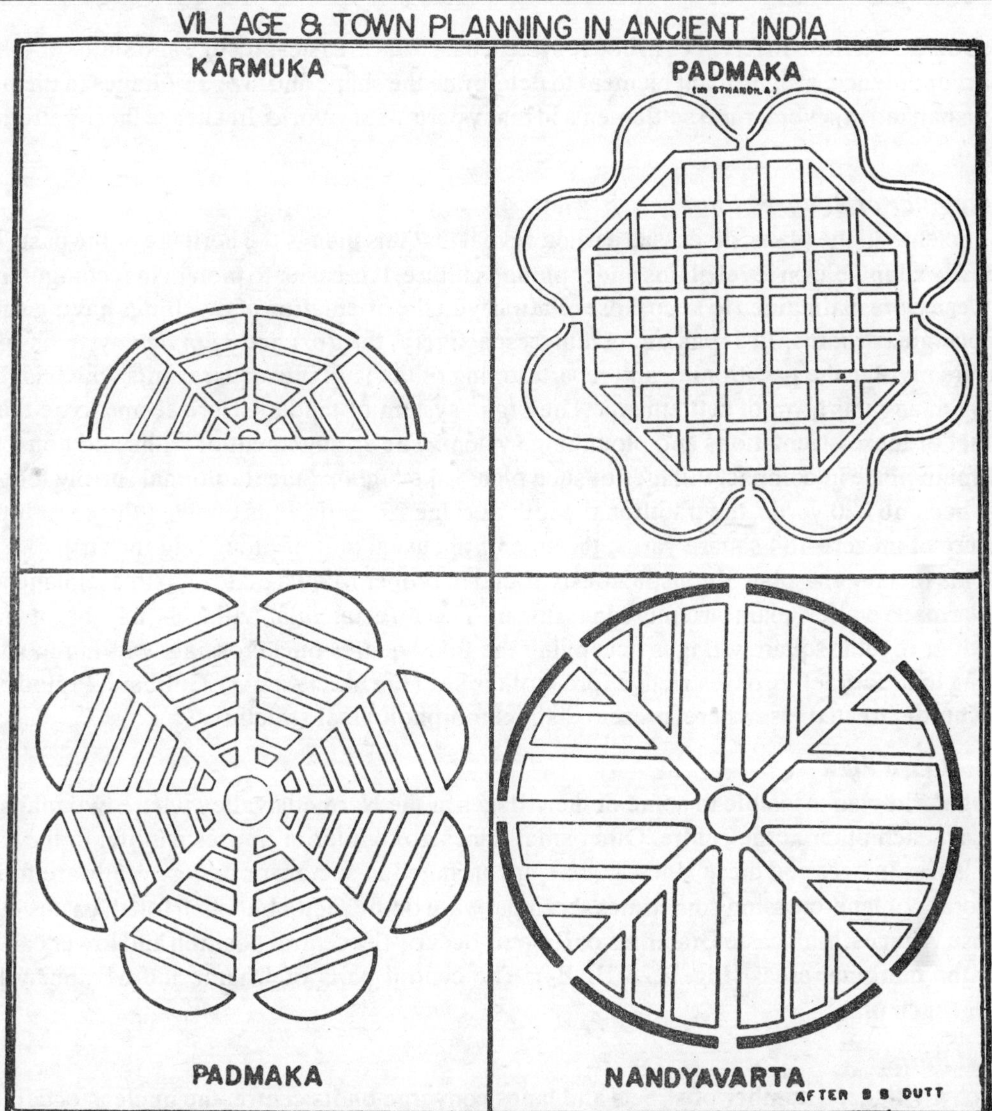

Figure 4.23

obliterated, modified, during the long period of history and only relics are visualized in the form of fortresses or walled villages. The patterns visible in the field, on the large-scale maps, cadastral maps and referred to in records present little conscious planning of rural settlements. Yet, we find an arrangement in the internal structural elements as well as external outlines of the villages. The compact villages so conspicuously found in the middle Ganga valley, in the Malwa region and elsewhere, "present a definite layout and an unmistakable connection between the configuration of the site, surface water (river, tank, pond, well), the nature of soil, cultivation, groves and the shapes of the fields."[22] These patterns are closely related to cart tracks, roads, mosques and temples, the cultural elements and also to the physical environment of the dwellings like site. Caste communities based on *jajmani* system play their own part in occupying separate sectors

and so do the vertical differences in house system based upon caste, prestige and status of villager. Impact of defence, a significant element to determine the shape and size of villages in the past, is still visualized in several rural settlements in many parts of the world. Let us see these patterns one by one.

Rectangular or Squared Plan

The ancient village plans, discussed earlier, reveal that this plan is the heritage of the past. These are easily adaptable on level plains under plough culture. It is easier to plough in rectangular plots and these were maintained to keep close relation with the orientation of dwellings having squared or rectangular rooms. In Japan and China respectively, the *Jori* and *Han den* systems of land measure involve the partitioning and repartitioning of the land into square units which is related to the rectangular form of settlements. The *bigha* system of land measure seems to be the end-product of these orientations and ploughing system. The arrangement of paths and houses find maximum place in compact villages of such plan. Like *bigha*,[23] the traditional furrow long (furlong) became 220 yards, the traditional width of ridge 22 yards, thus evolved the common land measure of an acre 484 square yards, the area of the usual unit of ploughing the strip.[24]

This rectangular plan is conspicuously found in proper Malwa plateau, Nimar upland and in the Narmada valley plain around Maheshwar. These rectangular villages may be of natural growth or regular square villages occupying the four squares on a crossing, varying in size according to the attractive or restrictive forces of the site (Fig. 4.24 A_1-A_5). Guljhara, Piplod Khurd and Khurda, treated elsewhere, present distinct morphological structure.

Chess Board Plan

A rough grid plan is visible in some of the villages in the Narmada valley where two main lanes intersect each other at the centre. Other small lanes go to interior houses parallel to the former main lanes. In between these lanes, houses are arranged in sectors or castes. Wells are found in one corner of lane-crossing sometimes serving a ward or the sector but open for all castes people. In these villages, high caste Brahmins or Rajputs occupy the central position and lower castes inhabit the marginal areas (Fig. 4.24 B_1-B_5). The central parts of Dharar and Manpur villages present such plan.

Radial Plan

In such a village, a number of streets and lanes converge on its centre, the nucleus occupied by Patel's or landlord's *garhi* (big house) or a market place or some temples of *Shiva* or *Hanuman* (the Hindu Gods). Most of these villages are old in origin representing the ancient aggregation of maximum possible houses under the protection of *garhi*. The well situated in the centre also serves the villagers (Fig. 4.24 C_1-C_5).

Dopple-Dorfer Pattern

Villages separated by roads, streets, small rivulets or ponds present double or sometimes treble nucleation, particularly in the level plain of the Narmada valley and in northern plateau region of Malwa. Settlements like Bhugore and Bhilkheri (Shujalpur) and Datana-Matana (Ujjain) seem to have grown by colonisation upon the edge of the other. Other examples are Damkhera and Bardia Surta, Batholi Tajpura (Maheshwar), Dival-Gujaria Khera (Khargone), Rampura-Gadaria-Rupadeh (Seoni-Malwa) and Nimach-Malona, Barkala-Charkhera (Harda) (Fig. 4.24 D_1-D_5).

Strassendorfer

Some villages working as rural markets are linked with the neighbouring towns by road and lie on both sides of roads or streets and present street village plan. Sometimes houses arranged in line along an open space resemble same pattern particularly, found in Gond inhabited areas of Betul. Such pattern is visualized in the Narmada valley as well as on Nimar upland (Fig. 4.24 E_2-E_5).

Linear Plan (Reihendorfer)

Some settlements develop in one direction like kellendorfer or strassendorfer and include Dickinsons' marschhufendorfer (marsh village), waldhufendorfer (forest villages), thukolonien and gutskolonien (estate settlements). Attractive forces encourage linear growth and restrictive elements of marsh, forest or highland prevent expansion in other sides and linear plan extends along the track or pathway leading to ferry point or big villages (Fig. 4.24 F_1-F_5).

Double Linear (Angerdorfer)

In the Narmada valley plain of Hoshangabad, some villages occupy high ground spreading in one direction in two lines separated by cart tracks or open space leading to field and forest (Fig. 4.25 J_1-J_2).

Elongated Plan

Drypoint villages develop along the high level surface restricted by floods or dissected topography form two sides and form elongated shape. Sometimes houses aligned along the stream for the advantage of water front present such forms. Matkuli Mongra (Sohagpur), Hari Dhana (Betul) (Fig. 4.25 E_1-E_3) and others in the Narmada valley along the river represent well-developed elongated plan. Morphological structure of Matkuli village treated elsewhere gives spatial expansion of settlements in between river and *nala* (Fig. 4.31).

Hollow Pattern

An open or unbuilt space, a pond, high ground or *satti* (structure, platform, temple in the memory of a pious lady) or temple or big banyan or *peepal* tree occupying the central place in a settlement of compact form resembles such plan visualized in many parts of the world, here exemplified by Kajalkheri (Hoshangabad), Dalchi (Barwaha), Piranpur (Mungoli) (Fig. 4.25 A_1-A_3), and Barauda in Jaora (Ratlam).

L-Shaped Pattern

Sometimes at the junction of a main road and a minor street or track, two rectangular blocks of houses meet at right angles. The smaller block represents new growth due to attractive forces applying in one side greater force and restrictive forces fixing them to extend in one direction. Chatarkhera (Hoshangabad), Churia (Betul), Kodhur (Khandwa) (Fig. 4.25 $B_1$1 - B_3) and Dogaha Kalan in Khurai and others in the Narmada valley in Udaipura and Hoshangabad along the river represent such plan.

T-Shaped Plan

In some villages, a smaller limb extends towards cultivated fields at an angle to give the L-shape a new form resembling T. Such a limb also develops from a main rectangular or elongated form

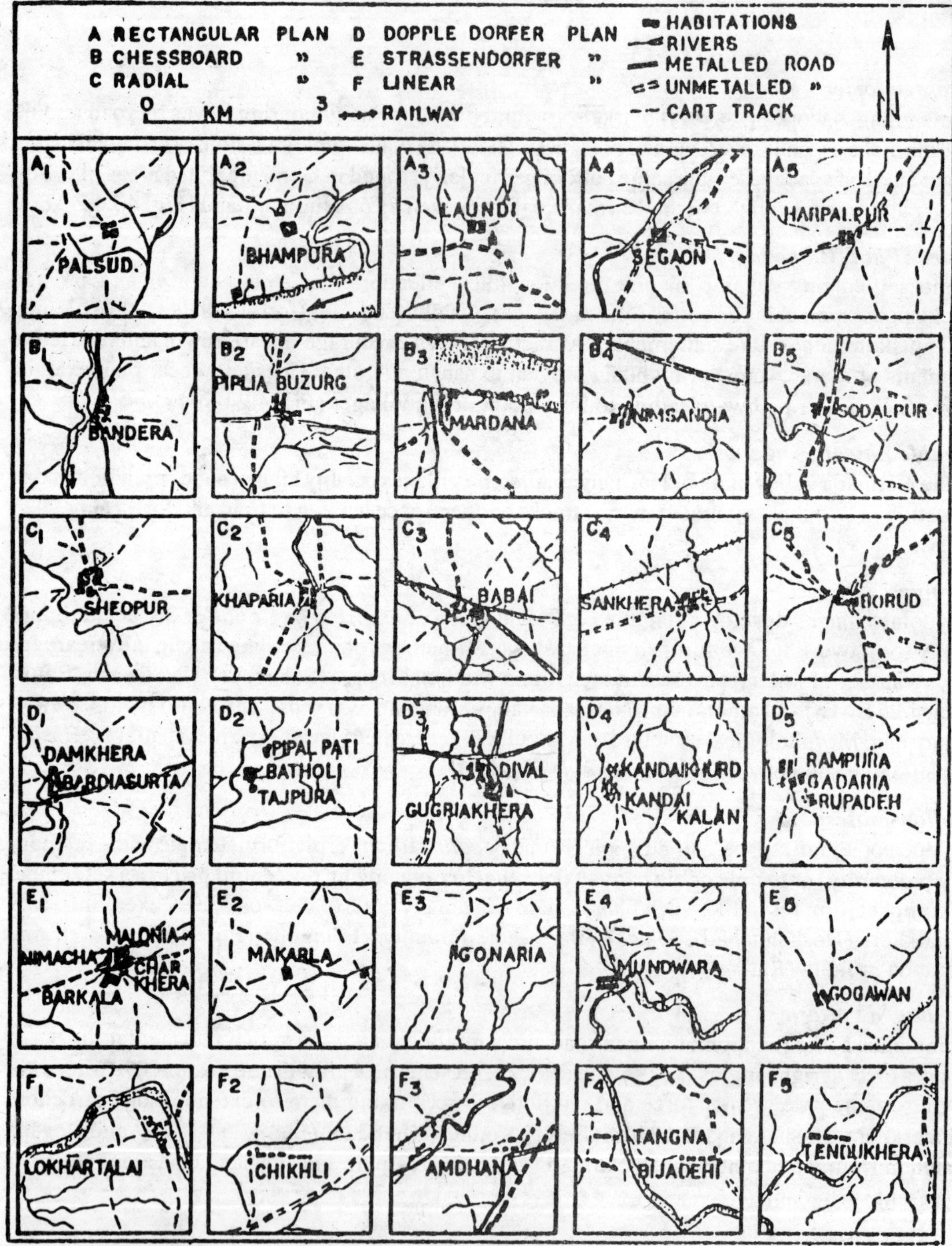

LAYOUT OF VILLAGE-HABITATIONS

Figure 4.24

LAYOUT OF VILLAGE HABITATION

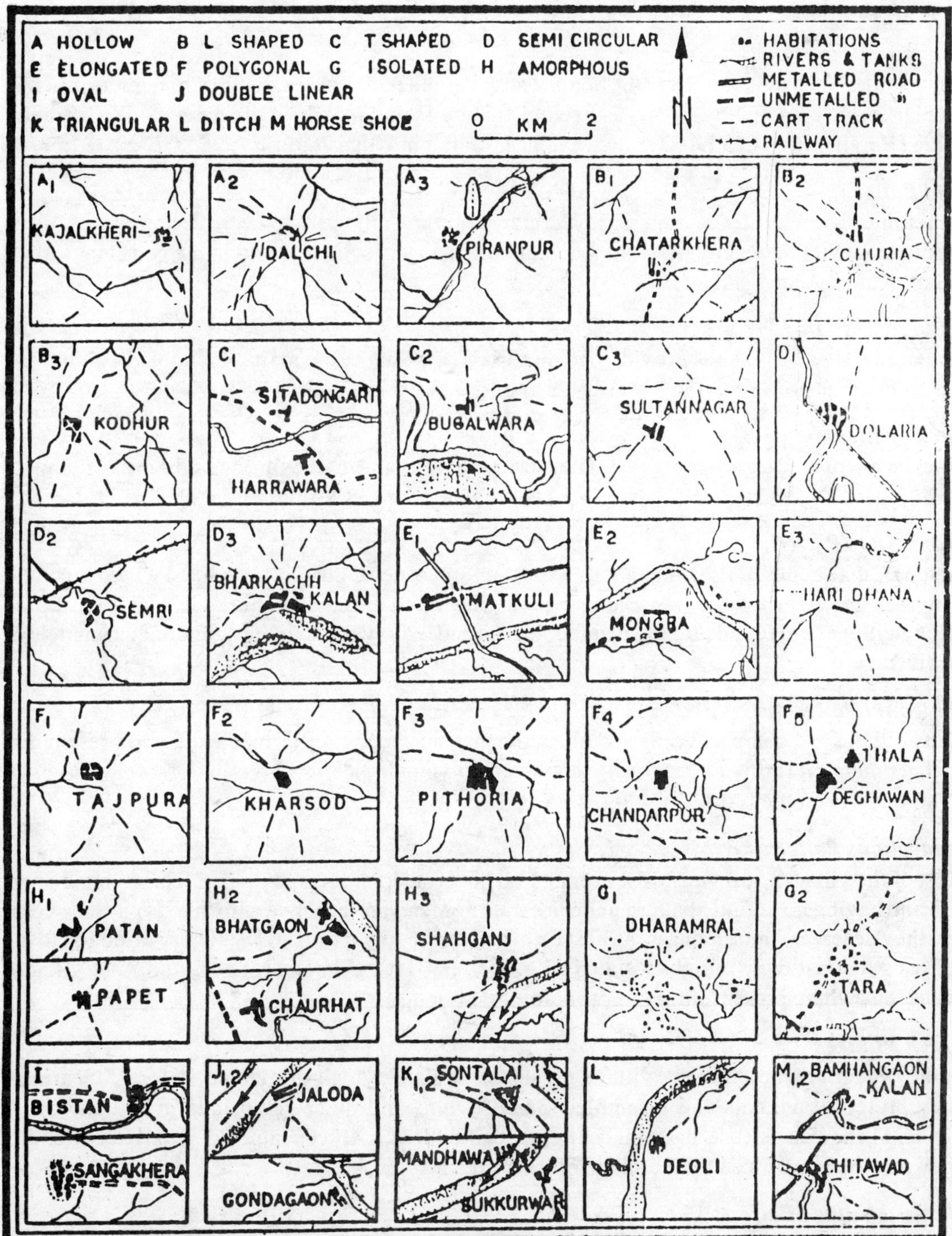

Figure 4.25

of village into T-shape following the terrain. Sita Dongari etc. are citable examples (Fig. 4.25 C_1-C_3 and Fig. 3.1a).

Semi-Circular Plan

These settlements develop along the bend of streams and the crescent shape of meanders in semi-circular form separated by streets as exemplified by Dolaria, Semri (Hoshangabad), Barkachh Kalan (Bareli) (Fig. 4.25 D_1-D_3) and Maniar in Ballia in Uttar Pradesh.

Oval Pattern

Sometimes restrictive forces determine the extent of some villages to take oval shape with houses huddled together to occupy maximum available space particularly found in the Narmada valley and on Nimar upland (Fig. 4.25 I_1-I_2).

Triangular Plan

Sometimes sites or villages provide peculiar triangular shape, the main block forming the base and other extensions growing towards the apex as shown in Figure 4.25 K_1-K_2.

Ditch Walled

Defence has played significant role for constructing walls and ditches around villages of compact form, especially in Guna and Sagar districts, showing distinct forms (Fig. 4.25 L).

Horse-Shoe Pattern

On the arcuate bends of river meanders, a special form of settlement is visualized which is named as horse-shoe plan village like Bamhangaon Kalan and Chitawad (Fig. 4.25 M_1-M_2). Some oblong villages are found along the higher levees and oxbow lakes or the abandoned channels or the rivers.

Polygonal Pattern

Many old big and compact villages both on the plateau and in the Narmada valley represent distinct geometrical form of hexagon, octagon and polygon indicating aggregation of dwellings of diverse castes on the fertile soil (Fig. 4.25 F_1-F_5).

Amorphous Pattern

Most of the villages, grown amidst irregular physical surroundings, with hamlets having dispersion and having no definite pattern under a single nomenclature, hence amorphous pattern seems best they deserve. Amorphous is the best form in interior countryside where every direction to the field is street/pathway is rightly stated (Fig. 4.25 H_1- H_3). Udaigir, Mandu, and Aser villages treated elsewhere present similar morphological structure.

Green Villages

Dudley Stamp recorded many village greens in England which originated in forest clearings. They protected animals and resembled Bantu *Kraals* and other enclosures in settlements in Africa. These also acted as pastoral centres, social centres, market centres, defensive centres etc. They may be recognized by the shape of their green (Figs. 3.2, 3.3)

Planned Village Pattern

A few 'model' villages are planned to get definite shape. These are also called 'garden' villages in England mostly for providing residence to industrial employees. New model villages/settlements in India organized by non-government organizations as well as government colonies represent planned pattern. The *Kolkhozy* of the former U.S.S.R. presents another types of layout plan for agricultural organizations. The communal settlements of Israel and Coliery settlements in mining areas show planned character in shape. New ideal villages are coming up on Indian landscape with various amenities and institutional structures depicting planned layout.

Sample Villages

Now we can visualize some of these patterns with the help of structural details of the following villages:

Guljhara: Cultivator's Village in the Narmada Valley

Guljhara exhibits rectangular plan with few exceptions of additional growth along the highway of recent origin which is bound to take D-shape along the Maheshwar road in near future (Fig. 4.26A). The community structure presents sectorwise spatial occupations. Bhils form a separate hamlet near the forest (60 in number), only one Muslim household lies by the road. Brahmins and cultivators occupy the core of the village, businessmen are along the road and agricultural and service class people on peripheral areas each separated by *kachcha* lanes and a few concrete streets. The ginning and pressing mills of cotton in extreme south are distinct morphological features. Mostly engaged in agricultural operations, villagers depend also on manufacturing, household industry and a few on trade and transport. Cash cropping and manufacturing will soon change the morphological conditions of the villages in the south.

Piplod Khurd: A Nimar Upland Village

The village (21°48'N—76°17'E, Population 2,973) lies on the Nimar upland about 17 km south of Khandwa along the metalled road running to Burhanpur. A *nala*, tributary to the Abna river, flows in the north along the village land boundary. It derives its name from the Piploda State, the counterpart village Piplod Khas lying about 30 km in the east. Like Dharar village of Malwa plateau, this village was also preoccupied by aboriginals who were relegated by the state grantees to the marginal areas. It is a compact rectangular village, a typical settlement of the Nimar upland. The *garhi* (landlord's palace) named as *bari* and *chhoti* reminds us about the two clan members round whose dwellings aggregated other Rajputs of closer kindred or from relations or others as helpers and dependents.

The village is now electrified and flour mill and pumping sets are coming up as innovations. With 3,133 acres of total, 2,869 acres of cultivated land devoted to *jowar*, cotton, groundnut, wheat and others in order of importance, a few orchards of orange, lemon and papaya, about 100 acres of forest and 50 acres under fallow land, the village exhibits a true rural landscape of the region (Fig. 4.26B).

Khurda: A Mixed Type Missionary Village

Situated in a depression between hills of the Vindhyas, drained by the headwaters of the Ajnar river, the village (21°23'N—75°39'E; Population 1,233) lies 1.5 km south-west of Khurdi, a road bus terminus, 8 km from Manpur, the market village. A *kachcha*-cum-concrete road joins the village with Khurdi. Three hamlets of Christians, Gujars and Bhils have grown at intervals having cultivated fields in the neighbourhood surrounded by forested hills on the boundary. The mission-

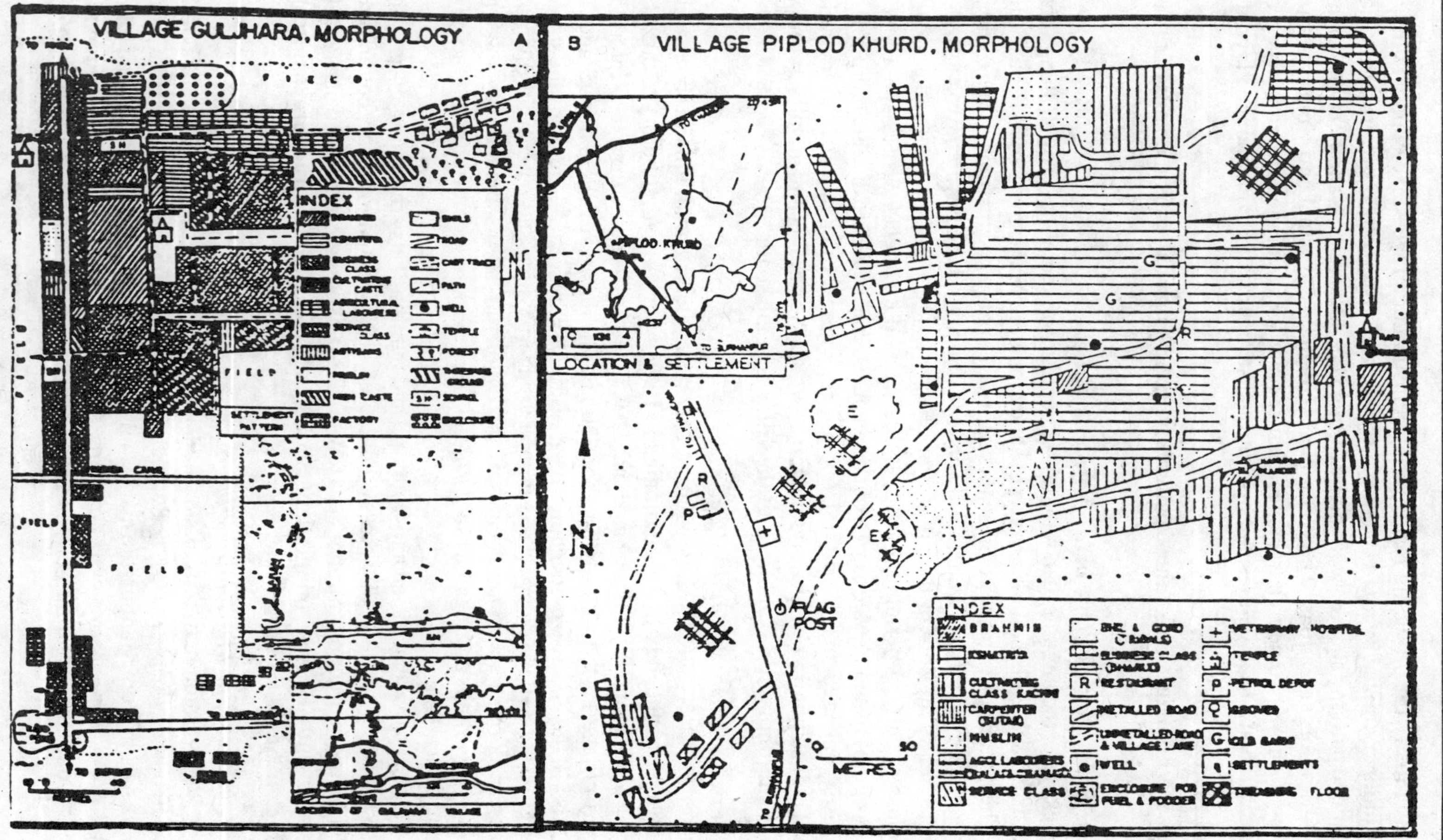
VILLAGE GULJHARA, MORPHOLOGY
A
INDEX
FIELD
SETTLEMENT PATTERN
B
VILLAGE PIPLOD KHURD, MORPHOLOGY
PIPLOD KHURD
LOCATION & SETTLEMENT
FLAG POST
METRES
50
INDEX
BRAHMIN
CULTIVATING CLASS
CARPENTER
MUSLIM
AGRI. LABOURERS
SERVICE CLASS
RESTAURANT
METALLED ROAD
WELL
ENCLOSURE FOR FUEL & FODDER
VETERINARY HOSPITAL
TEMPLE
PETROL DEPOT
SETTLEMENTS
THRESHING FLOOR

Figure 4.26

ary sector is well-planned having residential quarters, health centre, schools, hostel, church, tubewell and wells within easy reach by streets and roads. Gujar houses assemble haphazardly varying in space, size and shape with temples in the north. Bhils occupy separate space quite different in outlook and layout. Two houses of businessmen are later additions (Fig. 4.27).

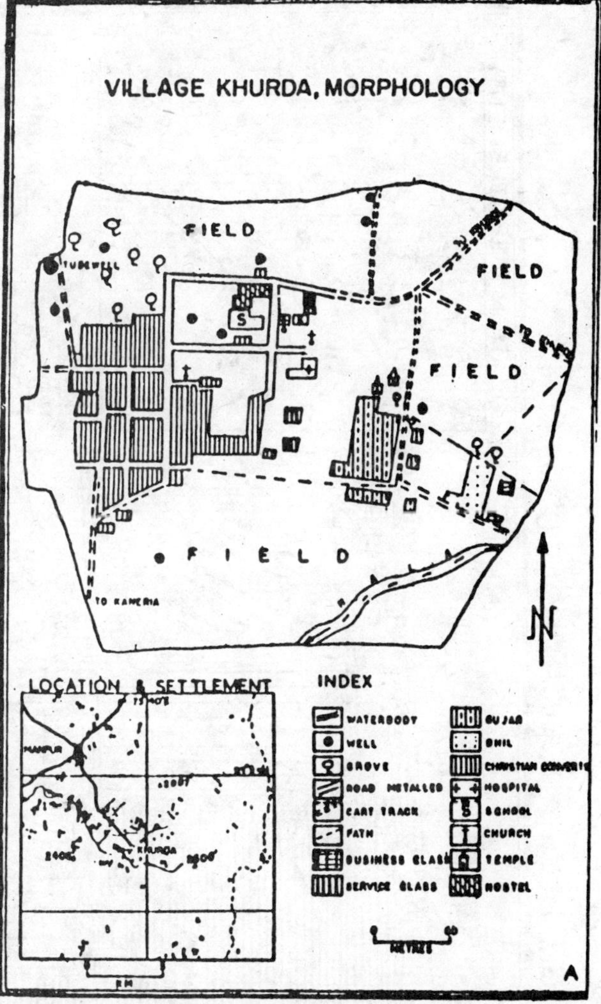

Figure 4.27

Dharar: An Ancient Village

The village (23°15'N—75°12'E, Population 3,975) is a squared compact settlement located on the Mahi-Maleni divide, 11 km south-east of Ratlam on Ratlam-Badnawar road. The village was originated by some Hindus about 1,900 years ago as is evident from Mahakaleshwar temple of 89 *Vikram Samvat* but its real growth in the present form came after Rajput occupation in the seventeenth century, as a Jagir village, under the Ratlam chief Ratan Singh. It was a tehsil headquarters till 1974 when Ratlam usurped its place. Dharar is a corrupt form of Dhadamar named after a grand victory against invaders during the historical period.

The village, as a revenue unit, consists of six other hamlets based upon castes like Bhil, Kolambi and Balai, far apart from the main nucleus. One is concerned here with this central settlement presenting a chessboard plan (Fig. 4.28), the main road and street running from the highway to the Tejaji temple. Other streets run at right angle connected by zigzag lanes which divide caste sections. *Hanuman Mandir* (the *garhi*) lies in the centre and the core of the village around it is occupied by the Brahmins and Kshatriyas. A detached aggregation along the main road depicts signs of new dispersion. It is also remarkable that Bhils, the original settlers, have been relegated to one corner separated by lanes.

Manpur: An Administrative and Market Village

Manpur village (22°25'N—75°37'E, Population 3,939) lies along the National Highway 3, 21 km south of Mhow and 44 km from Indore, on the plateau at a point whence the Vindhyan scarp breaks its height and level surface ends into rugged hilly terrain (Fig. 4.29). Though originally es-

VILLAGE DHARAR, MORPHOLOGY
(UKALA) WATER SPRING
LOCATION & SETTLEMENT
RATLAM
DHARAR
TO DHAR
TO UJJAIN
0 KM 10
INDEX
BRAHMIN
KSHATRIYA
CULT. CLASS
BUSINESS CLASS
AGCL LABRS.
SERVICE CLASS
CARPENTER
RAJGIR
BHIL
POTTER
MUSLIM
ROAD MET
CART TRACK
PATH
WATERBODY
WELL
UKALA
FLOURMILL
THRASHING GD.
TEMPLE
COOP CENTRE
GROVE
SH SCHOOL
PG PANCHAYAT GHAR
PO POST OFFICE
DISPENSARY
S SHOP
RESTAURANT
TEJA JI
HANUMAN MANDIR
BALAI
CHAMAR
MAHAKAL
MANDIR
SHIVA
DEO NARAIN
JAIN
RANOLA MANDIR
OTLA SHITLA MATA
0 METRES 50
N

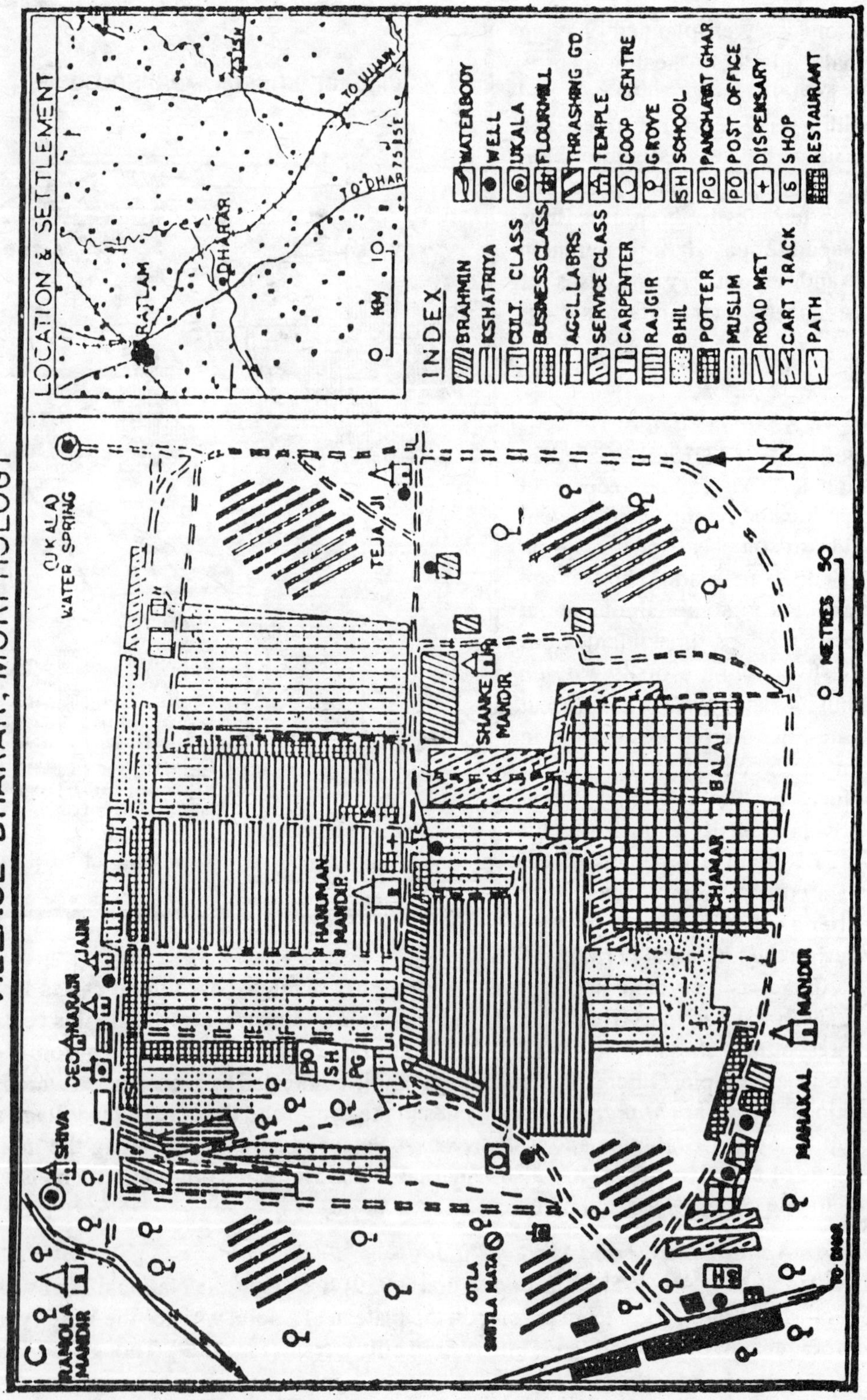

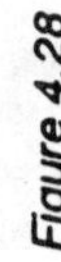

Figure 4.28

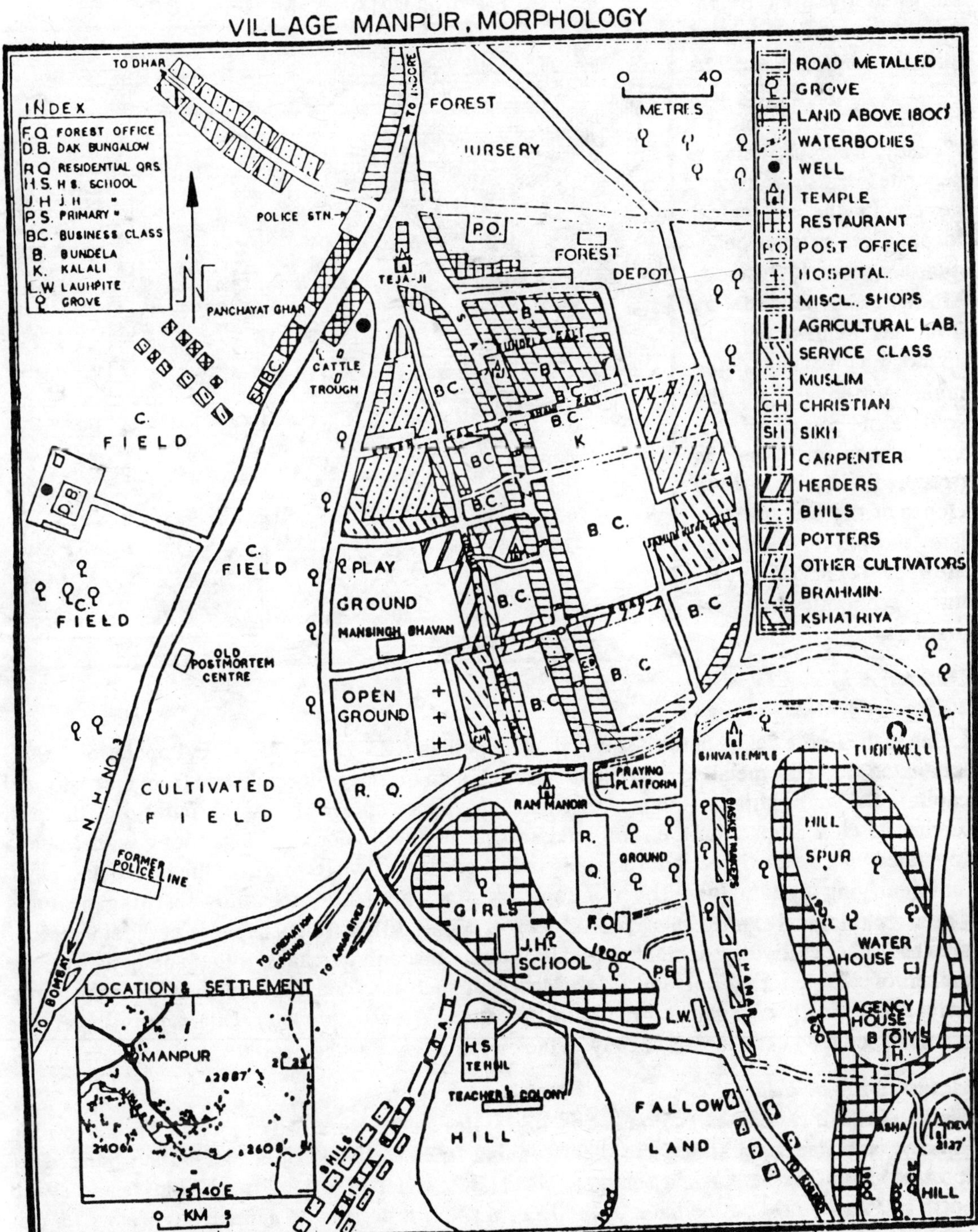

VILLAGE MANPUR, MORPHOLOGY
ROAD METALLED
GROVE
LAND ABOVE 1800'
WATERBODIES
WELL
TEMPLE
RESTAURANT
POST OFFICE
HOSPITAL
MISCL. SHOPS
AGRICULTURAL LAB.
SERVICE CLASS
MUSLIM
CHRISTIAN
SIKH
CARPENTER
HERDERS
BHILS
POTTERS
OTHER CULTIVATORS
BRAHMIN
KSHATRIYA
INDEX
F.O. FOREST OFFICE
D.B. DAK BUNGALOW
R.Q. RESIDENTIAL QRS.
H.S. H.S. SCHOOL
BC. BUSINESS CLASS
B. BUNDELA
K. KALALI
L.W. LAUHPITE
TO DHAR
FOREST
NURSERY
METRES
POLICE STN.
P.O.
FOREST DEPOT
TEJA-JI
PANCHAYAT GHAR
CATTLE TROUGH
FIELD
PLAY GROUND
MANSINGH BHAVAN
OLD POSTMORTEM CENTRE
OPEN GROUND
CULTIVATED FIELD
FORMER POLICE LINE
RAM MANDIR
PRAYING PLATFORM
SHIVA TEMPLE
TUBEWELL
HILL SPUR
GIRLS
J.H. SCHOOL
WATER HOUSE
AGENCY HOUSE
TO BOMBAY
LOCATION & SETTLEMENT
MANPUR
H.S.
TEACHER'S COLONY
HILL
FALLOW LAND
BHILS
75°40'E
KM

Figure 4.29

tablished by Man Singh, whose ruined 'Bhavan' still lies there, it got impetus during the British rule as a centre of the Agency, Manpur, being a separate British territory, governing the strategical location and as tehsil headquarters, recently shifted to Mhow. Surrounded by hills, the nearest being a spur of the great knot of the main Vindhyas, in the south-east corner of the map whose lower part is occupied by Agency House of the past, the village morphology reflects the impact of historico-culturo- economic transformations.

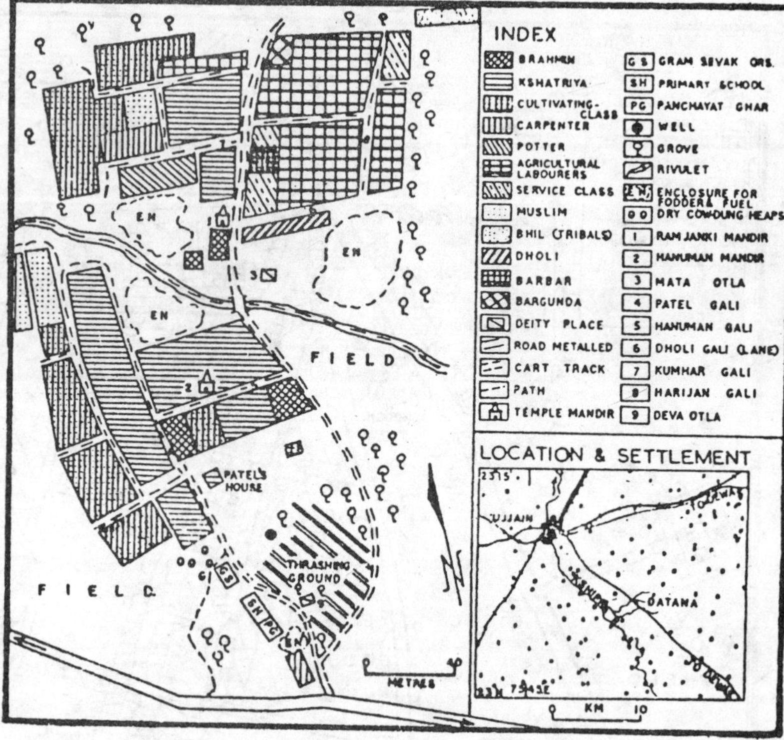

Figure 4.30

Datana: A Mixed Type Village of Malwa Proper

Lying in the fertile valley of the Kshipra river, the village (23°12'N—75°47'E, Population 1,097) is situated along the metalled road running from Ujjain to Dewas, 9 km distant from the historical capital of Avanti, Ujjain—the seat of Mahakal whence spread the Aryan culture of the past having its clear impact on the rural landscape. The dopple-dorfer village along with Matana separated by a *nala* originating from a big tank, appears to owe its origin to the feudal grant system signifying 'duttam' (given over) to some Jagirdar whose descent has now lost his genealogy. The morphological expressions of the settlement (Fig. 4.30) exhibit occupance of the site by Rajputs and other cultivators including Muslims either through purchase of the land or as revenue makers of later periods. The small *nala* bisects it into halves as does the *kachcha* road in the northern section. Mostly engaged in agricultural operations, a few employed in Ujjain, the villagers are not unaffected by cash- nexus society of the city or *shahar* as they call it.

Matkuli: A New Village

Matkuli (22°32'N—78°29'E, Population 1,803) lies on the crossroad of metalled roads joining Pipariya and Panchmarhi and the other running to Chhindwaa, on a plateau surrounded by forested hills of the Satpuras in Sohagpur tehsil (Hoshangabad), 23 km from Pipariya and 29 km north of Panchmarhi on the bank of the Denwa river. It derives its name from *Meth-Kuli* (inhabited by contractors and labours) engaged in forest clearing and road construction during the last century. Primarily occupied by Gond Thakurs, it was inhabited by other caste people on the

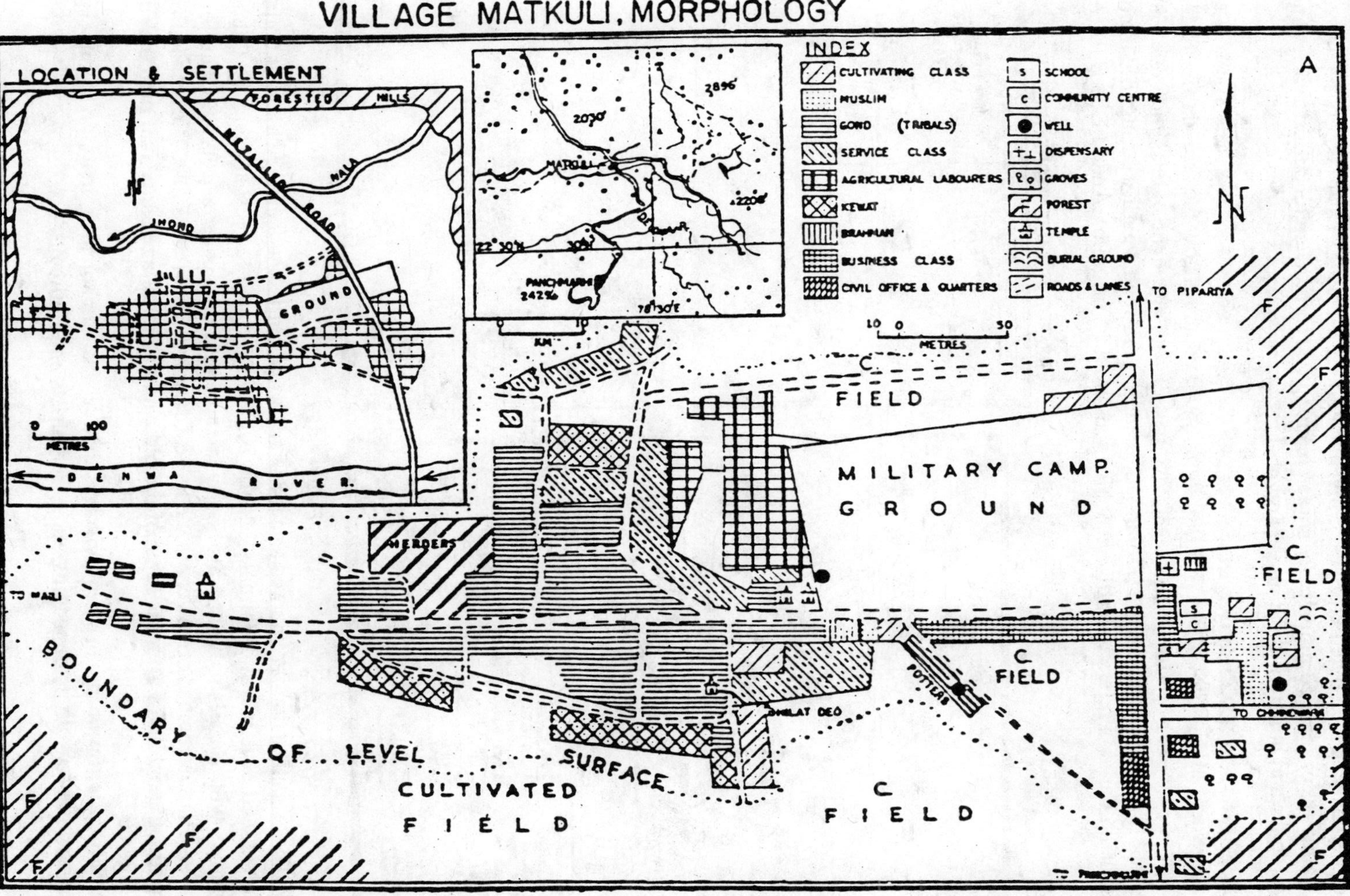
VILLAGE MATKULI, MORPHOLOGY
LOCATION & SETTLEMENT
FORESTED HILLS
METALLED ROAD
NALA
JHORD
GROUND
0 100 METRES
DENWA RIVER
2030'
2896'
MATKULI
2208'
22°30'N
PANCHMARHI
2425'
78°30'E
KM
INDEX
CULTIVATING CLASS
MUSLIM
GOND (TRIBALS)
SERVICE CLASS
AGRICULTURAL LABOURERS
KEWAT
BRAHMAN
BUSINESS CLASS
CIVIL OFFICE & QUARTERS
SCHOOL
COMMUNITY CENTRE
WELL
DISPENSARY
GROVES
FOREST
TEMPLE
BURIAL GROUND
ROADS & LANES
A
TO PIPARIYA
10 0 50
METRES
C
FIELD
MILITARY CAMP
GROUND
HERDERS
TO MALI
POTTERS
BHILAT DEO
TO CHHINDWARA
PANCHMARHI
BOUNDARY OF LEVEL SURFACE
CULTIVATED FIELD
F

Figure 4.31

basis of purchase of land by enterprises or revenue makers. As usual, caste sectors separated by lanes, pathways or some common place spread in elongated form. General outlook varies and so the size, space and height of the houses (Fig. 4.31).

Mandu: A Village of Political Origin

The village (22°20'N—75°25'E, Est. 1986, Pop. 2,808) occupies now the ruined fort of Mandu (2,270' or 667 metres), 36 km south of Dhar, on the southern scarp-bend of the Vindhyas. Mandu is a corrupt form of *Mandap Durga* (looking like canopy) or Mandavgarh, a stronghold from the earliest days. Farishta refers to traditions which tell about its origin by Anand Deo Bais (A.D.

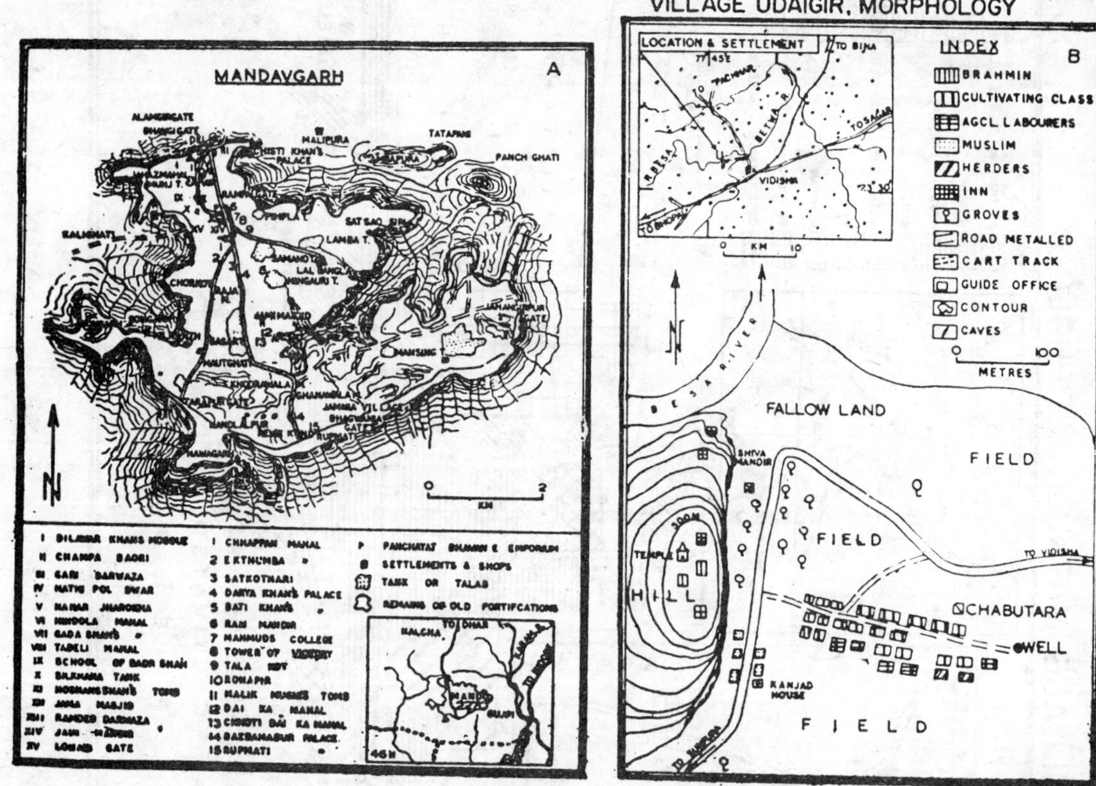

Figure 4.32

531-574) but it is true that it remained a scene of seize and battle between the chiefs of Gujarat and Malwa, and Muslims and Parmars. Mandu is closely related to Hoshangshah and almost synonymous with Baz Bahadur and his highly talented musician consort Rupmati. The forest around the village remained often very thick; its best days have, however gone. The archaeological department now looks after the ruins of the old capital and village panchayat runs the rural work (Fig. 4.32).

The village is now occupied by cultivators, shopkeepers, tongamen, agricultural labour class, stock raisers and few others depending upon the tourists and limited trade.

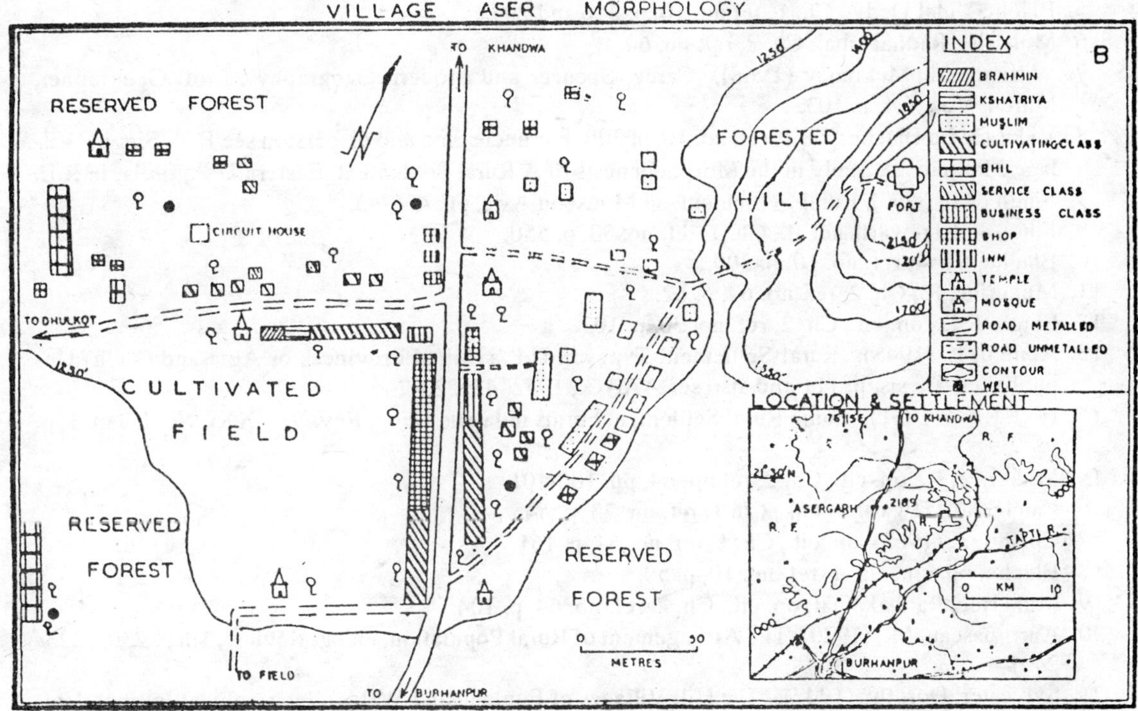

Figure 4.33

Aser: A Forest Village Reminding Past

Situated on the lower slopes of the famous Asergarh hills, occupied by ruined fort of the same name along the road running from Khandwa to Burhanpur, 48 km from the former and 18 km from the latter, in Burhanpur tahsil, the village is a typical forest village of mixed caste (Fig. 4.33).

Udaigir

It derives its name from the Udaigir caves having Jain and Hindu statues. It seems that the old village was demolished by bigot Muslims and the village flourished later on during the British rule. Inhabitants are mostly cultivators, stock raisers or herders and agricultural labourers. *Kachhi* is the dominating caste which is followed by *Gaderia* (Fig. 4.32).

References

1. Ahmad, E. (1965), 'Bihar: A Physical, Economic and Regional Geography, Ranchi University Press, p. 270.
2. Doxiadis, C.A. (1968), 'Ekistics, An Introduction to the Science of Settlements, New York University Press, p. 33.
3. Finch, V.C. et al., Ch. 1, ref. no. 33, p. 552.
4. Demangeon, A. (1925-26), Agricultural Systems and Schemes of Distribution of Population in Western Europe, The Geographical Teacher, Vol. 13, pp. 119-205.

5. Blache Vidal De La, Ch. 1, ref no. 10, p. 316 and 299.
6. Mukerjee Radhakamal, Ch. 2, ref. no. 64.
7. William, M. Mckinney (1968), 'Carey, Spencer and Modern Geography', Prof. Geographer, March, Vol. XX, p. 103.
8. Vidal De La Blache, Ch. 1. ref. no. 10, p. 300; For nucleation and dispersion see R.Y. Singh, 'Village Mahjuda: A Study in the Morphogenesis of A Rural Settlement, Eastern U.P., India, in R.L. Singh et al. (eds.), Rural Settlements in Monsoon Asia, pp. 436-43.
9. Finch and Trewartha et al., Ch. 1, ref. no. 33, p. 550.
10. Blache, Ch. 1, ref. no. 10, p. 300.
11. Mukerjee, R., Ch. 2, ref. no. 64, p. 62.
12. Singh, R.L., op. cit., Ch. 2, ref. no. 30, p. 103.
13. Ahmad, E. (1948), 'Rural Settlement Types in U.P. (United Provinces or Agra and Oudh) Unpublished Thesis, p. 111 and also see AAAG., 1952, 42, 223-246.
14. Hall, R.B., (1931), 'Some Rural Settlement Forms in Japan, Geog. Rev. Vol. XXI, No. 1, Jan. 1, p. 98.
15. Mukerjee, R., op. cit., Ch. 2, ref no. 64, pp. 100-101.
16. Finch and Trewartha et al., Ch. 1, ref. no. 33, p. 545.
17. Chisholm, (1962), op. cit., Ch. 1, ref. no. 64, p. 161.
18. Blache, op. cit., Ch. 1, ref. no. 10, p. 59.
19. Mukerjee, Radhakamal, op. cit., Ch. 2, ref. no. 64, p. 104.
20. Aurrousseau, M., (1920), The Arrangement of Rural Population, Geog. Review, 10, p. 230: (223-240).
21. Sylvester, Dorothy (1947), 'The Hill Villages of England and Wales, Geographical Journal, Vol. CX, p. 76.
22. Ahmed, E., (1948), Settlements in U.P., Agra and Oudh, op. cit., ref. no. 13, p. 133.
23. In the north of the Narmada river the India *Bigha* is of two types 'Kachcha' and Pukka. Originally it was based on a square each side of which is a certain number of paces or haths or (cubits) Vide Report of the Weights and Measure Committee (19/13- 14), Simla, p. 35. *Bigha* is sub-divided into *Biswa* and *Biswansi* (Dhur or Kattha). One *Bigha* = 20 *Biswa* and one *Biswa* = 20 *Biswansi* = one Lattha^2 (5½ haths now standardized at 8¼ feet). The Pukka or standard Bigha is 3025 square yards or 5/8 acre. *Bigha* in Malwa Region (Madhya Pradesh) varies from ¼ to 5/8 of an acre (0.101-0.253 hectares).
24. Mitchell, J.B., Ch. 1, ref. no. 52, p. 110.

5

Distributional Pattern of Rural Settlements

Introduction

In the beginning, we saw that rural settlement geography concerns with who build/inhabit what, where and how. It does emphasize the core of geography the variation always visualized through distribution of any phenomena. Here our focus is on distributional pattern of settlements. As already discussed, the occupance of rural landscape is the outcome of diverse physical, economic and historico-cultural phenomena interacting simultaneously, the rural settlements show variations in their distributional pattern, both even and uneven, and also in shapes and sizes in different part of the world. It is also remarkable that study of distribution is multi-level and multi-scale concept. it is the multi-scale analysis which gives clear view of the distribution on a small scale through large scale maps. The interactions with physico-cultural forces become obvious at local level large scale maps, e.g., between settlements and in relation, to various sites. Distribution reflects, how settlers select some sites, avoid others, spread and saturate a region in various stages or occupation and the time gap, in what fashion, where.

The approaches involved in studying distribution are simply: (a) analysis of size, form and function, (b) analysis of density, spacing and dispersion, showing relation with settlement processes and giving details of 'where' at all levels. We discussed about form in previous chapter. Now it is better to emphasize size, density and spacing which reveal distributional aspects clearly, i.e., areal variations showing varied type of concentration and dispersion in degrees. With a view to understanding and approving 'the distribution is the key to process' as stated by Sauer, we take examples from the Malwa Region (India).

Size and Density of Rural Settlements

The size speaks about the nature of soil, topography, socio-economic background of the culture group of a particular area. The factors responsible for compact, hamleted and other type of settlements have already been discussed in chapter four. Here the picture of villages categorized according to population provides general view of the Region. The census categories are: (i) Small villages having population (below 500), (ii) Medium villages (500-999), (iii) Large villages (1000-1999), (iv) Big villages (2000-4999) and (v) Very big villages (5000 and above) (Fig. 5.1A). With a few exceptions, all the districts show tendency towards growth in size, specially, of medium and large categories. Big villages have shown remarkable growth in Mandsaur, Ratlam, Indore, Nimar and Shajapur. Very big villages have come up in Indore and West and East Nimar. This reflects a change in rural structure, mainly due to industrial growth and development of transport facilities in recent times. A comparative percentage distribution of villages and population in each size group as shown in (Fig. 5.2A) and diagram showing classification of vil-

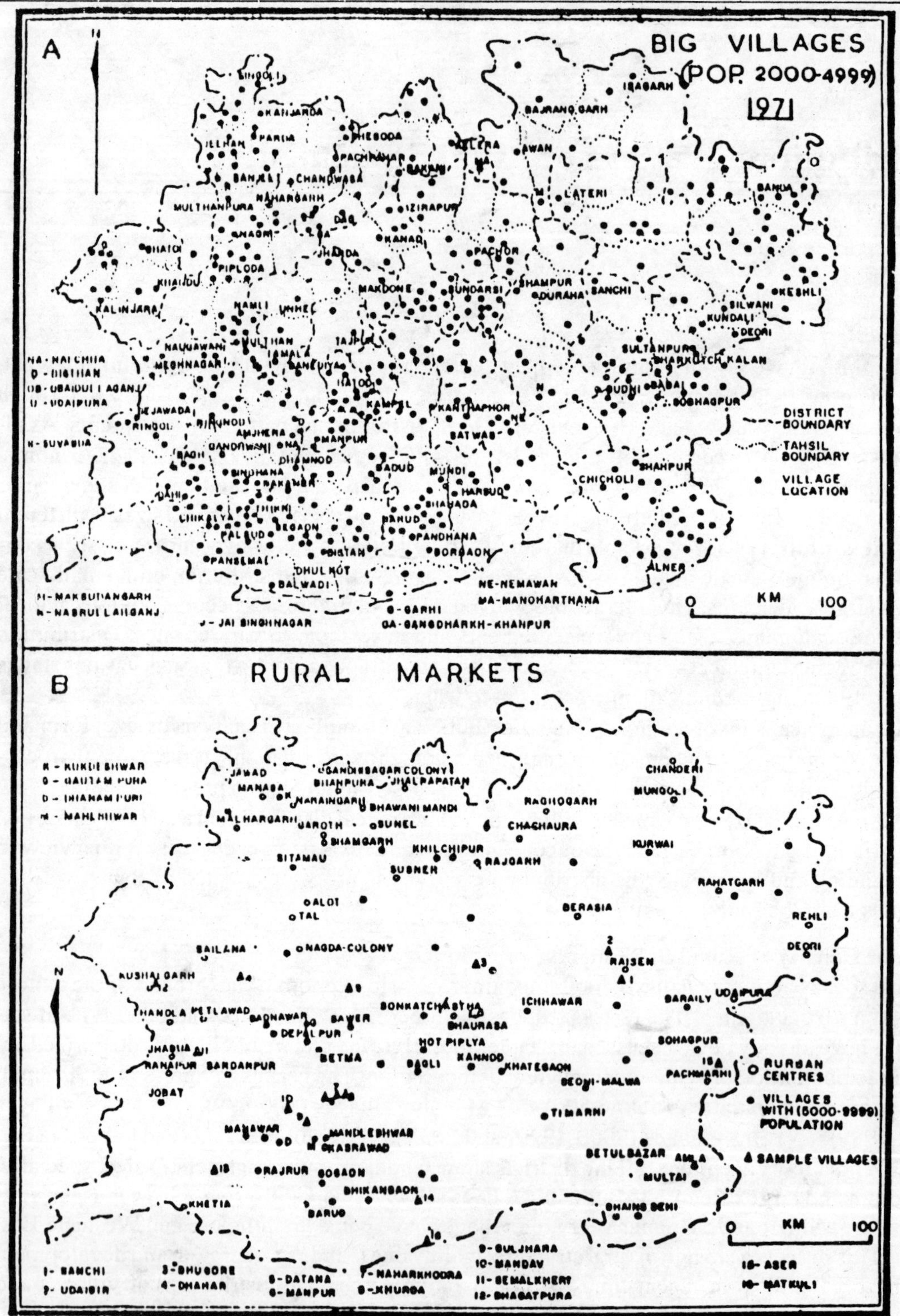
A
BIG VILLAGES
(POP. 2000-4999)
1971
DISTRICT BOUNDARY
TAHSIL BOUNDARY
VILLAGE LOCATION
0 KM 100
B
RURAL MARKETS
RURBAN CENTRES
VILLAGES WITH (5000-9999) POPULATION
SAMPLE VILLAGES
0 KM 100

Figure 5.1

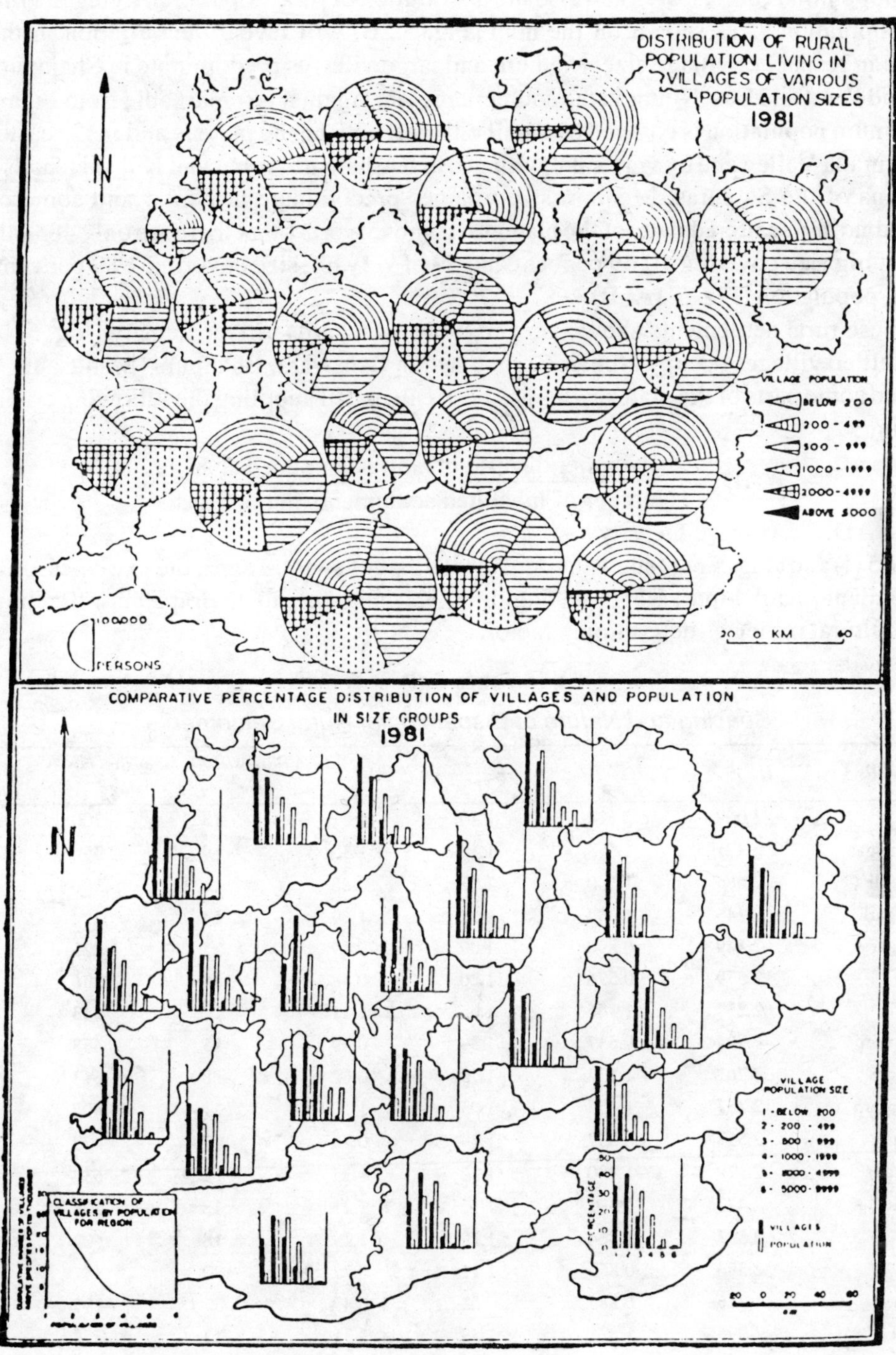
DISTRIBUTION OF RURAL
POPULATION LIVING IN
VILLAGES OF VARIOUS
POPULATION SIZES
1981
VILLAGE POPULATION
BELOW 200
200 - 499
500 - 999
1000 - 1999
2000 - 4999
ABOVE 5000
100000
PERSONS
20 0 KM 40
COMPARATIVE PERCENTAGE DISTRIBUTION OF VILLAGES AND POPULATION
IN SIZE GROUPS
1981
VILLAGE
POPULATION SIZE
1 - BELOW 200
2 - 200 - 499
3 - 500 - 999
4 - 1000 - 1999
5 - 2000 - 4999
6 - 5000 - 9999
VILLAGES
POPULATION
PERCENTAGE
CLASSIFICATION OF
VILLAGES BY POPULATION
FOR REGION
20 0 20 40 60

Figure 5.2

lages by population for total area and also the distribution of rural population living in villages of various population sizes shown on the map (Fig. 5.2B) will reveal the variation in the rural landscape in respect of village size. Medium and large villages predominate in Shajapur on the plateau and West and East Nimar in the southern region. Again it is remarkable from Figure 5.3A that maximum population is covered by small villages, both on the plateau and in the eastern part of the Narmada Valley and by very small villages in Kushalgarh, Jobat and Kukshi tehsils and on the margins of the Satpuras. Medium size villages predominate in Nimar and some parts of Hoshangabad and scattered parts of the plateau. It is note-worthy that there are only 485 inhabited villages of big size covering 10.69 per cent and 39 of very big size covering 1.87 per cent of the total rural population (Fig. 5.1A, B).

All these rural settlements show also variations as regards village density (Fig. 5.4A), the densely settled villages occupy Nimar, Garhi tahsil in Banswara, Bhanpura (Mandsaur), Multai (Betul) and some parts of the plateau; this has been calculated adopting the following co-efficient of grouping:

$$AD = \frac{\text{Number of rural inhabitants in the Tahsil}}{\text{Number of inhabited settlements in the Tahsil}}$$

When AD = Average Density

Table 5 (i) and (Fig. 5.5A) show the density of villages per 100 Km^2; the extremes, obviously seen in Sailana, Khilchipur, Rajgarh, Bagidora, Kushalgarh and Jhalrapatan, reflecting upon physico-cultural milieu as determining factor.

Table 5 (i)

Spacing and Nature of Dispersion of Rural Settlements

S.No.	Tehsils	Hs	rO	rE	RN	Villages/ 100 km^2	Density/ village	A/N (in km^2)
1.	Guna	3.009	1..694	1.40	1.21	15	300	7.8
2.	Ashoknagar	2.471	1.553	1.15	1.35	19	396	5.4
3.	Mungaoli	2.686	1.100	1.25	0.88	16	300	6.5
4.	Raghogarh	2.245	1.244	1.05	1.19	24	292	4.4
5.	Chachaura	2.149	0.890	1.00	0.89	25	325	4.0
6.	Jawad	2.579	0.576	1.20	0.48	18	336	5.5
7.	Nimach	2.257	1.166	1.05	1.11	22	443	4.5
8.	Manasa	2.794	0.637	1.30	0.49	15	458	6.9
9.	Bhanpura	3.761	1.172	1.75	0.62	8	613	4.5
10.	Malhargarh	2.257	1.155	1.05	1.10	21	498	4.5
11.	Garoth	2.557	0.857	1.19	0.72	17	473	5.7
12.	Mandsaur	2.579	1.380	1.20	1.15	17	637	5.9
13.	Sitamau	2.471	1.391	1.15	1.21	18	508	5.5
14.	Jaora	2.557	1.464	1.19	1.23	18	602	5.7
15.	Alot	2.396	0.855	1.11	0.77	20	451	5.0
16.	Sailana	1.726	0.385	0.82	0.47	37	197	2.7
17.	Ratlam	2.998	1.821	1.39	1.31	13	754	7.8
18.	Khachrod	2.557	1.297	1.19	1.09	17	541	5.7
19.	Mahidpur	2.418	1.355	1.12	1.21	19	447	5.1

Contd...

20.	Tarana	2.396	0.910	1.11	0.82	20	517	5.0
21.	Badnagar	2.729	1.803	1.27	1.42	15	567	6.5
22.	Ujjain	2.396	1.366	1.12	1.22	20	476	5.0
23.	Thandla	2.321	0.778	1.08	0.72	21	510	4.7
24.	Petlawad	2.224	0.927	1.03	0.90	22	376	4.3
25.	Jhabua	2.171	0.697	1.01	0.69	28	378	4.1
26.	Jobat	2.493	0.789	1.16	0.68	18	583	5.4
27.	Alirajpur	2.751	0.448	1.28	0.35	15	463	6.6
28.	Badnawar	2.729	1.410	1.27	1.11	15	555	6.5
29.	Sardarpur	2.149	1.210	1.00	1.21	15	536	6.8
30.	Dhar	2.278	0.943	1.06	0.89	23	333	4.5
31.	Kukshi	2.772	0.748	1.29	0.58	15	700	6.7
32.	Manawar	2.418	0.930	1.12	0.83	20	546	5.1
33.	Depalpur	2.579	1.620	1.20	1.35	17	569	5.8
34.	Sawer	2.450	1.607	1.14	1.14	19	551	5.2
35.	Indore	2.676	1.476	1.24	1.19	17	790	6.2
36.	Mhow	2.353	0.861	0.11	0.08	22	586	4.8
37.	Sonkatch	2.514	0.807	1.17	0.69	18	465	5.5
38.	Dewas	2.192	1.257	1.02	1.11	23	471	4.2
39.	Bagli	3.020	1.288	1.40	0.92	12	440	7.9
40.	Konnod	3.106	1.386	1.44	0.95	12	510	8.4
41.	Khategaon	2.772	1.561	1.29	1.21	15	418	6.7
42.	Barwaha	2.450	1.493	1.14	1.31	20	502	5.2
43.	Maheshwar	2.450	1.653	1.14	1.45	20	518	5.2
44.	Barwani	2.149	1.010	1.00	1.01	27	613	4.0
45.	Rajpur	2.815	1.349	1.21	1.03	15	788	6.9
46.	Kasrawad	2.579	1.584	1.20	1.32	17	512	5.8
47.	Sendhawa	2.471	0.954	1.15	0.83	20	672	5.3
48.	Khargone	2.600	1.101	1.21	0.91	16	737	5.9
49.	Bhikangaon	2.643	1.353	1.23	1.10	16	588	6.1
50.	Khandwa	2.697	1.137	1.25	0.91	16	643	6.3
51.	Harsud	2.471	1.092	1.15	0.95	19	487	5.3
52.	Burhanpur	2.149	0.810	1.00	0.81	18	728	4.0
53.	Susner	2.622	1.275	1.22	1.03	16	526	6.0
54.	Agar	2.418	1.355	1.12	1.21	19	534	5.1
55.	Shajapur	2.471	1.507	1.15	1.31	19	598	5.3
56.	Shujalpur	2.751	1.766	1.28	1.38	15	616	6.6
57.	Khilchipur	1.891	1.624	1.38	1.19	32	309	3.1
58.	Rajgarh	1.827	1.147	1.35	0.85	35	334	2.9
59.	Biora	2.171	1.364	1.01	1.35	24	365	4.1
60.	Sarangpur	2.321	1.534	1.08	1.42	21	506	4.7
61.	Narsingarh	2.246	1.258	1.04	1.21	23	445	4.4
62.	Lateri	2.600	1.331	1.21	1.10	18	311	5.9
63.	Sironj	2.332	1.319	1.09	1.21	21	318	4.8
64.	Kurwai	2.117	1.761	1.48	1.19	22	378	3.9

Contd...

65. Basoda	2.396	1.498	1.11	1.35	20	407	5.0
66. Vidisha	2.321	1.117	1.08	1.09	21	401	4.7
67. Berasia	2.396	1.343	1.11	1.21	20	325	5.0
68. Sehore	2.514	1.498	1.17	1.28	18	424	5.5
69. Huzur	2.418	1.366	1.12	1.22	21	334	5.1
70. Ashta	2.450	1.493	1.14	1.31	19	482	5.2
71. Ichhawar	3.030	1.424	1.41	1.01	19	402	8.0
72. Nasrullaganj	3.073	1.301	1.43	0.91	12	475	8.2
73. Budni	3.181	1.406	1.48	0.95	14	454	8.8
74. Raisen	2.676	1.426	1.44	0.99	17	346	6.2
75. Ghairatgang	2.536	1.192	1.18	1.01	21	335	5.6
76. Begamganj	2.996	0.877	1.07	0.82	22	286	4.6
77. Goharganj	2.794	1.066	1.30	1.09	15	362	6.8
78. Bareli	2.643	1.513	1.23	1.23	17	481	6.1
79. Silwani	2.514	1.392	1.17	1.19	23	266	5.5
80. Udaipura	3.009	1.442	1.40	1.03	12	507	5.2
81. Harda	2.493	1.299	1.16	1.12	19	417	5.4
82. Seoni-Malwa	2.514	1.111	1.17	1.95	18	458	5.5
83. Hoshangabad	2.514	1.158	1.17	0.99	17	590	4.9
84. Sohagpur	2.375	1.221	1.10	1.11	21	377	4.9
85. Bhainsdehi	2.643	0.590	1.23	0.48	16	466	6.1
86. Betul	2.321	0.886	1.08	0.82	22	532	4.7
87. Multai	2.662	0.598	1.22	0.49	17	593	6.0
88. Khurai	2.224	1.051	1.03	1.02	24	426	4.3
89. Banda	2.375	1.935	1.10	0.85	20	503	4.9
90. Sagar	2.375	1.023	1.10	0.93	20	497	4.9
91. Rehli	2.149	0.690	1.00	0.69	25	357	4.0
92. Pratapgarh	2.280	1.092	1.06	1.03	22	313	4.8
93. Ghatol	2.220	0.474	1.03	0.46	23	435	6.9
94. Garhi	2.220	0.639	1.03	0.62	23	702	4.3
95. Banswara	2.010	0.958	1.43	0.67	29	394	3.6
96. Bagidora	1.950	1.068	1.41	0.72	30	499	3.3
97. Kushalgarh	1.750	3.904	1.31	0.69	38	301	2.6
98. Khanpur	2.420	1.400	1.12	1.25	20	473	4.9
99. Jhalrapatan	1.950	1.847	1.41	1.31	30	320	4.1
100. Aklera	2.010	1.444	1.43	1.01	29	335	3.2
101. Pachpahar	2.480	0.977	1.15	0.85	19	477	5.3
102. Pirawa	2.400	1.021	1.11	0.92	20	437	5.2
103. Gangdhar	2.420	1.400	1.12	1.25	20	448	4.3
104. Akhalkuwa	2.751	0.448	1.28	0.35	15	430	3.8
105. Dhulia	0.471	0.954	1.15	0.83	20	355	3.8

Note: For explanation of the symbols see text, i.e., Hs = $1.0746\sqrt{A/N}$ etc. Tehsils of Jhalawar (Bakani, Manoharthana and Dag) and Achnera in Chittorgarh have been merged with other Tehsils; Maharashtra in parts has been treated here in two names, i.e., Akhalkuwa and Dhulia.

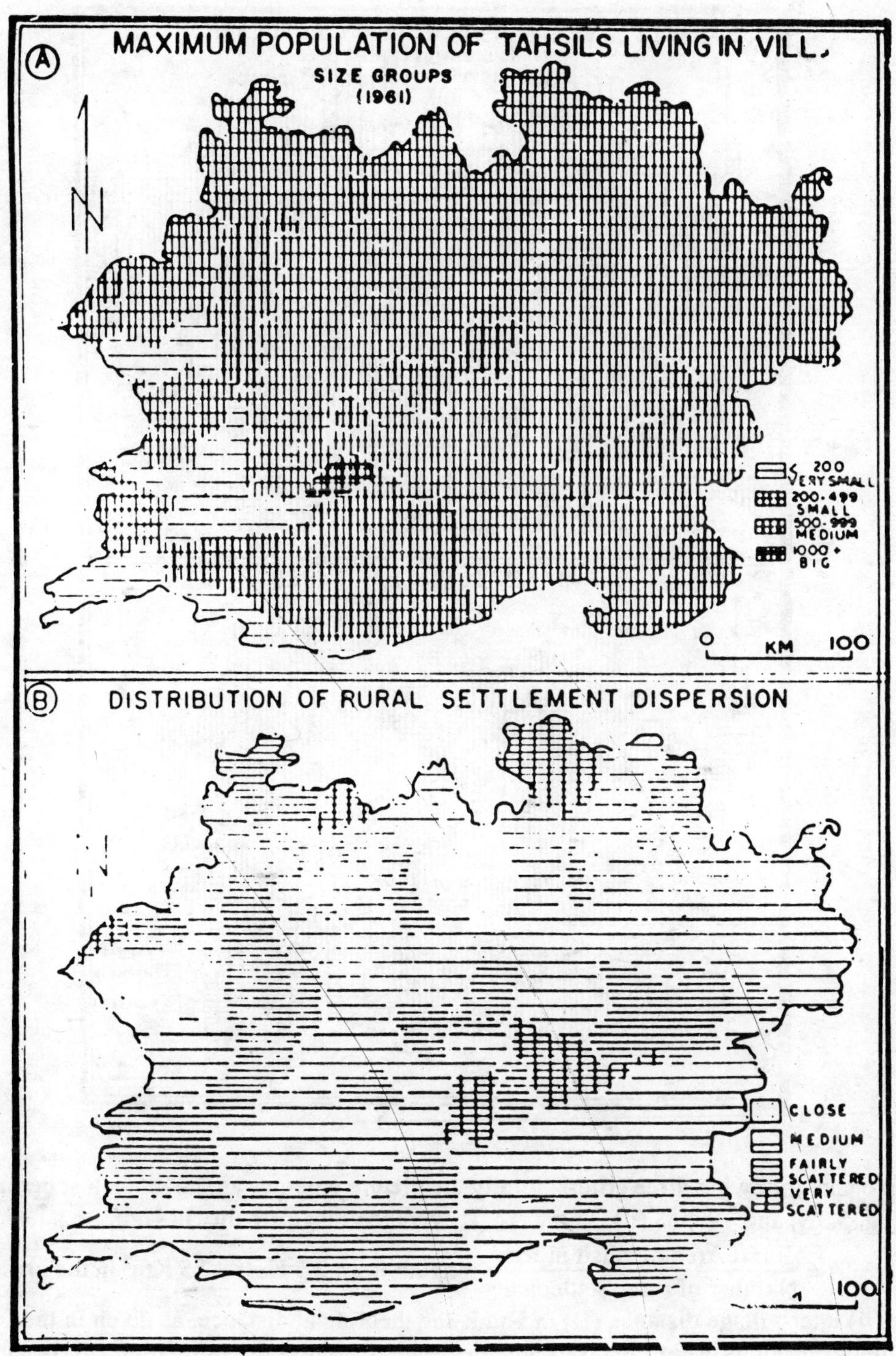
Ⓐ MAXIMUM POPULATION OF TAHSILS LIVING IN VILL.
SIZE GROUPS
(1961)
N
< 200
VERY SMALL
200-499
SMALL
500-999
MEDIUM
1000 +
BIG
0 KM 100
Ⓑ DISTRIBUTION OF RURAL SETTLEMENT DISPERSION
CLOSE
MEDIUM
FAIRLY
SCATTERED
VERY
SCATTERED
100

Figure 5.3

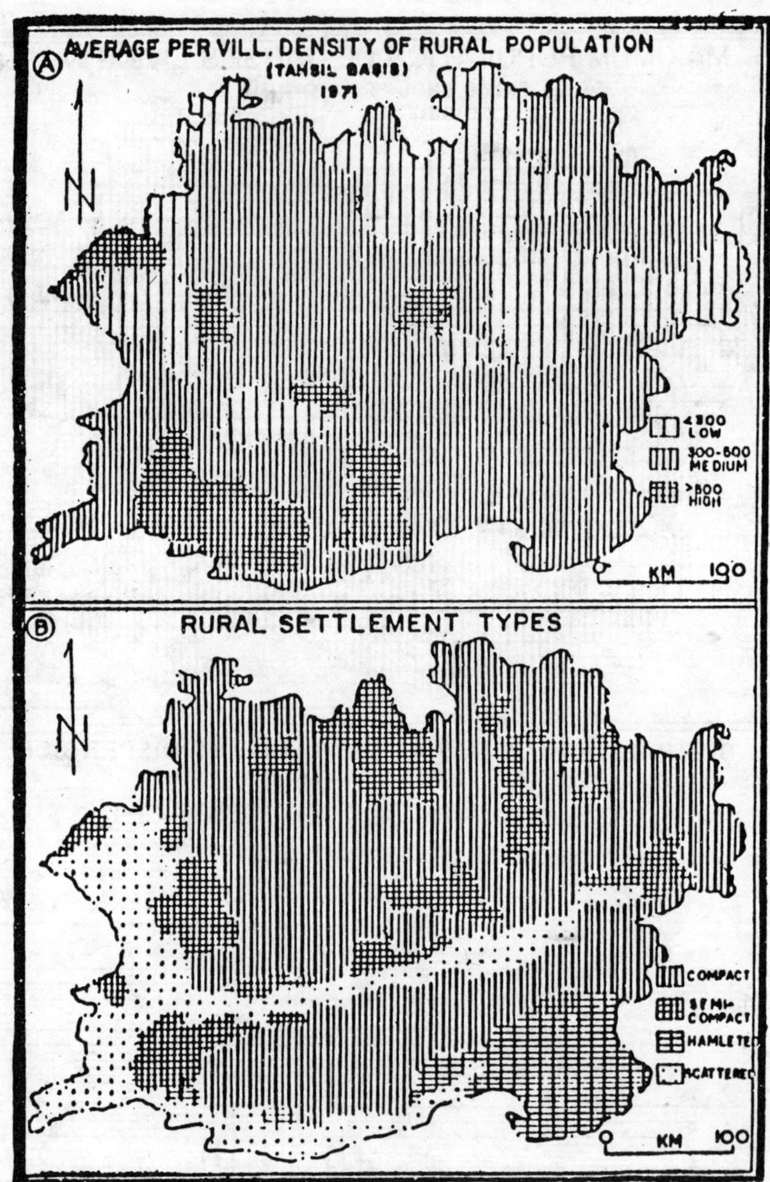

Figure 5.4

If we take following three criteria jointly the picture emerges as shown on a superimposed map (Fig. 5.3B) and Table 5 (ii). These are (i) average village areality in Km^2, i.e.,

$$\text{Areality} = A = \frac{\text{Rural Area of tahsil in Km}^2}{\text{Number of rural Settlements}}$$

ranging from 2.5 Km^2-12.5 Km^2 in the present example; (ii) inter-village distance (D) in Km is the theoretical distance, as given in the formula below, between points in hexagonal arrangement and 'd' is the density of settlements per unit area in Km^2, A = area and N = number of settlements.

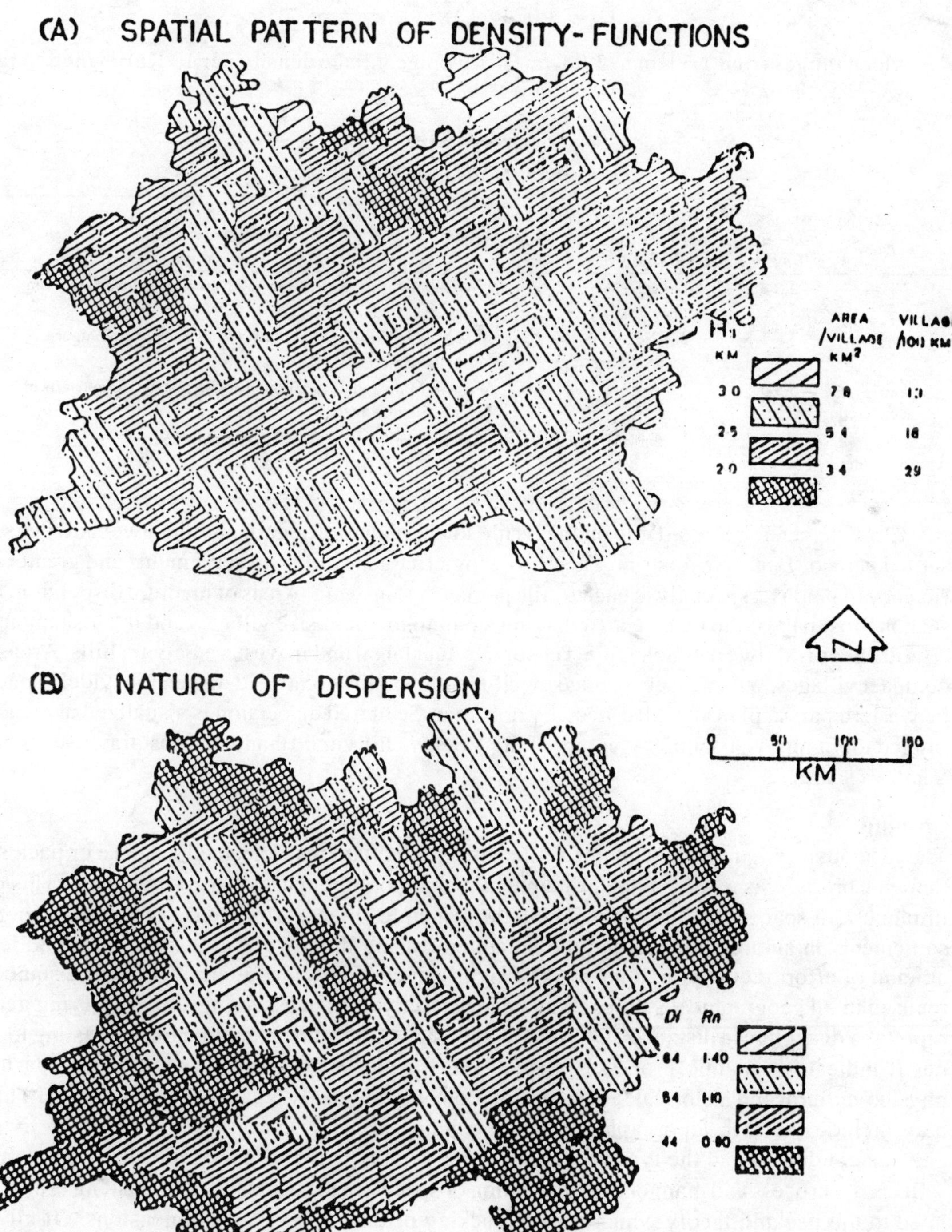
(A) SPATIAL PATTERN OF DENSITY-FUNCTIONS
H_1
KM
AREA /VILLAGE KM²
VILLAGE /100 KM²
3 0
7 8
13
2 5
5 4
18
2 0
3 4
29
N
(B) NATURE OF DISPERSION
0
50
100
150
KM
DI
Rn
84
1·40
64
1·10
44
0·80

Figure 5.5

$$D = 1.0746\sqrt{A/N} \text{ or } \frac{1.0746}{\sqrt{d}}$$

which ranges from 1.5 Km to 3.5 Km; (iii) average village density per 10 Km^2, where it ranges from <1.5 to >2.5.

Table 5 (ii)

Dispersion of Village Distribution

Degree of Dispersion	*Average Village areality (in Km^2)*	*Average Village Density in 10 Km^2*	*Inter Village Distance in Km*	*Main Areas*
1. Close	2.5-3.5	Above 2.5	1.5-2.0	Lower plain of the Kali Sindh and Newaj interfluves and Banswara, Sailana Tehsils.
2. Medium	3.5-5.5	2.0-2.5	2.0-2.5	Mostly eastern and central Malwa Plateau Western Satpura, Hoshangabad.
3. Fairly Scattered	5.5-7.5	1.5-2.0	2.5-3.0	Western Malwa Plateau, Some parts on plateau, Some parts of Vindhyas and Nimar.
4. Scattered or (widely spaced)	Above 7.5	Less than 1.5	Above 3.0	Hilly portion, on Vindhya and Bhanpura Tehsil

Close dispersion is available on the fertile lower plain of Rajgarh and Jhalawar and densely settled parts of Banswara district. This shows high frequency of rural settlements and greater efficiency in landuse, specially in each fertile pocket in Banswara. Areas of medium dispersion, are seen in most part of the plateau area, having small to medium size villages and in Hoshangabad (Harda, Seoni-Malwa and Sohagpur Tehsils), Betual tahsil and in western Satpura hills. Areas of compact villages, with densely packed dwellings show fairly scattered dispersion widely spaced on western part of plateau and, especially in Nimar. Scattered dispersion is visualized in areas of rugged topography, a common feature of the Vindhya hills and Bhanpura area, traversed by the Vindhya scarp.

Spacing

The idea of spacing must occupy the settlers in a particular area. The need to space or pack settlements properly is related to the principle of making optimum use of space available. This optimum use of space is also connected with the principle of least effort[1], viz., the best spacing of settlements in an area implies that the inhabitants using them will, on the whole, spend least amount of effort required in doing so. The significance of spacing in terms of linear distance is realised in all geographical studies. Watson is perfectly right in assuming and identifying geography as a discipline in distance[2]. Obviously, spacing is not a static phenomenon as existing today but it indicates dynamic processes responsible for present spacing of settlements. Various physico-cultural and historical factors in isolation or combinedly create a rural landscape. These may include the soil, topography drainage conditions, land tenure system, mode of living, defence conditions and the type of settling group with a particular level of technology. It also reflects the process and manner of organisation of space in a particular region. Spacing is also related to the packing theory which studies packing of things in various dimensions. Of all the polygons, which cover a surface without overlapping, hexagon is the most compact. It approaches most closely the circle, the most compact of all figures, on a two-dimensional surface and also facilitates best nesting.

The theoretical basis of transforming the density of settlements into spacing is provided by an ultimate development of serial hexagons. Supposing the hexagonal arrangement of settlements, the distance from a settlement to any one of the six other settlements surrounding it is $D = \frac{1.0746}{\sqrt{d}}$, where D is theoretical distance between points in hexagonal arrangement and 'd' is the density of settlements per unit area (Km^2)[3].

The computation of density functions as shown in Fig. 5.5A for 105 tehsils in Malwa Region reveals the following salient features of the gross pattern of spacing:

(i) Moderate spacing (≤ 2.00 Km): The value of spacing ranges between 1.75 Km (Kushalgarh) to 1.95 (Jhalrapatan, Bagidora) covering Khilchipur (1.89) and Rajgarh (1.83) in the north. It covers only 0.44% of the total area. This represents the tribal area in the west having scattered settlements and semi-compact structures in the north. The per village population pressure varies from 197 (Sailana) to 388 (Bagidora) and per village area is 3.4 Km^2. Number of villages per 100 Km^2 ranges between 30 in Bagidora to 37 in Kushalgarh.

(ii) Moderately High Spacing (2.00-2.5 Km): The value of spacing under this category ranges from 2.01 (Aklera, Banswara) to 2.53 (Ghairatganj). Major area (57.12%) comes under this group. Number of villages per 100 Km^2 varies from 18-29 and per village population ranges between 313 (Pratapgarh) to 702 (Garhi). Per village area varies from 3.4-5.4 Km^2.

(iii) High Spacing (2.3-3.00 Km): This spacing ranges between 2.51 (Sehore) to 2.79 (Kukshi). It covers 35.04% of the total area and inhabits 13-18 villages per 100 Km^2. Per village population varies from 311-790 while per village area ranges between 5.4 Km^2-7.8 Km^2.

(iv) Very High Spacing (>3.00 Km): The value of spacing ranges between 3.00 (Bagli) to 3.7 (Bhanpura). It covers 7.4% of the area. Number of villages per 100 Km^2 ranges between 8-13 and per village area is >7.8 Km^2.

The analysis shows that spacing and size do not reveal a direct correlation rather they appear to be inversely correlated in some parts. The failure of the application of the spacing and size relationship can perhaps be explained, to some extent, by taking into consideration rural density which implies the utilization of potentialities of the resources of the area and other historico-political lineaments influencing the pattern of evolution of the human occupance of the region, and the settlements as such. It leads to a valid generalization to the effect that both rural density and size of villages separately, are inversely correlated with the spacing of the villages. The most parts of Banswara district and southern part of Pratapgarh tahsil present a typical area of low and very low values. In this *bagar* area isolated hillocks and large number of small valleys have acted as repulsive and attractive tracts respectively with reference to human occupance. The high concentration of population lineating along the valleys, where fertile strips of land are available, and which have protection from invasion and battles creating turmoil in the area, resulted in the establishment of small and closely spaced settlements. The valley lineation of settlements has a striking association with low and very low values of spacing. The fact is dramatically revealed in the tahsil of Kushalgarh which has a very low value of spacing. In this area the rural density is moderate to high and the size of rural settlements is moderate to small.

Similarly, Aklera and Jhalrapatan tehsils in Jhalawar district and Khilchipur and Rajgarh (Rajgarh) form another small cluster of low and very low values of spacing. Characteristics of this tract are the small scattered villages lineated along the affluents of the Parbati, Parwan and Kali Sindh. These spread over the physiographic unit locally termed *Pathar* (stony) or *Upermal* (higher plateau) in which population is concentrated on the deep black soil tracts in the river valleys. Rural settlement density here is only medium.

The study indicates that the areas having close spacing are favourable for establishment of infrastructures, cheaper administration, ease in development of facilities according to available threshold of population in the Plateau and Narmada valley region with local variations. The hilly parts, with moderate spacing but scattered settlements, pose problems for provision of socio-economic services i.e. road, water supply, electric supply, institution and public health facilities etc.

Dispersion

Many patterns in human geography can be viewed as sets of points (settlements). These can be measured and their dispersion[4] in relation to random spacing will show degree of regularity. The measurement involves a form of nearest neighbour analysis[5]. As sample study let us see the cases of Malwa Region/Chiraigaon Block to measure the degree of dispersion. It is assumed that points (settlements) are distributed randomly in accordance with a poisson probability function, where it is supposed that any point has the same chance as any other point of occurring at a particular place (area), and any place has the same chance of receiving a point as any other place, and the location of each point has not been influenced by that of other points. By definition, "complete randomness is the midpoint of the continuum of spatial patterns extending from complete clustering to complete uniformity"[6] (Fig. 5.6). The formula for computing randomness (RN) is: $RN = {}^{ro}/_{rE}$, where ro is the observed mean of nearest inter village straight line distance, rE the expected distance $= {}^{0.5}/\sqrt{d}$, where d = village density; thus, $RN = 2\,ro\sqrt{d}$. This RN value is used as a measure of the degree to which observed distribution approaches or deviates from random expectation. The value of this statistic ranges from 0.0 (complete concentration) through 1.0 (random) to 2.1491 under conditions of maximum spacing. Distributed in hexagonal pattern each individual point or settlement (except those at the periphery of the distribution) will be equidistant from six other individual settlements; also the mean distance to nearest neighbour will be maximized and will have the value $\frac{1.0746}{\sqrt{d}}$. The formula for the mean distance to nearest neighbour expected in a randomly dispersed population of specified density seems first, to have been derived by Hertz[7].

The significance of the departure of ro from rE can be correlated with variance (V) for further testing which is computed by a mathematical expression:[8]

$V = \frac{(4-\pi)}{4d\pi} = \frac{0.0683086}{d}$ in which if the rE value is larger than the V, the distribution is termed regular; if the V is larger than the rE, it is termed clustered; if V = rE, it is termed as random, i.e., the variance-mean ratio is one. The significance test of departure can be made through the statistic of standard variate of normal curve[9] also, the formula being:

$$C = \frac{ro - rE}{\partial rE}$$

Where C is the standard variate of the normal curve, and ∂rE is the standard error of the mean distance to nearest neighbour in a randomly distributed population of the same density as that of

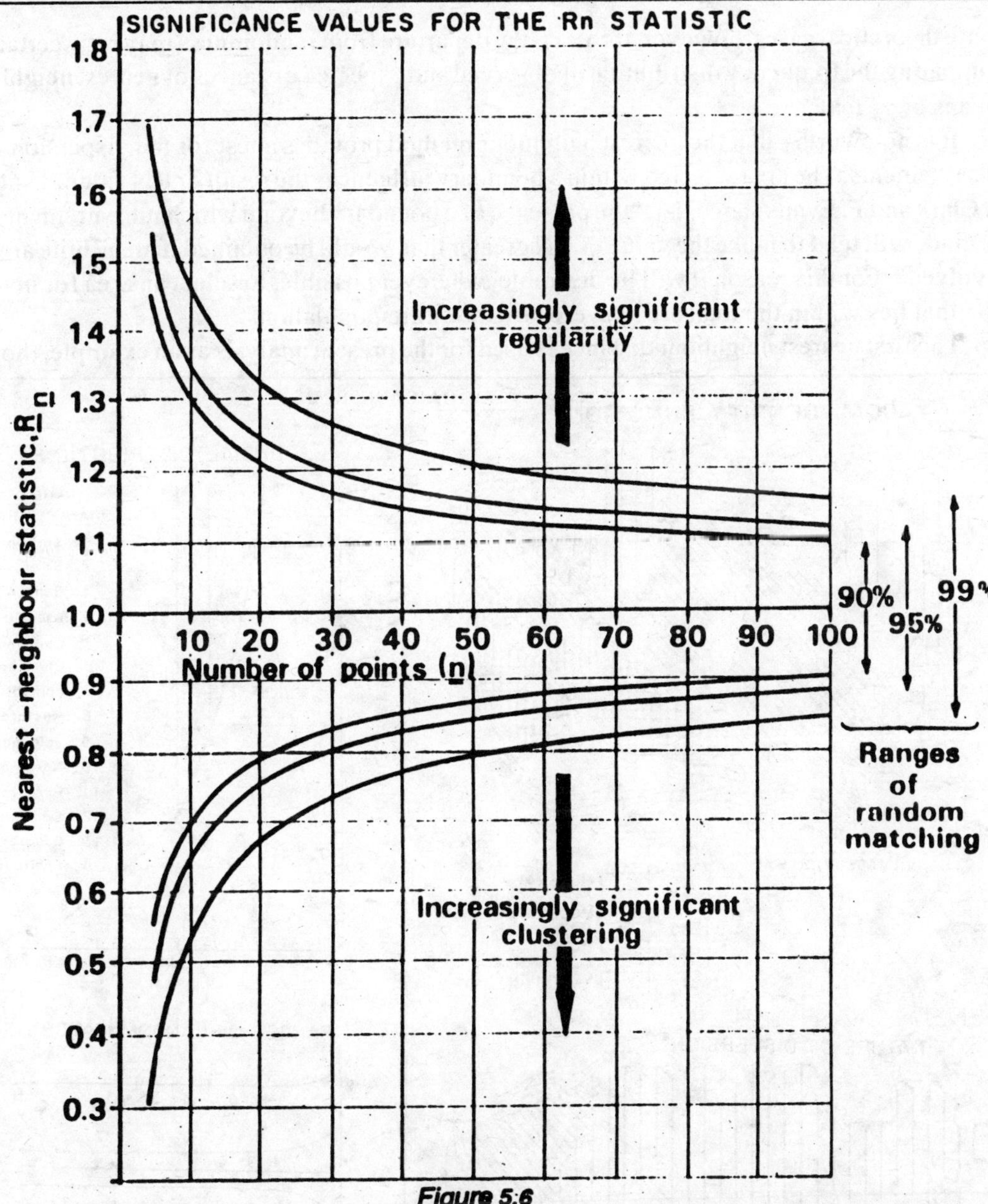

Figure 5:6

the observed population. The greater the difference between the observed and expected average distances, the larger the value of C, i.e., the greater the probability that the discerned pattern is non-random (Fig. 5.6). This $rE = \frac{0.26136}{\sqrt{nd}}$ where n is the number of total villages in the areal unit and δ = density of villages per Km^2. The upper and lower ranges of random matching at the 95% probability level will be computed with the help of rE, i.e., equal to $(\frac{2\partial rE \pm r_E}{r_E})$. The C values 1.96 and 2.58 represent respectively the 5% and the 1% levels of significance for a two tailed test. In

some theoretical cases, however, if ro = rE the departure from randomness may be ascertained by comparing the frequency distribution of observed and expected distances of nearest neighbour by means of χ^2 text.

It is noteworthy that the nearest neighbour method provides a test for the dispersion pattern of settlements. The area selected within a boundary influences the result or RN value. That is way P. Clark and F. Evans stated that "the presence of a boundary beyond which measurement cannot be made will tend to make the value of RN greater than would be obtained if an infinite area were involved". For this reason it will be desirable, wherever possible, to select an area for investigation that lies within the total area covered by the entire population.

The first nearest neighbour distance is used for the present analysis as an example, though its

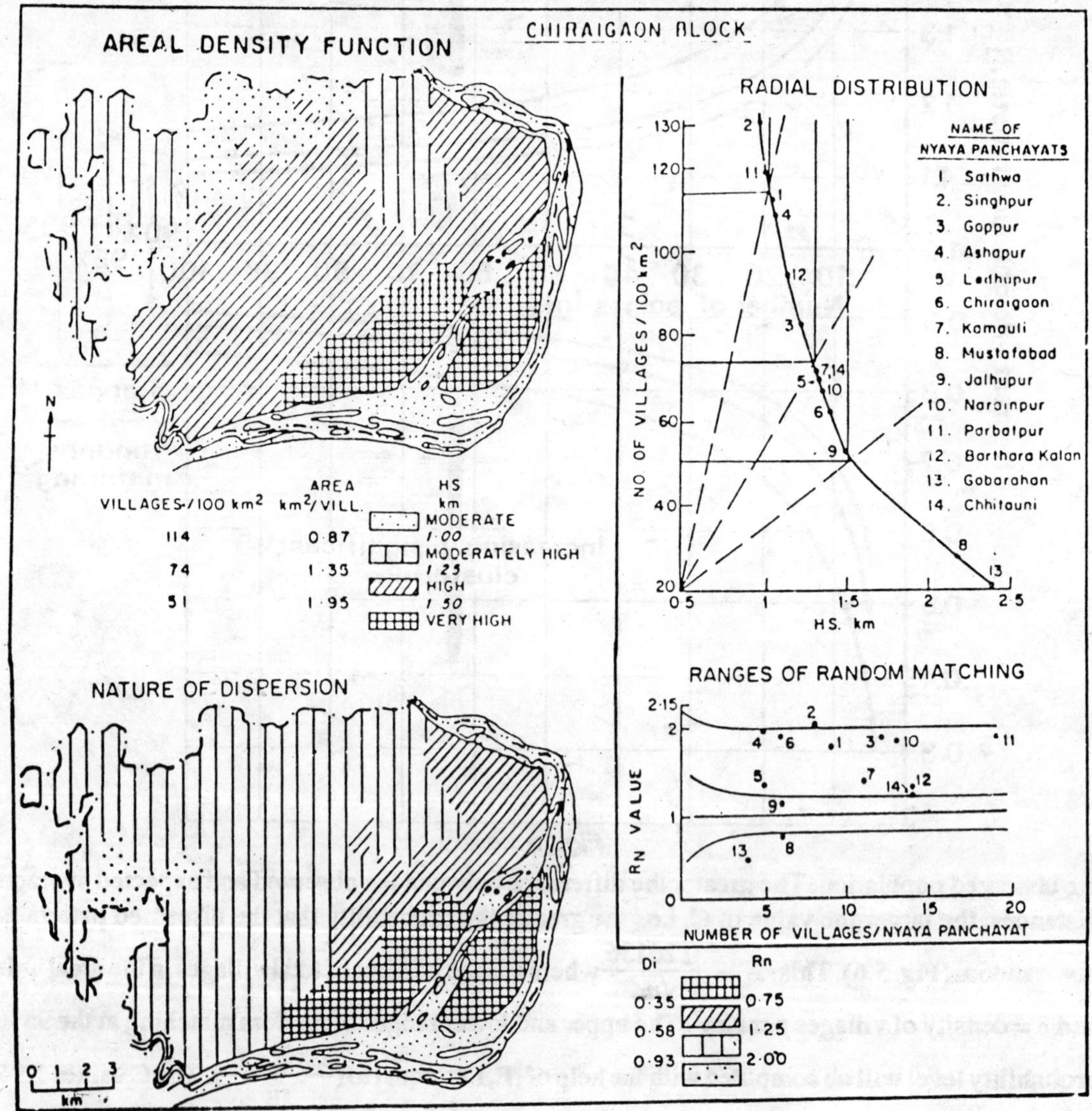

Figure 5.6(a)

drawback is that "a repeated pattern would yield a low value of RN even when the pattern may appear dispersed"[10], but in the case of uniform distribution the method is suitable. "Measures of more than first order should be adopted to minimize the severity of the problem"[11].

The quadrat sampling technique 'provides a way of overcoming the problem of size of area, but there are still some questions as to the proper size of the quadrat used to measure the frequency of points'[12].

Table 5 (iii)

Dispersion of Settlements in Chiraigaon Block

S.No.	Name of Nyayapanchayat	Expected Distance (rE)	Hypothetical Spacing (Hs)	Observed Distance (rO)	Rn Value	Di
1.	Sathawa	0.473	1.02	0.861	1.82	0.844
2.	Singhpur	0.438	0.94	0.902	2.06	0.959
3.	Goppur	0.554	1.19	1.058	1.91	0.889
4.	Ashapur	0.479	1.03	0.953	1.99	0.925
5.	Lerhupur	0.603	1.30	0.790	1.31	0.608
6.	Chiraigaon	0.639	1.37	1.252	1.96	0.914
7.	Kamauli	0.594	1.27	0.820	1.38	0.646
8.	Mustafabad	1.012	2.17	0.719	0.71	0.331
9.	Jalhupur	0.693	1.49	0.776	1.12	0.520
10.	Narainpur	0.612	1.32	1.114	1.82	0.844
11.	Parbatpur	0.459	0.99	0.872	1.90	0.881
12.	Bartharakalan	0.519	1.12	0.675	1.30	0598
13.	Gobaraha	1.107	2.38	0.531	0.48	0.223
14.	Chhitauni	0.595	1.28	0.720	1.21	0.562
	Total Average	0.603	1.30	0.903	1.50	0.695

The first example of the Malwa Region shows clear picture of dispersion in a meso-region (Fig. 5.5A, B and Table 5 (i)). The present example pertains to a block (Chiraigaon) in Varanasi district in the middle Ganga Plain in India (Fig. 5.6A). The results of various indices computed by Dinesh Singh (Department of Geography, Banaras Hindu University, Varanasi) are shown in Table 5 (iii). On the basis of Rn value dispersion of settlements at nyayapanchayat level has been classified in four categories:

(1) **Clustered** (0-0.75): It covers Mustafabad and Gobaraha nyayapanchayats having widely spaced big compact settlements on dry points, hence, about 50 villages in 100 Km^2, with areal coverage of approximately 2 Km^2 per village and very high hypothetical spacing beyond 1.50 Km. Flood conditions have restricted further permanent nature of dispersion of daughter settlements.

(2) **Random** (0.76-1.25): Jalhupur and Chhitauni nyayapanchayats fall under this category. Here, the number of villages per 100 Km^2 varies from 52 to 74; the observed inter village distance varies from 0.72 to 0.78; areal coverage from more than 1.35 up to 1.95 Km^2 per village, and high spacing from 1.26 to 1.50 Km. The tract is less affected by floods. A few settlements show clustered distributional pattern.

(3) **Low** (1.26-2.00): Here the observed inter village distance varies form 0.67 Km (Bharthara nyayapanchayat) to 1.25 Km (Chiraigaon nyayapanchayat). It covers the maximum part

(55%) of the study area having moderately high spacing; the areal coverage ranging from 0.88 to 1.35 per village, and number of villages per 100 Km^2 from 75 to 114. Semi-compact to hamleted settlements have occupied the fertile level plain.

(4) **High** (2.00): It covers the villages of only Singhpur nyayapanchayat with observed inter village distance of 0.90; moderate spacing less than one Km; the areal coverage up to 0.87 Km^2 per village and that being more than 114 villages in 100 Km^2. On local regional basis, however, dispersion increases from the Ganga flood zone towards western border merging with Cholapur Block.

There appears a positive correspondence between areal density function and nature of dispersion, specially, where Hs and Rn values are being compared. It is found that the area having moderate spacing (1.00 Km) records high dispersion (1.90 Rn). Moreover, the area with high spacing, recorded least dispersion while in the moderate case, both indices are positively related.

The analysis indicates the trend of dispersion towards regularity, as experienced in big river valley plains. Computation shows, that empirical variance mean ratio is always smaller than 1, and mean is more than variance, hence, Dacey's "Regular Poisson Probability Law" seems more appropriate in this case[13]. It can also be tested by the value of intensity of random disturbance[14] (Di), which is always less than 1.

Though Pinder states that 'the more extensive the area taken around a given distribution, the lower will be the RN value[15], it is not applicable in the present example. It is, however, worth remembering that, other things remaining the same, the RN value will tend to decrease with increasing area. Smith, rightly states that any value for RN could be produced simply by selecting the right area, so this technique must be used with care.

Spatial Regional Distribution Pattern

The previous discussion reveals, clearly, that the occupance of rural landscape is the outcome of diverse physical, economic and historico-cultural phenomena interacting simultaneously; the rural settlements show variations in their distributional pattern, both even and uneven, and also in shape and size in different area. It would be convenient to study these relationships within the frame of physical division of a region as example. Let us see the three broad subregions of Malwa Region[16].

The Malwa Plateau Region: It is admitted that distribution of settlements and density of population in a particular area exhibit different pictures. For instance, Indore district has higher density than that of Ujjain but inter-village distance is less in the latter. The reason may, easily be ascribed to the compactness of villages and concentration of populations in some places in the former.

Similarly, a lot of difference is visualized in the even and uneven distribution of settlements. A careful study of the maps (Fig. 5.7A, B) will reveal that the fertile plateau proper, extending from the Mahi divide up to Betwa-Sind Basin, illustrated in parts, presents even distribution of habitations, be it the Chambal Basin, Kali Sind, Kshipra, Chambal, Parbati or Sind Basins lying far apart from each other. Here, the physical and cultural settings have combined to present homogeneity in rural landscape. Compact and big villages occupy the fertile as well as almost level plain and interfluves since historical past (Fig. 5.4A, B). Intervillage distance varies from 2.3 Km to 2.6 Km. But, wherever this tract has been traversed by hills, uneven distribution can easily be visualized (Fig. 5.7A/C). Shaded parts in A and B and the eastern part in C present

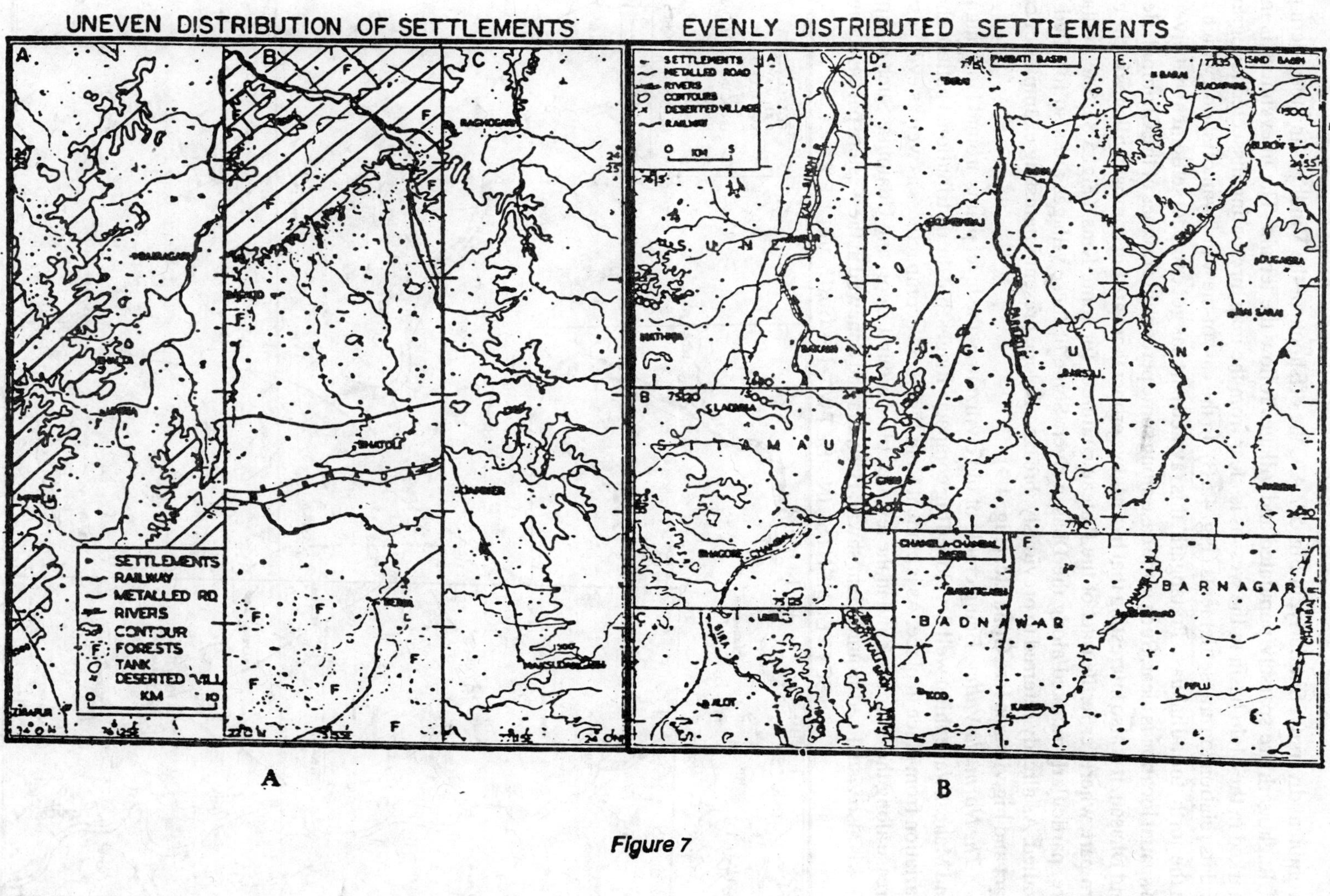
UNEVEN DISTRIBUTION OF SETTLEMENTS
EVENLY DISTRIBUTED SETTLEMENTS
SETTLEMENTS
RAILWAY
METALLED RD
RIVERS
CONTOUR
FORESTS
TANK
DESERTED VILL
KM
SETTLEMENTS
METALLED ROAD
RIVERS
CONTOURS
DESERTED VILLAGE
RAILWAY
KM
PARBATI BASIN
SIND BASIN
SITAMAU
BADNAWAR
BARNAGAR
A
B

Figure 7

prominent diversity. Similarly, in Fig. 5.7 A/C the offshoots of the Vindhyas in the eastern part of Raghogarh are sparsely populated and villages follow the terrain. The unevenness is more marked in the Mahi basin in the west as is clear from the map, presenting dissected topography and its relation to rural settlements (Fig. 4.5B). In the east of the Vindhyan offshoot, which runs in the north, form Jhabua to Pratapgarh, this ravined part has got compact settlement but diversity in spatial location is clear. Such is the case along some perceptible ravines of the Chambal, Betwa and Dhasan. It is also interesting that like Malwa proper there are big compact villages in the eastern part, wherever fertile tract of the Plateau continues for some Kms. (Fig. 5.8). Such villages are, particularly marked along the Dhasan river. Some of these villages are also fortified and walled. As already referred to previously, breaks-of-slope present interesting examples of compact and big villages like Gona etc. (Fig. 4.9).

The Narmada Valley: Being cradle of old civilization, the level plains around Hoshangabad and Maheshwar exhibit well developed big compact villages, but the distributional pattern shows variation from place to place. As is evident from Figure 5.9, compactness as well as evenness increase along the river bank and in the levelled plain around Deori and Udaipura. Such compactness is also visualized around Maheshwar, Barwaha and Sanawad in the western part. Even in the

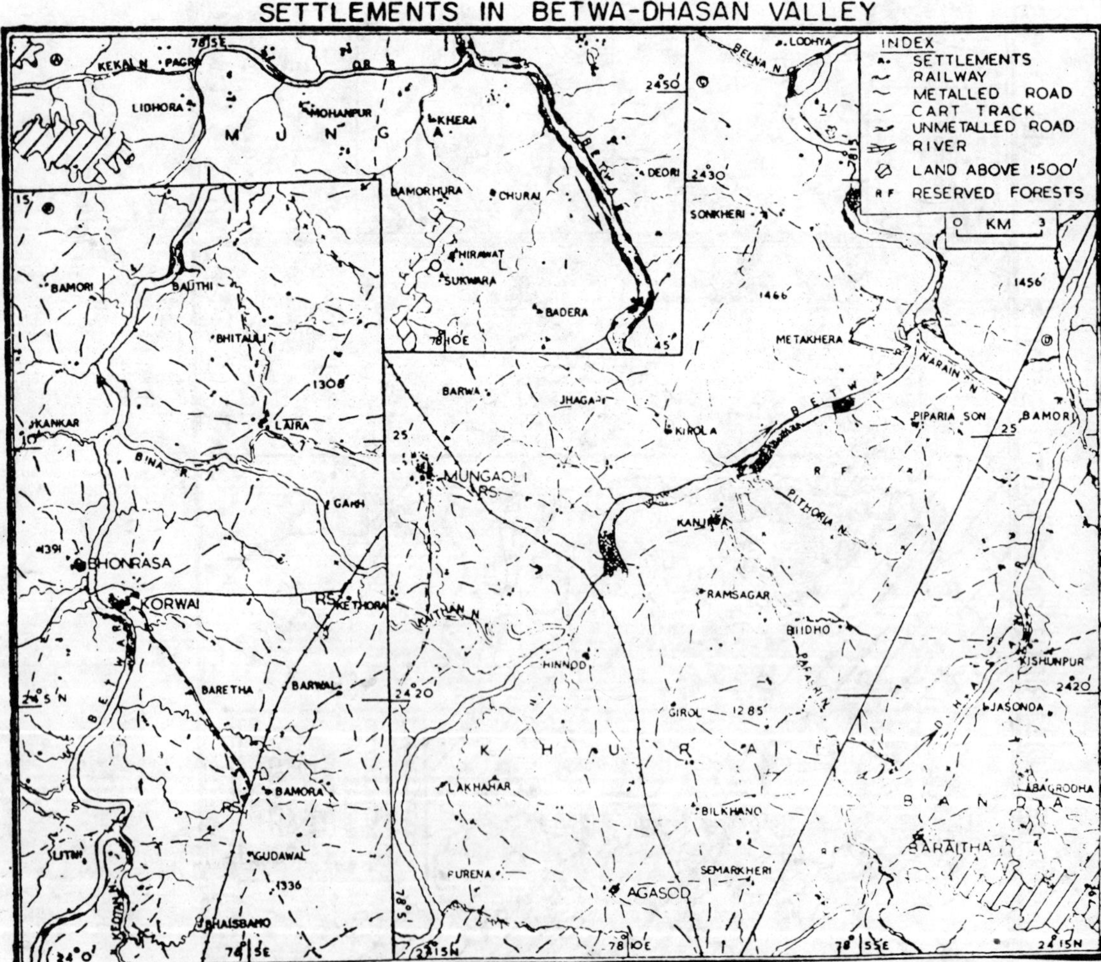

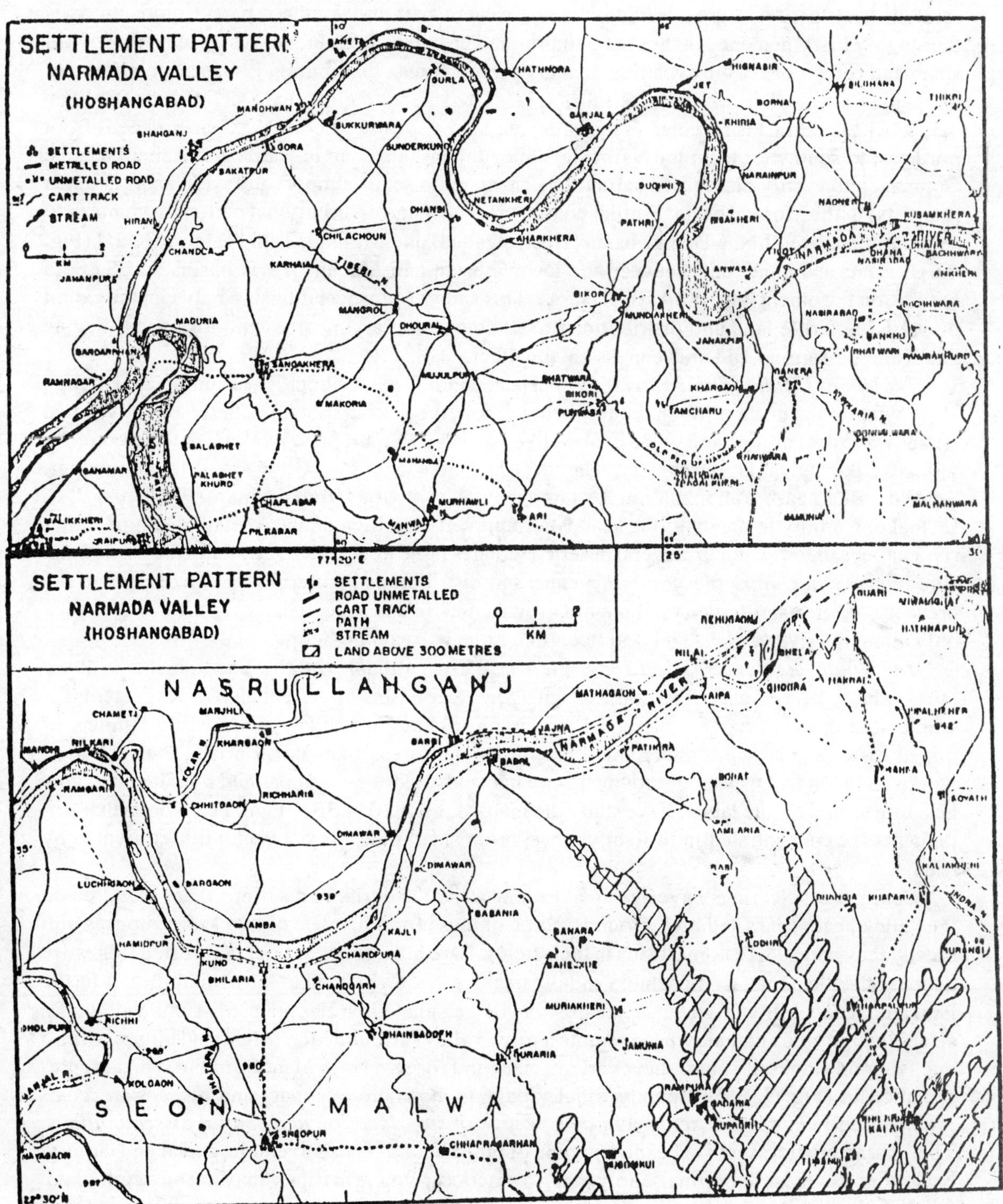
SETTLEMENT PATTERN
NARMADA VALLEY
(HOSHANGABAD)
SETTLEMENTS
METALLED ROAD
UNMETALLED ROAD
CART TRACK
STREAM
KM
HATHNORA
SURLA
HIGNABIR
JET
BORNA
THIKRI
MANOHWAN
SUKKURWARA
BARJALA
KHIRIA
SHAHGANJ
GORA
SUNDERKUND
SAKATPUR
NARAINPUR
NETANKHERI
DHANSI
PATHRI
KUSAMKHERA
CHILACHOUN
KHARKHERA
CHANDCA
KARHAIA
TIBERI N
ANWASA
NARMADA
RIVER
BACHHWARA
ANKHERI
JAMANPURA
MANGROL
BIKORI
DHOURAI
MADURIA
NASIRABAD
BARDARKHAN
SANGAKHERA
JANAKPUR
BANKHU
RAMNAGAR
MAKORIA
BHATWARA
KHARGAON
TAMCHARU
BALABHET
MAHANDA
PALABHET KHURD
CHAPLABAR
MURHAWLI
ARI
MALHANWARA
MALIKKHERI
PILKABAR
77°20'E
SETTLEMENT PATTERN
NARMADA VALLEY
(HOSHANGABAD)
SETTLEMENTS
ROAD UNMETALLED
CART TRACK
PATH
STREAM
LAND ABOVE 300 METRES
KM
NASRULLAHGANJ
REHUNAOWU
NILAI
MATHAGAON
NARMADA RIVER
AIPA
HATHNAPUR
CHAMETI
MARJHLI
KHARGAON
JAJNA
BARRI
BABRI
PATHRRA
RIL KARI
KOLAR R.
RAMGARI
CHHITGAON
RICHHARIA
SOYATH
DIMAWAR
AMLARIA
LUCHIRAON
BARGAON
DIMAWAR
BABANIA
KAJLI
DHANGIA
KHAPARIA
HAMIDPUR
AMBA
KUND
BANARA
CHANDPURA
LODHIRI
BHILARIA
CHANDGARH
MURIAKHERI
RICHHI
DHOLPUR
BHAINSADOOH
JAMUNIA
KURARIA
KOLGAON
RAMPURA
SEONI MALWA
SHEOPUR
CHHAPRAGARHAN
22°30'N

Figure 5.9

same district there is a great variation in the eastern part and southern part. Compactness is thoroughly lost when one reaches the Satpuras and the tribal areas in the west. Frequency of hill spurs and forests break the evenness in many parts. Uneven distribution is also seen in western Narmada Valley, where dissected terrain has restricted the settlements to level fertile tracts (Figs. 4.5, 4.10). A contrast is revealed in the valley, upland and hill settlements as one proceeds from northeast to southwest from the Narmada Valley in Hoshangabad to Harda and Harsud tehsils. Compact and evenly distributed habitations change into semi-compact and wide apart *Dhanas* (hamlets) in the Morand basin. Similar contrast is seen in the distributional pattern from north to south as visualized in the Denwa basin (Hoshangabad) and Morand, Tapi basin of Betual (Fig. 4.6), on the one hand, and between the Denwa basin and Machna Tawa basins and Satpura Divide, on the other (Figs. 4.6A, B, C, 4.5A). This shows a close relationship between the extent of available fertile land and distribution of settlements in varying sizes and forms, on the one hand, and uniformity and unevenness on, the other.

The Nimar Upland: Drained by the Goi, Deb, Kundi-Beda, Chhota Tawa and Machak rivers, all flowing to the north through the fertile black soil, the tract is spotted with the big towns like Khandwa and Khargone and urban centres like Barwani, Rajpur, Sendhwa etc., and big compact villages like Julvania, Deshgaon, Barud, Chhegaon, Sirsoda, Ghogaon, Mohammedpur, Shahada, Bhamgarh, Pandhana and Rustampur etc. It is obvious from the map, (Fig. 4.8A, B, C, D) that uniformity in the distributional pattern prevails and big compact villages occupy either river valleys or fertile tracts. Several deserted villages indicate scarcity of water in the hard strata. But diversity in compactness and unevenness in distributional pattern is visualized due to the presence of forests, reserved or of natural growth, and hills in several places. Uniformity is seen only along the river valleys and deserted villages increase on higher parts.

The Vindhyas, Satpuras and Betul Plateau: Distributional pattern of settlements in these areas exhibit clear impact of terrain. Except a few river basins of more than two Km extent, the whole area presents rugged, dissected topography. These basins are occupied by hamlets of mixed caste people, while other small basins, by the tribals like Bhil, Bhilala, Patlya, Baler, Korku and Gonds. Dispersed settlements are unevenly distributed, separated by hill spurs, gorges, forests and ravine lands. If we study the maps (Figs. 4.10, 4.5B), it will be obvious that settlements are concentrated in th river valleys, or on small plateaux between hills, cultivated by tribals.

Sometimes, clearings have been made along a river and tribal huts (Tapro) are scattered on the valley head, spurs and high grounds; some of these form hamlets of two to five houses but, mostly they spread like homesteads in their fields. Bare hills, ravines, thickly forested ridges are devoid of settlements. Compactness and dipersal are closely related to the availability of fertile land and accessibility of water in streams. A village situated on flat plateau, or in a valley of a sizable extent, and another lying in remote narrow valley surrounded by forest clad hills, or a third one lying on slopes of spurs, show varying sizes and forms as is evident from the typical representation in (Fig. 5.9). But purely tribal village is, nowhere, compact and *dispersion seems synonymous with a tribal settlement irrespective of size, location and spatial disseminations*. This characteristic, seems to be the outcome of multifactors related to ethnic, social and cultural background of these aboriginals. Polygamy, a practice in vogue in tribes, may not be overlooked.

But, the distributional pattern of settlements, in the eastern part of the Satpura hills and Betul plateau, differs from their counterpart in western Satpuras and in the Vindhyan hills. Here, hamleted settlements lie away from the streams and compact to semi-compact, villages are found along rivers (Figs. 4.5A, 4.6). Traversed by hills and having deeply cut ravines and dense jungles, gorges, steep scarps and rugged topography, the region, presents unevenly distributed habitations; this however, is particularly noticeable in upper Machna, Morand, Denwa and Ganjal basins. The pattern, itself, speaks about the later occupation of remote areas and the primary settlement zones lying around Betul, Multai etc., a habitat predominantly, of Gonds.

A Regional Comparison and Contrast in Spacial Distribution Pattern

Various environmental factors affect the variation in the arrangement of settlements. But, these factors in conjunction with culturo-historical and socio-economic factors (land productivity, tenure system, extent of cultivable land, culture or caste group, ethnic relationship, mode of living, diversification of activities, security conditions and hold of *Jajmani* system, India, etc., have determined the degree of spatial diffusion, homogeneity and variation in size and form. A comparison, between one valley settlement and another, and also between plateau settlements and valley settlements or plain settlements, on the other hand, will reveal that perceptible variation is visualized throughout the world settlement system. Here is an illustration from Malwa Region, on the basis of empirical evidences in the field, study of toposheets and data available in censuses and settlements reports.

A glimpse at settlements in the Betwa Valley (Fig. 5.8) reveals, that big villages lie widely spaced and other small villages scatter in between almost on regular space. Some of these big market villages have forts, are walled and all have temples and wells. Cart tracks radiate from such agglomerations to all other settlements. This leads to believe that during the medieval period Rajput and non-Rajput clan settlements occupied primarily, these centres and disseminated, later on, due to increase in population, political pressure, ethnic relations and other factors related to landuse and land tenure system. Some of these parent villages were made *tappa* centres during the Mughal and British periods. The same fact is revealed by the arrangement of these parent or mother settlements and other sister settlements in their surroundings on the Malwa Plateau in the Chambal-Mahi basin (Fig. 4.4). Big villages, like Madopur, Rubiya, Baroda, Amla, Jalar, Kharsod, Multhan Tilgara, Barmawal and Bilpank, have developed under Jagirdari system of princely states of former days. Other centres are later disseminations due to histo-culturo-economic factors discussed above. It is notable, that this was the central place where several immigrational waves, have swept, during historical period, the aboriginals and established the Hindu social order based upon Jajmani system.

The distributional pattern, visualized on the Nimar Upland (Fig. 4.8), speaks of the same diffusional process, though of later origin. Here, big size villages remind us of the defensive role, they have played during the period of anarchy. As the clearings advanced, new settlements spread all over the area, inhabited now. But, a close study of the distributional pattern in the Narmada Valley, particularly in areas of Sheet No. 55J/1, 46N/16 must reveal, that majority of villages of medium size occupy the tract almost equally spaced, except those, bordering the Narmada banks. Here, the settlements, with their peculiar sizes and forms and morphological similarities, tell their story of natural growth since hoary past out of socio-economic condensation based upon functions. Noteworthy is the fact, that centripetal forces, working under Rajput and non-Rajput clan settlements leading to nucleation, and centrifugal forces working under the same but for occupying new clearings, were mostly responsible for variation in Malwa Plateau settlements; while socio-economic condensation, based upon functions, for the Narmada Valley settlements. The age old caste system, based on functions, has played major role in establishing several villages of caste predominance. Such settlements, in the form of hamlets (Dhana), are, conspicuously, found on Betul plateau.

Characteristics of New Settlement Distribution and/in Pioneer fringe Areas

As already discussed in Chapter Three the theme confined to the process of occupance and whereabouts of the varied settlements. Again, we saw the distribution pattern, particularly, in Indian part. Now, let us see recent distributional aspects within a span of last five decades or so. Farm village was the characteristic type of rural settlement throughout the Third World countries with certain exceptions. Europe contained both, dispersed and nucleated settlement types with complicated intermingling and distributions; U.S.S.R. saw village (agglomerated) type distribution while the United States, mostly farmsteads scattered throughout the plains. Exceptionally, the aboriginal settlements were widely spaced in Northern America.

During modern times, the picture is changing alongwith new world order, the technological advancement, spread of innovations through media, atmosphere of free and secure living conditions, changes in land ownership or allotment or new lands to individuals, groups and communes and establishment of new habitations through resettlement process, rural market development along roads, shop-cum residences near recreation/tourist spots or resorts and so on so forth.

Environment or ecology oriented distributional patterns, firstly, concern with changes in stream courses and settlement on the left tract, with varied use, under farming. Such distributions abound in big meandering river flood plains. Simultaneously discernible are permanent settlements on the vast plains, well secured by mud-dams, thrown along flooding rivers, i.e., Ghaghara, Ganga, Koshi etc. Dykes and polders, in the Netherlands, present another form of distributions.

Forest cutting, was and is responsible for inducement to settlement distribution of forest margins, and even in the core of vulnerable jungles on hills, plateaus and river valleys. New plough runs on each and every slope of hills/mountains, where a Bhil, a Korku, a Gond, an Oraon or an Amhara or Oromo and other sons of soil survive in tiny huts or small hamlets. Not less in number are the hutments of forest cutters, forest produce collectors/gatherers, workers engaged in lumbering, sawing and allied activities, both in tropics and temperate zones. To this may be added the watchmens, forest guards with their attached quarters, various *ashrams* and development centres of NGO'S/Voluntary Organisations, i.e., Banbasi Ashram, Mirzapur, India.

Similar distributions are coming up in pioneer areas of Usarland (Fig. 6.7), swampy margins, new plantations and agricultural large scale farming. New large scale cadastral maps or 1:63,360, 1:50,000 small scale maps (toposheets), show strong deviation from previous spread of build up areas and are spotted on no-man's land.

The market mechanism, ease in transport and supportive partial employment, has brought roadside villages out along the road in the form of market centres in embryonic stage and such '*Corridor distribution* of shop-cum residence' is common along good motorable roads. In some areas, tea stalls, coffee stalls, groceries or bars attract travellers/settlers and one by one new shops add to grow it into a hamlet.

Road crossings or rail-road-crossings are new additions with market type developments and all bus-stands, along highways in India, show new settlement distributions, i.e., Saini,

Chaudagra, Aurai, Kachhawa Road are examples along G.T. Road. Other type of developments are, heavy vehicle or Truck halt-spots coming into the form of linear distribution with one or two restaurant, pumpsets, repair shop for vehicles, a petrol-pump and pan (betel leaves) shops etc., seen conspicuously along highways.

Wherever new allotments have been made for settlements, the landscape is changing. It may be Gram Samaj land or common land of a village, rehabilitation site, forced settling site, or resettlement sites in Malaysia, Bolivia, Sri Lanka, Eastern Siberia, Israel, Iraq, Sudan, Ethiopia or occupied Kashmir or Morocco, Algeria (of different political set up) or even Australian or New-Zealand's vast open plains. The Tibetan pioneer areas and western part of China are being settled politically, hence new distributions. Sometimes, these are planned, while in others, haphazard.

Refugee rehabilitation sites show another type of peculiar settlement distribution in Sri Lanka, Tamil Nadu (India), Pakistan (Afghanistan), Iraq border Zone, Jordan, Sudan, Chad, Vietnam, Thailand, Bangladesh, Kenya and many other Third World countries? To this may be added refugee camps of natural catastrophe-stricken settlers now in millions.

Rehabilitation site settlements are seen now scattered in all civilized parts of the world along with Multipurpose Projects of hydle-irrigation development schemes. Some of them are highly problematic raising human right issues, i.e., Narmada Project in India, Chernoble (USSR) etc.

The distribution of colony type (Government planned) settlements, are new additions, wherever the hand of development reaches. These are canal site, dam site, hydle sub-station site or factory site, fertilizer, cement, sugar or some manufactured good's factory site, processing site—all with attached colonies of settlements, hence, modernized and well planned, rural as well as urban, in character. New markets also develop in front of, or close to factory site, hence, '*Corridor extensions*' between two big centres like Kanpur and Lucknow.

The pioneer areas,[17] like arid parts of deserts (Rajasthan), coastal areas, high mountain ridges, snow affected thawing tracts, are areas of sparse settlements but here too, new distributional patterns are seen. The Indira Gandhi Canal area, Nagev in Israel, North Eastern Siberia, North Canada—all show new extensions of settlements.

It is noteworthy that one should not lose sight of the fact that, due to varied adaptations with ecology, man leaves some parts unpopulated, hence, deserted settlements, which affect the distributional pattern in vast areas of mining, forestry etc., and at micro-level, near the abandoned projects, factory sites, brick- kiln sites, landslide sites or flood sites. Similar deserted sites are the hard-hit areas by hurricanes, earthquakes, Volcanic eruption and change of river courses.

Of course, there would be newer distributional dot-maps for human habitations near space-sites, hotel and resort sites, military encampment sites, arms and ammunition sites and still newer 'peace centres' of intellectuals, academics to have gatherings regarding free and less-polluted habitat distribution of homo sapiens.

References

1. See Zipf, G.K. (1949), Human Behaviour and the Principle of Least Effort, 1965 ed. Hafner, New York.
2. Watson, J.W. (1955), 'Geography A Discipline in Distance' Scot. Geog. Mag. Vol. 71, pp. 1-13.
3. Mather, C.E. (1944), A Linear Distance Map of Farm Population in the U.S., AAAG, 34, 173-180;

see also M.F. Dacey, 'Analysis of Central Place and Point Patterns by a Nearest Neighbour Method, Lund Series (B) in Geog. 24 (1962): 55-76; J.P. Cole and C.A.M. King, Quantitative Geography, London, John Wiley and Sons Ltd., 1968, p. 490.

4. Stone, K.H. (1968), 'Multiple Scale Classification for Rural Settlement Geography, Acta Geographica (Helsinki) 20 No. 22: 307-328; for Pattern analysis see, J.C. Hudson, Pattern Recognition in Empirical Map Analysis Jl. Reg. Sc. 9, (1968), pp. 189-199.
5. See Clark, P.J. and F.C. Evans (1954), "Distance to Nearest Neighbour as a Measure of Relationship in Population' Ecology 35: 445-453.
6. Dacey, M.F. (1966), 'A County Seat Model for the Areal Pattern of the Urban System, Geog. Review 56, pp. 527-542.
7. Hertz, P. (1909), Uber den geigenseitigen durch semittlichen Abstand Von Punkte, die mit bekannter mittlerer Dikhte in Raume angeordnet sind, Mathematisch Annalen 67: 387-398.
8. Dacy, M.F, (1965), Order, Distance in an Inhomogeneous Random Point Pattern, coand., Geog., 9: 144-153.
9. Clark and Evans op. cit. ref. no. 5; see also L.J. King (1969), Statistical Analysis in Geography, New Jersey: Prentice Hall, pp. 99-100.
10. Getis, A. (1964), 'Temporal Land Use Pattern Analysis With the Use of Nearest Neighbour and Quadrat Method' AAAG, 54: 391-399; also see Getis, A. and Boots, B. 'Models of Spatial Processes', Cambridge University Press, Cambridge, 1978: 26-31.
11. See Barr, B.M., I.J. Lindsay and E.R. Reinelt, 'Pattern of Urban Spacing in the USSR, Journal Reg. Sc. 11 (1971): 221- 224; also N.B.K. Reddy 'Refinement of the Nearest Neighbour and Reflexive Neighbour Analysis; Ind. Geog. Jl. 48, (1973): 1-9.
12. Smith D.M. (1977), 'Patterns in Human Geography' Penguin Books Ltd. England: 180-188.
13. Dacey, M.F. (Modified Poisson Probability Law for Point Pattern More Regular Than Random; Annals Asso. Amm. Geog. 54 (1964): 559-65.
14. Dacey M.F. and Tung Tzehsing (1962), "Identification of Randomness in Point Pattern", Jl. Reg. Sc. 4: 83-96—the intensity of random disturbance is measured by the normalized index (Di), where $Di = \frac{ro}{(1.0746/\sqrt{d})}$.
15. Pinder, D.A. and M.E. Witherick (1972), "The Principles, Practice and Pitfalls or Nearest Neighbour Analysis", Geography 57: 277-288.
16. For other Studies see R.L. Singh (1955), Evolution of Settlements in the Middle Ganga Valley, National Geog. Jl. Ind. Vol. I,: 82-97; also see R.P.B. Singh (1977), Clan Settlements in the Saran Plain, N.G.S.I., Res. Pub. No. 18: 65-91.
17. See for other studies H.N. Nitz, Settlement Processes and the Evolution of Settlement and Field Farms in the Himalayan Foreland of Kumaon (North India), 12-23; Khoo Soo-hock and Voon Phin Kheong, 'Origin and Characteristics of Agricultural Settlements in Peninsular Malaysia, 52-68; Mario Hiraoka, Landscape Changes in a Pioneer Region: The East Bolivian Example 69-81; E. Ehlers, Land Consolidation and Farm Resettlement in the Federal Republic of Germany: 121-133; Carl Rathjens, Interrelations of Settlement Land Use and Forest Exploitation in Eastern Afghanistan, 134-139; David Grossman, The Grographical Significance of the Settlement Process the case of Israel: in Robert C. Eidt, Kashi N. Singh et al. (eds.) (1977), 'Man, Culture and Settlement', Kalyani Publishers, New Delhi.

6

Morphology

Origin and Growth of Morphology

The inherent principle of village morphology is the human instinct of gregariousness. As stated in Chapter two and three, the origin and purpose of village envisage various factors, which are also potential forces for providing momentum to the dynamic morphology of a settlement. To have a comprehensive holistic view of settlement, it is now essential, to deal with the morphogenesis[1] and morphological structure of rural settlements. Besides the geometrical shape, which is visualized through airview or on a well drawn map, as one aspect of the form of a settlement, the internal arrangement of lanes, houses, with varied relationships, provide another aspect, named as morphology, hence morphological structure. This morphological structure of settlements/villages, as concrete expression of human activity in space, involves five principles of settlement formation, advocated by Doxiadis (Fig. 1.1). His hypothetical frame for any settlement consists of four parts: (i) Homogeneous parts, (ii) Central part, (iii) Circulatory part and (iv) Special part. Various spatio-temporal transformations do occur, but these parts are always visible in any settlement or Ekistic unit (Fig. 6.1a). These basic parts, are closely associated with the dimensions of height, length, width and time, which are best explained by morphological analysis of the settlements/villages.

The internal morphology naturally involves analysis of (a) structural morphology and (b) social morphology. Of these, the former concerns with the description and interpretation of relationships evolved, e.g., (i) lane to lane (ii) lane to house and (iii) house to house; the latter, deals with the varied dwellings group, community structures and land or spaces. These relationships show innumerable variations at micro level as discussed in the sequel.

(i) The lane to lane relationship reveals many invisible dimensions of settlements. The length, breadth and level speak about the physico-cultural aspects of the settlements. The alignment and intersections of sub-lanes, exhibit the historical stage and process of occupance, and in most of the cases, the culture of the settler. The linear continuity, narrowness or wider space with zigzag serpentine passage in big settlements, remind us, the age and manner, of settling process. Simultaneously, the drainage outlets, the drains, coming out of houses, reveal, in many cases the directional aspects of houses. The wider, sometimes, paved streets, tell the touch of development efforts. Timing space as well as spacing time, is, best explained through these lanes, during summer or rainy season, when whole or a portion of lane is used by bullock carts, modern vehicles, on foot passers-by or rain water or permanent drains. These also play a role in providing space for children's, inter alia, hide seek games. The level of lanes, tells about the type of settlement, i.e., site and situation, whether it is in a plain, plateau, hilly terrain, a valley with multifarious con-

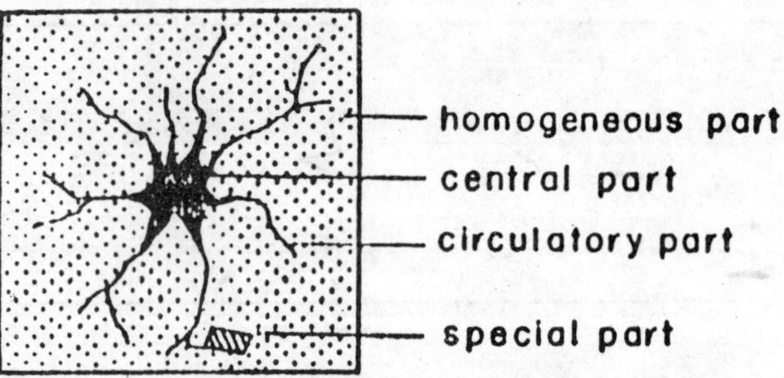

a village consists of :

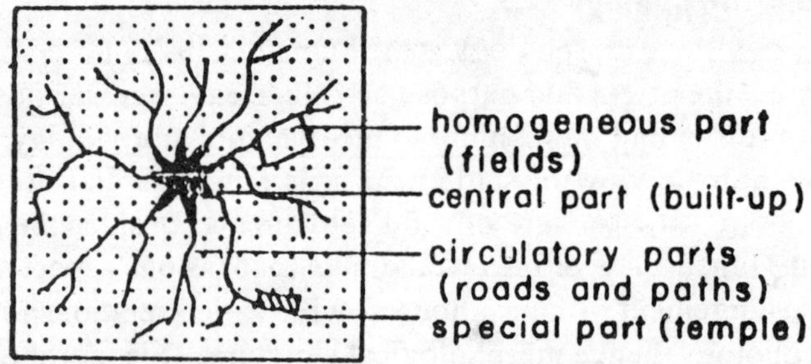

the built-up area of the village consists again of :

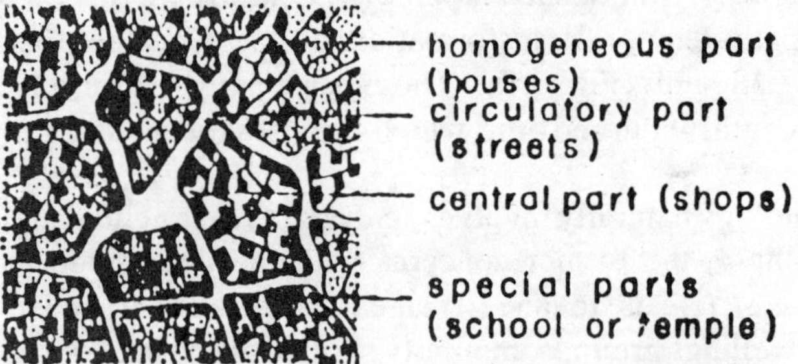

(after C.A. Doxiadis)

(Basic Parts of a settlement)

Figure 6.1 (a)

figuration, and also up-down alignments. Encroachments, so conspicuously observed at places with bends, tell the story of, not so pleasing, arrangement by strong but robust settlers. Sometimes, wide streets, interconnected with sub-lanes, serve as thorough passage and exhibit a planned layout. It is during various ceremonial occasions that the importance of lance is realized *enmasse*, as a common space to be best planned to improve the quality of life. Many a sanitation and health attribute is linked with the type of lanes.

Thus, streets as well as lanes, become visible arteries of the anatomy of settlement, which, if planned, provide lamp posts, lamp poles, sign boards, drainage lines, route for man and animals,

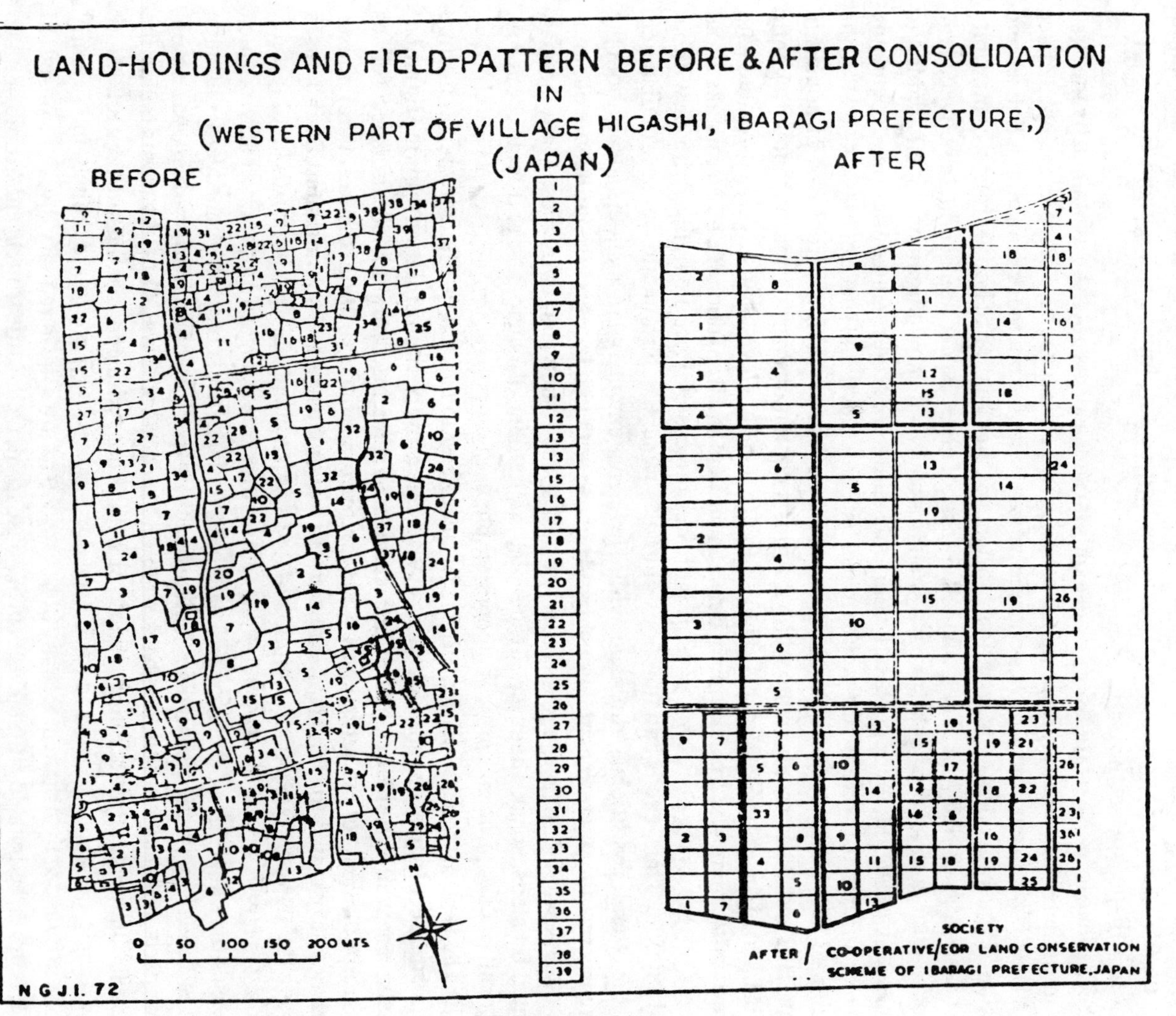
LAND-HOLDINGS AND FIELD-PATTERN BEFORE & AFTER CONSOLIDATION
IN
(WESTERN PART OF VILLAGE HIGASHI, IBARAGI PREFECTURE,)
(JAPAN)
BEFORE
AFTER
0 50 100 150 200 MTS
N
N G J.I. 72
SOCIETY
AFTER / CO-OPERATIVE/EOR LAND CONSERVATION
SCHEME OF IBARAGI PREFECTURE, JAPAN

Figure 6.1(b)

vehicle, water pipes, sunny and shady side space and, above all, a common space for both, haves and have nots, according to time and need. This living space is, however, not so functional on the same level in hamlets or isolated habitations, where it is offset by enough of space. Its functions, forms and layout-all vary in oriental and accidental world, on one hand, and old and new settlements, on the other. Any comparison, between Chinese and Indian Village and European or American Village, speaks the truth.

(ii) The lane to house relationship, also, exhibits other aspects not to be explained by the first. Sometimes, lanes extend after house construction, at others houses find place in the open space along a lane. So, this relationship goes on, side by side, with the internal expansion of houses and extension of lanes outside. On this relationship depends the situation of house groups, community wise or caste wise or clan wise. The backwall or front of house, space and height, in between lane and house door, and level of sub-space, sometimes steps, all show alignments well adapted to local needs. Here again, the aspects of health and sanitation, privacy and pollution, depend and vary on/according to, level and distance between lane and functional space of house as well as the condition of lane/street. Here again, the level of lanes is lower than the front part of houses in Plateau, Hill and Valley settlements while it forms a continuous part of house front with gentle slope in most of the Plain Settlements. The difference in height level is positively correlated with the age of settlement. The space, lying in between the lane and front door of a house, speaks about the status of the occupants; sometimes, it indicates the caste of people living, with or without animal support. Thus, needs and functions of house owners, determine the space and distance. Often, the overall conditions—drainage, width, level, pavement, of lanes/streets speak about the community residing there. The relationship of a house with two lanes is also indicative of status of the owner, whether occupying a corner, or vast space in between two lanes. Many houses, separated by steps, speak about type of people, the number of occupants, and their economy. Streets and houses of *bazars* present a common picture.

(iii) The house to house relationship varies according to the whims of the owner. It is more a cultural than ecological phenomena. We can visualize a few common relationships in alignment and distinct as well as form, i.e., internal structural arrangements. The study of this aspect relates to the morphogenesis of the settlement. A big house compound, partitioned into several houses according to expansion to clan members, denotes one of the original settling sites. Such houses may have the same entrance in the compound towards lane; and sub-spaces are divided, further, according to family houses. But the relations remain the same as regard intra-family affairs. Such big houses may have many common side and backwalls, hence, compact with several entrance doors. In densely populated/settled settlements, lack of space, between two houses, is common. In some parts, houses have common back walls and separate side walls but, the fronts facing the street, stand in linear fashion, either straight or with bends, with gaps for outside contact. Many houses, facing the opposite lanes, have adjacent backwalls, then courtyard, hence, inter family relations influenced by distance. Density of house also follows the hereditary divisions of settled parts. It is the directional locational aspects of house front, well, cattle trough and temple or place of worship, etc., which determine the layout of houses. House may remain separated by open space to provide enough space for privacy and multifarious uses. The distance, from house to house, depends, sometimes, on the owner's caste to maintain ritual or social sanctions though exceptions are there. Defence (specially theft) plays important role in layout of house fronts facing back of other house. But sometimes, house, constructed by owner, forfeiting/or avoiding the benefit of inter-house cordial relations, exhibits, his whim only.

The social morphology is, however, influenced to a great extent, by the relationships of house groups, the lane, open space, the temple, the pond or the village 'Dih', in some cases, village deity etc. Community sectors, divided by lanes/street, form a separate entity; in others, each house may show its own entity. The arrangement of caste wise hamlets, the distance, the direction-all speak about the social space, hence, influencing social morphology.

While discussing the variation, both spatial and temporal, in the morphological expressions of these rural habitats, it is worth recapitulation the evolutional stages, associated with the socio-economic and culturo-political organization of the community. The tradition, cultural traits, aspirations and value systems of the people govern the rural settlement forms and, if one has to appreciate the settlements, he must try to see the country 'with the eyes of the first settlers, and with those of the long line of heirs, that link them to us'. The same view has been expressed by Sorre in Volume 3 of the 'Tondements where he suggested that every life style tended to inscribe itself in a typical habitat form. In the case of rural settlements, he showed, how work rhythms, agricultural regimes, social structure and economic activities were related to house types and village patterns. The discussion in foregoing pages serves as background to understand morphology. How these forms originate? In chapter two we discussed in detail the models applicable for settlement occupance. Now, we can elaborate the nucleation and diffusion of settlements responsible for morphology. The case in hand is Mahjuda village of Varanasi district (India).

Nucleation: Nucleation, here, refers to morphological development at one site while diffusion gives the expansion of the same at other sites.

Evidences corroborated by traditional legends, folklore and the presence of ruined mounds of the old *Bhar* settlements in Bhori (after Bhar), the neighbouring village south west of Mahujda, speak about the expropriation of the Bhars and its occupation by the Maunas Rajputs. An outpost of the Bhars seems to have been established at the site, now deserted, and called *Dihwa* and *Nonra*, just facing the old site, across the Nadi Jhor (*nala*) (Fig. 3.11). However, these Rajputs, originally inhabiting the Bhori village, occupied and adopted narrow strip cultivation in the southern part of the present village; the northern part lying under forest, and much of the aboriginal cultural landscape was obliterated and transformed; chandrabedhi tanks were constructed in the eastern part. It was, during the period between A.D. 1550-1750, that most rapid rise of arable farming, dominating over forest culture took place and also involved the foundation of new settlements, partly, due to attracting pulls, like availability of arable land, water supply, forest land for fuel and grazing and building material etc., and partly, due to growth of population and further segmentation. Most of the land of old site was donated to the priestly community (the Brahmins) and the Rajputs shifted for better prospects, in different directions, the present site being one of them. The occasional flood limit played major role in site selection. The *Dih** or the old site, afterwards, became the pivotal point, round which, revolved the whole activities of settlements of later origin. Rajputs, as a dominant caste, occupied the original site along with others (Figs. 2.15a, 2.17, 3.12a). To it accreted agricultural labourers to perform various activities regarding forest cutting, cleaning, ploughing and cultivation; other menial caste people, like the

* The *Dih* is still considered an auspicious site and victory of Rajputs over Bhars is commemorated on Holi festival, the day of victory, by sacrificing pigs as they were object of veneration of Bhars.

Nonia, to help in farming and salt making and carrying goods on he-buffalo; ironsmith and wood workers, to help in agricultural activities like supply of implements and building materials and other social and ritual nees; *Bhunj* for frying grains* ; *Bania* or tradesman as supplier of provisions and goods; tailors to sew clothes; washermen to wash clothes; barbars to cut hair and perform rituals and other ceremonies; *Kahars* to serve water for daily use as well as for other services; Milkmen for stock raising; potters to supply pots for daily use as well as for ceremonial gatherings and rituals and tiles for roofing buildings; and herders to supply blankets as well as for sheep manuring in fallow plots. Kayasthas shifted to the settlement at a time, when land tenure system during the British period changed and most of them, working as officials in revenue departments of Banaras State, could purchase some of the land holdings from the Rajputs. The priestly community occupied its own original share as well the land donated to them for their professional performances.

Thus, the people of diverse castes flocked together for earning their living upon the produce of the arable and other land under the dominant Rajput lineage supremacy[2], the only corporate political group in the territory (Bhadohi) and others (were) rendered to a non-corporate and non-political status[3].

Once, the site was inhabited by diverse castes, the needs of farming and communal life articulated a strong sense of cooperation among them[4]. The *Jajmani* system prevailed and worked through a process of steady assimilation and acculturation. Strip cultivation along with irrigational limit increased in space and by seventeenth century, the compact settlement grew with caste sections of various groups, still holding their different appellation, i.e., *Babhanan, Sonaran, Jadwan, Nonian, Chamarauti* etc. Two *khors* (wide path for animals and outlet for rain water) in the west and south served the main purpose of road and link for village to outside. Other paths ran westward to the nala, northward to forest and eastward to tank.

Morphological Changes and Dispersion

During varied phases of evolution the hamletization took place on the basis of secular, religio-ritual and then socio- economic diffusion model. The main factors contributing to diffusion and changes in morphological structure were: (i) distintegration of joint family into nucleus one, (ii) loosening of clan and caste solidarity, (iii) socio-economic changes in land holding system, (iv) less effective role of religio-ritual model, (v) removal of the need for defensive agglomeration, (vi) technical improvement in water supply conditions, (vii) improved transport, (viii) diversification of occupation, and (ix) immigration etc.

Thus, the main or the mother settlement (Fig. 3.12a) rectangular in shape during first phase, developed into polygonal pattern with distinct internal form rajputs of the first joint family occupy the southern section, Brahmins are in the east and Goldsmiths in between them. Western part is inhabited by *Bhunj*, Washerman, *Banias*, Muslims and *Nonias*. North of the Rajputs are *Kayasthas* Barbers and *Kahars*. In the *Uttar Patti* (north zone) are scattered some later arrivals like the outcaste *Brahmin, Nonia, Kshatriya*, iron-smith and wood workers and beyond them, the northern skirts, are occupied by the Rajputs and Milkman. A separate (*basti*) settlement unit is inhabited by the *Chamars* in the east of the main settlement, separated by a big pond, which originated due to extraction of mud used in buildings. Settlement no 2 is purely of Rajputs, no. 4

* Fried grains were given as ready breakfast or meal for the farm labours and other workers.

of milkmen, no. 5 and 6 of milkmen and shepherds, no. 3 in the north-west of milkmen, the central hamlet no. 3 and 4 being inhabited by milkmen, *Rajputs* and Potters, etc. Unit no. 7, along the road in the north, is recently being occupied by Scheduled Castes and *Nonia*, no. 7 in the west of the road by Washermen and *Bhunj* and *Bania*. Mushhar's huts occupy the northern margin of the land near jungle.

Recent morphological additions are maternity centre near unit no. 7, seed and fertilizer store in the northern most point along road and shops (by all caste people) along the road, even beyond primary school and community centre in the south towards Bhori.

In general, new changes, mainly due to technological advancement, are responsible for morphological transformation. Briefly, the overall effect is as follows:

Transport means are replacing on foot passengers. People now depend more on bicycle, rickshaw, auto-rickshaw, trolley, pick-up trucks, jeep car, bus, motor cycle, motor bike, motor boat and passenger craft. Farm land to settlement distance is minimized. Footpaths are changing into feeder roads, hence, farm produce easily reaches house. Houses in the main settlement are being left and shifted as shop-cum houses along roads, hence, street- settlements spot each and every corner of densely settled Asian parts. Mechanized transport has attracted market villages with linear houses, strung out on either side of the road, in more than a Km in length. Such type of relocation of settlements is now a trend setter.

Water transport facilities are not far behind. In south east Asian countries, village morphology is changing with water transport conditions. River bank villages of big size are replacing the long house. Pile supported pathways are giving way to dock like structures; boat docking facilities are being altered and the morphology too. The rubber plantation has given rise to *small holder* settlements in Malaysia. Likewise, *Kampung* settlements along a river, along a canal or road, along a *Permatang* (raised beach), the FELDA settlement and *rumah banjir*, as pioneer settlements, exhibit new morphology on rural landscape. In America (U.S.A. and Canada) larger villages are coming up with complex morphology.

Another new features on rural landscape are the homestead type arrangement of houses near allotted plots after settlement process of land holding consolidation in India. Pumping sets, (electric/diesel) and other equipments and devices of mechanization add new dimension. Disintegration of joint family system has helped in such morphological extensions.

It seems, the old traditional village living would be replaced by farmstead and hamlet type living pattern with greater mechanization and dependence on secondary and tertiary activities.

Land Tenure System and Morphology

A geographer can not ignore the study of land tenure system which plays significant role in the regional distribution of settlements. The present morphology of villages is the end product of old tenure system, hence, a brief account of the same. The evolutional phases of rural settlements are closely related to the type of land tenure-adopted during a particular period by the village community with its dynamic forms. In the course of early settlements, the clearing of the dense forests itself provided a union of families into villages[5]. The waste, adjoining the village, was not the common property of the village, any more, than it is at the present day. And consequently, in early times the boundaries between village and village were rarely, if even, defined. It is only reasonable to suppose that from the earliest times of tribal settlement, the several tribal or clan areas were jealously guarded. All traces of early customs show the villages in India just in the same condition, in this respect, as raiyatwari villages. A village of this (i) system was occupying 'Khalsa' land, i.e., the land under the Crown, owned and supervised by the land lord, whereas the (ii) joint village was supervised by Patwaries (village record keepter = Lekhpal) for collection of revenue, although, the ownership belonged to individual cultivator. Most of the villages in erstwhile states, were of the first type. Taking however, the average sized village, there is little in external appearance to distinguish the 'joint' from the 'raiyatwari' form[6]. It was just possible that different tribes preferred different climates and, if they inherited diverse customs, one may find peculiar tenures in one place, which do not occur in another. Among the Rajputs or other tribes, which had adopted a monarchical constitution, it is common to find that the heads of the branch families held subordinate (territorial) titles (as Rawal, Thakur etc.); and there was regularly understood method of territorial rule in the Raja's Central Dominion, and those of the other chiefs, lying round. The subjects of each, were bound to allegiance to the chief, and the chief, to the Raja[7]. The cultivated area was divided into plots according to the member of heads of the families in the village, and each family received the produce of its share. In case of division, the land was equally divided among all sons, though sometimes, the eldest son might get an extra share, which differed according to place and time[8]. The raiyatwari villages, for which the proprietary titles were in 1860 conceded to '*Patels*', '*malguzars*' and the like, will have the same ending; the sons and grandsons of the proprietor will (or may) hold 'in common' after the death of the first grantee,and as shares multiply, there will, probably, be a minute subdivision[9].

The following things were common to influence and give their stamp on the rural landscape in Central India. The twelve '*baluteder*' or '*hakdars,*' who constituted the village staff, were important in the village community. They formed the village corporation, the key to morphology. Here too, the land tenures fell into two classes, 'Khalsa' or land held directly by the Darbar (Court) and alienated land held in Jagir, Muafi etc. 'Khalsa' lands were held either on '*ijardari*' or '*Khatedari*' tenure. In the first instance a village or several villages were held by an ijardar or farmer, who was responsible for the assessed revenue less a fixed commission. In the second case, the cultivator held directly from the State without the intervention of a middle man. Now, only two categories (i) bhumidhari and (ii) Sirdari, control the landscape.

In northern Indian parts also, *Bhaiyachara*[10] system of land tenure prevailed, in which, acquired territory was equally divided among the initial colonizers. In other cases, *Pattidari*[11] system (in which ownership of land by clan families and payment of revenue by the community) worked, always conducive to agglomeration, hence, morphological structure by multi-caste people of *Jajmani* system. Thus, behind each type of morphological structure there was a system of *Jati* (caste), *gotra* (clan) and Kula (kinship), subtly inter-linked with land system.

Land Reforms

During the present century (20th) new land reforms are the rule in both, capitalist and communist countries. Land reforms of Soviet Union, China, Albania, Ethiopia remind us about State ownership of the land and resettlements in pioneer areas according to allotments, either as collective or cooperative farms, in China as communes, in Ethiopia under Peasant Associations. Each has its marked implications on rural landscape. North Korea, Cambodia, Vietnam and a few other African, Latin American countries are perceiving new horizons. In non-communist countries, land reform programmes vary nationwise. Japan saw redistribution of land after World War II. Israel has got its own resettlement strategies of the Kibbutz, Moshav, Moshav Shitufi, and

Moshava. During Revolutionary Government's regime Ethiopia saw new reforms through Associations and '*Ras*' or land lord's land was confiscated and redistributed.

In India, since Zamindari Abolition Act could be implemented, internal restructuring took place. New ceiling imposed on family holdings and tenancy reforms are showing impact on village living system. There is change in field system after consolidation of land holdings (as in Japan Fig. 6.1b) as well as in social structure, hence, morphology, specially, due to increase in residences or nucleus families. With the advent of tenancy reform and Panchayati Raj (in Uttar Pradesh particularly) *Gram Samaj* or village land is being allotted to landless people, who, in addition to forming new hamlets, are intermingling with other caste people including scheduled castes, obviously, loosening the bond of Jajmani system, referred to in religio-ritual Model. The permanency of right, guaranteed through new land tenure, is a pull to attract plot holder to its new location.

The resettlement villages of Malaysia present new examples. Since the implementation of Asiatic Land Tenure and Indian Representation Act of 1946, Indians were prevented from purchasing more land. This resulted into densely populated parts as well as dense housing.

Rural landscape of Bolivia is changing with the coming of Japanese immigrants from Ryukun, which occurred due to agrarian reform in 1953. The Okinawan settlements, located in Santa Cruz area of Eastern Bolivia, exhibit examples of changes taking place along the foot hills east of the Andes.[12]

Socio-Spatial Structure

An analysis of the community structure in relation to space would provide better understanding of morphology. We saw, nucleation was responsible for evolution of morphology in the main compact settlement of Mahjuda village. Now, the analysis of hamletization, would give insight into micro-level details of socio-spatial structure. The factors, enumerated, started showing impact during first phase when one of the Rajputs moved towards north and occupied most of the area lying in north eastern portion of the village territory after partition of the land. The newly established part was named as *Uttar Patti*, being located in the north. Further division in joint family system brought fragmentation of holdings but, still, the land was held by the clan members and the forest land was common land under the supreme hold of Rajputs. Second unit of settlements, on new site, of Rajputs again, developed near a big well, hence, the hamlet named as *Inaraha* from Inara (well). This became one of the three wells which remained main source of water till recently. During this phase other Rajputs, belonging to the main joint family, were holding their outpost or occasional homestead (Chhawani) at third site near orchards, fields and jungle under its command. At this stage the occasional flood limit had become a rare limit and shifted westward due to the cutting of *Bhita* in the west and consequent improved drainage condition. When family members increased, and irrigation limit shifted northward, it became essential to settle in the centre to minimize the production cost.

Population pressure and location of woodlands and pastures in the marginal areas, forced the stock raising caste to leave the compact settlement and a new hamlet grew in the centre. Such a cluster, purely based upon caste (of Ahirs) also grew in northwest. The former, being settled around a member of the main clan descendant, was named as *Purwa* meaning a hamlet-second settlement of the main in order of importance-and the latter, as *Taliya* being settled along a small *Tal* (water depression). To this unit accreted the potters, who were provided fallow land to settle around the well, already built by the settlers of the third phase.

When the third phase settlers were occupying the central and northwestern parts, some of the milkmen were busy with their temporary occupation of the site no 4 in the north and when they became able to purchase some plots, they shifted there. Water supply was made by a new well constructed in the north on the margin of the forest and, in the central part, and forest gave fuel and grazing ground in their neighbourhood.

During this period two outcaste Brahmins and two Rajputs made their separate dwellings as most of their land was in the western part of the village. Flood condition had slightly improved and it was possible to take even *Kharif* crop in eastern fields.

During this phase continuous drought conditions resulted into crop failure and the Rajputs (dependent on agricultural labour) could not pay the revenue, and some of the plots were again occupied by a Rajput of higher clan hierarchy on the paying of arrears to the Banaras State Officials. Thus, a separate small unit, almost adjacent to the third central unit, grew with three dwellings in course of time.

During British regime, transport facilities improved and pressure of population forced the settlers to seek employment in cities. Some of the milkmen, along with others, sought employment in Calcutta and after earning some money purchased some of the plots from Rajputs (who spent more than they saved) and occupied the fifth site around a well, newly constructed by a person named Ajmer, the settlement being called *Ajmer Ka Inara*. To this site also shifted a harder from the main settlement, as it was difficult for him to carry his sheep, to and from the pastures or forest through the arable lands along narrow paths. Other milkmen too, found it difficult, to drive their cattle through the *Khor* without trampling the crops which occasionally led to disputes and also, to cover the long distance daily. Thus, they completely left the original site which is now being occupied by the goldsmiths.

Another group, mostly dependent upon tenancy system and suffering form the pressure of population, occupied the site in between the road and the settlement site no. 5. Milkmen, who could earn money outside, separated themselves from their joint families and settled here on their own plots. By this time the last irrigational limit had been reached and new wells were constructed in various sectors (Siwan). Carpet-money and earnings from Bombay made them follow agricultural operations paying higher bids for plots surrounding their site.

During seventh phase (1950 onwards), economic changes showed obvious impact on socio-spatial scattering. Village Panchayat headed by *Gram Pradhan*, village chief, provided Gram Samaj land (common land) to many landless people, who settled along road (Mostly *Nonia* and *Chamars*) south of central unit of phase no. 3; another member from business class, who started selling of fried rice (lai) in the local market, and some washermen, left the old site due to congestion and settled in the west of the main site, along the road. Some other caste people also are occupying road sides through purchase of land to develop it into a market of varied type of shops and in some cases, shop-cum-residence. *Chamars* (Harijan) the scheduled caste, have also occupied the north eastern jungle area in the name of Ambedkarnagar. Two Rajputs have shifted to their consolidated *Chaks* (Plots) in the north and west.

Thus, the religio-ritual model and secular model, which worked in congregating varied caste people, at several sites in sectors maintaining proper distance from the main settlers, are losing their hold and economic diffusion model is proving stronger in effect.

But, in interior villages away from the roads, the age old morphological structure prevails. Scheduled caste people are still segregated from the main settlements. We take some more examples of structural arrangement in the following settlements taken from Malwa Region on the basis of purposive sampling. The maps (Figs. 4.26, 4.27, 4.28, 4.29, 4.31, 4.33, 3.12a to 3.16 and 3.17 to 3.32) from other parts) are self explanatory exhibiting community structure as well as other morphological features of rural landscape. For other spatial structures of settler's habitations the following treatment present better explanation.

Caste and Segregation

We observe in morphology the caste or sub-caste wise sectors, the phenomenon of closed clusters of houses-generally of closely related agnatic kins, with surprisingly varied type of densities in different sectors; also group wise limits of the base or roof of various elements of settlements, i.e., disposal of dead, water source, cultivations on various occasions. Various factors enable a group to exercise some sort of segregation in some form or the other. These are invariably the age, sex, natal versus conjugal, that is, born in versus married in and ourselves versus outsiders. A few community structures are separately allotted to men and women, having different scales, specifications, treatments and elements like windows, etc. The same structures may have different elements, spaces, furnitures etc. earmarked to be used primarily by each sex. Burial grounds, dormitories, dancing grounds show another type of sex segregation. During womans' periods of confinement, for dying men, we do perceive separate space and structure. Segregation of residences among various castes, their mobility in various parts, particularly, to water sources, community buildings and spaces (Chaupal) during functions, feasts and festivals or even fasts-all reflect social segregation castewise/religion wise. Even social status hierarchy is reflected in the siting and situation of such residences. Often, there are three things, segregation, aggregation and segmentation.

The segregation of human and cattle living structure is manifested in varied ways culturally.

The tendency to have separate sub-areas can be attributed to caste hierarchy, ideas of impurity and pollution, the need for certain occupations to have room for carrying out the different processes and to other cultural factors. Even the Bhils are divided into endogamous subdivisions. They have settlements of mixed population, where sometimes, allied tribes like Dhanak and untouchables live.

Farmer's Dwelling and Farms

Since the location of farmer's dwelling is functionally related to the arable fields, pastures, water sites and woods, it is presumed that, with a few exceptions, the farmer occupies a place in a compact habitation, separated from his farm by a number of objects interposed in between. These may be other farmer's residences, village paths, water bodies, waste lands, gardens or fields belonging to other farmers. A farmer's land holdings scatter in the village territory in many or one direction but often, at a distance ranging from a few meters to some Kms. Fragmentation of the holdings, alongwith other obstacles, add new problems to the distance covered. Farm-dwelling relations are greatly influenced by the degree of fragmentation, scattering of plots, pattern of operation, irregular and circuitous pathways, elongation of village shape as well as of plots, obstructions caused by physical features like rivulet, hillock and ravines and lack of roads. But despite these, the farmer lives in the compact habitation not to face them under duress, but because of the compensation, he enjoys provided by aggregation. A farmer's dwelling is not only a resting place, but a centre of multi-variate activities, which he does, seemingly his own, often, common with others. He breathes the air, sleeps, walks, gossips, quarrels and prays not only in his dwelling but in the village, and because of the village. At each step, in the walk of life, he is mostly a mutual cooperator for articles ranging from needle and spade to bullocks, carts and a host of others, based upon reciprocal relations of functions, both vertical as well as horizontal. Farmer's social space, thus, outweighs his economic space. Yet, his physical distance creates economic strain and adds substantial loss to his accountless budget.

Here, it is noteworthy that expansion in settlement, due to the occupance by the member of various castes, primarily predominated by cultivating castes, stock raiser and then by service class, in later stages, was closely related to forest clearing and ownership of the land for crops, pastures and woods in common, each occupying a widening ring round the compact morphological structure of the day. Arable land was, obviously, not all, the village needed, in fact the extent of the arable land in any one village was ultimately limited not as a rule, by the extent of suitable soil for cultivation, but by the proportion of the land of the community, that must be left in grass to feed the beasts needed to pull the plough.[13] Woods provided not only grazing ground, but also, food and raw materials for farm implements and small but simple furnitures and hunting place to the self-sufficient villager of earlier times. It was just possible that a barn was established for storing grain or fodder, and an enclosure (*Khala*) for cattle, and a hut or *tapro* for busy seasons, which grew into small hamlet. Such hamlets, sometimes, under able leadership, asserted rights, and separate settlement, of different size and shape from its neighbour, flourished. The extent of soil, with little variation in fertility, was responsible to provide symmetrically spaced settlements of a definite size and shape with their land boundary running paralled to the residential one. The earlier settlers, when ousted by the Rajputs or Non-Rajput invaders, occupied the area widely scattered in wilderness (mostly in Central India) which was less fertile at that time; and this led to the variations in size and shape of the farm and compact dwelling groups.

The arrangement of settlement and land boundary, evolving simultaneously alongwith fragmentation of holdings, based on the right of inheritance, has led to variations in the distance of dwelling and farm, which also varies, form region to region and from one settlement to another within the same region. Presuming that the farmer occupies a central location in a settlement of some sample villages, following variations are visualized in farm dwelling distance on the basis of method, discussed below, as depicted through Table 6 (i).

Table 6 (I)

Village farm Distance in a Few Villages in Malwa Region

Village Name	*Distance in Metres*	*Village Name*	*Distance in Metres*
Dharar	1,272	Khurda	1.713
Datana	2,516	Piplod	2.739
Bhugore	2,135	Matkuli	1.378
Udaigir	1,376	Ajnad	2.127
Sanchi	2,387	Bamankheri	2,714
Dhamnod	1,108	Bhilkheri	2,109
Guljhara	1,209	Manpur	2,737

Intra-Village Spacing

We may take examples form the Malwa Region and the Northern Plains. Spacing has been computed with four assumptions and a simple forumla.

It is assumed that:

(a) the villages in any areal unit are of equal size with hexagonal shape of the village land,
(b) whole population of the village lives in compact settlement situated in the centre of the area,
(c) every plot of the village is accessible in a crow flight fashion,
(d) inhabitants do not cultivate any plot outside their village boundary.

The formula for intra village distance stands:

$$Vfd = 0.5373\sqrt{A/N}$$

Where Vfd = Village dwelling to farm or boundary distance
A = Area of unit
N = Number of settlements.

The computation regarding the Malwa region is shown in Table 6 (i).

It is clear that farm-dwelling distance varies from 1,108 to 2,737 metres. This variation increases according to the shape and size of the villages lying in forest, in the Upland of Nimar and others lying in rugged terrain of Sagar, Guna districts and in the Mahi basin. As shown in the Figures. 6.2, 6.3 and 3.9, the elongated shape of the village boundary of Sanchi and Udaigir, location of residential site of Bhugore in one corner and central position of Matkuli, present varied picture of relationship between farm and dwelling, shape of residential unit and village limit and other features of morphological expression.

The average intra-village distance, in Bhadohi district (Uttar Pradesh) at nyayapanchayat level, is 538 m (0.538 Km) which is less than the national average, i.e., 1120 m (1.12 Km). Here the computed data are classified in five categories:

(1) Very low distance (<500 m): It is found in 501 villages of 32 nyayapanchayats, covering an area not less than 32.96%. Variation ranges from 372 m in Chhatmi to 498 m in Vari. This area extends as a narrow belt in middle northern and southern parts endowed with fertile soil and well developed market centres.
(2) Low (500-600 m): Such nyayapanchayats spread (36.15% of area) in the middle part, where fertile soil and early development of transport facility, are main pull factors. Distance varies from 509 m in Tilanga to 550 m in Aurai and 595 m in Bisapur.
(3) Medium (600-700 m): Though nyayapanchayats of this group scatter throughout the Tahsil, yet, north western part exhibits main distribution. It covers 92 villages, with an area of 12.05% of the total, and distance varies from 600 m in Kurauna to 621 m in Ramnagar, 662 m in Darwasi and 690 m in Darunaha. These are Usar and Tal areas of the Tahsil with average fertile soil.
(4) High (700-800 m): 57 villages of this category spread in flood effected Khadar and Tal area covering 10.30% of area. Distance varies from 704 m in Jathi to 784 m in Patti Bejaon.
(5) Very High (800 m and above): This category covers 36 villages covering 8.09% of the area in Varipur, Deegh, Ibrahimpur and Ajaypur nyayapanchayats. Flood conditions and Usar land margins are deciding factors for greater distance.

Distribution of Plots and Sizes

Though distribution of landholdings is a cultural phenomena, which depends upon, the type of land tenure during occupance, hereditary rights and choice of the owner, yet the variations in size, are related to drainage conditions, irrigation facilities, nearness to the inhabitation, type of crop rotation, use of implements, status of cultivator and alos individual whims. Once a farmer inherited scattered fragmented holdings, the number of plots increase in next generation, and this becomes an unending process. Still, the soil, its type, fertility and spread, slope of the land, type of tenure system, adopted locally and seasonally, and socio-economic and cultural status of the farmer, determine the field pattern and size of polts. In figure 6.2, Dharar plots show fragmentation of plots rectangular in shape, small in size near the residential unit and bigger on the margin. But the plots, used since long, due to its nearness to Ujjain, Mandav and Dhar, the old historical centres-are smaller in comparison to the plots of Matkuli village of recent origin. Similar pattern is found in Datana and Bhugore and Udaigiri. Cultural impact is also visible in Khurda village, where recently, Missonary workers have brought square to rectangular pattern instead of long strips and irregular plots, found elsewhere. Effects of 'Goind' land or nearness to residential site is visible in most of the villages. Effect of *nala* and terrain is also visible in Udaigiri and Matkuli. Thus, size of plots near residential units, obviously, reflect the multiple use of land under crops, through minimization of distance and effort, with increased frequency in between dwelling and plot and establishment of seasonal work rhythm well adopted to household work and sowing, weeding, watching, carrying, harvesting, keeping (thrashing, winnowing, sacking etc.) etc. miscellaneous operations needed, involving maximum number of family members.

Settlement—Farm Distance: Space Relationship

Now, we can discuss the relationship between distance and landuse, the link which determines the work rhythm of the farmer, the chief tool, to bring morphological change in internal spatial pattern of the settlements. Everywhere he seems to be making some adjustments in the spatial pattern of this operations to economise effort[14]. Most of the cultivators follow intensive cultivation in the plots lying adjacent to residential units, which yield double crops of vegetables, cereals and fruits. The 'Zone of intensive cultivation, observes Chisholm', is composed of small or minute properties, which are fragmented and dispersed and mostly derive from basehold concession[15]. It is a common feature that maize, cotton, potato, fodder crops, vegetables and cereals are grown on well drained plots near the settlement site, other foodcrops in th second ring, and millets on the marginal land. This is because frequency of travel, care of crop and labour put into the plot, and transportation cost, determine the economic rent. Residing in the central cluster, the villager, is at a minimum economic distance from his scattered field.[16] Farmer's customary practices to satisfy his needs should not be overlooked. The cultivator, during ploughing and harvesting season, is bound to take his meal in the field often, carried along with him or carried by his family member. Farm product is taken to barn through bullock cart or tractor trolley, which need a track, an enclosure for fodder, and labour often engaged in driving, maintaining these all; these harmoniously blended, increase the economic cost of production. Hence, distance must be thought of as economic distance, not merely physical distance; it is the cost incurred and not the distance in so many km. which matters.[17] This economic distance increases, where one evaluates the labour, input involved in other agricultural operations like manuring, ploughing, harvesting and giving protection from animals, predatory birds, theft and host of others. Economic distance, should also be considered in relation to crop yield, which diminishes as the distance of farm from dwelling increases. This fact hinges upon the consideration, that the farmer will accept a less in-

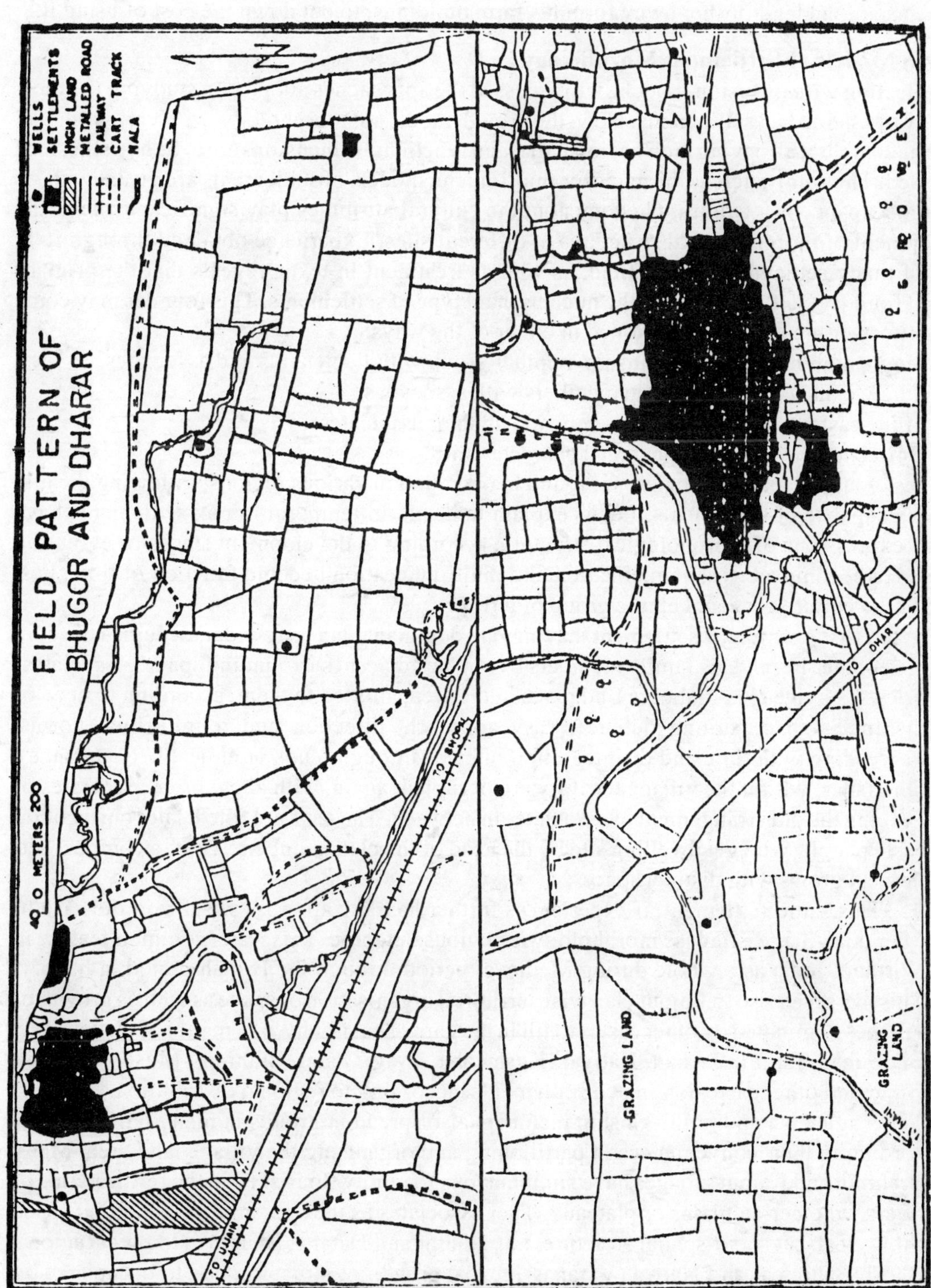
FIELD PATTERN OF
BHUGOR AND DHARAR
WELLS
SETTLEMENTS
HIGH LAND
METALLED ROAD
RAILWAY
CART TRACK
NALA
METERS 200
TO UJJAIN
TO BHOPAL
TO DHAR
GRAZING LAND
GRAZING LAND

Figure 6.2

tensive use of the land further away form his farm buildings, to cut down the cost of using it.[18]

Growth Models of Settlement Morphology

While dealing with diffusion models, we discussed the approaches adopted in studying the morphology of established settlements. Now, the growth models of morphology, with various nuclei or one nucleus, but all having their socio-spatial and functional dimensions are to be hypothesized and tested. Thus, uni-nucleus, bi-nuclei or multi-nuclei models of settlements are visualized. As human occupance is a cultural phenomenon, the cultural attributes play significant role in the development of morphological structures at different sites. Experience obtained through field study of many settlements in the field, as well as treatment in texts, reveals that the primary original founder (settler) becomes the nucleus in all type of settlements. This founder may come in a territory or the land to be occupied in either of the ways:

(a) Single dominant clan and kinship member group with lieutenants and associates.
(b) Single clan and multi-kinship members with associates.
(c) Multi-caste and clan-kinship members with their associates.
(d) Uni-clan tribes with unique racial characteristics.

These four alternate strategies, are found in operation in various regions, following the historical occupance of settlements. Let us explain in detail. In temporal frame, settlements have various expressions of morphological structure, according to development stages or evolution phases. Here, compactness, hamletization and multi-nucleation become function of time, best suited to the culture zone and ethnic group of territory.

(a) In the first example, a settlement, having one dominant clan as founder, occupies the core area of the site, and his family members live in the adjacent surrounding space. Associates-priests, service class, labours find place in the area, allotted to them, according to need of the time—space suiting defence, easy approach, direction and religio-ritual norms. Proceeding with time and disintegration of clan (through feuds or amicable occupance), other sites, within the village territory are occupied, again, with a few more associates or keeping the old arrangement of associates in between. The gaps are filled, later on, by other caste people, who get dwelling site by the head of the clan members. Thus, a compact settlement grows with distinct spaces.

This same settlement, if experiences further hamletization, as we saw in the case of Mahjuda village, sitewise morphology is obvious outcome. This was a common feature in Northern India as a whole during Medieval period through the British period in history. This has given rise to Rajput clan wise territorial organisation of space as well as growth of villages dominated by other castes to fill in the gaps. That is why, as a matter of fact, we see, Bhumihar, Kurmi, Sachan, Katiyar, Kushwaha, Tyagi, Patel, Brahmin, Muslim, Jat and Gujar and other caste dominated settlements, according to regional distribution.

(b) The single clan and multi-kinship members also spread in groups in many territories according to their conveniences in partitioning and organising the village land area. Many Brahmin and Rajput villages have simultaneously, jointly flourished in the fertile plains of rivers, whether on plains or plateaux. Ther associates as they assembled in allotted space show clear-cut socio-spatial structure, i.e., Dharar and Datana, Bhugore (Malwa Region), Bhori, Bahraichi and Natwa (Varanasi) reveal growth of structure, due to occupance by these people alongwith their associates in a compact settlement, i.e., of uni-nucleation.

FIELD PATTERN OF VILL. (A) MATKULI (B) DATANA (C) UDAIGIR
(A)
TO PIPARIA
(B)
CAMP GROUND
TO DEWAS
N
SHOOTING GROUND
DENWA R.
0 40 200
METRES
R. BETWA
WELLS
SETTLEMENTS
HIGHLANDS
METALLED ROAD
CART TRACK
NALA
PLOT BOUNDARY
(C)

Figure 6.3

Such settlements are, later fillings, and spread in spaces provided by, original territorial organisers to their associates, or the land obtained through Muafi, Jagirdari or grants.

(c) The multi-caste and clan-kinship groups occupy many big settlements, in river plains in Eastern India (Bihar), Malwa Plateau and southern peninsular parts of India. This occurred, in places, where various caste people in kinship groups, occupied an village area and spread alongwith their inmates, associates or later settlers. Naini in Bihar (Fig. 6.4) is the best example. Here evolved the morphological structure by Rajputs (Gautam, Kakan, Amethi and Bais), and Brahmins belonging to Mishra and Tiwari sub-caste groups. Other caste people have timely supported the 'Jajmani system' through their sectoral growths. Similar growth is seen in Mahui and Majhanpura in Saran Plain (Figs. 6.5, 6.6). This combination may be of Bhumihar and Rajput, Kurmi and Ahir, Rajput and Brahmin, Jat and Gujar, or others according to the type of diffusion and spread. In some areas it may show, multi-muclei arrangement.

(d) Uni-clan tribal group morphology develops according to racial characteristics of tribes concerned. For Gonds (Matkuli) and Bhils (Naharkhodra) represent two examples. The kinship groups, living in huts at separate isolated sites, have distinct structural growth.

The study of newer settlements, on usar and forest margins, reveals, that morphological structure is still coming up on the basis of one of the conditions explained through models.[19] It is obvious, that in later type of growth, mostly new entrepreneurs-belonging to all earning castes-are changing the morphological structure. As an example we may take Janakpur settlement (Fig. 6.7) on a usar margin, started by Yadav family sine 1951 and now, it is a well developed hamlet of about 20 houses. Still, other arrivals are awaited.

Man-Land Ratio and Caste (Jati) Ranking: A Changing Perspective

The study of man-land ratio, hinges upon, the historical background of the settlement occupance, in a particular area. As most of the old world countries, show evidences or humanization through various tribal clans, it would be easy to approach taking examples from Indian part. The Rajput clan ascendancy has been responsible for settlement occupance during Mughal period and onwards, with changes here and there with changes of chieftains, hence, taluqdars, proprietors and tenants. Under *Raiyatwari* or *Bhaichara* system of land tenure, various clans were in possession of the settled part, even during the British period, which more or less still continues, of course, witch considerable impact of the Zamindari Abolition Act in North. While studying the records one finds, without any surprise, that in Eastern Uttar Pradesh (Awadh) about 58 per cent of the land in Sultanpur, 55 per cent in Pratapgarh, excluding 10 per cent under proprietors (Primarily *taluqdars*), and about two thirds in Faizabad district remained under *taluqdari.* Elsewhere, the *Bhaichara* system (joint village land tenure) was evolved (as discussed earlier) in which the entire clan area is held in common by the members of a single clan. *Ain-i-Akbari* (1959 A.D.) reveals that, Rajputs paid 75 per cent of the total land revenue and shared responsibility with Brahmins or Muslims for an additional 15 per cent, as shown in table 6 (ii).

As the figures show, the Rajputs enjoyed dominance in land possession during Mughal period; but new landowners increased in number as well as in variety of castes, firstly Brahmin, Bhumihar, Muslim and Bania, Kayasthas (tables 6 (ii), 6 (iii), 6 (iv), 6 (v), 6 (vi) and Figs. 6.8, 6.9) and then lastly, after Independence, the yadavs, Kurmies and host of others, as member of settlement units sharing the space in morphology. If we see the man-land ratio of a particular village,

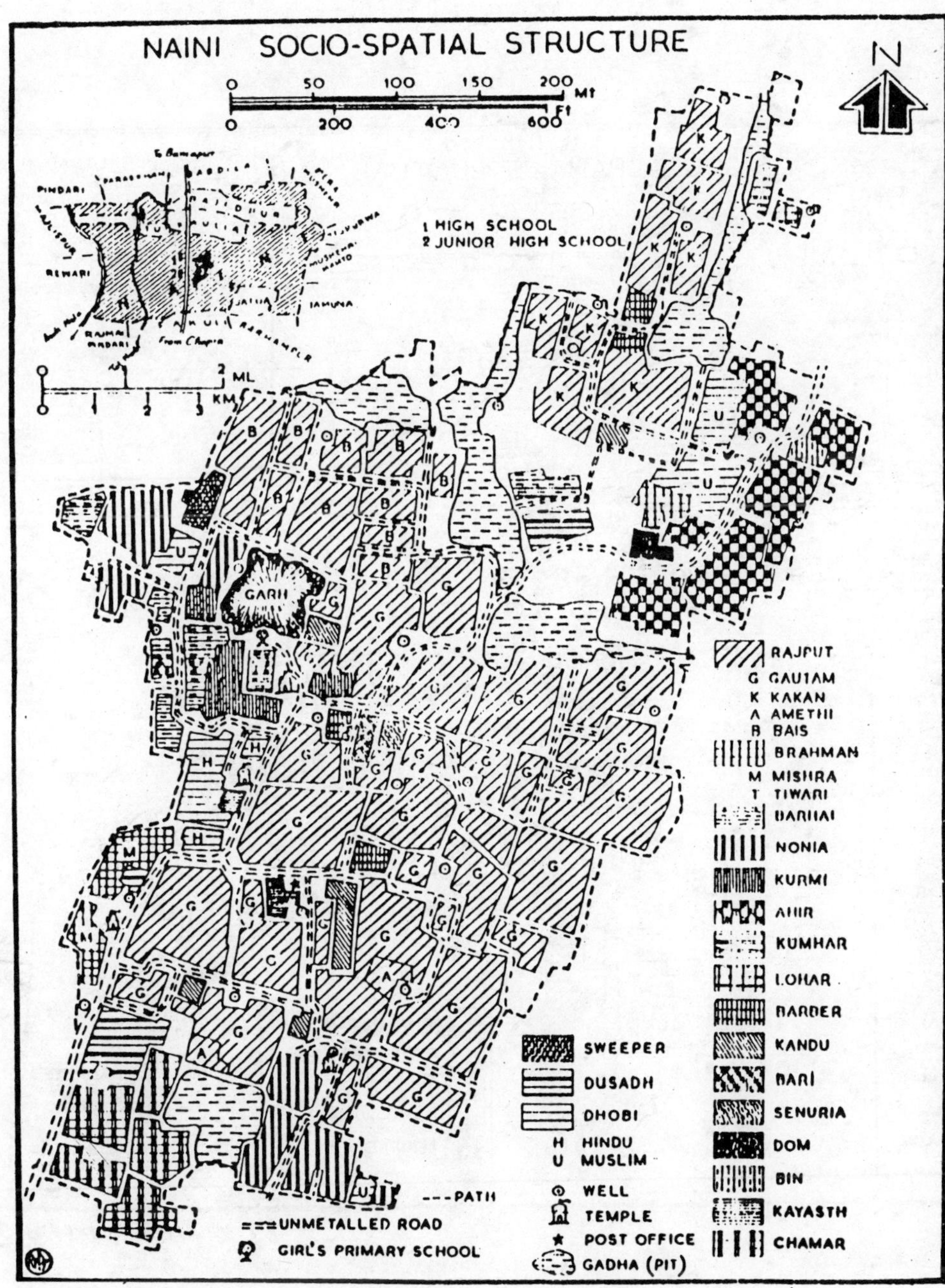

Figure 6.4

it becomes obvious, that many non-Rajput castes are the purchasers of land from Rajputs, hence, possession reflected, in the possession of village settlement site also, in shape of sectors or hamlets.

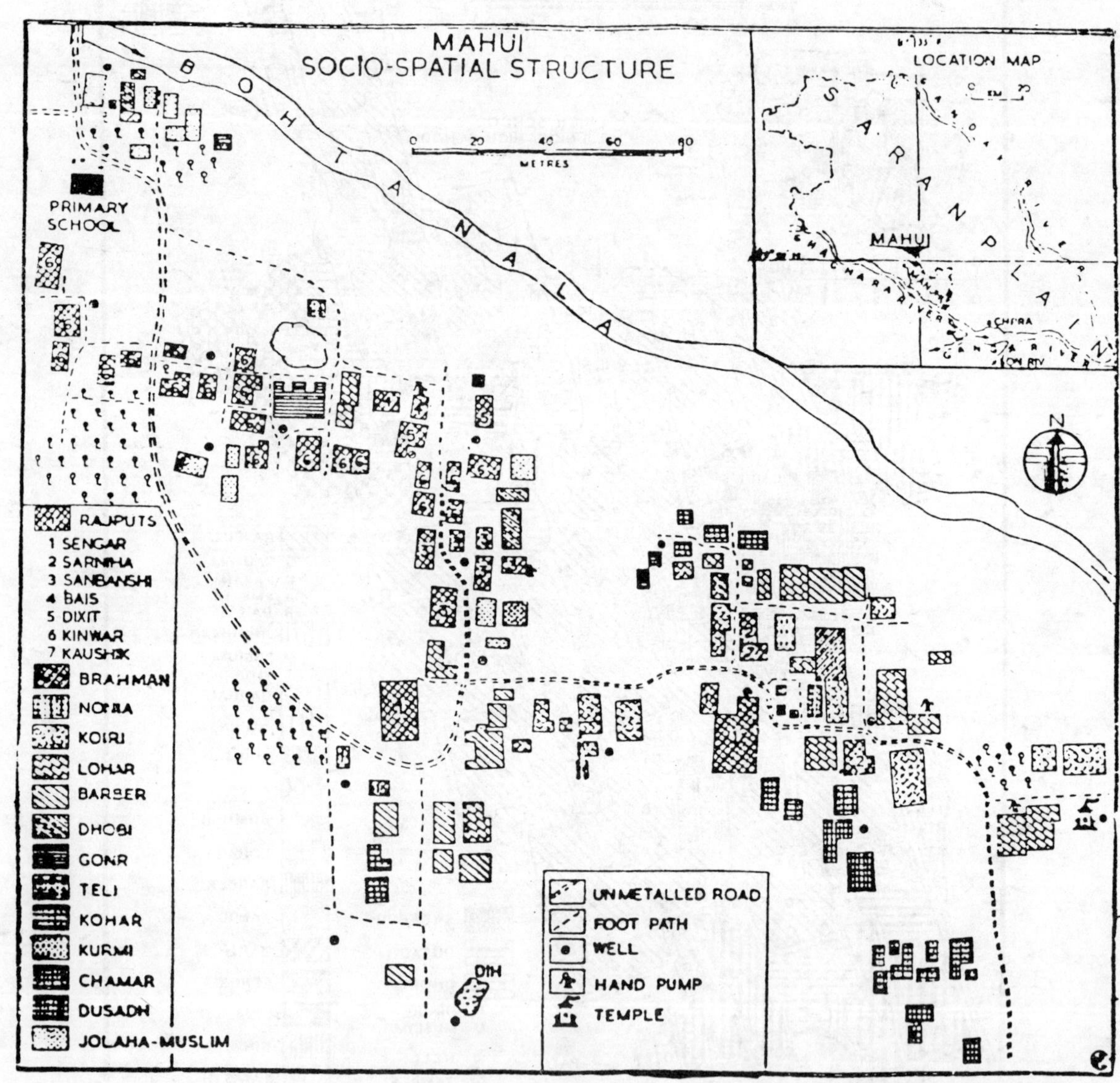

Figure 6.5

A look at the disintegration of joint family, and distribution of land during two centuries, makes the point clear (Fig. 6.10). The clan member (6 household members), occupying 125 acres of land in A.D. 1800, increases in number up to 36 (with hereditary rights), hence, ratio comes down to 1:3.47, which would be only 1:2 during 21st century.[21]

Table 6 (ii)

Castewise Payment of Land Revenue in Percentage (Ain- i-Akbari, A.D. 1596[20]*)*

Caste/Distt.	*Jaunpur*	*Ghazipur + Ballia*	*Banaras*	*All Districts*
Rajput	64	39	16	50
Brahman and Bhumihar	6	59	79	30
Brahman	18	—	5	11
Muslim	5	—	—	3
Muslim-Rajputs	6	—	—	4
Others	1	—	—	1
Unknown	—	2	—	1

Table 6 (iii)

Castes of Zamindars of Seven Parganas—1789-90

(in Percent)

Caste/Pargana	*Katehar (Varanasi)*	*Kolaslah (Benaras)*	*Majhwa (Mirzapur)*	*Haveli (Ghazipur)*	*Zaheerabad (Ghazipur)*	*Kopah (Ballia)*	*Mungra (Jaunpur)*	*All Parganas*
Rajput	76	62	90	3	5	14	55	29
Bhumihars	6	10	—	17	55	59	10	31
Brahmins	6	10	5	10	8	13	10	9
Muslims	—	4	—	59	16	4	5	18
Kayasthas	2	—	—	2	—	—	5	1
Other Hindus	6	14	5	9	16	7	10	11
Unknown	4	—	—	—	—	—	5	1

Source: Cohn, B.S. ref. no. 20, p. 68.

Table 6 (iv)

Land Ownership by Castes in 1885

(in Percent)

District	*Rajputs*	*Brahmins*	*Bhumihars*	*Banias*	*Muslims*
Ghazipur	26	12	26	3	13
Ballia	74	7	8	2	2
Jaunpur	39	15	—	4	29
Varanasi	37	—34—		13	8
Azamgarh	35	11	15	—	23
Gorakhpur	22	26	10	—	7
Basti	31	33	4	—	8
Faizabad	44	23	—	—	22
Sultanpur	76	—	—	—	17
Pratapgarh	83	7	—	—	6

Source: Computed from Various Settlement Reports.

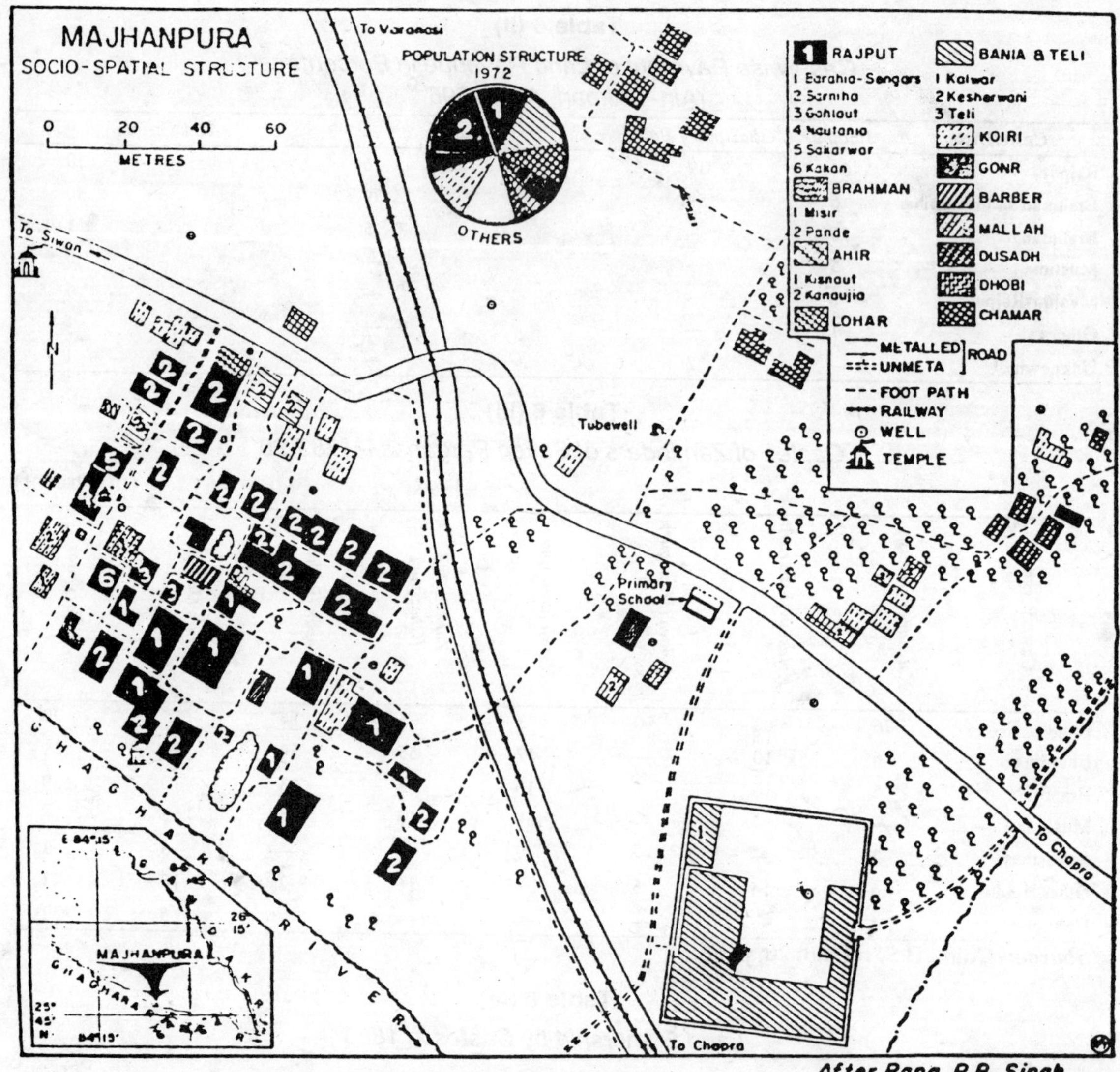

After Rana P.B. Singh

Figure 6.6

The current sale and purchase of land data regarding Umaraha and Barain villages (Varanasi) approve of the fact.

The table reveals that Rajput and Brahmin are the main sellers and Kurmi, Ahir, Bania and Muslims are main buyers, hence, change in economic conditions and status. This decides to a great extent the rank in society, i.e., hierarchy in society. Kurmi, Ahir, Muslim and Bania are raising their status and change is perceptible in their outer appearance of house structures, hence, change in occupied space as well as morphology. Sometimes, these purchasers are occupying land holdings away from main settlements, as new sites, hence, a hamlet in embryonic stage. Often, these neo-rich are coming out of congested village built up area and making construction on valuable cropped lands, hence, further change in structure as well as form.

A household wise study[22] reveals, that 83 per cent of total households, are under 5 acres of landholding and 62 per cent in the size of < 6 persons, with holding of >2.5 acres (table 6 (vii), Fig. 6.11). Thus, man-land ratio with its downward trend dependent upon nucleus family is more responsible for change in spatial structure too.

Table 6 (v)

Land Transfer (Umaraha) 1980-90

Caste of Sellers	*Total Number*	*No. of Sellers %*	*Caste of Buyers*	*Total Number of Buyers*	*Total No. of Buyers %*
Rajput	22	46.82	Kurmi	16	34.06
Kurmi	10	21.28	Bania	6	12.78
			Chamar	4	8.51
Kayastha	4	8.51	Ahir	4	8.51
Brahmin	3	6.38	Muslim	3	6.38
			Kohar	2	4.25
Sonar	3	6.38	Sonar	2	4.25
			Rajbhar	2	4.25
Chamar	2	4.25	Kohar	2	4.25
			Gareria	2	4.25
Rajbhar	2	4.25	Rajput	2	4.25
			Brahmin	1	2.13
Ahir	1	2.13	Halwai	1	2.13
Total	47	100		47	100

Source: Personal Survey in the Field.

Table 6 (vI)

Land Transfer (Barain) 1980-90

Caste of Sellers	*Total Number*	*Sellers's %*	*Cast of Buyers*	*Number of Buyers*	*Buyers's %*
Brahmin	18	60.00	Ahir	11	36.69
Ahir	4	13.34	Brahmin	6	20.00
Nonia	4	13,34	Rajput	3	10.00
Rajput	2	6.66	Koiri	3	10.00
Bhar	1	3.33	Bhar	2	6.66
			Bania	2	6.66
Pasi	1	3.33	Gosain	1	3.33
			Kohar	1	3.33
			Nonia	1	3.33
Total	30	100		30	100

The table shows that uneconomic land holdings (>2.5 acres) are expected to feed 75 per cent of the households. Naturally, their livelihood is supplanted by other secondary activities. This change leads to migration, selling of land, desertation of old site, and occupance in new area, hence, visible changes in morphological structure. Table 6 (viii) given below shows that in Sunderpur village (Varanasi) Figure 6.12, Brahmin, Koiri, Bania, Musalman are the main lan-downing castes. Dhobis (scheduled caste) rank third only. It is enough to prove upward movement of poor caste/class people. Koiris (backward) stand second.

Table 6 (vii)

Households (20% sample) Classified by Cultivators and Size of Holdings

(in Percent)

Size of Holdings (Acre)	Size of Households (Members)					
	1	2-3	4-6	7-9	10	Total
< 1.0	1.95	7.72	13.93	4.28	1.46	30.04
≥ 1.0	1.25	6.00	14.04	6.95	3.29	31.53
≥ 2.5	0.52	2.60	7.92	5.77	3.88	20.69
≥ 5.0	0.20	0.80	2.79	2.59	2.50	8.88
≥ 7.5	0.06	0.20	0.89	0.94	1.20	3.27
≥ 10.0	0.02	0.14	0.49	0.59	0.91	2.15
≥ 12.5	0.02	0.08	0.20	0.27	0.51	1.08
≥ 15.0	1.03	0.08	0.32	0.45	0.97	1.85
≥ 30.0	0.01	0.02	0.06	0.06	0.18	0.33
≥ 50.0	0.01	0.02	0.03	0.04	0.08	0.18
Total	4.07	17.66	40.65	22.64	14.98	100.00

Source: Computed from Distt. Census Handbook, Saran, 1971, Part X C.

Table 6 (viii)

Man-land Ratio and Caste Ranking—Chak Sunderpur

Caste	Population		Land Ownership (in acre)		Per Head Ownership (in acre)	Per Acre Population	Rank
	Total	Percent	Total	Percent			
Brahmin	339	21.39	88.75	54.49	0.252	3.55	1
Koiri	205	12.93	40.32	26.62	0.196	5.08	2
Bania	165	10.41	7.50	4.77	0.045	22.00	6
Harijan	185	11.76	4.37	2.78	0.023	42.33	9
Muslim	155	9.78	4.28	2.72	0.027	36.21	7
Tailors (Muslim)	196	12.37	2.00	1.27	0.010	98.00	10
Nai (Barbar)	85	5.36	2.18	1.39	0.025	38.99	8
Dhobi (Washerman)	30	1.89	3.28	2.08	0.109	9.15	3
Bhunj	65	4.10	0.20	1.12	0.003	32.5	11
Pasi	62	3.91	3.12	1.98	0.050	18.87	5
Shepherd	45	2.84	4.37	2.78	0.097	10.29	4
Bind	28	1.77	—	—	—	—	—
Carpenter Blacksmith	25	1.58	—	—	—	—	—
Total	1585	100.00	157.37	100.00	0.099	10.07	—

Source: Personal Investigation.

In another example, the computed statistics [table 6 (ix)] of the six villages have been plotted (Fig. 6.13) which clearly shows, the gradient line of man-land ratio, where different castes may be placed in the hierarchy, by order/rank in the village. The castes are arranged according to their rank and are plotted accordingly. The curves clearly show, a wide gap in the hierarchical system.

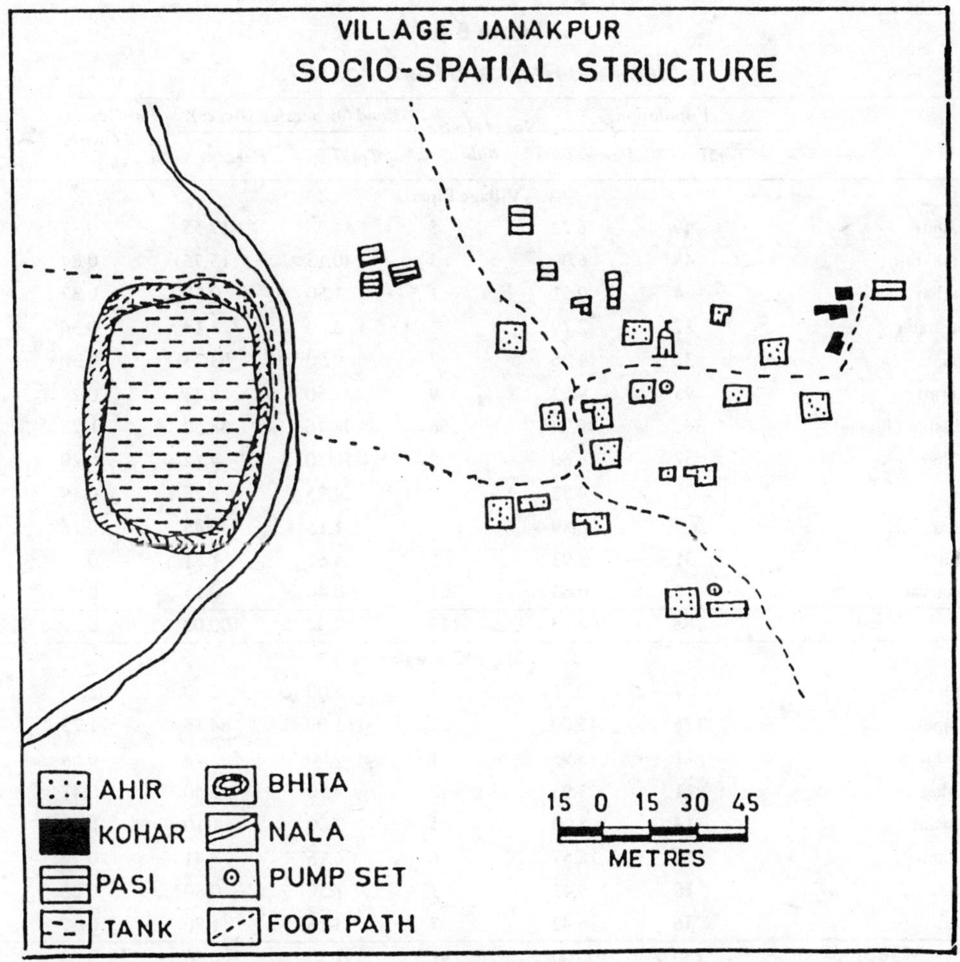

Figure 6.7

Generally, in most cases, the Rajputs are at the top [see table 6 (ix)], only because of their relatively large land ownership, while on the other hand, backward castes like Dharkar, Pasi and Chamar, have a lesser share [see table 6 (ix)]. It is notable, that in spite of first rank in the caste hierarchy of the orthodox-social scale, Bhahmins are not at the top, only due to less share in land ownership in addion to their dependency on the higher castes, along with deep invlovement in the ritual activities.

In most part of the Northern India, selling of land is a practice in vogue, in upper caste people, the reason being: to meet the marriage cost, maintenance of standard of living and reluctance in agricultural operations. Data regarding two village near Varanasi are examples.

The age old caste ranking, though outwardly, is still, on caste basis/hierarchy, yet, due to change in land ownership and other earnings, the first address in the form of *namaste*, *namaskar*, *salam* or synonyms in regional languages or hallow, does not, invariably follow hierarchy or caste. Now, Brahmins are ready to shower, boons of well being, welfare, flourishing life trends, on neo-rich Ahir, Kurmi or other backward caste people, before they salute them. And, yes, they do shower it beforehand.

Table 6 (ix)

Man-land Ratio and Ranking, 1979

S.No. and Rank	Caste	Population Total	Population Percent	No. of House-hold	Land Ownership (Acres) Total	Land Ownership (Acres) Percent	Per Capita Land Owner-ship	Per Acre Population Pressure
	A. Village Piparia							
1.	Rajput	49	6.22	5	44.74	17.55	0.91	1.09
2.	Brahamin	48	6.09	5	40.15	15.75	0.84	1.19
3.	Barhai	4	0.51	1	1.50	0.59	0.37	2.67
4.	Dushadh	22	2.79	3	8.00	3.14	0.36	2.75
5.	Nai	32	4.06	7	9.50	3.73	0.30	3.37
6.	Kurmi	75	9.52	9	21.50	8.43	0.29	3.49
7.	Muslim (Julaha)	388	49.24	66	98.16	38.50	0..25	3.95
8.	Kahar	52	6.60	8	10.50	4.12	0.20	4.95
9.	Teli	75	9.52	9	14.75	5.78	0.19	5.08
10.	Bhar	7	0.89	1	1.15	0.45	0.16	6.09
11.	Lohar	31	3.93	5	4.62	1.81	0.15	6.71
12.	Dharkar	5	0.63	1	0.40	0.15	0.05	12.50
	Total	788	100.00	117	254.97	100.00	0.32	3.09
	B. Village Khararaich							
1.	Teli	2	0.71	1	5.00	2.70	2.50	0.40
2.	Rajput	126	45.00	21	161.00	84.16	1.23	0.78
3.	Brahmin	11	3.93	1	7.00	3.73	0.64	1.57
4.	Kohar	11	3.93	2	4.50	2.40	0.41	2.44
5.	Muslim	14	5.00	1	2.00	1.10	0.14	7.00
6.	Chamar	52	18.57	6	6.15	3.41	0.12	8.45
7.	Kahar	18	6.43	3	1.50	0.80	0.08	12.00
8.	Pasi	46	16.43	7	3.15	1.70	0.07	14.60
	Total	280	100.00	42	191.30	100.00	0.68	1.46
	C. Village Chikania							
1.	Brahmin	92	31.19	6	81.00	77.40	0.88	1.14
2.	Rajput	4	1.35	1	2.75	2.63	0.69	1.45
3.	Pasi	6	2.03	1	2.15	2.05	0.36	2.79
4.	Ahir	30	10.17	2	7.00	6.69	0.23	4.28
5.	Koiri	10	3.39	2	2.25	2.15	0.22	4.44
6.	Bhar	9	3.06	1	1.50	1.43	0.17	6.00
7.	Lohar	7	2.37	1	1.00	0.95	0.14	7.00
8.	Teli (Kalawar)	7	2.37	1	0.75	0.73	0.11	9.30
9.	Thathera	10	3.39	1	1.00	0.95	0.10	10.00
10.	Khatic	25	8.47	3	1.35	1.29	0.05	18.52
11.	Chamar	80	27.13	13	3.50	3.35	0.04	22.86
12.	Kumhar	7	2.37	1	0.25	0.24	0.03	28.00
13.	Mallah	8	2.71	1	0.15	0.14	0.02	53.33
	Total	295	100.00	34	104.65	100.00	0.35	2.82

Contd...

			D. Village Nabipur				
1. Saithwar	181	20.49	21	172.15	48.90	0.95	1.05
2. Kurmi	77	8.72	16	37.55	10.62	0.49	2.05
3. Brahmin	20	2.26	3	9.00	2.55	0.45	2.22
a. Mishra	7	0.79	2	5.00	1.42	0.71	1.40
b. Shukla	13	1.47	1	4.00	1.13	0.31	3.25
4. Nai	18	2.04	4	7.00	1.99	0.39	2.57
5. Ahir	61	6.91	10	22.20	6.31	0.36	2.75
6. Kayastha	5	0.57	1	1.76	0.50	0.35	2.84
7. Chamar	143	16.19	43	45.22	12.84	0.32	3.16
8. Bhar	24	2.72	4	7.00	1.99	0.29	3.42
9. Kahar	27	3.06	4	7.75	2.20	0.29	3.44
10. Kohar	25	2.83	4	7.00	1.99	0.28	3.57
11. Teli	85	9.63	15	14.75	4.19	0.17	5.78
12. Lohar	24	2.72	3	4.10	1.16	0.17	5.85
13. Nonia	132	14.95	24	12.65	3.60	0.10	10.42
14. Muslim	61	6.91	9	3.90	1.11	0.06	15.62
Total	883	100.00	164	352.03	100.00	0.40	2.51
			E. Village Bisara				
1. Rajput	106	11.10	9	146.00	51.36	1.38	0.73
a. Bais	9	0.97	1	13.50	4.75	1.50	0.73
b. Kaushik	97	10.13	8	132.50	46.61	1.37	0.67
2. Brahmin (All Ojhas)	8	0.85	1	4.25	1.50	0.53	1.88
3. Ahir	127	13.30	14	35.15	12.36	0.28	3.61
4. Koiri	132	13.80	16	33.08	11.64	0.25	3.99
5. Teli	37	2.84	2	5.75	2.02	0.29	4.69
6. Gosain	6	0.63	1	1.25	0.44	0.21	4.80
7. Chamar	34	3.55	5	6.50	2.29	0.19	5.23
8. Dusadh	13	1.22	2	2.15	0.76	0.16	6.05
9. Kahar	45	4.71	7	5.50	1.93	0.12	8.18
10. Mallah	213	22.28	31	24.60	8.65	0.11	8.66
11. Barhai	65	6.80	10	7.45	2.62	0.11	8.72
12. Lohar	55	5.75	6	5.60	1.97	0.10	9.82
13. Nonia	50	5.22	3	3.50	1.23	0.07	14.29
14. Khatic	71	7.43	9	3.50	1.23	0.05	20.29
15. Nai	5	0.52	1	—	—	—	—
Total	957	100.00	126	284.28	100.00	0.30	3.33
			F. Village Muriari Khurd				
1. Saithwar	315	56.15	35	259.63	89.38	0.82	1.21
2. Ahir	18	3.21	2	3.25	1.19	0.18	5.54
3. Lohar	21	3.74	3	3.75	1.27	0.18	5.60
4. Nai	42	7.49	5	6.50	2.23	0.15	6.46
5. Kahar	4	0.71	1	0.50	0.17	0.12	8.00
6. Chamar	161	28.70	25	16.75	5.76	0.10	9.61
Total	561	100.00	71	290.38	100.00	0.518	1.93

Based on Personal Survey.

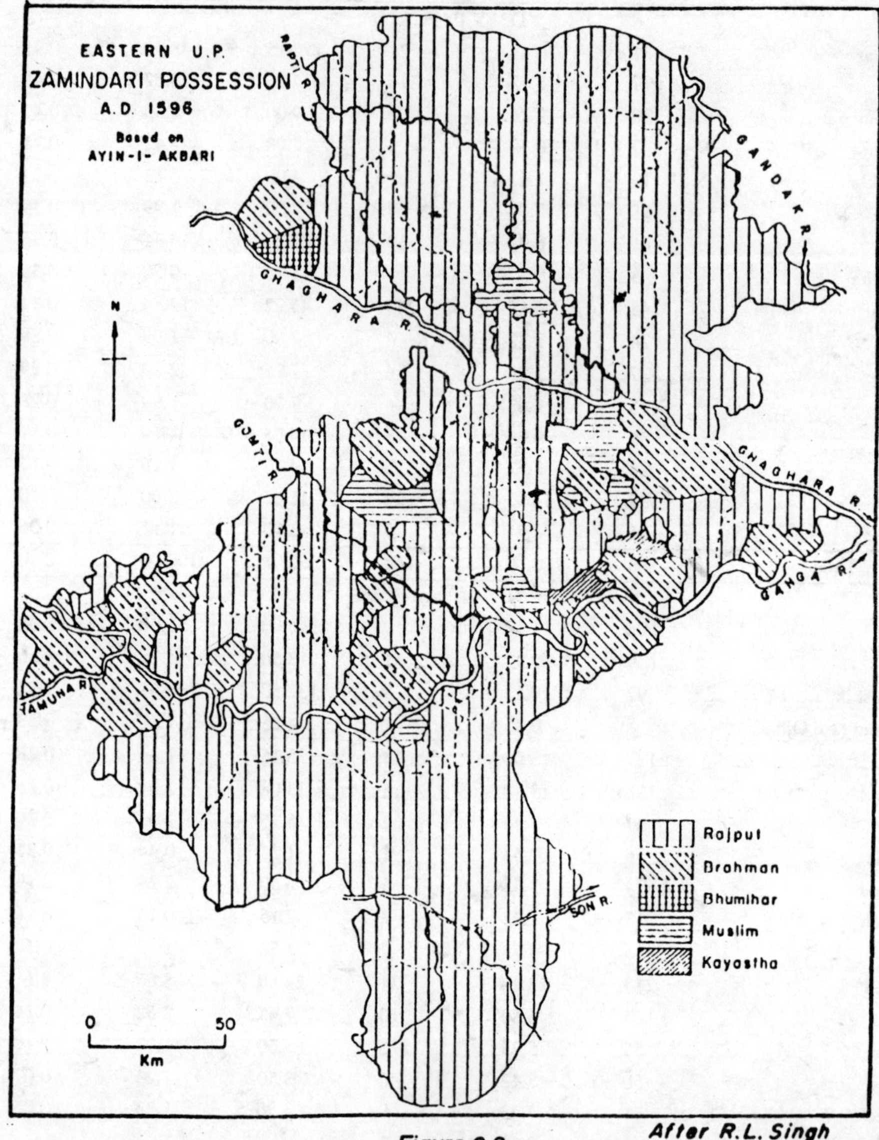

After R.L. Singh

Figure 6.8

Not only in behavioural approach, but in sharing the space, the type and size of house alongwith their attachments, the neo-rich show clear impact. Most of the land owning caste groups are being given due respect by the society. The norms of *Jajmani* system are losing significance.

Morphological Layout/Patterns

In Chapter four we discussed the settlement patterns, having some geometrical form. The examples given, exhibit such patterns in Malwa Region. Here we see another example from Ethiopia. Tefkee, Gesese and Dima-Meta-Moghley settlements are typical in size and structure, expressing the culturo-ecological milieu.

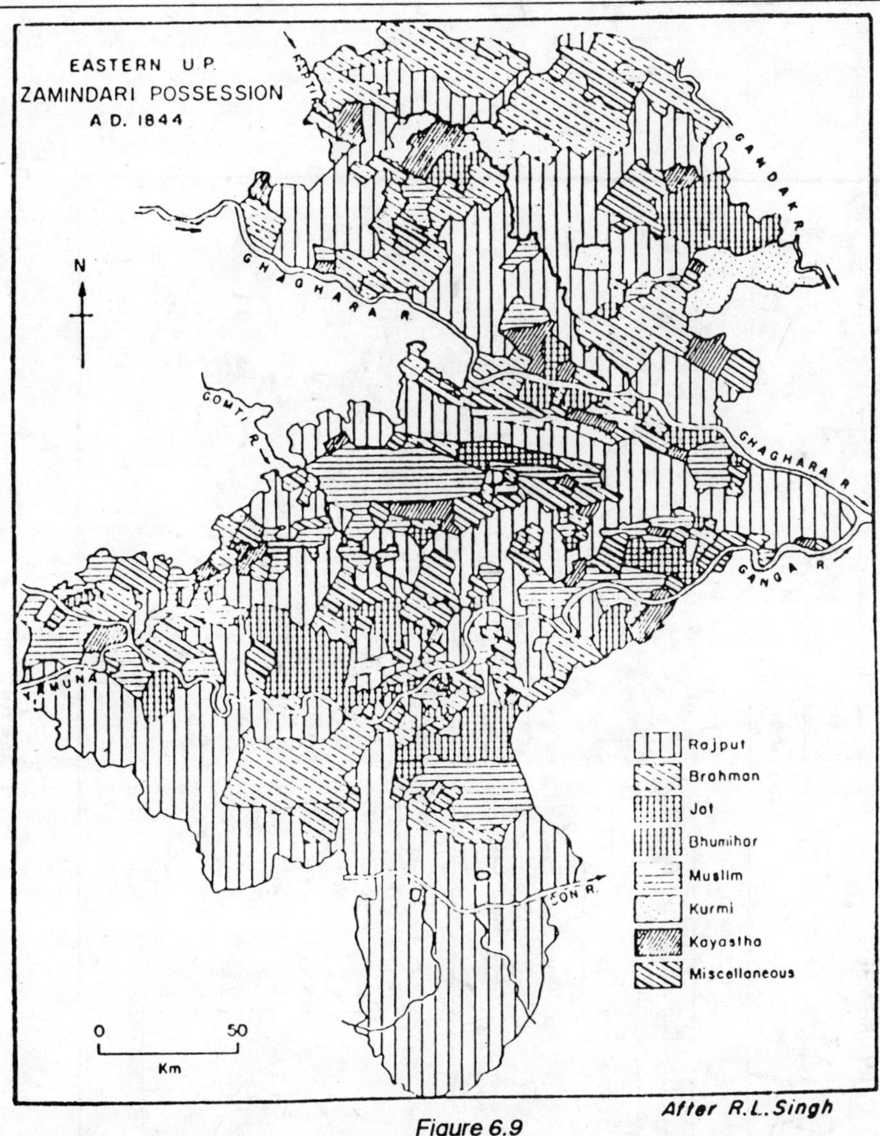

Figure 6.9

Gesese on Mountain Summit

It is a homestead type settlement about 3 km. north-west of Sebeta, a small service centre for farmer's association (Wereda centre), lying at a distance of 30 km. from Addis Ababa in south-west direction, below Moghley Mountain The clusters of houses/huts, occupy the flat summit extending from three to 5km., having spurs running towards lowland from high Moghley.

The settlement with its areal limits, occupies the flat summit, having rolling fields, tapering towards divides of small rivers, as spurs, offshooting from the high Moghley Mountain in the north (Fig. 6.14). The western boundary is formed by the river Fincha-flowing 150m below, at an elevation of 2200m, through interlocking spurs. In the south, extend higher ridges, with steep slopes, further away facing the lowland. The eastern side, has gentle slope, and is, easily connected by footpath, going to Sebeta. Narrow foot path/mule path runs downwards, through the

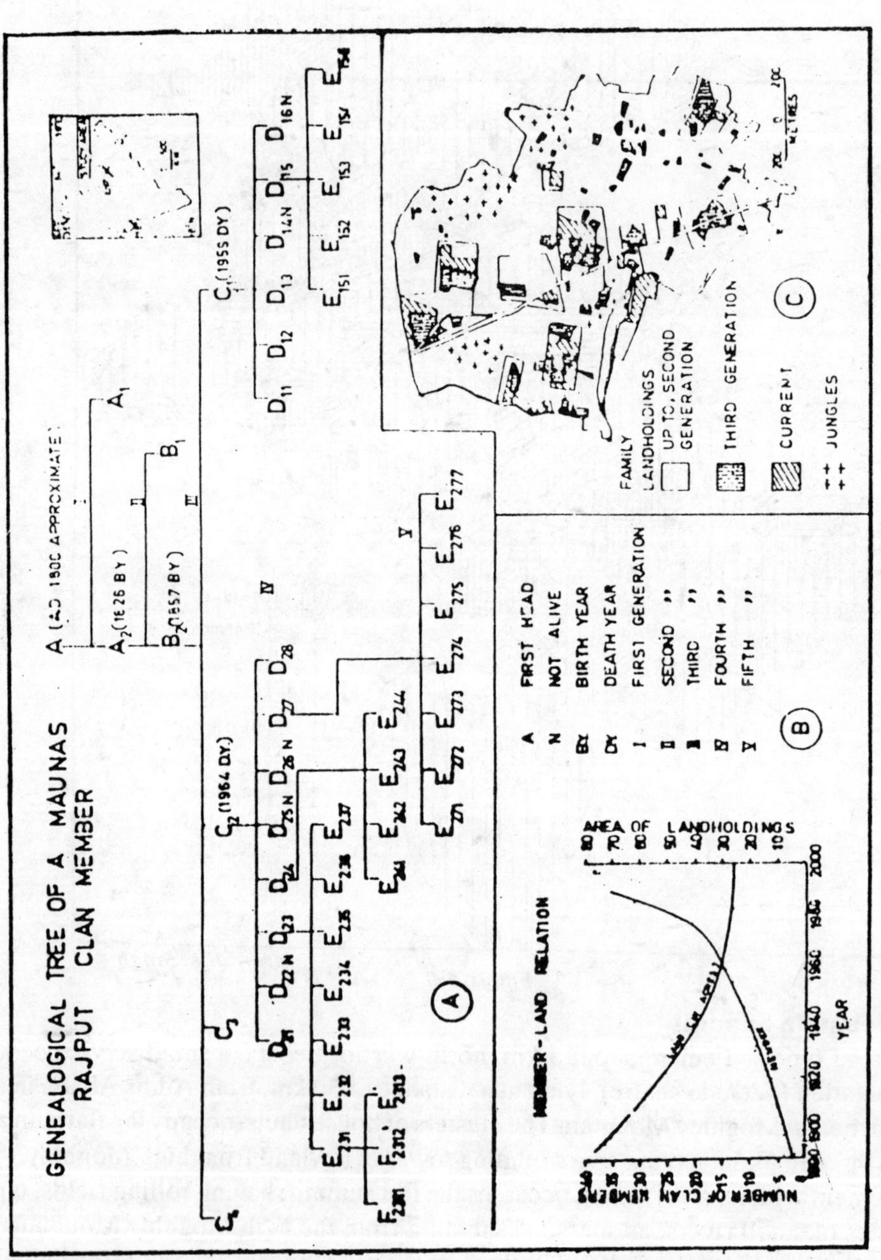
GENEALOGICAL TREE OF A MAUNAS RAJPUT CLAN MEMBER
A (AD 1800 APPROXIMATE)
A2 (1826 BY)
A1
B2 (1857 BY)
B1
C4
C3
C2 (1964 DY.)
C1 (1955 DY)
D21 D22 N D23 D24 D25 N D26 N D27 D28
D11 D12 D13 D14 N D15 D16 N
E231 E232 E233 E234 E235 E236 E237
E151 E152 E153 E154 E155
F2311 F2312 E2313
E241 E242 E243 E244
E271 E272 E273 E274 E275 E276 E277
A
MEMBER-LAND RELATION
NUMBER OF CLAN MEMBERS
AREA OF LANDHOLDINGS
YEAR
LAND (IN ACRES)
MEMBER
A FIRST HEAD
N NOT ALIVE
BY BIRTH YEAR
DY DEATH YEAR
I FIRST GENERATION
II SECOND ,,
III THIRD ,,
IV FOURTH ,,
V FIFTH ,,
B
FAMILY LANDHOLDINGS
UP TO, SECOND GENERATION
THIRD GENERATION
CURRENT
JUNGLES
METRES
C

Figure 6.10

flanks of the spurs, to Meta Beer Factory, located in the valley, beyond. Now deforested, the habitat holds only remnants of old original vegetation-a few big trees, acacia with umbrella like canopy, and scrubs scattered in patches. Relicts of stems of big trees still break the monotony of uniform ploughed surface. Divides are badly eroded, with clear cut formations of all sorts of gullies, which represent typical examples of erosion, in black soil. Slopes are sometimes, covered with acacia, eucalyptus, bushes and long grasses and sometimes, with crops or elsewhere as barren land. Settlers have tried to exploit the nature, without keeping in mind the future generation. Soil erosion, is a bad example, and inhabitants are providing helping hands to the agents of weathering and erosion, through cultivation, forest cutting and grazing.

After rains, they take millet, maize, rapeseed, wheat and tef. Long grasses serve as readily available fodder, hence, no care for collecting grain stalks. Heaps of fodder grass, when dry, maintain supply during exceptionally, dry season. Remarkable feature, is the ploughing of slopy fields, twice or thrice during January-May, the temporary fallow period. Slopy fields are, then, full of soil clods or basalt boulders. All crops remain unirrigated, but drinking water they bring from streams, fed by seepage, through mountain foothills. A diversion channel along the Finacha, a stream below, serves as drinking-cum-irrigation purpose of Meta Beer Factory area. Cattle, following the slopy and rocky, zigzag paths, go downwards to the channel for drinking water, daily. Oxen, cows, ass, mule, goat, sheep and horses all live together in fields, forests and sheds.

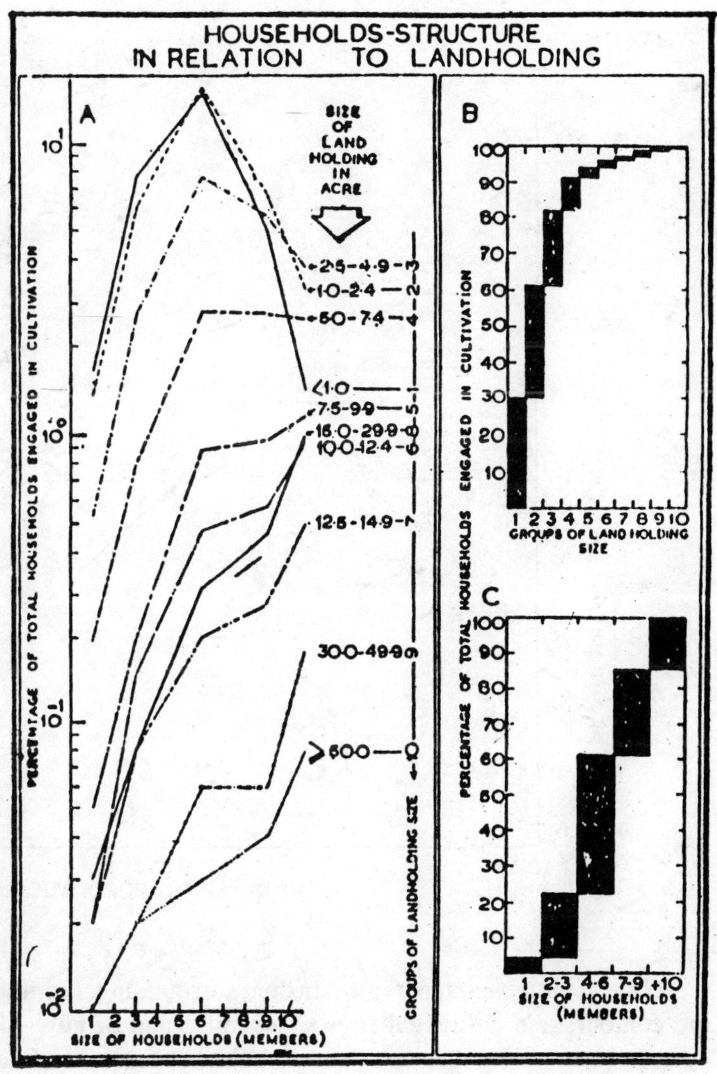

Figure 6.11

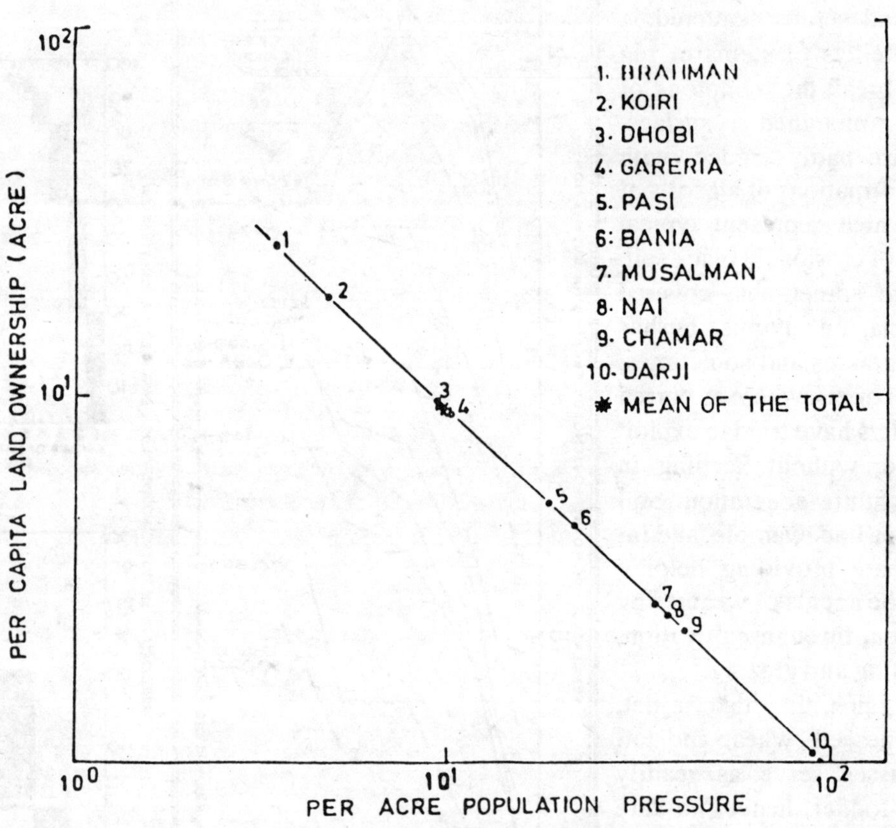

Figure 6.12

Gesese settlements are typical in their surrounding. From summit towards the stream, following contours and cultivated slopes, several group of huts, hug to the divide, with fences and hedges, surrounding them. Fach household, having two to five huts, has one gate at the outskirts of the enclosure, often covered with tin or thatched roof. Huts, with conical roofs, but four facets below, have the thick fences of wooden logs and leaves, thorny twigs, cleverly interwoven. These are sometimes, multifunctional; but the rich ones have separate huts for sleeping, kitchen and shed along with courtyard, set apart, to serve their optimal need. The compound sometimes, has, kitchen garden or stimulant crop, called *gasa.* The building material is, all wood and grass, the walls, always plastered with mud, mixed with cow-dung. Lack of white ants, plus regular annual repair make them durable, for years together.

Inhabitants (311) all Christians, are stout and sturdy and seem to be hardworking in fields. They cultivate, their own fields or the land brought under peasant Association, just after Revolu-

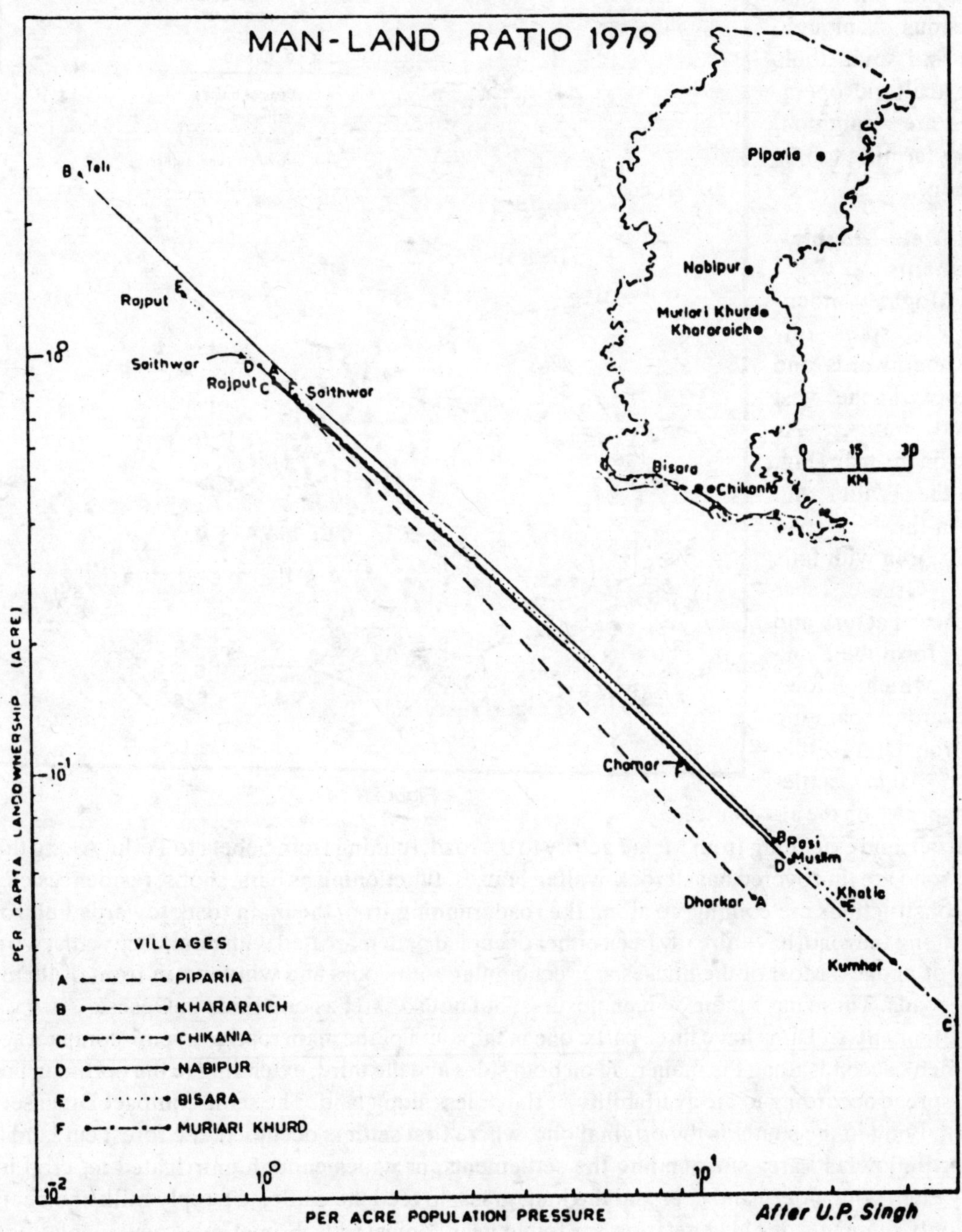
MAN-LAND RATIO 1979
Piparia
Nabipur
Muriari Khurd
Khararaiche
Bisara
Chikania
0 15 30
KM
B Teli
E Rajput
Saithwar D
Rajput C
F Saithwar
Chamar F
B Pasi
D Muslim
Dharkar A
Khatic E
Kumhar
C
PER CAPITA LANDOWNERSHIP (ACRE)
PER ACRE POPULATION PRESSURE
VILLAGES
A PIPARIA
B KHARARAICH
C CHIKANIA
D NABIPUR
E BISARA
F MURIARI KHURD
After U.P. Singh

Figure 6.13

tion, on wage basis, or as sharers. Oxen and indigenous plough, sickle and small tools for agricultural operations, are common. Poultry farming too, is common.

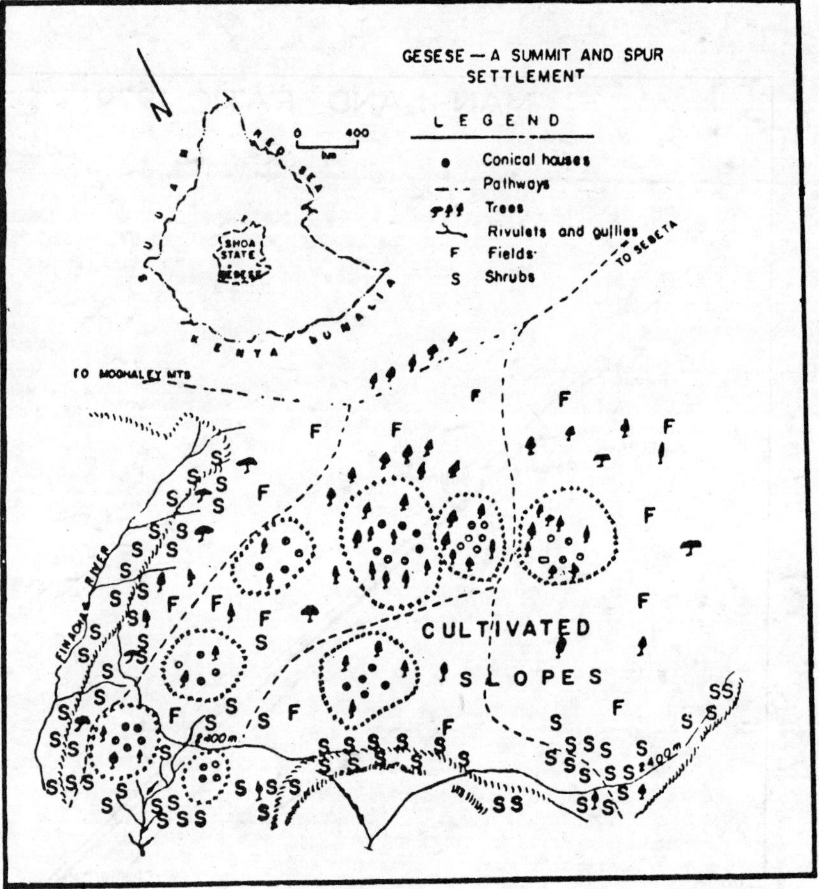

Figure 6.14

Dima-Meta-Moghley Settlements

From Moghley mountain peak spurs offshoot southwards and merge with the vast lowland area. As shown on the map (Fig. 6.15) the Wajitu and Finacha-the two streams, join with falls below Gesese near meta Beer Factory and jointly, form the Dima river, which flows southwards, separating Meta from Dima settlements. Meta settlements spread, on the almost level land extending from Meta Factory to the road, running from Sebeta to Tefki. Along the feeder road are tin covered basalt rock-walled houses, functioning as bars, shops, residences etc. New constructions are coming up along the road, running from the main road, towards Fulaso. Plots, along the road, have already been either occupied or demarcated with boundary walls, wire fences or hedges. Most of the houses are rectangular with doors and windows in front of them, facing roads. These have their own enclosures, but not so safe, as one finds in Gesese.

Settlements of Dima have three parts: one in the south of the main road as a semi-compact arrangement, second, along the main road on both sides and the third, extending in the north, on the spurs, spread according to the availability of flat or less slopy land. The semi-compact Dima settlement, lying in the south, is the original one, where first settlers occupied, the forest cut lands. The fertile lowland area surrounding the settlements, provides enough unirrigated *tef* crop to supply them with *injera* and *beer* and the long grass, to feed the cattle, to supply milk and beef. Now, only remnants of old vegetation are found near conical huts. Sometimes, new plantations occupy some of the fields. With the growth of population and new cuttings, and opening of road, a few settlers moved towards road and there is expansion along the road, in linear pattern. These houses, along the road, are different in form, size and constructional material. While wooden log and grass predominate in the former, rock walls and tin covers are common in the latter. Mostly, they are rectangular and sometimes, with two storeys. Vast cultivated area surrounds this settlement, with alternate arrangement of new plantations of wood trees.

The continuum of Similar habitat extends towards higher spurs, reaching Moghley mts. Homesteads scatter according to contour. Sometimes, single isolated huts occupy less extensive flat land. All settlements have their own hedge, door covered with shade of tin, one dog sitting and watching, while the owners work in the field. Cattle have separate hut/shed in the same compound. Use of tin is, now, the sign of status. Seldom these houses have ventilators. Newly built houses have windows, mostly in frontside. As one proceeds upward on spurs, the size of houses is reduced, but height of the wall, from plinth, remains almost the same. Mostly rectangular in shape, houses are clean and often supplied with small furnitures, cots and household utensils. Walls, made of wooden logs, are plastered with mud mixed with cow dung. The use of tin, easily fixed with logs by iron nails, is enough to withstand slow blowing wind without any storms. The heat of the thirteen months of Ethiopian sunshine, is compensated by the cold wind of the highlands, blowing throughout the year, hence, no oppressive temperature under the tin roof, even inside the house during noontime.

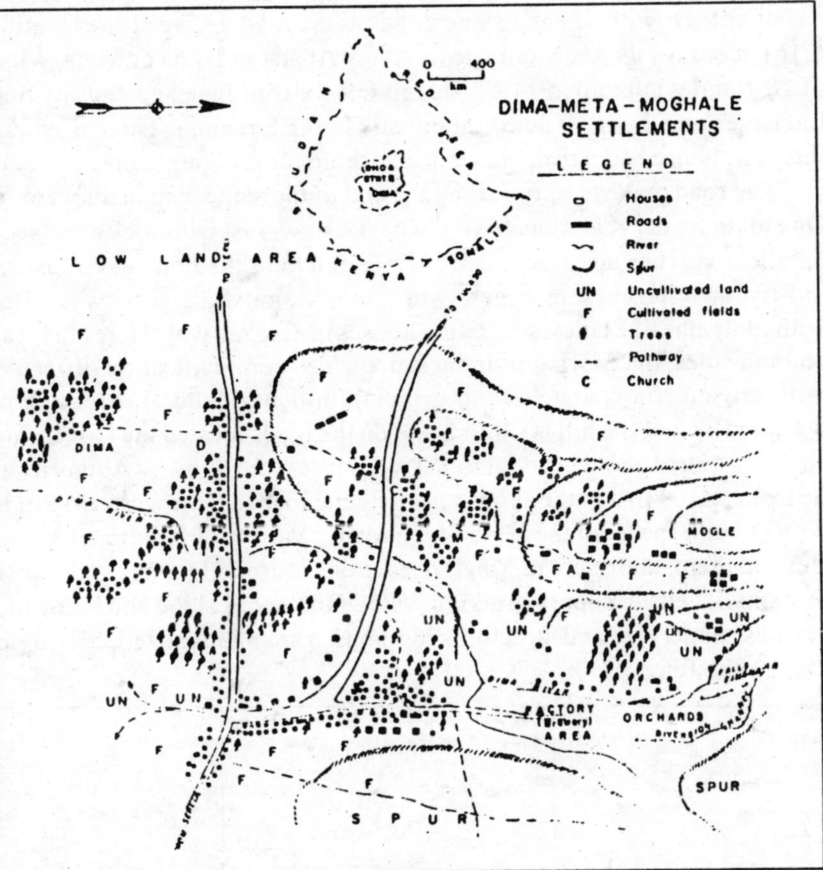

Figure 6.15

Tefki Settlement

Tefki is a typical market centre at a distance of 45kms from Addis Ababa (Population 2003;1244 male, 759 female) in the southwest, located in the midst of fertile lowland, along the highway, running to Jimma. Functioning like a small town in the area, it originated from a small rural market centre, established by local landlords (Ras = Zamindars), for exchange and sale of local produce. The whole surrounding landscape is a granary of Teff, hence Tefki, The lowlying area, on three sides, is flooded during rainy season, and now, is devoid of forests. In the south lies the basalt hillock, with a gentle slope, towards the road. Lying at an elevation of about 2000m, (Fig. 6.16), it enjoys the same climate as Addis Ababa or Dima or Meta, with a summer temperature of 18°c and winter up to 14°c. The rainfall starts in June and ends by September, but rainy days too have some hours of sunshine-mostly in the forenoon. There is enough sunshine throughout the year, hence more than adequate sunshine for growing crops.

The road makes a curve along the end of the slope, and demarcates flood free built-up area. One main feeder road runs from the centre upwards, with rocky surface, and crosses the hill. A parallel road runs up to the break of slope and joins the first one. Houses, spread along the roads, mostly separate, but sometimes, with common side walls. In between, lies the main built up area, with footpaths like lanes, separating houses in a zigzag way. Here are located main market places, on both sides, the Sewing training school, Telecommunication office, Women's flour grinding mill, private clinic, kebele flour grinding mill, agricultural extension office, and bars. On the western flank of the hill is Church and on the top is located the Government. House, once Italian House—a stronghold headquarter. Two centres for Highway Authority and Peasant Association lie in the east. Most of the shops run along the road. On the western skirt is an Elementary School with enough space. In the north of the road, a variety of functional houses, occupy the first line. Beyond them, there spread, small residential houses. Here one gets dense eucalyptus trees and a few small wells to supply drinking water. On the hill slope and below it, there scatter houses of various shape, size and structure. 283 houses are nationalized, 550 are privately owned and 60 under subletting.

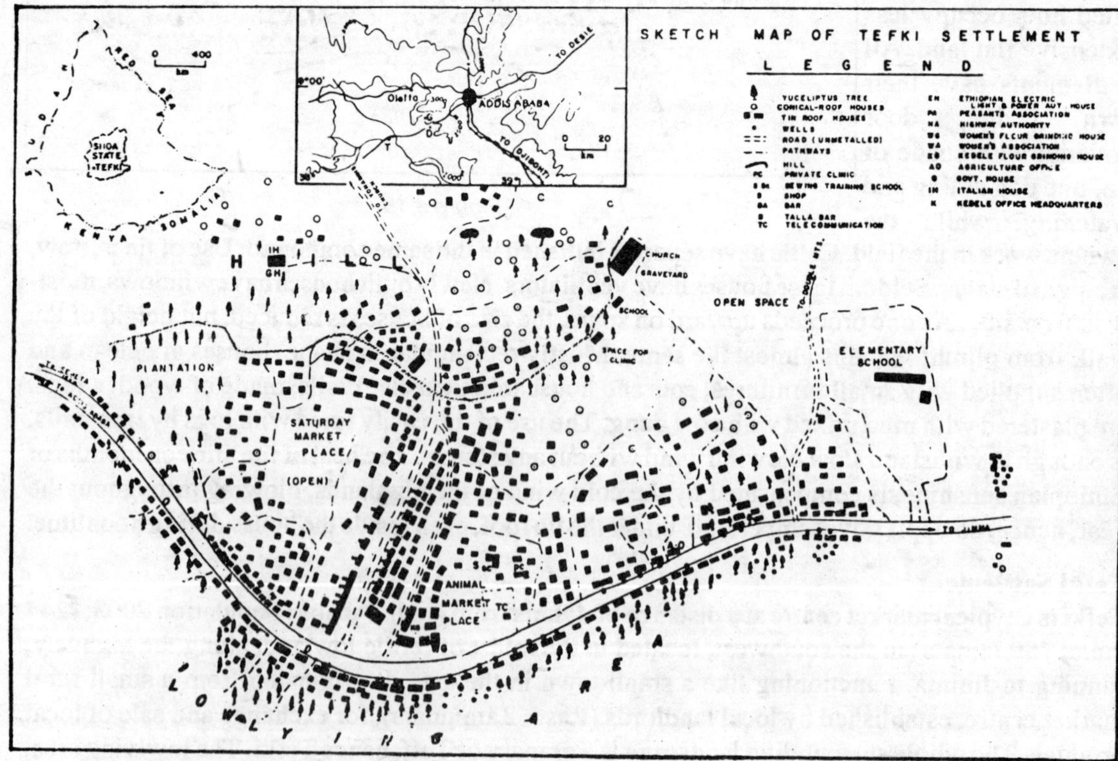

Figure 6.16

About 20 per cent of the houses are rock-walled and tin-roofed with wooden log partitions in between. Houses in the west and east have wooden log walls, thatched roofs and fences, conical huts occupy open spaces on the outskirts. Houses, lying on margins and open spaces, have enclosures, surrounded by hedges or wooden logs. Only a few houses have prototype second storey in the central part.

The market place is an open space, surrounded by houses. On Saturday people assemble here from far-off areas, to purchase grains, clothes and other articles of daily use. Traders come from bigger towns to sell clothes and fashion goods. The animal market place is surrounded by wooden logs, with entrances here and there, and partitions for the sale of sheep, goat, mule and horses etc. On the southeastern skirt new plantations occupy hill slopes, while acacia and eucalyptus dominate the landscape in the southwest.

With its Kebele headquarters, along the main road in the north, and Peasant Association building in the south, Tefki serves as administrative centre, also. There is women Association building in the central part, where women workers assemble and look after development activities. The only institution for education is the Elementary school up to 8th Standard. For further study children have to go to Sebeta about 15km. One more school has been started for lower classes near church building. Along the main road several *Talla* bars and two bar-cum-restaurant serve the visitors. Only 33 persons are engaged in Govt. service, 38 are tailors, 14 in organizations, 1506 in different trades, 52 school going children, 200 secondary school students.

References

1. Singh, R.Y. (1972) 'Village Mahjuda:A Study in the Morphogenesis of A Rural Settlement, Eastern U.P. (India) in Singh, R.L. et al. (eds.) 'Rural Settlements in Monsoon Asia', Proceedings of I.G.U., Symposia, Varanasi and Tokyo, pp. 234-240.
2. For the concept of 'Dominant Caste' see Ch.2 ref. no. 92; See also K.N. Singh, op.cit. Ch. 2, ref. no. 75, p. 205.
3. Singh, K.N. Ibid.
4. Mukerjee, R.K. (1940), Man and His Habitation, London, p. 61, also see R.L. Singh, Ch. 2 ref. no. 28, p. 75.
5. Baden, Powell, B.H. (1896) 'The Indian Village Community' Longman's Green & Co., London, p. 51.
6. Ibid, pp. 11-23.
7. Baden, Powell, B.H. (1899) 'The Origin and Growth of Village Communities in India' Swann Sonnenschein, London, p. 28.
8. Rhys, Davids, Buddhist India, p. 48.
9. Baden, Powell, ref. no. 7, p. 302.
10. Badan, Powell, B.H. (1974) Land Systems of British India, Vol. I, Delhi Oriental Publishers:162-163.
11. Baden, Powell, B.H. (1972), The Indian Village Community, Delhi Cosmo Publications:29,340.
12. Hiraoka, M. (1977), Ch. 5, ref. no. 14, pp. 69-81.
13. Mitchell, J.B., ref no. 88, Ch. 1, p. 112.
14. Ibid, p. 49.

15. Chisholm, M. (1969) 'Rural Settlement and Land Use, An Essay in Location' London, pp. 102-108 (particularly 55).
16. Ahmed, E., ref. no. 13, Ch. 4, p. 232.
17. Chisholm, M., ref. no. 15, Ch. 6, p. 30.
18. Ibid, p. 27.
19. See B.B. Singh (1976), Spatial Organisation of Settlement in Some North Indian Villages:214-223 in R.L. singh et al. (eds.) 'Geographic Dimensions of Rural Settlements', NGSI, Res. Pub. No. 16 in which he has tried to bring models of growth but they only explain the phases of morphological structures expressed through nucleation and diffusion.
20. Cohn, B.S. (1969), 'Structural Changes in Indian Rural Society 1596-1885' in Land Control and Social Structure in Indian History (edited by) R.E. FRYKEBERG, Madison, University of Wisconsin Press, p. 56.
21. Singh, R.Y. (1987) 'Geographic Dimension of A Clan Member During Two Centuries' Rural Systems, Vol. V, No. 3 Sept. pp. 207-213.
22. Singh, R.P.B. (1977), Clan Settlements in the Saran Plain, NGSI, Res. Pub. No. 18, pp. 130-131.

7

Shape Analysis

Introduction

In early periods of evolution of any occupance, the territory of movements of a group, is undefined. Common lands, lying in between, define the boundary of shifting nature, based on tradition and might of the settling being. This is, equally applicable, in the case of herbivores or carnivores, which roam about within certain physical limits, hence, a perceptual space, well adapted to avoid confrontation, becomes a bounded or closed space. The movements for earning the living, through hunting, collecting, gathering or primary productions are limited in that very closed space. Later on, it becomes territory for a particular occupying group, named tribe, in literature. Tribal territories, still, abound in number in several human occupance areas of the world. But, cultural growth manifestations result into various religions, whose boundary transcends the living space, culturally. It is the fixed territorial boundary, either a segment of kinship region or otherwise occupied, which is named as village, the geographer is most concerned with. Since village boundary evolves, simultaneously alongwith land occupance surrounding a settlement, it automatically, coincides with the adjacent village boundary, following the best practical possibility of being packed in space through various natural and man-made forces in operation. The boundary becomes a hill, *nala*, wasteland or some visible prominent vegetable group first, and then as time passes, a demarcated man made boundary with pillars or other symbols, fixed on the land. This becomes the bounded space of village within which the rights and obligations of settlers are defined. In most of the countries such boundaries are defined and recorded to be produced on maps cartographically. These coinciding boundaries, present before us, shapes of village territories, having regional variations in size, area and packing in space.

Within this bounded space the settlers establish habitations of various type, showing again, variations in size, shape and form, as discussed earlier. Here, human organization of bounded space is expressed through various interactions and manifestations. One obvious concrete expression is, the residential built-up area with all sorts of community sectors, and the other being agricultural landscape in the form of fields or other sources of primary production, i.e., mining, fishing, etc. The bounded shape of settlements has already been discussed, now we come to approach the study of shape of the village boundary as such.

Why This Analysis?

It is not a futile exercise, we are going to have. Shape, in itself, speaks enough of the whole trend and type of humanization of earth. In nature, the best occupance of space is through a geometrical shape, i.e., hexagon or its other forms 'polygons' with more than four sides. This is well demonstrated through cobwebs or beehives or ant hill spaces.[1] The deviation from this natural norm indicates, that some cultural factors have been responsible at various stages of evolution. Study of deviation, causing variation is our aim (geographer's goal). Why this shape distribution is not triangular, rectangular or even hexagonal? The answer will reflect, cultural-ecological forces in operation since occupance of a culture area. We can compare the boundaries of the United State's states with that of China or India, similarly, Parish boundaries in Europe and that of villages in South east Asia or a tribal village and a non-tribal counterpart in any region. The difference in shape will explain the factors in background-political, administrative, historical, religious etc.

Bunge, rightly, concludes that whether we use metrics describing surfaces, polynomials, fourier series of Taylor series or devise a classification and subjectively assign shapes to it like ox-bow, circular, rectangular etc., the problem remains that, in the first case, the measures reflect more than shape, as they include orientation also; in the second common method, classifications are often vague and assignment of shapes, to the various categories, lacks confidence. That is why, this first theorem states that, any simply connected shape can be matched by a polygon of any number of sides whose sides, are of equal but variable length. We shall deal with the qualities of polygon in sequel.

Approaches: (a) Qualitative/Classical (Shape versus Pattern)

The shape of settlements, the outer morphological expression, having geometrical forms, has been discussed in Chapter 4. The approach concerns, with the various similarities of geometrical forms observed in field or mapped on topographical sheets or cadastral maps. This approach, first applied by German geographers, is a classical one and has been followed by many a writer, elsewhere. Here, we emphasize another quantitative approach, better termed as *Geometrical approach.*

Shape Analysis: (b) Quantitative Approach

Christaller's model of distribution of centres in any uniform space, with several lattice arrangements, gives the idea of hexagonal spatial distribution of settlements. Lösch also dealt with the packing of centres in the colonization of a plain, leading to hexagonal arrangement. (Fig. 7.1).

The idea is, however, based on the elementary packing theory.

In a territory, having various shapes of village boundaries, the efficient division can be best explained in two ways: (i) having efficiency of movement and (ii) having efficiency of boundaries.

The first, involves distance minimization in between centre and outer margin, the second, is measured by

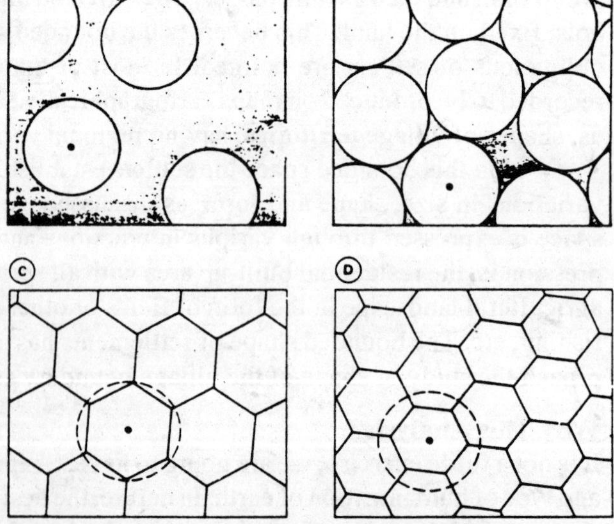

Figure 7.1: Packing of centres in the colonization of plain to give hexagonal territories. *Source*: Lösch, 1954, p. 110.

perimeter length of the territory. Figure 7.2A shows that circle is the economical of the regular polygons, because it is a regular polygon with an infinite number of sides and vertices. The two parameters, plotted in Figure 7.2B, reveal that, with increase in side, efficiency increases; more so in case of decagon. The hexagon is about four fifths as efficient as the circle, both in terms of radial distance and perimeter. Thus, circular arrangement of packing a space, however, is not without defects. In circular packing, either some areas remain unused, or there is overlapping. As regards hexagonal tessellation, one of the commonest criticisms is, that it is far too rigid and abstract. Still, following the works of natural scientists, hexagons are much used in models of settlement structure.

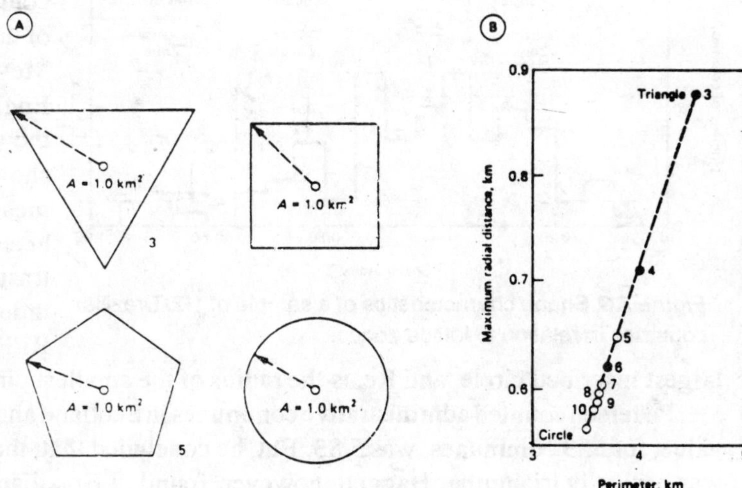

Figure 7.2: Efficiency of alternative types of regular polygon in relation to distance from centres and perimeter length. The numbers indicate the number of sides to the figure, while the solid circles denote shapes which will form a regular tesselation. A = area.

Measurement of Shape: A Review

The concept of shape measurement started from the work of Thompson in biological sciences[2]. In geomorphic studies Miller, on the basis of quantitative expression of the shape of the river basin, used basin circularity ratio[3]. The ratio is expressed as, $\frac{4A}{\pi \times p^2}$ where A = Area of the basin and P is permeter. Hagget, drawing samples from Brazil, examined the packing characteristics of hundred sample counties. He used shape index, (s) to measure that shape, which is expressed as the ratio of the area of the village or county (A) to the area of the circle with the longest axis (L) having a perimeter of πR^2, so that

$$S = \frac{A}{\pi R^2} \text{ or } \frac{4A}{\pi L^2} \text{ or } S = 1.27 \frac{A}{l^2}$$

where A = area of the county in km²

L = long axis of the county drawn as a straight line connecting the two most distant points on the perimeter.

Here the multiplier, 1.27 is computed to adjust the shape index ranging fom 1.00 (a circle) to zero in elongated shape. As shown in Figures 7.2 and 7.3, the values are 0.42 for triangular, 0.64 for square and 0.83 for hexagonal regular lattices of Coxeter.

The contact numbers on any boundary, also, provide a measure for shape of villages or counties. Haggett took the Brazilian coastal counties and recorded contact numbers. Here, the mean

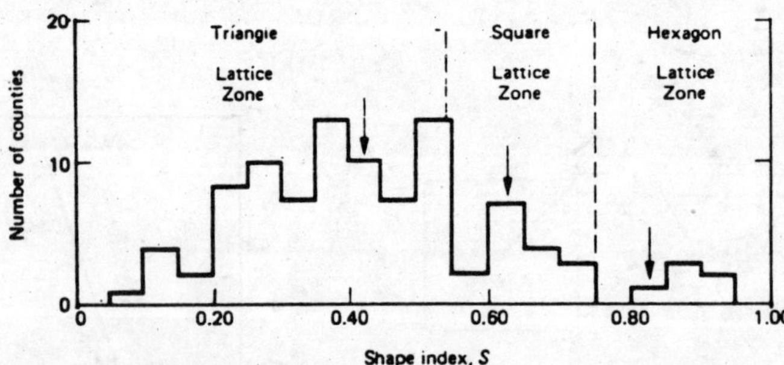

Figure 7.3: Shape characteristics of a sample of 100 Brazilian countries in relation to lattice zones.

contact number was 5.71, and one out of three counties, had six neighbours. Meyer and Huggett measured English Parishes east of Swindon on the basis of contact numbers, as shown on Figures 7.4 and 7.5 with a mean value of 5.5. The shape has been attributed to, the factor of contrasting relief. They also used, shape index of compactness, defined as Ri/Rc, where Ri, is the radius of the largest inscribed circle, and Rc, is the radius of the smallest circumscribed circle[4] (Fig. 7.6).

Pedersen counted administrative communes in Scotland and of Fyn in Denmark. The average value, for 553 communes, was 5.83. But, he concluded that, the administrative net in Denmark, was basically triangular. Haggett, however, found in Brazilian counties that higher population density areas were more closely packed, i.e., higher contact number. He examined this relationship in counties of Santa Catarina State, based on data for nine decades, and found that contact numbers increased from 3.50 in 1872 to 5.22 in 1960.

Rasheed,[5] in Bangla Desh, computed shape of 19 districts, taking the measurement of longest and shortest axis, and developed an index of departure from geographic centre, but its applicability to rural areas is yet to be tested. Many other researchers, like Gibbs, Simmons, Boys and Clark, Wilkins and Shaw, have also worked in measurement of shape, particularly, in urban areas, where cultural factors are the only determining ones of shape.

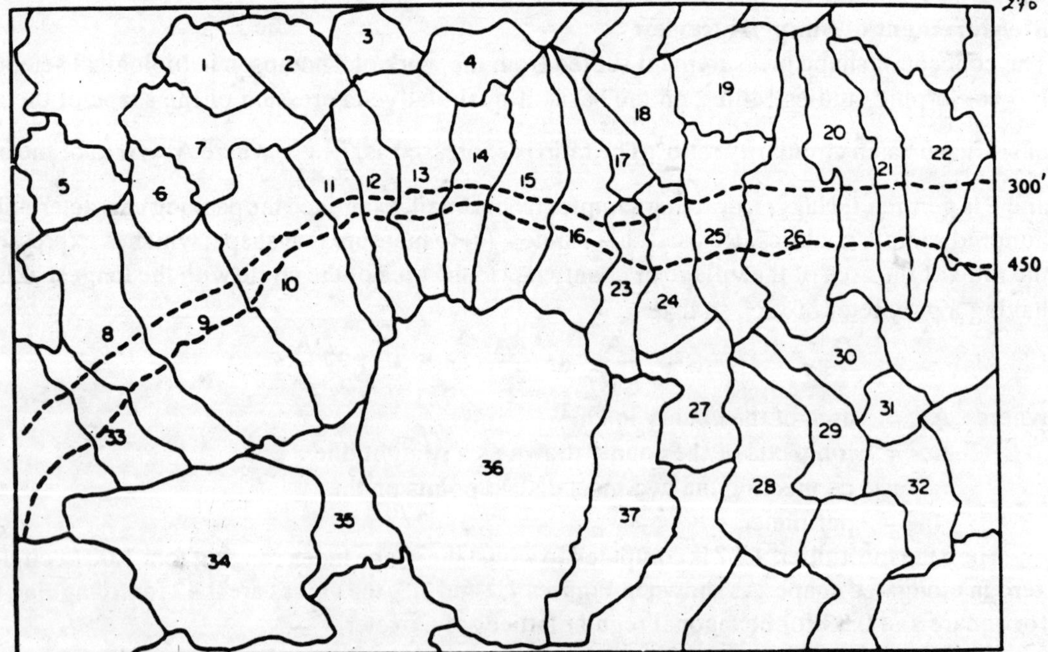

Figure 7.4: Parishes east of Swindon.

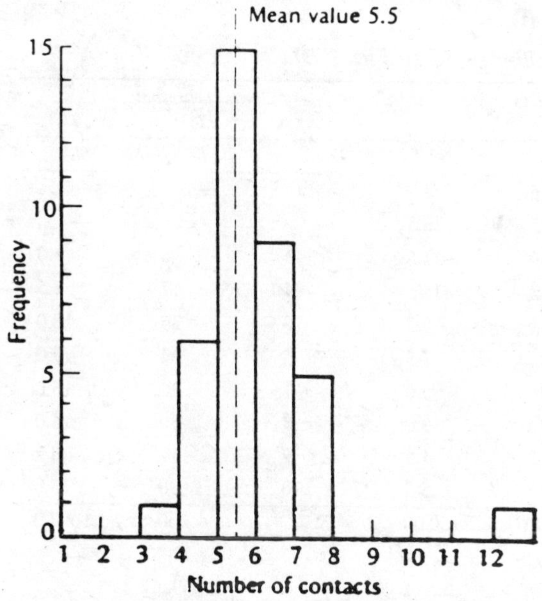

Figure 7.5: Parishes east of Swindon

Rana P.B. Singh did good exercise in shape analysis in his work. He also tried to transform shape into Dirichlet regions.[6] His findings are clear from the map (Fig. 7.7). Applying Miller's formula, he finds that, there is general trend from elongation towards square and the area, does not show the gaps among groups of frequency distribution of shape index, as in the case of Brazilian counties. Here, the mean of contact numbers is 4.5, only, showing that, rectangular system of village boundary is more common; ancient villages have circular shape and big sizes.

Singh and Singh,[7] taking a hypothetical case of a settlement with its nucleus along a river bluff, simulated phases of its growth. The idea behind this notional simulation was, that linearity has its own limitations and during its evolutional phase the settlement takes circular or curvilinear shape in suitable growth conditions. The phase wise growth of a settlement having C = 0, through different periods, up to C = 1 (the full fledged stage), as shown in Figure 7.8, is manifested in hamletization and cluster formation. Further, coalescing together of clusters or having independent separate growth of hamlets, depends upon local conditions. The growth situation is represented by $C = 1^{n+1}$, in which C = circularity index, n = time, +1 = spatial development. $C = 1^{n+m}$ represents further growth, where m = further growth trend.

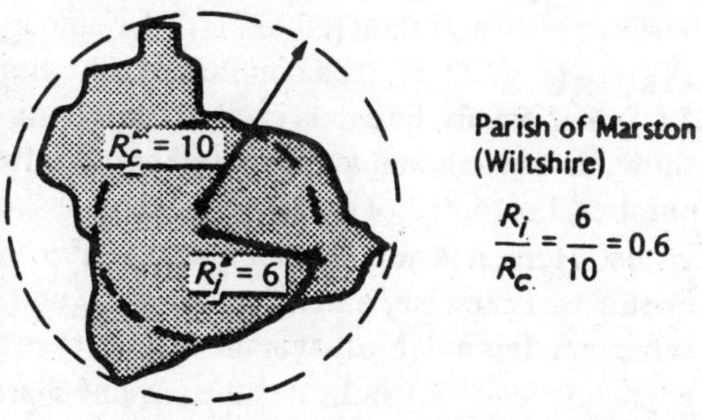

Figure 7.6: Deriving the index of compactness

A study, conducted on Gorakhpur district by Singh,[8] based on Miller's formula, reveals good results in Indian environment. Here, 200 villages (i.e., 5% of the total) have been selected on the basis of purposive random sampling from the Gorakhpur district. The computed results [Table 7 (i)] show that, in real sense, settlements do not exist in the exact lattice zones. The mean S value (0.54) indicates the maximum frequency (about 50%) near the triangular shape. Additionally, taking the limit up to square lattice, this frequency reaches 77.5 per cent (145 villages) marking considerable preponderance of square shape (Fig. 7.9A); it may also be supported through visual impression. In fact, the main causative factor, for such growth, has been the rectangular division of land, evolved in ancient India, i.e., *Bigha system.*

Only 7.5 per cent (15 villages) of sample villages, exhibit shape near to circle, while only about 4 per cent villages have recorded hexagonal shape [Table 7 (i)].

Table 7 (i)

Shape Characteristics of Villages (See Fig. 7.5)

Shape Index (S)			*Contact Index (C)*			*Contact Number (T)*		
Group	*f*	*%*	*Group*	*f*	*%*	*Group*	*f*	*%*
0.0-0.1	7	3.5	<1	16	8.0	—	—	—
0.1-0.2	11	5.5	1-2	65	23.5	—	—	—
0.2-0.3	23	11.5	2-3	49	24.5	3	6	3.0
0.3-0.4	30	15.0	3-4	23	11.5	4	17	8.5
0.4-0.5	30	15.0	4-5	11	5.5	5	36	18.0
0.5-0.6	32	16.0	5-6	7	3.5	6	34	17.0
0.6-0.7	24	12.0	6-7	10	5.0	7	20	15.0
0.7-0.8	23	11.5	7-8	6	3.0	8	30	15.0
0.8-0.9	5	2.5	8-9	3	1.5	9	17	8.5
0.9-1.0	15	7.5	>9	10	5.0	≥10	30	15.0
Σ	200	100.0	Σ	200	100.00	Σ	200	100.00
$\bar{x}$	0.54	—	$\bar{x}$	2.91	—	$\bar{x}$	6.865	—
χ^2	43.90	—	χ^2	191.30	—	χ^2	30.64	—

Source: Author's observations.

Among other shape characteristics, contact number (T) and contact index C (Contact number/area) are important [table 7 (i)]. A comparative look at village frequencies according to S and T, gives (Fig. 7.9 A, B) a contrasting situation; geometrically it has been found (S values, table 7 (i)) that square lattice is common, (having 4 contact number) but the observed frequencies, show, that hexagonal lattice is rather more frequent, as supported by the mean value of contact number, i.e., 6.865. The corresponding association of these indices are further analysed using χ^2 test. Here, it is notable that culturo-environmental conditions are mostly responsible for such contrasts. Likewise, other parts of India and even some other countries, e.g., Brazil reveal the same fact. It is notable that in the present case the frequency histogram does not record any range-gaps, this tendency indicates the variant character of village shapes, which may be further supported by the values of contact index.

Statistical Testing of Shape Indices

The observed frequency distribution of shape, contact number and contact index (Figs. 7.9 A, B, C), may be further compared to the expected frequency, with an assumption, that the region lies in invariant environment, as well as, every group has equal chance of probability. For such inter-relationship χ^2 test is the most useful technique. The χ^2 values of the above attributes (S, C, T) have been computed as 43.90, 30.64 and 191.30 respectively. Comparing these values to the tabulated values successively at 9, 9 and 7 degrees of freedom (df), it has been found that, even at 0.1 per cent probability level, the null hypothesis "that due to invariant environment there may not be any change in frequency distributions" has not been acceptable. This statement gives much emphasis upon the environmental control, which is the basic characteristic of the Poisson distribution, mathematically expressed as,

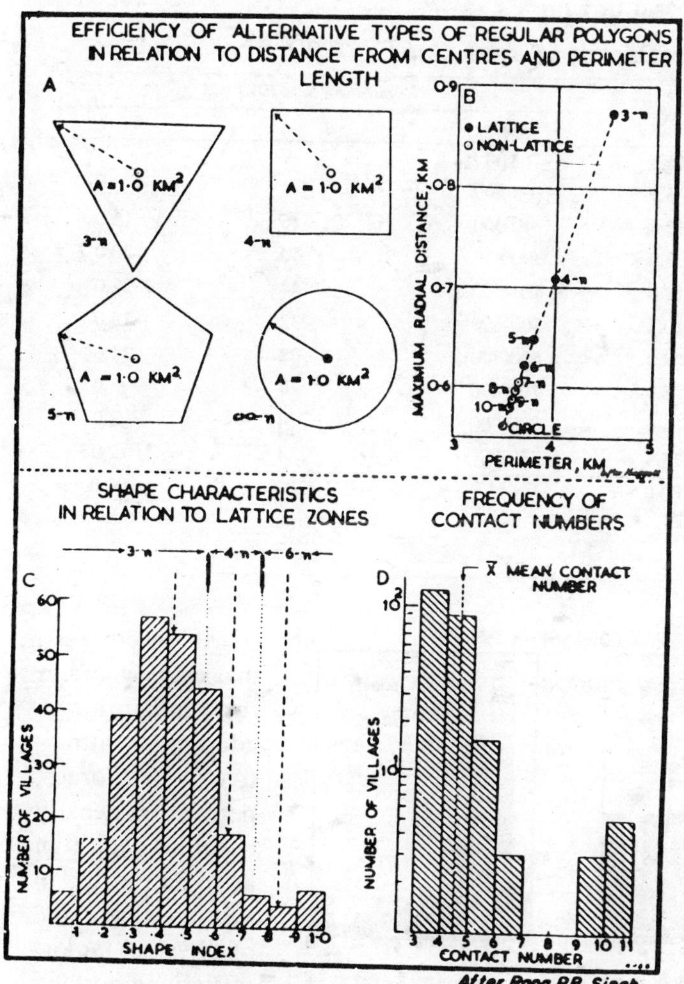

Figure 7.7

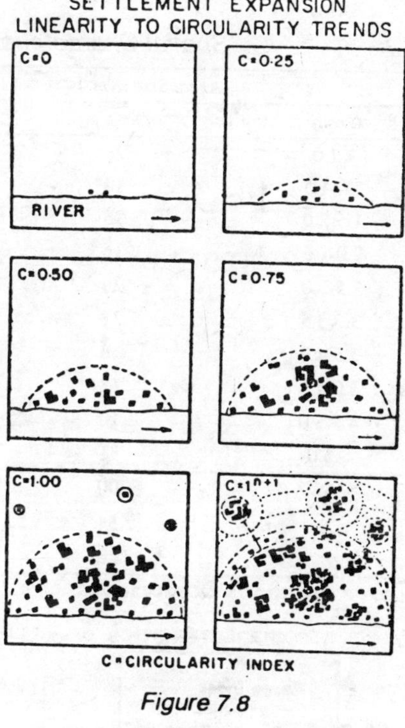

Figure 7.8

$$P(X:\lambda) = \frac{e^{-\lambda}\lambda^{x}}{x!} \text{ for } x = 1, 2$$

where the parameter (λ) is the expected number of points per sample area and x, is a defined random variable. Since the village samples are taken within the assumption, that the location of each village is independent of the location of any other point, the model of Poisson distribution will be applied successfully.

Shape Attributes Versus Size of Villages

The associationship, between area and population attributes in the context of shape, presents a revealing picture. The scatter diagrams, (Fig. 7.9 D, E) showing relationship of contact index, population density and areal size of 200 sample villages, do not show any significant correlation among these attributes, as the region lies in the fertile plain of the Ganga Valley. Similar to Brazilian counties, it may be noted in some areas, that more closely packed areas have relatively higher population density and, therefore, they have a higher contact number than highly populated areas. But, in an Indian environment one may not generalize, absolutely, that the increasing trend of population density will be followed by the higher contact index (Fig. 7.9D) as well as the areal size (Fig. 7.9 E). This may only be applicable in a larger area especially in time frame, as Haggett has generalized, taking Santa Catarina State of Brazil.

Table 7 (ii)

Spatial Characteristics of Sample Villages (See Fig. 7.9D, E)

Areal Size (Km^2)			Population Size 1971		
Group	*f*	*%*	*Group*	*f*	*%*
< 1.0	28	14.0	< 100	9	4.5
1.0-1.5	13	6.5	100-200	9	4.5
1.5-2.0	25	12.5	200-300	26	13.0
2.0-2.5	16	8.0	300-400	40	20.0
2.5-3.0	26	13.0	400-500	44	22.0
3.0-3.5	21	10.5	500-600	32	16.0
3.5-4.0	18	9.0	600-700	22	11.0
4.0-4.5	12	6.0	700-800	10	5.0
4.5-5.0	10	5.0	800-900	4	2.0
> 5.0	31	15.5	> 900	4	2.0
Σ	200	100.0	Σ	200	100.0
$\overline{X}$	2.54		$\overline{X}$	484	
χ^2	24.0		χ^2	100.7	

Source: Author's Observations.

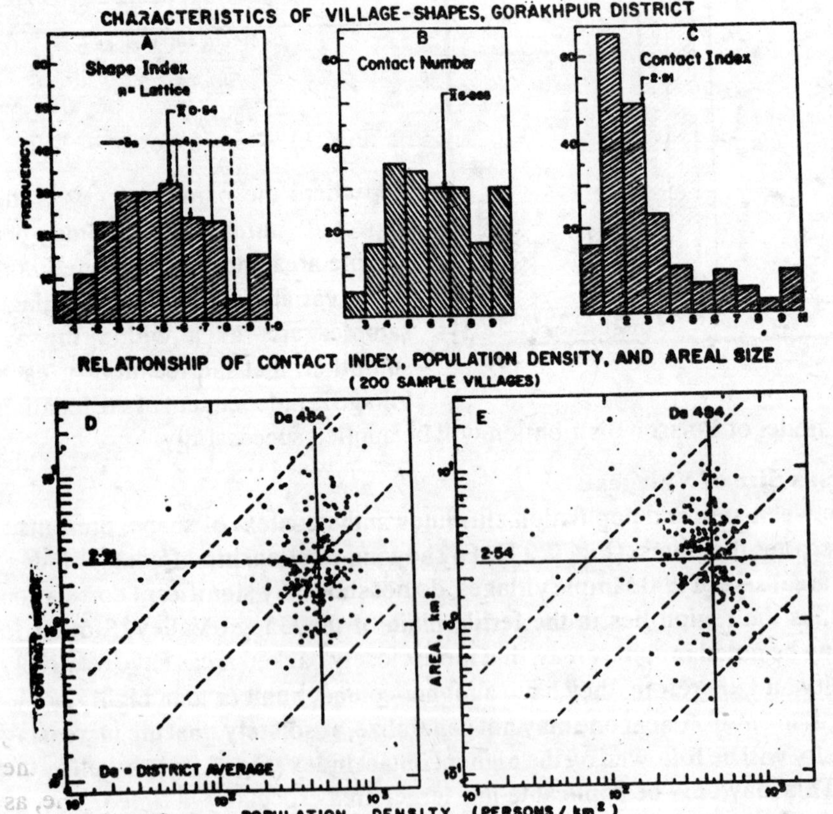

Figure 7.9

It is obvious, that everywhere in rural India, due to additional attractive forces, population density becomes very high at some places. In this concern, role of physical factors is very important. In the areas, subject to annual inundation, there appear villages with elongated shape, while in the areas having limited space for settlement expansion, population density becomes too high in time span.

The relationship between observed and expected frequency distribution of areal size, population-size [table 7 (ii)], shape index and contact index, has always recorded < 0.1% probability of significance at 9 *df*, it means, that the frequencies are generated by chance instead of any fixed rule. Similar situation can also be visualized for the frequency distribution of contact number of villages, which also record 0.1 per cent of probability level at 7 *df* [table 7 (i)].

Shape Transformation

The concept of transforming village shapes is analysed within two perspectives of constructing serial polygons-making *delaunay* triangles and *cellular* nets, the hexagons. Although its root goes back to mid nineteenth century (1850), when mathematician Dirichlet introduced the concept of serial polygons, the detailed properties have been studied later on by D'Arcy Thompson (1917). Such space-exhausting polygons are known as 'Cellular net' in geography, 'mosaics' in ecology, 'Thiessen polygons' in meteorology, 'Dirichlet' or 'Voronoi' polygons in mathematics.

The fundamental characteristics of these polygons within two assumptions of their validity are: (i) the area within the intersecting boundary lines of the polygons lies near to the enclosed centre than to any other centre, and (ii) a centre dominates all areas lying geometrically nearest to it.

References

1. The writer observed hexagonal territorial pattern of ant hills on both sides of the road running between Metahara and Awash extending more than 50 kms. in length in (Ethiopia).
2. Thompson, D'arcy W. (1917), Abridged Edition 1961, on Growth and Form, Cambridge:102-25.
3. Miller, V.C. (1953), A Quantitative Geomorphic Study of Drainage Basin Characteristics in the Clinch Mountain Area Virginia and Tennessee, New York:Columbia University Department of Geology (Ph.D. Dissertation). His ratio is, the ratio of circumference of a circle of same area, as the basin, to the basin perimeter.
4. See Iainr Meyer & Richard J. Huggett (1979), Geography:Theory in Practice Book one 'Settlements', Harper & Row, Publishers:116-119.
5. Rasheed, K.B.S. (1972), 'An Examination of the Shape of the Administrative Districts of Bangladesh, Geografiska Annaler B, 54:104-108.
6. Singh, Rana P.B., Ch. 6, ref. no. 22:150-160.
7. Singh K.N. & Singh Rana P.B. (1975) "Some Methodological Components in Rural Settlement Research" in 'Readings in Rural Settlement Geography' by R.L. Singh et al. (eds.) NCSI, Res. Publication No. 14, pp. 36-37.
8. See Singh, U.P. (1980) 'Geographic Dimensions of Rural Settlements in Gorakhpur District (U.P.), Ph.D. Thesis submitted to B.H.U. under the guidance of present author, pp. 122-138.

8

Rural Dwellings

Introduction

The earliest dwelling of *Homo erectus* was the cavesite in Africa, most probably, "at Choukoutien. But caves and rock shelters were not the only places for human habitations. Most of the settlement sites were in the open. The earliest evidence of housing, reflects on pit dwellings, dug into the ground, oval-to-near-rectangular in shape. Thus, there is allusion in the phrase 'Caveman era' to the cave as the first human habitation".[1] The pit dwelling, took several evolutionary forms, discussed in the sequel and, these, in turn, inherited diverse nomenclature, though always synonymous to house or dwelling, as treated below.

Through dwellings, man could easily adapt to the environment, and his occupance spread in varied ecological conditions. His dwellings are exceedingly varied in the raw materials used, in the climatic conditions (winds, temperatures, precipitation, seasonalities) being countered, in their sites, and in their forms and functions. "Men, today, erect shelters of bamboo and tropical leaves, build with boughs, twigs and mud, with bones and stone, grass sod and tamped earth, adobe and brick, timber and metal and ice. Men situate their shelters in swamps, over the edge of lakes, streams, and canals, by the shore, on hill slopes and mountain ridges, in open grasslands and in tropical clearings. The shelters may house, single family or a dozen, side by side, under one roof; it may be set apart in isolation or built as one of a cluster".[2] The shelters are now underground, too, and are positively being established in space.

The preceding discussion leads us to study the "core of the settlement geography (which) is the building's, where are they and why are they there?"[3] The another is, however, concerned here not only with buildings or human habitations meaning "a place of abode or settled dwelling",[4] but other structures related to them, too. In India a census house was defined in 1911 as "Any structure other than a dwelling house; such as tent pavilion, temple, *serai*, etc., or a site, camping ground, ghat, etc., to which a separate number has been fixed, and the dwelling place of one or more families, with their dependents and resident servants, having an independent entrance, whether that entrance be from a road, gallery, balcony, corridor, courtyard or otherwise".[5] A census house in 1961 was "a structure or part of a structure, inhabited or vacant, or a dwelling, a shop-cum-dwelling or a place of business, workshop, school etc., with a separate entrance".[6] It shows that definitions are everchanging, but always emphasizing structures with entrance.

Ancient Indian Concept

A permanent dwelling is referred to in literature as *Vastu*[7] a word derived from Sanskrit root *Vas* (meaning to reside). Similarly, *Griha*[8] meant a single hut or solitary house and apartment to be used as shelter or place of residence, other synonymous terms like *Gaya*,[9] *Agara*,[10] *Geha, Ud-*

vasita, Vesma, Sadma, Niketana, Nisanta, Pastya, Sadan, Bhavan, Mandira, Nikaya, Nilaya, Alaya etc., all indicated a residence[11]. The cottages of the sages and mendicants were named as *Parnshala* or *Utaja*; of wild tribes *Pakvana* or *Sabralya*. The building, however, named as *harmya*, includes *Prasada, Mandapa, Sabha* (assembly hall), *Sala, Prapa* and *Aranga*.[12] The houses of ancient India always possess a particular site, selected on the basis of religious sanctions by some priests, having auspicious direction of doors, alignment and layout of corners and rooms, plus attached structures, dealt with in proper sections.

Rural Buildings

The rural houses, form one of the essential facts of unproductive occupation[13] of the rural landscape; provide one, with clues regarding the complex relations between man and his environment, represent the cultural heritage of the past and the survival of tradition[14] and reflection of the social state.[15] But unfortunately, the focus on buildings, (which) is to provide a clearly definable core, is inadequately studied and known[16] and, particularly, very little progress is made in India.

The buildings are, however, distinguished in three groups.

(i) Primitive building: It most simply, refers to that produced by societies defined as primitive by anthropologists;[17] People have very few building types, a model with few individual variations, built by all;

(ii) Pre-industrial Vernacular:A greater, though, still limited, number of building types, more individual variations of the model, built by the tradesmen;

(iii) High style and Modern:Many specialized building types, each building being an original creation (although this may be changing), designed and built by team of specialists.

Though the buildings/houses can be studied in various ways, the best approach is to look at them chronologically-tracing the development over time, either of techniques, forms and ideas, or of the thoughts of the designer, or one can study them from any specific point of view. The author agrees with Rapoport that, the specific task is to select features of the house, which seem most universal, and to examine them in different context, so that one can best understand, what it is, that affects the forms, taken by dwellings and group of dwellings, and also, 'what it is, that so easily, enables one, to tell, often, at a glance, the area, culture or even sub-culture to which a dwelling/settlement belongs.[18]

Keeping in view the specific task referred to earlier, the discussion in the sequel relates, to the phases of development and essential features, having various forms, sizes and functions of a few regions. As the term form, points towards the forces, that create house form, implicit or explicit, it is proper to give a brief account of the two alternate theories of house form.

(i) ***Physical Determinism***: Supporters of this view advocate, that for thousand of years factors like climate, materials, site, defence, economics and religion, have determined the character of buildings. But, observations in the field reveal, that presence of similar factor can also result in very different house forms, and similar forms can be built in the presence of, and due to, different factors. Mostly, these factors can be termed as modifying factors rather than form determinants. Moreover, "Man was a symbol making animal before he was a tool making animal, that he reached specialization in myth, religion and ritual, before he did in material aspects of culture, and that, ritual exactitude came before exactitude in work.[19] In short, house form is not a result of physical forces or a single causal factor, it is something else or cultural.

(ii) ***Socio-cultural View***: The basic idea, behind this view, is that people with very different attitudes, (cosmological, symbiotic and exploitative) and ideals respond to varied physical environments. During this process, various changes and differences, in the interplay of social, cultural, ritual, economic and physical factors, create spatial variations. As such, the socio-cultural forces become primary and the others remain secondary or modifying. There is truth in the latter view. Because, what is more significant, is the vision, that people have, of the ideal life. In short, houses and settlements are the physical expression of the *genre de vie*.[20]

Thus, rural houses of a particular region, present diversity in form, size and functions, as well as, balanced adaptation, to the physical and cultural environment of the area. But at micro-level, one finds resemblances in dwellings and 'none of these facts is surprising in itself, for after all, men, the world over, use ingenuity to solve their material problems and, in so doing, employ a fundamental common sense. When needs are dire 'necessity becomes the mother of invention' and it is, therefore, not to be wondered at that the influence of environmental features is reflected in man's works in a similar way in different localities.[21] The natural environment, the wood, earth or stone and climate, have determined mostly the building materials and the form of the roof. The houses are constructed out of local materials, available or easily imported. On the basis of field observations the impact of building's genius is visualized, not only in the general aspects of these dwellings, but also in the doorways, wall paintings, and other carvings on wooden supporters and simple architectural designs. Thus, the dwellings, the 'most universal elements of cultural landscape,[22] having a highly 'significant place in the geographical hierarchy of phenomena,[23] depict in any region, the symbol of its regionalism, expressive of both its distinctive physical milieu, as well as, socio-economic structure.[24]

Development Phases and Present Dwellings

Men, passing through the socio-economic development phases, developed houses in form, size and functions (Fig. 8). House forms evolved through successive stages, corresponding to social and cultural differences of the occupants, showing general complexity in indigenous structural designs with the increase of time. Evidences of Palaeolilhic to Mesolithis period of occupation reveal varied type of development in structures. Tracing the stone Age settlements Jayaswal's[25] brief account presents a vivid picture in India (Fig. 2.5). Evidences of circular stone alignments, which seem to be protective device, or wattle huts or wind breaks, are found in Bagor, Banas basin, in Rajasthan. Similar alignments, having 2.25 to 5.00 m diameters, were traced from Barmer. Excavations at Chirand, near the confluence of Ganga with Son, show two types of dwellings: (i) pit-houses with roofs, and (ii) Circular structures with 2 m diameter. Their floors were paved, and walls were made of clay or mud plastered over a bamboo screen, from outside and inside. Like the Eastern Zone, the Northern region community in the Valley of Kashmir and Punjab (Burzhom site near Srinagar), practised the construction of mud/mud brick houses. Similar pit dwellings were also reported from the Neolithic localities of northern China. In South, in Sangankallu Ia one room circular house (having 5m diameter) was, perhaps, made of wood and bamboo. Here, during the second phase (c.1800-1500 B.C.) circular hutments, made of perishable material, are carefully made, as exemplified by Tekkal Kota I site, which presents, a circular structure with round post of 3" thickness, and placed at an interval of 9"-11" distance with a full plan aligned within a diameter of 18′ and levelled mud floor. The existence of house, built with mud brick and some sort of fortification, is evidenced from Nagda and Kayatha (Madhya Pradesh). At Navadatoly (Madhya Pradesh), the structures- residential and otherwise-were round

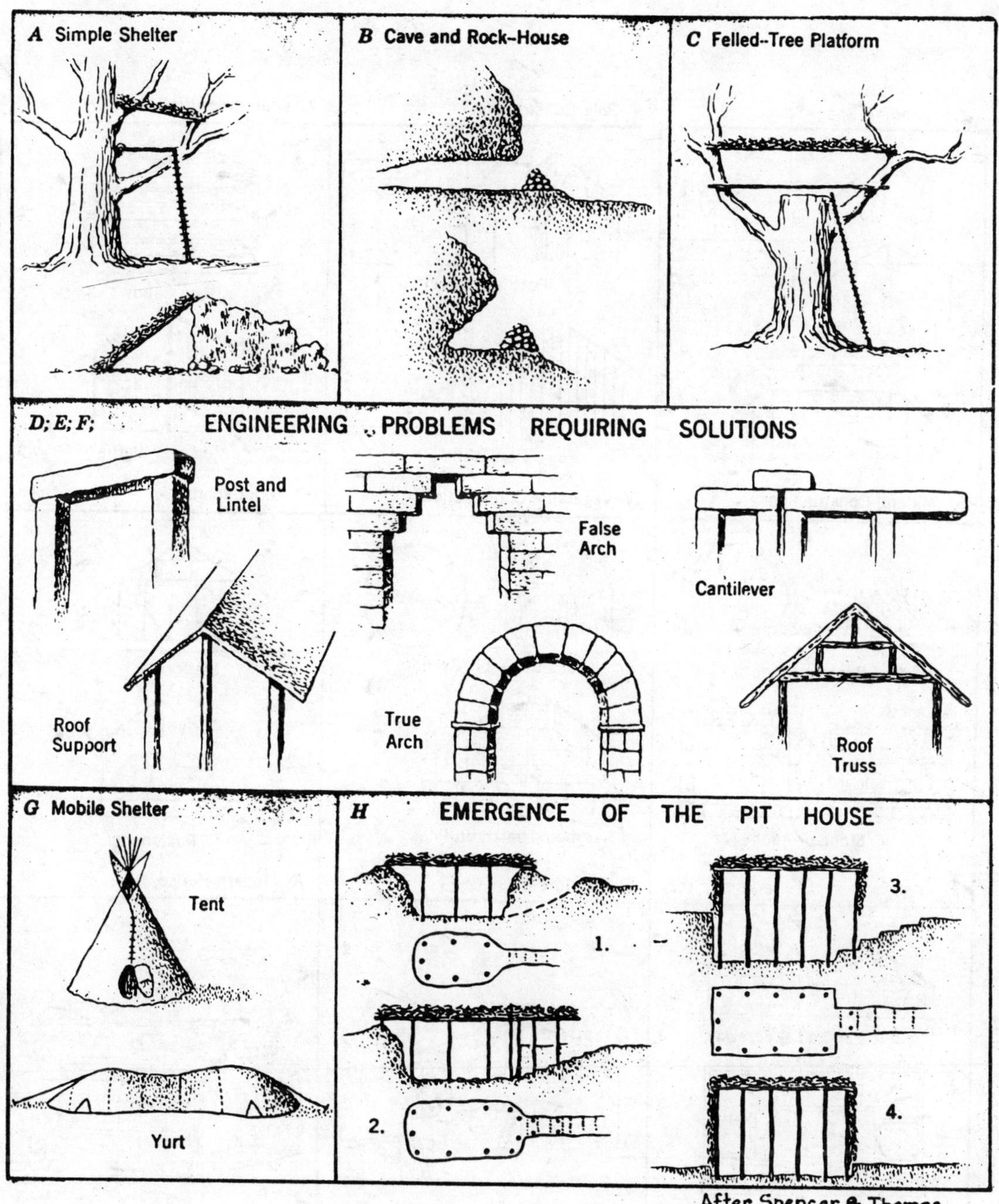

Figure 8.8: Elements of Housing Systems.

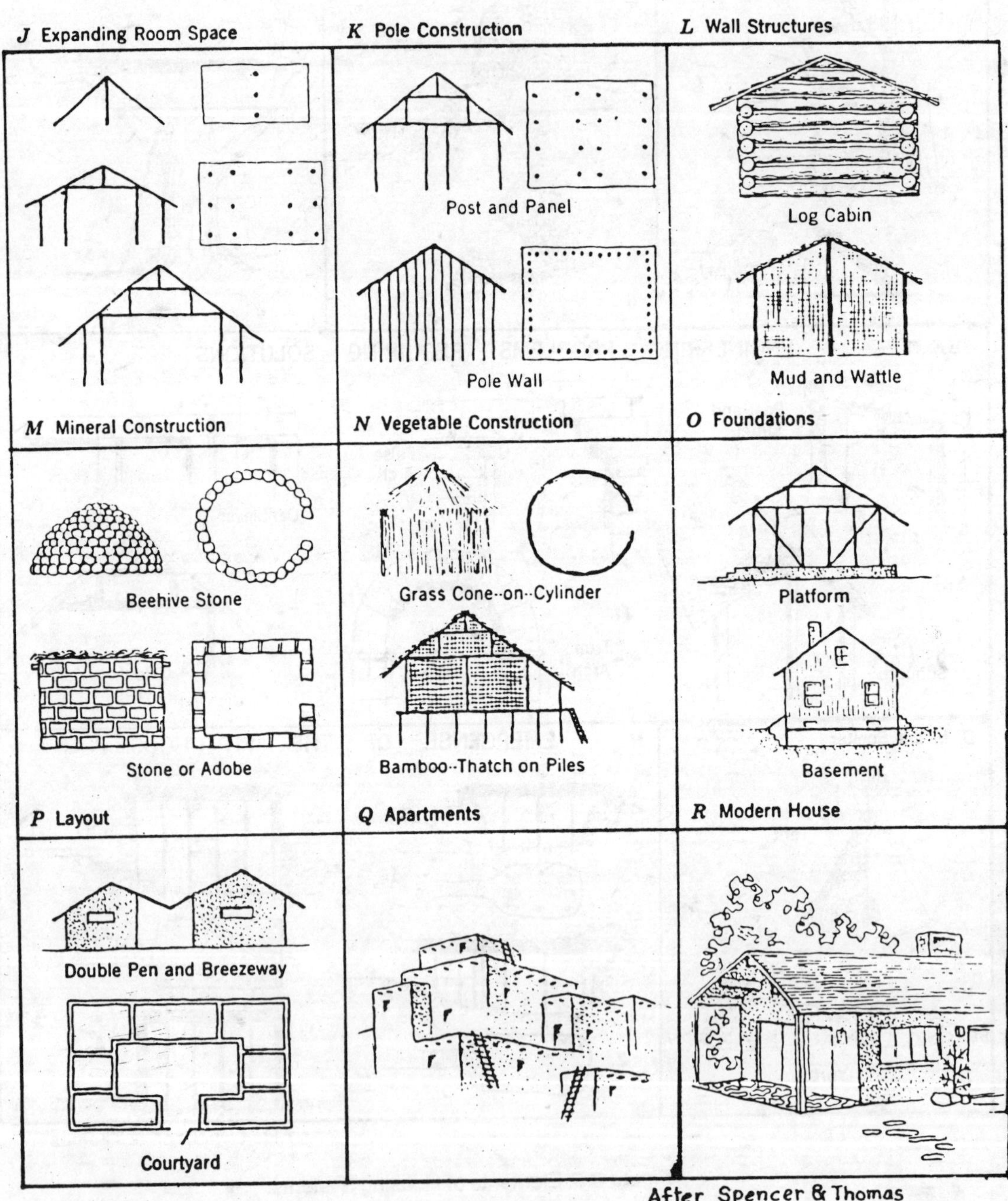

After Spencer & Thomas

and rectangular, their average size being 10′ in diameter when round or 10′ × 7′. These structures were built with round wooden posts, ranging in thickness from 4" to 9".

Bagh and the imaginative Udaigir caves, *inter alia*, bespeak the Neolithic occupation, but are discarded as being called the first form of human dwelling,[26] 'instead of the pit dwelling (which), was a northern hemisphere form, that may have begun during cold period in the Paleolithic Age.[27] Beside, the wattle and daub dwellings included reeds, twigs and small branches interwoven, and stones or rock cut boulders; and the 'substance dictated',[28] the form rather multiplicity of forms, all adapted to their environment.[29] The Neolithic architecture, alongwith fortification, palace, store house, factory, and temple building blossomed quite fully and diffusion of technologies moved rapidly to many parts of the world. Then, followed the diversification of structures for auxiliary buildings for purposes of storage, penning, sheltering of animals and development of workshop.

The circular or rectangular structures were, later on, arranged in threes or fours around a square or rectangular space, taking shape of courtyard, "which offered best protection for the cattle"[30] and was multi-functional in nature.[31]

Varied cultural traditions are responsible for specialization in forms because of considerations like, the religious motifs, directional facing, inclusion of shrines, focusing on sacred objects, siting of fire place or kitchen, aspects of sanctity, requiring the structures for such diverse purposes as, child birth, age ceremonies and rituals, need of defence and also the whims. We here examine a few examples.

Pueblo Houses

In America the ancient Pueblo Indians,[32] who had no metal tools, written communication or the wheel, built multi-storied, solar efficient houses strong enough to last centuries. Anthropologists say the great houses of *Chaco* canyon, where thousands of Indians may, have worked in 10th century, New Mexico, were built with windows, that caught the winter sun, but were shaded during the hot summer. Chaco architects constructed most of the houses, even having hundreds of rooms, using the sheer sandstone cliffs of the canyon as the back wall. The lower wall of the houses were built several feet thick and were designed to support the walls of the upper story, each made thinner and lighter, than the one below. Doors and windows openings were aligned from floor to floor and stone steps, as well as wooden ladders, connected the different levels. The walls, themselves, were made of thick blocks of stone and mud mortar, covered on the outside with a veneer of thinner slabs of rock that were often arranged in simple patterns.

Ceilings and floors were made of cross beams, covered with willow mats and mud. One of the great houses has 26,000 beams alone, each cut and carried from a Ponderosa forest, 40 km away. The ceremonial buildings were round, with built in benches, that could have held hundreds of spectators. Some had upper level rooms with windows, that overlook the stage like centre, much like private theatrical boxes of today.

Anthropologists say, these *Kivas* were riddled with tunnels and hidden doorways, that would have been used in mystical ceremonies of the ancient Indians.

Wooden Houses

Brunhes accounts for different houses in forest clearings of northern and central Europe. Regarding houses in France he narrates: 'To the north of Berne, the house is completely covered by its roof, as by a hood, the roof is like a cap of thatch or wood coming down to within six feet of the ground and almost hiding the walls. It descends on four sides with a steep and regular slope and the house, cannot breathe the fresh air from any of its sides. It is difficult even to catch a glimpse of the foot of the floor, or in some cases, the edge of a window, between the lower edge of the roof and the ground. Here is a description by Emmanuel de Mortonne of a wooden house in a different region a long way from the Swiss Plateau, the Paringu massif, in the Southern Carpathians: "The architecture of the *Stina* is of the simplest. The walls are, generally, formed of unsawn tree-trunks, resting on corner pillars set in the ground. The air passes freely through the unplugged interstices. Sometimes, there is a kind of basement made of unmortared stones. The roof, two or three times as high as the walls, is placed on top like a lid, which can be taken off and is shaped like a boat, with a straight keel and front and back faces. It is made of wooden laths, nailed one over another like, slates.

Mud/Stone Houses

Brunhes gives details of two type of houses: (i) Mud houses in lower Nile region and (ii) Stone houses in southern upper region. Such developments are common in most parts of the world, where mud and stone are available. It is the advent of specialized agriculture and industrial growth, which made men switch over to other forms than the universal huts. It is to be emphasized again, that during later period, these huts were arranged in threes or fours around a rectangular or square space[33] taking shape of courtyard, 'which offered best protection for the cattle'[34] and was multi-functional in nature. The increase in number of bands, population, and changes in socio-economic conditions, brought structures, ranging from small beehive units to store houses, temple, fortifications and palaces. In nutshell, "The technologies and styles of architecture increased, as did the materials employed, becoming elaborated into a bewildering variety and wealth of cultural forms in which, regional diversity became extremely marked".[35]

Essential Features of Houses

Courtyard (Vehra in Punjab, Bakhal in Malwa), is the most distinguishing feature of the rural house in the northern Indian settlements, in particular, and everywhere in general. This represents rectangular open space of diverse site, size, shape, situation, function and surroundings depending upon the need, available space or only the whim of the occupants.[36] Its situation and layout are also an indication of status of the occupant. It is worth noting, that courtyards are, rarely, fully surrounded by walled rooms, like those visualized in the Ganga Valley or others found in the plains of China, Nigeria and elsewhere within tropical regions. Even in old type *Garhies*, the door opens in front of gallery leading to courtyard. This may be ascribed, to the use of the latter, for cattle, which could be easily, safely kept, fed and milked there, even by women, specially at night. The most common occurrence of the courtyard is in the back side, where it is surrounded by an inner Verandah, attached to the main dwelling or by the walls of these rooms, and an outer wall, rarely having a door as found in modern type dwellings (Figs. 8.1 and 8.2) Sometimes, it has separate rooms for fodder and fuel or other household articles like earthen pots, loom, cattle shed or kitchen. Potter's furnace, fuel-wood and also ass find their place in such courtyard. Modern houses have lavatories, bathrooms and store rooms, well adjusted in such courtyards. The front side courtyard is surrounded by inner verandah, walled rooms on two or three sides, a verandah on a front side with a gallery, or by only a wall with a front door (Fig. 8.1/5B). In tribal houses,

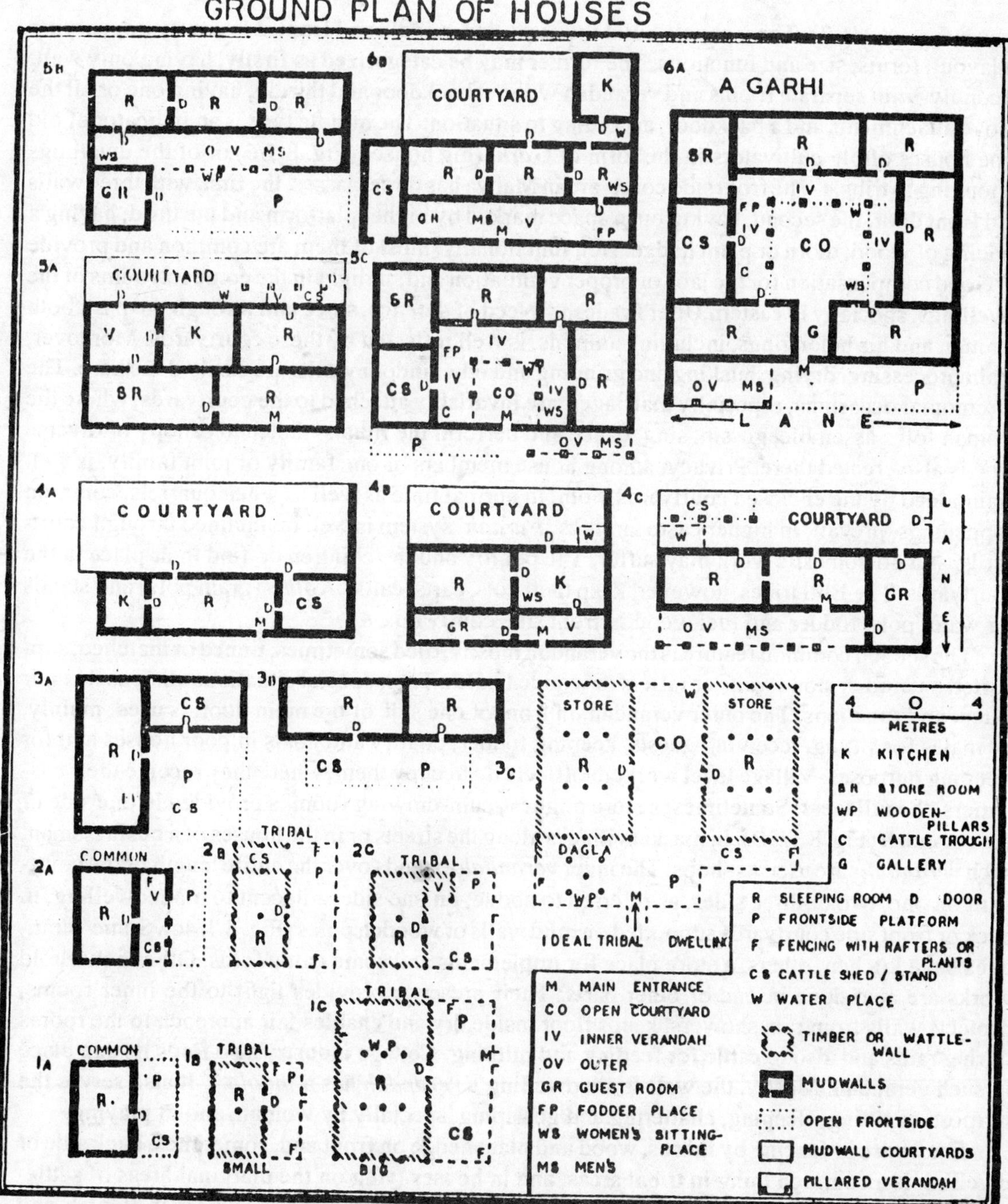

Figure 8.1

the open space between two dwellings, surrounded on back side by wooden or thorny hedges, serves the purpose of courtyard (Fig. 8.1./3c). The poor dwellings, mostly, one to two roomed, have open front side courtyard, one third to a meter higher than the street or lane level, often well marked by raised earthen platform or hedge, which also demarcate the dweller's right on front space (Figs. 8.1/1-3). Thus, people build the back side, middle and front side courtyard, varying in layout, forms, size and functions. The former may be categorized as firstly, having only wall, secondly, with separate rooms and verandah without backdoor and thirdly, having one or all the above attachments and a backdoor, according to situation. The middle type is an indicator of old type houses of big cultivators in the form of *Garhi* (big house) (Fig. 8.1/6) or of the dwellings belonging to tribals. The front side courtyard in Malwa has three classes, the first, with three walls and front door, the second, having open space marked by higher platform and the third, having a fencing of wood, thorn or plant hedge. But, functionally, most of them are common and provide a "Good compensation for the lack of proper ventilation and sunlight in the compact rooms of the dwellings, specially in eastern Utter Pradesh." Need of defence, since and through the past, both for men and his belongings, including animals, is well reflected by these courtyards. Moreover, grain processing, drying, husking and grinding and other indoor works are easily done here. The ceremonial occasions, especially marriages, are invariably attached to the courtyards, where the woman folks assemble, gossip, sing, dance and perform the rituals; thatched canopy of diverse type is also erected there. Privacy, among house members of one family or joint family, is well maintained by the enclosed courtyards, both, in normal time as well as when quarrels, common happenings, prevail. In higher caste families '*Purdah*' system is well maintained through courtyards, and no domestic work may suffer. The poultry and the children do find their place in the courtyards. The Bhil tribes, however, keep their cots, carts, cattle, *Kothis* (grain pots) and stands for water pots, fodder and fuel wood in front side courtyard.

The second common feature is the verandah mostly, tiled sometimes, tinned or thatched, supported on mud or stone walls or rafters or wooden poles. Their special situations vary, as do their extent and functions. The outer verandah, in front of one side of the main door, is used, mainly, by males for sitting, receiving guests, keeping fodder, poultry and goats in poor houses and for sleeping purposes. Village level workers/officers do occupy them, where they receive their customers, the villagers. Sometimes, a store or guest-cum-drawing room is provided in one side of the verandah (Fig. 8.1/5B). In market villages along the streets or in the houses of a businessman, such *verandahs* are used as shops. The inner *verandah* extends over the entire length of the courtyard on one, two or three sides, as referred to above; on one side, adjacent to main dwelling, in back or front side courtyards supported on mud walls or wooden poles (Fig. 8.1/4c). Some verandahs have kitchen, others, a store place for implements and some cattle folds. Other household works are also done in one or other parts. Their presence provides light to the inner rooms, protects walls from rain showers, keeps floor inside dry and enables fair approach to the rooms during rains and also to cattle for feeding and milking. Cottage industry also finds its due place in such verandah. Mostly, the well-to-do dwelling's *verandah* has a *jhoola*.[37] It also serves the purpose of sitting, sleeping, chattering and gossiping, specially by woman, and of playing.

Enclosure or fencing by thorns, wood and plant hedge on front and, sometimes, back side of dwelling is a common thing in tribal areas, and in houses lying on the marginal areas of settlements, everywhere where protection is needed and privacy demanded. *Ghers* in Punjab and western Utter Pradesh, *Khala* in Madhya Pradesh, (specially in Nimar) are its varieties. In Madhya Pradesh, such enclosures, a piece of land surrounded by fencing, at separate places around the settlement, is common. This is used for protection from wild animals, stray cattle and thieves and also, to keep fodder, fuel, implements, carts and other articles of agricultural use.

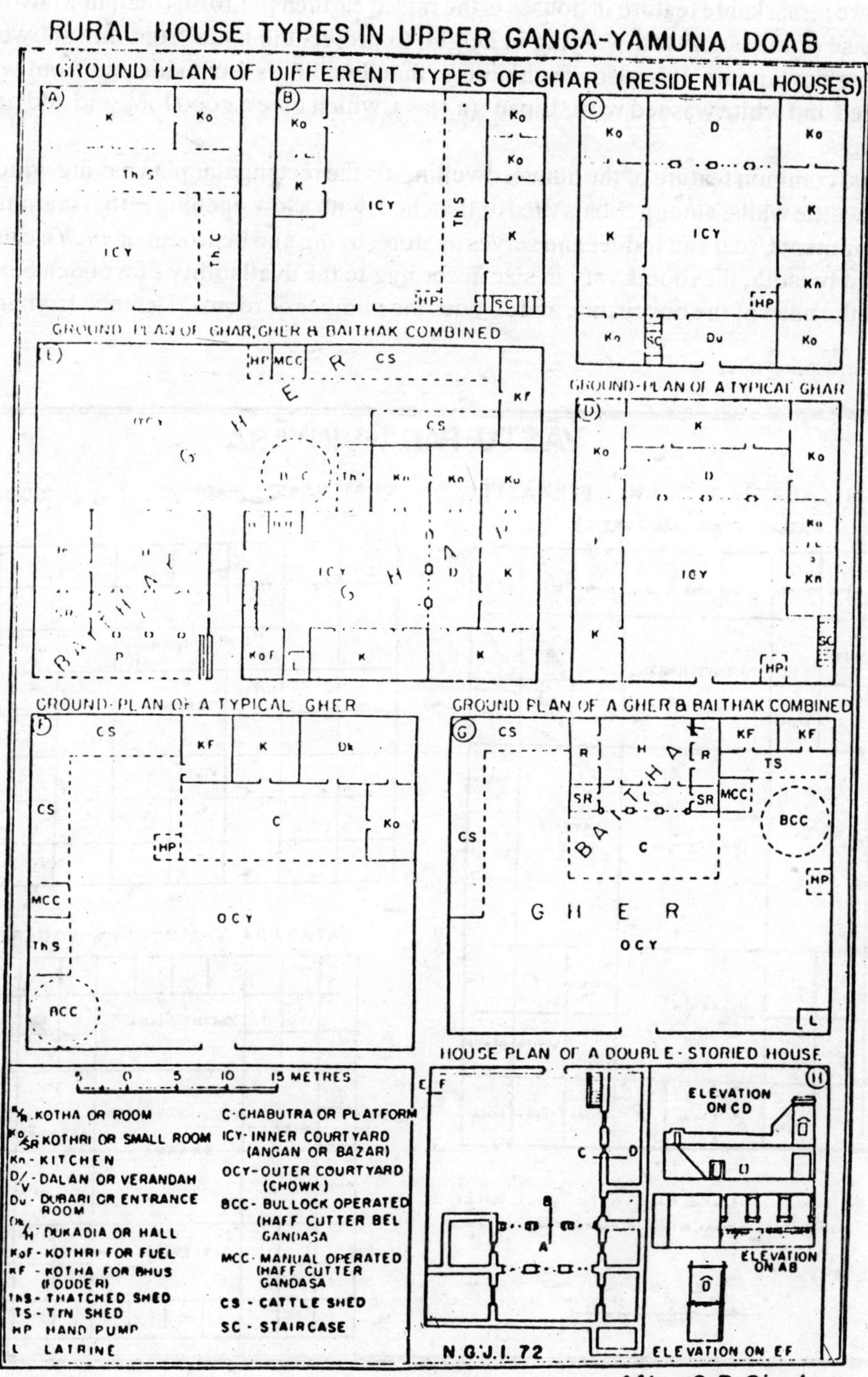
RURAL HOUSE TYPES IN UPPER GANGA-YAMUNA DOAB
GROUND PLAN OF DIFFERENT TYPES OF GHAR (RESIDENTIAL HOUSES)
GROUND PLAN OF GHAR, GHER & BAITHAK COMBINED
GROUND-PLAN OF A TYPICAL GHAR
GROUND-PLAN OF A TYPICAL GHER
GROUND PLAN OF A GHER & BAITHAK COMBINED
HOUSE PLAN OF A DOUBLE-STORIED HOUSE
ELEVATION ON CD
ELEVATION ON AB
ELEVATION ON EF
5 0 5 10 15 METRES
K/R - KOTHA OR ROOM
Ko/SR - KOTHRI OR SMALL ROOM
Kn - KITCHEN
D/V - DALAN OR VERANDAH
Du - DUBARI OR ENTRANCE ROOM
Dk/H - DUKADIA OR HALL
KoF - KOTHRI FOR FUEL
KF - KOTHA FOR BHUS (FODDER)
ThS - THATCHED SHED
TS - TIN SHED
HP - HAND PUMP
L - LATRINE
C - CHABUTRA OR PLATFORM
ICY - INNER COURTYARD (ANGAN OR BAZAR)
OCY - OUTER COURTYARD (CHOWK)
BCC - BULLOCK OPERATED CHAFF CUTTER BEL GANDASA
MCC - MANUAL OPERATED CHAFF CUTTER GANDASA
CS - CATTLE SHED
SC - STAIRCASE
N.G.J.I. 72
After S.P. Singh

Figure 8.2

One more remarkable feature in houses is the raised earthen platform (otali in Malwa) along the lower base of the outer wall, varying in height, to protect the latter from rain showers, rain waters during downpours. It is also worth noting, that dwelling's front side and front walls are well plastered and white washed with 'Lipan' (a clay), which give a good look and add beauty to rural buildings.

The most common feature of the human dwellings is the rectangular plan having windowless mud walls, wattle walls; among tribals tiled or thatched, with a low opening, often crammed with meager equipments, fuel and fodder and serves as store, living and bedroom or even a cattle fold. In length and breadth, the rooms vary in size according to the availability of wooden beams and rafters, and the need of the occupants, and so does the number of rooms. Defence from invading

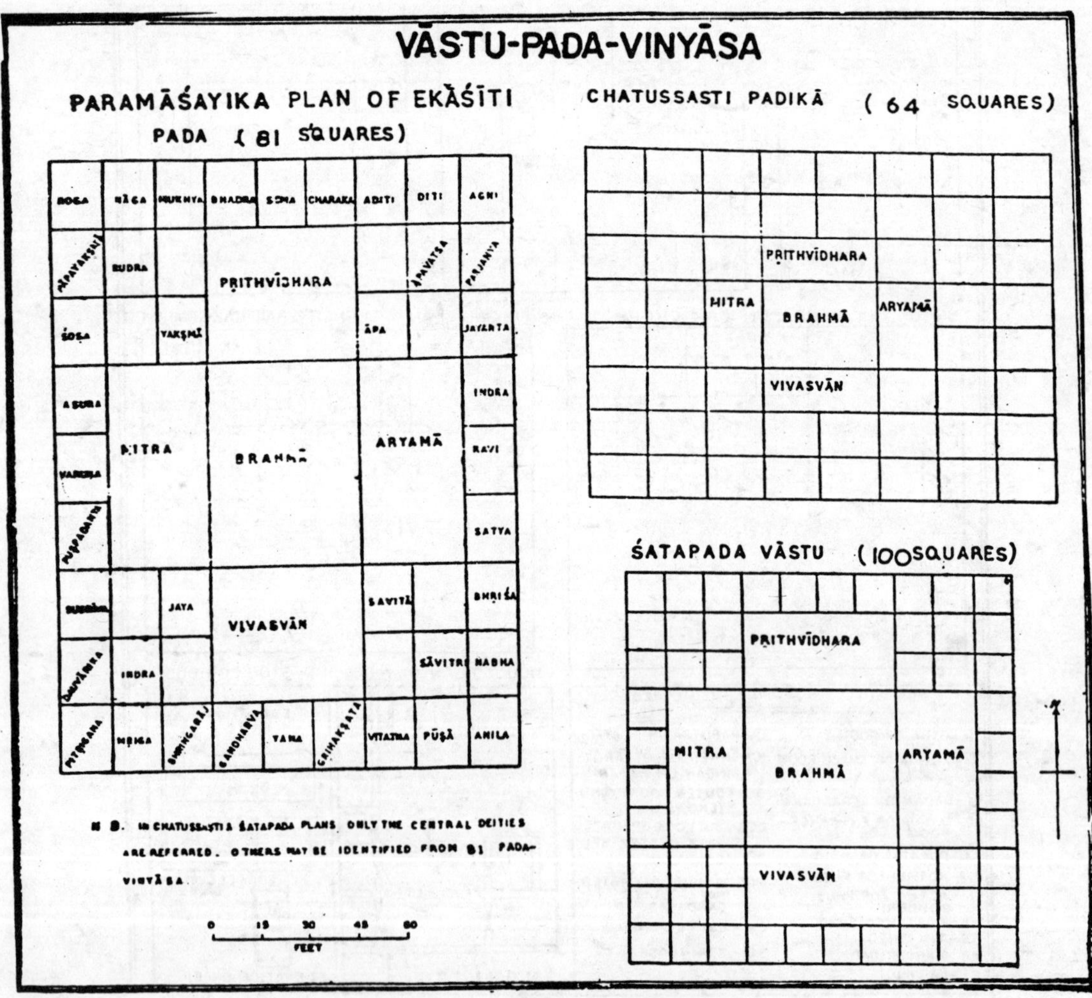

Figure 8.3

elements, thieves, monkeys and other wild animals, as well, as inauspiceous surroundings, are responsible for lack of window or ventilators or holes in dwellings.

Ground Plan and Layout of Houses

The evolution of ground plan of rural dwellings, visualized in the region, reveals that rectangular pits or caves took the form of several huts surrounding a common courtyard, which was primarily occupied by a tribal class, a joint family and, in later times, by a single family, belonging to any caste, having various types of accommodation according to the need and status of the occupants.

In India the old Hindu literature refers to the various house types based on *Vastupadvinyasa.* The present houses are relict of and modifications of the same. The Puranas as well as astronomical literature speak about the graphical nature of ground plans, divided into squares/rectangles. There is mention in the matsya Purana that each deity presides over a particular square. As depicted through (Fig. 8.3) the plan is named as follows:

(1) Ekasiti Pada having 81 squares, (2) *Chatussasti* Pada, having an area divided into 64 equal squares and (3) *Satapada*, having 100 equal squares. The aim of such layout plan was to select sites for specific purposes. As shown in map (Fig. 8.4) the 16 rooms are specifically allotted to

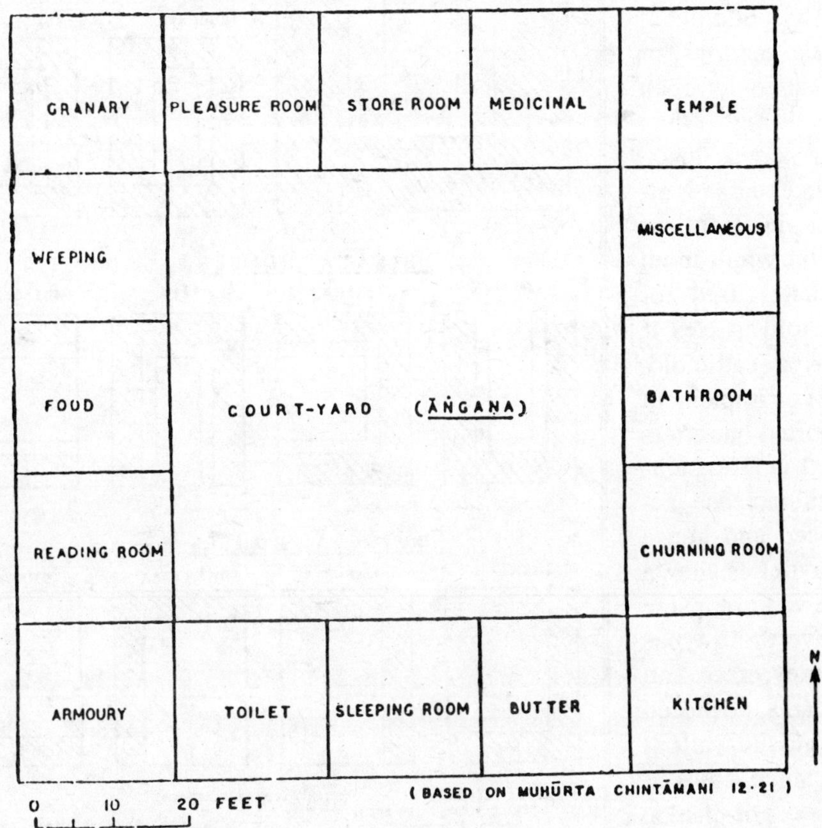

Figure 8.4

particular purposes.

Matsya Purana refers to S̄alā buildings for common people and recognizes four kinds of such s̄alā (winged) houses as shown on the map (Fig. 8.5) and given below.

(1) *Chatus̄salā* Houses (four winged) are of five types named as *Sarvatobhadra, Nandyavārta, Vardhamānā, Ruchaka,* and *Swastika.*

(2) *Trisala* House is categorized as *Dhānyaka, Suksetra, Visalā* and *Paksaghna.*

(3) *Dvisala* Houses are named as *Subha, Yamsūrya, Dhānyaka* and *Dhana.*

(4) Ekasala Houses having only one wing were most common inhabited by poor people.

The basic one room dwelling (Fig. 8.1/1A, B, 2A, B) varies in size from 3m × 12m × 4m having (15m^2-35m^2) floor area. Such a house has, either a partition, usually found in tribal houses of Bhils, or no partition inside, and raised platform, sometimes, well demarcated by additional platform on the margins, or by fencing, or only open front side, a little higher than the field or street level. Sometimes, a verandah is attached either in front or either side of the width about 2.5m in breadth, used for storing household articles, if walled, or as a cattlefold, fodder or fuel or implement store, if supported on rafters (Fig. 8.1/2A, 3A). The number of rooms increase according to need and house changes its layout as shown on map. The rooms, inside the house, have proto types of a second storey, erected on wooden beams, placed transversely into the walls at one meter distance, covered by wooden pieces or planks. In case of a second storey

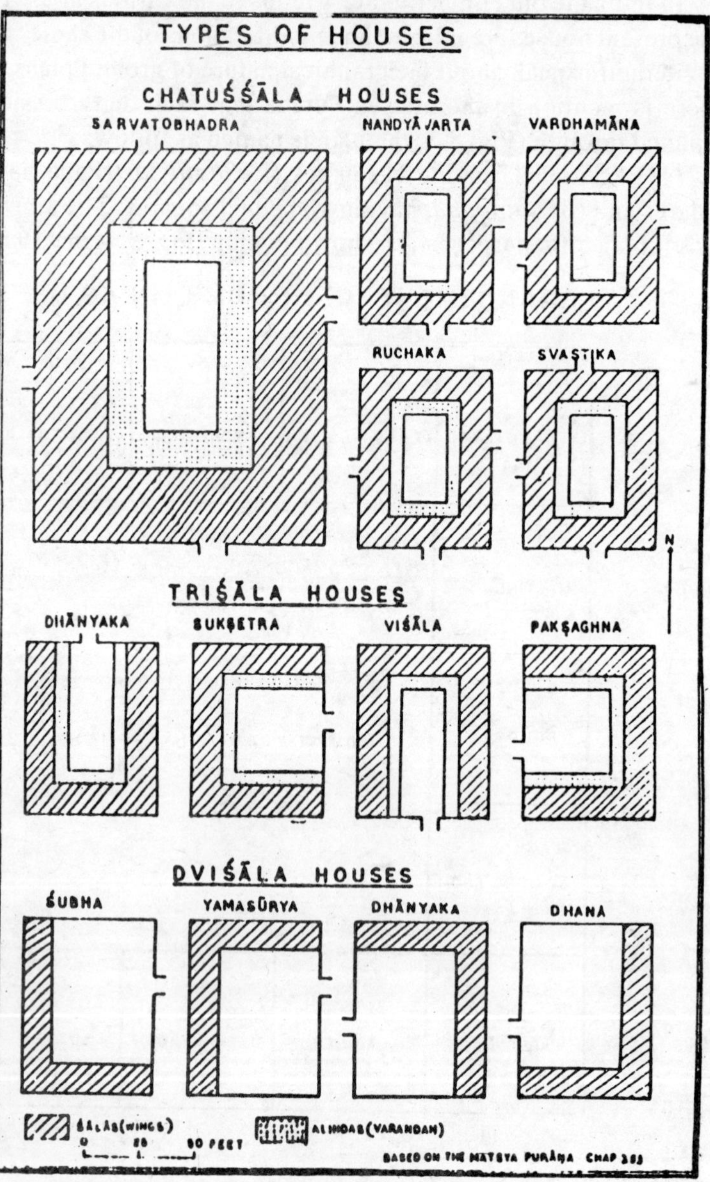

Figure 8.5

those beams are placed closely. Sometimes, these beams are extended in the verandah and these extensions are used for keeping household articles. The inner *Kotha* is approachable through wooden stair cases, being often used as store or sleeping room. The non agriculturists, like businessman and other high caste people, have such '*Kothas*' of multi-functional types.

Only a few old type big houses or '*Garhis*' (in Malwa) have separate plans, varying in the arrangement of additional rooms for catalyzed and kitchen. It is noteworthy, that a separate *Baithak* or *Dalan* (guest house), wholly used by males is common in northern Indian settlements. The common dimensions of big houses, having middle type courtyard, are 16m × 12m but in a few dwellings 20m × 16m are also seen.

It is remarkable that, in layout, mostly groups of adjacent houses, either cluster round one common inner yard or form double rooms of houses, the backwalls of which form straight lines. In such layouts the dwellings, standing back to back, have one common and straight back wall, but the front walls form an irregular line, reflected by zig-zag lanes. These back wall lines can best be explained by the need for protection, on the one hand, and by development phases, indicating later additions during successive periods of village settlements. Such a layout, having common back and side walls, is fully demarcated in community wise sectors, usually found in the rural villages, which provide definite market pattern. The protection measures, taken into consideration and adopted since long, over balance the directional aspects as well as auspicious aspects in the general layout of dwellings in the southern Indian parts and no particular directions carry more weight. While wells are not dug in the south side of dwellings in Northern Indian Plain, in southern part, they have no directional relations. Similarly, other attachments occupy the available space irrespective of auspicious considerations. But, separate houses, generally, have easterly and northerly doors. In Northern Indian plains, in particular, houses have courtyards oblong in shape from north to south, best suited to get winter sunshine. Observations reveal the fact that,the influence of *Brahmanization* and *Aryanization* is more visible around religious centers like Varanasi, Ujjain, Ayodhya, Mathura, etc., where people, avoid southerly aspect of the houses, invariably follow '*Udyapan*' inauguration or entrance ceremony. Along sacred rivers, people avoid sleeping with their feet towards them. The further away one goes the less attention is paid to these auspicious considerations, varying in degree as well as quantity. But the aboriginals follow the directions of their priests.

Now, we may discuss the structural features of dwellings.

(a) Foundation and Floors of Dwellings

Geological background and building materials play major role in determining the foundation because the common one storeyed, low walled houses require foundations a few feet deep, varying from one-third meter, both in mud and stone walled houses, to 1 meter for wooden post dwellings. It is notable that upper caste people, in particular, lay foundations according to '*pind*' or '*Garbh*' the size of which is fixed by priests on the basis of astrological calculations. Wooden posts, in tribal dwellings, are invariably fixed with murrum and boulders. The floor of the house is, generally, '*Kachcha*', which is levelled, after being rammed with hard murrum and plastered with clay and cow dung. Plastering by cow dung or clay mud (Lipan) keeps the house clean, good looking, free from germs and rat holes. The level of the main rooms is about one-sixth meter higher than the verandah level or courtyard which are also kept higher than the door level in front of the house. This front side too is kept higher, varying from one-sixth to 1 meter from the field or lane level. The courtyard slopes towards the main drain, which opens in one convenient side of the house, following its situation and site. The front side of the house has a gentle slope towards lane or open space or hedge, except in market villages, where the front wall or fence forms street limit.

(b) Walls and Roofs

Mudwalls predominate the dwellings, in most of the rural country area and, irrespective of size and plan, their construction remains the same, everywhere. After foundation being laid, walls are run up with damp mud, prepared out of local soil muddled with water, sometimes by the buffaloes, applied in successive layers of 25 to 30 cm in height, with a time gap, required to get the damp layer hardened enough to support another layer. Sometimes, they use sandstone and wooden planks (after 3 m height) to make the wall durable and other successive layers are put to required limit and form. These walls are plastered with cow dung mixed with grass, straw and dust and thick coating is provided to save them from rain showers. it is common practice to repair the walls after rains, i.e., just before '*Deepawali*' (the light festival) in most of Indian houses. Mention here must be made of the practice of protecting house walls from rains. At the base they provide '*otali*', raised ground, about half meter high throughout the outer wall. Similarly, pegs are fixed in outside walls. From hemp, a sort of mat, about 15m thick, is made just sufficient in size to cover the exterior of the walls, which has to take the pressure of rain showers. The mat is hung on pegs and removed after the monsoon is over. In some areas pulse (Tuar), Arhar stalks (Cajanus indicus) are used for such protection. The stone walled houses, are still lower in height, and constructed by boulders of basalt, sand stone etc., arranged one after another, sometimes, having mortar in between.

The common single tenements of tribals are built out of the materials locally available, no cement, brick or lime is used in such constructions; it has a *Kachcha* floor and there is no sink in the house, no bathroom, washing or bathing place, inside or attached to the house. Wooden posts (ballis) of about 16m diameter are fixed at a distance of 1.5 to 2m. from one another in five rows, the rows on both the extremes are used for fixing the bamboo mats to serve as walls. The height of the posts, in other 3 rows varies from 2m to 2.3m. A horizontal beam (a wooden balli of 16 cm diameter) is fixed joining the posts in each of the three middle row. On the beams are fixed small posts to serve as the members of the truss, on this scaffolding, *purlins* (wooden ballis 10 cm to 12 cm in diameter) are fastened by wire, nails, etc., and rafter (Sagtis of 7.5m diametre in Malwa) are then fixed on the *purlins* by means of wire, nails. The distance between one rafter and another is about 22 cm. Now, the frame of the roof is prepared, which is covered by '*sarali*' weeds or leaves or grasses, etc. Country made flat or semicircular tiles are laid on the roofs. The walls are made of, either bamboo mats, which are fastened to the exterior row of wooden posts and later plastered with clay and cow dung, or wooden rafters and leave serve as wall materials. The door frame is made of the straight wooden rafters of bamboo splinters, interwoven with nails, and removable on hinge (Fig. 8.1/2B, 3C).

Thatching process is more or less the same in both types of roofs, be it tiled or thatched, though varying in materials used and height they achieve. If one compares, one dwelling with another on regional basis, it becomes clear that "climate expresses itself through the form of its roofs".[38] Gables on walls support *mangari* or ridgepole on two sides, which is supported in the middle by a number of thicker beams, fixed transversely in the walls, sometimes, direct in touch and sometimes, through 'Bel', another wooden supporter, fixed between beam and the ridge pole. The latter is available from local woods. The space, between ridge pole and pot of the wall, is covered by transversely fixed rafters, bamboo pieces or thinly split tree trunks. They project beyond the wall, half meter in other parts, and up to 1m in Eastern Utter Pradesh upto eaves, where wooden 'Dasa' is fixed transversely, along the eaves, to make it symmetrical. The whole framework is then covered with bamboo splinters, '*tuar*' stalks, thin rafters, fastened with strings and nails, and made smooth with grass, *palash* leaves (Butea monosperma) and mud, ready to support tiles of both types, the flat and semi-cylindrical which form ridge and channel, combinedly or severally, to run off the rain water. it is remarkable that higher walled dwellings of the Ganga Valley, have separate single or double secondary supporters (Ghoria) to eaves. Stone walled houses, when thatched with stone slabs or tins, have less steep slopes and strong supporters resulting into narrow rooms.

The wattle and daub dwellings, supported by rafters, are thatched with grass and plant leaves, fastened with strings with the wooden or bamboo framework.

(c) Other Features

'Dagla' (tanda) is a common feature lying by the side of a tribal dwelling in Madhya Pradesh (India). It is a raised structure of wooden '*ballis*' at a height of 2m to 3m, thatched with wooden rafters, put transversely; open on all sides, where fodder is stored and cattle staked, or is sometimes, used as sleeping place (Fig. 8.1/3C).

Similarly, '*Bittha*' '*Upraur*' (a heap of cow dung cakes) is made by piling up cakes and covering it with leaves thatch, in all parts of rural countryside, varying in size and form as well as season.

(d) Architectural Features and Internal Arrangement

Some of the low caste people have distinctive fancy pattern on the exterior of the walls generally painted by 'geru' (red chalk) or white clay (Kharia mitti) which give picturesque view. Designed 'Dasa' (supporter), locally called '*Sobawati*' in Malwa, adds beauty to the symmetrical eaves in most of the well-to-do houses. In eastern Utter Pradesh, eaves, supported below by double 'Ghoria' and 'Dasa', look more symmetrical and attractive and exhibit status of the owner. Similarly, carving on pillars, doors and wooden wings, create distinction between houses, especially, those lying in market villages. Beautifully carved teak pillars of Chettiars (Tamil Nadu) and Haveli's *otlo, parsal* and *ordo* (Gujarat) present the grandeur of wooden carved mansions and lofty pillars. Well carved and tar coloured black pillars are, mostly, used in verandahs. Pillars and doors in 'Baithak' of northern Indian houses are, invariably, designed and carved.

In tribal or poor houses one finds all culinary articles, earthen bins or '*Kothis*' or '*Kadgi*' of wood or grass, for storing grains, and cots etc., the clay oven (Chulha), cooking utensils (tapelas), '*thalis*', iron sauce pan (kadhai = kadahi), a '*karhachi*' (a big spoon), '*tawa*' pitchers, '*musal*', '*gatti*', '*okhali*' (husking and grinding device) and '*topla*' (basket) etc., are other articles. A net of grass fibre, called '*sinka*', is suspended from roof. '*Matka*', water place of wooden structure, is common. Bows & arrows find their separate place. In other dwellings of a well-to-do or medium class occupants, one finds a few cots, boxes, '*Jhoola*', grain bins, a few wooden furnitures, almirahs, agricultural implements, utensils, '*Lipan*' and other house-hold articles, arranged or scattered at several places.

House Types

Variations occur in dwellings according to the building materials, available and used, which are mostly determined by natural environment. Similarly, *genrede vie* determines the size, form and function, and both the factors (i.e., physical and cultural environment) combinedly, give a regional characteristic to the dwellings. House types are classified on the following basis.

(1) Building material applied
(2) Size and shape
(3) Socio-culturo-economic status. Let us see one by one.

1. House Types Based on Building Materials

(A) Walls: (i) mud (ii) stone (iii) brick (iv) timber (v) Wattle

(i) *Mud* is the most common material, available from all type of soils, varying in texture and colour. It is also the widespread oldest material used in houses of old civilizations. The vernacular buildings, involving family labour and neighbours cooperation, are, everywhere, available with mud walls. Even, the ordinary dweller runs up wall out of his own labour. It is also convenient to repair and build, when required, without any extra payment to mason, by giving periodical coating, plastering and thatching. Mud walled houses also are cool during summer. But, the disadvantages are also many-effects of dampness, white ants, dirty nooks and corners, time and labour consuming, space consuming, less durability are negative aspects.

(ii) *Stone* or basalt boulders or rock cut pieces are widely used in such areas, where proximity/nearness, availability in greater amount and portability are favourable factors. Sandstone providing hilly zones, volcanic plateau zones exhibit examples of such houses in abundance.

(iii) *Brick* walls are now covering the country side with the increased use of coal as baking material. It's role in construction cost, durability, space saving and maneuverability is obvious. The oldest evidences of houses are available in brickwalls of archaeological finds. It has other form of uses too (a) Mud mortar, as cementing material, is widely used in country side (b) various other cementing materials as mortar are used since ancient times. Now cement is covering the market in rural country side too. (c) Unbaked kachcha brick is also used for low height walls, but, popular in poor class owners.

(iv) *Timber or wooden* wall houses were, and are, common in forest areas of the world. In many a hilly parts of the world, where rocks are available in abundance, the labour cost, required to cut them of precise size, and in transporting them, is outbalanced by the easily gathered wood just near the dwelling, to which the tribals are well accustomed. Examples abound in Bhil areas in Central India and rural country side in Sweden, North America (folk log houses of Mexico), Italy and Brazil etc.

(v) *Wattle* wall is the product of terrain, forest cover, i.e., availability of material almost without cost and long earned skill among the owners, of mostly, aboriginal occupied areas, particularly, Vindhyas and Satpuras in India. Gonds and Bhils, mostly, reside in such houses. Their small dwellings occupy even the slopes and summits of the hills. Almost scattered in home steads, such '*tapro*' may, easily, be run up with the forest wood logs, bamboo and reed, available in profusion, first near the site, wherever, they make clearing to settle.

(B) *Roofs* may be of (i) tile (ii) thatch (iii) mud+other material (iv) Tin (v) Stone slab (vi) Wood

(vii) brick+others.

(i) Tiled roofs are common throughout the world. Two types of tiles, semi-cylindrical and flat are used for covering houses with varied sizes and forms. By and large, the size is larger in Northern India Plain and shorter in other plateau and hilly areas.

(ii) Thatching is original shelter making skill, still prevalent, in most of the poor class settlers. All sorts of walls are covered by thatch, be it stone walled houses of Portugal, or timber walled dwellings of Brazil, South East Asia and North America and mudwalled houses of India. Even conical houses of Africa, show a variety of thatching skills, particularly, in Abyssinian Highlands. Date palm leaves also serve thatching along with other grasses, leaves, twigs etc.

(iii) Mud thatching often mixed with cow dung, is common in Western part of India. In western part of Utter Pradesh, such houses mark the horizon in each settlement. Its occasional plastering is enough to provide safety from rains.

(iv) Tin roofed houses are increasing in number, according to innovation diffusion, in climatically suitable areas; countries lacking in storm or strong speedy winds, are using tins in rural as well as urban areas. Ethiopian market centres exemplify it well. Tin sheds are easy in construction, and slops in rural areas, are switching over to its use, everywhere.

(v) Stone slabs or flakes are being used since ancient times in mountain, hill and plateau areas. Sandstone, lime stone and slate-slabs make durable roofs after being cut and designed according to need. Temple, mosques and churches, invariably, show its *in toto* presence.

(vi) Wood as roof material is common in temperate forest zone, where wooden slabs, carefully superimposed and joined with rounded corners, protect house from snow water.[39] In tropical part too, wooden strips form roofs covered with tin or water proof materials.

(vii) Bricks make flat and smooth roof in the form of lingers mixed with iron rods and cement, a practice in vogue, in modern type rural houses, particularly, in rural market centres.

2. *Size and Shape as Basis for Classification*

The author here presents empirical study conducted in Malwa Region in India. Houses are grouped in five categories having various size, shape and accommodation, ranging from one room to more than five rooms. (1) The predominant group of one room dwelling shares 66.1 per cent of the region's total, occupied by 69.4 per cent persons, per household occupation number being 4.4, slightly less than the regional average of 4.87. The tribals, *balai, chamar*, most of the service class and small cultivator-cum-agricultural labour class people have such dwellings, lying mostly in hilly parts and marginal areas of the villages elsewhere. (ii) The poor and slightly well off people occupy two room dwellings, which cover 23 per cent of the regional total and accommodate 25.9 per cent population, having 5.5 persons per household. Here again one meets the tribals, agricultural labours, small cultivators and a few artisans and business class people having one main room, a verandah or a side attachment for catalyzed or other sheds required by the occupant. (iii) The lower middle class people comprising the peasants, carpenters, potters, business class, and a few of higher castes, occupy such dwellings, mostly of L-shape, having 6.6 per cent of the regional total and providing shelter to 8.6 per cent persons, who form a household of 6.2. (iv) Such dwellings, which have four rooms, cover only 2.2 per cent of the total and have 3.1 per cent population, the average household being 6.9. The middle class cultivators of upper caste, a few institutions come under this group. The houses having five or more than five rooms belong to rich persons, mostly being cultiv 11ors having *Garhi* or some institutions. This forms only 1.6 per cent of the total dwellings, occupied by 2.4 per cent persons with an average household of 7.3. This indicates several facts: (1) Most of the dwellings of the region are one roomed, where most of the people find shelter; (2) Very few dwellings have five or more than five rooms, and rich class people form very low percentage of the population; (3) There is positive correlation between accommodation and house hold strength throughout the region; (4) Number of occupants per dwelling has greater pressure in tribal areas, where more than 75 per cent live in one room dwellings; (s) Similarly, poor class people in other areas also have more than 5 persons per dwelling with only one room or two[40] (Fig. 8.6).

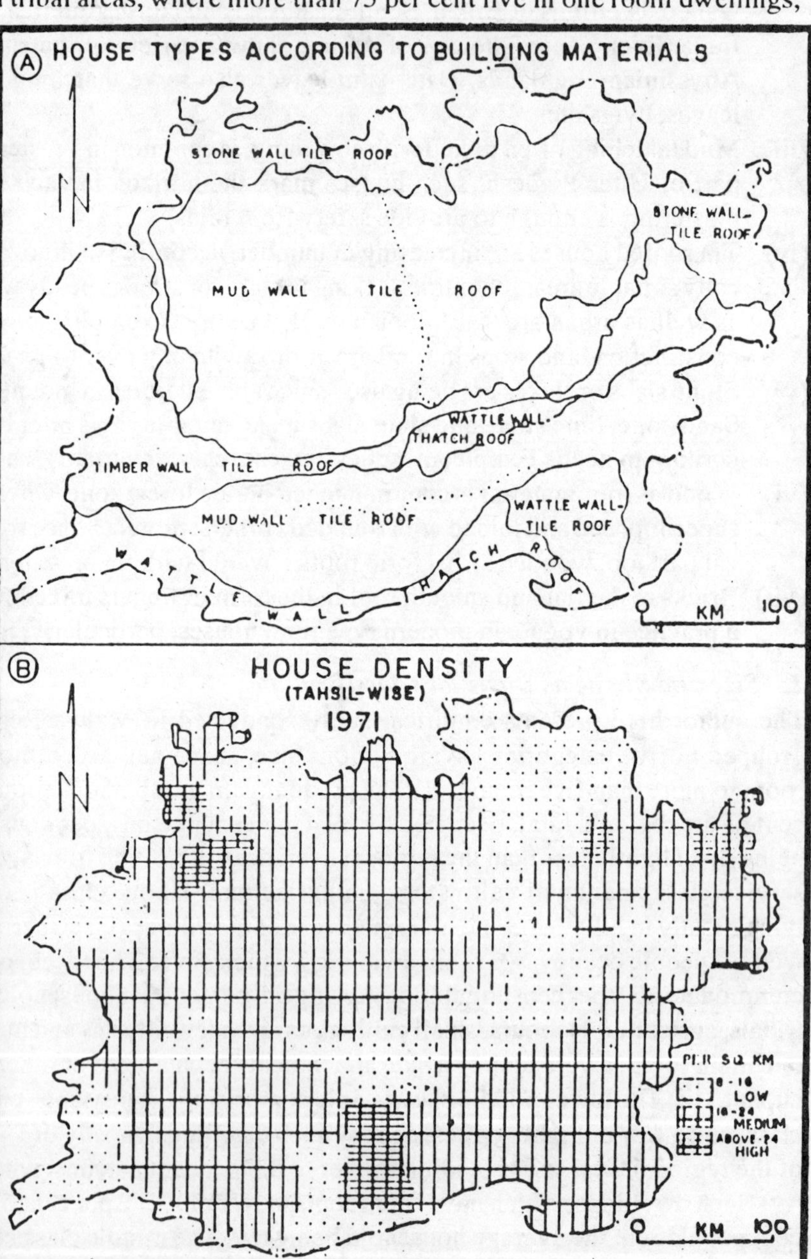

Figure 8.6

3. *House Type Based Upon Socio-Economic Status*

The study leads one to discuss about the part played by socio-economic conditions, which are best expressed in the size and shape of the houses in every region. It reveals that variation is visualized according to the cultural groups, including high caste people like *Brahmins, Rajputs, Kayasthas* and *Muslims*, particularly, *Shiyas* including *Bohras* and *Banias*, which have more spacious houses varying in vertical section also. Privacy, joint family relations, separate rooms required for cattle, store and guests, according to their cultural heritage, give various size, shape and plans, quite distinct from those of agricultural labour class, having almost no privacy or '*pardah*' on the one hand, and also distinct from tribal dwellings on the other. Thus, there are two groups: (1) The first including the occupants of superior status, both socially and economically or economically only, and the other, (ii) Tribal's group having close medium and poor contact with the superior group. The superior cultural group, mostly, occupies Plateau, Narmada valley and Nimar Upland Region and lives in mud or stone walled tiled dwellings, and the tribals, shelter themselves in timber or wattle walled and tiled or thatched dwellings, though mud and tile are taking the place of other materials with the increase in contract, forest clearing and rising income through various welfare schemes. The sub groups include: (1) *Gonds, Bhiala* and *Bhils* living outside hills; (ii) Medium group of *Bhils, Patlyas, Banjaras*, and Bhilalas of interior and, (iii) Poor or primitive group including *Bhils* of interior areas, *Korkus, Balers, Mankers* etc., living in the interior parts of the Vindhyas and Satpuras.

Vertical section in dwellings, mostly found in market villages or old villages of Plateau, Narmada Valley or Nimar, reflect the status of original *Jagirdars, Patels, Banias* or newly advanced business class. Such house types, sometimes, reflect lack of space, practice of privacy and 'Pardah' and also a compensation for cool air and sunshine, they provide to the dweller. It is remarkable that such double storeyed houses have no complete superstructure upon the whole base of ground floor, but only front side is provided with separate rooms for sleeping, store or a room for woman folk approachable through wooden, cemented or stone staircases from outside or inside.

Functions

Houses are also categorized according to the use to which they are put. The census organization[41] gives 13 categories, in all, which have been grouped here into four: (i) Dwellings including vacant houses. (ii) Shop-cum-workshop and, administrative, financial and educational institutions, (iii) Community centres and medical institutions and (iv) Others. These functions vary according to the need of a dweller, e.g., (i) Cattle shed, (ii) Implement shed, (iii) Grain store, (iv) Enclosure for sheep and goats, (v) Piggery sheds, (vi) Poultry shed, (vii) Labour shed near Brick Kilns or building constructions, (viii) Project site sheds for labour, sometimes, labour colony, (ix) Truck farming including vegetable and fruit stores, (x) Fishery tents or houses, (xi) Enclosures for fodder, cart and miscellaneous articles, (xii) Fuel store for keeping cow dung cake or dry wood and grain stalks, (xiii) Hay store, (xiv) Shed for pumpset, diesel set, (xv) Watching tents or wooden constructions on higher grounds to save crops from wild animals, birds, thief etc., (xvi) Inn or Dharmshala for staying by travelers, pilgrims or even traders, (xvii) Sheds-cum-restaurant along Highways as halt shelters, (xviii) Temple, mosque or church attached priest houses, (xix) Deity abodes, (xx) Other religious shrine-sheds for priest, *Panda* and *Pujari*, (xxi) *Bhuta-Preta* apparition (ghost) temples and attached shelters, (xxii) Horse stables, (xxiii) Elephant hall, and (xxiv) Dog rooms etc.

According to sample study the residential dwellings cover more than 62 per cent followed by others (about 30%); group two sharing 6.5 per cent and the rest coming under category No. 3. The percentage varies district wise, which reflects functional shift according to industrial and rural development. Similarly, the tenure status of sample houses[42] reveals, that about 91 per cent house hold occupy own dwellings of various functional groups, the rest being sheltered in rented buildings. About 75,500 persons have been recorded as houseless. If one realizes the pressure on one roomed dwellings this number would increase and cross the critical level.

A Gestalt View

In brief, house types are classified as follows: (1) Mudwalled tiled, (2) Mudwalled + mudroofed, (3) Mudwalled thatched, (4) Mudwalled with prototype wooden first floor, (5) Brick walled tiled, (6) Brick walled with concrete or brick slab roofed, (7) Brick walled thatched, (8) Kachcha brick walled tiled, (9) Kachcha brickwalled thatched, (10) Stonewalled tiled, (11) Stone walled thatched, (12) Stonewalled slab/flake roofed, (13) Timber walled tiled, (14) Timberwalled thatched, (15) Timber walled wooden roof, (16) Wattle walled tiled, (17) Wattle walled thatched, (18) Wattle-daub dwellings, (19) Cave Dwellings, i.e., at Carriers (near Paris), Spain, (20) Underground dwellings of Turkey and Spain, turfan (Gobi desert), (21) Loess houses in China namely Fenghuo[43] settlement, (22) Long houses of Sarawak, (23) Atoni houses,[44] (Fig. 8.7), (24) Pueblo Indian' houses in New Mexico, (25) Pastoral tents, (26) Sod houses of Eskimo, Alaska, (27) Igloo of Eskimo, (28) Bamboo pile house of Cambodia, (29) Batak pile dwelling sumara,

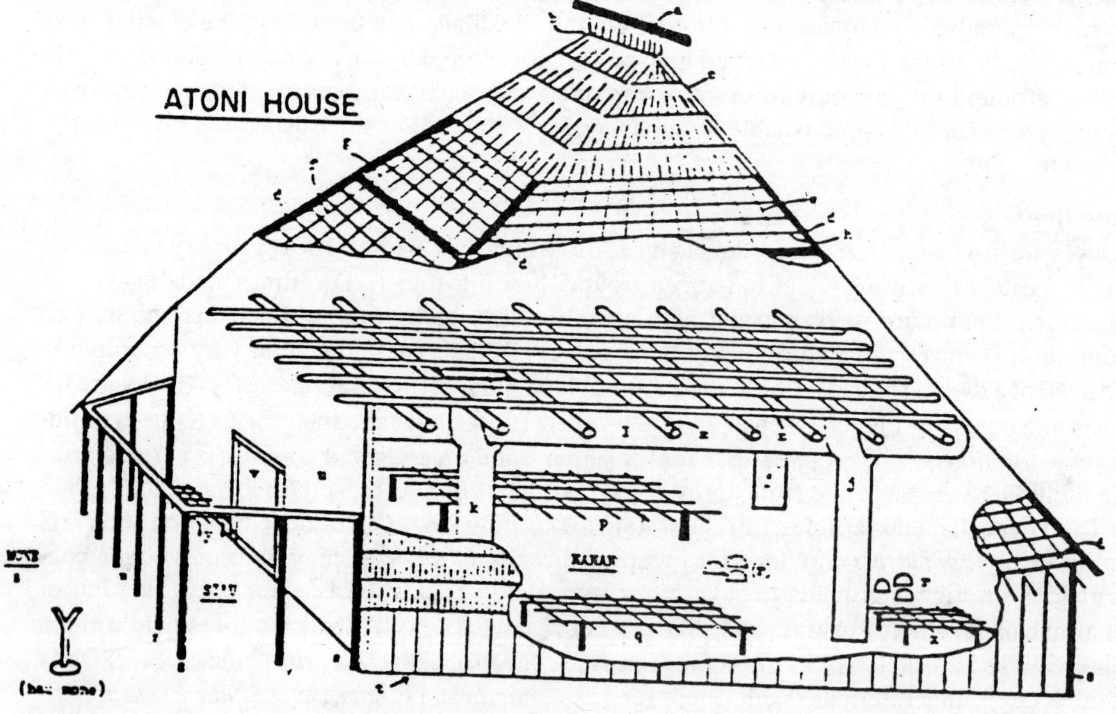

Figure 8.7. a. ***fuf manas***, 'sun cranium'; b. ***fuf ai***, 'fire cranium'; c. ***hun***, 'grass' (thatch roof); d. ***suaf bidjaekase***, 'horse spar'; e. ***suaf benaf***, '***benaf*** spar'; f. ***suaf susuf***, '***susuf*** spar'; g. ***aka'nunu***, 'pillow'; h. ***tak pani***, cross-spar; i. ***tnat oe***, 'hold water' cross spars; j. ***ni ainaf***, 'mother post'; k. ***ni ainaf*** (nakan), 'mother post' ('head'); l. ***atbat***, beam; m. ***kranit***, cross-beam; n. ***nesa***, rafter; ***otoi***, 'entrance' (attic); p. ***harak ko'u***, 'great platform'; q. ***harak tupa***, 'sleeping platform'; r. ***tunaf***, 'hearth'; s. ***ni manu***, 'chicken post'; t. ***haef*** 'foot'; u. ***piku***, 'wall'; v. ***eno***, 'door'; w. ***toi***, 'entrance' (outer section); x. ***harak manba'at***, 'egreement platform' (serving platform); y. ***harak***, 'platform'; z. ***mone***, 'outside; male' (yeard).

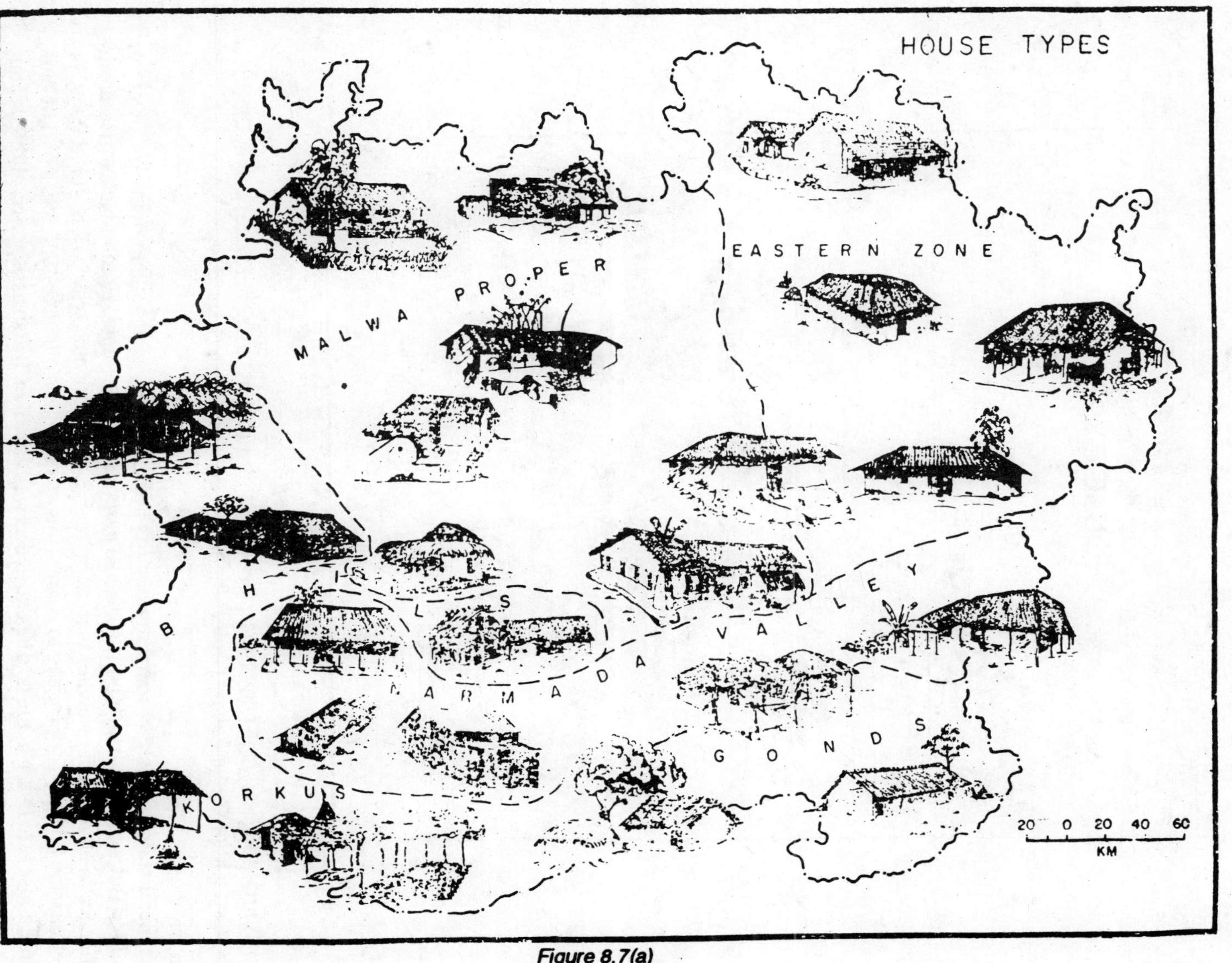
HOUSE TYPES
EASTERN ZONE
MALWA PROPER
NARMADA VALLEY
BHILS
GONDS
KORKUS
20 0 20 40 60
KM

Figure 8.7(a)

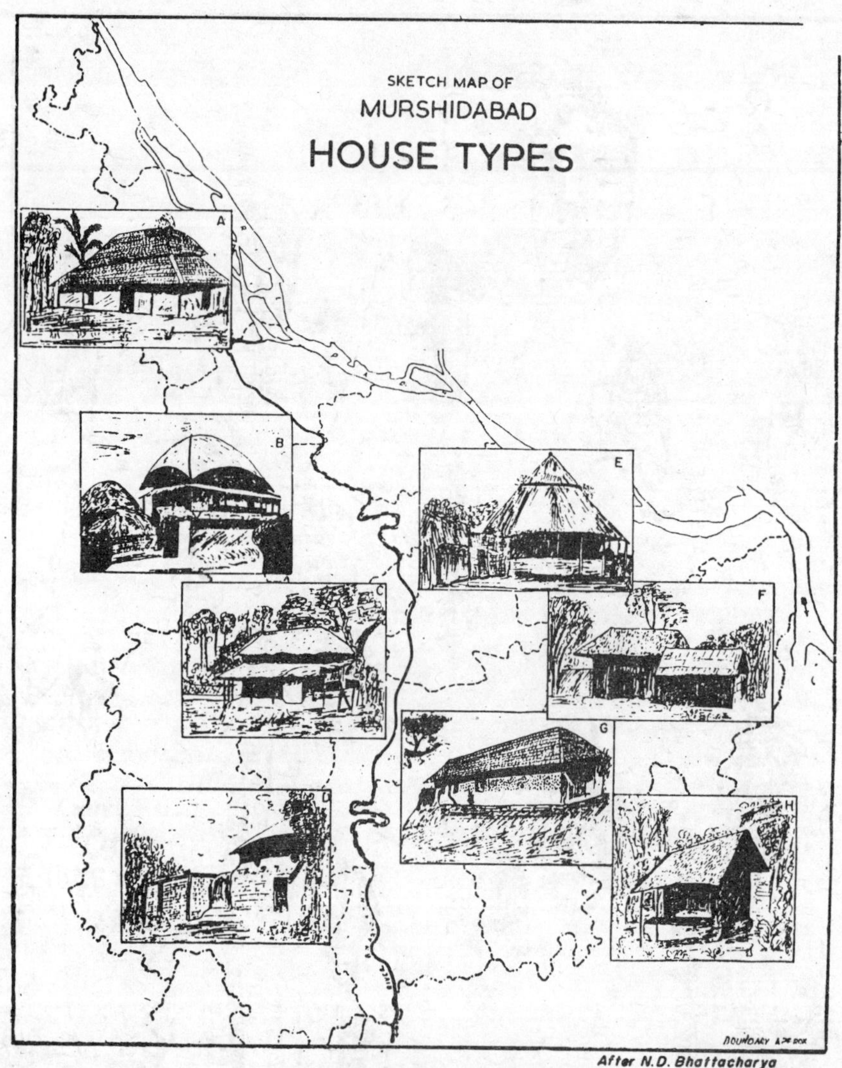

Figure 8.8

(30) Yurt, Mongolia, (31) Clay house, Syria, (32) Conical huts, Africa, (Togo) and in Ethiopia, (33) Cart tent of Gadia *Luhars* (Ironsmiths), (34) Boat house on (Figs. 8.7a-8.20).

House Versus Home

A general statement is that rented building is house for the occupant and home for owner or builder. But, such building, if built, for rental purposes are not homes. Home attaches greater significance to attachment of owner to it, as builder as well as owner, who builds, for not only his lifelong stay but also for progeny to come. Home symbolizes our ancestors. It is a part of ours, while house is to live, a home is to be married as well as to live. It also has specific allotted rooms or space for specific purposes, i.e., for worship, marriage, rituals, kitchen etc. The whole settlement becomes a setting for the life of home. But in other case, the house is regarded as the total

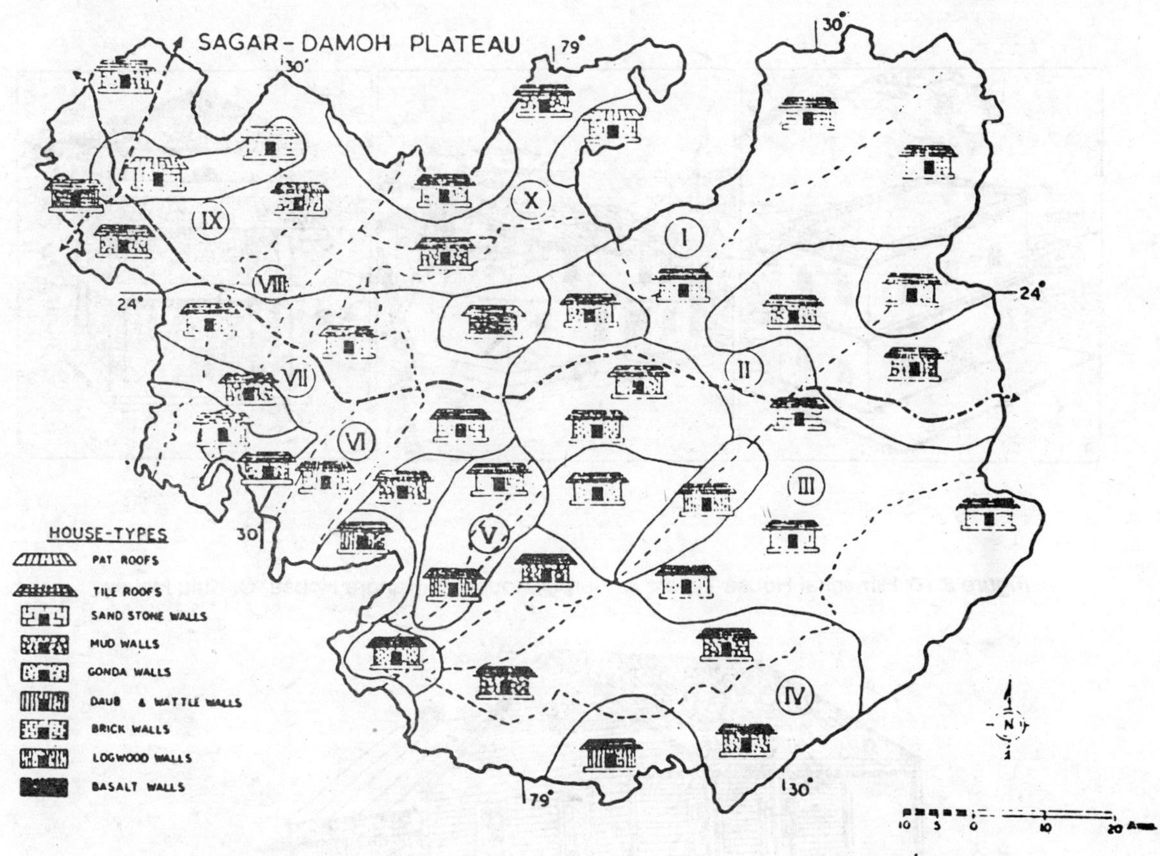

[- - - - Physiographic Boundaries]
[—Limits of House types.]

Figure 8.9. (I) The Rajpura Plateau, (II) The Haveli, (III) The Bearma Basin, (IV) The Selwara-Jamunia-Chikhali Highlands, (V) The Abchand-Naharmau Highlands, (VI) The Sagar-Jaisinagar Highlands, (VII) The Dhasan Basin, (VIII) The Rahatgarh-Malthon Highlands, (IX) The Badar-Bina Doab, and (X) The Dhamoni-Shahgarh Highlands.

setting for life, and the settlement only as "Connective tissue,[45] almost 'waste' space, to be traversed and secondary in nature. Home is a dwelling place, a fixed residence of family or household, a native land, where one feels at home, knowing and being familiar with every thing there; hence, home coming, home sickness, home made, home rule, home work, home like-popular terms and also those having no home or homeless. Likewise, one has home-village, a settlement, where he and his kins, were and are born, and will born.

It is only homes in country side, which show, impact of family structure, kinship and caste and find full expression of *genre de vie*. It is here that we can talk about basic needs, family life, position of women, privacy and social intercourse—all well adapted to owner's attitudes. Here only, one can expect the economic, protective, religious, adductive, social, affectional and status giving services available to a group life or family life. The shared occupancy of a home by a num-

Figure 8.10: Himachal House Types: A. Nurpur House, B. Kangra House, C. Kulu House.

Figure 8.11: Built-in porch type.

Figure 8.12: Built-in porch type.

Figure 8.13: Attached porch type.

Figure 8.14: Open passage type; double log pen.

Figure 8.15: Single log pen.

Figure 8.16: Midwestern or "i" type..

Figure 8.17: Shotgun type.

Figure 8.18: Bungalow type.

Figure 8.19: Trapper type.

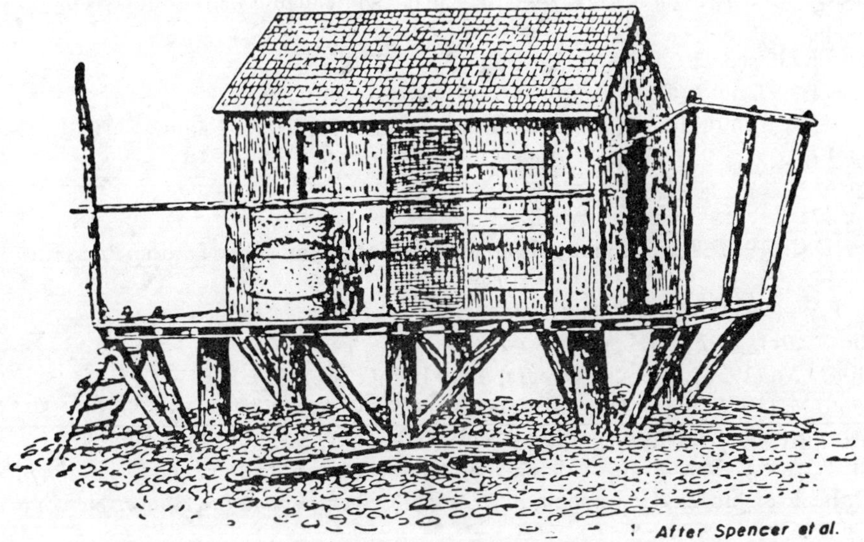

Figure 8.20: Oysterman type.

ber of family members allows each member the use of several rooms. It is commonly accepted, that the home life of an individual, affords him quite different satisfactions, from those gained or sought in his activities, elsewhere. To sum up 'The marketable man is never the complete man in his uniqueness, and conversely, the whole man is never marketable.[46]

References

1. Spencer, J.E. & Thomas W.L. ref. no. 1, Ch. 1, p. 133.
2. Ibid, p. 93.
3. Stone, K.H. (1965), The Development of a Focus for the Geography of Settlement, Economic Geography, Vol. 41, p. 347.
4. Webster's New International Dictionary II edition, G. Belland Sons Ltd., London, 1959, p. 1122.
5. Census of India, 1911 p. 7 (Vol. 17), Census of India Agency Report and Tables.
6. Census of India, 1961, Part II-A, General Population Tables Vol. VIII, M.P. 4.
7. Rig. I 154-5; Atharva, III, 12; Matsya, 252, 11; Agni 247.1.
8. Bhag. Vol. 1,2.
9. Rig I, 74, 2; Atharva 1, 27.4 etc.
10. Atharva, IV, 36.3.
11. Pandey, R.B. (1951), Vikramaditya of Ujjain, Shatdal Prakashan, Banaras, p. 220 quoting the Amarkosha, p. 11, 22.
12. Manasara, III 7; cf. Dutta, B.B. (1925), Town Planning in Ancient India, Calcutta, pp. 1-2.
13. Brunhes Jean, ref. no. 3, Ch. 2, p. 39.
14. Singh, R.L. (1957), Typical Rural Dwellings in the Umland of Banaras, India, N.G.J.I. Vol. III, Pt. II June, p. 52.
15. Blache, op.cit. see Ch. 2, ref. no. 2 p. 304.
16. Stône, K.H. ref. no. 3, Ch. 8, p. 355.
17. Rapoport, A. (1969), House Form and Culture, Prentice Hall, INC, Englewood Cliffs, N.J., pp. 3-7.
18. Ibid, p. 17.
19. Ibid, p. 45.
20. Ibid, p. 47.
21. Money, D.C. (1967), Introduction to Human Geography, University Tutorial Press Ltd., 9-10, London, p. 34.
22. Bryan, P.W. (1933), Man's Adaptation of Nature, London, p. 133.
23. Brunhes, J., ref. no. 3, Ch. 2, p. 33.
24. Houston, J.M. (1953), A Social Geography of Europe, p. 109.
25. Jayaswal, V. (1976), Examining Settlements in Stone Age India, pp. 89-96 in R.L. Singh et al. (eds), Geographic Dimensions of Rural Settlements, N.G.S.I., Res. Pub. No. 16.
26. Raglan, L. (1963), The Origin of Vernacular Architecture, in 'Culture and Environment' edited by Foster, I. LL & Alcock, L., London, p. 273; Idem, 'Temple and the House' New York, Norton, 1964, p. 196.
27. Spencer, J.E. & Thomas, W.L. ref. no. 1 Ch. 8, p. 133.
28. Blache Vidal De La, ref. no. 2, Ch. 2, p. 238.
29. Brunhes, J. ref. no. 3, Ch. 2, p. 48.
30. Havel, E.B. (1915), Ancient and Medieval Architecture of India, London, p. 12.
31. See for detailed study of courtyard R.L. Singh (1957), ref. no. 14.

32. Pueblo Indian's Solar Efficient Houses, Indian Express, 7.4.87 (UNI), New York.
33. Brown, P. (1965), Indian Architecture, Buddhist and Hindu Periods', p. 3.
34. Havel, E.B. (1915) op.cit ref. no. 30.
35. Spencer J.E. & Thomas, W.L. ref. no. 1, p. 133.
36. Rectangular Pattern is a symbol of optimum arrangement of privacy space in terms of audible straight line distance for identification of specific sound as well as object beyond a certain boundary/hedge etc. It is the simplest geometrical form of a layman.
37. Jhoola (Wooden rectangular plank, tied with strings on four corners, hanging by wooden beams, put transversely on walls or poles) is a common feature of Malwa, Gujarat and Rajasthan and some parts south of the Narmada in India.
38. Brunhes, J. ref. no. 3, Ch. 2, p. 86.
39. Ibid, Plates VIII to XI.
40. About 2000 houses of 16 sample villages and 30 random villages have been surveyed from various representative zones of the region, and the material after sifting was plotted and superimposed, which gives the regional pattern.
41. Census of India, 1961, Vol. VIII, part IV-B, pp. 6-27.
42. Ibid, pp. 44-73.
43. 'The Future Lies in Mud' by Anil Agarwal, Indian Express 13.3.83.
44. Chandhoke, S.K. (1991) (ed), Human Habitation-culture Environment Interface, SPA & Har Ananad Publications etc., see C.E. Cunningham on "Order in the Architecture pp. 327-356.
45. Rapoport, A. ref. no. 17, Ch. 8, p. 70.
46. Hocking, W.E. (1929), Human Nature and Its Remaking, Yale University Press, New Haven, pp. 304-306.

9

Rural Service Centres and Markets

Growth Centre Concept

The concept, though borrowed from the concept of Central Place Theory, got significance due to emphasis on micro-level planning in India. The three elements of the theory, i.e., (i) urban centres, (ii) the hexagonal arrangement of their market areas, and (iii) transport network, are sought in non-urban hierarchy, in the form of, firstly, the service centres secondly, their zones of influence, and thirdly, the movement patterns at lower level. It is presumed, that the essential features of the main constructs of the theory, can be easily applied at lower levels, with certain modifications. The theoretical framework, derived from Central Place Theory, helps in identifying growth centres of various orders. The simple definition of the term, growth centre, is that "It is an urban core with a rural hinterland, capable of growth." It is a core, because, it serves its surrounding territory with services available in it, as well as, employs many from its service zone. It is obvious, that the role and nature of growth centre, depends upon the type of development region, to which it may belong. Friedmann gives four types of such regions named as frontier, downward transitional, upward transitional and the core regions. According to empirical studies, growth centres, in the first two types of regions, cater to the provisions of services such as education, health, communications, transport, finance, trade, extension and retail services. Some centres may also provide administrative, judiciary and law and order services. In the third type, the growth centre, would be the centre having a potentiality to absorb the new investment leading to renewal. In the last type, it serves as a counter magnate and is capable of taking some of the function away from its central core, thus, easing the tension, felt at central core, i.e., decentralization of services.

Thus, a growth centre, is a logical extension of a service centre on the continuum of settlements, based on functional characteristics. At one end of it, one comes across a set of dependent settlements and at the other, there is a regional centre, which may be termed as growth centre. In between, one finds, an array of central villages and service centres.[1]

The genesis of growth centre concept, is traced into growth pole theory of Perroux[2] and Boudeville, but in true sense, its merits were argued by, *inter alia*, Green[3] and Taylor, who think that, these centres are supposed to provide, stimulation of economic growth and generation of employment, the diffusion of innovation, especially induced innovation, the provision of adequate services for the hinterland, especially, those related to basic needs, such as, education, health, water, power and housing etc., coordination of government and local development planning and effective interaction of local ideas and initiatives.[4] Misra, rightly states that, growth centres are located at favourable points, where from, inducement for growth can be provided through selective, diversified and decentralized provisions of infrastructure and overheads. These points, being closer to the people, prove to be more suitable, for injecting the elements of growth and welfare, at lowest level. Experience shows that, trickling down of benefits, from such centres to surrounding settlements, is natural process. Keeping in view, the maximum diffusion of innovations and benefits, the rationalization of spatial organisation of settlements, at this rural level becomes necessary, e.g., number, size and spacing of these centres in a region. For a well linked hierarchically arranged growth centre, i.e., optimum location, one looks towards the Central Place Theory.

The Central Place Theory

Walter Christaller (1893-1969), a German scholar, submitted his dissertation on the structure of settlements in the Southern Germany in 1932 to the University of Erlangen. He was influenced by the locational theorists like J.G. Kohl, Johann von Thunen, Alfred Weber (Christaller's former teacher) and also the settlement geographer Robert Gradmann. His works got greater recognition in the 1940s and 1950s, when scholars in the United States, realized their value.[5] The gist of Christaller's theory, stripped of details and elaborations (given in the sequel), is as follows:

(1) A central place is located at the centre of the minimum aggregate travel distance, provides functions and services to its complementary zone, as well as minimum cost, to the customers, and the maximum profit to the sellers.
(2) Hierarchy of central places exists, where higher order places provide functions, which the lower order places do not have. But, the reverse may not be true. The higher order places provide functions, in addition to, what the lower order places have.
(3) Unique functions to the higher order places have wider area of influence, than those which are common.
(4) Higher order places command a larger area than the lower order places, i.e., former have higher degree of centrality.
(5) The higher order places are widely spaced and fewer in number.
(6) The higher order centres, not only possess, unique function but also, a larger number of establishments, providing lower order ubiquitous functions than the lower order places. This is, because the customers minimise the travel distance cost by shopping, both, higher order and lower order goods in the same place.
(7) Hierarchy of central places develop with each order of centre nesting the lower order centre. The nesting of lower order centres, within a hexagonal complementary zone, is determined by three principles: (i) marketing, (ii) traffic, and (iii) administrative.

The basic concepts of the theory, can be best explained, through the study of movements, networks, nodes, hierarchy and surfaces (zones of influence) as successive stages. The core of the Central Place Theory is, thus, formed by six basic concepts[6] as enumerated and explained below.

(1) *Centralization as an ordering Principle*: Christaller propounded, that services tend to concentrate around certain points, which are more important, rather than around, other points.
(2) *The Central Place*: It is the most important aspect of the theory. It provides goods and services to an area larger than itself. The Central Place is determined by its centrality in the region. There are area bound and point bound places or settlements around it. The number of central functions performed, the size of the population served by these centres, determine the rank, of course, according to a notional scale of ordering, hence, higher and lower order

places.

(3) *The Importance and Centrality*: The importance of a settlement, is not the sum total of its inhabitants, but rather of their combined economic efforts. It may be that correlations exist between size of population and degree of centrality.

(4) *The Central Functions*: These functions are those, which by their nature are available in a few places but are availed of by a number of places. Thus, central functions are non-ubiquitous. The degree of a function is supposed to vary, inversely, with the frequency of its occurrence. The higher order central functions, belong to higher order Central Place, and the lower order functions, belong to a lower order central place or an auxiliary central place. These functions are trade, banking, administration, education, commerce and transportation.

(5) *Complementary region*: While a central place is one, where an importance-surplus exists, a complementary region is one, where an importance-deficit exists. The former balances the latter through functions and services.

(6) *Economic Distance and the Range of A Good*: The spatial supply of, and demand for, goods and services are determined by factors like freight, storage cost, loss of weight and the time; in the case of passenger movement, by travel cost, travel time and discomfort perceived by the consumer. Proceeding further from the Central Place, the cost of travelling to the central place, besides the cost of goods and services on arrival, is so great that consumer demand is reduced to zero. This *distance* is called the range of a good or upper limit. Likewise, any good or service, has a threshold of demand or size of market area, which is the minimum number of consumers required to support a business (Fig. 9.1). A primary school or a local grocery has a low threshold, whereas a Higher Secondary School or a departmental store has a high threshold or lower limit. It shows, that each good or function, has its own characteristic range, which may vary from one central place to another. The upper limit is a *spatial index*, determined by the farthest distance from the central place; the lower limit is a *quantity index*, determined by the minimum number of people required to support that function in the central place.

Christaller's Centrality of an urban centre, however, was defined as *the ratio* between all the services provided there, (for both, its own residents and for visitors from its complementary region) and the services needed just for its own residents. Centres with high centrality supply many services per resident, and those, with low centrality, few services per resident. Christaller

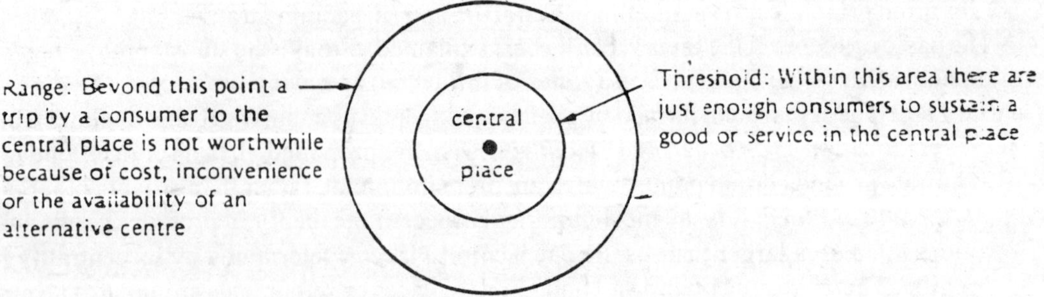

Figure 9.1: The threshold and range of a good or service

discovered in his study that the number of telephones provided a useful indicatoı for the range of central goods available in a town. With the telephone data he defined the centrality of a town, as equal to the number of telephones in the town, minus the town's population multiplied by the average number of telephones per population in the towns' complementary region, e.g., a town of 25,000 with 5000 telephones in a region with 1 telephone for every 50 people would have an index of 5000- 25000 (1/50) or 4500. This index, basically, measures the difference between the expected level of services (required in a town to serve its residents) and the level of services actually measured within the centre. But, later on, the two concepts of *range of a central good* and *market size threshold*, discussed earlier, proved to be the basis of his theory.

Complementary Regions and Hierarchy

On the basis of two concepts of range and threshold, it is now possible to see, how an hierarchy of central places, supplying goods of different orders, develops (Fig. 9.2). In the stages of colonization of the area, the arrangement of central places follows, the best suited geometrical form, triangular lattices tessellation, thus, giving final hexagonal pattern. Five assumptions precede such a pattern:

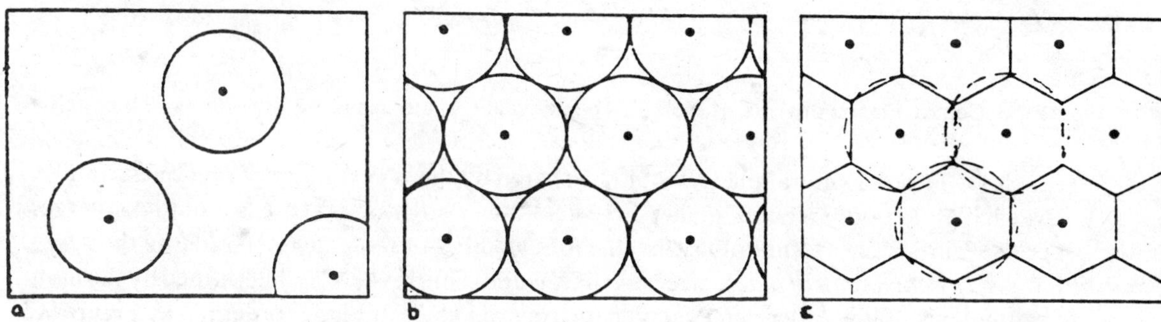

Figure 9.2: Stages in the development of hexagonal market areas (a) Isolated central places in an area of low population density (b) Population growth leads to increase in number of central places—market areas touch (c) Further population growth means that, to pack central places even more densely, market areas have to overlap and hesagons are produced.

(1) The region should form an isotropic plain with a homogeneous distribution of purchasing power,
(2) Central goods must be purchased from the nearest central place,
(3) The Central place's complementary zone must coincide the plain boundary,
(4) Consumer movement must be minimized,
(5) No excess profits may be earned by any central place.

If this pattern is observed at lower level, for successively lower order goods and central places, down to the lowest order ones, one gets a complete hierarchy of centres and market areas. The main features of such an hierarchy, obviously, emerge as follows:

(1) Each lower order central place, would be located, midway between three higher order central places,
(2) Each higher order central place would have, six next lower order ones around it-one on each of the six points of its hexagonal market area,

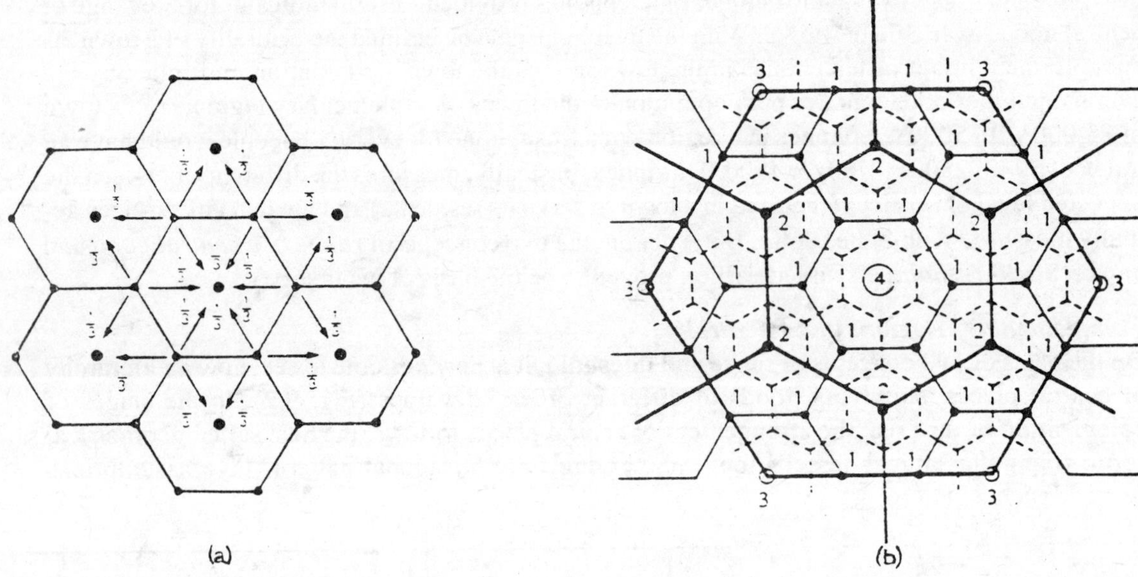

Figure 9.3: Central Place networks (K = 3) (a) The derivation of the 3 in K = 3 (b) The K = 3 hierarchy

(3) Each lower order central place, would be shared by three next higher order ones, and

(4) At each higher order central place, three next lower order market areas would converge.

It is also Christaller's terminology that *the total number of settlements (including the centre itself), served by each central place, is termed its K value*. This K value, is determined by the number of settlements of low order places served by a central place or higher order place. Figure 9.3

Figure 9.4: More central Place networks
(a) The derivation of the 4 in K = 4 (b) The derivation of the 7 in K = 7

shows that a first order centre provides goods and services for one third of the population of six settlements as well as its own population, it, thus, serves the population equivalent of three settlements, i.e., K=3. This, provides efficient marketing, and in its most simple form, allows consumers in the lower order centres, to choose between three competing central places, hence, *market optimizing case* or *marketing principle* of Christaller. The K=4 network is the most economical arrangement for traffic flow, i.e., *traffic optimizing* situation (Fig. 9.4). The lower order centres lie along straight lines between higher order centres. A central place serves one half of the population of six lower order centres and its own population, i.e., in total it serves (6 × 1/2) + 1 = 4 places, hence, K=4 hierarchy. In an administration-optimizing situation, there is clear-cut separation of the higher order centre and its neighbouring lower order centres. The central place serves, the entire population of six lower order places, plus its own population, hence, K = 7 hierarchy[6a] Fig. 9.5. These were called by Christaller as fixed-K hierarchies, because, the same fixed relationships hold at all levels of the settlement hierarchy (Fig. 9.6).

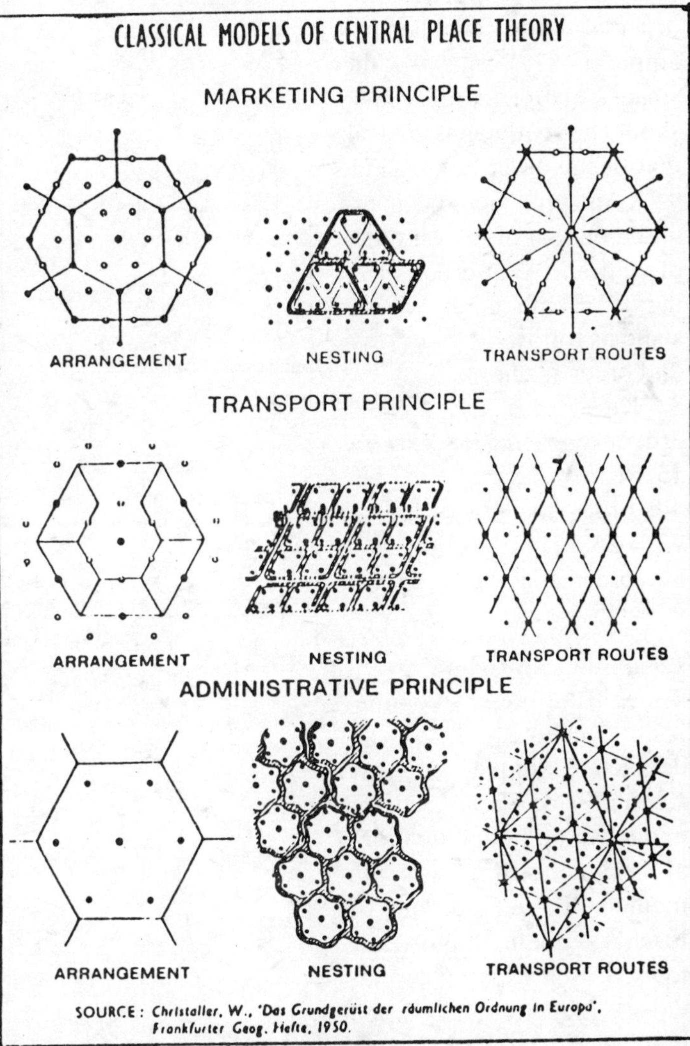

Figure 9.5

For calculating the number of central places expected in each order, following successive subtraction and division method simply works. If K=3 and settlements are 81 in number, the predicted number of central places of each order (to the nearest whole number) would be:

1st order = 81-81/3 = 54
2nd order = 81/3-81/9 = 18
3rd order = 81/9-81/27 = 6
4th order = 81/27-81/81 = 2
5th order = 81/81-81/243 = 1

The average spacing, between centres of each order, will become greater with increasing order of settlement. For example in a K=3 network the spacing of higher order centre should be 1.7 times as great as that of the order below (Fig. 9.7). Any predicted spacing is based on that of lowest order of centre. If first oider spacing is 5 km., others would stand as follows:

2nd order spacing = 5 x $\sqrt{3}$ = 8.7 Km.

3rd order spacing = 8.7 x $\sqrt{3}$ = 15.1 Km.

4th order spacing = 15.1 x $\sqrt{3}$ = 26.2 Km.

5th order spacing = 26.2 x $\sqrt{3}$ = 45.4 Km.

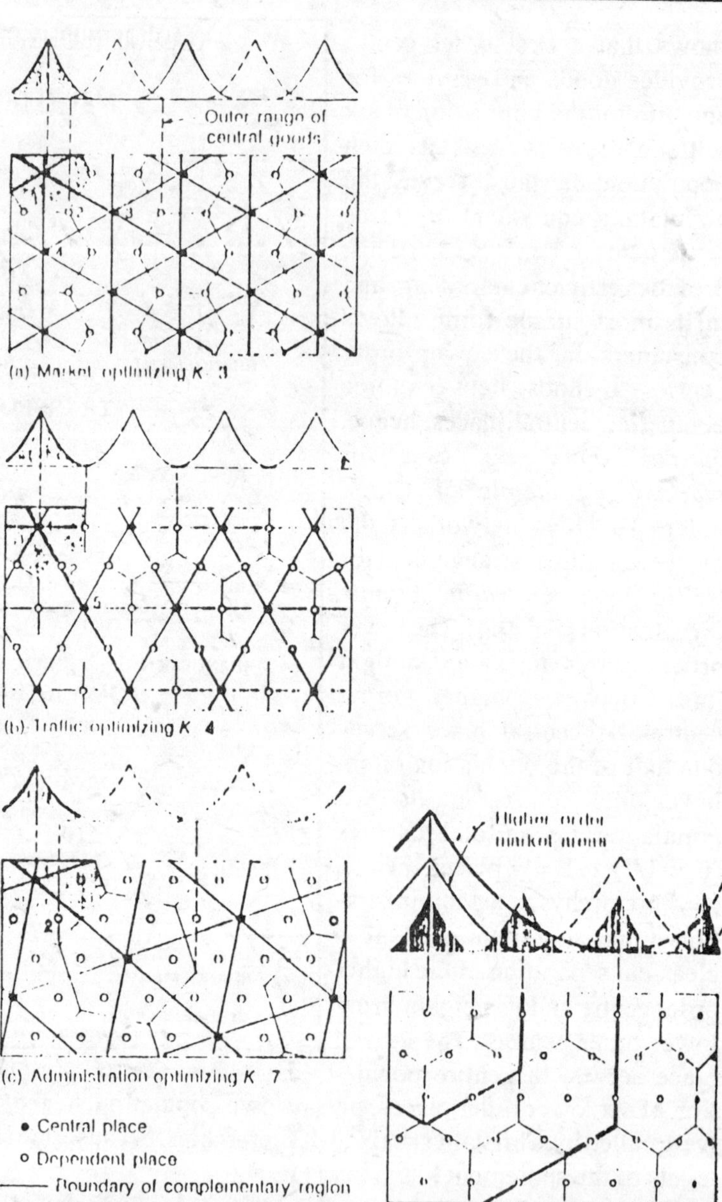

Figure 9.6: Alternative principles of organization in the Christaller model. Settlements can be partitioned in one of three basis ways, (a), (b), or (c), by enlargning and rotating the hexagonal cells. The cells can then be grouped hierarchically to give tiers of higher-order centres; for example, (d) shows higher-order centers in a traffic-optimizing (K = 4) hierarchy. Note the way in which lower-order centers "nest" whthin the market areas of higher-order centers in a manner reminiscent of sets of Russian dolls.

Löschian Landscape

Though the present volume, is not concerned, much, with detailed critique of the Central Place Theory, yet, for understanding the operational characteristics of the method, a brief account of losch's modifications follows. Lösch used all K networks together and varied their size. The K=3 system was used for the commodity with the lowest threshold requirement, then the K=4 for the next largest threshold requirement, then K=7 and so son. One can understand this process by imagining that the fixed K=3 network is drawn on a map. The K=4 network is now drawn on an overlay of transparent tracing paper and pinned to the K=3 map by a single thumb tack through the

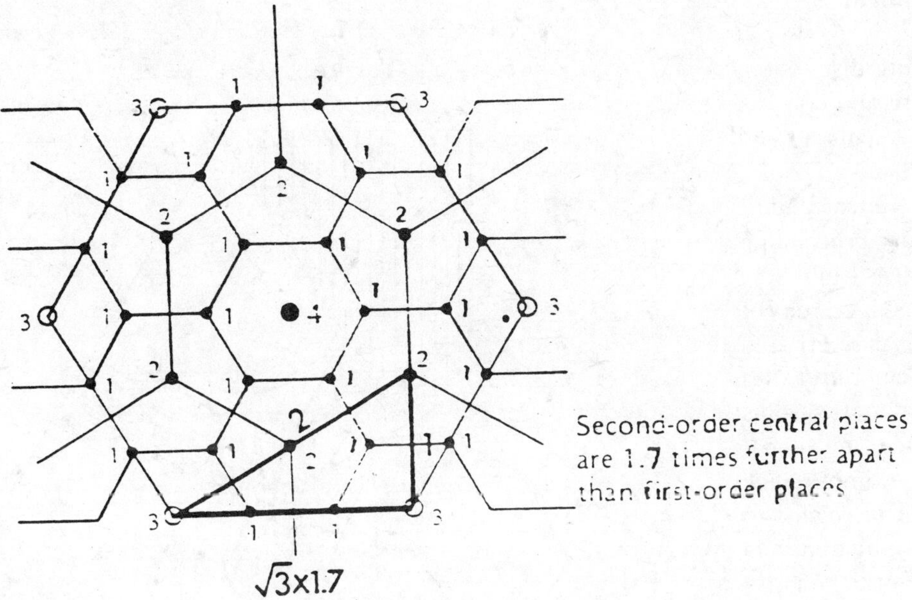

Figure 9.7: Spacing in a K = 3 settlement hierarchy

common central place. By rotating the overlay, many major places, on both the K=3 and the K=4 paper, are made to coincide. For example, if we have a K=3 school system and a K=4 hospital system, we try to rotate the overlay so that high school and the Doctor's hospital, both, coincide in the same locations, rather than being split between two. Lösch went on to add the K=7 and still higher K network to the map, always trying to get as many services as possible to overlap in the same locations.[7]

Rotation, thus, produces 12 sectors of which six offer many services and the remaining six offer few services. Lösch called these *city rich* and *city poor* sectors respectively (Fig. 9.8).

Thus, Christaller's hierarchy, consists of several fixed tiers, in which all places, in a particular tier, have the same size and function, and all higher order places perform all the functions of the smaller central places. *In Contrast*, the Löschian hierarchy is far less rigid. It consists of a nearly continuous sequence of centres rather than distinct tiers. So, settlements of the same size need not have the same function (e.g., a centre serving 7 settlements may be either a K=7 central place or a centre where, both, a K=3 and K=4 central place coincide) and larger places need not perform all the functions of the smaller central places.[8]

The hexagonal territories in a Löschian landscape is clear from the map (Fig. 9.9a, 9.9b).

Lösch's landscape was criticized by Walter Isard for failing to take account of variations in population density. The economic landscape produced, when variations in population density are considered, is clear from map (Fig. 9.10); there is a set of irregular sized polygons, each containing the same number of people, smaller ones being found nearer city centres.[9]

Lösch also marks an attempt to introduce economic equilibrium conditions, but Beckmann finds these inadequate.[10]

Identification of Hierarchy

The foregoing discussion, on the nature and concept of growth centres and Central Place Theory, provides sufficient understanding for proceeding towards measuring the centrality and hierarchy of settlements. As referred to earlier, the centrality of a place is equal to its surplus of importance, i.e., equal to the relative importance of this place in regard to region belonging to it. It is the outcome of the quality and quantity of functions performed by a settlement. These central functions, are available in a few settlements, but, are availed of by a number of settlements. Obviously, the degree of importance of a function, is supposed to vary inversely, with the frequency of its occurrence. The level and types of functions, both, affect the quality of a central function.

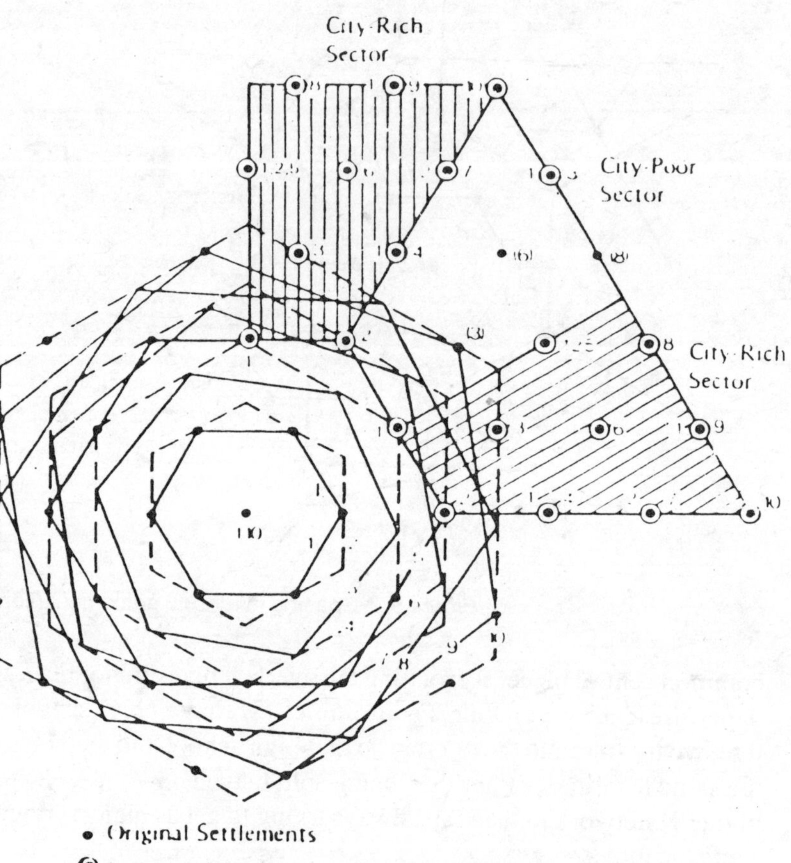

Figue 9.8: The ten smallest possible market areas

Thus, the hierarchy of settlements, is closely associated with the hierarchy of central functions. This functional hierarchy is decisive in measuring centrality, which needs measurement of the level and number of functions available in a centre. Let us discuss its various aspects.

(a) *Methods*: Various *methods* are used to measure the centrality of functions and settlements and their hierarchy. These are: (i) Scalogram analysis, (ii) Population threshold and ranking of central places and functions, and (iii) Ranking of settlements on the basis of hierarchy of function.[11] We may digress a little, to consider other aspects of hierarchy, before coming again to a tested method to be adopted for study.

(i) Rank Size Rule

Functional hierarchy and rank size rule are also closely related to the spatial distributional pattern of settlements in rural landscape. Relation between the rank of a settlement and its size, and

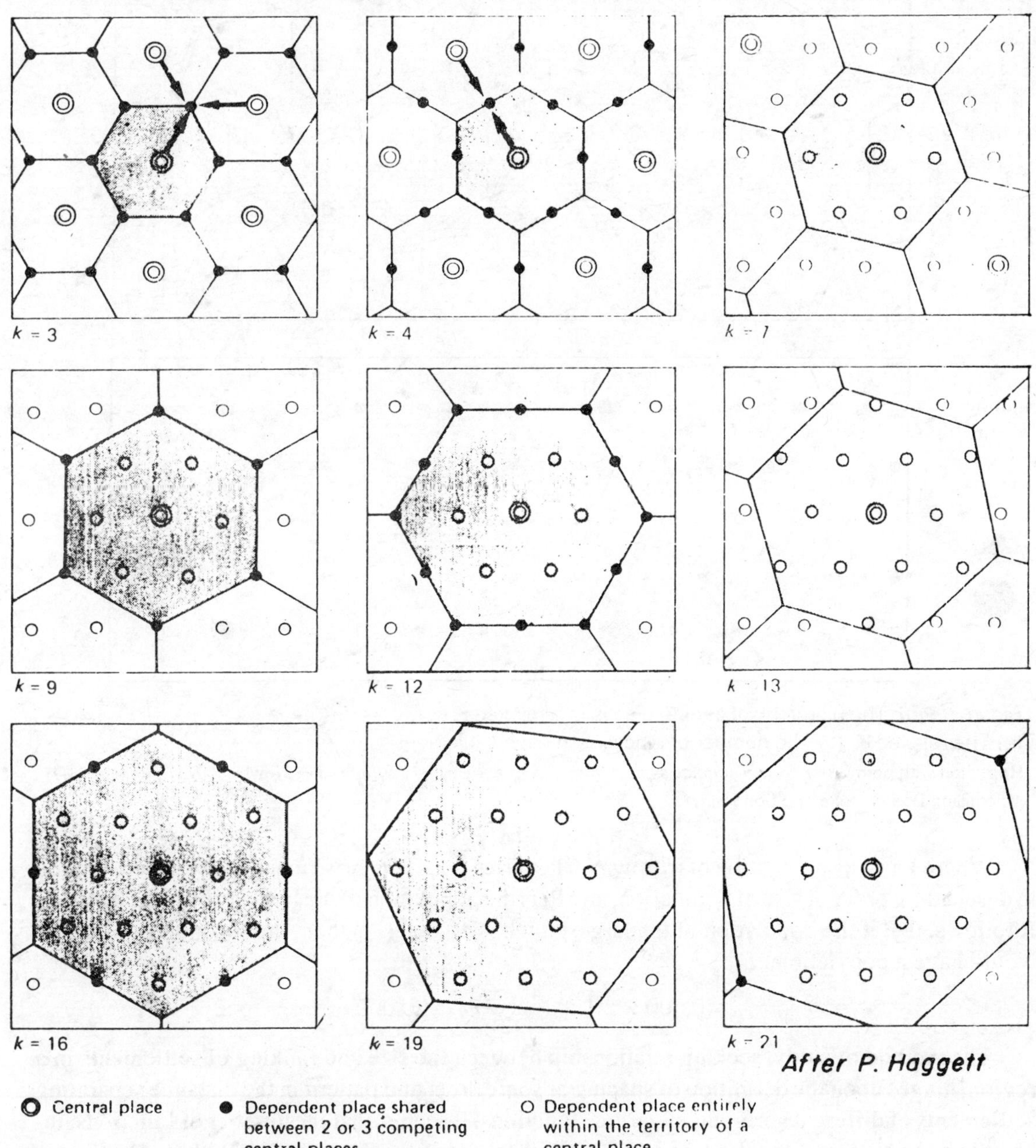

Figure 9.9(a): Nine smallest hexagonal territories in a Löschian landscape.
Source: Lösch, 1954, p. 118.

another of different level, was sought by many scholars at the dawn of 20th century. Zipf and Averbach, in their study discovered such a relationship, which is stated formally as *rank size rule* as shown by the following formula:

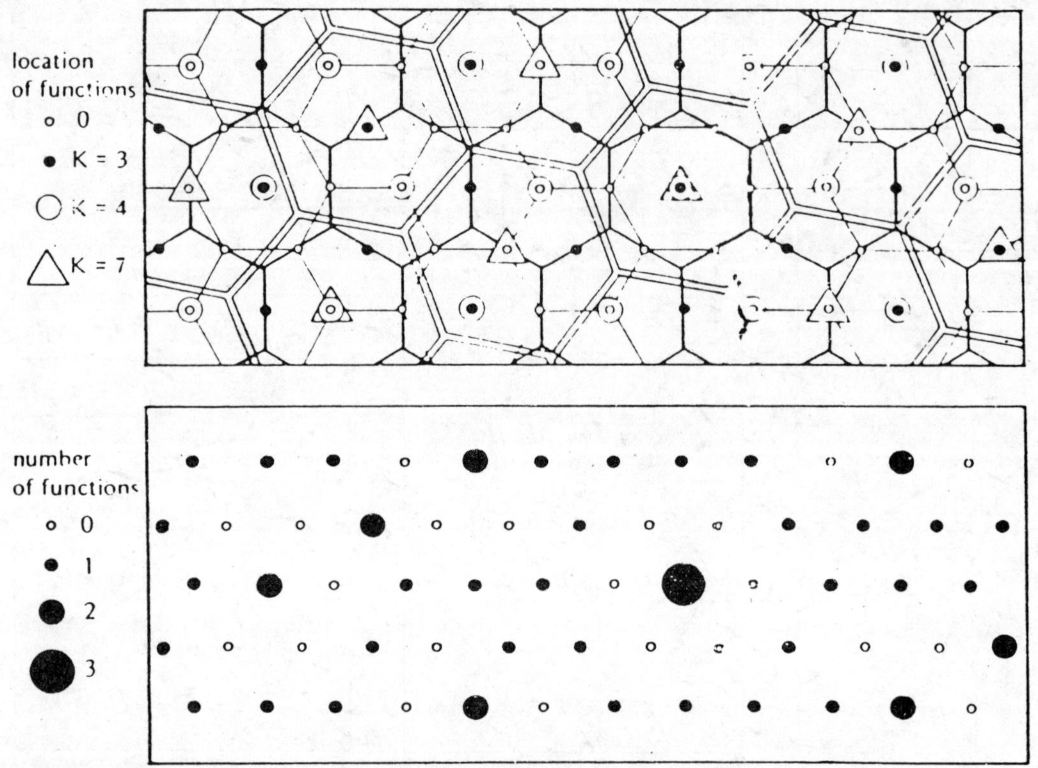

Figure 9.9(b): The hierarchy of central places in a relaxed K network
(a) The relaxed K, (b) The number of functions in each settlement
Reprinted with permission from *Techniques in Human Geography* by P. Toyne and P. Newby (1971) published by Macmillan, Basingstoke and London.

$$Pn = P_1(n)^{-1}$$

Where Pn is the population of nth town in the series 1,2,3,...n, in which the towns are arranged in descending order of size of population, and P_1 is the population of the largest and primate town. It follows, that if the population of the largest town is 40,000 (P_1) then, the second town in rank would have a population of

$$40{,}000 \times 2^{-1} = \frac{40{,}000}{2} = 20{,}000$$

The method of study, seeking relationship between the size and ranking of settlements in a region, hinges upon the definition of spacing or some order and pattern in the distance separating settlements of different sizes and of various functions. It seems, that the number of functions, increases in the settlements of larger size. Some of these functions are not regularly found but, some may be selected as best indicators of settlement hierarchy, i.e., primary school, post office, number of shops etc. Thomas and Gibbs, investigated the problems regarding some towns, and showed a positive association between the logarithms of distance and population size. King (1961), however, in his study of 162 towns and non-central places, discovered that spacing of the latter was less predictable. Similar studies have been made by Stafford (1963)[12], Berry and Garrison (1958) and by Gunwardena (1964) in Sri Lanka. The problem of continuous variation,

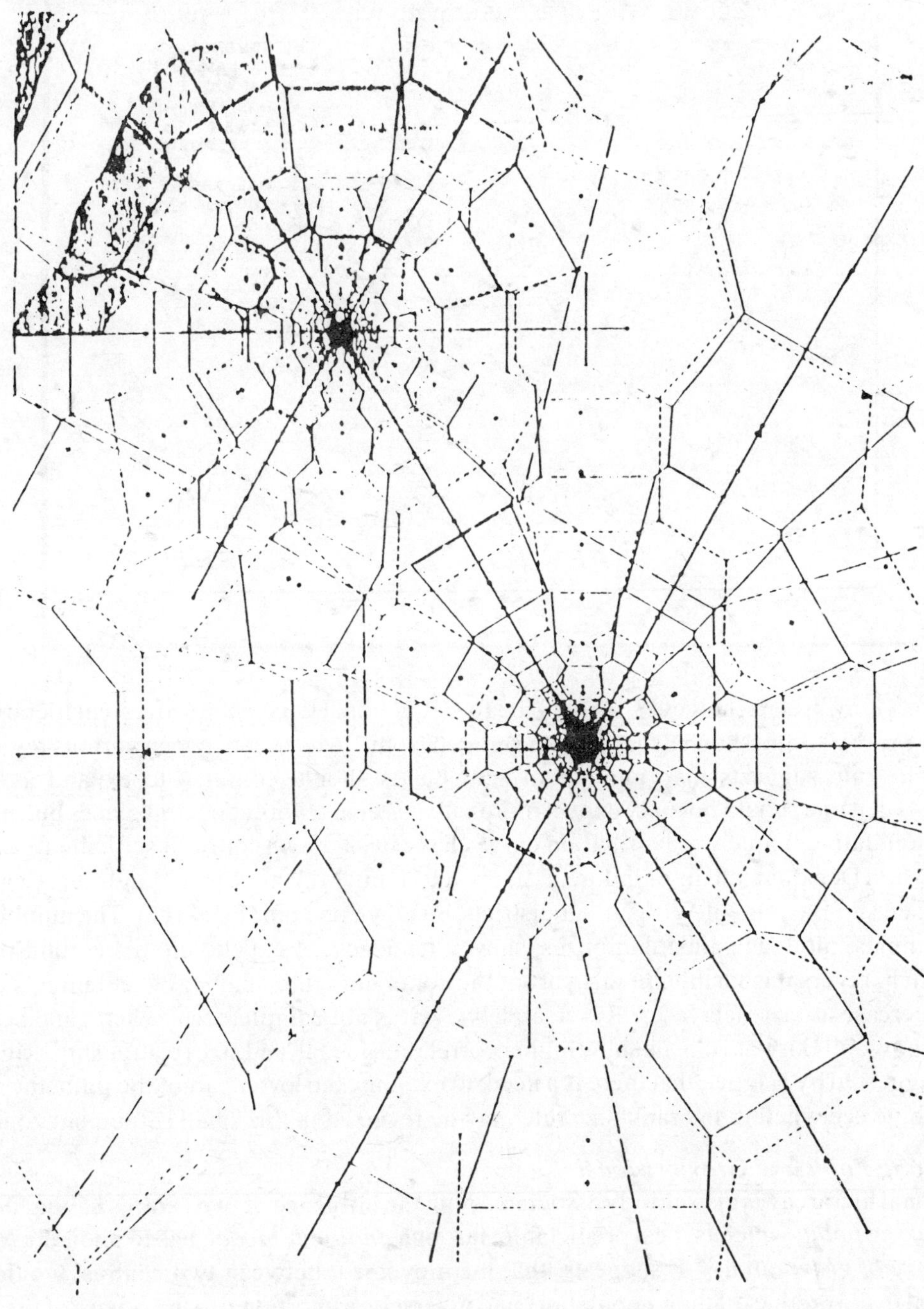

Figure 9.10

found between village and hamlet functions, has been discarded by Hagget and Gunwardena,[13] who suggest that one may view the threshold of any function as the middle point of its *entry zone*. This technique was used by Gunwardena for a number of settlement functions in the southern part

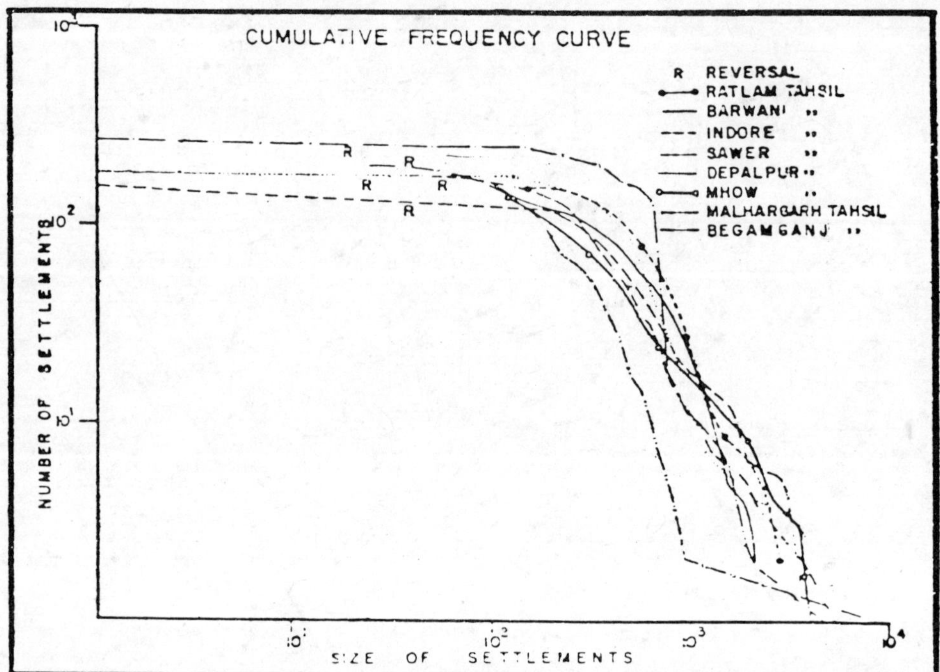

Figure 9.11

of Sri Lanka. Gunwardena, however, recognized four functional tiers in the settlement hierarchy, in southern Sri Lanka and showed that K-value ranged from 1.6 to 11.0 between various regions.

Thus, the rule suggests that, number of settlements should continue to expand as size decreases, so that one should not only expect more villages than towns or central places but, more hamlets. Cumulative frequency distribution curves have been drawn for rural settlements of Indore, Sawer and Depalpur tahsils of Indore; Ratlam of Ratlam; Malhargarh of Mandsaur; Begamganj of Raisen and Barwani of West Nimar districts as shown on map (Fig. 9.11). The number of rural settlements, plotted against their sizes, show a tendency, to expand up to a certain limit, beyond which, reversal is visible. In this part of the continuum, the number of settlements continues to decrease as size decreases. Reversal, however, is not complete, anywhere, and settlements of Mhow and Barwani tahsils show higher correlation in rank and size relationship. Rightly has been suggested by Hagget, that there is a need, to examine the lower part of the limb, the sub-village limb, to see whether the rank-size rule may be reversed in this small settlement zone.

(ii) Breaking Point and Gravity Model

The functional hierarchy is also closely associated with the influence of two centres having *interaction breaking point*, which is, best predictable, through *analogue model*, based upon the *Newtonian theory of gravitation.*[14] It suggests, that the movement between two centres, would be proportional to the product of their population, and inversely proportional to the square of the distance, separating them, as shown by the given formula:

$$M_{ij} = \frac{P_i P_j}{(d_{ij})^2}$$

Where, M_{ij} is the interaction between two centres, i and j, of population P_i and P_j respectively, and d_{ij} is the distance between them. Reilly developed this formulation as the *Law of Retail Gravitation* to find the interaction breaking point. He assumed, that the number of people, a town attracts to its shops, depends, inversely, on the distance between a person and the town, and directly on the town's population. If a person gets choice to purchase from the two towns, he will go to the town with the largest size/distance quotient, since, this town exerts the stronger 'pull' on the person.

P. converse, in 1949, modified Reilly's law, to predict the breaking point, which demarcates the theoretical boundary between the two market areas. This is calculated from the formula:

$$D_j = \frac{D_{ij}}{1 + \sqrt{P_i/P_j}}$$

Where D_j= breaking point between town i in kilometers from j; D_{ij} = distance between town i and j; P_i=Population of town i (large) and P_j=Population of town j (small).

We can also demarcate the sphere of influence as shown on map (Fig. 9-12). This also helps in predicting the movement of people or goods between a set of regions. The shopper patronizes the nearest centre.

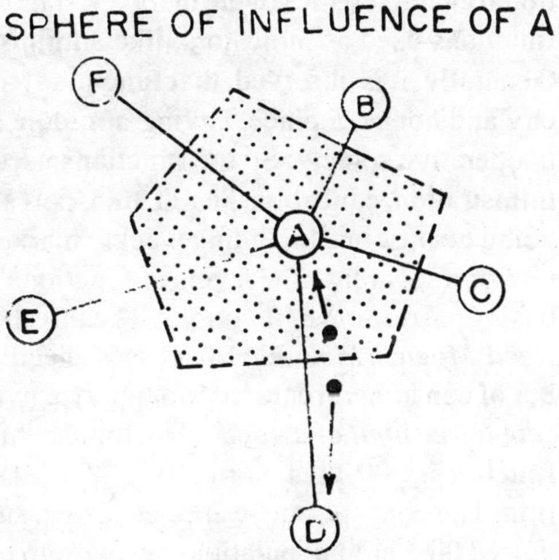

SPHERE OF INFLUENCE OF A

Figure 9.12

D.L. Huff, in 1962, presented a model which predicts the productivity of consumer trips from several towns to several shopping places. In statistical form the formula stands:

$$P_{ij} = \frac{\dfrac{S_j}{T_{ij}}}{\displaystyle\sum_{j=1}^{n} \frac{S_j}{T_{ij}\lambda}}$$

Where P_{ij} = probability of a consumer at point of origin it travelling to centre j

s_j = Size of shopping centre

T_{ij} = journey time from i to j

λ = (Lambda) is an exponent or constant. It is the power to which 'distance' is raised and varies inversely with the order of a good. Consumers are prepared to travel long distances in order to purchase furniture; therefore lambda would be low.

$\sum_{j=1}^{n}$ = Statistical notational short hand instruction to add all values for the j centres, starting with j=1 and ending with j=n, where n is the total number of j centres.

It is noteworthy, that while converse's formula establishes only the 0.5 probability line (breaking point) between two centres, Huff's model shows the decline of pulling force of the various centres with distance.

If we consider the applicability of these methods, it is clear that they are best suited for delineating complementary zones in the urban hierarchy. For lower order settlements and planning for growth centres in rural country side the third method is most suitable and tested in several areas.

(b) *Ranking of Settlements on the Basis of Hierarchy of Functions* This is based on the operational characteristics of the theory, so far discussed. Hierarchy may be determined by considering functions used as indicators, like administrative status, health, transport and communications. Generally, it is observed, that functions tend to cluster around certain levels of functional hierarchy and hence, a place, having a middle school should have a sup-post office, a bus stop or a cooperative society. So the functions used as indicators, in the present empirical study, are administration, education, health, transport and communication, trade and finance, the total number being twenty-one including weekly market, which plays an enormous role in the retail trade pattern of rural areas. The levels of functional hierarchy have been determined and identified on the basis of *threshold of functions*. The thresholds of functions have been determined on the basis of *Reed, Muench Method,*[15] discussed ahead. Population threshold is defined as, the minimum number of consumers required to support a given service and is identical with the classical concept of '*the lower limit of a good*'. The logic behind the concept is that, if the population threshold of a function is 300, then, normally, all the settlements having that population should have that function. The concept can be applied also in such cases, where no single settlement may have the required threshold population, but a group of settlements considered together may have it. So, the practical implications vary according to local conditions.

Population Threshold

For the estimation of population threshold three simple popular methods are in vogue: (i) Entry point (ii) Statistical Median and (iii) Reed, Muench Method. While, in the first the population sizes may not represent the *true threshold* of the function, as it is based on single observation; in the case of under developed areas, where stress is on achieving optimum standard of availability, in terms of unit area and unit population (saturation with facilities), this method could be adopted. The second method suffers from over estimation of the value in the case of lower order functions, it is more appropriate in the case of higher order functions. In the third method, population threshold can be calculated in an objective way by applying the formula of *Median Population threshold* T_{50} or the middle point of functions '*entry zone*'.

This method is the best for underdeveloped areas, where the resources are limited, and judicious utilization of the resources is the main consideration.

An alternative method is suggested by S. Balkrishna, according to which, the threshold is that population level for which the percentage of larger settlement having the function and the percentage of smaller settlements having the function differ to the maximum extent. By testing on the data utilized in the case of Sri Lanka (by H.G.) he could find its utility limited.

G.K. Mishra enumerates three difficulties in using Reed, Muench method and suggests use of *heuristic algorithms* for constrained as well as unconstrained location-allocation. The method is worth testing (see B.S. and C.D., V. 9, March 1975, 1).

Functional Gaps

The significance of the concept of hierarchy, based upon threshold is in the identification of functional gaps in a regional settlement system. It becomes the aim of the planner to find out, how many settlements in the region are having a population of 300 or more and also, how many of them do not have the function. The population threshold enables to propose, that all settlements having higher population than the 'threshold', and yet not having the function, should have it. It is generally observed that population requirements of some functions under such services as health, communications and trade have high threshold levels. In such cases, if a group of settlements satisfies both the threshold and range of goods, then the planner may easily recommend the deployment of those functions to that group of settlements and unnecessary duplication in the deployment of services may be avoided. Thus, the functional gaps, may easily be identified in a regional system, and with priorities properly fixed on a scientific basis, socio-economic facilities may be deployed at the best possible locations.

Indicators

While selecting the functions used as indicators it was observed, that, generally, non-policy functions tend to concentrate in settlements, where a set of policy functions are made available. Hence, most of the functions, in the test, are policy functions.[16]

Applying the Reed, Muench Method it became obvious that the functions tend to cluster themselves within definite population size group and tend to form four levels of hierarchy. The lowest group, having a function has the tendency to be found in population size between 300-800; the second group tends to cluster between population size of 800-1250; the third group tends to cluster between 1,250-3,500 and the fourth group, at a population size of more than 3500. After determining the levels of functional hierarchy, it is attempted to quantify them by giving appropriate *weightage* for each level. The *median points* of functions, in terms of population size, are considered as the basis. These entry points are weighted or scores are allotted to each of the central functions. The first level as, a base, is awarded a score of 1, the second a value of 4, the third level a score of 10 and the fourth level a value of 15. All functions belonging to a particular level are considered to have equal importance. For example, a middle school, a dispensary, and a post and telegraph office-all are of equal importance in the regional context. In the vertical organisation of settlements, if a settlement has a primary school, it has scored a value of 1, while on the other hand, if it has a middle school, it has been awarded a score of 4 and if it has a H.S. school, it is allotted a score of 10. The *weightage* awarded to a particular level has been multiplied by the quantity of a particular function at that particular level. Thus, centrality scores have been calculated for all the settlements of Depalpur Tahsil (Indore, Madhya Pradesh). Beside, the settlements, which have developed functions belonging to all the five categories, have been given an additional score of four:settlements; representing four categories, gained three more to their score and so on. This method presents diversity index.[17] Similarly, unweighted scores are also allotted and a control has been maintained. Switching from weighted to unweighted scores does not lead to any dramatic change. There are no shifts in the ranking of the settlements.

Hierarchy Levels

None of the functions used as indicators occur in 56 settlements; 62 settlements have a score of 1; 14 have a score of 2; 22 have 3; 8 have 4; 7 have 7-10; 2 have 10-20; one has 40-60 and two have 60-100. It is clear that settlements fall in to four groups, i.e., first, second, third and fourth order respectively. The first order group has been divided in to A and B categories, though arbitrarily.

The classification shows that the system is hierarchical and there are three places of 4th order, 9 of third, 12 of 2nd, 36 of first (B) and 68 of first order (A) (Fig. 9.13a,c). The distribution is of dispersed type as the distances between the groups are greater. The hiatus, between the three big market centres, with more scores and the rest, is noteworthy. One may easily point out to the large number of 'embryos' (98 settlements having score of 1-3) and venture a hypothesis, that central place system in Depalpur is expanding and locational gaps are to be filled up.

Besides four orders one may discern 9 levels of hierarchy. If one observes the functional distribution in these settlements, it is clear that with a marginal change in the variety of functions performed, there is a very substantial increase in the number of points scored by the successive settlements. This depicts that centrality is being positively affected by the level of functions performed, rather than the variety of functions available. Rangewasa and Betma are examples. Thus, it may easily be hypothesized, that if the number of services performing a particular function is high and if the function is performed at a higher level of functional hierarchy, then the settlement performing the function scores more points.

Centrality and Population Size

Fig. 9.13b presents relationship between centrality scores and population size in the region. The correlation has been worked out for settlements having more than 3 scores with the help of Spearman's correlation coefficient method; it has worked out to be 0.94. There is very high correlation between centrality and population size in the region and there is also break in population size group in centrality scores.

Multiple Criteria Centrality

Scholars like Dickinson, Smailes, Brush and others in India have applied composite index derived on the basis of a few assumptions simply found in developing Third World too. These are institutions, services and commercial population. This Coi (Composite Index) can be computed on the basis of mathematical formula expressed as:

$$S_j = \frac{\frac{T_{pj}}{n}}{\sum_{j=1} T_{pj}} \times 100 \qquad \text{(i)}$$

Where S_j = Score value for Jth function (weightage)

T_{pj} = Threshold population of jth function

n = Number of functions used as indicators.

For explaining the formula better let us assume another function X_{ij}:

$$\text{(a) } X_{ij} = \Delta S_j \qquad \text{(ii)}$$

Now, if the j th function belongs to the i th settlement and

(b) $\Delta X_{ij} = o$, if the function does not belong to the i th settlement.

The functionality index for the i th settlement can be computed as

$$F_i = \sum_{J=1}^{N} X_{ij} = X_{i1} + X_{i2} + X_{i3} + \dots\dots\dots + X_{in} \qquad \text{(iii)}$$

After calculating the functionality index one can easily find out C_i and W_i values by using formula:

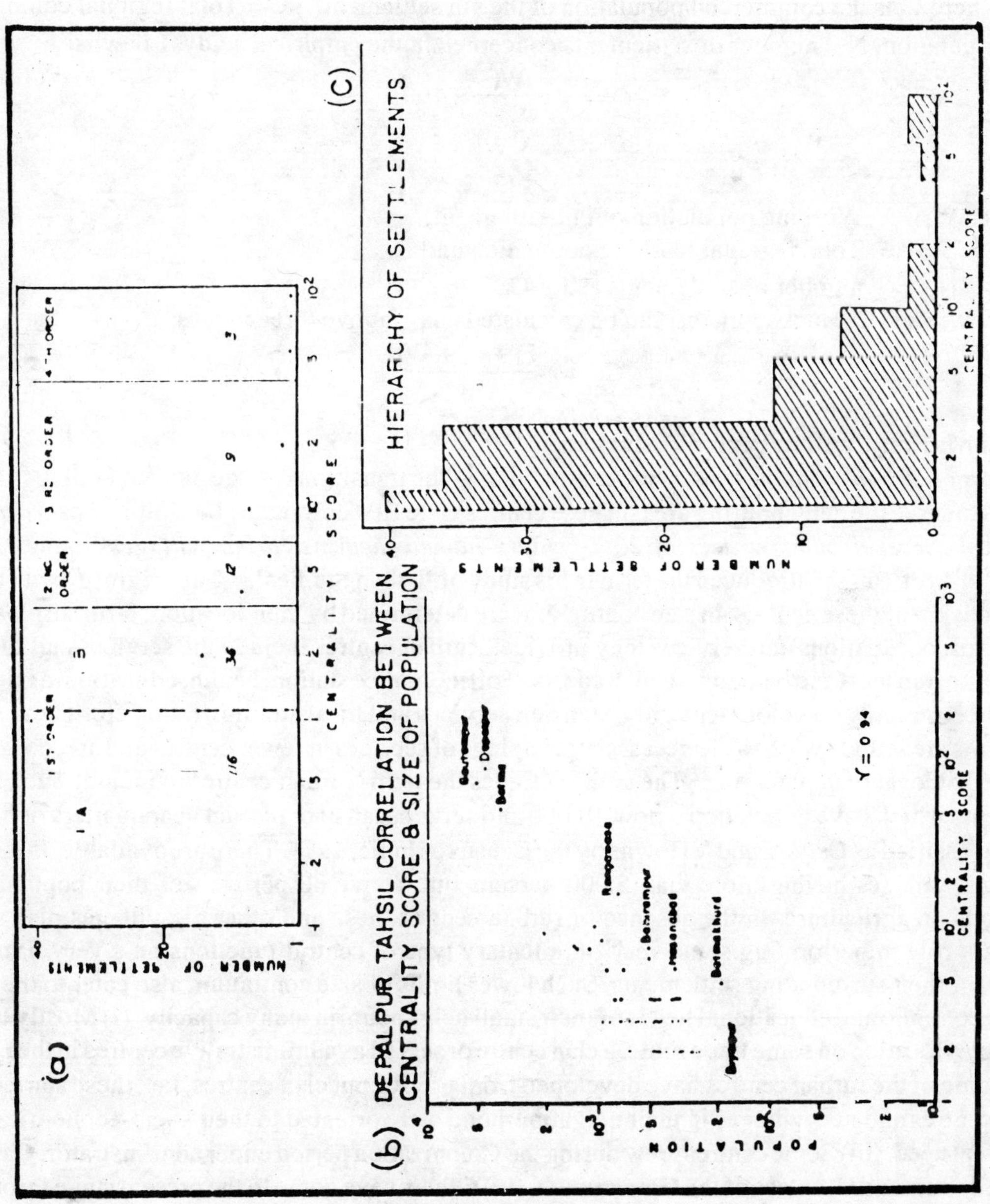
(a)
1ST ORDER
2ND ORDER
3RD ORDER
4TH ORDER
NUMBER OF SETTLEMENTS
CENTRALITY SCORE
(b) DEPALPUR TAHSIL CORRELATION BETWEEN
CENTRALITY SCORE & SIZE OF POPULATION
POPULATION
Y = 0.94
CENTRALITY SCORE
(C) HIERARCHY OF SETTLEMENTS
NUMBER OF SETTLEMENTS
CENTRALITY SCORE

Figure 9.13

$$C_i = \frac{C_i}{\sum_{i=1}^{N} C_i} \times 100 \qquad \text{(iv)}$$

Where C_i is the commercial population of the i th settlement, $\sum C_i$= Total regional commercial population, N = number of settlements concerned in the empirical study. Likewise,

$$W_i = \frac{W_i}{\sum_{i=1}^{N} W_i} \times 100$$

Where W_i = Working population of i th settlement,
$\sum W_i$= Total regional working population and
N = number of settlements as for C_i.

Now, Coi (Composite Index) can be calculated using above three values:

$$Coi = \frac{F_i + C_i + W_i}{3}$$

Rural Market Centres/Periodic Markets

The term '*rurban*' connotes, a service centre lying in the transitional stage between villages and towns to serve the neighbouring areas. These centres were first designated by Golpin[18] as '*rurban centres'. Several other writers of 20th century named them as 'urban villages*'[19] and 'sub town'.[20] Prof. Singh introduced the term in his study of 'Urban Studies'.[21] The origin, growth and relationship of these centres, in size continuum, are determined by their location, farm surpluses, non-farm occupations and services they provide. Rurban centres include the services and functions like transport and banking, retail trade, post office, police station, health, education, agricultural, Community Development and Extension services and local administration etc. These settlements are found owing to the necessary groupings of services in fewer centres and are, usually, located at local road junction.[22] The author utilizes the term 'rurban centre' to include such settlements which have population below 10,000 and serve as tahsil or district headquarters or have been classified as Class V and VI towns by the Census of India, 1971. There are available, in some regions, villages having more than 5,000 persons but, above 80 per cent of their population depends on agriculture. In the absence of rurban centres these and other big villages play significant role in performing some very rudimentary type of central functions on a very limited scale for their surrounding settlements. Such lower limits of size continuum also cater to the social, economic and educational needs of their small neighbours in many capacity: (i) Mostly they occupy a location on some trade route, a clan centre or served as administrative centres in the past. (ii) Some of the rurban centres have developed from pre-Rajput clan centres, i.e., these started as clan centres and new villages in their neighbourhood were oriented to their socio-economic and political need. (iii) Some centres grew during the Colonization period under administrator, Chiefs and Thakurs and Grantees of the Government. (iv) Others have come to the present stage through changes in socio-economic conditions, mostly, serving as administrative centres in the near past. Morphologically, they include civil offices like Tahsil, Block, Post Office, Police Station, Dispensary, educational institutions, some medical practioner's residence, flour and oil and ginning or rice husking, dal (pulse) making mills. Shop's of general retailers and general merchants occupy road-crossroad or lie near bus stop or railway station. Narrow lanes, sometimes, paved with bricks or boulders or made of concrete, lead to the interior where houses seem huddled up due to lack of space. If they be on the bank of a river, all the streets coverage towards a crossroad leading near or direct to *ghat*. However, they have potentials to serve their surroundings, keeping in pace with the dynamic changes to be brought in the rural socio-economic structure.

Periodic Markets[23]

As discussed above, these service centres have periodic markets '*hat*' of multi-variate type for supplying cattle, fodder, grains, furnitures and other things of rural use. Their periodicity is well arranged and every day in the week is observed a market day within accessible service area. Thus, they work as collecting and distributing centres, as chief foci of economic, social and cultural activities of their surrounding regions.

Approach

While dealing with weekly markets in Indian countryside (Tamilnadu) Bohle[24] expresses two approaches adopted in studying the spatio-temporal structure of market place trade: (1) firstly, the aggregate view of spatio-temporal mobility patterns,[25] and (ii) secondly, the individualistic approach.[26] The basic assumption is that spatial structures and spatial processes are logical outcomes of the interaction between environment and cognitive processes of human actors.[27] But the consumer behaviour, approached from aggregate point of view, got less support during mid-seventies and disaggregate view of market behaviour is preferred, and is also relevant to the context of Third World Countries. According to Bohle, one of the most characteristic features of a periodic market system is the fact, that both, consumers and traders are regularly involved in a market decision process. He finds that the important factors, which contribute to the diversity of trader's and consumer's market behaviour, are the variations amongst the individual market participants, in their capital, scale of operation, type of commodity or services offered or purchased, place of residence, social rank (caste) sex, and specific combinations of occupational activities and economic spheres.[28] This is because these centres, in the form of rural markets, fulfill all the basic needs of the rural people, as such, they are downward terminus for manufactured goods and the upward entry point for the farm produce that flow through the regional marketing system.[29] They serve as nuclei of exchange and barter, places of entertainment, worship, meeting friends and getting news from beyond the sphere of village.[30] Moreover, it is at the rural markets that the village microcosm touches the greater external world, where rural milieu represents a cross section of the country gentry of various social grades and strata.[31]

Factors/Attributes

Analyzing on the basis of multi-dimensional attractiveness attributes and preferences the most significant attributes become clear. These are: (i) accessibility of the market, (ii) size of turnover, (iii) price level for traders, and (i) quality of goods, (ii) variety of commodities available and (iii) the atmosphere of the market for consumers. Thus, it also became obvious that socio-psychological factors play a major role in decision making process. Bohle concludes, rightly, that 'An individualistic interpretation of the spatio-temporal movements of people and goods is, therefore, indispensable, to reach a more comprehensive understanding of the nature and organization of a periodic market system.[32] His model regarding Market Rotation of Mobile Traders regarding

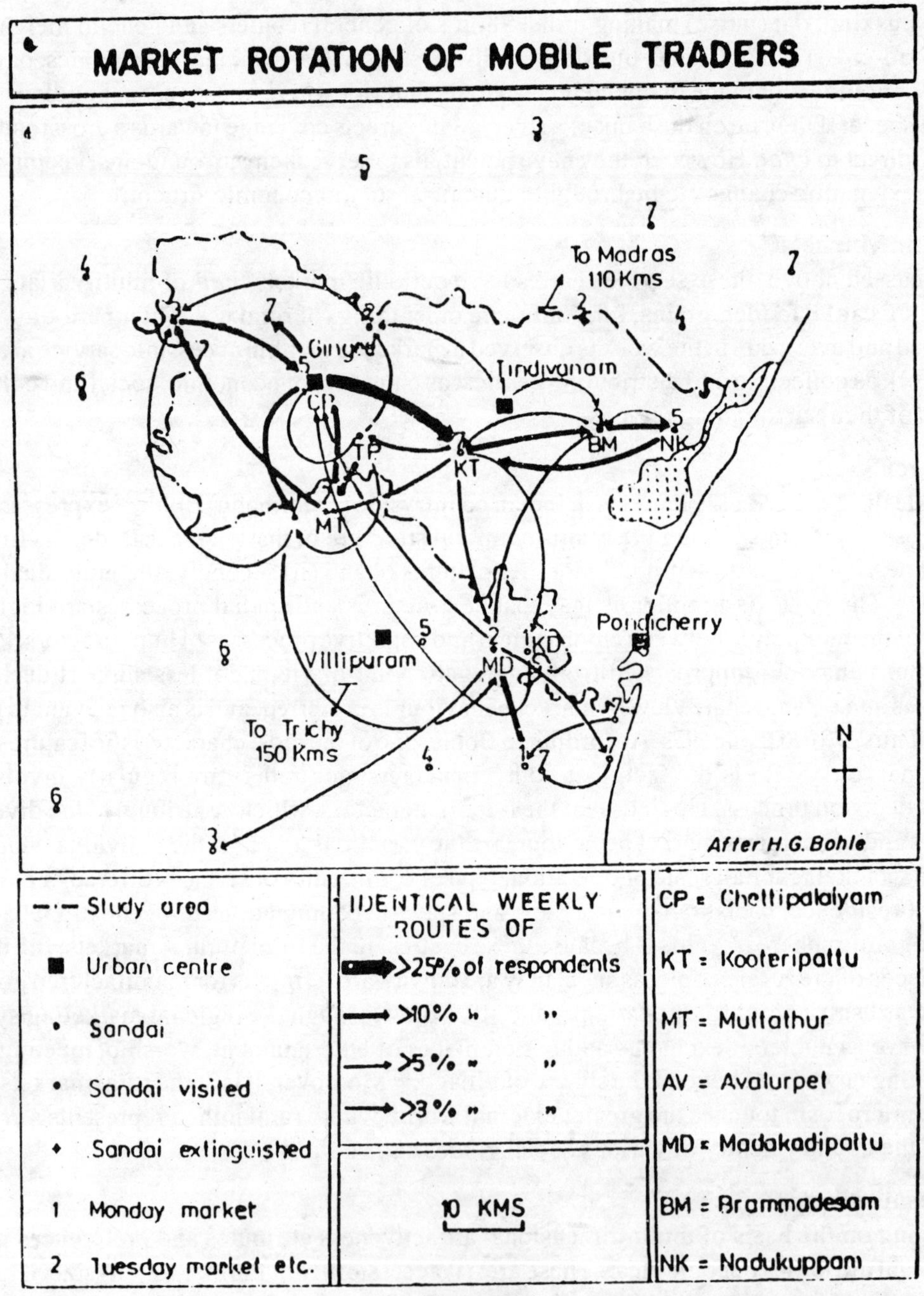

Figure 9.14

***Sandai*=Shandy from (Santhai a Tamil word) (central place) is commendable (Fig. 9.14).**

Stages

Applying an individualistic approach, Singh tried his Stability Theory, which defines stages of instability and stability of rural Central Places. During first stage, such centres originate as the

places of weekly, biweekly, monthly or annual fairs without permanent shops or dwellings for sellers at the market site, more than 75 per cent of these sellers being producers themselves. In general, the shape/size of the service area of the centre is circular. During second stage, the fluctuation in the number of traders and consumers, between market days and non- market days, becomes smaller. Many shops are settled, magnitude of goods and services increase as also the phenomena of market capture takes place, hence, weaker markets decay or are extinguished. Construction of brick and cement shops is common. In third stage, prosperity brings more buildings, wholesale dealers, vehiclular means of transport, instead of beasts of burden or carts, and elongation of service area along arteries of transport. The superimposed features, the railway or roads act effectively. Members of joint family in rural areas (agriculturists) handicraftsmen, artisans and others settle through immigration. In the last stage, the central place attains stability with stable number of traders/consumers on all days of the week. It stops to capture other bazars. Such central places are common in the Northern Indian Plain. In arid Rajasthan Zone these bazars are, still, in first stage. Lower agricultural productivity of land, lower range of surplus marketable goods, lower density of population, longer distances to cover (spacing of settlements), are responsible for weekly markets. In Yorubaland,[33] these centres have been classified on the basis of their functions, in the distributional chain as follows:

Classification

(1) feeder markets, which overlap into subsistence trader,
(2) bulking centres, which are marked by subsistence trade in which the small amounts brought at feeder markets or elsewhere, carried directly by the producer, are combined into fairly large loads by traders,
(3) the major markets, which are marked by the presence of money traders, who buy the bulked loads of subsistence traders and,
(4) large trade centres, where the produce is distributed along similar market lines.

Periodicity

Likewise, these are categorized as: (i) urban daily markets, (ii) the urban nightly markets, commencing at dust and continuing upto about 10 P.M., (iii) the daily rural markets, (iv) the rural periodic night markets, and (v) rural periodic day markets. Generally, the stagewise arrangement of such markets is fixed as one day (weekly), biweekly and daily. In some parts (specially developed North), Sundays are non market days. The diurnal variations occur according to type of schedule, i.e., morning or evening hours. Fairs, usually annual, are also under this title, if marketing is kept in view. They are based on religious, social, recreational and economic factors of a region, often as a milieu. They follow the production rhythm, and rest periods of rural folk, linked with religious sites, having spatio- temporal locations in a meso or macro region. In Indian condition, such fair markets (specially in Northern Plain) have wider socio- economic value for the area concerned.

Specialized Markets

Some market centres specialize, in one particular commodity, available in sizeable quantity. The commodities vary from livestock (Sonpur in Bihar, Dadri (Ballia in Eastern Uttar Pradesh), Bateshwar in Western Uttar Pradesh and Sagar, Madhya Pradesh) forest produce (Damoh (Madhya Pradesh), rice (Nohta in Eastern Malwa Plateau), handloom clothes (Erode, Shandy in Tamilnadu, Khalilabad in Uttar Pradesh, etc.) to leather goods, fruits and other items, used in different parts of the world. This is because, these are available there on a large scale, engaging larger number of people including the larger number of skilled persons, available.

The range of commodities varies in various developing parts from spices to food stuffs, clothing, footwears, vessels, bangles, jewellery, forest produce, garden produce, livestock, toys and implements etc.

General distribution of periodic markets follow the simple pattern such as:

(i) they are mostly located away from railways and roads,
(ii) the second largest number is along branch roads,
(iii) lowest number near railways.

Grain Market Centres need special mention, usually, classified in three categories: (1) Bazars or Hats—The name denotes a primary market centre dealing in commodities, generally, required by rural persons. These are sometimes, regulated and controlled by village Panchayats or Peasant Associations (as in Ethiopia). (2) Mandis—At taluq or Tahsil level such secondary market centres deal with whole sale transactions. These are centrally located and regulated by local bodies. (3) Ganjs—The wholesale markets at rail heads work as terminal centres and are controlled by local bodies or UDAS (Urban Dwellers' Association).

An Example

A study, conducted in Ethiopia (Africa) in Kembata and Hadiya districts (Awraja), is based on five variables: (i) Organization of periodic markets in space and time, (ii) the integration of market functions at different levels of market hierarchy, (iii) the availability of goods and services demanded by the people, (iv) purchase of goods and services from periodic markets at relatively cheaper prices, and (v) the capacity of retail trade to earn livelihood and to absorb the rural exodus in areas, where scarcity of farm land prevails. The role of periodic markets would be limited, if market place in the *awraja* do not show efficiency in these five ways. The study reveals that 60 per cent of the oldest markets were formerly military camps. A nearest neighbour index RN, calculated, gave a value of 1.04, indicating a random distribution. The periodic market system has a seven day cycle with predominance of Saturday markets. More or less, all market days in the system are less complementary to one another. As a result, clashes or overlapping of market schedules are the major features of market periodicity in the *awraja*. During feudal regime, by the virtue of being under the controls of feudals, the locations of markets and the days of meeting had been decided by the will and whim of the administrators. In addition to the feudal political system, the religion and traditions of the people, have been influencing the locations of markets, the days of meetings and, even, the market functions. The Churchyards are the focal points. Most of the markets, following a cult, are held under big trees. A linear relationship exists between the size of resident population and the number of central functions. 63 per cent of the market items are agricultural products, 17 per cent imported and 19 per cent miscellaneous services. The periodic functions of markets show less integration and less respect of the market hierarchy with irregular distribution of items in different market places. This is attributable, to subjective factors prevailing in people out of tradition. The average direct distance travelled is 9.47 km. 98 per cent of the traders are retailers and 89.9 per cent of the retailers are farmer traders. About 6 per cent of the traders own pack animals. The movements are mostly horizontal, i.e., between markets of the same order. The pattern of trader's movement in different orders indicated the first and second orders, as important wholesaling centres, and the third and fourth orders, as retailing centres. The prices of agricultural items increase, as one approaches the main road. Market places are favoured by 74 per cent of the consumers in terms of availability of items and preferred by 25 per cent in case of fair prices of offered items. The mobile traders like market periodicity for the very fact that it has a virtue of concentrating demands in specific places of specific days.

The role of rural service centres would be greater, if corrective measures are adopted to avoid weaknesses, existing in the periodic market system.[34]

References

1. Sen L.K. et al. (1971), Planning Rural Growth Centres for Integrated Area Development-A Study in Miryalguda Taluka, NICD, Hyderabad-p. 17.
2. Perroux, F. (1955), Economic Space, Theory and Application, Quarterly Journal of Economics 64, pp. 90-97.
3. Green, R.J. (1966), The Remote Countryside-A Plan for Contraction, Planning outlook, 1, pp. 17-37.
4. Taylor, D.R.F. (1979), Role of Functions of Lower Order Centres in Rural Development in R.P. Misra, General Editor, Rural-Urban Migrations, UNICARD, Nagoya, pp. 265-291.
5. See for details John E. Brush (1953), The Hierarchy of Central Places in Southwestern Wisconsin, The Geographical Review, Vol. 43 pp. 380-402; Ruthedge Vining (1955), A Description of Certain Spatial Aspects of an Economic System, Economic Development and Cultural Change, Vol. 3, pp. 147-195; Carlisle W. Baskin, (1957), A Critique and Translation of Walter Christaller's Die Zentralen Orte in Suddeutschland, unpublished Ph.D. Thesis, University of Virginia; also on W. Christaller (1933), The Central Places in Southern Germany (translation- 1966), New Jersey; John D. Nystuen, (1959), Geographical Analysis of Consumer Movements and Retail Business Locations (1) Theories (2) Empirical Patterns in Cedar Rapids, Iowa, and (3) A Simulation Model of Movement, Unpublished Ph.D. Thesis, Deptt. of Geography, University of Washington; Berry and William L. Garrison (1958), Recent Development of Central Place Theory, Papers and Proceedings, Regional Science Association, Vol. 4, pp. 107-120; Briyan J.L. Berry and Allan Pred (1961), Central Place Studies:A Bibliography of Theory and Applications (Philadelphia, Regional Science Research Institute; Iainr, Meyer and Huggett, R.J., ref. no. 4 Ch. 7 pp. 11-23; B.J.L. Berry (1967), Geography of Market Centres and Retail Distribution, New Jersey, Ch. IV; P. Haggett (1965), Locational Analysis in Human Geography, London; William Bunge (1962), Theoretical Geography, Lund Studies in Geography, pp. 128-148; M.F. Dacey (1965), The Geometry of Central Places, Geografiska Annaler, B. 47-2, 113; K. S.O. Beavon, (1975), Christaller's Central Place Theory: Reviewed, Revealed, Revised, Johannesburg University of Witwaterstrand, Deptt. of Geography and En. Studies, Res. Paper No. 15; also B.J.L. Berry (1967), Geography of Market Centres and Retail Distribution, Englewood Cliff, Prentice Hall.
6. Paramhamsa, V.R.K. (General Editor) and L.K. Sen et al. (eds.) ref. no. 1 Ch. 9, pp. 23-24.

6a. K indicates the span of control of higher order centres, while k (small letter) is also used in central place hierarchy. This k is known as the bifurcation ratio. It denotes the number of lower order settlements served by a higher order centre, e.g., for a K = 3 network, k = 2, thus, k = K-1.

7. Haggett, p. (1972), Geography:A Modern Synthesis, Harper and Row Series in Geography, New York, p. 370.
8. Ibid, p. 371.

9. Meyer, I. and Huggett, J. ref. no. 4 Ch. 7, p. 19.
10. Bunge W., ref. no. 5, p. 135.
11. Lalit K. Sen et al. ref. no. 1, pp. 81-96.
12. Stafford, H.A. Jr. (1963), The Functional Bases of Small Towns, Econ. Geog., Vol. 39, April, p. 173.
13. Haggett, P. and K.A. Gunwardena (1964), Determination of Population Threshold for Settlement Functions by the Reed, Muench Method, Prof. Geog., pp. 166-169, Vol. XVI, No. 4.
14. The Original formula is

$$F = G \frac{M_i M_j}{d^2}$$

Where F is the force exerted on two masses M_i and M_j at a distance d apart, and G is a universal constant known as the constant of gravitation. Thus, two planets attract one another with a force determined by the gravitational law. The relationship is adopted to the attraction between towns and other social phenomena.
15. Haggett P. and K.A. Gunwardena, ref. no. 13; see L.J. Reed and M. Muench (1938), A Simple Method for Estimating Fifty Percent End Points, American Journal of Hygiene, Vol. 27, pp. 493-497.
16. The functions of which the Government can take a direct action (Indian Condition) are preferred and referred to as policy functions; the rest are called as non-policy functions.
17. Folk, S. (1968), Central Place Systems and Spatial Integration in Nilgiris and Coorg (South India), Collected Papers, Denmark 21st I.G.U. India.
18. Galpin, C.G (1915), The Social Anatomy of an Agricultural Community, Research Bulletin 34, Agricultural Experiment Station of the University of Wisconsin.
19. Dickinson, R.E. (1932), The Distribution of Functions of Smaller Urban Settlements in East Anglia, Geography, 17, pp. 19-31; see also S.L. Kayastha and B.N. Singh (1981), Spatial Strategy For Integrated Rural Area Development:A Case Study of Ghazipur Tahsil (Uttar Pradesh) India, NGJI, Vol. 27 Parts 1 and 2:30-40.
20. Smailes, A.E. (1944), The Urban Hierarchy in England and Wales, Geography, 29, pp. 41-51.
21. Singh, R.L. (1955-56), Urban Hierarchy in Umland of Banaras, Journal of the Scientific Research, B.H.U., Vol. VI, (2), p. 191.
22. Singh R.L. and Singh S.M. (1960), Mungra Badshahpur:A Rural Settlement in Ganga Ghaghara Doab West, The N.G.J.I., Vol. VI, p. 119.
23. See S. Plattner (1975), Rural Market Networks, Scientific American, 232-5:66-79 also B.G. Tamaskar (1966), The Weekly Markets of Sagar-Damoh Plateau, N.G.J.I., V. XII, I, pp. 38-50.
24. Bohle, H.G. (1981), Spatio-Temporal Decision Making in South Indian Weekly Markets:An Investigation Into Consumer-Trader Perceptions and Preferences, N.G.J.I., Vol. XXVII, 1 and 2, pp. 1-13.
25. Hodder, B.W. (1969), Markets in Yorubaland, in:Ibadan University Press, pp. 1-109.
26. Symanski, R. and Webber, M.J. (1974), Complex Periodic Market Cycles, in A.A.A.G., 64:203-213.
27. Golledge, R.G., Brown, L.A. and Williamson, F. (1972), Behavioural Approaches in Geography:An Overview, Australian Geographer, 12 p. 76.
28. Bhole, H.G., ref. no. 24, p. 6.
29. See S. Plattner, op.cit., ref, no. 23.
30. Singh, S.M. (1966), The Stability Theory of Rural Central Place Development, NGJI, Vol. XI, Part 1, p. 14.
31. Singh, K.N. (1962), Rural Markets and Rurban Centres in Eastern Uttar Pradesh-A Geographical Analysis, Ph. D. Thesis (Unpub.), Deptt. of Geography, B.H.U. Varanasi, p. 273.

32. Bohle, H.G. ref. no. 24, p. 13.
33. Hodder, B.W. (1965), Distribution of Markets in Yorubaland, Scottish Geographical Magazine, 81, p. 48.
34. Alemayehu Lirenso (1982), The Functional Role of Periodic Markets in Economic Development:The Case of Kembata and Hadiya, Ethiopia, Deptt. of Geography Seminar Paper based on IDR Res. Project:1-21.

10

Integrated Planning and Rationalization of Rural Settlements

Transformation of Villages Versus Transitional Phases of Changes

Earlier, we discussed about the internal changes in social behaviour in Chapter three, distributional changes in Chapter five, and morphological in Chapter six. Now, we take the holistic approach and have an appraisal of the transitional phases of the rural settlements obtained through various agents. A geographer, like other scholars concerned with settlements, observes some commonalties in rural living system of any part of the world. Obviously, the villages and village living system, both, are undergoing changes, visible or partly visible to a member in society. Traditionally the villages are viewed as a settlement, where man takes birth, lives and dies; the village community is conceived to operate via "family-centred, parent controlled, continuity seeking institutions and ideologies".[1] These villages do experience change, but slow, in the term of changes in family structure, village council and social patterns. It is discernible, that production technology has always been the primary moving force in generating changes in agricultural operations or other forms of primary production. But, new attractions, of better standard of living for improving the existing levels of living, do bring change in village family, e.g., clothing, housing, education, home furnishing, use of energy, travel patterns, social mores and consumption of various goods. In India, now, the scenario obtains predominance of uneconomic holding, a third of the agricultural population reduced to the level of agricultural labourers, a large portion of the non-agricultural rural population also, living in a precarious condition dependent on the prosperity of agriculture, also a substantial section of even the owners of land and tenants, on medium or small sized forms: struggling hard for survival on meagre agricultural production. Other changes are: larger political units becoming viable from the improved system of communication; printing and other technical media of linguistic and visual communication supplementing a reliance on oral communication; an interdependence coming into being between communities, that previously were separated from and independent of one another; formal schooling replacing tribal initiation; inherited status giving way before achieved status; occupations becoming more skilled and specialized; salaried employment in industry and elsewhere, starting to spread and impersonal labour relations dominate, and sharper distinctions arising between work and leisure.

Factors

There are regional variations in the factors responsible for rural village life. Common factors work as agents of change in south east Asian parts, typically different from other areas. Spencer enumerates eight of them, considered as most significant.

(1) Public Health Conditions are improving. In many Third World countries better sanitation, drinking water supply, disease control and other public health programmes have proved to be most significant producers of changes, (2) Better means of transportation and communication provide contacts within reach in interior most rural villages, (3) Involvement of State in rural uplift, (4) Electrification, (5) Education programmes, (6) Better marketing system provides deeper penetration into the rural hinterlands of all kinds of consumer, processor and producer goods, (7) Spread of settlements in gap areas or empty spaces of the past, and (8) Increase in mobility conditions and simultaneous impact of contact as well as urbanization.[2]

Cultural Change

Due to population growth, the visible change is in settlements growing larger. Longevity and migration to cities, both are conducive to change in age structure of children and elderly adults. Likewise, range of activities, is not confined to primary production. People engage themselves in public works programme, processing of goods, manufacturing, part time agriculture, catering to urban markets, community services and transport services. There is less shared 'public life' in even south or south east Asian parts. City dwellers, often, visiting home and village commuters are conducive to a new sort of social life in villages, too. This changes also the traditional social cohesion and brings new community structure, particularly that of nuclear family. The effective local leadership of village community is being replaced by officials of Govt. Projects and Administration. Several types of dissensions, party alignments, and caste structure based divisions have set in deterioration in traditional structures resulting into confusion in village living system. Most significant changes occurred in countries adopting cultural revolution through land reforms, i.e., China, North Korea, Vietnam, Ethiopia, etc. in communist countries and Japan, Israel, India, Indonesia, etc. elsewhere.

Similar changes, in cultural aspects, are visible through electrification and mechanization. People in rural areas are switching over to new type of domestic housing with cement, concrete, tin and iron rods and plywoods. Thus, transformation process is on and villages are passing, through a transitional phase, ready to response planning efforts. The confused state, however, needs rationalization and, here, geographer will play its demanded role in future.

Need for Planning

The distribution of farmstead, inter alia, newly created hamlets and refugee camps, the best layout of roads, location of service centres, construction of poor people demonstration houses and planning of houses/buildings are the problems, which could be solved by the coordinated and cooperative efforts of geographers, rural sociologists and socio-economic planners. The 'settlement geographer can (best) suggest the alterations in the pattern of roads and the distribution of services, that can make the transformation least painful.' One may study them under the following subheads: (i) Planning, in relation to locational efficiency of landuse, marketing, living conditions etc., (ii) in relation to current economic well-being and social dynamics and demands of modernization, (iii) the service villages and rural service centres as agents of rural change, (iv) the infrastructural development for rural uplift including planning. But, before discussing about the planning, one must see, what the real settlements are as social units, what is their social dynamics, rural-urban relationship and change strategy between traditional society and modernity. What are structural elements of social organisation? What should be the cohesive yet viable unit for planning and rationalization? What is the ecological basis of Planning? Let us discuss them first.

Village As Social Unit

The rural society in India in the form of village, as a social unit, is assumed, since long, a community which has 'a strong base in historical and even present fact'.[3] Isolation of the villages, the Jajmani system and caste and kinship, are three bases, on which, the feelings of community focusing on the village, have rested. The author has already discussed in detail the isolation factor in preceding chapters. Traditionally, India has been served by the Jajmani and Hat systems. In the former system the primary, secondary and tertiary sectors of the social economy are interlocked; persons or families under various sectors are bound by mutual economic and social duties and obligations; and the 'Entire social fabric is interwoven under these behavioural value system'.[4] Yet, both, the Jajmani and the Hat systems have been fast breaking down with the changed political, economic and territorial organizations on the one hand, and assertion of new social value system on the other. The third base of the village community, caste and kinship, largely, determine the function, the status, the available opportunities as well as the handicaps of an individual. Caste differences, even determine, the difference in modes of domestic and social life, also types of house and cultural patterns of the people, which are found in the rural area. It has fixed the psychology of the various social groups and has evolved, such minutely graded levels of social distance and superior inferior relationships, that the social structure looks like a gigantic hierarchic pyramid. "This institution, though, subjected to mortal blows from economic political, ideological and other forces, yet, even, in its death agonies, is still, having its grip over the rural social life".[5] There is an evidence that caste, as a system, is losing its grip. The change is in the attitudes of the castes, which now work to improve themselves and to raise their social standing; it is not in the direction of dissolving the system. "In some respects, caste consciousness has become even worse".[6] But it seems probable that,in the course of time, the nation will swallow up the caste, that the customary restrictions will be gradually modified till the social system becomes again, one of classes, as it was in Vedic times. There are no doubt, customs that should go, customs that are definitely harmful, customs, that in modern conditions, have become ridiculous. But, "These are more accidental excrescences that can be removed without harming the substance of the caste system. Because, what is required is a pruning knife, not an axe.[7] So, to, properly, unravel, the causes of the octopus like stranglehold of the caste system, is very urgent for the proper comprehension of the life processes of rural society in India and also for laying down the lines of its future development.[8] Like caste system, family and familism too, impress their stamp on the entire rural structure.[9]

Social Requisites of Economic Development

The question stands boldly: "Can a superstructure of modernization be built on a foundation, that retains all the essentials of the traditional order?"[10] Culture, being an adaptive mechanism, reacts to every change in the natural and social environment, which result into certain inevitable changes in the social and cultural milieu. So, a sound strategy of planned change, must be based on recognition of social complexities, on anticipation of cultural barriers and on a variable approach to the mechanics of implementation. Unfortunately, the economic infrastructures of modernization have been, carefully, identified, but the position, in respect of the social and geographical infrastructures, is not the same. If one observes carefully, the road to economic development, especially, at the critical "take off" stage, is hard and requires considerable sacrifice and even privations. Only emotional preparedness to undergo these self imposed sufferings is, therefore, necessary. In sum, the ideological-motivational-institutional-organizational framework of the developing (rural) societies will have to undergo a thorough overhaul, if they have to take any rapid strides in the direction of modernization.[11]

Rural-Urban Relationships

"The seething cauldron of rural life is neither to be treated as a passive, quiet backpool of urban society nor to be treated as an auxiliary appendage of dazzling metropolis. It has to be studied in its own magnitude and significance".[12] Undoubtedly, "The new urban society is being grafted into the traditional rural society... resulting in to a new rural urban configuration."[13] But, the forces of change, which may be potent, when viewed from the city, quickly, lose their impact, when spread over the vast number of villages, that have to be affected. More than this, there are buffers,[14] rurban centres discussed in Ch. nine, which attenuate and divert this impact, as it moves against the grain of traditional urban-rural relationships. Some of the religious centres are exceptions, i.e., Varanasi, Ujjain, Puri etc., as their religious sphere of influence is so wide and extensive, that it has penetrated in to all parts of the Indian regions. Otherwise, "It is a common experience of academics and administrators that people residing in the suburban villages, by and large, are super sensitive, cynical, and tend towards normalcy, as compared to those, belonging to villages in the interior: "By a curious design of social dynamics these suburban villages act as buffers between the urban-industrial centres, on the one hand, and the vast rural areas, on the other. They also function as shock-absorbers between the tow areas.[15]

Structural Framework of Rural Settlements in Future

A common question before a planner is regarding the type of community, which is likely to emerge in rural areas. In view of the changing socio-economic structure of the villages and emerging situations in rural India, V. Nath[16] foresees important changes in its physical structure and socio-economic composition. Population pressure, physical and favourable social factors, will compel the inhabitants to form new villages, on sites, away from the much prized agriculturally productive land, lying just outside the settlement. Homestead fashion will arise in well irrigated areas. The pattern of settlements in such areas is, therefore, likely to become more open and dispersed, with large number of new villages and homestead settlements developing, side by side, with older, tightly nucleated villages, which would themselves be expanding. There will be growth of larger villages and small towns into rural 'service centres' with the progressive agriculturation of the small and medium villages and the concentration of the rural artisans and other non-agriculturists in those centres. He maintains that, this trend would generate technological advance in both the agricultural and service centre economics, as both, would be serving each other in a more efficient way. The increased agricultural production and rising rural incomes and standard of living, would not only help accelerate the marketing and distributive activities of the service centres, but would also enable them to attract various processing industries. The size of the centres and the number of dependent villages would, however, vary in different districts. The trend will be to form markets along arteries near crossings, bus stop sites and other attractive sites. Thus, rural society would consist of a large number of villages or homesteads, predominantly, agricultural and a much smaller number of service centres having mixed population of artisans, servicemen and also a few cultivators.

Ecological Basis of Planning

It is needless to emphasize that, how far ecological problems are dealt with, has, now, become, a criterion of social progress and an index of civilization's level of culture. Here comes geographical research with its great potentialities for a comprehensive approach to study the natural and social phenomena. This comprehensive potential can be fully employed, precisely, in the course of interdisciplinary ecological research at grassroots levels. The substance of the main scientific trends of ecological research or inquiries in geography can be defined as follows: (i) control over changes in the environment caused by human activity (anthropogenic monitoring), (ii) scientific, geographical forecasting of the consequences of the impact of economic activity on the environment; (iii) prevention, mitigation and elimination of elemental natural calamities, (iv) optimization of the environment in the natural technical systems created by man (Ursul, 1983, p. 200).

The ecological inquiries are concerned with, as a prerequisite, the study of ecosystem more precisely termed as 'geoecobiota, (Gerasimov, 1984). Our concern with 'ecosystem' as a basis for planning is, now, very much in vogue, particularly, in reaction to recent literature on the impending doom of the universe, if ecological 'laws' continue to be disobeyed (Commoner, 1971; Meadows *et al.*, 1972). It means, the mankind must maintain, the most commonly used, ecological balance which requires 'an exchange between ecosystem components:animal life, plant life and physical or inorganic elements (Lassey, 1977, p. 12). The maintenance of ecological balance, in itself, envisages: (i) preservation of ecological integrity so as to provide a continuing supply of life supporting resources, (ii) efficient and appropriate landuse, (iii) healthy (UNEP, 86) living conditions, (iv) aesthetically pleasing environment, (v) effective social, economic and governmental institutions, (vi) improved human welfare, (vii) physical structure and adapted landscape of pleasing design, and (viii) comprehensiveness. If all major factors affecting human impact on the environment are to be considered in planning, a comprehensive or holistic viewpoint is necessary. (See R.Y. Singh et al. (eds) Planning In Integrated Rural Environment (1988), Deep & Deep Publications, p. 34).

Search for Unit Area of Development or Community and Inter Village Relationships

As V. Nath concludes, the primary community, in rural India is today constituted, not by the 'Village' (settlement), but by the members of a single caste living within a village. But the service centres, referred to above, with their constituent group of villages would constitute, Says Nath, a real community. The first and the main objective, for a planner, is the search and identification of a real community. Here comes on the forefront, the geographer, who can, best, locate them, spatially. The question is, what should be the territorial extent of such a community or a more cohesive, yet, viable area of development? Rural sociologists may cooperate with the settlement geographer, and the latter, would undoubtedly locate "where" they are and 'where' they ought to be.

The block centred growth, considered to be ideal, under Community Development Programme, was evaluated by Balwantrai Mehta team for Democratic Decentralization. The committee recommended for the jurisdiction of the Panchayat Samiti, the principal unit of local government at inter village level, also, to be coextensive with that of the block, and that of the Zila Parishad with the district. But, the form was never given the content. Failure resulted, because, the village is too small an unit of development, the block is too large and unwieldy...and it has no roots in history nor, social or economic growth.[17] Also, the size was arbitrarily determined. Viability of the centre, which aspect is one of the essential premises of rural development and centre building in each area for an integrated rural development, was ignored, and choice of location of the block headquarters was hung on political expediency of local leaders or unimaginative local officials.[18] It is clearly mentioned in a note prepared by the C.D. Department, Government of India, that, whereas the concept of block remains valid, the development effort, looked at from the point of view of organized community backing, necessarily, remains diffused. The Department had, therefore, drawn up a scheme to locate rural communities around potential *growth centres*, in terms of an area, with an economic base, and a range of population, sufficiently large to support a package of economic and social services, so that, the process of development is sustained and accelerated through the common interest and energetic support of the people.[19]

It is also experienced that 'as the pursuit of individual interest, within and outside the village, has become more common, the influence of the community over its members has diminished.'[20]

Moreover, the rural development efforts, so far, have only helped to further differentiate the village community. The COPP Team report said, "It is difficult to know how the community spirit can be whole heartedly evoked under the existing system of agriculture in which there are marked inequalities. The result of the plan has been to accentuate the inequalities".[21] It leads to the fact, that the inter-village level of territorial unit, with its wider social and economic base, would be the nearly self-sufficient social and economic unit. 'A larger than village spatial unit is imperative for, even, the minimal operational scale of economic forces.[22] Indeed, there is community of communities, but it is envisaged that, as technological changes take place in agriculture, and as transport facilities improve, the unit of effective Community Organization will become larger. Gradually, the operational area of local planning and decision will become a group of villages, rather than the individual villages.[23] This type of functional organization, above the village and below the block level, could strengthen the governmental discharge of duties and could also delimit the effective range and scope of the responsibility of the local communities for their own economic and social advancement. This would also have spatial advantages as well as better coordination in the functioning of the various agencies. It may also bring industrial decentralization and reverse the flow of human and material capital, which now streams from the rural to the urban sector. Communist China is doing it by coercive measures. India and (other democratic Third World countries) have to do it by economic inducement and persuasion.[24]

Experiences show that there is evidence to the existence of inter-village levels of integration within the micro-region and only a neighbourly-nexus could provide the basis of inter village cooperation, which the block can never hope to stimulate. Even in the past "Intimate links, economic, religious and social, existed between neighbouring villages.[25] Sri Jayaprakash Narayan proposed to constitute regional communities of neighbouring villages as an integral community and pleaded that, this regional community should be recognized as the basic unit of planning and for joint activity in agriculture and industrial production.[26] Such a regional community may be active as cognitive social unit and have a size analogous to the present Nyaya Panchayat area.

The study of inter-village locality group also, leads one to the notion of establishing small towns[27] or uni-service centres (suggested by Prof. R.L. Singh, comprising 10-25 villages, the pattern depending upon topography), service centres[28], urban centres[29], small towns[30] or locational centres[31] named by different authors. These uni-service centres will act as cells of modernization, promote new type of functional leadership, would be inspired by the value of nationalism and secularism, which will put new life into the spatio-political institutions in their zone of influence. "These locational centres, will develop into store houses of information and radiate innovations at a much faster rate, and at the same time, bring about equalization process to all sections of the people.[32]

Planning Service Villages and Rural Service Centres as Agents of Rural Change

The foregoing discussion reveals, that uni-service centres would work as new focal points and agents of rural change. A three tier arrangement, thus, becomes clear in the structural framework of rural settlements, already proposed, in the schematic hierarchy of settlements (Figs. 10.1, 10.2), i.e., a dependent village at lower level, central village at higher level and service centre on the top. A more or less hexagonal pattern will emerge around such service centres. Having fixed locational priorities, these emerging centres would fit in, both, the traditional as well as emerging spatio-temporal frame. As India's population is on the threshold of an agricultural, non- agricultural and rural urban continuum, "These centres would emerge to take their legitimate position in the locational functional hierarchy, of population centres.[33] Selection of such centres, however, is to be made continuously impartially, unbiased and without having any prestige attachment, political or religious. Some settlements have enjoyed historico-cultural significance in the origin, evolution and intensification of the settlement net in the region.[34] Such settlements may be selected as central villages or rural service centres for centre building purposes. Their socio-economic development would require less expenditure and effort than creating a net of wholly new centres, almost superimposed, on the existing landscape. Selection of settlements, according to proposed schematic hierarchy, and establishment of basic civic and institutional services and facilities, would necessarily bring social, economic and cultural changes, and modernization in countryside, without inflicting the age old traditional pride and heritage of the area. Moreover, a form of decentralization may be devised, which may assure, integrated development of all sections of the village community, and through it, of rural society as a whole. To the extent that this is achieved, the easier it will be to secure, a larger measure of interaction between the rural, urban and industrial economics for the country as a whole.[35]

Spatial Strategy of Service Centre Approach

As the geographic space is concerned with the environment, in which man lives, acts and rests,[36] any attempt on his part to achieve the rationale environment, through welfare approach,[37] involves the consideration of the following four aims, which control and regulate the quality of life in integrated form: (a) maximum of contacts, (b) minimum of efforts, (c) optimum of space, and (d) quality of environment.[38] As the 'Settlement system is a spatial framework of the social and economic activities',[39] it is proper to identify service centres as growth centres of different orders which maintain the organization system in a given space.

With a view to considering space as planning unit referred to earlier and as a bounding territory for action, service centre approach has been applied in hierarchical level; in fact, service

MODEL PATTERN OF SPATIAL INTEGRATION & FUNCTIONAL COORDINATION FOR DEPALPUR TAHSIL (Malwa Region)

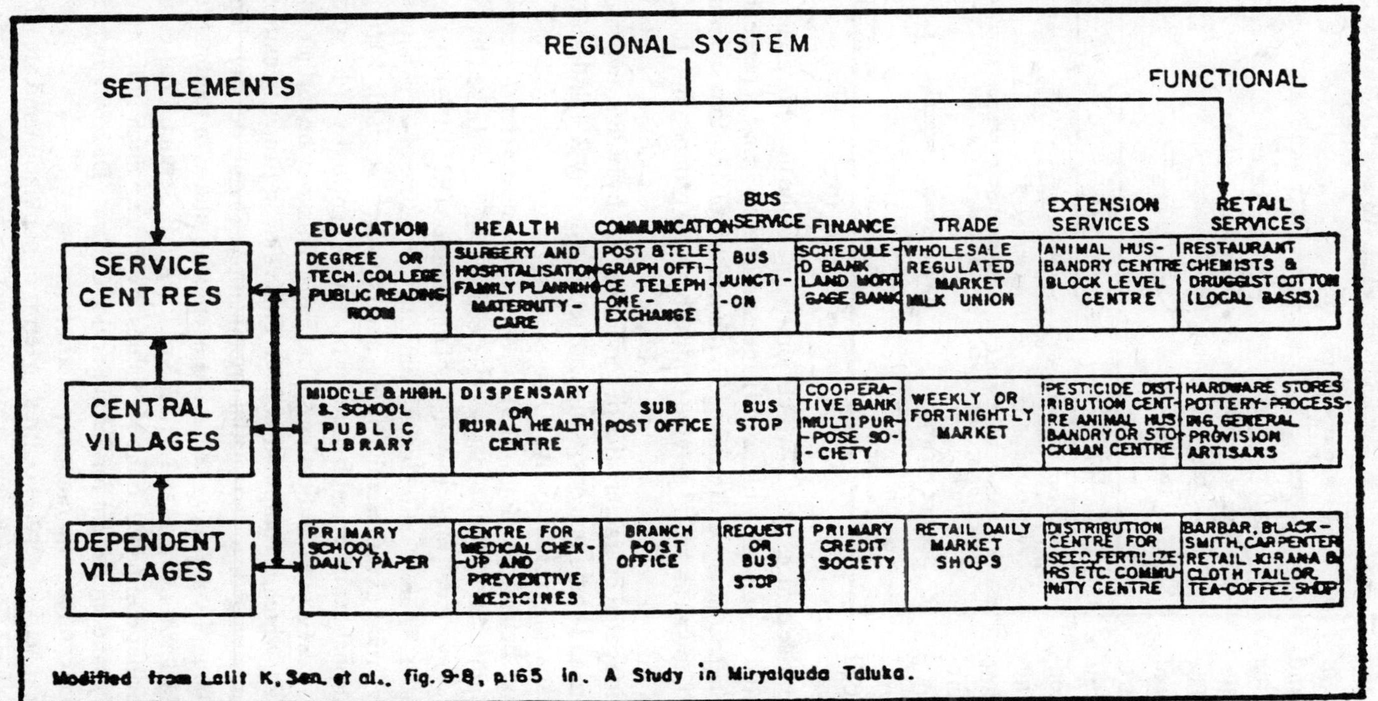

Figure 10.1

centres have been recognized as the nodal centres of communication and change, which balance the settlement system. The level and capacity of a service centre, depends upon, the economic efficiency, in terms of functional magnitude and functional distinctiveness. With this analogy, the service centres are grouped into two classes-

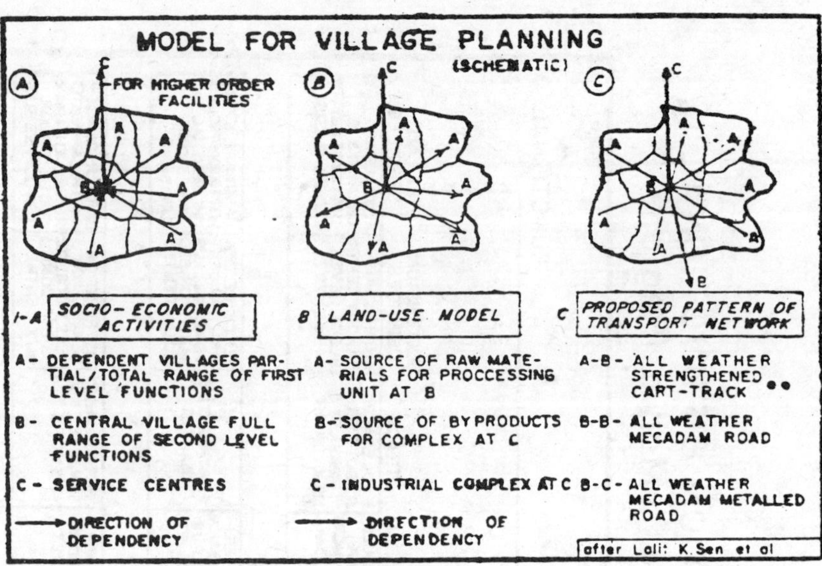

Figure 10.2

towns and rural service centres (RSC)-which, jointly, make the total hierarchy of service centres, which is represented by centrality index (Ci), measured (a) in terms of percentage share of commercial population (secondary and tertiary activities) to the total regional commercial population. On the basis of Ci, towns and rural service centres both are grouped into four classes (Fig. 10.3 and Table 10 (i)).

For measuring spatial characteristics of service centres by orders, two situations, have been visualized-random and homogeneous, which are represented by RN (index of randomness), and Hs (hypothetical spacing) respectively.

The locational behaviour (Fig. 10.3) of service centres, clearly, shows the impact of topographical conditions. Higher order service centres are inter-linked by National and State Highways. On regional level, random pattern of distribution (RN 1.08-1.10) is clearly visualized but it varies by order. There is quite distinct similarity in nature of dispersion of towns and rural service centres by orders as represented by RN and Di values (see table 10 (i)). The comparison, of observed and probable numerical frequency of service centres by order, shows pressure in the highest and the lowest groups, indicating spatial gaps. This may be further clarified by the convergent Ratio (CR), which is computed as 2.08. This value indicates transitional ecological setting of the region having distorted spatial organization. Taking density- function as base, the hypothetical spacing of centres, by order, has been computed. On regional level Hs values are recorded as 39.24 km for towns and 31.53 Km for Rural Service Centres respectively; these values may be further compared to the Hs values, by order, which indicate clustered trend for Towns and nearly random pattern for Rural Service Centres (Di 20.94 and 45.60 respectively). Rest of the service centres form random pattern.

The service capacity of service centres, in terms of population and area, has been computed on the basis of the K=3 Christallerian net, which is applicable to a maximum extent in the region. It has been observed that the highest order service centres have relatively very high capacity (on

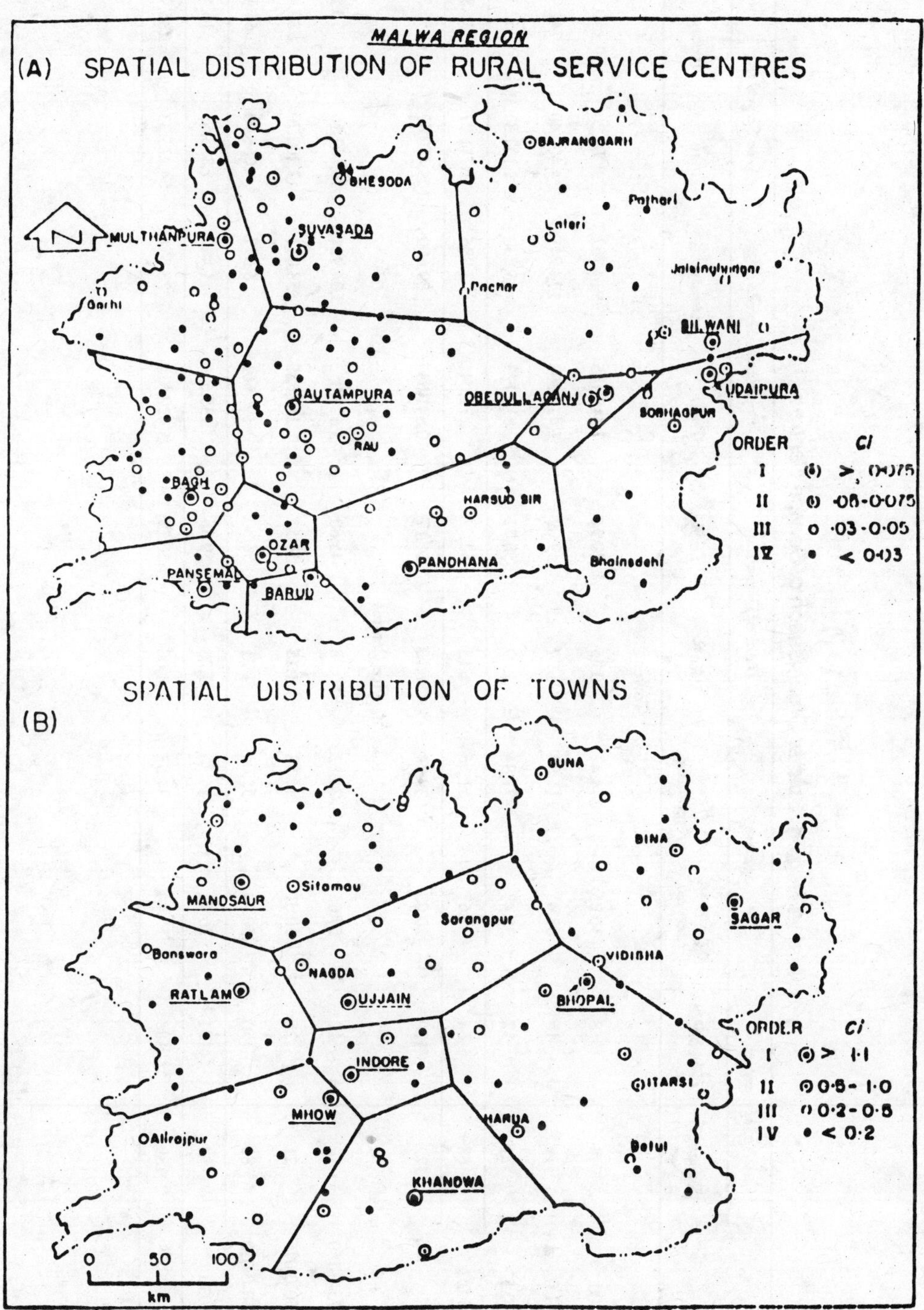
MALWA REGION
(A) SPATIAL DISTRIBUTION OF RURAL SERVICE CENTRES
BAJRANGGARH
BHESODA
SUVASADA
MULTHANPURA
Lateri
Pathari
Pachor
BILWANI
UDAIPURA
GAUTAMPURA
OBEDULLAGANJ
SOBHAGPUR
RAU
BAGH
HARSUD SIR
OZAR
PANDHANA
PANSEMAL
BARUD
Bhainsdehi
ORDER CI
I >, 0·075
II ·05-0·075
III ·03-0·05
IV < 0·03
SPATIAL DISTRIBUTION OF TOWNS
(B)
GUNA
BINA
MANDSAUR
Sitamau
SAGAR
Sarangpur
Banswara
VIDISHA
NAGDA
RATLAM
UJJAIN
BHOPAL
INDORE
ITARSI
MHOW
HARDA
Alirajpur
Betul
KHANDWA
ORDER CI
I > 1·1
II 0·5-1·0
III 0·2-0·5
IV < 0·2
0 50 100
km

Figure 10.3

Table 10 (I)

Malwa Region: Spatial Organisation of Service Centres

		No. of Centres		*Spacing*		*Index of Dispersion*		*Population Served*		*Area Served (Km²)*	
		Existing	*Probable*	*rO Km. Observed*	*Hs Km. Hypothetical*	*Rn*	*Di %*	*Total*	*Average*	*Total*	*Average*
					Towns						
I	> 1.00	8	8	30.25	144.47	0.45	20.94	7,318,105	914,752	73,204.20	9,150.50
II	0.5-1.0	14	16	68.45	115.84	1.27	59.09	2,439,368	174,241	24,401.40	1,742.96
III	0.2-0.5	31	32	39.48	77.84	1.09	50.72	813,123	26,230	8,133.80	262.38
IV	0.15-0.2	68	64	27.63	52.56	1.13	52.57	271,041	3,986	2,711.27	36.87
		122	120	20.08	39.24	1.10	51.17	10,841,637	89,600	108,450.67	896.29
					Rural Service Centres						
I	0.075-0.150	12	12	57.05	125.12	0.98	45.60	3,659,053	3,04,921	36,602.10	3,050.17
II	0.050-0.075	21	25	50.61	94.58	1.15	53.51	1,219,685	58,083	12,200.70	580.99
III	0.030-0.050	62	50	30.99·	55.04	1.21	56.30	406,561	6.557	4,066.90	65.60
IV	< 0.030	94	101	26.62	44.70	1.28	59.56	135,520	1,442	1,355.63	14.42
		189	188	15.84	31.53	1.08	50.25	5,420,819	28,682	54,225.33	286.91

an average level a town serves 914,752 persons and 9150.5 Km^2 and a Rural Service Centre, 304,921 persons and 3,050.17 Km^2 of area) while the lowest order centre has a very low servicing capacity (on an average a town serves 3,986 persons and 39.87 Km^2 of area, while a RSC serves 1,442 persons and 14.42 Km^2 area). Such variations show a critical stage of developing economy.

To minimize the spatial gaps and to develop a balanced spatial organization it would be better to make provision of infrastructural coordinates at smaller levels, so that the service efficiency of small order service centres is to be maximized up to optimum level. At present the service zones show (as represented through the Dirichlet[40] polygons) an unbalanced form, which could be reduced through the additional development of service centres in the gap areas.

A Model for Spatial Integration and Functional Co-ordination of Settlements

In preceding pages (Ch.9), the author has already discussed about the hierarchy of functions as well as settlements in the sample study area of Depalpur Tahsil. Spatial integration involves, an exercise in filling the locational gaps and attempting to combine the different parts of the settlement system in a coherent pattern. It is evident, that three classes of functional hierarchy were related, not only to the size of population within which they tended to occur, but were also associated with space preferences or choice, shown by the villagers for interaction with other settlements for their socioeconomic requirements. Also, the tahsil area may be divided in to many sub-regions, each consisting of a group of villages, small and big, acting as dependent settlements on a central village for their socio-economic facilities. These central villages, in their turn, along with their service areas, come under the zone of influence of a higher order service centre like Gautampura, Depalpur and Betma. This presents spatial three-tier organization. Though, from the point of view of functional jurisdiction, central villages will be responsible for the provision of a certain level of socio-economic facilities to the settlements within not more than 50 Km^2 of area and about 4,500 population, the service centre like Betma, will be responsible for the provision of these facilities to its own dependent area, and in addition, will have some higher order facilities for catering to the demand for them for a certain size of area and of population. Such a pattern[41] of integration and co-ordination (Figs. 10.1, 10.4, 10.5) and table 10 (ii) & (iii) is based on the following assumptions:

1. That, the region needs to change from a traditional society into a modern (appropriate technology oriented) industrial society based on democratic decentralization under the framework of Community Rural Development Programme.
2. That, change is to be planned by and through the government without recourse to coercion with the best possible people's participation.
3. That, it is a continuous, gradual process and requires to keep a long range perspective in view.
4. That, in identifying a region, the totality of development process should be taken into account, rural and urban being integral elements of the development process.
5. That, there may be local variations in the size of area and population at each level of hierarchy based upon topographical conditions of the region.

Thus, the model provides an advisory plan for development of the facilities to those concerned with planning. It will also reduce the regional imbalances in the provision of socio-economic facilities and will give way to a situation of controlled imbalance. Newly created centres will carve out their own zone of influence. Since, all the central villages will be connected with the dependent settlements by a network of carttrack and with either of these three service

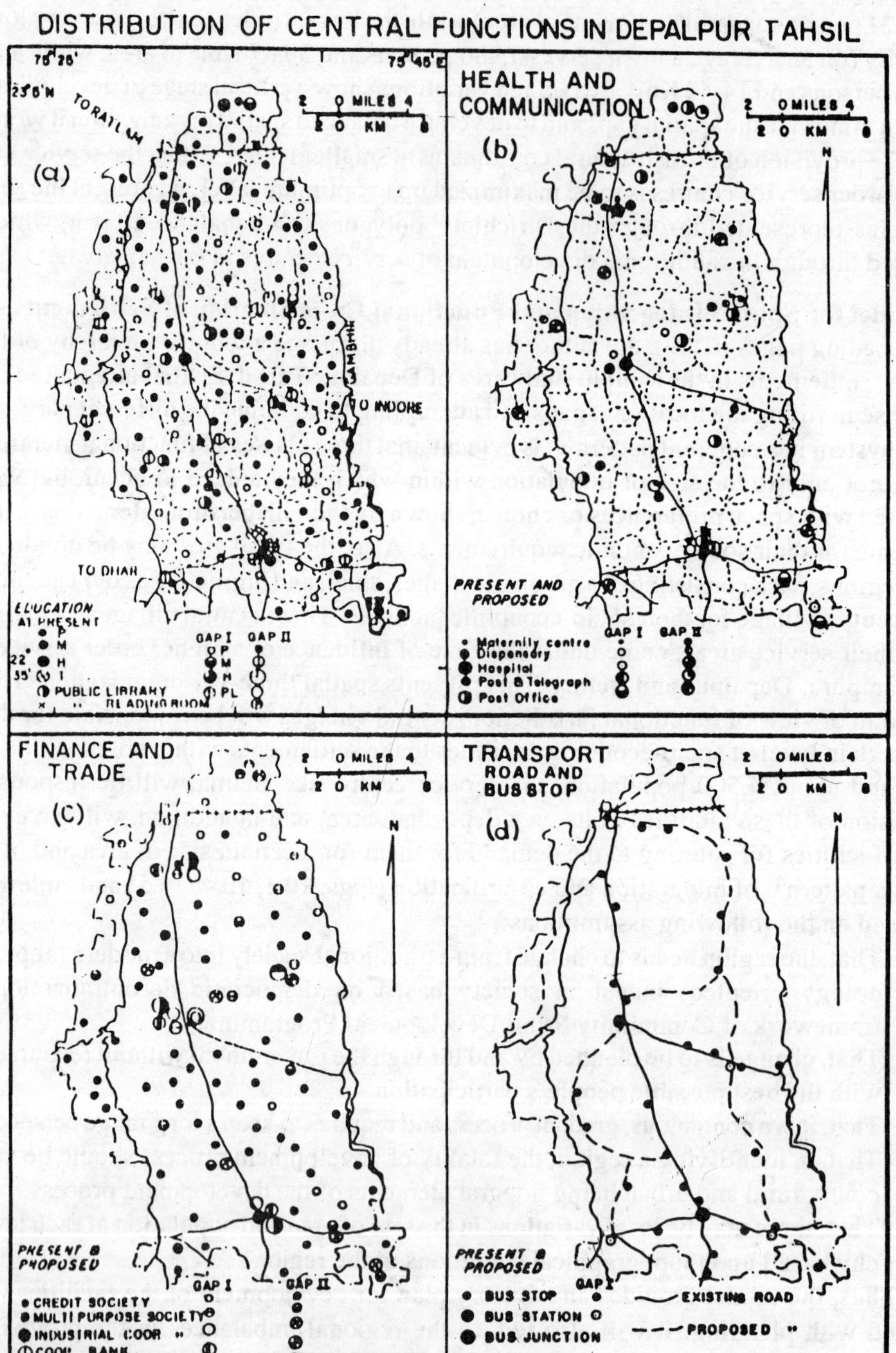
DISTRIBUTION OF CENTRAL FUNCTIONS IN DEPALPUR TAHSIL
(a)
TO DHAR
O INDORE
EDUCATION AT PRESENT
P
M
H
PUBLIC LIBRARY
GAP I GAP II
HEALTH AND COMMUNICATION
(b)
PRESENT AND PROPOSED
Maternity centre
Dispensary
Hospital
Post & Telegraph
Post Office
FINANCE AND TRADE
(c)
PRESENT & PROPOSED
CREDIT SOCIETY
MULTI PURPOSE SOCIETY
INDUSTRIAL COOP
COOP. BANK
WEEKLY MARKET
LAND MARTGAGE BANK
TRANSPORT ROAD AND BUS STOP
(d)
PRESENT & PROPOSED
BUS STOP
BUS STATION
BUS JUNCTION
EXISTING ROAD
PROPOSED
2 0 MILES 4
2 0 KM 6
N

Figure 10.4

centres by all season roads, the interaction will be immensely facilitated. There are 18 settlements proposed to act as central villages for 173 dependent settlements. Each service centre will serve about 6 central villages and each central village, about eight dependent settlements (Figs. 10.1, 10.4, 10.5).

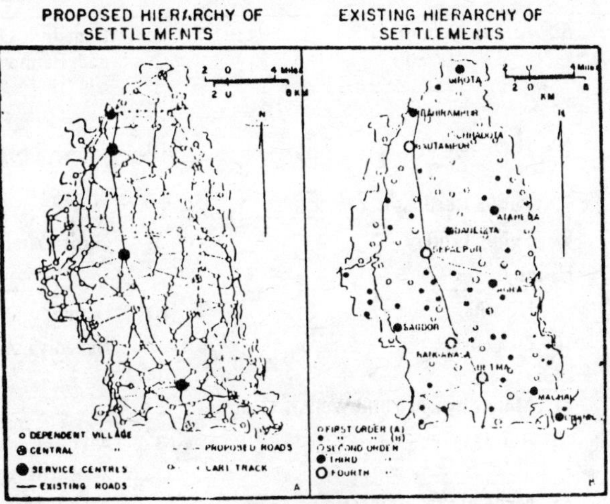

Figure 10.5

A Model for Locational Efficiency of Landuse and Marketing

Keeping in view the discussion in chapter 6, regarding the farm-dwelling and landuse space relationships, and the corrective measures adopted in preceding paragraphs, an attempt has been made, to describe the best line of research, which should be taken up for further strengthening the locational model, identified and developed earlier; one may call this area of research a 'locational efficiency model' with the help of which, it is possible to predict the location of industry in the region. Location of such industry, specially in central villages, will help in guiding the direct participation of the dependent settlements in the development of the centre's secondary sector consisting of processing and manufacturing of raw materials or agro-based industries. The research requires, however, a detailed study of the landuse pattern, production of major crops and its linkage with the factory and markets and the ties between the centre and its dependent settlements at micro- level. Coming to its operational characteristics, one must remember the identification of locational gaps, corrective measures adopted to fill those gaps. The tables 10 (ii) and 10 (iii) contain a list of proposed central villages out of which one may easily pick up the future locations for the processing industry. As these weight-losing industries are located on the resource base and have locational advantages, the central villages or a selection of a few from among them, will serve as location points for the establishment of processing unit.

Table 10 (II)

Allotment of Scores to Indicators
Proposed Central Functions

Functions	*Scores*	*Gap (i)*	*Gap (ii)*
A. Administration			
1. Tahsil Headquarters	10	Nil	Nil
2. Block Headquarters	10	—do—	—do—
3. Police Station	10	—do—	—do—
B. Education			
4. Primary School	1	Chandan Khedi, Karoda, Mendakwas, Jalalpura, Ujalya, Shahpura, Bhidola, Khatwadi, Chiman Khedi, Ahirwas, Khedi, Baroda Panth, Amli, Sikandri, Karodiya, Ajanda, Ram Badodiya	Bhanwargarh, Salampur, Thalariya, Panth Badodiya, Dhaniya, Mundipur, Bhamakheda Kharsoda, Garhi Billoda

Contd...

5. Middly School	4	Banediya, Girota, Ataheda, Dhannad, Betma	Chhadota, Machal, Agra, Gokalpura, Kanwasa, Jalodiyapar, Arodakot, Sagdod, Ghata Billod, Chatwada, Karodiya
6. High School	10	Nil	Ataheda, Rangawasa, Dhannad Betma, Ataheda
7. Public Reading Room	15	Nil	Betma, Ataheda
8. Public Library	3	Girota, Ataheda, Dhannad, Betma	Jalodiynpar, Karodiya, Ghata Billod
C. Health			
9. Hospital	10	Betma	Nil
10. Dispensary	4	Banediya, Ataheda, Dhannad	Jalodiyapar, Kanwasa, Agra, Aurangapura
11. Maternity and Child Welfare Centres	2	Nil	Depalpur, Betma, Ataheda
12. Rural Health Centre	3	All Central Villages as given in Table (ii)	
13. Medical Practitioner	1	All Villages having Middle School	
14. Animal Husbandry Officer (A.H.O.)	1	—do—	
D. Communication and Transport			
15. Post and Telegraph	4	Betma	Ataheda, Rangawasa, Girota
16. Telegraph Office	2	Nil	Nil
17. Post Office	3	Machal, Dhannad	Ghata Billod, Aurangpura, Jalodiyapar, Khireli, Farkoda
18. Bus Stop	3	Girota, Ataheda, Dhannad, Chhadota, Tolawli, Chander	Sejwani, Thalariya, Sagdod Panth Badodiya, Sunela Dharmat
Sub Station	—	Machal, Agra	Bahirampur, Ghata Billod
E. Finance and Trade			
19. Cooperative Bank	2	Nil	Depalpur, Betma, Gautampur, Ataheda
20. Cooperative Society (Credit Society)	2	Neori, Tolawali, Jalodiyapar, Dharmat, Rudrakhiya, Atyana	Bahirampur, Naulana, Pilawali, kali, Bachhoda, Ralatya Phulan, Kandra, Semda, Chiklonda, Alawada, Lalendi, Rayatpura, Chandan Khedi, Amli, Jalalpura, Karki, Gulawat, Kali Billod
(Multipurpose Society	2	Gautampura, Depalpur, Banediya, Girota, Ataheda	Machal, Dhannad, Ghata Billod, Rangwasa, Agra, Sagdod, Jalodiyapar, Kanwasa, Farkoda, Katkoda
(Industrial Society)	2	Gautampura, Depalpur	Machal, Dhannad, Rangawasa, Girota, Gokalpur, Banediya (having 10 industrial units)
21. Weekly Market	10	Girota (Saturday), Ataheda (Tuesday)	Nil
Land Mortgage Bank	—	At Depalpur	

Table 10 (iii)

Proposed Hierarchy of Settlements

Service Centres	*Central Villages*
Depalpur, Gautampura, Betma	Girota, Bahirampur, Chhadota, kanwasa, Farkoda, Jalodiyapar, Jalodiya Panth, Bahediya, Ataheda, Sagdod, Rangawasa, Agra, Neori, Aurangpura, Ghata Billod, Machal, Kali Billod, Dhannad

When functional gaps will be removed, the dependent settlements will not be more than 5 to 6 km from such centres. All these settlements will be connected by the shortest distance cart tracks or all season village roads (Fig. 10.5). Weekly or fortnightly markets will be complementary to the existing markets in service centres. This pattern will cut short the economic distance, assure the farmer to get a competitive price for his product, provide easy and timely approach to the extension agencies like centres for seed, fertilizers, pesticides, credit, loan and also the civil facilities like schools, hospitals and retail services as shown in Fig. 10.2A. Besides a model location of socio-economic activities, the second part (Fig. 10.2b) shows the site for the location of the processing unit in relation to its dependent settlements. Proper survey of cropping pattern and production figures, will assure the timely supply of the produce, to the unit, and also competitive price, to the farmer. The integration of the socio-economic overheads, with the processing units, will bring stability to the area, served, and also, to the centre. These two models point, automatically, to a third one, regarding transportation network. The central village must have connections with dependent settlements by at least strengthened cart-tracks. The transportation network, however, will require co-operation and coordination of planner and executing authorities in relation to inter-village and inter-regional distances. The central village will also be connected with other neighbouring centre and with a centre of greater importance by all season roads (Fig. 10.2C). This will facilitate timely, and quicker supply of products to and from the central village. The type of road will, however, vary according to the local needs and finance available for constructing the infrastructures.like bridges and culverts. The model for Farkoda, in between Gautampura and Depalpur service centres, will present all the three conditions, referred to above.

Planning the Infrastructural Development

The discussion, in the preceding pages, included spatial strategy and the inter-village planning, leading to the indentification, location and development of centres belonging to the higher level of three-tier organization. Now, the lower base village needs proper study. The village is the product of a social, cultural, economic and physical balance. A village planner or "Any planner, can be likened to the rider of a cycle, who has to maintain a balance on the rear wheel of practical issues and the front wheel of theoretical understanding".[42] There are two interlocking concepts, of the community and of the rural environment, related to the planning of development of a village. The village, as a physical structure, forms part of the rural environment. But, the physical planning is but one aspect of total planning. Social, economic, administrative and physical planning form one integrated activity. This integration is, however, unrealized as yet. A planner must be aware of the dimension of time in preparing and executing his work, because, villages are an inheritance from the post, exist in the present, and have a potential in the future. "The planning process involves six main stages, indentified as, data; particular problem situation; philosophic framework; insights/concepts/principles relating man to environment; environmental objectives; over all design of development; and the plans one makes to govern stages of growth."[43]

As regards the relation of man to environment, he must be considered a part of the biosphere. Within the framework of a prevailing philosophy, man and environment adapt to each other's needs which may be grouped into four major systems. It is the keys to the control of the village systems, which will form planning principles. The four main systems of the village (on physical components) consist of:

i) System dealing with cattle and other domestic animals, bullock carts and fuel.
ii) System which deals with agricultural production and exchange, irrigation and distribution.
iii) System relating to social and industrial communal life.
iv) System relating to their shelter, housing and small activities. The fourth system, with which a geographer is mostly concerned, may be for convenience, expanded into three subsystems given below:
   (a) This includes houses used according to various needs and functions; class and caste factors interact in determining location of houses.
   (b) It suggests compounds and yards.
   (c) This system consists of several overlapping activities and functions, i.e., need for gossip and social spaces, meeting spaces at compound level, water facilities, shady trees and pedestrian movement etc. If one analyses, through the aid of subsystems, a concept of habitat becomes clear. Now, the satisfaction of the housing need will be a major component of the village development programme. Coming to environmental objectives, one observes, that each system can absorb slight changes, which do not distort the system as a whole, i.e., bullock cart can be given rubber tyred wheels and could not be replaced by tractors. It has also been experienced that communities develop according to a cumulative, one way sequence and pass through three stages.

Firstly, any transformation of a subsystem of a settlement needs contact with larger settlements, hence, inter-village planning. The next stage, concerning overall development design, reveals the fact, that, the strategy of welfare oriented village planning, is directly concerned with rural development including village agriculture, community development, local construction, rural industries and the co-operative movement. So, one has to see the interweaving process of development of greater unit while determining the shape and form of physical structural development of a village. The last stage is concerned with the plans to govern the stages of growth, that is, how to shape in time and space the gradual transformation of a village. This will require the evolution of a way of guiding the village development through the establishment of performance standards,[44] governmental plan of actions and an order of growth and form in terms of directions, principles and spatial organisations to govern the physical growth of the village. Now the policies for public action could be set up and priorities be fixed.

For example, for the low cost housing technology, a theme of significance faces many problems, which require a multifaceted approach considering (i) planned utilization of land (ii) increased indigenous technical knowledge and skills, (iii) increased use of indigenous building materials, (iv) promotion of labour intensive construction technologies, and (v) the development of suitable public policy and finance mechanisms. The interdisciplinary interaction among architects, economists, engineers and social scientists may search out the solution to these well.

The general hints[45] for settlement planning are as follows:- (1) topography, (2) foundation soil, (3) ground water, (4) quality of soil, (5) surface drainage and sewage disposal, (6) main direction of the wind, (7) economic section and location of fields, meadows and pasture grounds, (8) documents required for planning, (9) arable land and livestock numbers, (10) old buildings, (11) village traffic, (12) water and power supply, (13) structure of village population, (14) modern agricultural machines and implements, (15) hygiene and the prevention of epidemics, (16) fire protection, (17) labour safety and prevention of accidents, (18) recreation needs, (19) privacy and religious ceremonies.

But, one cannot proceed and operate as planner, unless one has a parallel concept of the development of a spatial theory. Space theory in physical planning is concerned with three dimensions, i.e., a housing site having base, sides and roofs. It involves social, caste space and economic space on a hierarchy of spaces, all having primary and public use. Thus, social relationships give physical dimensions through family groups, movement and access patterns and constructional order.

The implementation of plan requires exercise of skill, according to a set of principles, to be guided by environmental conditions, referred to above as plan process theory and plan implementation.

At all level of village development planning, however, the object of planning will be "to ensure progress through establishing change with order and ensuring order through change" [46]

Grassroots Approach

Besides service centre planning and deployment of facilities according to identified spatial functional gaps, what the poor countries need most, is the grassroots approach in planning and implementation. The basic principle is (i) to contact unto the last, (ii) to discuss and enquire unto the last, (iii) to persuade unto the last for involvement after conviction, and (iv) during all these processes to retain the will to make the facilities (quality of life) reach unto the last. Because, the old saying goes, 'where there is a will, there is a way'

Following these principles house to house family wise survey is the prerequisite for micro-level village/settlement planning. The themes of the survey, very clearly, are regarding basic needs, food, shelter, clothing, then recreation, religion, education, health and community behaviour. Community and settlement, rather, hamlet wise plan should be prepared by all Govt., NGO, and village people jointly, taking into its ambit, the spectrums containing resources and implementational aspects.

Transformation of Rural Settlement System

The rationalization of rural settlement system aims at its transformation. In this regard, one must be fully convinced, that each step (march forward), use of spade or sickle, adaptation of innovation, practice, dietary habits, will to change, and implementation, come under transformatory processes. It is, therefore, obvious that RHT involves various transformatory processes, though interlinked, having dichotomous system of components, which need interpretation/explanation. The dual arrangement of physical and cultural components/processes would be misgiving because, any change, and more so a transformation, happens to be the outcome of simultaneous interaction of human society and nature. Yet, for the sake of understanding and better explanation, we may have the following taxonomic form, represented through the Figure 1.8. The existence of natural landscape (Geoecobiota) is manifested through various channels and further developments result into the present rural habitat system. The second model (Figure 10.6) symbolizes the

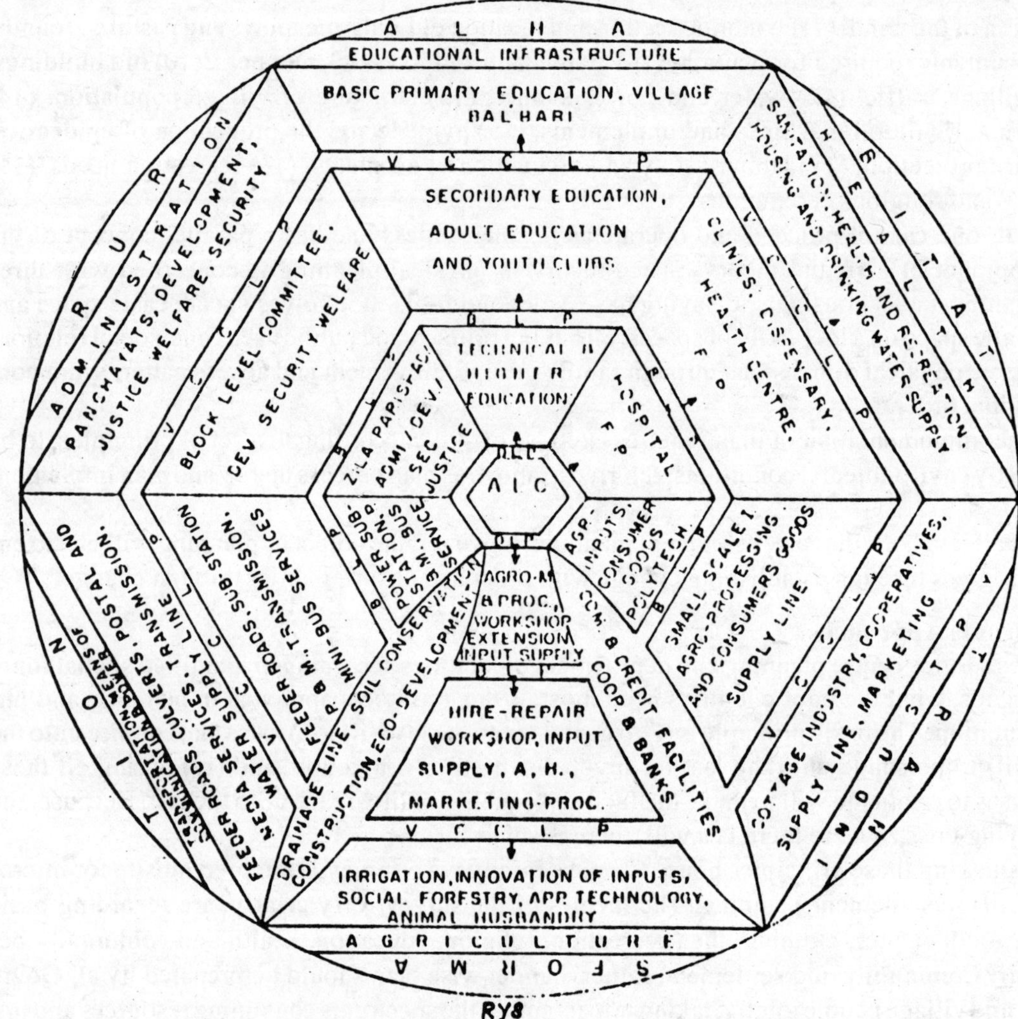

VCCLP—Village Community/Cluster Level Planning
BLP—Block Level Planning
DLP—District Level Planning
ALC—Apex Level Coordination

Figure 10.6

processes of rural habitat transformation.

It emphasizes upon the grassroots approach for planning with due care to eco-development and decentralization of administrative and development activities. The vital village community-level sectoral but integrated development envisages, the spread for growth points, providing each facility according to local needs. Block level growth centres, based upon the former growth points, respond to the secondary and tertiary activities. The district level growth centres, playing vital role in processing and marketing the products and supplying inputs, will be coordinated through development agencies. Projects of soil conservation, drainage and constructional works cover the whole gamut of planning, starting from village up to district level ready to absorb and

employ the labour (skilled as well as unskilled) as per demand, mostly, in agricultural activities and infrastructural development. Credit and commercial facilities, must have a continuous chain, from village level up to the apex level, either through cooperative banks or both (cooperative and nationalized banks). The ecodevelopment, covering each level, means rational development of the environment, better termed, as ecologically justified development (Frolov).[47]

Human Settlements Approach

The sections dealing with various approaches (i.e. service centre, grassroots and finally transformation) help in switching over to global human settlements 'only one earth'[48] model. This approach sees man-in totality-in work, in play at home and in relationship with nature and the environment. Its objective is, to ensure the spread of development efforts-the quality of life-to the people. The UNEP agreed, to quote here, during its meetings, that the main objectives of a determined new effort for development and improvement of human settlements technology should be to (a) identify a global network of leading institutions in the field of human settlements technology, which will be organized on an ecosystem and regional basis, (b) establish the necessary mechanisms for coordinating and promoting the activities of these institutions (research information, implementation of projects), (c) collect, disseminate and make all data in the field, readily available, (d) promote the use of environmentally, sound technologies which, due to their very nature, will help countries and communities become self-reliant.

For global settlement planning one has to think in terms of NEW (National Economic Welfare) instead of G.N.P. as a measure of development. To achieve this, one must overcome the five preconceived 'ideas' of: (i) historic determinism, (ii) economic determinism, (iii) technological determinism, (iv) Centre- periphery Theory, and (v) the Theory of Equilibrium. Man has to accept, not only the principle of planet earth as one unit but also 'planet as one in the economic sense'. Rightly it has been emphasized that "Although some politicians, some industrialists and others would like to create a dichotomy between human settlements and the natural environment, there is none."

References

1. Charles Medge, (1974), The Relevance of Family Pattern in the Process of Modernization in East Asia, in Robert J. Smith, (ed), Social Organization and the Application of Anthropology, Essays in Honor of Lauriston Sharp, Ithaca Cornell University Press, p. 171.
2. See Spencer, J.E. (1977), The Transformation of Traditional Rural Village, pp. 160-169 in Robert C. Eidt, K.N. Singh & Rana P.B. Singh (eds), Man, Culture and Settlement, Kalyani Publishers, New Delhi.
3. The New India:Progress Through Democracy, New York, Planning Commission, Govt. of India, 1958, p. 42.
4. Wiser, W.H. (1936), The Hindu Jajmani System, Lucknow Publishing House, Lucknow, India; see also Beidelman, T.O. (1950), A Comparative Analysis of the Jajmani System, Monograph of the Association of Asian Studies, VIII (J.J. Augustin) Locust Valley, N.Y.) and Kolenda, P.M. (1933) 'Toward a Model of the Hindu Jajmani System' Human Organisation, Vol. 22, pp. 11-31.
5. Desai, A.R. (1961), Rural India in Transition, Popular Book Dept., Bombay, 7, p. 12.

6. Prasad, N. (1970), Change Strategy in a Developing Society, India, Meenakshi Prakashan, Meerut, Preface III.
7. Blunt, E.A.H. (1969), The Caste System of Northern India, S. Chand and Co., Delhi-Lucknow, p. 253.
8. Desai, A.R. op.cit. ref. 5, p. 13.
9. See R.Y. Singh (1978), The Malwa Region:Rural Habitat System, Structure and Change, op.cit. ref. no. 34, Ch. 1, for detailed account on 'Structural Elements of Social Organisation in Rural Settlements' as well as on 'Social Dynamics, Society and Modernity' pp. 168-169.
10. Dube, S.C. (1968), Formulating the Goal of Change, p. 46 in "Some Aspects of Social Changes in India (eds), Kuppuswamy, B. & Mehta, P., Sterling Publishers (P) Ltd., Delhi-6, p. 16.
11. Ibid, p. 53
12. Desai, A.R. ref, no. 5, pp. 1-2.
13. Pandhanadhikar, K.C. and J. (1970), Determinants of Social Structure and Social Change in India, and other Papers, Bombay Popular Prakashan, p. 50.
14. Lambert, Richard (1962), The Impact of Urban Society Upon Village Life, p. 117 in India's Urban Future (ed.) Turner Roy, Berkeley, University of California.
15. Prasad, N., op.cit. ref. no. 6, p. 196.
16. Nath, V. (1962), The Village and the Community, p. 144 in Turner Roy (ed.) India's Urban Future, ref. no. 14.
17. Mukerji, B. (1961), Community Development in India, Bombay, Orient Longmans, pp. 181-182.
18. Singh, K.N. (1966), A Case for Small Towns in Regional Planning in India, p. 210 in R.L. Singh (ed.) Applied Geography, NGSI, Varanasi-5.
19. Quoted in Pilot Projects for Integrated Area Development, Foundation and Council for Social Development, New Delhi May, 1969, mimeo).
20. Singh, Tarlok (1964), Towards an Integrated Society, Orient Longman, p. 165.
21. Report II, p. 88.
22. Singh, K.N., ref. no. 18, p. 209.
23. Singh, Tarlok (1962), Problems of Integrating Rural, Industrial and Urban Development, p. 333 in Turner Roy (ed.) 'India's Urban Future, op.cit. ref. no. 14.
24. Shanti, Tangri (1962), Urbanization, Political Stability And Economic Growth, in India's Urban Future, op.cit. ref. no. 14, p. 217.
25. Srinivas, M.N. (ed.) (1960), India's Villages, London, p. 6.
26. Jaya Prakash Narayan, 'Plea For Reconstruction of Indian Polity'.
27. Johnson, E.A.J. (1965), Market Towns and Spatial Development in India, NCAER, New Delhi, footnote 1, p. 87.
28. Nath, V. ref. no. 14, p. 153.
29. Mukherjee Radhakamal (1963), Man and His Habitation:A Study in Social Ecology, Bombay Popular Prakashan, p. 181.
30. Nath, V. 'Regions for Planning' The Journal of Public Administration, XII (No. 1). 11.
31. Department of Community Development, Government of India, Note on Pilot Projects in Growth Centres (April, 1970).
32. Ibid.
33. Singh, K.N. op.cit., ref. no. 18, p. 217.
34. Morphological Study of a Few Villages in Chapter Six would clarify.
35. Singh, Tarlok, op.cit. ref. no. 23, p. 334.
36. Leszezycki, S. (1974), The Factors of Space and Its Role in Todays Economics, p-30 in K. Secomski (ed.), Spatial Planning and Policy, Theoretical Foundations, Waszawa, Polich, Ac. Sc.
37. See for masterly explanation Smith, D.M. (1977), Human Geography:A Welfare Approach, Edward Arnold (Publishers) Ltd., London, pp. 1-16.

38. Doxiadis, C.A. (1969) 'Ekistics, An Attempt for a Scientific Approach to the Problems of Human Settlements' in Science and Technology and the Cities (eds.), Committee on Science and Astronautics, U.S. House of Representatives Washington, D.C., U.S. Govt., p. 9.
39. Koloszar, M. (1975) 'Interrelationship Between Settlement Strategies, Systems and Socio-economic Development in 'National Settlement Strategies, East and West, (ed.) Harry Swain Luxemberg:I.I.A. S-A. Cp.-75-3, 68.
40. See G.L. Dirichlet (1850) 'Uber die Reduction der Positiven Quadratischen Formen mit drei unbestimmten gangen Zahlen' Jl. fur die reine and angewandte Mathematick, 40, 204-34 (esp. 216-20).
41. Modified from Sen, L.K. et al. op.cit. Ch.9, ref. no. 1, p. 165.
42. Oaklay, David (1965) 'Village Planning a Theoretical Approach' p. 35 in "The Rural Habitat" (eds.), David Oklay and K. Raman Unni. School of Planning and Architecture, New Delhi.
43. Oklay, David "Planning Village Development:An Enquiry into Method" p. 47 in the Rural Habitat", ref. no. 42.
44. Oklay David, op.cit. ref. no. 42, p. 111.
45. See for details Johannes Jahne (1978), 'Technical Fundamentals, Construction Practice in Rural Areas Part II, Specially part IV in "Principles and Practice of Planning Villages and Proposals for Rural Building Projects", Asia Publishing House, Bombay.
46. Okaly David op.cit. ref. no. 42, p. 40.
47. Frolov, I.T. (1983), The Marxist Leninist Conception of the Ecological Problem in 'philosophy and the Ecological Problem in 'Philosophy and the Ecological Problems of Civilization', (ed.) A.D. Ursul, Progress Publishers, Moscow, p. 42.
48. See Gwen Bell (ed.) (1976), Strategies For Human Settlements:Habitat and Environment, The University Press of Hawaii Hondolulu, p. 180.

Plates

A House in Eastern U.P.

A Potter's House in Ganga Valley, U.P.

View of Central Rural Dwellings in the Central Part of Dhamnod Village (Narmada Valley)

Thatched Cattlesheds are Common Features in Tribal Forest Areas: A View From Aser (Khandwa).

Back View of a Bhil House in Semalkheri (Jhabua)

Scheduled Castes have Seperate Hamlet: A View from Manpur Village.

A Rafterwalled Dwelling of a Poor Service-Class Man; Pig-House is Attached
A View from Mathia (Sagar), M.P.

A Bhil House in Bhagatpura (Kushalgarh) in Rajasthan.

Stonewalled and Slab Covered Houses are Common Features in Jhalawar;
A View From Chhatarpur Village.

Index